NELLY SACHS, FLIGHT AND METAMORPHOSIS

Stanford University Press
Stanford, California


*Flight and Metamorphosis* was originally published in German under the title *Flucht und Verwandlung. Nelly Sachs, Schriftstellerin, Berlin/Stockholm* © Aris Fioretos and Suhrkamp Verlag, 2010.

All quotations translated into English by Tomas Tranæus, except where otherwise specified.

This book has been published with the assistance of The Europe Center at the Freeman Spogli Institute for International Studies, Stanford University; The Jewish Theatre, Stockholm; The National Library, Stockholm; gewerk design, Berlin; Kulturstiftung des Bundes, Halle an der Saale; Stiftung Lotto, B, Deutsche Klassenlotterie, Berlin; Riksbankens Jubileumsfond, Stockholm; Svenska Akademien, Stockholm; and Deutsche Akademie für Sprache und Dichtung, Darmstadt.



Printed in China on acid-free, archival-quality paper.

Designed by gewerk design, Berlin
Typeset by Ola Wallin in Minion 10,6/14

Library of Congress Cataloging-in-Publication Data
Fioretos, Aris, 1960- author.
[Flucht und Verwandlung. English]
Nelly Sachs, flight and metamorphosis : an illustrated biography / Aris Fioretos ; translated by Tomas Tranæus.
pages cm
"Originally published in German under the title Flucht und Verwandlung."
Includes bibliographical references and index.
ISBN 978-0-8047-7530-4 (cloth : alk. paper)
ISBN 978-0-8047-7531-1 (pbk. : alk. paper)
1. Sachs, Nelly, 1891-1970. 2. Sachs, Nelly, 1891-1970--Criticism and interpretation. 3. Poets, German--20th century--Biography. 4. Jewish women authors--Germany--Biography. I. Tranæus, Tomas, translator. II. Title.
PT2637.A4184Z64313 2011
831'.914--dc22

2010050159

ARIS FIORETOS

# NELLY SACHS, FLIGHT AND METAMORPHOSIS

AN ILLUSTRATED BIOGRAPHY

TRANSLATED BY TOMAS TRANÆUS

STANFORD UNIVERSITY PRESS

STANFORD, CALIFORNIA

1

# CONTENTS

"You will have understood ... my repeated wish that I want to disappear behind my work, to remain anonymous ... I would like to be fully extinguished — just a voice, a sigh for those who wish to listen."

Nelly Sachs in a letter to Walter A. Berendsohn, June 25, 1959

## FOREWORD

2

How to approach a writer who spoke of tragic events in her past, but avoided concrete circumstances? A writer who, in the first epitaphs to her "dead brothers and sisters," preferred to use initials rather than full names? Who, early as well as later in life, burned poems and letters she felt were too frank, too private? In short, a writer who wished to disappear behind her work?

For Nelly Sachs, texts had to speak for themselves. No knowledge about the person behind the work was necessary; in fact, it could be threatening. Although she understood writing as an act of devotion which ultimately left no other mark than the traces of passion, her considerable correspondence — around 4,000 extant letters — shows how concerned she was that details of her private life should remain private. There are usually good reasons for respecting a writer's wishes regarding such matters, and rarely any bad ones. Yet at the same time as Sachs withheld facts about the background to her work, she said that she was doing so. With one hand she pointed to what the other hand was hiding. This double gesture is significant. Perhaps it says something about how she viewed the interplay of life and letters.

In her correspondence with the Germanist Walter A. Berendsohn, Sachs repeatedly urged caution regarding information imparted in confidence. In order to underline the urgency of her request she used a drastic turn of phrase: if her friend were really going to write the proposed study of her life as a writer, he must understand that she wanted to be "extinguished" as a person. Sachs could hardly have been unaware that the German verb *ausschalten* sounded as if it came straight out of the Nazis' vocabulary — that "diction of the Third Reich" or "lexicon of inhumanity" of which Victor Klemperer, Dolf Sternberger, and others amassed evidence after the war. Why did she use such a charged term? Was it in order to state emphatically the limits of what Berendsohn could include in his book? A demand that he concentrate on the work and leave everything else to "the reporters from the celebrity press," as she also wrote? Or was it in fact a straightforward declaration of a more general problem: how to give expression to the defenseless without risking new exposure? Did she fear that the inclusion of biographical data would obscure the import of the poem and, paradoxically, cause more pain to be inflicted? "The heartrending tragedy of our destiny will not and must not [...] be diminished by the many items of information which are wholly unnecessary in this context."

No doubt such considerations, and others, played a part. Still — "extinguished"? Despite its metaphorical proximity to the chimneys of the crematorium ovens, and despite its kinship with a verb such as the Nazi term *gleichschalten* ("leveling"), *ausschalten* may have suggested something else as well...

During the first year of their Swedish exile, Sachs and her mother lived at temporary addresses. In October 1941 they were able to move to an apartment

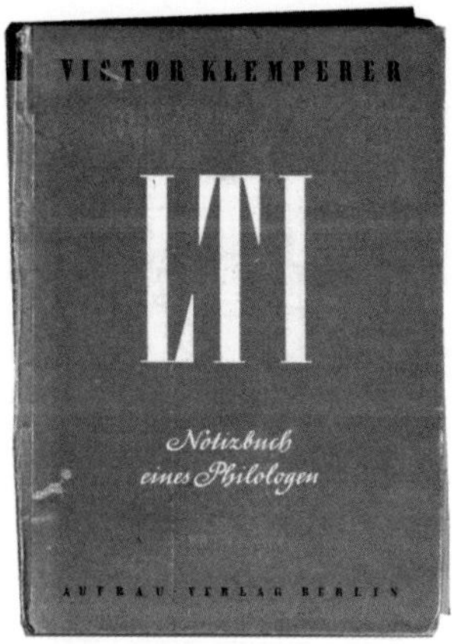


3

4

of their own, in a building in Bergsundsstrand on the south side of Stockholm. Located on the ground floor, it consisted of one room and a kitchen, and was dark and cold. According to notes made later, it was occasionally filled with the stench of sewers. After seven years without sunlight, in August 1948, the pair were able to move to a one-room apartment measuring 41 square meters, with a kitchen and dining alcove, a couple of floors higher up in the same building. Here Sachs would spend the rest of her life. Until her mother's death in February 1950, she devoted most of her time to caring for her. What small income she earned came from translations of Swedish literature, mostly poetry. Only at night could she write her own work — in the dark, as her mother would otherwise wake up.

This is the prototypical setting for Sachs' poetry: alone with the alphabet at night. She felt literally "thrown into an 'Outside,'" as she put it to the literary critic Margit Abenius. Although she may have been in a world governed by social conventions, she wasn't part of it. Paradoxically situated, hers was an eerie sphere, bound up with the dead and the sorrow they left behind. Much later, in a letter to her French translator, Lionel Richard, Sachs would term this her "Nightly Dimension." *Ausschalten* meant this, too: with the light extinguished, the person behind the work was no longer visible. Yet she was there all the same. The night was illuminated by the one thing that mattered: the writing. Whatever else there was, it should remain in the dark.

This study is devoted to the interplay between life and letters, inside and outside in a body of work neglected by critics in recent years. Hence it is also concerned with Sachs' self-image. Her development as a poet is remarkable not least because she began the memorable part of her œuvre when she was over fifty years old. During the quarter-century that followed, her poems became ever more convincing from a critical point of view. Literary history boasts few such examples, if any. How was this development made possible?

The self-image that Sachs created from an experience of loss and parting, flight and metamorphosis, was predicated on the notion that the poems came to her, that they were dictated by horrific circumstances which forced her to speak. "The words came and broke forth in me — to the edge of annihilation," she said in an interview on Swiss television in 1965. This image fits in with the vision of a poet with an Orphic mission. It is furthermore easy to identify traits which are traditionally perceived as feminine. Sachs is less active than passive. She does not compose poems, but rather is overwhelmed by them. She is more receiver than sender.

Sachs' literary estate shows that she rarely rewrote or edited her texts. Many of them were printed in versions nearly identical — bar the odd word or comma — to the original. Yet must that mean she was a mere medium without intent — a handful of strings moved by the divine wind? At the same time as the circumstances following her escape from Nazi Germany were far from comfortable, she conscientiously worked in the service of poetry. She had submitted texts to newspapers and periodicals already in her youth. After her flight she contacted Swedish writers and critics and began almost immediately to translate their work into German. Despite her isolation she built, over time, a wide-ranging "network of words" (*Adernetz der Sprache*, literally, 'vascular system' or 'capillaries of language') with coordinates near and far, among the living and the dead, exiled writers and representatives of the younger generation. And during the difficult years of the 1960s, scarred by the effects of persecution during the Nazi years, she was periodically committed to psychiatric clinics in whose protected setting she wrote what are perhaps her most powerful works, the "glowing enigmas" and the late dramatic poetry.

This study dwells upon such contradictions and upon other ones. Even if Sachs saw herself as a "battleground," it was in her that the words broke forth — and they did so "to the edge of annihilation." The same convulsions with which she was born as a poet also extinguished her as a private individual. In the end the words glowed from the inside. Like enigmas, they illuminated without explanation. Thus implying that a different sort of reading was required: one that doesn't assume the meaning of a poem is a treasure to be unearthed and exported. Inaccessibility was part of its appearance. As was obscurity.

May the following pages contain enough of the latter for Sachs' poems to gleam as only they can.

**TEXT** Dedication, IdWdT (NSW:I) · Klemperer, *LTI. Notizbuch eines Philologen*, Berlin 1947 · Sternberger, Storz och Süskind, *Aus dem Wörterbuch des Unmenschen*, Hamburg 1957 · Berendsohn · For letters to Berendsohn 06/25/1959 and Abenius 03/17/1958, see Briefe 140 and 125 respectively · Letter to Berendsohn 09/07/1959, ABerendsohnD · The apartment is described in a letter from Elvan Johansson 05/27/1980, ADinesen · "Weitere Aufzeichnungen,", NSW:IV · Letter to Richard 01/30/1968 · Interview with Werner Weber, broadcast on Swiss television 11/10/1965 · The *Adernetz der Sprache* occurs in the poem "Da schrieb der Schreiber des Sohar," Unww (NSW:II) · GR:I–IV, NSW:II · For the image of the writer as "battleground," see letter to Gunnar Ekelöf 07/05/1965, Briefe 216 | **IMAGE 1** Nelly Sachs in 1960 (Photo Anna Riwkin, KBS) · **2** Bergsundsstrand 23, 1991 (Photo Esbjörn Eriksson, KBS) · **3** Victor Klemperer, *Lingua tertii imperii* 1947 · **4** Dolf Sternberger, Gerhard Storz och W. E. Süskind, *Aus dem Wörterbuch des Unmenschen* 1957

Li

# IN THE GARDEN OF PARADISE

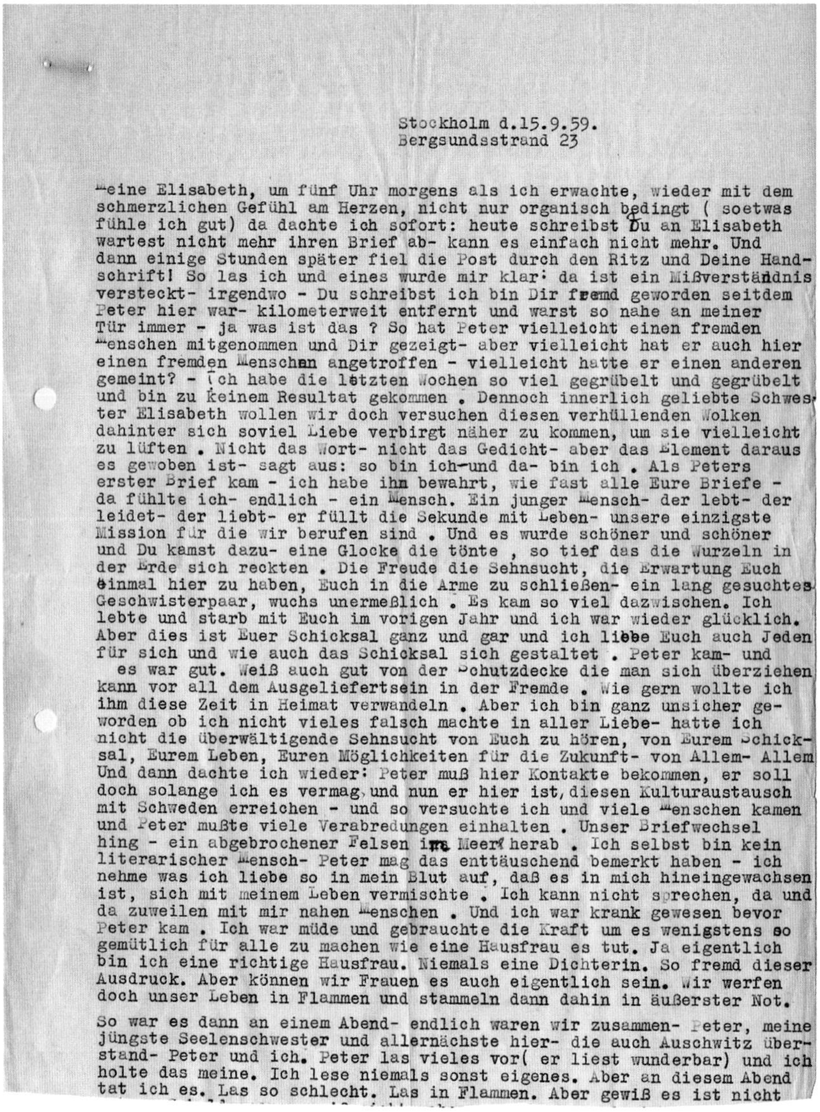

Stockholm d.15.9.59.
Bergsundsstrand 23

Meine Elisabeth, um fünf Uhr morgens als ich erwachte, wieder mit dem schmerzlichen Gefühl am Herzen, nicht nur organisch bedingt ( soetwas fühle ich gut) da dachte ich sofort: heute schreibst Du an Elisabeth wartest nicht mehr ihren Brief ab- kann es einfach nicht mehr. Und dann einige Stunden später fiel die Post durch den Ritz und Deine Handschrift! So las ich und eines wurde mir klar: da ist ein Mißverständnis versteckt- irgendwo - Du schreibst ich bin Dir fremd geworden seitdem Peter hier war- kilometerweit entfernt und warst so nahe an meiner Tür immer - ja was ist das ? So hat Peter vielleicht einen fremden Menschen mitgenommen und Dir gezeigt- aber vielleicht hat er auch hier einen fremden Menschen angetroffen - vielleicht hatte er einen anderen gemeint? - Ich habe die letzten Wochen so viel gegrübelt und gegrübelt und bin zu keinem Resultat gekommen . Dennoch innerlich geliebte Schwester Elisabeth wollen wir doch versuchen diesen verhüllenden Wolken dahinter sich soviel Liebe verbirgt näher zu kommen, um sie vielleicht zu lüften . Nicht das Wort- nicht das Gedicht- aber das Element daraus es gewoben ist- sagt aus: so bin ich-und da- bin ich . Als Peters erster Brief kam - ich habe ihn bewahrt, wie fast alle Eure Briefe - da fühlte ich- endlich - ein Mensch. Ein junger Mensch- der lebt- der leidet- der liebt- er füllt die Sekunde mit Leben- unsere einzigste Mission für die wir berufen sind . Und es wurde schöner und schöner und Du kamst dazu- eine Glocke die tönte , so tief das die Wurzeln in der Erde sich reckten . Die Freude die Sehnsucht, die Erwartung Euch einmal hier zu haben, Euch in die Arme zu schließen- ein lang gesuchtes Geschwisterpaar, wuchs unermeßlich . Es kam so viel dazwischen. Ich lebte und starb mit Euch im vorigen Jahr und ich war wieder glücklich. Aber dies ist Euer Schicksal ganz und gar und ich liebe Euch auch Jeden für sich und wie auch das Schicksal sich gestaltet . Peter kam- und es war gut. Weiß auch gut von der Schutzdecke die man sich überziehen kann vor all dem Ausgeliefertsein in der Fremde . Wie gern wollte ich ihm diese Zeit in Heimat verwandeln . Aber ich bin ganz unsicher geworden ob ich nicht vieles falsch machte in aller Liebe- hatte ich nicht die überwältigende Sehnsucht von Euch zu hören, von Eurem Schicksal, Eurem Leben, Euren Möglichkeiten für die Zukunft- von Allem- Allem Und dann dachte ich wieder: Peter muß hier Kontakte bekommen, er soll doch solange ich es vermag, und nun er hier ist, diesen Kulturaustausch mit Schweden erreichen - und so versuchte ich und viele Menschen kamen und Peter mußte viele Verabredungen einhalten . Unser Briefwechsel hing - ein abgebrochener Felsen im Meer herab . Ich selbst bin kein literarischer Mensch- Peter mag das enttäuschend bemerkt haben - ich nehme was ich liebe so in mein Blut auf, daß es in mich hineingewachsen ist, sich mit meinem Leben vermischte . Ich kann nicht sprechen, da und da zuweilen mit mir nahen Menschen . Und ich war krank gewesen bevor Peter kam . Ich war müde und gebrauchte die Kraft um es wenigstens so gemütlich für alle zu machen wie eine Hausfrau es tut. Ja eigentlich bin ich eine richtige Hausfrau. Niemals eine Dichterin. So fremd dieser Ausdruck. Aber können wir Frauen es auch eigentlich sein. Wir werfen doch unser Leben in Flammen und stammeln dann dahin in äußerster Not.

So war es dann an einem Abend- endlich waren wir zusammen- Peter, meine jüngste Seelenschwester und allernächste hier- die auch Auschwitz überstand- Peter und ich. Peter las vieles vor( er liest wunderbar) und ich holte das meine. Ich lese niemals sonst eigenes. Aber an diesem Abend tat ich es. Las so schlecht. Las in Flammen. Aber gewiß es ist nicht

1

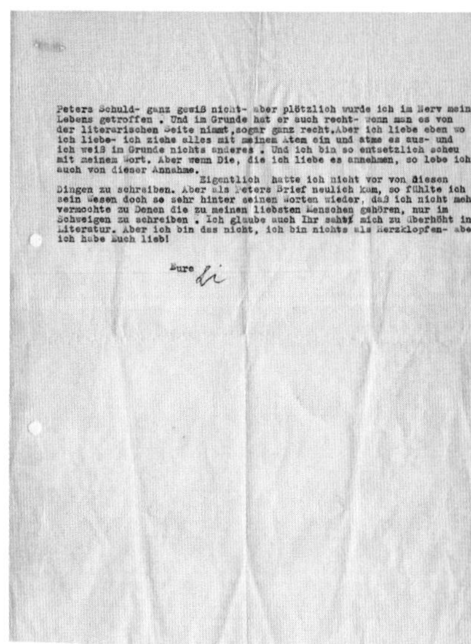

Peters Schuld- ganz gewiß nicht- aber plötzlich wurde ich im Nerv meines Lebens getroffen . Und im Grunde hat er auch recht- wenn man es von der literarischen Seite nimmt, sogar ganz recht. Aber ich liebe eben wo ich liebe- ich ziehe alles mit meinem Atem ein und atme es aus- und ich weiß im Grunde nichts anderes . Und ich bin so entsetzlich scheu mit meinem Wort. Aber wenn Die, die ich liebe es annehmen, so lebe ich auch von dieser Annahme.

Eigentlich hatte ich nicht vor von diesen Dingen zu schreiben. Aber als Peters Brief neulich kam, so fühlte ich sein Wesen doch so sehr hinter seinen Worten wieder, daß ich nicht mehr vermochte zu Denen die zu meinen liebsten Menschen gehören, nur im Schweigen zu schreiben . Ich glaube auch Ihr saht mich zu überhöht in Literatur. Aber ich bin das nicht, ich bin nichts als Herzklopfen- aber ich habe Euch lieb!

Eure Li

**"A REAL HOUSEWIFE"**

In a Swedish postwar novel, now forgotten, a picture is painted of the disappearing sense of security that many Berliners were forced to experience during the 1930s. The narrator has traveled to the capital of the new German Reich. There she visits a poet of Jewish extraction who lives with her parents "in a house in Tiergarten with a small garden filled with flowers and shrubs and little dwarf trees. It was an unexpected idyll in the middle of the big city. And the family was peculiarly Goethean: musical, literary, refined. Among beautiful furnishings in harmonious rooms we sat talking about poetry and poets, as if we were really in a eighteenth-century salon."

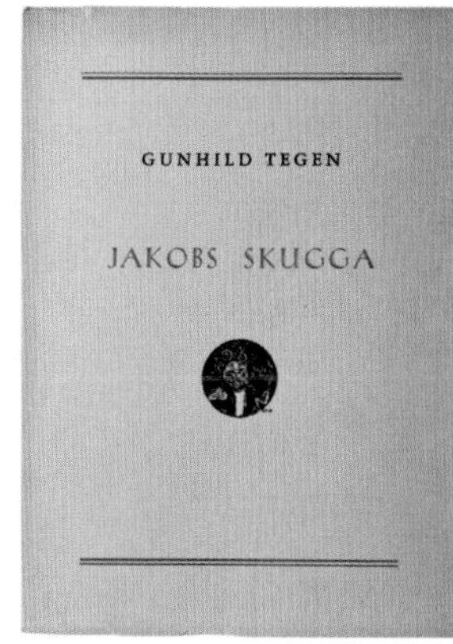


2

Published in 1953 by the author herself, Gunhild Tegen's roman-à-clef *Jakobs skugga* (Jacob's Shadow) was written during the first months after the war, under the influence of the 600 interviews she and her husband, the philosopher Einar Tegen, and a team of interviewers had held with refugees. About twenty of these were transcribed in the anthology *De dödsdömda vittna* (Testimonies of the Condemned) that appeared the same autumn. The Berlin poet at the center of the story — calm and dignified, with dark hair and "large, dreamy roe-deer eyes" in which "the shadow of angst" could be glimpsed — is named "Nell Bartholdi." One day, the narrator muses, that may become "a name posterity will remember..." Even if Tegen's novel itself offers few reasons for posterity to recall it, the narrator was not mistaken. Following a flight "at the eleventh hour," arriving in Stockholm together with her sick mother, the poet who received Tegen in Tiergarten would be remembered as Leonie Sachs, commonly known as Nelly.

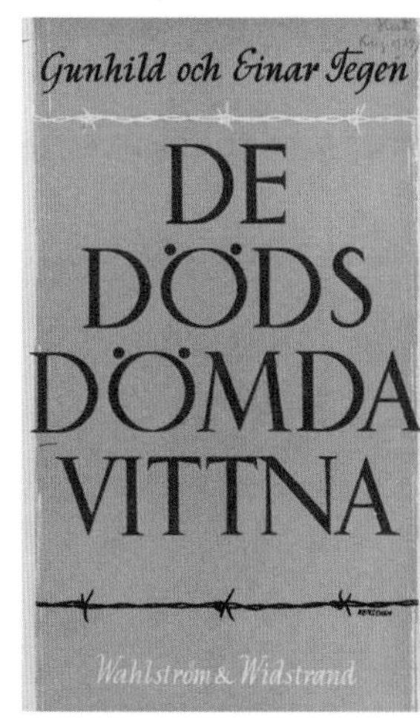


3

Born on December 10, 1891, as the only child of an assimilated German Jewish family, Sachs described herself in less grandiloquent terms. "I have never been a poet, you know," she told literary critic Margit Abenius after the war. "To this day I've never owned a desk — my manuscripts are here in the kitchen cupboard." A year and half later she had earned enough money to be able to buy her first bookshelves, but she still maintained, this time in a letter to her friend and colleague Elisabeth Borchers: "As for myself, I'm not a literary person. [---] Actually, I'm a real housewife. Not a poet at all. That expression seems so foreign. But can we women actually be poets? After all, we throw our lives on the fire and then stand there, stammering in deepest distress."

Even if these assessments are not borne out by her mature work, they suggest a matter-of-factness enlivened by irony as well as the dedication which characterized most of what Sachs undertook. The fact that her personal copy of Tegen's housewifely novel, still extant at the Royal Library in Stockholm, shows no signs of having been read might be considered an instance of historical justice. For "a real housewife" the kitchen table would do as a writing surface. In truth, the cupboard where her manuscripts were kept along with glasses and crockery was a writing case in disguise.

**TEXT** TegenJ, 52, 53, and 58 · TegenD · For letters to Abenius 03/17/1958 and Borchers 09/15/1959, see Briefe 125 and 150 respectively | **IMAGE 1** Letter to Elisabeth Borchers 09/15/1959 (DLA) · **2** Gunhild Tegen, *Jakobs skugga* 1953 · **3** Einar och Gunhild Tegen, *De dödsdömda vittna* 1945

## FOUR SQUARE METERS OF UNIVERSE

4

Nobelpristagare skapar i ett rum på fyra kvm

AB 7/12 -66

5

A round table and a bench with a box underneath. A bed with a pink blanket. A light green bookshelf. A Bakelite telephone (with the number 684843) and a lamp. Curtains. A typewriter. "This is where the Nobel laureate in literature, Nelly Sachs, who turned 75 on the very day of the Nobel festivities, sleeps, eats, and works."

In connection with the tributes a quarter of a century after her flight to Sweden on May 16, 1940, Sachs received many visitors in her one-room apartment with a dining alcove in south Stockholm. One of the callers was a reporter from the *Aftonbladet* evening paper, by the name of Bernt Nilsson. He happened to visit the day after Samuel Josef Agnon, with whom Sachs shared the prize, had been there with his wife and the Israeli ambassador — "That turned into a party in the big sitting room." When the reporter rang the doorbell the following day he stepped into "an atmosphere of lingering hangover. The sherry bottle was still on the table and Nelly Sachs hadn't had time to put everything the photographers had moved back into place." The article he wrote after his visit was illustrated with a photo of the laureate sitting in the alcove she called her "cuddy" due to the view it had over the waters of Liljeholmsviken. The tiny space lay beyond the kitchen with its gas cooker and sink. Four square meters was all that was needed to create a central point in the universe. This was where she ate and slept, this was where she wrote on a portable Mercedes typewriter, which to her visitor sounded "like a stone crusher, but types very clearly."

**TEXT** Bernt Nilsson, "Nobelpristagare skapar i ett rum på fyra kvm," *Aftonbladet*, 12/07/1966 · For Sachs' "cuddy," see e.g. letter to Erik and Karin Lindegren 01/16/1963, Briefe 202 | **IMAGE 4** Sachs' "cuddy" in 1970 (Photo Harry Järv, KBS) · **5** "Nobelpristagare skapar i ett rum på fyra kvm," *Aftonbladet*, 12/07/1966 · **6** Sachs' typewriter (KBS)

## UNDER THE PROTECTIVE BLANKET

When her international acclaim grew towards the end of the 1950s and Sachs' name appeared with increasing frequency in the press, not least in connection with the prizes and awards of which the shared Nobel Prize would be the most significant, she tried to limit what was made public about her life before the flight. To friends such as the Finno-Swedish composer Moses Pergament and his German wife, Ilse, she would write, for example: "Together with my beloved mother I spent 8 years in Berlin trembling in fear of the Gestapo and receiving daily threats and blackmail attempts in the mail. I have seen a beloved person, mortally wounded, break down before my eyes." But such information must

6

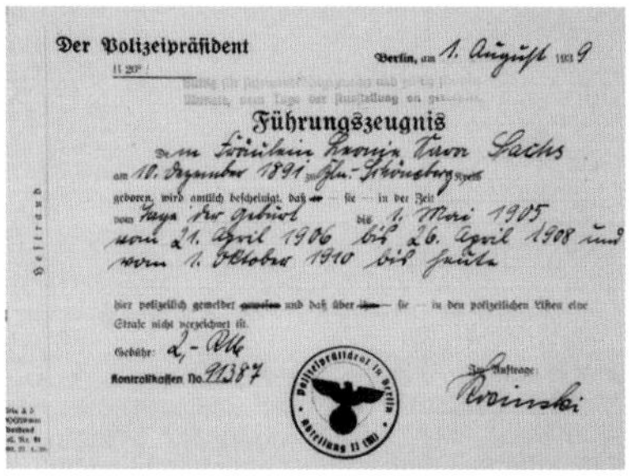

Der Polizeipräsident

Berlin, am 1. August 1939

Führungszeugnis

Dem Fräulein Leonie Nelly Sachs

am 10. Dezember 1891 zu Bln.-Schöneberg

geboren, wird amtlich bescheinigt, daß sie in der Zeit

vom Tage der Geburt bis 1. Mai 1905

vom 21. April 1906 bis 26. April 1908 und

vom 1. Oktober 1910 bis heute

hier polizeilich gemeldet und daß über sie in den polizeilichen Listen eine Strafe nicht verzeichnet ist.

Gebühr: 2,- RM

Kontrollkassen No. 91387

Im Auftrage:

Rosinski

7

remain in the private sphere; in sharing it, she had to be able to count on her friends' sense of discretion.

On the one hand, Sachs felt persecuted again, which led to repeated internments at psychiatric clinics during the last ten years of her life. On the other, she could not understand why her works should have to be read in the light of tragic events in her private life. In the letter to Borchers quoted previously she stressed: "I am also very familiar with the protective blanket one can pull over one's head when feeling exposed in a foreign country." Later statements about the background to her literary œuvre, which she preferred to couch in enigmatic terms or skillfully phrased reticences, must be interpreted in this context — as a means of protection against exposure.

At a time when Sachs had spent only a few years in Sweden, when she was still unknown save for the odd review here or there, she did, however, tell Walter A. Berendsohn at length about her years in Berlin. Among other things, she mentioned the tragic love of a seventeen-year-old girl for a (hitherto unknown) man — an acquaintance which, according to statements in letters, was resumed in the 1930s and lasted until the "holocaust years of the Hitler era." From the essay Berendsohn wrote on the basis of these statements — "Ekstatischer Aufstieg" (Ecstatic Ascent) — it emerges that the first meeting most likely occurred in 1908, probably during a stay at a spa in Bad Reinerz in Riesengebirge, possibly Marienbad, which ended in disaster. The young girl reacted with a refusal to eat so inconsolable that it required medical treatment. Police registration records show that she wasn't resident in Berlin from the end of April 1908 until October 1910. Most likely she was staying at a private clinic in Hagenstraße 43–47 in Grunewald which was run by a family friend, the psychiatrist and neurologist RICHARD CASSIRER (1868–1925). (At this time Grunewald was not yet part of the administrative district of Berlin.) The psychiatrist who feared that the unhappy girl would starve herself to death noted that he had never seen a case which more fully confirmed Heine's words in *Romanzero*: "And my tribe is the Asra / who die when they love." When the patient showed him some poems she had written, he advised her to continue writing. Perhaps poetry would prevail where medicine had failed. For the first time, writing became a matter of survival — or rather of living on — for Sachs.

8

9

**TEXT** Letter to Ilse and Moses Pergament 05/05/1960, APergament · For letter to Borchers 09/15/1959, see Briefe 150 · Letter to Berendsohn 09/07/1959, ABerendsohnD · BerendsohnE, 15 · The absence from Berlin is recorded in the Police Chief's Record of Conduct (*Führungszeugnis*) 08/01/1939, ASachs · Heine, "Der Asra," *Romanzero*, Hamburg 1851 | **IMAGE 7** Copy of Sachs' *Führungszeugnis* 08/01/1939 (KBS) · **8** Richard Cassirer, around 1910 (HUB) · **9** Hagenstraße 43–47 in Berlin-Grunewald in the 1930s (Museum Charlottenburg-Wilmersdorf, Berlin)

## ONCE UPON A TIME...

Sachs' experiences as a seventeen-year-old make up the original trauma of her life, perhaps also of her work. In the years that followed the crisis she wrote poems, prose stories, and pieces for puppet and marionette theater. Some texts dealt with unhappy love, but most of them subsumed the experiences in a general doctrine of melancholy and wounded innocence, of partings and tears. Extant works show a growing technical skill, particularly in terms of rhymes and meter, but few instances of stylistic individuality and even fewer of thematic originality. The title of an album from the 1930s, whose handwritten poems are decorated with dried flowers and ornamental drawings, roundly captures the world with which Sachs associated her writing well into maturity: "Unser Paradiesgärtlein mit Schwalbengezwitscher" (Our Little Garden of Paradise with Swallows Chirping).

The model for this pristine Eden is still on display in Frankfurt am Main. In the city museum there is a painting by an anonymous artist, executed around 1410 on a wooden panel measuring 26 by 33 centimeters, usually referred to as *Paradiesgärtlein* (The Little Garden of Paradise). In contrast with other pain-

10

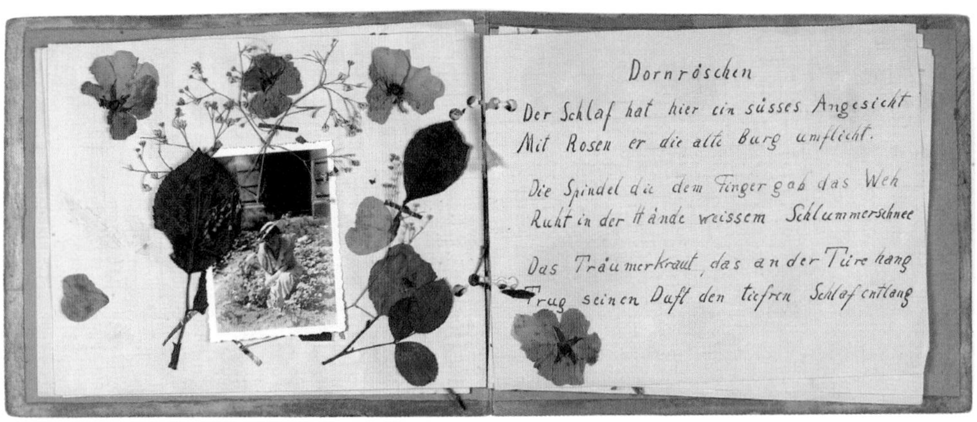
Dornröschen
Der Schlaf hat hier ein süsses Angesicht
Mit Rosen er die alte Burg umflicht.
Die Spindel die dem Finger gab das Weh
Ruht in der Hände weissem Schlummerschnee
Das Träumerkraut, das an der Türe hang
Trug seinen Duft den tiefen Schlaf entlang

11

tings on the same theme — Mary in the rose garden — the Virgin is not depicted in the middle of the image, but left-of-center and in the upper part of the painting, seated at a table with a plate, a glass, and some fruits. She is shown from the front, as convention required, but her head is turned downwards, her gaze avoiding the viewer. The reason is simple: in her hand the Virgin holds a book. She may still be in paradise, yet in her thoughts she is elsewhere. Even if it doesn't provide outright escape, reading offers a means of mental removal. The body inhabits the organic world of plants and animals, while the spirit dwells in the immaterial world of dreams and imagination. While Mary is absorbed by words, the saints pick cherries (Dorothy) or lean over a well symbolizing the source of life (Barbara). A third saint (Catharine) holds a psaltery whose strings the Infant touches. In front of the Archangel Michael, who according to tradition guards the entrance to Paradise, is a fettered monkey, while a small dead dragon lies at Saint George's feet. Evil has been vanquished, but traces of the intrusion remain. Behind the two male figures, Saint Oswald holds the trunk of a tree — perhaps it is that of knowledge. The painting was one of the earliest to depict flowers and herbs in a naturalistic manner. The same goes for the twelve birds around the fortified walls, symbolizing the twelve tribes of Israel and their dispersion around the globe.

Even if this anonymous *hortus conclusus* is displayed on a museum wall in Frankfurt, the question is whether for Sachs the original wasn't in fact located in the Prussian capital...

Following the wedding in 1890 of the thirty-two-year-old engineer GEORG WILLIAM SACHS (February 7, 1858–November 26, 1930) and his still teenage bride MARGARETE, née Karger (June 9, 1871–February 7, 1950), the family lived during the first few years after their daughter's birth at Maaßenstraße 12. The father was of Eastern Jewish, the mother of Western Jewish extraction. After a few years in the Schöneberg district, they moved to Bellevue in Tiergarten in 1894, an area which was becoming popular at that time with families of the upwardly mobile bourgeoisie, and which — as the lawyer Sammy Gronemann would later recall — became known as "the poor West" (*Nebbichwesten*) in popular Jewish parlance due to its location between the slums around Alexanderplatz to the east and the noble districts of Charlottenburg, Wilmersdorf, and Grunewald to the west. "In Berlin, Eastern Jew and Western Jew were not so much geographical as chronological concepts," Gronemann elaborated. "Quite often you would get Jews who had arrived from the east settling first in one of the above-mentioned streets [around Alexanderplatz] and eventually, after having achieved a certain prosperity, moving on to the more distinguished district of Bellevue, the upper-middle class area, and then, all the while climbing the social ladder, changing their address to Charlottenburg and becoming Western Jews."

For fifteen years the family lived at Lessingstraße 33 (today number 5). The

12

13

property which gave onto the Spree canal had a private garden that included a pavilion and a fountain. From the 1911 edition of the *Adreßbuch*, the family's home was given as Siegmundshof 16. At this time about 16,000 inhabitants of Jewish extraction were registered in Tiergarten, which was the equivalent of 5.5 percent of the district's population. The Sachs residence at Siegmundshof was a *bel étage* apartment with two drawing rooms (one red and one yellow), a study and a ladies' room, a loggia, and a glass-enclosed veranda. A few houses away lay a synagogue belonging to the orthodox congregation Adass Jisroel, but the Jewish families in the area were predominantly liberal-minded and belonged to the main congregation in Levetzowstraße on the other side of the canal. In later written recollections, the family's maid from 1929 until 1931, Lina Schubert (née Schoegel), noted that in addition to the many rooms and drawing rooms there was "a very spacious winter garden with many house limes and plants, an idyllic water grotto with a little fountain and goldfishes. Nelly very much liked to spend time there, planting new cuttings from the large house limes in pots and feeding the goldfish, etc."

The girl who grew up in protected *Nebbichwesten* was not wanting for much, perhaps only company. In particular, the garden at the back of the house was important. Its raked paths were edged by elder bushes, the lawn was decorated with flowerbeds of roses and tulips, and in one corner was an arbor where the nursemaid would sit. A gardener looked after the herb garden and vegetable patch, trees and shrubs provided shade as well as fruits and berries. For a time the girl kept a pair of white rabbits in a cage (they appear in the childhood account "Chelion" from the 1930s, as "Arabella" and "Prokop"), and there were other animals living at the back of the house as well. This was as close as one could get to a paradisiacal garden in the hectic city of stone and asphalt. Many years later, however, when Berendsohn wanted to summarize her childhood, Sachs would only let him use some rather elliptical statements: "Very lonely and introverted. Grew up with animals, deer, goat, dogs, given as company to the child by the very animal-loving father. At night in dreamed dance movements followed the exceptionally musical father's fantasies for piano. Thought out poems and stories in her mind. Had inherited this disposition from her mother. Exceedingly shy at school. Told no one about the secret writer notion. A gloom hovers over the teenage years. A fate befalls the seventeen-year-old and it lasted until the holocaust years of the Hitler era. Real source of her later writing."

From the legend-like description it emerges that Nelly's was a protected, not to say over-protected, childhood. For three years she attended the Dorotheen-Schule at the intersection of Wilhelmshavener Straße and Turmstraße in Moabit. Following two years' private tuition at home — likely administered by the strict "governess" who is said to have locked the girl in a closet when her parents were out for the night and who is called "Ulla" in "Chelion" — there were five years at Hélène Aubert's "higher school for girls" at Brückenallee 6. The secondary school lay a few minutes' walk from home and provided tuition in everything that was required of a housewife-to-be. From the autumn of 1905 until the following spring, however, Sachs was at a boarding school in the country, where her parents had sent her. Evidently she was not expected to become educated in any deeper sense during her formative years. Unsurprisingly, given her literary interests, she felt increasingly alien. In temperament, too, she differed from the other pupils, who were busy preparing themselves for their roles as housewives or society ladies. "Scared at school that it would show one was different," runs the description in the unpublished prose work "Briefe aus der Nacht" (Night Letters) from 1950–1953. Perhaps the pubescent pupil felt that she was different because of her background, or for other reasons; at the very least, she seems to have been afraid of being found out as a poet.

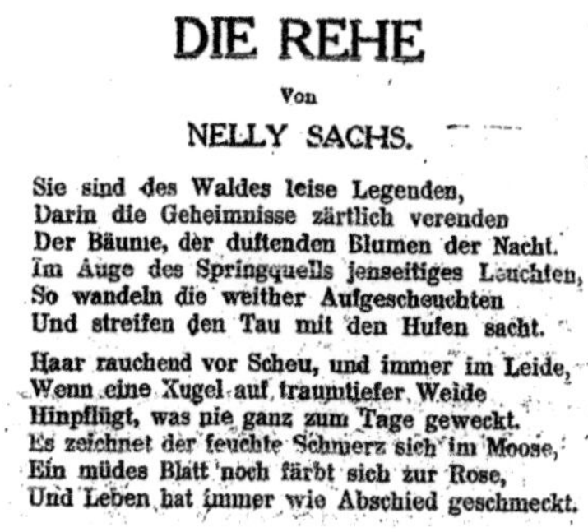
DIE REHE

Von

NELLY SACHS.

Sie sind des Waldes leise Legenden,
Darin die Geheimnisse zärtlich verenden
Der Bäume, der duftenden Blumen der Nacht.
Im Auge des Springquells jenseitiges Leuchten,
So wandeln die weither Aufgescheuchten
Und streifen den Tau mit den Hufen sacht.

Haar rauchend vor Scheu, und immer im Leide,
Wenn eine Kugel auf traumtiefer Weide
Hinpflügt, was nie ganz zum Tage geweckt.
Es zeichnet der feuchte Schmerz sich im Moose,
Ein müdes Blatt noch färbt sich zur Rose,
Und Leben hat immer wie Abschied geschmeckt.

14

As a teenager, too, Nelly appears to have had just about everything — except company. Her mother was busy with the home, her father with the business. That left the animals in the garden. The large apartment is reported to have had a library stocked with the usual classics, but also "a collection of the sacred texts of the world's peoples," as Sachs later told the journalist Egon Kötting, and which came to represent the collected wisdom of the world. If Margarete awakened an interest in poetry in the teenage Nelly, her father indulged in recreational music-making — "for the notes that Father plays are a rehearsal for the heavenly music," as "Chelion" has it, whose reminiscences appear to be of a childhood such as Sachs preferred to imagine it. And while she shared some of her mother's chores and danced to her father's piano pieces in the evening, she seems, like the Virgin in Frankfurt, to have preferred fleeing to literature — that secret realm of the lonely.

The poem "Die Rehe" (The Roe Deer) was first printed in the *Berliner Tageblatt* on February 26, 1933, but had been written many years earlier. The text is made up of two stanzas of verse rhymed in the style of the period (as with other early poems, it is reproduced here without rhyme and meter):

> They are the silent legends of the forest, / Where secrets end on a sensitive note / The legends of the woods, the night's scented flowers. / In the eye of the wellspring a light from beyond, / Thus they roam frightened from afar / Slowly stroking the dew with their hooves. // Fur steaming with fear, and always in danger, / When a bullet drawn dream-deep / Pierces what never had time to awaken — / Moist pain imprinted on the moss, / A tired leaf yet colored crimson, / And life has always tasted of parting.

During her Berlin years Sachs would write verse in this bittersweet vein. Even after her father's death from cancer in the late autumn of 1930, following many years' care at home, her poetry continued to feature deft rhymes set to comfortable meter. The picture of her childhood years which would later emerge

15

in letters to friends and acquaintances was similarly suffused with an idealized glow. And mythologized. Nonetheless, on closer reading, neither the private correspondence nor the poems written before the flight conjure up an intact world in which the clocks are frozen in the non-time of legends, despite a shedding of trees' leaves as abundant as that of the mourner's tears. Rather, Sachs made use of another convention: that of the threatened idyll. Her *hortus* was possibly still *conclusus*, but its walls were neither insurmountable nor impenetrable, its barriers far from safe. The innocent deer with their "fur steaming with fear" suffered in the knowledge of the impending danger. The future had nothing good in store. Even in the early texts, life bore the hue of parting. Existence consisted of leave-taking.

**TEXT** "Unser Paradiesgärtlein mit Schwalbengezwitscher," AWosk · Gronemann, "Erinnerungen," quoted in *Jüdisches Leben in Deutschland*, ed. Monika Richarz, Stuttgart 1979, 406 · Heinrich Silbergleit, "Zur Statistik der Jüdischen Bevölkerung Berlins," *Zeitschrift für Demographie und Statistik der Juden*, 1927, nos. 9–12, 134 · Schubert:1 · "Briefe aus der Nacht," NSW:IV · The quote from a conversation with Kötting in November 1958 appears in Dinesen, 35 · "Chelion," ASachs · BerendsohnE, 15 · "Die Rehe," FG, 246 | **IMAGE 10** The Sachs family in 1892 (DLA) · **11** "Unser Paradiesgärtlein mit Schwalbengezwitscher," poetry album (DLA) · **12** William Sachs in the early 1880s (DLA) · **13** Margarete Karger, married Sachs, in the late 1880s (DLA) · **14** "Die Rehe," Berliner Tageblatt, 02/26/1933

## MOTHER, FATHER, CHILD

The characteristics ascribed to her father by the adult daughter were classically patriarchal: he appeared strong, reliable, enterprising. Her mother's attributes were equally stereotyped: she was tender, loving, subservient. One might also say: granite and wave. Blazing will and docile emotion. Or, why not, *Eisbein mit Sauerkraut* and diet food with herbal extracts. But William Sachs' sense of beauty made him something more than a Prussian engineer "of the Mosaic faith" but no religiousness; and his wife's ironies made her something other than a pious woman of good family who turned wife and mother before she had time to become an adult. Some letters from the period before the marriage have been preserved, in which the future spouses flirt on the threshold of seriousness: "My sweet little you," William wrote in the summer of 1890, "you ask if I think of you, if I long for you?" There follows a poem which William hints is by his own hand:

> When quiet slumber / Has barely closed my eyes, / The image slowly slips / Into my dream. // But with the morning's dream / It never fades away: / For I bear it in my heart / Throughout the day.

"My dear little you," wrote the betrothed from the Pyrmont spa, "Barely have I received your letter, which made me happy to my heart, before I promptly sit down at my desk to speak with my little Willie." Delightedly she tells him that

16

17

she liked the story of an image saved by the dream and then borne in the heart all day. "You see, my treasure," she continued, "my senses are still the same in this prosaic life. Receptive to poetry, and yet it is remarkable that I prefer a certain Herr William Sachs' story to all others, even those of my Heine. Such are the changes that time brings." Margarete had identified the text as one of the songs from Heine's "Die Heimkehr."

The "prosaic life" which followed on the wedding was hardly devoid of poetry, even if what poetry there was seems to have been mostly of another sort than Heine's. Margarete was the fourth child of five of the merchant MENDEL MAX KARGER (1824–1876) and his wife FEODORA, née Meyer (1845–1896). Her father died when she was five years old. Both her mother and her mother's mother, AMALIE MEYER, née Lessing (1825–1912), were alive fifteen years later when Margarete had her only child. Having previously been living next to her daughter, Amalie now moved in with the young family. There is reason to assume, then, as the biographer Gabriele Fritsch-Vivié does, that Nelly's first years were spent in an environment shaped by three generations of women, with the concomitant continuity and identification. And that men, conspicuous mostly by their absence, belonged to a world beyond the walls of the home.

18

William was the oldest child of ADOLF SACHS (1827–1911), a manufacturer of Eastern Jewish origin who in 1868 had founded "A. Sachs, Rubber and Gutta-Percha Products" at Leipziger Straße 33 in the Jewish textile quarter. His son trained as an engineer and entered the firm early, helping to expand it with his business sense and inventiveness. The firm's last year at number 33 on Leipziger Straße was 1907; in the 1918 edition of the *Adreßbuch* it is listed a few buildings farther along the street, at number 51 near the distinguished Dönhoff-Platz. William, however, had gone independent already in 1894/1895 by founding "A. Sachs & Sons, Rubber Products Manufacturer" with headquarters at Lessingstraße 33. The building belonged to the Karger family and had been transferred to Margarete a few years previously — possibly as a dowry. In 1907 William's youngest brother ALFRED (1863–1942) opened a branch around the corner, at Bachstraße 2, while one of the two middle brothers, RICHARD (1859–1932/1933), took over their father's firm after his death in 1911. The other middle brother, ALEXIS (1862–1924/1926), was a part-owner for a long time. The selection of goods included everything from raincoats of crude rubber and shoe soles of gutta-percha to advanced medical and technical instruments. With time the family became known as the "Rubber Sachses" of Berlin.

**TEXT** Letter from William Sachs 07/06/1890, reply from Margarete Karger 07/07/1890, AWosk · Heine, "Wenn ich auf dem Lager liege," *Buch der Lieder*, Hamburg 1827 · Fritsch-Vivié, 20 · Address books from Berlin | **IMAGE** **15** Father's monthly tram pass, 1901 (KBS) · **16** "A. Sachs, Gummi- und Guttaperchawaren" in Leipziger Straße, 1934 (Photo A. Vennemann) · **17** William Sachs x 3, 1920s (KBS) · **18** Nelly Sachs, late 1890s (DLA) · **19** William Sachs with roe deer, around 1900 (DLA)

19

20

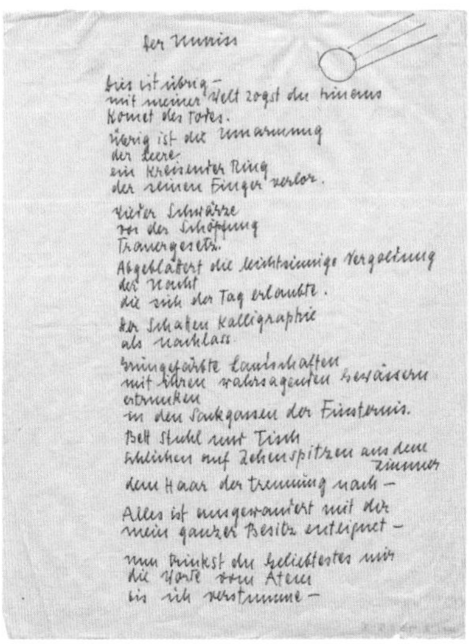
Der Umriss

Dies ist übrig –
mit meiner Welt zogst du hinaus
Komet des Todes.
Übrig ist die Umarmung
der Leere
ein kreisender Ring
der seinen Finger verlor.

Vieler Schwärze
vor der Schöpfung
Trauergesetz.
Abgeblättert die leichtsinnige Vergoldung
der Nacht
die sich der Tag erlaubte.

Der Schatten Kalligraphie
als Nachlass.

Tränengefärbte Landschaften
mit ihren wahrsagenden Gewässern
ertrunken
in den Sackgassen der Finsternis.

Bett Stuhl und Tisch
schleichen auf Zehenspitzen aus dem Zimmer
dem Haar der Trennung nach –

Alles ist ausgewandert mit dir
mein ganzer Besitz enteignet –

nun trinkst du Geliebtester mir
die Worte vom Atem
bis ich verstumme –

21

## THE CALLIGRAPHY OF SHADOWS

Many years after her parents' death, during the difficult year of 1960, Sachs wrote a poem about remains, which was given the title "Der Umriß" (The Outline). The first stanza reads:

> This remains — / with my world you departed / comet of death. / What remains is emptiness' / embrace / the circle of the ring / which has lost its finger.

In the upper right-hand corner of the manuscript she drew a circle with three rays extending at an angle up towards the right. It is clearly a depiction of a comet (or as it is also known in German, a *Haarstern*, a "hair star"). Each of the final three stanzas ends with a dash — as if the punctuation were imitating the celestial body's fringed tail:

> Bed chair and table / steal on tiptoe from the room / behind the hair of parting — // Everything went with you / all I possessed was seized — // only you my beloved / drink the words from my breath / until I am struck dumb —

Possibly the poem is about the man Sachs had purportedly met again towards the middle of the 1930s and who had died during the war. But it is more likely to be about her mother, whom she often described as her "most beloved." Indeed, Sachs used her mother's wedding ring to draw the circle. The finger that once bore it may have been "lost." Everything the narrator "possessed" may have been seized. Loss and absence may be the only things that remain when one's breath had been emptied even of words. For the poem, that is, all that remained was to embrace the emptiness left over — an "outline" as fine as a strand of hair, black and elusive. Or as the text has it: "The calligraphy of shadows / as legacy."

**TEXT** "Der Umriß," FiS (NSW:II) · For the information on the poem's date of origin, see Lennartsson, 65 | **IMAGE 20** Sachs' parents' wedding rings (JMB) · **21** "Der Umriß," typescript (KBS)

## RAPTURE AND DISTRESS

The seventeen-year-old who fell in love with a (married? older? perhaps homosexual?) man was enraptured. "Love pulled her along like an overpowering force of nature," her friend Bengt Holmqvist wrote some time after the Nobel Prize in an essay based on extensive conversations with Sachs. It "permeated her whole being, and seemed — in an irresistible, joyful ecstasy — to 'break through the prison walls.'"

The quoted expression suggests a view of loveless existence as a prison from which the young woman tried to break free. The word *Kerker* (prison) occurs only once in Sachs' poetry, in *Flucht und Verwandlung* (Flight and Metamorphosis) from 1959, where the poem "Schlaf webt das Atemnetz" (Sleep Weaves the Net of Breathing) depicts a related context:

> Sleep weaves the net of breathing / holy script / but no one here can read / except the lovers / who flee out / through the nights' singing / swirling prisons

For a teenager who saw love as both a force of nature and a liberation, who demanded that devotion be absolute, being abandoned triggered a shock. The young Nelly reacted forcefully. She stopped eating, refused sustenance, became increasingly thin. What remained when the beloved one had abandoned her? Perhaps an outline.

"Only after a prolonged crisis," Holmqvist remarks, did she decide "not to choose Karoline von Günderrode's path (Bettina von Arnim's epistolary novel was one of her favorite books). She lived on in a state of deepened loneliness, with a reinforced sense of being different; but, at the same time, in the unforgettable experience of love — even 'hopeless' love — as a mighty, all-transforming force." This love disaster was so earth-shattering that it would give rise to aftershocks more than half a century later... During and after the acute crisis of 1908–1910 writing came to play an important role, perhaps the most important of all. Where both parents and psychiatrist failed, words worked. Possibly because poetry could formulate love without replacing it. Possibly because poetry was loyal to both the beloved and the loss of him. Possibly because it was capable of depicting the very emptiness itself. It would be some time, however, before words had more than a therapeutic function. In younger years Sachs still used conventional imagery in which personal experiences were given a universal form. Romantic poetry provided the necessary trappings — tried and tested images or symbols with whose help she could render emotions in a way that made them comprehensible and therefore interchangeable. Thus her fate was made a little less unique, she was made a little less alone. The person who wrote poetry about partings and tears was seeking "an explanation, a world view, in which her lot could be seen as something more than utterly meaningless," opines Holmqvist, seconded by Sachs. As yet her will to understand was greater than the will to grasp — or "embrace" — emptiness.

It wasn't until many years later that Sachs would find a language which didn't erase the irreplaceable experience — an idiom of devotion that didn't limit itself to illustrating the great themes of poetry (Love, Death, Longing) but tried to present them in exemplary fashion. The distress of the seventeen-year-old at being abandoned was still there, like a wound waiting to become "readable," as the late poem "Immer wieder neue Sintflut" (Always a New Deluge) would put it. When, later in life, Sachs spoke about the source of her poetry she would almost always invoke this early trauma, but she would also cloak it in vagueness. "As the source of my endeavor, to take on poetically our people's greatest tragedy," she remarked, for example, in a letter to Berendsohn, "suffice it to hint at a personal fate which in the Hitler years led to a martyrdom. Everything else should and must be allowed to remain in obscurity." Her fate should appear, but only in hints and suggestions — everything else must stand aside for the poetic statement. That was the only way to make the wound readable, as a pain whose inaccessible source carried on throbbing, like background radiation. The distress never ended, it merely took on other forms.

This strategy of simultaneously indicating and withholding was applied in several respects. When, after the war, Sachs wrote about "Israel's body" in what is arguably her most famous poem, "O die Schornsteine" (O the Chimneys), she was turning to readers prepared to engage with the text. A handful of suggestive indications must suffice, the rest was down to empathy. The representativeness that her poetry shows particularly in the first collections, *In den Wohnungen des Todes* (In the Dwellings of Death, 1947) and *Sternverdunkelung* (Star Eclipse, 1949), has to do with this effort to include the reader. To be sure, the ambitions are soaring, and there is reason to ask how a survivor is ever going to be able to share the fate of the victims. But Sachs' poetic voice did not primarily want to speak for the suffering and deaths of six million people, which is how her work has typically been interpreted. Hers was a poetry, rather, that wanted to make the reader internalize the inconceivable pain. Even if the damage could not be undone, the wound had to be made "readable." This required a feeling for that which defied comprehension as well. Emptiness had to be given an outline.

22

It is as if Sachs sensed a difference between two ways of approaching a text: the interpreter's and the reader's. Where the former sought an underlying basis that might explain the trauma, the latter was concerned with its consequences and the fact that explanations alone were never enough. That made love the natural ally of sorrow. For Sachs, ultimately, only those who love would seem to be true readers. Less curious than attentive, they seek to "flee out" to the place where existence is readable if not comprehensible. They wish to make themselves at home in an Outer region which can never be fully embraced by the intellect, but where loneliness, night and death do not hold them back either.

**TEXT** Holmqvist, 27 · "Schlaf webt das Atemnetz," FuV (NSW:II) · Letter to Berendsohn 09/07/1959, ABerendsohnD · "Immer wieder neue Sintflut" (NSW:II) · "O die Schornsteine," IdWdT (NSW:I) | **IMAGE 22** Nelly Sachs in her late teens (DLA)

## PRACTICE MAKES PERFECT

Among William Sachs' inventions were some that would contribute to developing the nascent area of aviation, but also a prize-winning "muscle strengthener" which was patented on October 25, 1887, and sold to princes, noblemen and generals, ministers and bankers. Made up of a pair of wooden handles, a set of elastic cords and various hooks and rubber rings, the instrument could be ordered for 24 marks from the branch on Leipziger Straße 33. ("Ensure upon purchase that each rubber cord bears the imprint of German Reichspatent.") If the customer paid an additional reichsmark, he would also receive a brochure with thirty illustrations entitled *Die Heilgymnastik im Hause für Gesunde und Kranke* (Remedial Exercises at Home for the Healthy and the Ill), in which the inventor expounded the advantages of indoor gymnastics and provided detailed instructions for using the instrument for the purpose of "maintaining and improving health, as well as curing illnesses." (The brochure does not state a year of publication, but considering the ordering address it was probably published before the branch disappeared from Leipziger Straße 33 in the 1908 edition of the *Adreßbuch*.)

The general description of muscle-strengthening instruments included with the patent explained why Sachs' invention would last. The number of rubber cords could be varied, which meant that the "strength levels" could be adapted to the user's age and individual strength. In other words: unlike other instruments available on the market, Sachs' invention could be used by both men and women.

In his instructions the inventor — who when he wasn't riding or working on new patents was partial to playing the piano for his dancing daughter — emphasized that "only movement in life preserves life." Lack of mobility would inevitably lead to bodily dysfunction. Internal organs would lose their vigor, diseases appear, premature death could no longer be excluded. The advances in the area of physiotherapy made possible by the instrument had a clear advantage over dumbbells, wall bars, and medicine balls: "the majority of currently common gymnastic exercises merely allow the force of gravity to act on the bodily part in question, *consequently they do not fulfill the very important function of making the body sound and strong*. Physiotherapy requires the body to provide only so much power *as it can use to strengthen its muscles, without excessively stimulating or straining the nervous system*." Eventually Sachs' invention would become known as "the Expander" — a name which suggested both that the instrument was based on stretching movements and that regular use of it would increase the body's strength and reach.

Modern man's sedentary way of life and spiritual duties, in conjunction with an overly rich diet, led unavoidably to headaches, migraines, constipation, loss of appetite, and bouts of insomnia. But it could also result in "hypogastric suffering, hypochondria, hysteria, and melancholia, as well as low spirits and general discontentment." It is not known whether the inventor advised his unhappy daughter to use the instrument which should "not be lacking in any family or school." But if Nelly did use it, the first of the thirty-five suggested exercises may have been employed: "Grasp the instrument with both hands, as shown in the figure, and hold both arms stiffly outstretched in front of you, at chest height. Attempt to stretch the rubber cords, making use of all your muscle power. When the elasticity of the wires has been overcome, allow them

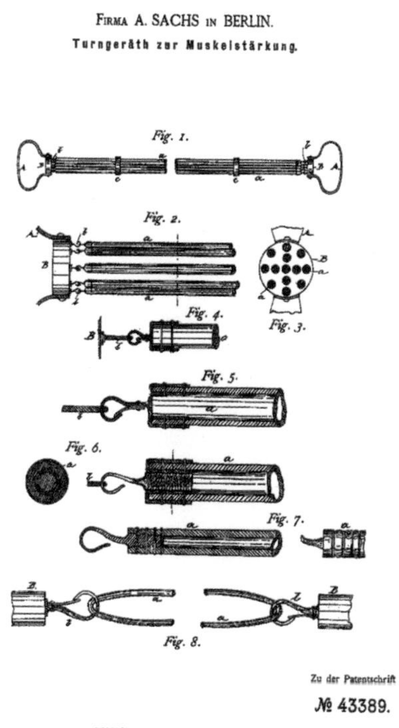


23

to return to their original position of their own contractive power by means of a gradual relaxation of the tensed muscle power and by allowing the hand to follow the movement with less resistance. Repeat this exercise 5 to 10 times, breathing deeply and forcefully in the process."

The exercise — which was said to be especially effective in cases of "muscular and nervous debility" — is unlikely to have been anything beyond a limited success with the inventor's lovesick daughter, but her later works show that stretching survived as a poetic principle. Lines and cords appear repeatedly in her texts, just as do the expansive veins and arteries of language. Strands of hair are the connecting links between Here and Beyond, washing lines can be turned into meridians and latitudes. In the 1950s Sachs' use of dashes increased dramatically as well, as if she wanted to set her entire poetry asway. In *Flucht und Verwandlung*, for example, this punctuation mark replaced almost all others. (Only two full stops survived in print, which may have been due to an oversight.) And in the dramatic poem *Beryll sieht in der Nacht* (Beryll Sees in the Night) from her last decade, one stage direction reads: "On the horizon the ark appears out of the mist, bearing the survivors of the final deluge. The image becomes gradually clearer. One sees: the ark is breathing, like a black lung cut out of the night."

Here the desire to break through to another dimension appears to have been accomplished. On the other side of the deluge a new world begins. Made of night and past, the vessel of creation is turned into a gigantic lung. At last, William Sachs' Expander had achieved cosmic proportions.

**TEXT** "Turngeräth zur Muskelstärkung," Kaiserliches Patentamt, Patentschrift Nr. 43389, Klasse 77: Sport, ausgegeben den 31. 5. 1888 · SachsW, 3, 3–4, 4–5, and 3, AWosk · *Beryll sieht in der Nacht*, ZiS (NSW:III) | **IMAGE 23** "Turngeräth zur Muskelstärkung," 1888 (DPMA) · **24** Illustrations from William Sachs, *Die Heilgymnastik im Hause* n.d. (DLA)

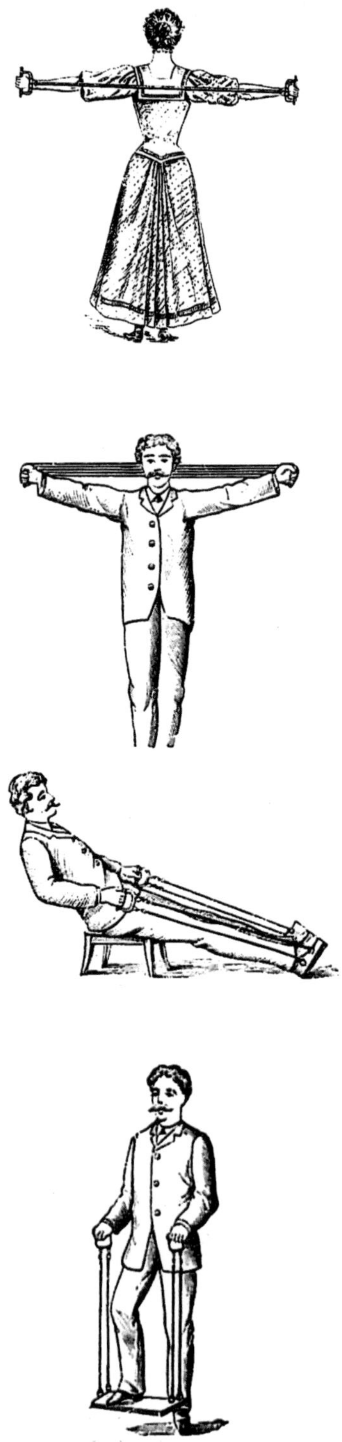

24

## THE COLOR OF PARTING

If the muscle-strengthening instrument — notwithstanding some success among hale housewives and sporty secretaries — belonged primarily in the masculine sphere of interest, there were other objects in Sachs' life which were explicitly affiliated with the female sphere. Among these was the so-called *Oblatenalbum* (scrapbook) which had belonged to her maternal grandmother and whose sentimental value was such that it was packed into the medium-sized brown suitcase that mother and daughter brought with them on their flight from Germany. In her younger years Nelly liked to leaf through the scrapbook pictures, which featured everything from rosy-cheeked children, noble soldiers, and nubile ladies to scenes out of the brothers Grimm and escutcheons from glorious German principalities of yore. Flower arrangements were juxtaposed with bottles of mineral water, birds with fishes. Playing cards were stuck in alongside initials, spirits from fables rubbed shoulders with putti. In one image Snow White lies in a glass coffin, in a couple of others Friday kneels before Robinson Crusoe and the dashing prince before Sleeping Beauty. Sachs is said later to have added new pictures to the collection, and she also wrote a verse picture book, "Auf ein altes Oblatenalbum" (To an Old Scrapbook), in which several of the scenes described were reproduced: dwarves and merry-go-rounds at fairs, puppet shows, tightrope walkers …

The prose story "Chelion" — which Sachs presented at a soirée held on the premises of the Jewish Women's Association in 1937 — describes a childhood which has much in common with her own. The title is an almost perfect anagram of her parents' pet name for their daughter — "Lichen" for Leonie — and the unpublished, 72-page typed manuscript contains several elements and themes that coincide with the family's actual circumstances. For example, the young protagonist's birthday is just before Christmas, the father's dog has the same name as William Sachs' St. Bernard ("Flock"), and the house with the leafy garden is only a stone's throw from the S-Bahn tracks, under whose arches — in Flensburger Straße — Jant the fishmonger has his stand.

Characterized by the same "painful color of parting" that emerges from Sachs' accounts of her own childhood, the text describes Chelion as an anxious girl afraid of many things in life, particularly of being abandoned. She asks the maid, Sophie, not to grind the spices to be used in the evening meal — "chervil, anise, and marjoram" — because they seem to be sighing and moaning and are perhaps dying. ("No need to worry, Chelion, spices have no feelings.") During a visit to the covered market with another maid, Magda, she kisses a fish the fishwife is about to kill. ("Is it in heaven now, the child asks in a trembling voice. I don't know, Magda says hesitantly, the lady put it in her bag.") Wandering through a Christmas market with her parents, the girl sees something gray and downy in the hands of a man — a bird. "Why does it have to die, the child asks as tears roll down her cheeks."

Although Chelion lives in a paradise, nothing is permanent, everything is ephemeral — herbs, fishes, birds. The color of imminent parting stains every action. Only the dream-world of fairy tales offers the promise of time reliably stopped in its tracks. This becomes particularly clear in the section headed "Das Oblatenalbum" (The Scrapbook). Here, a red scrapbook in which small pictures with captions have been pasted is at the center of events. Chelion is leafing through it together with her nursemaid, Teresa. "Now there is no place on earth that Chelion likes better to visit than the light green meadows of scrapbook pictures." Teresa explains what the pictures are of. Look, that's where Sleeping Beauty pricks her finger on the spindle. See, that's where the rose bushes grow up around the tower. "Spindle, Chelion thinks, and for her it is as if this word came steaming like a ship from foreign lands, with a cargo of fairies' veils." The scrapbook pictures have magical qualities. Perusing them doesn't just

25

conjure up another world, but transports the child to another dimension, free from partings. It may be that Snow White eats the poisoned apple and is placed in a glass coffin, but the girl already knows that the handsome prince will one day kiss her awake. Perhaps Sleeping Beauty will slumber for a hundred years, but on another page of the calendar she wakes up. In contrast with the transience in Chelion's world, that of the scrapbook is merely temporary.

The nursemaid, for her part, is reminded of her rural roots, which she had to leave in order to earn her keep in the city. The region she comes from also has green meadows and cottages and playing children. When she describes how on seeing the scrapbook pictures it is as if this lost world were once again before her eyes, Chelion climbs into her lap in order to see the cows mooing in her pupils. "It's only an expression," Teresa explains, laughing, "the little garden doesn't stick in your eyes, either, even though you play there every day." But the child insists. Even if the visions are transitory, they do have to re-create the world and therefore remain somewhere. She now begs Teresa at least to say that the meadows where she comes from are as green as those in the pictures, that the children wear the same flower garlands, and that the kitchen hand doffs his white cap when he collects the hens' eggs. No, no, the nursemaid replies, it's not like that. The meadows where she comes from are neither magically green nor do they glimmer as in a fairy tale. The child objects: "'But I once dreamt of a such a green meadow, Teresa, a boy with golden locks was walking across it, he was called Hellmut.' 'Yes, in dreams you may have seen something similar, but in reality it doesn't exist, I at least have never seen it.'"

It would be hard to claim that the critic identified as "t.," who reviewed the soirée for the *Jüdischer Rundschau* in 1937 and dismissed Sachs' lyrical prose tale as "schmaltzy children's emotions," misjudged the tenor of the text. Even if it is stuffed with clichés and some scenes appear borrowed from a rose-tinted *Heinrich von Ofterdingen*, even if the metaphors belong in pulp novels and the tone is sweet bordering on saccharine, the story still formulates a belief in the distinctiveness of literature which Sachs would maintain and which would soon enough receive a more ominous treatment. Poetry could not save what had been lost, but it might invoke the loss. "Words are evening," she writes in "Gebete" (Prayers), which began the cycle entitled "Leise Melodie" (Quiet Melody) from the early 1930s. If the yellow and red autumn leaves, the many tears and dusky moods in Sachs' first works had any purpose beyond confirming her familiarity with outmoded conventions, it was to testify to literature's secret pact with transience. Every invocation of presence was in fact a veiled farewell.

**TEXT** "Chelion," and "Leise Melodie," ASachs · "Auf ein altes Oblatenalbum," ADähnert:I · The signature "t.," "Rezitationsabend," *Jüdische Rundschau*, no. 74, 09/17/1937 | **IMAGE 25** Scrapbook pictures from "Das Oblatenalbum" (KBS)

## ETHEREAL MUSIC SET TO A MECHANICAL MELODY

"To travel with one's father," Sachs writes in "Chelion," "means a great deal to a little girl." Suddenly one's bodice is put on back to front, and furthermore seems to have gained a few buttons too many. One's hair can be worn loose, since a father's hand is too gentle to want to braid it. "O Chelion, little bird! You are allowed to pick at the adults' meals, to chirp in sweet summer serenity and to dance the bowing branches' dance under the shady willows."

26

The travelers visit a castle whose gates are opened by an elderly man with a raven on his shoulder. The place is old and decrepit and reminds the narrator of the sunken city of Vineta. The castellan, who goes by the name of Reinhold, takes the visitors to a pavilion in which a ticking can be heard — incessantly and from everywhere. It emerges that the pavilion contains instruments in which time and music are sleeping. "And he takes a tiny pink box with a picture of a child and lambs on it and begins to touch it with his fingers. Lo and behold, it begins to sing ever so beautifully and softly, it is the music of fairies which may be captured in it." On seeing the magical music box from whose interior ethereal music emanates, Chelion is transformed. "She is like a delightful flower that opens its whorl, swathed in dreams. Chelion has become a butterfly, in order to greet it."

Sachs herself could hear similar music when she opened the lid of yet another object which was packed into the brown suitcase: a music box made of dark wood and measuring 11.6 × 8 × 6.3 centimeters. The metal cylinder is sunk into the base; on the inside the following stanza is inscribed: "Go clad in the lily robes of innocence / crowned by earthly joy / And when you take pleasure in happiness / Think again of me at times." The music box had belonged to her father. On the inside of the lid is a picture of a young woman kneeling, wearing a white dress with a red bodice. The dress, the dark hair, and the red cheeks bring Snow White to mind. The woman is surrounded by flowers in large pots and holds her hands up like a Virgin. But the annunciation she is receiving is not the archangel Gabriel's message that she will bear the son of God, it is the music produced by the steel comb and the pins rotating at the bottom of the box. Possessed by the music, she too opens up like the chalice into which Chelion was transformed.

Among Sachs' early poems is one entitled "Eine alte Spieluhr spielt Menuett as Don Juan" (An Old Music Box Plays the Minuet from Don Giovanni), which was published in the periodical *Der Morgen* in January 1937, a couple of months before she read from her childhood account at the Jewish Women's Association. It is not about her father's music box but about another one, owned by his youngest brother Alfred who, according to a letter to Emilia Fogelklou-Norlind from the early 1940s, used to play it for his niece:

The notes play as in the evening's glow / Distant dream of an old dolls' game! / The pageboys cradle a rose stalk, / Banners ruffle and stream in the wind. // Puddles giggle and are gone. / Pause. When a rose petal fell, / Notes haunt a distant goal, / Aloft, they look like tears.

**Nelly Sachs:**

***Eine alte Spieluhr spielt Menuett aus Don Juan***

Wie im Abendschein die Töne gehn,
Fern im Traum, ein altes Puppenspiel!
Pagen halten einen Rosenstiel,
Windgekräuselte Standarten wehn.

Kleine Wasser kichern und vergehn.
Pause. Wenn ein Rosenblatt entfiel,
Töne geistern in ein fernes Ziel,
In den Lüften sie gleich Tränen stehn.

27

This is the soundtrack of the young Sachs' doctrine of parting. As the transient art form par excellence, music seemed fairy-like because it lacked substance. Each note perished the moment it was struck, each *gehn* (goes) was a *vergehn* (goes under) in disguise. But the ethereal tones remained a thing for fairy tales and legends, whose verses brought tears to the eyes. The metal cylinder with its carefully placed pins guaranteed that the melody would always sound — like a reminder of itself — and the memory of Autumn, Love, and Music thus remain immaculate. (There is still some distance to go to Baudelaire's anguish: "How piercing is not the dusk of autumn's days! O, piercing to the edge of pain!") In "Chelion," Reinhold finally puts "the old music box back in its place; the music in it has once again fallen into slumber." The recollections aroused by the melody have scattered. Yet it is enough to open the lid again for distant dreams to stir. In Sachs' old music box, innumerable sweet farewells slumber. It wasn't until after the war that she stopped popping it open.

**TEXT** "Chelion," ASachs · For the letter to Fogelklou-Norlind 07/18/1943, see Briefe 13 · "Eine alte Spieluhr spielt Menuett aus Don Juan," FG, 246 · Baudelaire, "Le Confiteor de l'artiste," *Le Spleen de Paris* (posthumously 1869), *Œuvres complètes*, ed. Claude Pichois, Paris 1975, vol. I, 278 | **IMAGE 26** William Sachs' music box (Catharina Engström's collection, Stockholm) · **27** "Eine alte Spieluhr spielt Menuett aus Don Juan," *Der Morgen*, 1937, no. 10, 459 (CM)

## NEVERMORE

The clearest expression of Sachs' belief in literature's bond with transience occurs in one of the last scenes in "Chelion." The protagonist is making tissue-paper roses together with Miss Ulla and her friend Ännchen. Ännchen has just bought a school copybook that came with some free scrapbook pictures. The girls are looking at the pictures. One is of a swallow with a rosemary twig in its beak, the other of an islet in the sea. Both bear captions in a foreign language none of them understand. Beneath the swallow is the word *Farewell*, beneath the islet *Nevermore*. Henceforth Chelion will "always in *Farewell* see a swallow flying with a rosemary twig in its beak, but in *Nevermore* she will gaze upon a gloomy moorland full of thistles and frozen rush and waves beating against the reef." If the former statement holds out the promise of future reunion, the latter confirms the definitive goodbye. In compressed form, the distinction reflects the difference between Sachs' early and late works. The texts written before her enforced emigration in 1940 may depict the passing of time with the help of moldering leaves and lines of swallows crossing the sky, but this is a transience marked by repetition. In Sachs' early poetry each autumn reinvents the end. After seven and a half years of "living under threat," as she would later describe life in the Third Reich, precious little of this credence remained. *Nevermore* had replaced *Farewell.*

The famous leitmotif from Poe's poem "The Raven" reappears in one other place in the œuvre. The dramatic poem *Versteckspiel mit Emanuel* (Hide and Seek with Emanuel), a "delirium of loneliness" from 1955, depicts the lonely Marie's longing for her youthful love who went to sea and never returned. She hears roaring in the water pipes and murmuring in the kitchen cupboards. She wonders if her beloved went "out with Ännchen in the martyr light" and begins to search behind the furniture. ("Wait — wait — perhaps behind the cupboard?") Increasingly confused, she bangs the doors and finally takes her own shadow for a "catfish" which she tries to catch:

28

> Whistle then, whistle — A creaking — at the top of the mast — hear it creaking — Hoist my chest oh how it stings — The salty breeze — no I don't put salt on my egg — Sssssss — Nevermore — and an eagle in a storm with its nest in its beak — exile — sea flight — roar flight —

Sssssss … *Nevermore* is the refugees' secret scrapbook picture.

**TEXT** "Chelion," ASachs · "Leben unter Bedrohung," NSW:IV · Poe, *The Complete Tales and Poems*, New York 1975, 943–946 · *Versteckspiel mit Emanuel*, ZiS (NSW:III) | **IMAGE 28** Scrapbook picture from "Das Oblatenalbum" (KBS)

## BAPTISM CERTIFICATES

Baptism certificates come in many forms. Those issued to writers are usually different from those that parents of newborns pick up at the registry office or from Jewish congregations. The facts of the present case: Sachs was issued her first certificate as an infant, her second thirty years later.

29

With her debut, *Legenden und Erzählungen* (Legends and Tales), the unoriginal phase of Sachs' œuvre culminated. The book was published in 1921, shortly before Sachs' thirtieth birthday, in a small edition by the practically unknown F. W. Mayer Verlag in Berlin (only two other titles have been confirmed: one Luise Tuckermann's *Gedichte* [Poems], and *Weihnachtsgedichte* [Christmas Poems], both from 1933). The book comprises six "legends" and half that number of "tales," which according to Sachs were partly written before the First World War and which testify to her admiration for Selma Lagerlöf. However, the *lieder* of the romantics as well as church legends also glitter beneath these sonorous wefts, confirming the writer's interest in German popular and chivalrous poetry — in Novalis, Tieck, and the brothers Grimm as well as later followers such as Mörike and Stifter. The tone hovers somewhere between myth and daydream. The props are symbolical, the action always fateful.

BREFKORT
CARTE POSTALE
PLATS FÖR SKRIFTLIGT MEDDELANDE
ADRESSEN ANB
SVERIGE
KUNGLPOST
20 öre
Fräulein Nelly Sachs
Schriftstellerin
Siegmundshof 16
Berlin

30

The mystically oriented love gospel that pervades the texts — and which has more to do with Christian edification literature than with Kurt Tucholsky's *Träumereien an preußischen Kaminen* (Reveries by Prussian Hearths) or Walter Benjamin's "Schicksal und Charakter" (Destiny and Character), to mention just two works by more or less contemporary Berliners published at around the same time — is most easily captured by means of the two quotations that frame the texts.

The first legend about the monk and Renaissance painter Fra Angelico takes its motto from Angelus Silesius' *Der cherubinische Wandersmann* (The Cherubinic Wanderer): "I know the image of God: his reflection he has etched / On all his creations, and you can recognize him there." Among the books Sachs left behind is an edition of the text much cherished by the romantics and cultically revered by pious readers. No year of publication is given, but a bibliographic examination reveals that it was published in 1913, as number 41 of the Insel publishing house's *Bücherei*. While the motto in Sachs' text could of course have been added at an earlier date, it does seem to suggest — as the biographer Ruth Dinesen has pointed out — that she most likely did not write the legend about the Dominican before the First World War. Later statements by Sachs, in letters to her publisher Siegfried Unseld for example, claiming that her first book contained "the schoolgirl legends of a fifteen-year-old" and "child works," may at any rate be regarded as somewhat bold in chronological terms . . .

If Sachs' debut opens with one of Silesius' famous alexandrines which emphasizes the divine imprint on creation, the final tale closes with a quotation no less well known. The story is devoted to the captive Silenus (the nominal similarity with the mystic from Silesia is unlikely to be incidental). A son of the poet-god Hermes and a nymph, Silenus was a therianthropic being, equal parts man and horse. Sachs rounded her text off with three words also quoted in *Gösta Berling's Saga*, which she had been given a German translation of on her fifteenth birthday: *Amor vincit omnia*. The rearranged words from Virgil's *Ecologae* x:69 are missing the conclusion *et nos cedamus amori* ("Love conquers all, so let us be conquered by love"), but for anyone acquainted with the young writer's tales there could be no doubt about the message. In contrast with Lagerlöf's novel, where the motto has an ironic lining, Sachs' use of it illustrates the conviction that a human being, in particular a woman, could only fulfill her (innate) mission in life by submitting to the dictates of love. Most of the texts in the debut deal with this heavily idealized mission. By shifting between the dealings between good and evil on the one hand, and the relationship between man and woman on the other, they seek to avert the alarming energies of sexuality with the help of the self-sacrificing love of God's "creations."

In November 1921 the author sent a copy of the book to her paragon. A few days later she received a postcard in reply, on which the Nobel laureate admit-

ted that she "couldn't have done it any better myself." It is uncertain whether the recipient caught the subtle irony. Many years later, in the earliest preserved letter to Berendsohn, Sachs declared the postcard her "treasure." But Lagerlöf's ambiguous kindness was unlikely the only reason she kept the eventually well-thumbed prize for the rest of her life. The postcard's address amounted to nothing less than a second baptism certificate: "Miss Nelly Sachs, Writer, Siegmundshof 16, Berlin." The Swedish writer had acknowledged the Berliner as a colleague. The title baptized Sachs a second time. From now on she could call herself *Schriftstellerin*.

**TEXT** LuE · *Aus des Angelus Silesius cherubinischem Wandersmann*, Leipzig n.d. (1913) · DinesenU, 107, footnote 22 · Letters to Unseld 03/15 and 04/27/1963, ASachs · Postcard from Lagerlöf 12/05/1921, AWosk · For letter to Berendsohn 09/12/1944, see Briefe 22 | **IMAGE 29** Nelly Sachs, *Legenden und Erzählungen* 1921 · **30** Postcard from Selma Lagerlöf, 1921 (DLA) · **31** "Das Oblatenalbum" (KBS)

## THREE SISTERS

The childhood conjured up in "Chelion" was no intact world. The main character appears innocent, but is everywhere reminded of the transience of life. Bittersweet or terrifying: for one who had learned to read it, doom was written on every petal and castle wall. After her mother's death in 1950 Sachs would speak more frankly about her childhood in the prose text "Briefe aus der Nacht." A note made in February 1951, for example, reads: "The little hell of the child's loneliness. The night's golden innards. These round suns with the black crosses. These horrific preparations for life's deathblow." The final sentence is characteristic: life is seen as a preparation for death. From the outset, existence is marked by the wound of finitude.

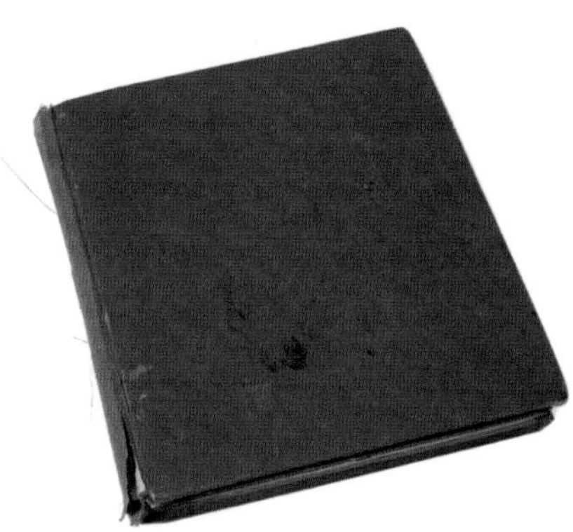

Not much is known about Sachs' early years. Her parents never had any more children. Possibly the extrovert father sought liaisons elsewhere, while the introvert mother found intimacy and support with her daughter and her own mother. But even if Nelly grew up as the over-protected child in a sibling-less home in Bellevue, and even if she seems to have associated the first years of her life with an overwhelming sense of loneliness, she was not socially shy, nor did she lack either relatives or friends of her own age. Among her many cousins was, on her father's side, MANFRED GEORGE (1893–1965), who was the youngest son of William's sister FELICIA (1861–1907) and who, after emigrating to Czechoslovakia in 1933, eventually became editor-in-chief of the German-Jewish weekly *Der Aufbau* in New York. On her mother's side was, among others, HEINZ MEYER (1907–1945), the son of Margarete's younger sister ANNA (1872–?), who would become a rabbi and whom Sachs mentions with obvious warmth in later correspondence. Heinz was considerably younger than her, however, and probably had no significance during her childhood and adolescence. The relatives got together in connection with birthdays and holidays, on which the families would pay each other visits. Following the love crisis of 1908–1910, however, Sachs began to make the new acquaintances of a maturing person. Among these were three women whose friendship would become particularly important. Eventually they would be declared “sisters.”

DORA JABLONSKI (1891–1942), who was the same age as Sachs, was the daughter of one of Margarete Sachs’ school friends, Elise Jablonski, née Eiseck. The family lived in smart Fasanenstraße in Charlottenburg and the older children — besides Dora there was WALTER (*1892), HILDE (*1897) and WOLFGANG (*1912) — often came to visit. William Sachs and Berthold Jablonski, who was a successful grain merchant with cultural interests, went on business trips together while the mothers indulged in what women of their class and background were expected to immerse themselves in: walks, tea parties, parlor games. Like Nelly, the eldest daughter, Dora, is said to have been an introverted soul with a feeling for art, music, and dance. In contrast with her friend, however, who never made a deprecating remark about her parents, she was regarded as a difficult daughter who countered her mother’s ostentatious bourgeois lifestyle by wearing a severe reform dress and, according to Eva Steinthal, a classmate of her younger sister, preferred to keep her head in the clouds. Many years later her middle sister, Hilde, claimed that she had been “utterly unerotic.”

In Dora, Nelly found a person of the same background and temperament as herself. She too sought an identity between the only roles seemingly on offer: those of virtuous daughter and future housewife. Their friendship offered them a selective sisterhood whose breadth and character they determined themselves. The teenage girls became friends at about the same time that Sachs suffered her first nervous breakdown. During the years that followed on the 1908 crisis they met daily, went on excursions together, and shared a passion for the arts. While Nelly appears to have preferred literature, Dora was a dedicated painter of mainly flower arrangements and landscapes. There is a photograph preserved from this period, most likely taken shortly before the outbreak of the war, in which Nelly is sitting in an armchair on a balcony while an unidentified friend perches on the armrest. Possibly it is Dora. Considering the fact that Nelly has taken the better seat and that her body language suggests familiarity with the place, the photograph was probably taken at Siegmundshof. It could be summer, though Nelly’s thick socks might suggest a day in the spring or early fall. The two women appear to have a bond but do not overemphasize their friendship. They are around twenty years old, a colluding pair offering restrained smiles to the photographer. While her friend wears a reform dress, Nelly is clad in a dress with a jacket and wears lace-up shoes. Both dress and appearance support Steinthal’s later characterization: “Mignon-like.”

31

32

According to Dora's youngest brother Wolfgang, who was occasionally allowed along to Siegmundshof, the two friends spoke endlessly about art and poetry. Considering the large age gap between him and his older sister, these conversations ought to have taken place after the World War — otherwise the boy is unlikely to have remembered them later in life. At that time Nelly and Dora were no longer teenagers, jointly absorbed by the mysteries of artistic creation, but adult women around thirty. The age says something about the artistic incubation period that Sachs was going through. On the one hand, her social environment and upbringing required that she socialize only with men who were either brothers or potential husbands; on the other, she had reached an age at which parents no longer dictated all of the conditions for her existence. That left art and literature as havens. Both Dora and Nelly still lived at home. While Nelly, pen and paper in hand, retreated into one of the rooms at Siegmundshof, her friend found refuge in the studio she shared with Steinthal until the latter's family lost its fortune during the financial turmoil of 1923. A couple of photographs from the 1920s show her in an almost identical pose: in one wearing a reform dress and a heavy necklace, standing in front of a lattice window, in the other wearing a cardigan and a discreet necklace, posing pensively by a low wall. In both, she rests her right arm in front of her and turns her gaze away. Although the dreamy attitude is typical of the period, it is hard to shake off the impression of a woman held back by circumstances, longing for a world beyond barriers and conventions.

33

34

A later statement by Steinthal throws a gloomy light on Nelly's existential situation. She is said to have become insufferable to both her parents and herself on repeated occasions, and to have been sent to a private boarding house — "not a clinic and not a hotel, something between the two." It is uncertain when this happened, even if the descriptions of the place she is said to have been sent to sound reminiscent of the private clinic that Richard Cassirer ran in Grunewald and which after his death in 1925 would be turned into a private hotel. After a few weeks away, Sachs would return home. Sometimes she was picked up by Dora, who clearly disliked her treatment by her parents. On one occasion, however, her friend sent her younger sister, which suggests that Sachs' stays away from home ought to have taken place at a time when Hilde was old enough to handle the task — which would reasonably have been in her fifteenth or sixteenth year, that is, after 1913. Thus if Steinthal's recollections are accurate, Sachs' life was marked by melancholy long after the crisis in 1908.

In 1926 Berthold Jablonski died. Although his eldest daughter no longer had to conform to her father's notions of a suitable wife, it would be another eight years before she married, in 1934. Her younger sister Hilde had already wed Otto Bental when Dora became the wife of HUGO HORWITZ (1876–1942?), fifteen years her senior. Her husband had been educated at home as a

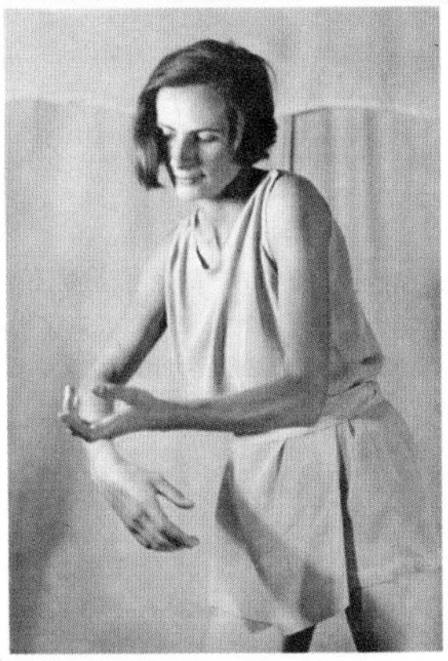
35

36

37

young boy and held no formal profession, but was regarded as an "intellectual" and was well versed in classic literature and philosophy, being particularly interested in Spinoza. If this is the same Hugo Horwitz that the city's *Adreßbuch* listed as resident at An der Fliegwiese 48 in Charlottenburg at the time, he was a doctor of philosophy and identified himself as a "writer." With the marriage, contacts between the friends became less frequent. But by then Nelly had already made the acquaintance of the woman who would mean most to her and whom she later declared her "life-saver."

GUDRUN DÄHNERT (1907–1976), née Harlan, was the grandchild of Sachs' former teacher Hélène Aubert. She came from a nationalistically minded, Protestant background characterized by anthroposophical ambitions. Soon after the Second World War she married the musicologist Ulrich Dähnert. Her father was an airplane manufacturer, and among her cousins was the actor and director Veit Harlan. The two women had met at the annual birthday party held at the Aubert residence, but it wasn't until 1929 that Gudrun felt ready to begin a friendship. At the time she was twenty-two and had recently completed training as a physiotherapist at Anna Hermann's physical education institute. Her parents had moved back to the family home town of Dresden, while their daughter, who had opened a private clinic in the capital, moved in with her maternal grandmother. There she met Nelly one day, who was paying a visit to her "venerated former headmistress," in the words of her friend in later written recollections.

Their meeting is notable not least because Sachs apparently remained in contact with her old teacher more than twenty years after having left a school life which in her own words had made her feel foreign and different. This is how Dähnert describes the apparition she met in her grandmother's sitting room: "There she was before me now, this fragile, frail creature. While she spoke to my grandmother she frequently and self-consciously adjusted the generous brim of her blue hat. I marveled then at her delicate little hands. With her almost black hair and her very pale skin she looked like a Snow White."

According to her identity papers Sachs was a mature woman of almost forty, but to her friend she seemed a timeless being — half shy schoolgirl, half fairy-tale princess. The tendency to legend-making is also noticeable in the report that her grandmother one evening many years earlier had heard a voice in her head, urging her to hurry to Nelly's side. A rushed cab ride to Siegmundshof later she found the girl "in bed deathly ill and totally emaciated." While it is true that Dähnert wrote down her memories only after Sachs' death, in the early 1970s, and almost certain that her recollections were colored by the perspective that the war, the flight, and the literary œuvre conferred, it is nonetheless remarkable how untouched the image of the suffering woman remained. The nuances are scant and simple: almost black hair, nearly white skin. Nelly is good but has been tested, a virgin as pure as Snow White. The pain of the love crisis is still there, but remains beyond words. The wound must be borne in dignified silence.

The day after the meeting at the Aubert residence the women saw each other again. After Nelly had read some poems out loud the friendship was sealed. "We were so naturally close to each other. She soon returned. We found that we were sisters." In a couple of photographs from the period Dähnert is seen in a bob, wearing a simple dress. She is in the middle of a movement which is as much a physical exercise as dance — an interest which should have appealed to the dancing daughter of an inventor of strength-training instruments. Despite the fact that they were separated by sixteen years, the sporty Gudrun immediately took on the role of protector of Nelly, who was nearly twice her age. Thus she would remain even during the hazardous years of the 1930s, when she showed courage on many occasions and, by means of a perilous journey via Göteborg and Sunne to Mårbacka and Stockholm in the summer of 1939, managed to secure the conditions for the departure that Nelly for various reasons had been putting off until it was nearly too late.

38

Important help during the preparations for the flight came from Sachs' third "sister": ANNELIESE NEFF (1910–1992), whom Dähnert had befriended when they became classmates in the second year. Neff was "almost always unhappy" and was described many years later as "slightly hysterical" by Dähnert's sister-in-law Liselotte Harlan in an interview with Fritsch-Vivié. To cheer up her former classmate, Dähnert brought her along to meet her new friend one day in May 1933. Perhaps Sachs' affectionate manner would have a "harmonic" effect on her. For her part, Neff described their meeting thus, in a later letter to Dinesen: "I made the acquaintance of my friend Nelly Sachs in May 1933 when, at twenty-five years of age, I had contracted my lifelong and already very serious but not yet defined illness, with much pain and a deep inner sorrow as well. — By the agency of my friend at the time, Nelly hurried to my house, stepped quietly into my room, where I was lying on the couch, sat down at the foot end and began to caress my hands. She said: You don't need to be sad anymore! Your sister is here!"

If Dähnert's interest in literature was general, Neff's was pronounced. She had studied German and Classical Greek at university and, like Sachs, she followed the theater scholar Max Herrmann's open romantics seminar and admired his wife, Helene, who had written a thesis on Goethe shortly after the turn of the century. For a time she also attended the literary evening classes for professionals which were given by Helene Herrmann at her private school until it closed in 1933. She kept it a secret, however, that she had "had the most frequent of contacts with the George circle," since her new-found sister had made it clear that she did not share the group's views on poetry. The reasons for Neff's suggested illness are not known, but may have contributed to her becoming blind later in life.

39

The account demonstrates that the roles could shift. If Gudrun was Anneliese's "friend at the time" but Nelly's protector, Nelly became Anneliese's savior and new friend: "I: constantly miserable and sick, she comforted me constantly, quickly wrote a poem for me to make me happy, and in her innermost self she bore the pain and fear due to the prevailing difficult circumstances, which I shared with her." Together the three sisters studied the romantics in depth, among them Novalis and Brentano, read the legends about the founder of Hasidism, Baal Shem Tov, and Martin Buber's translations of pious Eastern Jewish mystics. It isn't unlikely that Neff, who called herself "Ännchen" in letters to Sachs, partly inspired one of Chelion's classmates in the childhood account from the 1930s: "It is nice for Chelion that she had been able to help dry Ännchen's tears, she is very happy about that." (Sachs had, however, had a classmate whose name was Alix Neufeld but who was called "Ännchen" and who would be remembered in debut poetry collection's epitaph "Die Abenteuerin [A. N.]" [The Adventuress (A. N.)].)

In an environment where men were absent the women exhibited traits that contemporary gender roles would deem masculine. Gudrun acted like Prince Valiant — noble, moral, and Christian. She was a practical soul, the escort without make-up who carried both her and Nelly's umbrellas during walks in the autumn rain. Sensitive to her friend's vulnerability, she came to her aid in all weathers. Nelly, for her part, preferred wide hats and pearl necklaces, but nonetheless became a "hero" in Anneliese's eyes for hurrying to her succor when she was unwell, providing her with strengthening poems by her bedside. The women played active and passive roles, complemented each other and formed what Dinesen has called "a kind of order of sisters."

Arguably the demonic aspects exhibited by the George circle were missing. Nor is there any honoring of the fatherland, of either the inner or the outer kind, in which poetry would be the vessel of truth. But the Christian doctrine of self-sacrifice and brotherly love, and not least the belief in the purifying effects of death, provided a pattern which imbued actions with a purpose that greatly exceeded sordid material worth. The atmosphere created in the shadow of the catastrophe wasn't necessarily homoerotic (even if Neff, like several of Sachs' other friends, was lesbian), but could be described as homosocial. The sisters were united in their belief in the necessity of dedication and the unity of the heart. Or, as Neff would write much later about her friend's literary ambitions after the Holocaust: she "is now experiencing her further inner development in the realm of the dead, — no doubt 'blessed' — until, as fully expected — the gates open and the word of longing at the end of her *Simson fällt durch Jahrtausende* (Samson Falls through Millennia) is utterly fulfilled for her: 'Enter — enter!'"

Theirs was a sisterhood in preparation for the eternal communion.

**TEXT** "Briefe aus der Nacht," NSW:IV · For Dora Jablonski, see Dinesen, 84–88 · Dähnert, 226, 227 · Fritsch-Vivié, 62–63 · Letters from Neff 01/27 and 02/12/1982, ADinesen · Letter from Neff 02/12/1954 and "Chelion," ASachs | **IMAGE 32** Nelly Sachs with unknown friend in the 1910s (DLA) · **33** Dora Jablonski in the 1920s · **34** Jablonski in the 1920s (Ruth Dinesen's collection, Glumsø) · **35** Gudrun Dähnert in 1929 (Kurt Kehrwieder's collection, Bochum) · **36** Dähnert in the 1930s (Kurt Kehrwieder's collection, Bochum) · **37** Gudrun Dähnert (Kurt Kehrwieder's collection, Bochum) · **38** Anneliese Neff in the 1930s (KBS) · **39** Hélène Aubert, n.d. (Photo A. Michalowski, Kurt Kehrwieder's collection, Bochum)

## *RARA AVIS*

Towards the end of the 1950s, in a letter to the literary historian Käte Hamburger, who spent the Nazi years in Swedish exile, Sachs described how she had taken part in a meeting of the Swedish Authors' Association at which a newly instituted poetry prize was to be awarded. Moved to tears, she realized that the choice had fallen on "the *rara* refugee *avis*" in the guests' midst who had tried to spread Swedish poetry in the German language area. A couple of years later Sachs returned to this image in a letter to the German writer Werner Reinert. She was interned at the Beckomberga mental hospital at the time, and described the routine there and what a "mercy" her hospital room was. Then she added that a selection of Swedish translations of her poems had recently been published under the title *Flykt och förvandling* (Flight and Metamorphosis), and summed up: "The *rara avis* captured in a beautiful way."

Even if the designation referred to a poet and translator in exile, Sachs appears to have felt a special kinship with birds much earlier. In several cases this was linked to the artistic element of the ethereal: dance. Both Chelion and Lichen, light as swallows, liked to dance to their fathers' piano playing in the evenings. Already in Sachs' first book, *Legenden und Erzählungen*, dance played a significant part. In the story about "Der gefesselte Silen" (The Chained Silen) we learn of Beatrice, daughter of a Burgundian king who is struck by "a severe and mysterious illness. It was not that she suffered any evident pain, instead her suffering expressed itself as a kind of mild melancholy. She refused to eat or drink [---] and withered away more each day." Nothing seems to help the dejected maiden — not even the paradisiacal garden of flowers and herbs which is planted for her or the wild animals she is brought from foreign lands. It is not until "a young Syrian dancing girl, slave to a Frankish knight," performs at the court that a change can be seen. Barely older than fourteen, the girl has sleek limbs that glitter in the brown hues of the Saracens. "Sweetly spellbound one followed her, whose floating foot seemed to transform everything around it."

The image is reminiscent of the Spanish woman who appears in one of Rilke's poems, but in contrast with his Gypsy who "assured of victory, confident and with a lovely / welcoming smile," stamps out the flames after the flamenco she has let flare up, Sachs' dancer lacks all supercilious traits. Her art may enchant

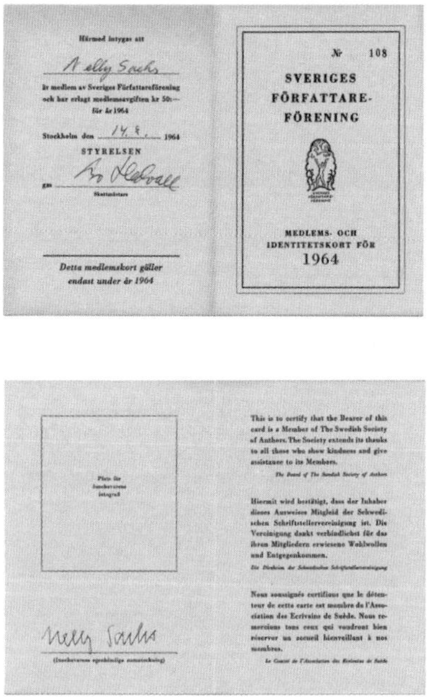
Härmed intygas att

Nelly Sachs

är medlem av Sveriges Författareförening
och har erlagt medlemsavgiften kr 50:—
för år 1964

Stockholm den 14.8. 1964

STYRELSEN

Skattmästare

Detta medlemskort gäller
endast under år 1964

№ 108

SVERIGES
FÖRFATTARE-
FÖRENING

MEDLEMS- OCH
IDENTITETSKORT FÖR
1964

Nelly Sachs

This is to certify that the Bearer of this card is a Member of The Swedish Society of Authors. The Society extends its thanks to all those who show kindness and give assistance to its Members.

The Board of The Swedish Society of Authors

Hiermit wird bestätigt, dass der Inhaber dieses Ausweises Mitglied der Schwedischen Schriftstellervereinigung ist. Die Vereinigung dankt verbindlichst für das ihren Mitgliedern erwiesene Wohlwollen und Entgegenkommen.

Nous soussignés certifions que le détenteur de cette carte est membre de l'Association des Ecrivains de Suède. Nous remercions tous ceux qui voudront bien réserver un accueil bienveillant à nos membres.

40

the onlookers, but she is actually a moth who drifts from flower to flower in search of the poppy that brings sleep. During the dance, however, something strange happens to Beatrice, who had been admiring the act. "Her pallid features gradually regained charm and youthful freshness, the small mouth opened slowly like a flower bud touched by the sun, but the large dark eyes shone with a mysterious glow." The chastely eroticizing metaphors underscore that the dance has awakened a distant longing. The reason soon becomes clear: "The young dancing girl had, at the sound of the flutes' lamenting melodies, begun to skitter like a little bird and at the same time swing her arms up and down like wings." In order that the reader not mistake the source of the pain, the narrator provides the explanation: "They all understood the meaning of what had happened and realized that she whose mouth was denied the ability to utter her pain had found another language. And they felt the deepest compassion for the bird caught in foreign lands, who in the midst of a party of high nobles had been gripped by longing for her homeland." The scene could have ended there — with a *rara avis* surrounded by noble people whose souls have been touched by the slave's aesthetically presented, agonizingly unutterable suffering. But Sachs took it further. While the onlookers slowly regain their composure and awaken as if from a stupefaction, the princess sinks to the ground. "Young Miss Beatrice, pale and unconscious, lay collapsed on the floor as if dying." Unlike the rest of the audience, her empathy with the dance was so complete that she took on the dancing girl's fate during the performance and now lay at death's door herself.

The subjects and the means vary, but for both the early and the later Sachs, art provided a doctrine of empathy. Beatrice is moved neither by the dancing girl nor by her suggestive dance — rather, she is overcome by an artistic representation based on the distance between a faraway homeland and chivalrous reality. It is the pain of parting which is the source of the emotion. For Sachs, art evoked the very longing it was based on. "After this event the princess descended into an even deeper melancholy than before, and no one would henceforth be able to coax the slightest word from her mouth, much less extract a smile from her lips."

As the seventy-year-old patient in Ward 29 at Beckomberga knew, and as the seventeen-year-old had been taught already by Dr. Cassirer at the clinic in Grunewald, words didn't offer relief so much as salvation. Even if they weren't spoken they could always be written down. The only thing that separated compassion from suffering was art.

**TEXT** Letter to Hamburger 01/06/1958, DLA · For letter to Reinert 04/27/1961, see Briefe 182 · LuEN, 230, 231, 231, 232, 232, 233, and 233 respectively · Rilke, "Spanische Tänzerin," *Sämtliche Werke*, Frankfurt am Main 1976, vol. 11, 531–532 | **IMAGE 40** Sachs' membership card for the Swedish Authors' Association, 1964 (KBS)

## MOVEMENT × 2

As Dinesen has noted, the account of the dancing slave calls to mind the Berlin dancer NIDDY IMPEKOVEN (1904–2002). In a famous photograph from 1920 she is performing barefoot, with a dark headdress and a matching shawl tied around her neck. Her short dress has been painted to look like it is made of feathers, the fabric covering hips, arms, and upper body. Lengths of fabric extend from her arms to her trunk, making it seem like she is spreading her wings to fly.

The subsequently famous dance piece "Gefangener Vogel" (Captured Bird), with music by Bruno Hartl, had its first performance at the opera house in Frankfurt in December 1918. The following year it was staged for the first time in Berlin. A contemporary critic — Hans Frentz — described, a few years later, an impression he shared with many: "In 'Captured Bird' the free body — transformed, one might say, into longing — tries with all its might to liberate itself from the burden which weighs down this altogether too young and frail creature, allotted a great gift. [---] Thus the idea for 'Captured Bird' comes from no less a person than her mother, and the young dancer has proceeded to give it this outstanding interpretation which has been indelibly imprinted on the soul of each and every person past whom this endlessly longing fledgling fluttered. One sat there in the cramped space and heard this life-cheated creature from the ether beat its wings against the bars. One was in the primeval forest and listened to its song bring infinite joy, and — woe betide us — one caught its distant, half-muffled cry as it was hunted and driven from its paradise . . ."

41

Impekoven put audiences in a state of bliss. She embodied the very same longing that she evoked in the theater. Thespianism already had its Duse, now dancing had its Niddy. Putatively girlish and natural, innocent and whimsical, her pieces lacked Valeska Gert's bitter ironies and Mary Wigman's expressionistic movements. Not a trace of Charlotte Bara's enigmatic gestures hovering between piousness and danse macabre. Impekoven was neither vixen nor priestess, neither *femme fatale* nor Mother Earth. Possibly she had something of the *garçonne* about her, but above all she was an enchanting girl. Of her could be said what a contemporary critic wrote about "Le Douanier" Rousseau's painting of a child (and whom Ernst Blass quoted in a portrait of Impekoven): "The baby is drastic. She has naked calves and naked arms . . ."

42

The words appear in an essay by the critic Theodor Däubler. In Blass' portrait, however, the conclusion is missing: "A fantastic experience and already a strong stylistic expression." The sentiment captures the prevalent view of Impekoven's dancing art. It was direct, frank, and ingenuous — a succession of sudden expressions, harmoniously brought together, that "begin from the beginning." Even if sexuality wasn't absent, its menacing edge was missing. Far removed from both voluptuous orientalism and clamorous metropolis,

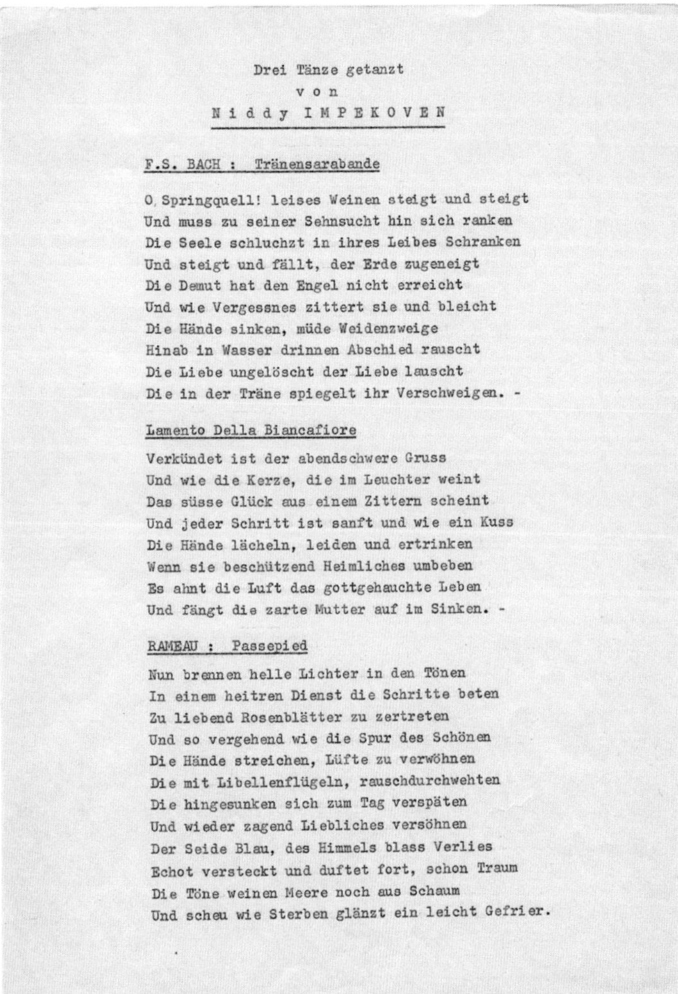

Drei Tänze getanzt
von
**Niddy IMPEKOVEN**

F.S. BACH : Tränensarabande

O, Springquell! leises Weinen steigt und steigt
Und muss zu seiner Sehnsucht hin sich ranken
Die Seele schluchzt in ihres Leibes Schranken
Und steigt und fällt, der Erde zugeneigt
Die Demut hat den Engel nicht erreicht
Und wie Vergessnes zittert sie und bleicht
Die Hände sinken, müde Weidenzweige
Hinab in Wasser drinnen Abschied rauscht
Die Liebe ungelöscht der Liebe lauscht
Die in der Träne spiegelt ihr Verschweigen. -

Lamento Della Biancafiore

Verkündet ist der abendschwere Gruss
Und wie die Kerze, die im Leuchter weint
Das süsse Glück aus einem Zittern scheint
Und jeder Schritt ist sanft und wie ein Kuss
Die Hände lächeln, leiden und ertrinken
Wenn sie beschützend Heimliches umbeben
Es ahnt die Luft das gottgehauchte Leben
Und fängt die zarte Mutter auf im Sinken. -

RAMEAU : Passepied

Nun brennen helle Lichter in den Tönen
In einem heitren Dienst die Schritte beten
Zu liebend Rosenblätter zu zertreten
Und so vergehend wie die Spur des Schönen
Die Hände streichen, Lüfte zu verwöhnen
Die mit Libellenflügeln, rauschdurchwehten
Die hingesunken sich zum Tag verspäten
Und wieder zagend Liebliches versöhnen
Der Seide Blau, des Himmels blass Verlies
Echot versteckt und duftet fort, schon Traum
Die Töne weinen Meere noch aus Schaum
Und scheu wie Sterben glänzt ein leicht Gefrier.

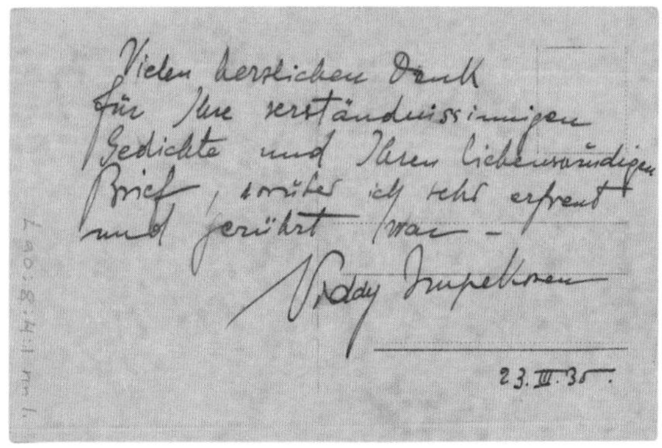

Vielen herzlichen Dank
für Ihre verständnisinnigen
Gedichte und Ihren liebenswürdigen
Brief, worüber ich sehr erfreut
und gerührt war –
Niddy Impekoven
23.III.35.

43

44

the movements remained sensual — drifting between longing and reverie. Sachs, it would seem, saw her literary work in a similar way. It is no surprise that Impekoven's pieces for "Old and New Dolls," her "Child Scenes" and "Waltz from A Thousand and One Nights" appealed to her to the extent that she wrote about them. Neff later recalled that she and Nelly went to "a very beautiful evening of dance" together, which at its earliest would have taken place in May 1933 — most likely a few years later, since Impekoven on March 23, 1935, sent her unknown admirer a postcard: "Thank you very much for your insightful poems and your kind letter, which made me very happy and were very moving." The picture was of the dancer wearing a sleeveless white dress and with a large black crucifix around her neck.

Sachs had probably sent her some poems with dance themes a short time earlier. There remain, at any rate, a handful of such poems from the period, most of which were published in *Der Morgen* in 1937 and contained allusions to works by Boccherini, Mozart, and Rameau. But there is also a text entitled

"Drei Tänze getanzt von Niddy Impekoven" (Three Dances Danced by Niddy Impekoven), which include a "Tränensarabande" (Tear Sarabande) after Bach:

> O well-spring! Quiet weeping rises and rises / And must cling to its longing / The soul sobs within the body's boundaries / And rises and falls, pulled to earth / Humility has not reached the angel / Which trembles and grows pale as if forgotten / Its hands drop, tired willow boughs / Into the water where parting murmurs / Unquenched, love listens to love / Trace its secret in tears. —

If Rilke linked his dancer with the element of fire — a haughty artist not unlike a tobacco factory worker, who stamps out the flames with nimble, rapping metric feet — Sachs instead associated dancing with water. The body was a vessel filled with longing. Moved by the music, tears sprang forth from the unfathomable source of longing, the sobs of the soul were expanded into the tidal movements that determine earthly life. Forever seeking the lowest level, this Archimedean point in life, water became at once the medium of origin and of parting. Even if the life of man be finite, inextinguishable love is reflected in his tears. As an artistic medium, dance was thus closest to water: fluid and transitory, it nonetheless produced a movement which did not perish.

45

Sachs would remain true to this high view of dance. Later in life she confessed to Berendsohn: "Already as a child my greatest wish was to become a dancer." She continued: "Dance became my form of expression even before words did. My innermost element. It was only the heavy fate which befell me that took me from this form of expression to another: the word!" In one of the epitaphs after the war, "Die Tänzerin [D. H.]" (The Dancer [D. H.]), she described feet which wander to the time of a sarabande — "For longing was your gesture." Dedicated to her friend Dora Jablonski, married Horwitz, the poem is one of many texts expressing the conviction that true longing is always extreme: the person yearning strives beyond the limits of the possible. Dance doubly transforms this craving into movement — both in space and sentiment. Thus it may, despite its fleeting nature, tie beginning to end and remain the "incipient longing / of distant days of creation —"

The last words are taken from the poem "Tänzerin" (Dancer) in *Flucht und Verwandlung*. The final dash — a longing gesture outstretched into empty space — surely was no coincidence.

**TEXT** Frentz, *Niddy Impekoven und ihre Tänze*, Freiburg 1930, 19–20 · Blass, *Das Wesen der neuen Tanzkunst*, Weimar 1921, 30 · Däubler, "Henri Rousseau," *Die weißen Blätter*, 1916, no. 2, 243 · Letter from Neff 02/12/1982, ADinesen · Postcard from Impekoven 03/23/1935 and "Drei Tänze getanzt von Niddy Impekoven," ASachs · For letter to Berendsohn 01/25/1959, see Briefe 132 · "Die Tänzerin," IdWdT (NSW:I) · "Tänzerin," FuV (NSW:II) | **IMAGE 41** Impekoven as ceramic figurine (The Wellinger Collection, Vienna) · **42** Niddy Impekoven as "captured bird," around 1920 (Photo Ninny and Carry Hess, DTA) · **43** Postcard from Impekoven to Sachs 03/23/1935 (KBS) · **44** "Drei Tänze getanzt von Niddy Impekoven," typescript (KBS) · **45** Impekoven in "Tear Sarabande" (Photo Ninni and Carry Hess)

Wie ich das Leben im „Hause William Sachs" sah im Jahre 1930.

Das Jahr 1929 ging seinem Ende zu. Zu Sylvester fuhr Gertrud nach Börnicke zu ihrer Mutter
und ich blieb bei den Herrschaften u. hatte am Neujahrstag dann frei. Morgens
wünschten wir uns ein gesegnetes, neues Jahr. Dem Herrn W. Sachs ging es so einiger-
maßen und nachdem wir Mittag gegessen hatten, verabschiedeten wir uns und
ich fuhr mit der S Bahn vom Bahnhof Thiergarten zum Alex u. von da mit dem 14 Bus
nach Weissensee, wo meine Verwandten wohnten. Meine Schwester u. Schwager waren
ja erst ein halbes Jahr verheiratet u. trotzdem luden sie mich oft zu sich ein,
damit wir immer verbunden waren. Gegen Abend fuhr ich dann wieder zurück nach
Siegmundshof 16. Frl. Nelly Sachs war, wie immer noch wach u. wir unterhielten uns
noch ein wenig, sie fragte mich, wie es meine Schwester u. ihren Mann so geht,
ja, sie nahm immer regen Anteil an unser Wohlergehen u. s. w. Wir wünschten
uns eine gute Nacht u. ich sehe sie noch heute im Geiste vor mir, mit ihrem
zarten, sehr hübschen Gesicht u. den großen, sprechenden Augen, das Haar legte
sich wie zarte Wellen um ihr Gesicht, es war in der Mitte gescheitelt u. hinten
zu einem schweren Knoten zusammengefügt im Nacken. Abends trug sie
damals einen dunkellila farbenen Morgenrock aus Sammt, dieser stand ihr
sehr gut. Dann besuchten eines Tages meine Eltern uns, aus Ballenstedt,
wo wir wohnten, waren sie zu Besuch bei meiner Schwester nach Weissensee unverhofft gekommen, um ihr neues Heim zu bewundern u. dann
eines Tages, am Nachmittag, klingelte es an der Haustür. Gertrud ging öffnen
und als sie wiederkam, strahlte sie mich mit ihren blauen Augen
an u. meinte, „Fräulein Lina, sie werden sich aber jetzt sehr freuen"!
Ja da hatte sie Recht gehabt, da standen auf einmal meine lieben
Eltern vor mir. Wie habe ich mich doch gefreut, das werde ich nie im
Leben vergessen, ich dachte zuerst, das wäre ein Traum. Dann kam Frl.
Sachs u. Frau Sachs, und sie begrüssten meine Eltern sehr herzlich, u.

46

## DEATH'S FLOWERING

When Sachs met Dähnert her father lay seriously ill with cancer. During the latter part of the 1920s he was cared for at home — by his daughter as well, who showed such dedication to the task that the doctor said she was a born nurse. But her father shook his head: "No, my daughter would expire with every dying patient." Relatives got the impression that the forty-year-old Nelly was completely devoted to her calling, possibly writing a little poetry now and then. A similar picture is painted by the family's maid, Lina Schoegel, who in some later recollections describes how the self-sacrificing daughter dressed her father's "cancer wound on his forehead, and when he had had a good sleep she brought him his breakfast herself and then read him many things, she was always around him and never had time to think of herself, which is something I have often quietly admired her for."

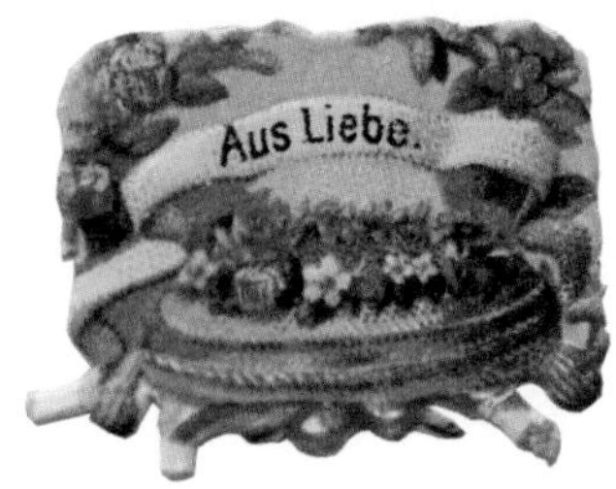


47

In her three accounts of her years with the family, the former maid gives an insight into life at Siegmundshof: "Miss Nelly Sachs' care for her father was moving, she made arm baths, I went to the pharmacy in Karl-Straße where they prepared everything Herr Sachs needed for his palliation. Sometimes they also took a taxi to Grunewald to see 'Professor Lazarus' in Winkelstraße, where he ran a sanatorium. Herr Sachs would receive radium radiation for the cancer wound on his forehead. When afterwards a new thin layer of skin had formed on top of the wound, we were all of us both happy and grateful. But unfortunately it would only last a short time. Miss Nelly suffered most, for she was very attached to her father and many were the mornings when her pretty, dark eyes were red-rimmed and swollen from crying. Already at that time she was burdened with suffering — for one likes a father and can't readily part with him — and so was her mother. Mrs. Sachs would also suffer biliary colic after such attacks, and then our worries doubled. Sometimes we didn't have a very easy time of it at all."

The oncologist who administered the treatment was probably university professor B. Lazarus at Winkelstraße 24. During his stays at home William Sachs would rest under blankets in the loggia while his daughter or the maid read to him from the newspaper. Sometimes his brothers Alfred or Richard would come to visit, on other occasions it would be his secretary, Miss Rehberg, with whom there is reason to believe that he had a long extramarital liaison. Repeatedly the patient had to go to Dr. Lazarus for radiation treatment; on these occasions his wife and his daughter would take turns spending the night at the sanatorium in Grunewald. At times the maid would also visit. When the patient wanted to rest, she went for walks with Nelly in Grunewald — "then she would quickly write down a poem, since she always carried a writing pad and a pen in her little bag." One Wednesday in November, when his daughter was on an errand and the company secretary was paying yet another visit, William Sachs died. Nelly received the news on her return an hour later. A neighbor of the family — the gynecologist HANS GEORG LIEBMANN (1886–1987), who had written his dissertation on rare laryngeal tumors and who had often seen to the patient — took her in his arms. "Nelly sobbed and said again and again that now she also wanted to die. The good Dr. L then uttered a sentence I have never forgotten: 'You won't die now, for death is something you must first become deserving of!'"

That was on November 26, 1930. The parting that Sachs had so often written poems about had become a reality. Yet there were still stanzas to be written. She had a few lines inscribed on the urn in which her father's remains were interred at the nondenominational cemetery in Berliner Straße in Wilmersdorf. Later she wrote "Inschrift auf die Urne meines Vater" (Inscription on My Father's Urn) which included the proclamation: "Down here we are but happenstance, / but up there we blossom!" With their romantic imagery, these lines are characteristic of Sachs' poetry during the Berlin years. Existence was literally an "earthly life" as she wrote in the unpublished drama "Ein Spiel vom Zauberer Merlin" (A Play about the Wizard Merlin) from the Christmas of 1940 ("It is not death, but it is love / That brings the greatest pain in this earthly life"). The only thing man could hope for in this boundless disarray of events was a connection with other rootlets. True flowering was possible solely up above, in the Elysian fields of the life to come. Death alone made language blossom.

**TEXT** Dähnert, 227 · Schubert:1 · Schubert:2 · "Inschrift auf die Urne meines Vaters," ASachs · "Ein Spiel vom Zauberer Merlin," ASahlin | **IMAGE 46** Lina Schubert, "Wie ich das Leben im Hause William Sachs sah im Jahre 1930," manuscript (KBS) · **47** Pictures from "Das Oblatenalbum" (KBS)

## A BOUQUET

Aside from the legends and tales, the dramas for marionettes and the pieces for puppet theater, Sachs mostly wrote poetry before the Nazi takeover. It was usually sentimental verses with animal and nature themes, prayers, devotional or dedicatory texts, sonnets, travel miniatures and dance poems. Swallows swept across the evening sky, sorrowful tears trickled down crimson cheeks. Weeping was the poet's secret ally. The world belonged to disappearance, he who spoke was intimate with liquidation.

48

A small number of poems show that Sachs was no stranger to a freer form, but these were usually epigonal exercises in sentimentality. In later conversations with friends and critics such as Berendsohn and Holmqvist she claimed that for a time she had given herself to a bold form leaning towards contemporary expressionistic poetry. On the advice of friends, however, these texts were destroyed so that the person behind them would not be regarded as mentally disturbed. "Already as a very young girl," Sachs later told Hans Magnus Enzensberger, "I tried a different direction, which lay very close to my inner self. My friends found them so incomprehensible (they mostly belonged to

49

the George circle) that I kept them quite secret and then burned them all before the Hitler escape." Still, she can't have been all that young if the friends who advised her against publication were close to the circle around Stefan George, for even if Sachs became acquainted with Jablonski before 1910, she didn't befriend Neff until after the ominous Reichstag election of 1933. And no explanation was ever given for why a "very young girl" would wait until she was at least forty years old before burning the poems.

It appears more likely that Sachs burned the material — if indeed it ever existed — because it seemed too intimate and unprotected. Indications of a less rule-bound poetry are not frequent in the early part of her œuvre. Yet despite the tidy rhymes to melancholy, words do flare up occasionally. Here and there are unexpected neologisms, and in hastily sketched phrases evincing as much nerve as tearfulness distant energies may be sensed. In these sudden moments it is as if Sachs has plugged her poetry into the power circuit of her later works. The bouquet of thunder buds and sprays of lightning the reader can put together from her pre-flight production includes such lines as: "Puddles giggle and are gone," "The shrill clock soars like sorrowed snow, / Plums abide the afternoon sun —," and "O breath-light prayer / of lunar glint," whose juxtaposition of different registers of perception demonstrates a certain skill. But it is in compound words that the poet of the exile years makes her clearest mark. In "Beyond-primed," for example. Or "tear-delayed."

**TEXT** Berendsohn, 19 · Holmqvist, 36 · For letter to Enzensberger 06/18/1961, see Briefe 185 | **IMAGE** **48** Dolls from the 1920s (from a private collection) · **49** Flowers drawn by Nelly Sachs (DLA)

## ROMANTICS

"Now Chelion has become one of the little girls in the scrapbook," Sachs noted in the childhood account from the 1930s, written at a time when the fairy tales had faded into memories. But even after her flight to Sweden she carried on ascribing suggestive powers to her grandmother's scrapbook pictures. In a letter to Carl Seelig after the war she thanked him for his gift — Brontë's *Wuthering Heights* in Gladys von Sontheimer's German translation from 1945. Adding that she too was a "romantic," she made reference to the scrapbook which had been bundled into the brown suitcase.

"Chelion" suggests that Sachs read events in her own past into several of the pictures in the scrapbook, some of which had been pasted there by her. Later she would browse the pictures in search of ideas for texts. For example, the playing card queens and jacks that turn up in several dramatic poems, including *Nachtwache* (Nightwatch), are difficult to comprehend without leafing through the scrapbook. "Genovefa" is the name given to a queen of hearts of whom a jack of hearts mysteriously declares: "I sacrifice her." And the fact that the blond Hellmut in "Chelion" has a name beginning with the same letter as the name of one of the male protagonists in this "nightmare in nine pictures" is probably as unlikely to be a coincidence as the fact that the only playing cards among the scrapbook pictures that aren't face cards are either sevens or nines which have the shape of the letter *H*...

But now we are in a different world, characterized by real partings.

50

**TEXT** "Das Oblatenalbum" and "Chelion," ASachs · Letter to Seelig 08/21/1947, Robert-Walser-Archiv der Carl-Seelig-Stiftung, Zurich · *Nachtwache*, ZiS (NSW:III) | **IMAGE 50** Scrapbook pictures from "Das Oblatenalbum" (KBS)

# THE GREAT ANONYMOUS

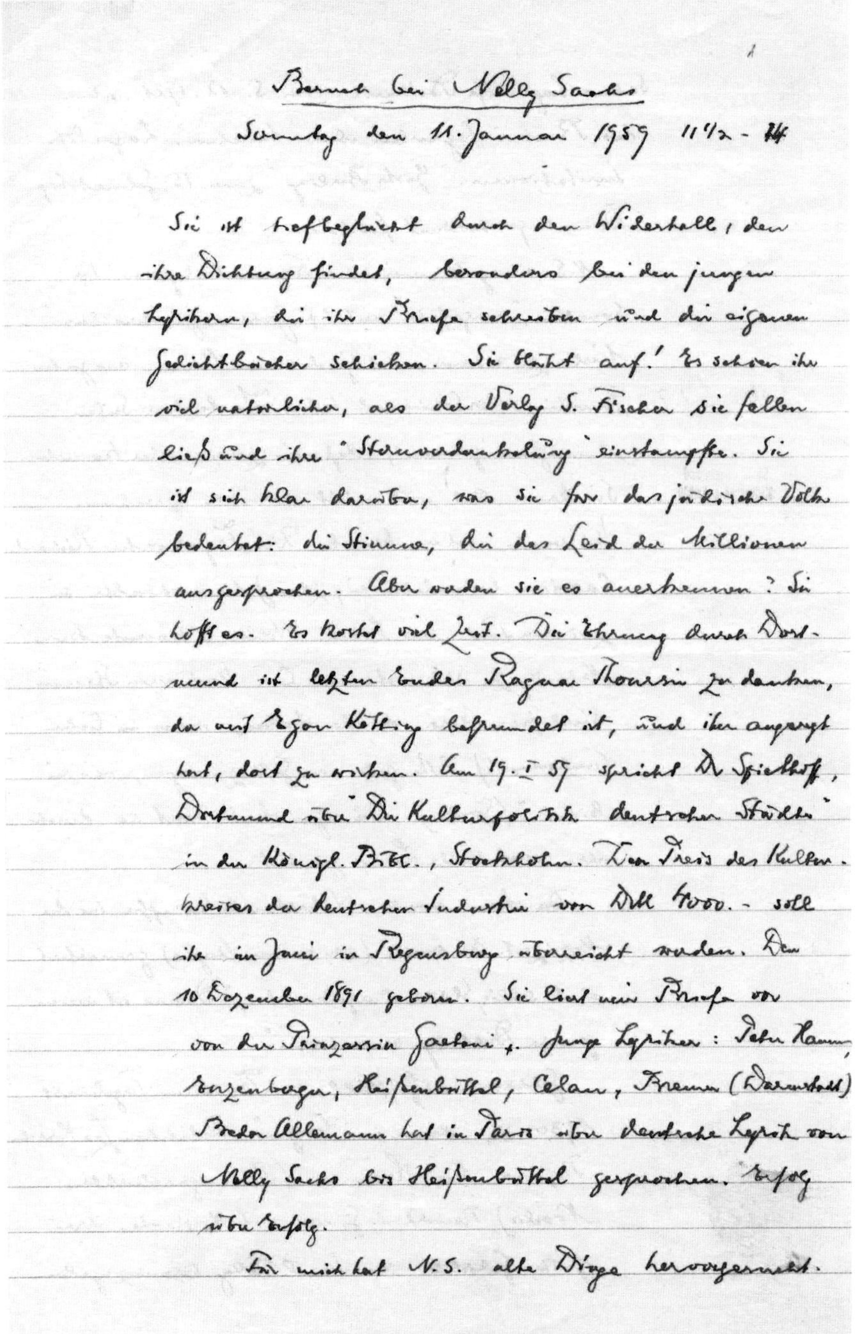

Besuch bei Nelly Sachs

Sonntag den 11. Januar 1959 11½ - 14

Sie ist tiefbeglückt durch den Widerhall, den ihre Dichtung findet, besonders bei den jungen Lyrikern, die ihr Briefe schreiben und die eigenen Gedichtbücher schicken. Sie blüht auf! Es scheint ihr viel natürlicher, als der Verlag S. Fischer sie fallen ließ und ihre "Sternverdunkelung" einstampfte. Sie ist sich klar darüber, was sie für das jüdische Volk bedeutet: die Stimme, die das Leid der Millionen ausgesprochen. Aber werden sie es anerkennen? Sie hofft es. Es kostet viel Zeit. Die Ehrung durch Dortmund ist letzten Endes Ragnar Thoursie zu danken, der mit Egon Kötting befreundet ist, und ihn angeregt hat, dort zu wirken. Am 19.I.59 spricht Dr. Spielhoff, Dortmund über "Die Kulturpolitik deutscher Städte" in der Königl. Bibl., Stockholm. Der Preis des Kulturkreises der deutschen Industrie von DM 4000.- soll ihr im Juni in Regensburg überreicht werden. Am 10 Dezember 1891 geboren. Sie liest mir Briefe vor von der Prinzessin Gaetani +. Junge Lyriker: Peter Hamm, Enzensberger, Heißenbüttel, Celan, Fremm (Darmstadt) Beda Allemann hat in Paris über deutsche Lyrik von Nelly Sachs bis Heißenbüttel gesprochen. Erfolg über Erfolg.

Für mich hat N.S. alte Dinge heraufgerufen.

1

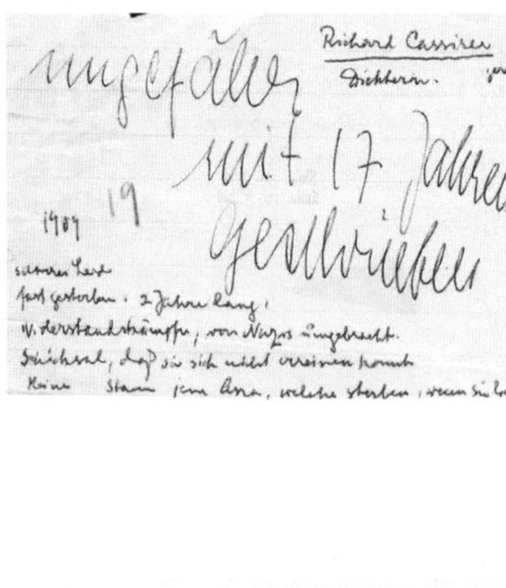

ungefähr mit 17 Jahren geschrieben

Richard Cassirer

Dichterin. gestellt

1909 19

schwere Lese

fast gestorben. 2 Jahre lang.

v. Verstandskämpfe, von Nazis umgebracht.

Schicksal, daß sie sich nicht vereinen konnte

Keine Stamm jener Arm, welche sterben, wenn sie lieben

## X = X = X

On a winter's day towards the end of the 1950s — it was the second Sunday of January to be exact, just before half past eleven in the morning — Sachs received Walter A. Berendsohn in her home in Stockholm's Södermalm district. Over the following two and half hours she told him about the years in Berlin, about the flight and the years that followed it, about the poems written by an unhappy seventeen-year-old and how and why it was that she sought, much later, a voice for the suffering of six million people. In the notes Berendsohn made afterwards he recorded, telegrammatically: "Love for a non-Jewish man of good family. Fate has made it mutually impossible for them to have each other. She cannot and will not talk about it. She became seriously ill." After a summary of the treatment in Dr. Cassirer's care in Grunewald, he concluded: "The man became a resistance fighter during the Nazi period. He was martyred (before my eyes) and finally killed. 'Out of this grew my entire poetic œuvre.'"

2

The account varies on other occasions, leading friends and acquaintances to assume that the man Sachs met as a teenager was the same person as the one she would later celebrate as her "dead bridegroom." In a letter written in 1948 to the Austrian writer and critic Friedrich Torberg, for example, she hinted at a "destiny that marked my whole life until '33," and which "ended, as I wrote in 'Prayers for the Dead Bridegroom.'" In a letter to the Swiss poet Rudolf Peyer she wrote, a decade later: "since my seventeenth year I have had a grievous fate, the meaning of which has remained hidden from me. It lasted until the time of our flight to Sweden [...]. It lasted until a terrible death." And in a letter to her friends Ilse and Moses Pergament she stated, in the following year: "I have seen a beloved person, mortally wounded, break down before my eyes."

More instances from her correspondence could be cited, or from statements made in conversations with friends and acquaintances. But the information itself is not as important as the fact that with time it acquired a formulaic, almost ritual character. Sachs had learned to say or write what was necessary in order to awaken interest but thwart inquisitiveness. It emerges from her conversation with Berendsohn that she put equals signs between the anonymous infatuation of her youth, the man she met in the 1930s, and the person who died during the war: x = x = x. By referring her entire œuvre to a source so overwhelming that there was no space left for any others, she provided the tragic details with a story familiar from both chivalrous poetry and romances. The still-smarting pain that was hinted at made further information an impossibility. A tactful interlocutor like Berendsohn had no choice but to treat the confidence with reverential silence. Nobody wanted to inflict further pain on Sachs by asking follow-up questions. It would have to suffice to observe that she remained true to the closing words in *Legenden und Erzählungen*: *Amor vincit omnia.*

**TEXT** Berendsohn, "Besuch bei Nelly Sachs, Sonntag den 11. Januar 1959 11½–14," ABerendsohnD · For letter to Torberg 08/01/1948, see Torberg, *In diesem Sinne. Briefe and Freunde und Zeitgenossen*, München 1981, 332 · For letter to Peyer 07/22/1959, see Briefe 144 · Letter to Pergament 05/05/1960, ASachs | **IMAGE 1** Walter A. Berendsohn, "Besuch bei Nelly Sachs, Sonntag den 11. Januar 1959 11½–14," Manuscript (ABerendsohnD) · **2** Walter A. Berendsohn in the 1950s (Photo Anna Riwkin, KBS)

## WHO TESTIFIES FOR THE WITNESS?

Berendsohn's notes deserve a close reading, however. Nowhere in them does Sachs say expressly that the men are one and the same. Nor does she claim the opposite. By simply identifying the original beloved as the source of her work she instead leaves it to the interviewer to draw his own conclusions. Later in life, recalcitrant fate is said to have reunited her with the acquaintance from her youth — "by means of a horrendous connection," as she has it in a letter to Abenius. The non-Jewish man of good family fought for an honorable cause for which he eventually had to pay with his life. Even if he was tormented before Sachs' eyes, he did not necessarily die in connection with this suffering. At least the quoted statement — "He was martyred (before my eyes) and finally killed" — does not allow for any definitive conclusion: the latter event does not have to have followed immediately on the former.

All the same, Sachs' choice of verb (*gemartert*) places the experience in a frame of reference with religious overtones. The martyr (from the Greek word for "witness") is someone who sacrifices his life for his beliefs. The only edifying aspect of the suggested tragedy is that it made Sachs' poems grow up. Once and for all she left the flowers and the creatures in the garden of paradise. Henceforth her poetry would bear witness — not so much to her own suffering as to that of others, the martyrs. Only thus could she react to Paul Celan's harrowing words: "No one / testifies for / the witness." With compassion.

**TEXT** "Besuch bei Nelly Sachs, Sonntag den 11. Januar 1959 11½–14," ABerendsohnD · For letter to Abenius 03/17/1958, see Briefe 125 · Celan, "Aschenglorie," *Gesammelte Werke*, Frankfurt am Main 1983, vol. II, 72

## CRIES, WHISPERS, AND TOMBIC SILENCE

Sachs' scattered statements about the unique love of her life have led to both cries and whispers. Some critics have ventured discreet guesses on the basis of the letters, other have preferred to speculate loudly (and fruitlessly) on rumors. One example will suffice. After having described Sachs' situation in the postscript to a posthumous volume of selected works from 1977, her correspondent and colleague HILDE DOMIN (1909–2006) returned to the question of the dead bridegroom in an essay which was said to contain "additional information about Nelly Sachs and her life and work": "During a stay abroad in 1977 I happened to meet a close relation of Nelly Sachs, whom we all believed was living quite alone in the world with her mother. As soon as I heard how close a relation this was, I immediately asked about the Gestapo arrest, and also about the beloved man. And in fact the conclusion I drew from *Die Suchende* [The Seeker] proved accurate: the two of them were arrested at the same time, in the course of a rendezvous in Steinplatz. Nelly Sachs had not been permitted to marry this man, as he was divorced and her father, an orthodox Jew, refused to give his approval."

As Fritsch-Vivié has pointed out, however, William Sachs was hardly an orthodox believer, neither is there any Jewish marriage law that prohibits marriage with a divorced person. The foreign journey, which took Domin to London, most likely brought her into contact with either Emmy Sachs, who was the daughter of William Sachs' younger brother Alexis and who had emigrated to Britain, or her husband, Tobias Brandt, who had emigrated via South Africa to Britain. The account of a Gestapo interrogation which Sachs gives in one of her rare prose pieces, "Leben unter Bedrohung" (Life Under Threat) from 1956, appears to have colored what her relations and closest friends believed they knew about her love. Possibly Sachs was alluding to the same event as Domin when she mentioned, in a letter to Abenius, "the old wound [which] by means of a horrendous connection had been ripped open again." But even this statement does not have to mean that the man in the 1930s was identical with the beloved from 1908. It *can* be taken to mean that a new but complicated infatuation led to a breaking up which was reminiscent of the experience from her youth and tore open the wound which had never healed...

Not even her friends Dähnert and Neff, who were close to Sachs during the period in question, were ever told the identity of the man. In her correspondence with Dinesen, Neff was only able to report that: "It was of course *a human being*, a man Nelly had become acquainted with at 17 years of age, in Bad Reinerz (Riesengebirge) where she was spending time with her parents. Nelly has merely hinted at this to me, and I can only relate to you a small proportion: marrying this immeasurably beloved person was an impossibility. Of necessity, his natural inclinations would preclude any such union. The two of them remained in contact throughout their lives, and this liaison formed the innermost core of her life. Thus he became, in the end, 'the dead bridegroom.'" Which says both everything and nothing. Dähnert, for her part, avoided speculating about the man's possible homosexuality and only noted after her friend's death that: "Lichen never [...] told me who the beloved was. When, last year, in July 1969, I tentatively asked her once again, she said: 'The only person who knew was my dear mother, and she took the secret to her grave.'"

Sachs remained faithful to x, or perhaps it was x, or possibly x, to the very end. The name of "the beloved" was buried along with her mother. Henceforth her "most beloved" would be the urn of love.

**TEXT** Domin, "Zusätzliche Information zu Leben und Werk von Nelly Sachs," *Text + Kritik*, 1979, no. 23, 42 · Fritsch-Vivié, 42 · "Leben unter Bedrohung," NSW:IV · For letter to Abenius 03/17/1958, see Briefe 125 · Dinesen, 63 · Dähnert, 227

**AN UNKNOWN QUANTITY**

What reasons did Sachs have for never revealing the identity — or possibly identities — of her beloved? Was the love platonic? Was it not reciprocated? Was the man a relative? Did he belong to the family's circle of friends and was he married? Did his "natural predisposition" force them apart? Did the parting have more to do with social conventions or so-called external circumstances? Was the man's identity kept under wraps out of consideration for his family? Or for Nelly's family? If so, why? Would an acknowledgement have put him in danger? Or someone else? Was the danger still there after the war? And if it was, was it of the same nature as before the catastrophe? Did the man's identity touch on something shameful? A self-inflicted failure or a personal shortcoming? A betrayal? Did he perhaps fight on the Nazi side, despite harboring political and ideological antipathies against it — like Hajo Klare, an "Aryan" who had two brothers in the SS and who, in order to ease his bad conscience, taught at Helene Herrmann's and Vera Lachmann's school for Jewish children in Grunewald, and was killed on the Russian front in the middle of the war? In other words: was the man, like "Peter" in Tegen's roman-à-clef, a soldier in the Wehrmacht? ("Nell, my little Nell! You never did get Peter! And he never got you! Once Hitler had come to power, an officer couldn't marry a Jewess. But he could become an officer. His father had seen to that. And now both Peter and his father lay deep in the black soil of Ukraine, one at Kiev, the other at Vitebsk…")

Questions and more questions… Once the smoke screens have been wafted aside, we're left largely with speculation. The only thing that can be said with certainty is that Sachs *wanted* the beloved to be known — yet only as "the dead bridegroom." She exposed a man whose identity she nonetheless withheld. Most likely he was not some made-up Prince Charming or palatable alibi for a person who wanted to evade owning up to other desires. He had lived. At least for a time in Berlin. Sometime during the war he died. Probably in 1943, possibly the following year. That is about all the sources can tell us. What the man — or men, as the case may be — most brings to mind is the sort of shadowy figure, cut from black cardboard and given rudimentary attributes, that appears in films such as Lotte Reiniger's *Das Ornament des verliebten Herzens* (The Ornament of the Infatuated Heart) from 1919, or *Die Abenteuer des Prinzen Achmed* (The Adventures of Prince Ahmed) from 1926. Or is he rather the empty space left where the figure was cut from the cardboard? Reduced to the intensity with which he is missed, he seems to be capable of being everyone and nobody — a placeholder for a passion which, unlike love,

3

survived war, separation, catastrophe. Under the heading "A… killed; the most beloved person; seen a beloved person… mortally wounded, break down; the horrific things that had happened to a beloved person" Dinesen cites twelve excerpts from her correspondence register in which Sachs makes remarks which *might* have to do with the anonymous lover. But these are insinuations, and it isn't even certain that they refer to one and the same person. In addition, they were made much later, between January 1957 and May 1960, over twenty years after the lovers saw each other for the last time.

Considering the time of the man's death, Sachs must have been informed of the tragedy after her flight. But how? In a letter? Over the telephone? By other refugees who had managed to escape? In a letter to Berendsohn, written a year or two before she demanded that personal information be treated with discretion, she described the background to the mystery play *Eli*: "so I would still like to tell you a little bit about how it was that I suddenly had to write it, this naked, smoldering chunk of human misery. I received a terrible piece of news — someone very close to me had died a true martyr's death." Possibly Sachs was speaking of the beloved x; possibly the information had to do with her cousin on her mother's side, the rabbi Heinz Meyer, who was said to have spent four days hidden in a coffin before he was deported to Theresienstadt on May 17, 1943. At first Meyer preached to the prisoners, but in the following year he and his family were taken to Auschwitz, where the gas showers waited. It emerges from letters to Dähnert that Sachs heard about her cousin's fate "via a lady who had previously been a prisoner in Theresienstadt." Was she informed about the dead bridegroom by the same ex-prisoner? Even if it can't be ruled out that her cousin was the beloved x of the 1930s — a circumstance that social conventions most certainly would have required be kept secret — he cannot possibly have been the object of the first infatuation. In 1908 the rabbi-to-be was but one year old…

Did the beloved work in Sachs' immediate vicinity? Shortly after the war she reestablished contact with her cousin Manfred George and his wife, Mary Graf, in New York. In a letter from January 1946 she described the years before her father's death: "Due to my father's serious illness, he died in 1930, I was tied for years to the home, due to my own unhappy fate, which left me unmarried, I withdrew ever deeper." In her memoir, the family's maid mentions Dr. Liebmann. This neighbor who lived a few floors up in the building "was about the same age as Miss Nelly." According to Lina Schoegel he saw to the patient and also took Nelly in his arms to comfort her when death finally came. Hans Georg Liebmann, who was in fact five years older than Nelly and had spent his school years elsewhere, was the son of the manufacturer Adolf Liebmann. In the 1920s he returned to Berlin and also visited the new apartment in Lessingstraße, where mother and daughter had moved after William Sachs' death. "He stayed to dinner and was also very taken with the new, beauti-

4

ful home, and spoke in very praising terms of it. But then he left again and I did not see him in our home after that. Perhaps he moved away from Berlin, to London I later heard." Other sources — among them Hilde and Otto Bental — maintain that Sachs spoke of Liebmann with striking warmth.

The last time Liebmann was registered at Siegmundshof was 1935; the following year he was listed in the city's *Adreßbuch* as resident at Bismarckstraße 102. After having been forced to sell the clinic he ran with a couple of colleagues in Tiergarten, he emigrated in 1936 to London. Difficulties in settling there led him to continue to New York the following year. There he practiced as a doctor until the end of the 1960s. Just like his former neighbor, he lived with his mother and remained unmarried until his death in 1987. Considering the fact that Sachs would write her most intimate love poems only a few months after Liebmann's emigration — and speak in them, among other things, about what distinguished being "in love from loving" (*Lieb von Liebe*) — the chronology would allow for the possibility that he was the beloved man, even if his long life after the war makes this considerably less likely.

On the other hand: would a concrete name make it easier to understand Sachs' poetry? Or why she designated longing the driving force behind her writing? Would the reader be brought closer to the hidden core of the texts? Should she or he not instead be asking themselves how omission came to be part of the way in which Sachs' poetry speaks? Did her unwillingness, perhaps her inability, to state a name have to do with something deeper — not with her life but with her work? To Dähnert Sachs wrote, after the war: "But it is my fate to be alone, as it is the fate of my people." Loneliness became the distinguishing mark of poetry. Without it, no poems. The wound that love had torn open in life must be made readable in the work, but only as the scar of abandonment: XXX.

**TEXT** For Hajo Klare, see Vera Lachmann, "Erinnerungen an Erika Weigand," *Castrum peregrini*, 1979, no. 138, 81 · TegenJ, 119 · Briefregister, 162 · For letters to Berendsohn 01/23/1957, Dähnert 03/20/1947 and 08/14/1948, as well as to George and Graf 01/27/1946, see Briefe 104, 40, 54, and 25 respectively · Schubert:2 · Schubert:3 · For the statement by Hilde Bental, see Dinesen, 81 · For information on Liebmann, see his records of reparations (*Entschädigungsakte*) no. 261 813, Landesamt für Bürger- und Ordnungsangelegenheiten Abt. 1 (EBB) | **IMAGE 3** Scrapbook pictures from "Das Oblatenalbum" (KBS) · **4** Stills from Lotte Reiniger, *Die Abenteuer des Prinzen Achmed* 1926 (Christel Strobel, Agentur für Primrose Productions, Munich)

### *MOID*

In Samuel Josef Agnon's short novel *Sippur Pashut* (A Simple Story) from 1935 there is a young woman named Bluma. The story takes place towards the end of the nineteenth century in the author's home town, the former Galician shtetl Buczacz — now Buchach — on the river Strypa in western Ukraine. An orphan, Bluma grows up in the Hurwitz family. But the rich relatives treat her badly

and force her to do the chores of a maid. Eventually, the son Hirschel falls in love with her, which leads to the sorts of complications that realist novels of the period were partial to exploring. In contrast, for example, with Sonia in Tolstoy's *War and Peace*, who stays and raises the children her beloved Nikolai has by another woman, Bluma leaves the hypocritical family. Opposed to the false morals of the Jewish middle class, she becomes involved with socialist circles. Towards the end of the story she even comes across as a feminist when she declares that "not every woman has to get married." In essence, Agnon's book is about Hirschel's attempts to forget his great love, but it is in Bluma that the writer created something rare in his œuvre: the portrait of an independent woman. In an epilogue Agnon promised to return to her in a future novel. Despite assurances that "much ink" would flow, however, he never wrote a separate sequel. Bluma remained an example — albeit an unusually spirited one — of what the characters in the book would have called a *moid*: a childless woman who had refused to marry or who hadn't found anyone by the age when convention required a person get married. In other words: a person from whom time has run away.

In this respect, the fifty-year-old woman who managed to flee Germany for Sweden was a *moid*. When tragic circumstances made marriage impossible she chose solitude. But Sachs did not let separation mean the end of love. On the contrary, poetry provided the medium in which the liaison could continue. There, the unknown man even became "bridegroom." With time Sachs would come to view her fate as exemplary for a whole people. Many of her texts — at first poems and stories, later dramas — do not merely deal with abandonment, but also try to extract from it a positive significance. Some set out expressly from the experience of being left, such as the cycle "Gebete für den toten Bräutigam" (Prayers for the Dead Bridegroom), while others more indirectly cover the sentimental range of solitude. Nonetheless the question remains whether the most intimate texts weren't written before the flight. In 1937 Sachs finished a cycle of fourteen poems in which she turns for the first (and last) time to the form often given to love in poetry: the dialogue. In these unpublished "Lieder vom Abschied. An den Fernen" (Songs of Farewell: To the Distant One) contact is established between a longing I and a distant You. The beloved may be in a faraway place, but dialogue is still possible. That is to say: the absent man may be addressed and thus be experienced in and by means of the very distance that separates the lovers.

5

The third poem, "Geliebter, hier sind Masslieben" (Beloved, Here Are Daisies), offers an example of the predominant register:

> Beloved, here are daisies / — A smile from meadows green — / The kiss has remained with them / With me only evening dew. // Beloved, here are violets / The quiet melody — / — Distant blue — a brief moment / It dreams itself as close

as never before. // Beloved, here is a dread / A breeze, a trembling grass / Take it, and you take my life / Stooped and wet with tears.

The props may be worn, the sentiments recognizable, but by playing off *Geliebter* (beloved) against *geblieben* (remained), *Veilchen* (violets) against *Weilchen* (brief moment), *Beben* (trembling) against *Leben* (life), Sachs nonetheless does what she can to depict unique love in the ready-made language of daisies. The distant beloved is "heard" in the remaining one, the poem's bouquet echoes in the vanishing moment when the self dreams herself near with the language of flowers. And life passes in expectant throbbing — a tension as lasting as longing, as brief as a "melody." All that remains is breath and grass atremble.

The self's eyes are orphaned when the sound of the beloved's footsteps have faded away. Although the heart sobs "lost," the lips are mute: "Like the amen after prayer / my heart but trembles the name." The beloved is forever hidden in the heart's chamber. His name sounds between heartbeats, in the trembling that keeps the self alive despite being made of absence. This is an *amour* without future, which cannot be repeated and will never come back. Before Sachs was forced to experience the refugee's *nevermore*, she had learned what it was to become *moid* — a stateless wanderer in the Republic of Love:

The swallow's words "abandoned" / Soar to a "nevermore."

**TEXT** Agnon, *A Simple Story*, New York 1985 · "Lieder vom Abschied," ASachs | **IMAGE** **5** Scrapbook pictures from "Das Oblatenalbum" (KBS)

## THE THOU, THE WIZARD, THE BRIDEGROOM, AND THE GREAT ANONYMOUS

There are many male characters in Sachs' works. Some are priests of rapacious religions, others have been chosen by God without knowing it. There are executioners, victims, and victims who become executioners. Some exude the ambivalent overtones of eroticism, while others are idealized and take on the traits of sterling knights … Among the figures who play a special role for love between the sexes is the enigmatic thou in some of the early sonnets and the distant beloved invoked in the 1930s "Lieder vom Abschied." The wizard Merlin features in texts spread throughout the entire œuvre, whereas the dead bridegroom is extolled in the prayers from the 1940s, and in the late dramatic poetry "The Great Anonymous" appears. Irrespective of whether these characters are shrouded in the veils of chivalrous poetry or private mythology, they are all incarnations of the relationship between the sexes and the marvels and pitfalls of togetherness.

**THE THOU.** In an undated sonnet — probably from the 1910s — Sachs writes:

As nuns carry their book of prayers / Devoted to only One, never seduced / By earthly desire not ever touched / Has my life abided in You alone.

The poem depicts a time when love was still intact and concerned "One" — which in this context can mean both "[m]y brother Death" and "God," since the poem's cross-references are ambiguous and some pronouns are headed by capital letters while others aren't. Yet more important than the lament over a life without desire and touching is the perspective: the speaker is speaking Afterwards. The description of the pious, never-seduced women serves as a contrast. The speaker who alone has been touched by desire is on the other side of innocence. God "releases what he strikes," and sent a cherub equipped with a "fire atom" who set longing ablaze. In this indivisible core the energy remains long after the attempts at fission. Even if the separation is a fact — the very prerequisite of the sonnet — the glowing particle survives all conceivable distances in time and space. Although the text is an element of a grieving process, on a deeper level it is a hymn to unconditional love.

In the following poem, the self wishes that the happiness that failed her will strengthen the beloved:

6

For you may my departed smile gleam / May your tears betide only me / May my forsaken joy now gladden you / The strength that failed me fortify your arm.

For someone who understands devotion in absolute terms, love can know no limits even if it has been wronged. Neither can pain. In the gospel Sachs preached in her early sonnets — unsurprisingly, it evinces common traits with the New Testament — no sacrifice is deemed too great, no suffering beyond the pale:

But faith has such a firm home in me / That I can swallow snakes without fear / As if love could not a poison fang humble.

But in spite of faith, devotion is not without shadows. Strangely enough, these have the capacity to be cast on the time *before* the self was struck by fate, on the untouched place in which she once was. After the loss she notes that she had a premonition of what was going to happen. Future unhappiness lay unreleased in the past. The self needn't even have raised its gaze in order to see in her inner eye how her being would be frozen at the sight of the beloved. But even if she had spotted the looming catastrophe in time, she would have been incapable of defending herself. Whether she wanted it or not, she had been chosen. Despite this fatefulness she affirms the catastrophe with every fiber of her being. It is the relationship which is over, not love. "If the soul be ordered to bequeath its treasures / What wealth it would reap as they went to you." The greater the loss, the richer the loneliness.

From this perspective it appears logical that the poem which was intended to process the pain instead keeps the flame alive. The sonnets render "[t]he greatest pain with a dark ring" — a magic circle that the self neither wants to leave nor believes herself capable of leaving. The sole option left is to keep the suffering alive after the beloved has disappeared. For the person who can grow rich only on loss, each new attempt to rephrase longing increases love's value. "Your countenance, wizard, dwelt in hiding!" it is stated at one point, "You [are] a vessel in which dark forces seethe." The poem is turned into a bottomless vessel from which the self's longing repeatedly surges. Its verses don't quench her thirst, but increase it. To this state can be applied the same words with which one of the sonnets characterizes Diana, the goddess of hunting: "Saved is she, never more recovered / Protected as a source, between malediction and mercy"...

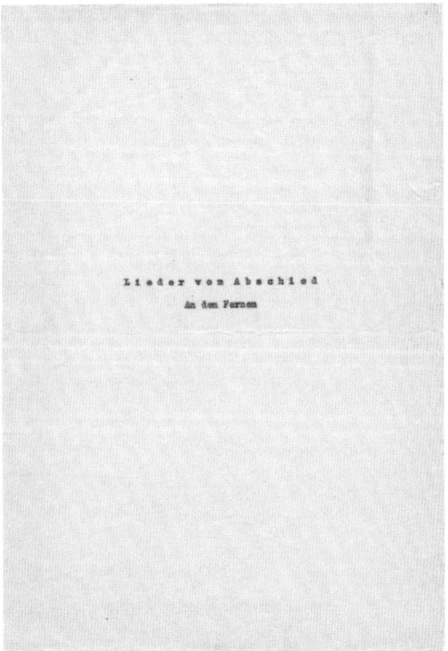
Lieder von Abschied
An den Fernen

7

**THE WIZARD.** In the mysterious regions of love, the contradictory place between mercy and malediction is traditionally occupied by wizards and seducers. In Sachs' library there is still a copy of *Die Geschichte des Zauberers Merlin* (The Story of the Wizard Merlin), where the two roles are amalgamated into one character. Translated by Dorothea Schlegel and published in 1911, the book is illustrated with a heliograph after a painting by the pre-Raphaelite painter Edward Coley Burne-Jones, *The Beguiling of Merlin*, from 1872–1877. The picture shows the helpless wizard caught in a briar while the ravishing but ambiguous fairy Nynianne (or Nimue or Viviane) reads from a book of spells. Merlin is the son of the Devil and a virgin. After growing up he becomes part of the court of King Arthur and takes his place among the knights of the round table. The good side of his double nature seems to have vanquished the evil one. But the angered father, who had hoped for a new Antichrist, sends Nynianne to him. The fairy shows "such devoted love that he becomes fully and completely and more and more enchanted and captivated by her." Thus she is able to coax the secret of the magic arts out of him. During an encounter by a briar Merlin rests his head on her lap. When he has fallen asleep she applies the magic she has learned and removes him to a place to which only she has access. Thenceforth it is in Nynianne's power to come and go as she pleases, while the wizard is captive in the invisible prison of disobliging love.

During the sixty years of her writing life, Sachs repeatedly returned to this story, as has been noted by Dinesen. (Sachs' literary estate includes a newspaper cutting from the *Frankfurter Zeitung* of July 5, 1936, which had originally been found in her edition of Schlegel. Under the headline "Merlin und der Teufel" [Merlin and the Devil], Victor Meyer-Eckart describes a "tale" which gave Sachs little peace.) In the sonnets of the 1910s, the beloved was expressly called a "wizard"; in the 1920s the theme was further developed in the story "Wie der Zauberer Merlin erlöset ward" (How the Wizard Merlin Was Freed); and after her arrival in Sweden she transformed the material into a theater piece — "Ein Spiel vom Zauberer Merlin" (A Play about the Wizard Merlin) —

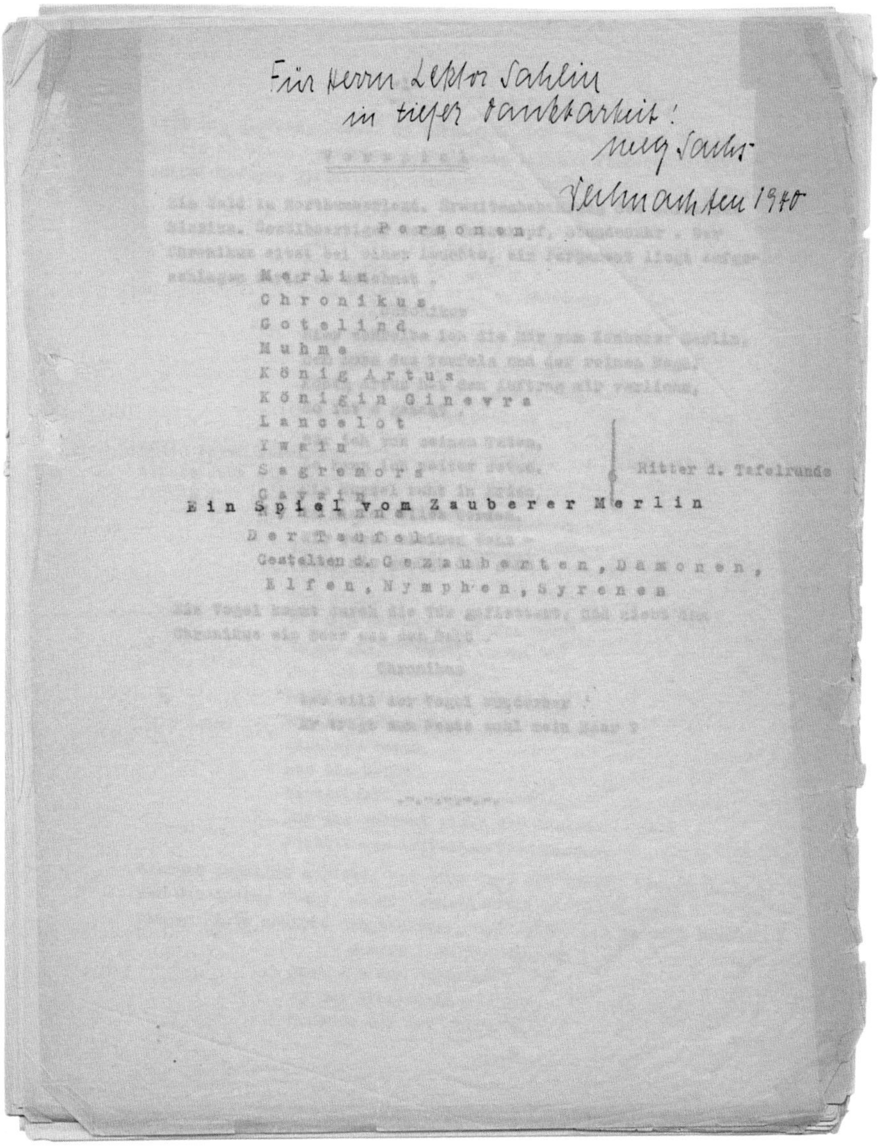

Für Herrn Lektor Sahlin
in tiefer Dankbarkeit!
Nelly Sachs
Weihnachten 1940

Personen

Merlin
Chronikus
Gotelind
Muhme
König Artus
Königin Ginevra
Lancelot
Ywein
Sagremors
Gaw[illegible]
[illegible]
— Ritter d. Tafelrunde

Ein Spiel vom Zauberer Merlin

Der Teufel
Gestalten d. Gezauberten, Damonen,
Elfen, Nymphen, Syrenen

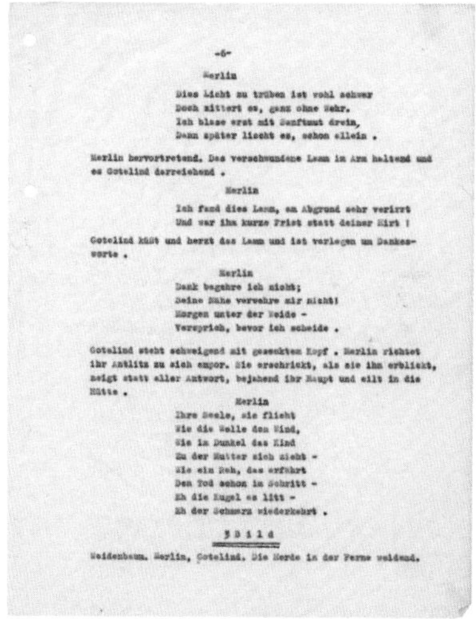

-6-

Merlin

Dies Licht zu trüben ist wohl schwer
Doch zittert es, ganz ohne Wehr.
Ich blase erst mit Sanftmut drein,
Dann später lischt es, schon allein .

Merlin hervortretend. Das verschwundene Lamm im Arm haltend und es Gotelind darreichend .

Merlin

Ich fand dies Lamm, am Abgrund sehr verirrt
Und war ihm kurze Frist statt deiner Hirt !

Gotelind küßt und herzt das Lamm und ist verlegen um Dankesworte .

Merlin

Dank begehre ich nicht;
Deine Nähe verwehre mir nicht!
Morgen unter der Weide -
Versprich, bevor ich scheide .

Gotelind steht schweigend mit gesenktem Kopf . Merlin richtet ihr Antlitz zu sich empor. Sie erschrickt, als sie ihn erblickt, neigt statt aller Antwort, bejahend ihr Haupt und eilt in die Hütte .

Merlin

Ihre Seele, sie flieht
Wie die Welle den Wind,
Wie im Dunkel das Kind
Zu der Mutter sich zieht -
Wie ein Reh, das erfährt
Den Tod schon im Schritt -
Eh die Kugel es litt -
Eh der Schmerz wiederkehrt .

3 Bild

Weidenbaum. Merlin, Gotelind. Die Herde in der Ferne weidend.

8

which she gave as a gift to Enar Sahlin at Christmas in 1940. Towards the end of her life she was again working on a dramatic piece, this time entitled "Merlin der Zauberer" (The Wizard Merlin), and another play from the same period, *Verzauberung* (Enchantment), centers on the meeting between a wizard and a girl. The material possessed a power to charm that Sachs apparently was defenseless against.

The earliest handling of the theme appears in a poem from the Berlin period, entitled "Merlin." A couple of the stanzas read:

> See now in the realm of air / Ever captured in the wind's harp / Crying in Ariel's expanse / A voice like wind and dream. // And these word ornaments / Would, until my magic pen / Rests in floral fulfillment / Bring you out in adornment.

As Dinesen has remarked, Sachs sought a way to get around the story's cursing of the wizard. Evidently she wasn't satisfied with the way the legend ended, wanting instead to release the wizard from the confinement of invisibility. He was still "ever captured in the wind's harp," as intangible as air or dreams, but the speaker in Sachs' poem is the same person as the author of it, and can therefore promise that as long as her "magic pen" does not rest her words shall long for the beloved. What the story's fairy prevented, the writer can restore: the poet adorns the desired one and lets him appear in language's enchanting robes. It may be that he has been stolen by another woman, but by means of the poem's ornaments he becomes visible again. If Nynianne dreamt the risky dream of a love object which would forever be only hers, Sachs gave herself to the hope of a love more intact than innocence.

When she returned to Merlin many years later, around Christmas in 1940, the emphasis had shifted. The artful seduction was gone and Nynianne no longer played a prominent role. Instead, the relationship between the wizard and the fair but orphaned girl Gotelind was at the heart of the story. As storms rage, "the shy, child-pious" girl kneels in prayer. Suddenly the door is thrown open and she fears death has arrived. But instead of the grim reaper it is Merlin who enters and proclaims: "It is not death, but it is love / That brings the greatest pain in this earthly life." The girl falls into the arms of the beloved and is taken away. In the next scene they are sitting by a well in which Gotelind's dead mother appears in a luminous mist. The girl asks the wizard to let her die at his feet, but he is gripped by her chaste yet unreserved devotion. As the mother's glow slowly dies again he feels his soul leaving him. He now realizes that only Gotelind can protect him and asks her to take pity on him. Henceforth she will preserve his soul "in the form of a star" in her innermost being. Then the wizard wraps his cloak around what is left of him and disappears into the air.

The events described are far from original. Still, it might be worth noting that Sachs separates good from evil by releasing the man's uncorrupted soul from his wicked body. It is not until then that Nynianne (whose name "means:

/ 'I do not want to'") appears and the drama's basic conflict can be played out. The third person in the love triangle turns out to be not a fairy but a nymph, who inveigles the weak-willed Merlin until he conjures everything under the sun — an ocean "he sprays with its white foam," coral reefs and monsters become visible, suddenly goblins with green hair fly through the air. As if these tricks weren't enough, icebergs and primeval forests, deserts and wild animals appear as well. In short: all of creation. Still the nymph isn't satisfied — she wants to see the Maker himself. "This my magic wand cannot show," Merlin apologizes. "That which breathes here, comes from silence." But Nynianne laughs and calls him a jester. What would his tricks be worth if they weren't able to manifest the very principle of creation? Her unbelief makes the wizard attempt the unforgivable and he "begins the invocation of the Supreme." A few pages later his hubris plunges everything into perdition. Suddenly the oceans rise and the mountains sink. Thunder and lightning. "Nothing is recognizable anymore."

When the dust has settled, Gotelind appears with the vicarious narrator of the drama, Chronikus. The action is summarized and given an instructive moral. When the maiden relates that she thought she could hear her beloved's voice in a dream, however, Merlin's soul is unexpectedly unloosed from her. Like a radiant star it floats through the air in the direction of the briar, where she at last finds him in the flesh too. The noble girl can now, once and for all, sink down by the wizard's feet at which lizards, weasels, and snakes are playing. "But I was glad to kiss the snake / It was my lord's playmate." Then she dies. Merlin has barely regained his soul when he understands the girl's sacrifice: it is about boundless love. "This is Gotelind, the shepherdess, who gave to me / Her heart; and for her love became a grave." Through the sacrifice he gains release and his soul leaves him — yet this time of its own accord, as a butterfly, and he is reunited with his beloved in the ether. Finally Merlin also dies, with a clear conscience.

9

Sachs would not maintain much of this piously conventional drama form in her later writing. The scent of roses and sweet doom had been aired out, the corsets and suits of armor mothballed, the melancholy strains had rung out forever. Even the magic tricks were cancelled — or rather: replaced with the singular conjuring of letters. But the belief in unconditional love lived on, understood as a force that can break through the barriers between dimensions, turn the invisible visible and transform a snakebite into a kiss of mercy. What unconditional love could not have in this world, it would get in the next — thus the message between the lines.

When Sachs returned to the theme during the final years of her life, the wizard no longer played the part of seducer, but he still possessed unimaginable powers. The short piece *Verzauberung* from the early 1960s shrinks the cast to three people: one "Tooth of Time" representing the grinding passage of transience, one "wizard," and one "girl." The last two are in a study which is transformed into an "ice-age cave" as soon as the wizard begins to speak and whose interior is recognizable from dramatic texts such as *Abram im Salz* (Abraham in the Salt) from the 1940s. *Verzauberung* has much of the nightmare. The set is minimal as in Beckett, virtually nonexistent. Seated on a chair center stage, the girl has been placed under hypnosis. The wizard leans his head back and asks her to open her mouth. Her posture hovers somewhere between hostage and Madonna — a *Pietà* resembling Duchenne de Boulogne's portraits of artificial ecstasy. Again and again the man urges the girl to describe what it is she is seeing. "I am blind!" she protests, but nonetheless describes visions which seem to be a result of his commanding as much as of any inner compulsion. That is to say, the text is that strangest of things: a drama in which nothing is shown. If the two virtually motionless characters are disregarded, what is being seen is rendered only in words — an inner scenery in which the power of imagination is being commanded yet never becomes translated into external events. Thus the invisible takes on form. As marked omission.

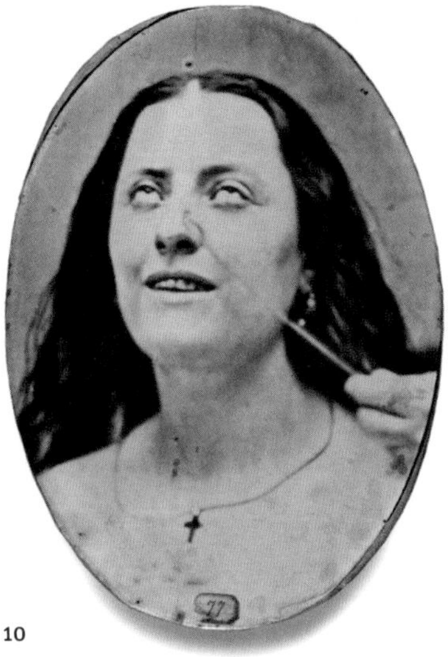

10

At first the hypnotized girl describes hunting scenes painted on the walls of the cave she thinks she's in: "A hunter steps out of the icy wall — he is dragging a dying stag by the antlers — and points the arrow at my heart — the stag raises its antlers and writes on my body: I give you my death —." In this nightmarish scenario the boundaries between dimensions are not definitive. The hunter can step out of the prehistoric painting, the sacrificial animal drawn on the cave wall can write directly on the girl's body, proclaiming that it is giving her its dying. And in the same way that the hunter sends arrows towards the stag, the wizard directs his "further" towards the hypnotized girl. By means of such ritualized invocation he finally calls forth the innermost and most painful visions. Now faces of air don masks "of forgetting," a piece of night is broken away from the ice, larvae lays eggs in nests of air. The wizard remarks that this must be a "black wedding" and wonders why the girl isn't struck dumb by her burning passion. To which she answers: "I sing in the flames — love — love — love —."

Sachs' drama is not about artful seduction, even if the hypnotist exercises a power over the girl she can't resist. Neither does the wizard appear to be identical to the lover, as he did in the legend piece from 1940. After a lifelong relationship with the Merlin theme, the only thing that remains is devotion. That is the true subject of *Verzauberung*. The drama deals with the ultimate love sacrifice — the kind that is consumed until only flames remain. What is being called forth in the fatal séance is definitive doom. In the last pages, nothing is holding the fire back any more, everything is love, and the "bridegroom" can rise "from longing's grave." He has become "an arrow," the girl recounts, "nothing but an arrow." The beloved whom she once buried in her yearning has been transformed into the pure direction of flames, as indicated by Cupid. When the hypnotist wakes her from her artificial sleep she gazes down at her empty lap and wonders: "My hands filled with earthly dust — / What is it?" To which the wizard replies: "Your bridegroom's mask —." All that remains of burning longing is the beloved's cover of dust.

**THE BRIDEGROOM.** Sometime during the first half of the 1940s, when the outcome of the war could be discerned, Sachs received the news that the man she had remained faithful to, despite pain and separation, had died. How and where is unclear, as is the way in which the news reached her. The only certainty is that in the winter of 1943–1944 she began a series of poems which she regarded as a passion cycle and grouped under the heading "Gebete für den toten Bräutigam." These texts are one of the cornerstones of the sepulcher of a book that appeared in 1947 and by means of which she came to be seen as the poet of Jewish victimhood, *In den Wohnungen des Todes.*

Despite the crucial significance which Sachs attached to her tragic infatuation in adolescence, and which she later claimed, in a letter to Friedrich Torberg, reached its culmination in the ten poems about the dead bridegroom, she opened her collection of poems with texts written in memory of another You: Israel. The entire first part, "Dein Leib im Rauch durch die Luft" (Your Body into Smoke through the Air), deals with the fate of the Jewish people. By means of the repeated apostrophizing of a collective singular which has been spread like smoke in the air, the intimate prayers for the individual are prepared behind a personal pronoun. "O lofty point of encounter in poverty's room," it is stated in a voice at times reminiscent of Rilke's:

> If only I knew what the elements mean; / They refer to you, for everything always refers / To you, I cannot help myself crying.

The tidy use of rhyming recalls the verse of the 1920s and 1930s. Despite a décor far from original — kisses, tears, sighs — the texts exude the matter-of-factness of prayer. The I speaking does not need to seek experiences or a language to paraphrase them with. On the contrary, the poems are characterized by a balance between distance and proximity: the dead one may have died recently, but it was a long time since his footsteps died away. "I can hear your footsteps / Each and every one has borne death," Sachs had written ten years earlier in "Songs of Parting." Now "the shoes have been torn off,"

> Your shoes were made of calfskin. / They may have been tanned, dyed, / The thing had pierced them — / But who knows where a last living / Breath lives?

The prayers of the 1940s try to preserve the final sigh, the beloved's last wisp of breath, in the sound of receding footsteps. Even if the shoes have been torn off and transformed into placeholders for emptiness, the abandoned one dreams of the mother animal's warm tongue licking the calf's skin. She remembers a man's hat and wonders what sand tasted the beloved's blood. She asks herself what his last gaze rested on. Was it a stone? Earth enough to fill a shoe? A puddle of water? The buckle of the enemy's leather belt? Despite mottos taken from Jewish mysticism and biblical allusions recalling the Jewish destiny, there is nothing in these poems claiming that the man died in a camp or because of his Jewish descent. Nor is the obverse established. The only certainty is that the beloved fell far from home, on foreign soil, possibly to an enemy bullet. In short: whoever he was and however he died, he too is a victim. In the last poem he is aptly given "the eyes of the hind." His status is imbued with female traits that unite him with the stag of myth and the eternal victim of the hunt.

The self in these devotional texts is seeking certainty in vain. She mumbles words that dissipate in the air. The prayers which were intended to conjure up the absent one are turned into farewells, lips are pursed but never meet the other's lips. Every sign alludes to the dead one, yet the poem's self is unable to interpret their meaning. Although death is a fact, everything remains speculation. Question: Is there anything left to save when unknowing seems to be the sole thing remaining? Answer: Only longing. "She who with kisses and tears and sighs fills the secretive rooms with air — / Is she perhaps the invisible earth?" The query is rhetorical. Sachs doesn't so much answer it as let it ring on. Thereby the poem is opened towards a dimension without name and address, which is at once on this side of death and on the other:

> O my beloved, perhaps our love has already yielded worlds in longing's heaven — / For which our breathing, in — and out, builds a cradle for life and death?

Sachs pins her hopes on the dash connecting fullness and emptiness. With its help would a cradle of longing be fashioned from the poem.

**THE GREAT ANONYMOUS.** In one of her last texts before international fame arrived in 1966, the unfinished drama "Der große Anonyme," Sachs returned for the last time to Merlin. Drafts show that she was seeking a form which could unite all the aspects she had come to associate with the material over more than fifty years of writing. Words, dance, and music together would give shape to a drama of deliverance with cosmic proportions. The ten-page text takes place in a ballroom where couples are dancing on the border between night and day. The lights are soon dimmed and we find ourselves in metaphysical regions. A woman's voice declares that she is going to dance to the end of the world and then open the door and disappear, while a man's voice wonders if that will be into life or out to death.

> I do not know / Perhaps in the green time / when wells have two exits —

Even if the woman cannot say what is on the other side, she is seeking the same source where pain was collected, fresh and strong, half a century earlier. As so often, Sachs was trying to give shape to the drama of recollection. Memories of events in the past would, paradoxically, lead forward, into the unknown. Perhaps the well did have two exits after all…

"Is it into green time you want to go," says a new voice, called "The nocturnal": "to the wizard Merlin, perhaps?" A few exchanges later he proclaims, this time "as a young page": "Remember — remember / see the green time in the woods in Dioflè." A thousand years are pushed aside as easily as old bones, the past steps out of the dark, the woman's voice turns into a girl who is rambling and hallucinating:

> I seek the place / where stars kiss each other / times embrace one another / I am 17 springs // sinking through the floor / where there's stomping and din / Old is trampled down / New is released / Darkness strikes against me

In this kaleidoscopic drama, new characters appear with each turn, only to prove to be facets of previous incarnations. This happens most clearly with some "dance worms" who follow on each other and are only kept separate by being numbered (from 1 through 6). The reader gets the impression that the voices don't come from a fixed place in space or are tied to a particular person — instead they overlap and amplify each other like the parts in a piece of music. In a similar way, tenses form separate currents in the same basic flow. The future lies stored in the past, yet elapsed events turn out not to be wholly in the past. A millennium passes in an instant, whereas an early love experience may last until long after death.

Even if both time and space shift, the axis around which events rotate is nonetheless made up of one and the same experience: the seduction of a seventeen-year-old girl one summer day in eternity. At this point she is not seeking either Merlin or a new dance partner, playing-card jacks or don giovannis, but a male character who is grander than all the shifting manifestations in which he has featured for half a century: "The Great Anonymous." The personified love which Sachs gave different forms without ever giving them a name has become an all-embracing principle. Namelessness is its designation, formlessness its shape. In a couple of instances this paradoxical character is called "conductor" as if to underline that although he does not make the air sing he still "controls the world" with its breathing and music. The formless creation is "a piece of night in which the world is embroiled." In a final colossal effort he is to be peeled out of the darkness. But this requires the girl's help: "embody my voice," he urges her, "wall me in inside the dungeon of your homesickness." And the choir provides the refrain: "We want to be beside ourselves / break open the shell —."

The poem's persona has finally taken on features of the bride of Christ. Without her, even the Great Anonymous would be powerless. (And without the poem, Creation would be valueless.) He needs her longing in order to become flesh and blood. In her last text about the centrifugal forces of love, Sachs is no longer writing about artful seduction, nor formulating any farewells or epitaphs. The drama's seventeen-year-old girl who rises up from the grassy spot where she had been resting finally releases her beloved from formlessness. Dancing, she molds his contours at her potter's wheel. The beloved may appear in many guises, but love — this "atom of fire" — remains the same, indivisible and intact. Out of the abandoned one a birth-giver has been wrought. It's even possible that she creates the Creator. At least that might explain the drama's final question:

> out of the night / What time is It?

The answer likely lies at the well's other exit.

**TEXT** *Die Geschichte des Zauberers Merlin*, Weimar 1911, 246 · Victor Meyer-Eckhardt, "Merlin und der Teufel," *Frankfurter Zeitung* 07/05/1936 · Dinesen, 62 · The sonnets are in ASachsS · "Lieder vom Abschied," ASachs · *Abram im Salz*, ZiS (NSW:III) · For letter to Torberg 08/01/1948, see *In diesem Sinne. Briefe an Freunde und Zeitgenossen*, Munich 1981, 332 · "Gebete für den toten Bräutigam," IdWdT (NSW:II) · *Verzauberung*, ZiS (NSW:III) · "Der große Anonyme," NSW:III | **IMAGE 6** Edward Coley Burne-Jones, The Beguiling of Merlin (1872–1877), oil painting. Courtesy National Museums Liverpool (Lady Lever Art Gallery, Merseyside) · **7** "Lieder vom Abschied," typescript (KBS) · **8** "Ein Spiel vom Zauberer Merlin," typescript (KBS) · **9** Scrapbook picture from "Das Oblatenalbum" (KBS) · **10** Duchenne de Boulogne, "Extase de l'amour humain," 1861 (simulation by Birgit Schlegel) · **11** Scrapbook pictures from "Das Oblatenalbum" (KBS)

11

# LESS AND LESS SPACE

1

### IN THE DWELLINGS OF THE PAST

After William Sachs' death the stately apartment in Siegmundshof became too big and too expensive. According to Dähnert he had tried to secure "a proper fortune" for his wife and daughter, well aware of how helpless his wife was in matters concerning the everyday "struggle for existence." But the hyperinflation of the 1920s and the stock market crash towards the end of the same decade had hit his assets hard. The safest option was to move back to Lessingstraße 33, which still belonged to Margarete. There they could live rent-free and subsist on the modest income which remained after running costs had been paid. After fifteen years with the firm, Miss Rehberg left her position as secretary without giving notice. For a time they were helped by an administrator, but he is said to have done most things wrong. When Sachs finally decided to deal with the accounts herself, they were in a chaotic state. Over the following year she came to grips with the finances, wound up the firm, and sold the properties her father had owned. After forty years as daughter, she assumed a man's social and financial duties. From now on she was her mother's life companion.

When the renovation of the apartment in Lessingstraße was finished, the furniture was reupholstered and then the move was organized. From the spring of 1931 widow and daughter were living in a considerably brighter — and judging from the color choices, more feminine — home consisting of "7 rooms 2 hallways 2 servants' bedrooms 1 kitchen," as it was later described in an enumeration of lost property which was submitted in connection with an application for damages in the 1950s. Here the paintings with nature sceneries, which in Siegmundshof had hung in gloomy drawing rooms, were displayed more to their advantage, and the heavy furniture from the old study was divided between several rooms in the new apartment. Sachs' own room — in which one wall was covered by white-painted bookshelves holding some 500 volumes — was in pink, while the other rooms were painted in pastel tones. Even the stairwell was given a facelift in pink, blue, and violet.

Only the office where the administration of the building was carried out remained a strict and businesslike world. While the other rooms had something ethereal about them, this was a geometric place with clear guidelines. In her memoir, Dähnert describes life there: "Li's bookkeeping was a sight to behold. Everything was handwritten by her with the utmost care. And she emphasized that one must never make a mistake in such a book. [. . .] In this small room was also her father's fabulous stone collection. On the floor just to the right of the door was an amethyst druse which measured about 30 centimeters across. Large crystals glittered in it. This was our bed of violet." In the office were kept not just William Sachs' business papers and precious minerals, but also reference works containing "the whole world." From now on, however, Sachs had to explore the secrets of the universe on her own. In the music room across the hallway, William Sachs' presence was also missing. The room contained the abandoned piano on which he used to improvise. Now silence reigned.

2

Forty years old, Sachs returned to the address where the garden of paradise had been. The animals were gone, but under the leafy fruit trees at the back she planted roses, other plants, and herbs. Around the front a small rock garden was laid out, by which she posed in some photos from the mid-1930s. For expertise she consulted Karl Foerster's botanical works, which would provide plenty of reading pleasure during the garden-less exile years as well. Once more in residence at Lessingstraße, Margarete prepared herself for old age. In William's absence, the home was turned into a mausoleum in pastel tones. Located on a quiet street on the fringes of the hectic metropolis, it offered a place where memory could be kept alive. Although Nelly had to look after her mother, who in time would show increasing signs of ill health (meals were reduced to a diet regime of fish, herbs, and puréed vegetables), she was no longer her father's carer and her freedom was all the greater. The future lay before her.

**TEXT** "Auflistung über die Verschleuderung" (D18), Akte 73 435, Margarete Sachs, 01/26/1956, Landesamt für Bürger- und Ordnungsangelegenheiten, Abt. I (EBB) · The information about Sachs' library appears in "Anmeldung wegen Verschleuderung einer Wohnungseinrichtung" (D16) Akte 73 435, Margarete Sachs (EBB) · EBB) · Dähnert, 228–231 | **IMAGE 1** Sachs towards the end of the 1930s (from a private collection) · **2** Karl Foerster, *Der Steingarten der sieben Jahreszeiten* 1936

## A DYING SYSTEM

The year before William Sachs died, Nelly could celebrate her first publication since her debut. On November 17, 1929, the editor of the cultural section of the *Vossische Zeitung*, Monty Jacobs, informed her that the poem "Zur Ruh" (To Rest) had been selected for publication from the material she had submitted, since it suited the time of year. If the author agreed, it would be published the following day.

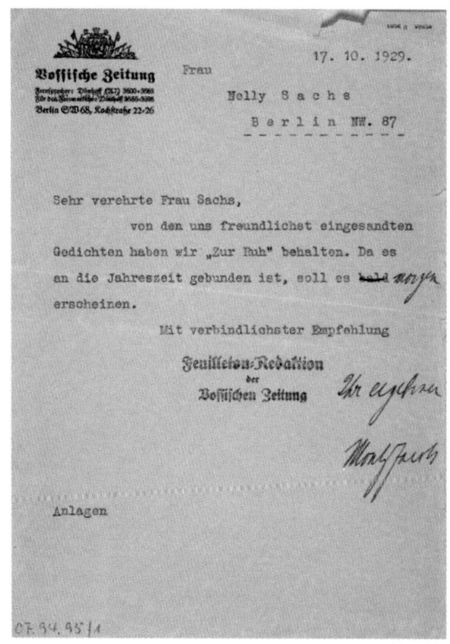

Vossische Zeitung

17. 10. 1929.

Frau
Nelly Sachs
Berlin NW. 87

Sehr verehrte Frau Sachs,
von den uns freundlichst eingesandten Gedichten haben wir „Zur Ruh" behalten. Da es an die Jahreszeit gebunden ist, soll es ~~bald~~ morgen erscheinen.

Mit verbindlichster Empfehlung
Feuilleton-Redaktion der Vossischen Zeitung

Anlagen

3

> Apples red fall in the summer lane / Green stars sink into lonely death, / The cart clatters upon rutted stone / Laying autumn's last remains — — / To rest. // Water yearned seeps to its tomb, / Softly cherished by a sea of flowers / The butterfly flits in the potato field / Nodding all the world's sleep — / To rest. // The buzzing of bees, the flaxen fount / Are joy enough, the cricket's grace / Now lit by beyond, / The cock will crow no more till day breaks — — / To rest.

The poem had little in common with the dominant literary climate in Berlin at the time — writings such as Brecht's *Hauspostille* (Manual of Piety), Tucholsky and Heartfield's pamphlet *Deutschland, Deutschland über alles* (Germany, Germany Above All), or, for that matter, Benn's *Gesammelte Gedichte* (Collected Poetry), which had been published some years earlier. But the prim rhymes and bittersweet tones will have been similar to what was being written for popular weekly magazines or desk drawers in 1929. Even if Dora, her friend from youth, had a brother who was close to the circle around George, and even if Neff, whom Sachs would get to know a few years later, sympathized with the group's lofty views on poetry, her own texts come across as finger exercises. She was still testing conventions and learning the craft; only rarely would she slip in a word or metaphor that showed the glint of the blade among the dense layers of images — as in the final stanza's "lit by beyond," for example, with its brief glimpse of 1960s poetry.

4

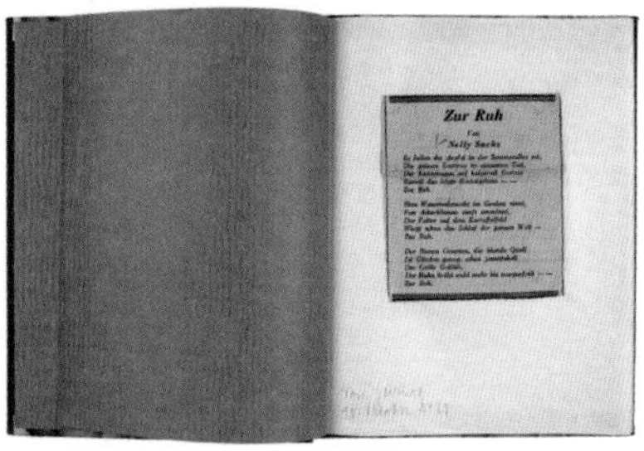


The writer of "Zur Ruh" observed decorum. As in other poems from the period, the text features variations on themes from her prose works which are implicitly knighted with the capital letter of noble values: Longing, Love, Transience… The red apples falling from the trees can be found in both the early puppet-theater piece "Der Jahrmarkt der Träume" (The Fair of Dreams) and in the later fairy-tale album "Die Apfeltraumallee" (The Apple-Dream Lane), the crowing cock can be heard in texts right up to the end of her œuvre. On the whole, Sachs spent her Berlin years recycling. Of the three hundred or so extant poems from the period up to the flight, many contain similar images and some even identical turns of verse. It is apparent that she was less interested in being original than in fulfilling the requirements she associated with a particular genre. The same rhyme can migrate from a nature poem to a travel miniature, tears roll in texts with animal themes as well as with devotional imagery, and in the lyrical poetry everything somehow seems steeped in departure. The texts show an urge for expression, but have no voice of their own. The words are still in the way. The question the reader ends up asking after getting through these texts is less *who* than *what* is writing… The title of the publication in the *Vossische Zeitung* hints at the probable answer: a dying verse system.

**TEXT** "Zur Ruh," FG, 247 · "Der Jahrmarkt der Träume" and "Die Apfeltraumallee," ADähnert:I | **IMAGE 3** Letter from Monty Jacobs 11/17/1929 (DLA) · **4** Scrapbook with pasted poem, "Zur Ruh," *Vossische Zeitung* 11/18/1929 (DLA)

## VISIT FROM A POETESS

"Zur Ruh" would be Sachs' last publication before Kurt von Schleicher stepped down as chancellor of the Reich on January 8, 1933, and Hitler assumed his position two days later. A couple of months earlier she had sent a selection of poems to the *Berliner Tageblatt.* Later she would also visit the editorial offices on Jerusalemer Straße in Berlin-Mitte. In her roman-à-clef Tegen turned this visit into an art revelation. The editor "Leo Huber" is bent over papers at his desk as usual when there is a knock at the door. "It is still summer, a scorching August day, when a young lady arrives with some poems. She is shy and pretty

Reg Vo E 2
73435

Anlage

Anfang der dreißiger Jahre begannen einige Kritiker und Literaturprofessoren auf meine Dichtungen aufmerksam zu werden. Ich hatte bisdahin meine schriftstellerische Tätigkeit verborgen gehalten .

Der Professor der Germanistik Max Hermann war einer der eifrigsten Fürsprecher. Zu ihnen gesellte sich der Kulturredakteur Monty Jacobs in der Voss.Zeitung, der Redakteur der " Neuen Rundschau Prof. Oscar Bie und der Redakteur des Berliner Tageblattes Leo Hirsch. Alle sind inzwischen verstorben. Max Hermann und Leo Hirsch wurden Opfer des Nazismus .

Im Jahre 1932 begann Leo Hirsch eine Auswahl Gedichte im Berliner Tageblatt zu veröffentlichen nachdem ich einen wunderbaren Brief von ihm erhalten hatte indem er mir eine große Zukunft als deutsche Lyrikerin prophezeite .

Im Jahre 33 wurde es mir verboten weiter zu veröffentlichen einige literarischen Zeitschriften veröffentlichten noch eine Zeit ohne meinen Namen zu drucken . Eine von Leo Hirsch und Prof.Hermann geplante veröffentlichung meiner frühen Gedichte in Buchform mußte unterbleiben .

Im Jahre 1940 im letzten Augenblick vor der Verschickung wurden meine im Jahre 1950 hier verstorbene Mutter und ich durch die Dichterin Selma Lagerlöf mit der ich lange im Briefwechsel stand und dem schwedischen Malerprinzen Eugen, nach Schweden gerettet .

Wir kamen völlig mittellos hierher und lebten von einer Einsammlung die literarische Persönlichkeiten in Schweden für uns veranstalteten . Auch die Mosaiska Församlingen Stockholm trug bis heute für unseren bezw. meinen Unterhalt bei .

Eine Zeitlang arbeitete ich an Übersetzungen für das von den Professoren Myrdahl und Tegen für intelektuelle Flüchtlinge ins Leben gerufene sogenannte Samarbets-Comité das schwedische Dichtung durch Übersetzungen im Ausland bekannt machen sollte .

Durch die schwere Erkrankung meiner Mutter die ich Tag und Nacht pflegte und meine dadurch bis zum völligen Zusammenbruch führenden körperlichen Zustand mußte ich diese Arbeit aufgeben und war nun völlig auf die Unterstützung der Mosaiska Församlingen in Stockholm angewiesen . Auch hat das Nobelcomité durch seinen Vorsitzenden den Dichter Anders Österling mir in Anerkennung mehrere Male Ehrengaben zuerkannt die bei der außerordentlich schwirigen Lage wo die Ausgaben für Ärzte und Pflege wuchsen eine große Hilfe darstellten .

Nach dem Tode meiner Mutter im Jahre 1950 erhalte ich von der Mosaiska Församlingen Stockholm 200 Kr. monatlich . Diese Zuteilung liegt von der jüdischen Gemeinde bestätigt bei den Wiedergutmachungsakten .

Ich habe herausgegeben im Jahre 1947 im Aufbau Verlag Berlin
Die Wohnungen des Todes Gedichte

Von Welle und Granit eine Antologie schwedischer moderner Lyrik in meiner Übersetzung

Im Jahre 1949

Sternverdunkelung Gedichte
beim S. Fischer Verlag Frankfurt a.M.

5

and has a Jewish name. He asks her to sit down on the other side of the desk and smiles his little embarrassed smile. She is so sweet, it's a shame to have to let her expectations down..."

Huber is a hardened editor who knows what unsolicited poems tend to contain. Clumsy rhymes and lopsided images are not for his publication, where "only first-class things" may appear. Even sweet smiles or beseeching eyes will fail to persuade him. Resignedly he looks down at the sheets, then lifts his gaze again and asks with narrowing eyes if he is meant to read them now. His visitor nods "like an anxious schoolchild." The editor senses that the occasion is "momentous" for her and decides out of politeness to have look at the poems right away. Except for a fly buzzing against a window pane and a typewriter clattering through the wall, it is silent. "Sheet after sheet he lays down on the desk. There are ten of them, each with a little poem. When he has finished he dare not look at her, he begins to read again — it could of course be that the girl is so pretty... But after the second reading he is certain — this is *art*."

6

The seasoned newspaperman who lowered his guard in Tegen's novel was LEO HIRSCH (1903–1943) and was not older than his visitor, but twelve years her junior. The Swedish novelist had met him during a trip to Germany in the 1920s and had stayed in touch. Hirsch himself would describe his acquaintance with the forty-year-old Sachs in a letter of recommendation to the publisher Karl Otto Bonnier in Stockholm. There he explained how "Miss Sachs" had sent him some poems in the spring of 1932. With the publication in the *Berliner Tageblatt*, doors were opened to other newspapers and periodicals. "When in 1933 the productive Jewish cultural forces began to be consolidated in Germany, the name of Nelly Sachs was one of the best." Whether this is Hirsch's bad memory, or the acute political situation in the run-up to the Second World War making him exaggerate tactfully, matters little. On September 13, 1932, he informed the unknown poet who had sent him her poems that one of them was going to be published. It wasn't until six months later, however, on February 26 the following year, that the two stanzas appeared in the newspaper. There are no further publications known from this period (although Sachs later stated, in a letter in connection with an application for damages in the 1950s, that "some literary periodicals published for a time without printing my name"). Six months would pass before she could register another publication, on July 9, 1933, followed by another on December 21. Both were printed through the agency of Hirsch. Then more than a year passed before her name again appeared in public, this time in *Jugend*, a weekly devoted to literary and artistic subjects. At that point the so-called *Gleichschaltung* (leveling) of German cultural life was already in full swing.

Through her earliest publications and those that would follow in papers available to Germans of Jewish descent during the 1930s — including the *Central-Verein-Zeitung*, *Bayerische Israelitische Gemeindezeitung*, and *Israeli-*

*tisches Familienblatt* — Sachs went from being an unknown *Schriftstellerin* to a published *Dichterin*. Hirsch played no small part in this. Evidently he took a liking to what he regarded as genuine art, and did what he could for the poet. Following the "leveling" of the *Berliner Tageblatt* as a result of the "publisher law" which came into force on January 1, 1934, he worked as dramaturge at the theater of the Jewish Cultural League as well as editor of its *Monatsblätter*, in which he occasionally published new poems by Sachs. When persecution increased during the latter part of the 1930s, Hirsch fought not just for civil rights which had been taken for granted barely a decade earlier, but also against poverty and illness. His wife suffered from serious rheumatoid arthritis; he himself had mouth cancer. (In his last letter to Sachs, one month after her flight, he added laconically: "I have in the meantime been relieved of half of my teeth.") When the Jewish Culture League was outlawed in the autumn of 1941, and Hirsch lost his job as the congregation's librarian, he was ordered to do forced labor. He died a year and a half later at the Jüdisches Krankenhaus on Iranische Straße in Berlin, as a result of illness and terror.

After the war Hirsch's mother filled in a form at Yad Vashem in Jerusalem giving the date of death as January 6, 1943 (which incidentally would have been around the time Sachs learned that her beloved had died). At that point the writer whom he had taken under his wing had already raised a memorial. The unpublished epitaph "Der Pilger" (The Pilgrim), which Sachs annexed in a letter to Fogelklou-Norlind four and a half months after Hirsch's death, bore the bracketed initials "[L. H.]." Here the misfortunes of the past transform what appears to have been a formal friendship, in which the polite plural "you" was used in correspondence, into an intimate I/you relationship predicated on sorrow:

> You came once with the morning sun. / The evening could only lend you its shadow. // In your eyes glowed only pillars of fire and desert sand, / And behind them in homesickness the ever promised land. // Who sent you out, you of the biblical era / To prepare the route back with nothing but longing. // Of dream and cloud has death been created. / But behind there stands Zion, behind the evening and behind the night.

**TEXT** TegenJ, 97-98 · Letters from Hirsch to Bonnier 06/08/1939 and to Sachs 07/05/1940, ASachs · Annex 01/03/1956 to account of damages to professional advancement (Schaden am beruflichen Fortkommen) (E2), Akte 73 435, Margarete Sachs, 01/26/1956, Landesamt für Bürger- und Ordnungsangelegenheiten, Abt. I (EBB) · Information regarding Hirsch from his mother 02/13/1957, Yad Vashem · For letter to Fogelklou-Norlind 05/23/1943, see Briefe 12 · "Der Pilger [L. H.]," NSW:I | **IMAGE 5** Annex 01/03/1956 to Nelly Sachs' account of "Schaden am beruflichen Fortkommen" (EBB) · **6** Leo Hirsch in the 1930s (AAdK)

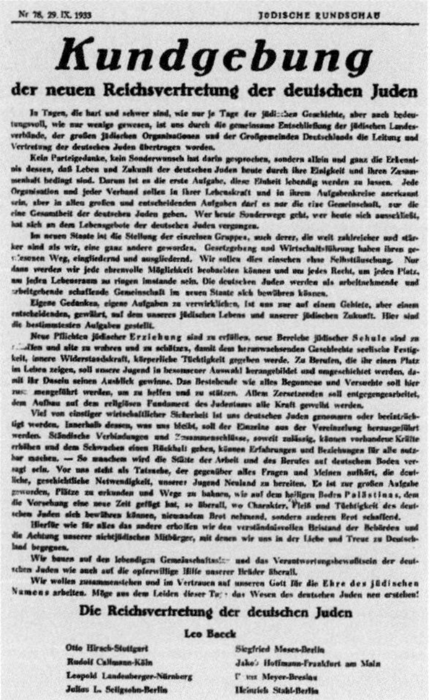
Nr 78, 29. IX. 1933 — JÜDISCHE RUNDSCHAU

**Kundgebung**

**der neuen Reichsvertretung der deutschen Juden**

In Tagen, die hart und schwer sind, wie nur je Tage der jüdischen Geschichte, aber auch bedeutungsvoll, wie nur wenige gewesen, ist uns durch die gemeinsame Entschließung der jüdischen Landesverbände, der großen jüdischen Organisationen und der Großgemeinden Deutschlands die Leitung und Vertretung der deutschen Juden übertragen worden.

Kein Parteigedanke, kein Sonderwunsch hat darin gesprochen, sondern allein und ganz die Erkenntnis dessen, daß Leben und Zukunft der deutschen Juden heute durch ihre Einigkeit und ihren Zusammenhalt bedingt sind. Darum ist es die erste Aufgabe, diese Einheit lebendig werden zu lassen. Jede Organisation und jeder Verband sollen in ihrer Lebenskraft und in ihrem Aufgabenkreise anerkannt sein, aber in allen großen und entscheidenden Aufgaben darf es nur die eine Gemeinschaft, nur die eine Gesamtheit der deutschen Juden geben. Wer heute Sonderwege geht, wer heute sich ausschließt, hat sich an dem Lebensgebote der deutschen Juden vergangen.

Im neuen Staate ist die Stellung der einzelnen Gruppen, auch derer, die weit zahlreicher und stärker sind als wir, eine ganz andere geworden. Gesetzgebung und Wirtschaftsführung haben ihren gewiesenen Weg, eingliedernd und ausgliedernd. Wir sollen dies einsehen ohne Selbsttäuschung. Nur dann werden wir jede ehrenvolle Möglichkeit beobachten können und um jedes Recht, um jeden Platz, um jeden Lebensraum zu ringen imstande sein. Die deutschen Juden werden als arbeitnehmende und arbeitgebende schaffende Gemeinschaft im neuen Staate sich bewähren können.

Eigene Gedanken, eigene Aufgaben zu verwirklichen, ist uns nur auf einem Gebiete, aber einem entscheidenden, gewährt, auf dem unseres jüdischen Lebens und unserer jüdischen Zukunft. Hier sind die bestimmtesten Aufgaben gestellt.

Neue Pflichten jüdischer Erziehung sind zu erfüllen, neue Bereiche jüdischer Schule sind zu schaffen und alte zu wahren und zu schützen, damit dem heranwachsenden Geschlechte seelische Festigkeit, innere Widerstandskraft, körperliche Tüchtigkeit gegeben werde. Zu Berufen, die ihr einen Platz im Leben zeigen, soll unsere Jugend in besonderer Auswahl herangebildet und umgeschichtet werden, damit ihr Dasein seinen Ausblick gewinne. Das Bestehende wie alles Begonnene und Versuchte soll hier zusammengeführt werden, um zu helfen und zu stützen. Allem Zersetzenden soll entgegengearbeitet, dem Aufbau auf dem religiösen Fundament des Judentums alle Kraft geweiht werden.

Viel von einstiger wirtschaftlicher Sicherheit ist uns deutschen Juden genommen oder beeinträchtigt worden. Innerhalb dessen, was uns bleibt, soll der Einzelne aus der Vereinzelung herausgeführt werden. Ständische Verbindungen und Zusammenschlüsse, soweit zulässig, können vorhandene Kräfte erhöhen und dem Schwachen einen Rückhalt geben, können Erfahrungen und Beziehungen für alle nutzbar machen. — So manchem wird die Stütze der Arbeit und des Berufes auf deutschem Boden versagt sein. Vor uns steht als Tatsache, der gegenüber alles Fragen und Meinen aufhört, die deutliche, geschichtliche Notwendigkeit, unserer Jugend Neuland zu bereiten. Es ist zur großen Aufgabe geworden, Plätze zu erkunden und Wege zu bahnen, wie auf dem heiligen Boden Palästinas, dem die Vorsehung eine neue Zeit gefügt hat, so überall, wo Charakter, Fleiß und Tüchtigkeit des deutschen Juden sich bewähren können, niemandem Brot nehmend, sondern anderen Brot schaffend.

Hierfür wie für alles das andere erhoffen wir den verständnisvollen Beistand der Behörden und die Achtung unserer nichtjüdischen Mitbürger, mit denen wir uns in der Liebe und Treue zu Deutschland begegnen.

Wir bauen auf den lebendigen Gemeinschaftssinn und das Verantwortungsbewußtsein der deutschen Juden wie auch auf die opferwillige Hilfe unserer Brüder überall.

Wir wollen zusammenstehen und im Vertrauen auf unseren Gott für die Ehre des jüdischen Namens arbeiten. Möge aus dem Leiden dieser Tage das Wesen des deutschen Juden neu erstehen!

**Die Reichsvertretung der deutschen Juden**

**Leo Baeck**

Otto Hirsch-Stuttgart — Siegfried Moses-Berlin
Rudolf Callmann-Köln — Jakob Hoffmann-Frankfurt am Main
Leopold Landenberger-Nürnberg — [illegible] Meyer-Breslau
Julius L. Seligsohn-Berlin — Heinrich Stahl-Berlin

7

8

## INSIGHT WITHOUT SELF-DELUSION

A few months after the Nazi takeover the "Reich Ministry for Popular Enlightenment and Propaganda" was founded under the leadership of a doctor of German literature from Rheydt in Nordrhein-Westfalen, Joseph Goebbels. Twelve days later, on March 25, the recently appointed minister declared to a group of radio executives and producers: "The Ministry's task is to carry out a spiritual mobilization. Thus it is, in the spiritual area, the same thing as the Defense Ministry is in the area of surveillance. [---] The spiritual mobilization is equally as necessary, perhaps even more necessary, as the material defense preparedness of the people." After a raft of new laws and ordinances during the spring and summer, and not least through the book-burnings which were organized around the country on May 10, it was clear to anyone who wished to remain up to date with developments that "Jewish" affairs were going to be singled out. On September 27 the law that would regulate the cultural life of the new German state came into force. The "Reich Culture Chamber Law" required citizens who wanted to create or consume culture to present an *Ariernachweis* (Aryan certificate). In effect this meant that Jews were prevented from participating in general cultural life. Six months later, on New Year's Day 1934, the "publisher law" began to apply, preventing Jews from publishing their work anywhere except in sanctioned papers. All that remained was to participate within the very limited scope of activities still permitted for "non-Aryans." Or write for one's desk drawer.

Two days after the "Reich Culture Chamber Law" had entered into force a proclamation was published in the *Jüdische Rundschau*, signed among others by Leo Baeck, the Rabbi of Berlin and a prominent representative of the country's liberal Jews. "At a time," it read, "that is as hard and difficult as any in Jewish history, but also significant as few times have been, we have been entrusted with the leadership and representation of the German Jews by a joint decision of the State Association of the Jewish Communities, the major Jewish organizations, and the large Jewish communities of Germany." Thus the "Reich Association of German Jews" was founded. From the announcement it emerged what the organization's particular concern was. The positions of individual groups had changed in the new state. There were groups that were considerably stronger and more numerous than "us," which required that individual thoughts and hopes be realized in a coordinated way, as otherwise the collective voice would go unheard. In order to secure the diversity and future of Jewish life, ranks had to be closed and an umbrella organization established. Only united would "we" stand strong in the face of coming challenges, politically and economically, socially and culturally — and be able to fight "for every right, for every place, for every *Lebensraum*." Anything else would be denial or wishful thinking. "We should realize this without self-delusion."

9

As yet the leadership did not realize that the more successful the organization was at bringing together separate, not infrequently conflicting wills in one organization, the easier it would be for those in power to watch over their activities.

**TEXT** For Goebbels' speech 03/25/1933, see Jutta Sywottek, *Mobilmachung für den totalen Krieg. Die propagandistische Vorbereitung der deutschen Bevölkerung auf den Zweiten Weltkrieg*, Opladen 1976, 23 · "Kundgebung der neuen Reichsvertretung der deutschen Juden," *Jüdische Rundschau*, no. 78, 09/29/1933 | **IMAGE 7** "Kundgebung der neuen Reichsvertretung der deutschen Juden," *Jüdische Rundschau*, 09/29/1933 (CM) · **8** Book-burning, May 1933 (BPK) · **9** Joseph Goebbels, 1934 (BPK)

## GHETTOIZATION

A few months earlier Hans Hinkel — who had been editor at *Völkischer Beobachter* and was active within the anti-Semitic "League for the Struggle for German Culture" — in his capacity as "state commissioner" at the Prussian Ministry for Science, Art, and Popular Education, had granted the founding of a "Culture League of German Jews." The man Goebbels later appointed "Special Commissioner for the Supervision of Culturally Active Jews within the German Reich" quickly saw the advantages of centralizing the arrangement of "non-Aryan" cultural expressions. The new organization came to be headquartered in Mommsenstraße 56, just one door away from the boarding house where Margarete and Nelly Sachs would spend their last months before the flight in 1940. The honorary chairmanship included, besides Leo Baeck, the religious philosopher Martin Buber, the literary historian and critic Arthur Eloesser, the artist and former president of Berlin's Akademie der Künste, Max Liebermann, and the writer Jacob Wassermann. Baeck led the department of humanities, while the playwright and theater critic Julius Bab ran the section for literature and theater. The popular lecturer and reader-aloud Ludwig Hardt managed the recitation evenings together with Edith Herrnstadt-Oettingen,

10

the musicologists Anneliese Landau and Alfred Einstein were in charge of the musical arts, and Max Osborn, former critic at the *Vossische Zeitung*, led the department of art history together with the art historian Hedwig Fechheimer.

In a proclamation from the late summer of the same year, published in *Der Schild*, the journal of the National Federation of Jewish Combat Soldiers, came a rallying call. To the question "What do we want?" the new leadership replied: "To give hundreds of people who have lost their jobs and been condemned to defeatism, we want to provide work, an existence, courage in life, resolve! To manifest the religious and relational kinship of the Jews! From our confession to Judaism in our moment of need build a proud consciousness for better times! See and experience works of art! Harden the spirit with those greater in spirit! Strive towards the goal of being an insightful, modest part of the greater whole, with the duty to feel and act for the common good! That is how we perceive the purpose of the *Culture League*. We all want to, we all have to join together in this! *One* league — *one* community — *one* will — *one* religion." With its plea for a hardened spirit and proud self-consciousness, the proclamation can seem both typical of its time and disquietingly close to the language prevalent in more unpleasant publications. But what were Jewish cultural practitioners to do in a period when their space was shrinking in every area? Anyone who couldn't, or wouldn't, emigrate was forced to make a virtue of necessity. Under the auspices of the new league, many of the artists who had been excluded from a cultural life to which they had been contributing as recently as six months earlier could be given the opportunity of work and of securing a minor income. In the long run, Jewish identity would thereby be strengthened and included as a cooperative part "of the greater whole" . . .

In the first year alone the league received 20,000 new members. A theater was opened in Charlottenstraße 92 — the first play to be staged was Lessing's *Nathan der Weise* (Nathan the Wise) — and over the following years, until the league's dissolution on September 11, 1941, hundreds of music and theater performances, evenings of readings and lectures, film screenings and art exhibitions were arranged in Berlin alone. In 1935 there were more than three dozen regional and local culture bodies numbering over 70,000 members; two years later more than 120 organizations — including synagogues and culture associations — belonged to the national league. Most performances were held in the capital, where they were an almost daily occurrence, but Hamburg and Frankfurt offered busy programs as well. Since activities were monitored and censored by the Gestapo, self-censorship was applied for preventive purposes. Individual program items had to be personally approved by Hinkel. And conditions got rapidly harsher: non-Jews were soon banned outright from attending or taking part in performances, and fewer and fewer works by artists regarded as particularly "German" were allowed, which led to an agitated discussion about what many considered a self-imposed ghettoization.

Huddled under the same umbrella were nationalists and liberals, communists and Zionists, the orthodox and the evangelically baptized, former combat soldiers and fervent pacifists, traditionalists and avant-gardists, often with nothing more in common than their classification as "non-Aryans." On the one hand there were those who, following the Berlin Rabbi Joachim Prinz, favored a Judaism freed from national and cultural barriers ("Bedouins, heroes, kings, prophets, minstrels"...) and who only sought "their own freedom." Anyone reading between the lines understood the implication: emigration and the founding of a Zionist state. On the other there were those who agreed with Hans-Joachim Schoeps, a conservative Prussian Jew and founder of German Vanguard, German Jews' Support Squad, who identified with the homeland even when this was to one's own cost. "Even if our fatherland rejects us, we remain prepared for Germany," he insisted in a pamphlet directed at Prinz. Opinion was divided among artists and intellectuals as well. Some held that the right thing to do under the prevailing difficulties was to concentrate on specifically Jewish subjects and concerns, while others regarded limitations as a self-imposed burden which only worsened the situation. In his short piece for the first issue of the league's *Monatsblätter* in October 1933, Buber tried to launch a third way without the stale flavor of compromise. Under the heading "Names Carry Obligations" he remarked that it was enough to take "the four words" that made up the organization's name seriously, separately and together — *culture, league, German, Jewish*: "no more is needed here."

11

Soon enough it turned out that only three of the words were permitted. In January 1934 the Gestapo objected to the Culture League's inclusion in the general directory of associations. The term "German Jews" was linguistically as well as culturally fallacious. There were no German or Polish Jews, and no Jews of other nationalities either — there were, simply, Jews. In order to avoid confusion it was important to separate this ethnic group from others. Nor was the league allowed to give 1933 as its year of establishment, since that year was reserved as year 1 in the history of the new Reich. Following a legal examination, Hinkel announced that he did not, however, see any obstacle to the organization's name being changed to "The Culture League for Jews in Germany," for example. At the members' assembly on April 26, 1935, it was decided that the name would be changed to "The Jewish Culture League" plus a regional specification (Berlin, Hamburg, Rhein-Ruhr, etc.). Only six months later, in November, a proud Goebbels declared: "The Reich Culture Chamber is now free of Jews. No Jew is any longer active in our people's cultural life."

The separation of "German" from "Jewish" — decreed as a policy of state and racially motivated — had become a reality. In less than two years, the Nazi bureaucracy succeeded in ghettoizing everything it regarded as Jewish. Or as Joachim Prinz noted in the *Jüdische Rundschau*: "We are living in a very peculiar cultural situation. [---] If one considers the fact that we no longer have a legitimate place within the German cultural landscape, due not so much to us as to its culture, then all of these things that we 'practice' in terms of culture stand out. We play Beethoven, Bach, and Mozart, we go back to Goethe and Hölderlin, we listen longingly to the great manifestations of these Germans. That is a good thing, and there is always something beautiful and touching about the return to old things. But what a spectacle, what a tragedy for people who live in an era without living *in* it."

The ghetto was no longer geographically defined as it had been in the Middle Ages. It was everywhere now, and it didn't stop at either linguistic or judicial borders — instead it offered its practitioners a life and an occupation in a place and time to which they were not seen as belonging. The mechanisms of exclusion had transformed existence into exteriority. For Prinz, only one conclusion was possible: "The fate of the Jew is fatelessness."

**TEXT** For the proclamation of the Jewish Culture League, see *Der Schild*, no. 15, 08/14/1933 · Prinz, *Wir Juden. Besinnung, Rückblick, Zukunft*, Berlin 1934, 173 · Schoeps, *Wir deutschen Juden*, Berlin 1934, 51 · Buber, "Name verpflichtet," *Monatsblätter Kulturbund deutscher Juden*, 1933, no. 1, 2 · For Goebbels' announcement, see *Jüdische Rundschau*, 11/19/1935 · Prinz, "Das Leben ohne Nachbarn – Versuch einer ersten Analyse: Ghetto 1935," *Jüdische Rundschau*, 04/17/1935 | **IMAGE 10** Hans Hinkel, 1933 (BPK) · **11** Joachim Prinz in the 1950s (American Jewish Congress, Washington)

12

## INTIMATES OF DEATH

Among the Jewish cultural associations in the new Germany, the one in Berlin was the biggest and most active. The leadership of the national league had its seat in the city, there was a theater, concert and lecture halls, newspapers and magazines, as well as a gramophone company. The prominent publishing houses were in Berlin, as were leading Jewish central organizations. Additionally, many actors, musicians, writers, and artists lived there — even if one of the association's stewards sent an irate letter to Tel Aviv as late as in 1937 complaining that should the city continue to recruit all the good musicians, it would soon be impossible to put together a respectable orchestra in the German capital…

During the latter half of the 1930s, the program leaflets also featured Sachs' name. Judging from advertisements and reviews this occurred (at least) in April 1936, in March or April and December of 1937, and in June and September of 1938. As a poet she was dubbed "a sensitive harpist," although the signature "t." in his 1937 review in the *Jüdische Rundschau* objected to the "saccharinity" which was said to characterize her prose text "Chelion." In a review published in the winter of the same year — which also contained a report about Jewish life in Stockholm — the criticism was repeated regarding the puppet theater piece "Der Jahrmarkt der Träume," which was described as "syrupy redundancy poetry." The writer was said to adorn "all fantasy figures

13
14
15
16

with her lyrical layer of icing." In September the following year "t." summarized Sachs' poetry as being "motherly in essence" — an analysis that the unmarried and childless poet may have found difficult to comprehend. There are no more mentions in the press after that. Excessive sweetness and heartfelt motherliness: as a storyteller Sachs came across as harmless, turgid, sentimental, while the same characteristics in her poetry made her a sensitive receiver of the refined music of the spirit.

Exceptionally Sachs would read her works herself, but usually they were delivered by the reader-aloud Erna Leonhard, better known by her stage name of Feld, who would be deported at the beginning of the 1940s and later remembered in an epitaph. In her first letter to Manfred George after the war Sachs recalled: "And then there were the years in Berlin when we, a small circle of writers read by Erna Feld-Leonhard, assembled, each time in renewed dread, whose turn would it be next. Kurt Pinthus, Jacob Picard were among them, I heard that they had been saved by going to America. Otherwise I don't think anyone had the good fortune of making it to another country." The circle also included now-forgotten writers such as Schalom Ben-Chorin (actually Fritz Rosenthal), Ilse Blumenthal-Weiß, Arthur Silbergleit, and Grete Striem-Boas. As well as Gertrud Chodziesner, better known by her nom d'artiste Kolmar, who had the same birthday as Sachs but was three years younger and in all likelihood was murdered shortly after her deportation to Auschwitz at the beginning of March 1943.

In a letter to the writer and critic Kurt Pinthus, who had mentioned her writing in an article covering the "Jewish poetry of the times" in the *Central-Verein-Zeitung* on April 9, 1936, and who managed to emigrate to America the following year, Sachs recalled: "The memory of the little band of intimates

**Veranstaltungen**

**Klavierabend Erich Landerer.** Der Klavierabend des Pianisten Erich Landerer im Brüdervereinshaus bereicherte den Eindruck seines letzten Auftretens in außergewöhnlichem Maße. In diesem Konzert wurde der eminent expressiv begabte Künstler zum selbstlos nachschöpferischen Betreuer des ihm anvertrauten Werks. Nach der flächigen Debussyschen „Suite bergamasque" entschieden wir uns für den Liszt der H-moll Sonate. Diese Sonate ist ein Gipfel seines Schaffens, in die er persönlichste Eigenzüge hineingelegt hat. Landerer trumpft mit dem herrisch selbstbewußten Grundmotiv auf, schlägt sich mit ihm durch das Gehege von Kapriolen, Figurinen und Läufen, die das Thema umspülen. Er läßt die strahlende Milde eines fromm-gläubigen Gesangs das Spielwerk durchbrechen, das weiter vorwärtstreibende Geschehen in Reflexen blenden und wuchtet diesen Gesang nach titanischen Anläufen, hymnisch glorifiziert, in den Raum. In anregendem Plauderton durchstreift er in der „Promenade" das Museum, sieht, erlebt Bilder, ein altes Schloß, von unheimlichen Geschichten umdüstert, ein schweres Ochsengespann, das im Schwanken der Last schwarze tiefe Furchen zieht, fröhliche Bilder von streitenden Kindern, gackernden Küchlein, kreischenden Marktweibern, düstergraue Katakomben, quälenden Hexenspuk, der schwindet im Blick auf das in der Sonnenflut sich aufrichtende Tor von Kiew, im schaukelnden Geläute der großen und kleinen Glocken, in verwehten Orgelklängen und der großen Weite des Raumes, der sich zur Gottgläubigkeit öffnet. So prägnant wie Landerer diese Bilder malt, so gab er Chopin in natürlichem Sentiment, im Glimmen seiner Harmonie, ließ er das pianistische Feuerwerk „Danse du feu" von de Falla mit Brillanz, Kraft und Präzision abbrennen. Ein herrlicher Abend, ein beglücktes Publikum; der einzige Mißton war der halbbesetzte Saal, der unserem kunstbeflissenen Publikum schlecht ansteht. Dr. Jakob Schönberg

**„Ungehörte Stimmen".** Erna Leonhard (Feld) und Leo Merten (Menter) warben am dritten Abend dieser Vortragsreihe für die Dichtungen von Paul Mayer, Elly Groß und Nelly Sachs. Paul Mayer ist zweifellos ein Lyriker von Rang; zum Vorrang einer Persönlichkeit fehlt ihm freilich ein unverkennbar eigener Ton. Seine zuweilen von Rilke beeinflußten Verse schwanken zwischen dichterischer Aussage und lyrischem Gesang, bleiben aber in ihrem Ringen um Formgeschlossenheit sowie um Weib, Welt, Gott und um Annäherung an biblische Gestalten bemerkenswert. Elly Groß vermag in seelenvollen, bezwingend schlichten Strophen und Prosazeilen von der knospenhaften Versponnenheit ihres Gefühlslebens als Blinde und zugleich von ihrer tapferen Lebenshaltung zu überzeugen. Nelly Sachs, sonst eine Harfenistin zarter Gefühle, enttäuschte in ihrem Puppenspiel „Jahrmarkt der Träume" durch eine süßliche Ueberlyrik, indem sie aus den Spielzeugschachteln alter Romantik Sagenfiguren wie Melusine, grünlockige Waldfrauen, ein Elfenfräulein u. a. hervorholte, ihnen „Prinzessin Schwalbe" sowie — Engel zugesellte und alle Phantasiegestalten mit Zieraten aus ihrem lyrischen Zuckerguß „schmückte". Erna Leonhard (Feld) und Leo Merten (Menter) ergänzten sich in erneuter Bewährung vorteilhaft: er dämpfte in kluger Zurückhaltung manchen Gefühlsüberschwang, sie kam zögernden Seelenerschließungen aufmunternd entgegen. So wurde der Abend ungleichwertiger Dichtungen zu einem unanfechtbaren rezitatorischen Erfolg. —t.

17

of death we once were, when Erna Feld-Leonhard held her reading soirées, still stands so very clear before my inner eye and is forever engraved on my emotions." And in a letter to the writer and lawyer Jacob Picard, who fled a few months before she did, she wrote, at the beginning of the 1950s: "During those nights, there in Berlin, death always stalking us, with the friends who will never come back to us here, there flowered in the darkness something one might perhaps call the Chassidic spirit, almost drowned in the clamorous din."

Not unexpectedly, Sachs in the postwar period saw her final years in her homeland in the light — or rather in the shadow — of the catastrophe. The saccharine verses were but a memory. Pain transformed the bittersweet stanzas into lyrical protocols of loss.

**TEXT** För For the information about a letter of complaint to musicians in Tel Aviv, see Henryk M. Broder, "Schätze in alten Pappschachteln," *Geschlossene Vorstellung. Der jüdische Kulturbund in Deutschland 1933–1941*, ed. Akademie der Künste, Berlin 1992, 25 · For the charge of "saccharinity," see *Jüdische Rundschau*, no. 27, 04/06/1937 · For the descriptions "a sensitive harpist" and "syrupy redundancy poetry," see *Jüdische Rundschau*, no. 101, 12/21/1937 · For the description "motherly in essence," see *Jüdische Rundschau*, no. 50, 06/24/1938 · For letters to George 01/27/1946, Pinthus 11/12/1946, and Picard 09/19/1951, see Briefe 25, 39, and 85 respectively | **IMAGE 12** Gertrud Kolmar and family in the 1930s (DLA) · **13** Ilse Blumenthal-Weiß in the 1930s (Miriam Merzbacher-Blumenthal's collection, Greenwich, CT) · **14** Erna Feld-Leonhard in the 1930s (KBS) · **15** Kurt Pinthus, 1925 (DLA) · **16** Manfred George in the 1940s (DLA) · **17** *Jüdische Rundschau*, 12/21/1937 (CM)

## CUT-OFF CULTURE

The members of the Jewish Culture League continually had to weigh their own independence against the Nazi regulatory strait-jacket. Before the premiere with *Nathan the Wise* in October 1933 they could still be found heatedly discussing if the repertory should represent the people's proud past and preserve their own more or less successfully assimilated identity, or if the offering instead should touch upon the current situation and strive towards "the new Judaism," as one of many unsigned opinion pieces had it: "therefore we regard it as important right from the outset to point to the fact that we as Jews also should not turn our gaze backwards to the past but ahead to the future; we do not want to console ourselves with the fact that 150 years ago Lessing wrote *Nathan the Wise*, instead we want to see how we might overcome Jews' distress today." To which the conciliatory league chairman Kurt Singer replied: "You see, as Jews we do not want to pursue politics in 'the Culture League' but create art which, beyond strictly limited axioms, can bear and draw aesthetic and stylistic criticism, not world-political criticism."

During the first half of the 1930s art still stood in opposition to politics, the eternal against the immediate. But the further the decade progressed, the more the selection was circumscribed. It wasn't long before the antagonism between aesthetic and ideological considerations proved illusory. Those interested were only allowed to visit events organized by "non-Aryans" for "non-

Aryans." The subject matter too had to classified as "non-Aryan" otherwise it would not be permitted. Preferably the themes should be Old Testament or comical; under no circumstances were they allowed to touch on current political events. The same applied to the works they were based on — comedies, piano pieces, cycles of sonnets — which, during the final few seasons before the catastrophe, were almost exclusively being written by people of the same descent as the audience.

A quick browse through the repertory demonstrates how quickly and radically it changed. With Lessing's drama of ideas, the director Karl Loewenberg could turn a plea for transcultural humanism into a religious drama which implicitly hinted at current political circumstances. It is likely, however, that many in the audience suspected they were in a temple. Nonetheless the final scene, in which Christians and Muslims march off to the palace while Nathan remains, alone, was rendered in such an ambiguous way that it allowed the critics to debate whether they had witnessed the true Jewish destiny or if the actors instead had shown that the cultural bonds between peoples stood above individual religious affiliations. Even if German-language classics were banned, it was still possible to stage Shakespeare, Molière and Ibsen, Shaw, Pirandello and Sholem Aleichem. Soon "Jewish" plays became increasingly common, however: shtetl romances, jeremiads with a liturgical tint, prophetic pieces about the destruction of Jerusalem… Jacob wrestled the angel, Golem marched across the stage in clogs. The more difficult circumstances appeared, the more popular light-hearted subjects became. The works of Shakespeare continued to be featured, but after a few years it was no longer the tragedies or historic plays but the comedies that were being staged.

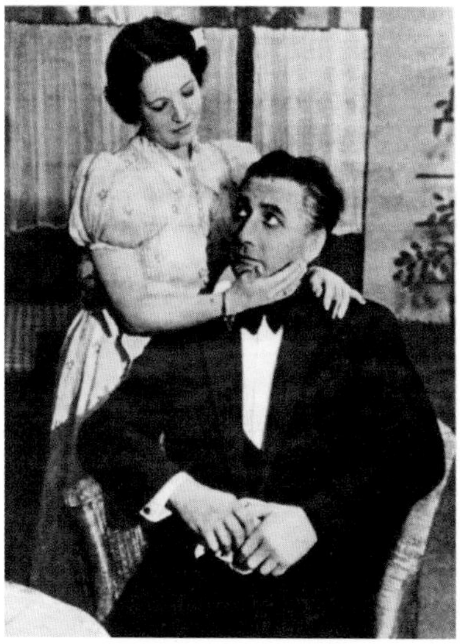
18

A representative example of the offering during the final years before the Culture League was banned is Ferenc Molnár's *Delila*. It is not improbable that this comedy in three acts was seen by the future writer of dramatic poems such as *Simson fällt durch Jahrtausende* or the unpublished torso "Das Haar" (The Hair). The play had its first performance in 1937, shortly before the author went into Swiss exile, and premiered in Berlin on April 4 the following year under the direction of Hans Buxbaum. Heinz Condell designed the set; the cast included Elfriede Borodkin as the dissolute and cunning waitress Ilonka, Walter Herz as her penniless betrothed, Jenny Bernstein as the wise wife Delila, and Fritz Wisten as a gray-haired Samson, the innkeeper torn between lust and duty, young desire and aged love. One reviewer of the play was Leo Hirsch, who in an article in *Jüdisches Gemeindeblatt* asserted: "Molnár's *Delila* is no biblical tragedy, but a modern comedy, Molnár's Samson is an innkeeper by the motorway between Budapest and Balaton [---], in short, everything here is theater, and moreover theater of the most appealing, savory kind." The reviewer found the playwright's modernization of the dramatic conflict particularly attractive. In Molnár's version, Samson is a Casanova past

SCHES GEMEINDEBLATT Nr. 15 / 10. April 1938

Molnars „Delila" Die Erstaufführung im Jüdischen Kulturbund

Fritz Wisten — Jenny Bernstein

Walter Herz — Elfriede Borodkin

19

his prime who runs an inn somewhere between capital and holiday resort. Despite his rounded cheeks and gray temples, he still believes he possesses power and allure, but in fact becomes "batted back and forth between two women." The charming Ilonka, who is full of flirtation and knowing looks, pretends to fancy him but is really after his recent lottery win. The real Delilah of the drama is the innkeeper's sagacious wife. Nobly she agrees to divorce him, demanding only her husband's savings as compensation for pain and suffering. But when the power over the money is transferred from Samson to Delilah, the waitress loses interest. "The finest, noblest trick by the theater wizard Molnár is that the wife, who agrees to divorce her innkeeper for the price of the ominous passbook, bestows this small fortune on her rival's bridegroom as a dowry; that is, to get to keep her husband."

The Bible's tragic story of Delilah, who seduces Samson and makes him betray the secret of his unnatural strength, is turned by Molnár into a relationship comedy with deftly redistributed traits. His version takes a number of liberties with the plot in the Book of Judges, such as doing away with the key scene. When Delilah obtains the passbook, her husband loses all his power to charm and needs neither haircut nor shave. Instead, in the final act, he buries his face ashamedly in his cravat. For his wife, who has already passed the money on so that the poor groom can marry the waitress, there is little more to do than stroke her husband gently on his gray crown. Those theatergoers who, like Hirsch, were pleased with *Delila* saw in it religious material turned into social comedy. The discussion within the Culture League seemed but a memory. To the extent that current issues were dealt with, this was, at best, between the lines. "In reality this piece by Molnár, too, is a fairy tale for adults," the reviewer wrapped up, "or, in fairy-tale-land a reality." Perhaps he imagined that the play's celebration of the love between Samson and Delilah contained a hidden appeal for composure between entities whose love had been such a one-way affair in the Bible. Perhaps the fairy-tale-like entertainment for adults gave him pleasure enough as it was. All that is certain is that Hirsch was "grateful for both."

The real tragedy was played out with more infernal tools than scissors. By means of endless new decrees and ordinances, Jewish culture was progressively circumscribed until, cut off, it had lost all power to assert itself.

**TEXT** "Warum Nathan der Weise?" *Jüdische Rundschau*, no. 59, 07/25/1933 · Singer, "Um die Tätigkeit des 'Kulturbundes,'" *Jüdische Rundschau*, no. 63, 08/08/1933 · Hirsch, "Molnárs 'Delila.' Die Erstaufführung im Jüdischen Kulturbund," *Jüdisches Gemeindeblatt*, no. 15, 04/10/1938 | **IMAGE 18** Scene with Fritz Wisten (Samson) and Jenny Bernstein (Delilah) in Ferenc Molnár's *Delila*, Theater Jüdischer Kulturbund in April 1938 (AAdK) · **19** *Gemeindeblatt der jüdischen Gemeinde zu Berlin*, 04/10/1938 (AAdK)

## THE QUESTION OF SPACE

The so-called "Jewish question" was, among many other things, one of space — geographically, legally, culturally. Who had the right to be where? How? And on what conditions? To which citizens did the law give room? Who could practice their profession without restrictions? To what extent was one the master of one's own assets? Or one's identity? Why was one allowed to be published? Who disposed of their own past as evangelically baptized, war hero, or nationalistically inclined?

Restrictions increased unrelentingly between January 1933 and the summer of 1940. The year after Margarete and Nelly Sachs emigrated, the yellow star ensured that it became impossible for Jews to seek protection even anonymously. There follow some dates along the downward spiral (borrowed from the historian Annegret Ehmann), until the point at which Germans of Jewish descent literally stood in their own way and, under the deadly logic of terror, had to be eliminated once and for all:

**1933** March 31: "non-Aryan" lawyers and judges banned from the courts; April 1: organized boycott of "non-Aryan" shops, lawyers' offices, and doctors' practices; April 7: beginning of the exclusion of "non-Aryan" civil servants, employees, and workers from public employment; April 25: "Law Against the Overcrowding of German Schools and Universities"; September 27: under the new "Reich Culture Chamber Law," cultural workers must present an "Aryan certificate," in effect preventing Jews from participating in cultural life;

**1934** January 1: the "Publisher Law" enters into force, preventing Jews from being published anywhere except in officially sanctioned newspapers;

**1935** July 25: Jews are declared "unworthy of the defense forces"; September 15: the "Reich Citizen law" is passed in connection with the party days in Nuremberg, laying the foundation for later Jewish exclusions;

**1937** January 1: "Aryanization" of Jewish shops and firms; July 16: restrictions on the issuing of passports to Jews;

**1938** April 26: forced registration of all Jewish assets; June 6: drastic reductions to the acceptance of Jewish asylum seekers; June 14: all Jewish business activity must be identified as such; October 5: Jewish passports are stamped with a J; October 27–28: by means of the so-called Poland Action, all Jews with Polish citizenship are forcibly deported; November 9–10: pogrom against Jewish shops and individuals (the *Reichskristallnacht*); November 12: Jews are gradually excluded from business activities, bans on Jews visiting theaters, cinemas, public events, and sports grounds; November 15: Jewish children banned from visiting municipal schools, more and more park benches have signs with pronouncements such as "Aryans only," "For Jews" or "Not for Jews"; December 6: Jews are banned from setting foot on government premises ("Jew prohibition");

**1939** January 1: all Jewish men must bear the name "Israel," all women the name "Sara"; January 30: Hitler announces "the annihilation of the Jewish race

20

in Europe" in the event of war; February 21: Jews are forced to surrender jewelry and objects made out of precious metals; April 30: tenancy rights are abolished for Jews; September 23: Jews are forced to surrender radios;

**1940** July 4: Jews in Berlin are only permitted to buy food between 4 pm and 5 pm; July 29: Jews are no longer allowed to have telephone jacks.

When the two last ordinances were imposed, Margarete and Nelly Sachs had already managed to get away to safety. After the move from the stately apartment in Siegmundshof to the smaller one in Lessingstraße, living conditions got progressively worse. In connection with "de-Judification" in the late summer of 1939 the pair were forced to move to a furnished room in Mommsenstraße 22 in Charlottenburg, in an apartment owned by a widow, Hedwig Rosenheim. In March the following year they moved again, to Pension Schwalbe farther down the same street (number 55). In eight years, the space they had at their disposal had gone from being an expensively furnished *bel étage* apartment to a spartan room in a pension. Earlier they had not been allowed to sit on the park benches in Tiergarten; now they weren't even allowed to visit the park. In a photograph taken after their arrival in Sweden, Margarete is seated on the edge of a park bench, with her daughter standing next to her. They are some hours and a thousand kilometers away from a world in which their presence ultimately had become an obstacle. At last they were no longer standing in their own way.

21

**TEXT** Annegret Ehmann, "1933–1945," *Juden in Berlin 1671–1945. Ein Lesebuch*, Berlin 1988, 242–243 | **IMAGE 20** German park bench, 1935 (BPK) · **21** By the radio tower, Berlin, 1940 (BPK) · **22** Unter den Linden, Berlin, 1937 (Photo Herbert Kraft, BPK) · **23** Margarete and Nelly Sachs after their flight (DLA)

22

## NEW ACQUAINTANCES

Among Sachs' significant acquaintances during the 1930s were the couple Max and Helene Herrmann, and their close friend and confidante, Vera Lachmann. In the account Sachs wrote in connection with her claim for war damages in the 1950s she pointed out: "At the beginning of the 1930s some critics and literature professors began to take notice of my poems. Until then I had kept my writing activities secret. The professor of German philology, Max Herrmann, was one of the keenest advocates." In one of the unpublished epitaphs from the earlier half of the 1940s, "Die Blutende [H. H.]" (The Bleeding One [H. H.]), Sachs recalled Herrmann's wife, while Lachmann came to play a significant role in connection with the flight.

MAX HERRMANN, born in 1865 in Berlin, studied German philology and history, presenting his thesis in 1889. Two years later he published a study of the thirteenth-century humanist Albrecht van Eyb, which gave him the right to teach at a higher educational institution. Due to his Jewish descent, how-

23

24

25

ever, it was thirty years before he received tenure at the university, in 1919. And it would be another decade before he could take up a full professorship, in 1930 — at the same rate of pay he'd had in his previous post. At that point he was sixty-five years old. From 1900 onwards, Herrmann held noted lectures in the history and theory of theater at the University of Berlin, earning renown as an interpreter of Lessing. He also taught the romantics. Sachs attended these open lectures — probably from the end of the 1920s, and as far as can be judged before she met Neff in May 1933. The same year that the First World War broke out Herrmann presented his main work, *Forschungen zur deutschen Theatergeschichte des Mittelalters und der Renaissance* (Investigations into German Theater History of the Middle Ages and the Renaissance) which, by expanding the analysis from exclusively text studies to the specific stage history of a work, came to lay the foundations for modern history of theater. During these years he also strived to free the discipline from German philology. His efforts bore fruit. In 1923 the world's first institute for the study of history of theater was founded in Berlin. Herrmann shared the leadership of it with his younger colleague Julius Petersen, known among other things as a publisher of Goethe's and Schiller's works, and one of the period's most prominent historians of literature.

In 1898 the then young, still unmarried Helene Schlesinger (1877–1944) enrolled at the university as a "guest listener" in German philology, philosophy, and art history, a full decade before women were allowed to study under organized circumstances at Prussian universities. She had recently graduated from an "upper secondary course for women" where she had been taught by the pedagogue and women's rights activist Helene Lange. In the same year she married the historian of theater, who was twelve years her senior. In 1904 HELENE HERRMANN was able to present her doctoral thesis at the university's German department, as the fourth woman ever to do so. The thesis, which had been supervised by the philosopher Wilhelm Dilthey among others, was devoted to "the psychological conceptions in the young Goethe and his period." An academic career was out of the question, so in 1907 she got a teaching qualification and proceeded to teach German, Latin, and French at the Falkschen Upper Secondary School. She continued to do research on the side, and also to write literary criticism. Together with her husband, Helene Herrmann supported younger academics and those generally interested in culture. Several former students — Neff among them — have testified to her pedagogic skill and ability to awaken and deepen in others an interest in literature. In one of the rare remaining photographs, a head-and-shoulders portrait, her gaze is arranged in the conventional manner, upwards at an angle and out of the picture. The gaze, the dark background and the white, toga-like dress she's wearing suggest a timeless spirituality spent with — or rather among — evergreen classics. Her eyes are tired, however; her gray head of hair is not particularly neatly combed. It is as if what went on in daily life could only be kept at a distance with effort. Much later a grandchild of hers, Renate Eastman, would say in conversation with the historian Levke Harders that Helene Herrmann "was always teased for not being completely composed [...]; her socks grew baggy and her hair hung in strands. She dropped things and walked around with her handbag wide-open. But it didn't seem to bother her."

Her husband appears to have been more organized. In photographs Max Herrmann looks lanky and imposing. His attributes are those of the learned man: wire-rimmed glasses, starched collar, a proper set of Prussian whiskers above his upper lip. Easton remembers him as "a man who looked rather frightening with his tousled hair and moustache, and a large, dark mole on his left cheek." All the same, he had "very, very soft hands." As the students at the university were preparing the book-burnings during the spring of 1933, Herrmann was one of few teachers to protest, in a missive to the Prussian Culture Ministry. The letter, dated May 1, was addressed directly to the minister, Bernhard Rust, and reveals much about how the nationalistically minded professor viewed the latest upheavals: "My sense of honor, which is deeply rooted in my ever maintained and manifested national German disposition, definitely opposes my pursuing my academic activity in a building where it is publicly said about those who belong to the community that I belong to due to my ancestry, 'The Jew can only think like a Jew; if he writes German, he lies,' and opposes it all the more definitely as it is my specific task to teach the German spirit to the students; I write German, I think German, I feel German, and I do not lie."

For reasons unknown Herrmann was not forced into retirement at the same time as other colleagues of Jewish descent, with reference to the euphemistic "Law of Restoring the Professional Bureaucracy," which stipulated an "Aryan" teaching staff. Dähnert has described how he entered the overcrowded lecture hall following the decision to purge the teaching staff: "Ladies and gentlemen, I would request that you leave the lecture hall, as I am a Jew. I am standing here of compulsion, as I have not yet been given notice." But instead of leaving the lecture hall, the students gave Herrmann a standing ovation. He was dismissed in September, however, and spent the remaining years researching and writing about Goethe in the face of ever greater hardship.

In the same year that her husband was stripped of his post, his wife opened a private school for "non-Aryan" children together with her former student and colleague VERA LACHMANN (1904–1985) — at first in the latter's apartment in Auguste-Viktoria-Straße in the southwestern district of Schmargendorf, later at Jagowstraße (now Richard-Strauß-Straße) in Grunewald. Up until the New Year of 1938/1939 the pair taught children aged ten to eighteen. A former pupil recalled many years later: "The tone at the school was distinctly German-patriotic, but anti-nationalistic and anti-militaristic. The school had

26

27

not been lucky in its choice of neighborhood. Himmler's house was nearby, and I still remember the two SS men standing guard." Lachmann herself recalled: "In order to have something to do and also because it had to be done, we rounded up lost children from the streets and opened a school. A cousin of mine gave me a chauffeur's quarters in the courtyard, and everyone, even the most distant aunt, brought in a table and a chair. And in the end we had a small school with about sixty pupils, boys and girls. It existed for about six years, and it was my salvation and what filled my life during the Nazi years. [---] But in the end, on January 1, 1939, it was prohibited once and for all."

During the final years it became progressively more difficult for Max Herrmann to do his research. The couple were forced to leave the large apartment in Augsburger Straße, where they occasionally held soirées. They sold their vast library and moved to a smaller, rented apartment in the Zehlendorf district. The professor's former student Ruth Möwius, who would publish works by both him and his wife after the war, remembers how the nearly eighty-year-old man was forced to walk on foot to the Deutsches Staatsbibliothek, having to take a long way around in the process since Jews were not allowed to set foot in Tiergarten. With the help of a special permit he was still able to use the library, but had to remain standing at the loans desk as Jews were refused chairs. In 1939 the couple moved to Helene Herrmann's niece, Käthe Finder, who lived in Charlottenburg and whose two daughters — Eva, married Ebert, and Hilde, married Alsberg — would flee to Sweden. In July 1941 Max Herrmann wrote to Lachmann: "What has filled me with particular joy is your acknowledgment that you fully understand that my thoughts are opposed to what is going on." He added: "The decision and its practical consequences would amount to a complete rupture with the innermost sides of my being, a relinquishing of all my means of subsistence." As a nationalistic German, and despite the repression, Herrmann could not countenance leaving a country whose regime couldn't stand him.

When the letter was sent Lachmann was already in America. After her emigration via Denmark and Sweden she at first taught at institutions on the East Coast, among them Yale University, where the father of her former student and friend, Erika Weigand, worked. Erika, a German American, had got to know Lachmann at the boarding school run by the reform pedagogue Paul Geheeb and his wife Edith Geheeb-Cassirer in Odenwald, Hessen, in 1930, where the thirteen-year-old had been sent for an exchange year by her parents. Three years later she returned to Berlin, where she spent the years until 1937 at the Jewish school in Grunewald — "learning and also teaching others," as Lachmann would write in a memoir. After her return to America, Weigand did what she could to help her Jewish friends and acquaintances leave Germany. (Her idealistic mindset made it difficult, however, for her to come to terms with the procedural, rule-bound handling of asylum requests, and when the full extent of the concentration camps became known she felt like an accessory. In 1946 she committed suicide.) Lachmann, who had read German and classical philology, earned her doctorate in 1931 with a thesis on the Old Icelandic saga about Hardar. Partly through the efforts of Weigand she was able to travel to New York, where she arrived on board the Swedish liner *Gripsholm* on December 6, 1939. Early in 1940 she purchased a large piece of land in North Carolina, and in 1944 founded "Camp Catawba" — a summer camp for boys between five and eleven years of age, partly with Odenwald as a model — together with her partner, the composer Tui St. George Tucker. Over the next quarter-century, they sung Negro spirituals instead of German folk songs, went hiking and read Schiller, Molière, and Chekhov around the campfire. In 1946 Lachmann was granted American citizenship. Three years later she was employed at Brooklyn College in New York City, where she remained until her retirement. When she died in 1985 she had published three collections of poetry with Castrum Peregrini in Amsterdam. Some of the texts were put to music by Tui St. George Tucker.

Life ended earlier for the Herrmann couple. On September 8 they were taken with Käthe Finder to a "collection camp" in central Berlin. The following day they were stripped of all their remaining savings. And the day after that they were deported to Theresienstadt. As far as can be determined, Max Herrmann died on November 17, 1942. In May 1944 his wife was transferred with a "work contingent transport" to Auschwitz, where she died on June 10 or 11 of the same year.

28

29

**TEXT** Annex 01/03/1956 to account of "Schaden am beruflichen Fortkommen" (E2), Akte 73 435, Margarete Sachs, 01/26/1956, Landesamt für Bürger- und Ordnungsangelegenheiten, Abt. I (EBB) · "Die Blutende [H. H.]," NSW:I · Levke Harders and Nadin Seltsam, "Spurensuche. Helene (1877–1944) und Max Herrmann (1865–1942)," *Zeitschrift für Germanistik*, 2010, no. 2, 307–323, from where most of the information has been taken · Dähnert, 234 · For letter from Herrmann to Rust, see Ruth Möwius, "In Memoriam Max Herrmann," postscript to Herrmann, *Die Entstehung der berufsmässigen Schauspielkunst*, ed. Ruth Möwius, Berlin 1962, 291 · For Lachmann's recollection, see Gabriele Kreis, *Frauen im Exil. Dichtung und Wirklichkeit*, Darmstadt 1988, 126–127 · For letter from Herrmann to Lachmann, see Stefan Corssen, *Max Herrmann und die Anfänge der Theaterwissenschaft*, Tübingen 1998, 84 · Beate Planskoy, "Erinnerungen an Vera Lachmann und an ihre Schule," *"Hier ist kein Bleiben länger". Jüdische Schulgründerinnen in Wilmersdorf*, Wilmersdorf Museum, Abteilung Volksbildung, Berlin 1992, 31–33 · Vera Lachmann, "Erinnerungen an Erika Weigand," *Castrum peregrini*, 1979, no. 138, 82 | **IMAGE 24** Max Herrmann in his younger years (©UB der HU zu Berlin; Porträtsammlung; Hermann, Max) · **25** Helene Herrmann in the 1930s (The Castrum Peregrini Foundation, Amsterdam) · **26** Vera Lachmann in the 1930s (Beate Planskoy's collection, London) · **27** Lachmann and Tui St. Tucker in the 1950s (Robert Jurgrau's collection, New York) · **28** Max Herrmann around 1940 (©UB der HU zu Berlin; Porträtsammlung; Hermann, Max) · **29** Helene Herrmann (?) in the 1940s (Renate Easton's collection, Goostrey)

## TIME OF TERROR

After her flight to Sweden, Sachs summarized her experiences during the final years in Berlin on three sheets of paper. This is one of her few published prose works, appearing for the first time in Swedish translation by the clergyman and writer Olov Hartman in the journal *Vår lösen*, affiliated with the Sigtuna Foundation, in October 1955. The following year she explained in a letter to Walter Euler: "The text contains the unimaginable things I experienced during the seven years under Hitler and the murder I endured of the person closest and most dear to me…"

When it was published in German in *Ariel*, in 1956, it was entitled "Leben unter Bedrohung" (Life Under Threat). Tersely and drastically, it recounts experiences of the National Socialist Reich. Among other things there is a meditation on time, in which Sachs analyzes the relationship between active and passive doing, the power of words, and the conditions of an era characterized by nivellization and witch-hunts. "Time under dictate. Who dictates? Everyone! Except those who are lying on their backs like a beetle before death. One hand takes away from me the time I wanted to spend with you. It takes from me this packet of seeds from which blue flowers would sprout without a shade of violet, already reminiscent of destruction." The division between perpetrators and victims is categorical: the former are in control of time, the latter have to submit to it. Where some see a baton, others see a cane. "Life under threat! The sky reflected in the polished belt buckle of one whose authority issues from time?"

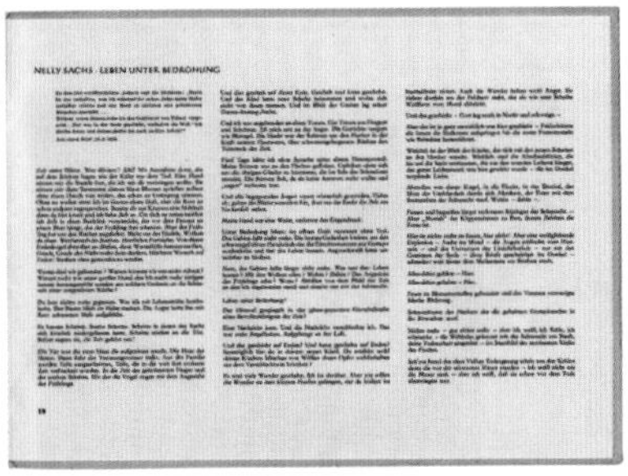
NELLY SACHS · LEBEN UNTER BEDROHUNG

30

As the shrinking canopy of sky suggests, not just time but space too is decisive. For one lying on his back on the ground, the sky appears like a bell jar: threatening and impenetrable. Fleeing to another dimension, outside of ordained time, seems impossible. Even the firmament appears forged of iron. In the distance the tramping of boots can be heard, the sound turning time's passage through space into a drilled rhythm. "There were steps. Powerful steps. Steps with which right had become established. Boots struck the door. At once they said, time belongs to us!" The boundary between public and private is no longer respected. Intimate space is under threat. The self's shelters can be breached anytime, anyhow, anywhere. Security exists only for others. "The door was the first skin to be torn away. The skin of the home."

In this world where both time and space belong to a tyrannical order, literature has little place. Novalis' blue flower no longer promises any miracles — least of all an escape to a world beyond barriers and regulations. In the rose garden the petals are wilting: "Spring has turned its back on us. Flowers from putrefaction." And like Gregor Samsa, who awoke from anxious dreams only to find that he had been turned into "vermin," the people in the text are on their backs, waiting for the fatal moment when time runs out. What remains is to hope for mercy. Sachs, however, gives this unforeseeable event a different meaning than what is usually intended in Christian faith, where God is supposed to give man the strength he needs to be delivered from death. In Sachs' mercy, on the contrary, is the "mercy of no longer having to exist. Supreme wish on earth: to die without being murdered."

In the existence depicted by Sachs there is no retreating to a safe haven, no shared writing of history, no language that keeps what it promises. Her auto biographical prose text — whose subjectless presentation suggests that it is not about acquiring but about losing a self — sets out from the individual in a time of terror. The Germany of the Nazis, like other dictatorships built on collective notions of the enemy, had no time for individual innocence. Under its logic, people belonging to a suspect minority were undesired and by extension superfluous. As a "non-Aryan," one's status as a subject was only interesting insofar as it could be turned into object. And as the creator of Gregor Samsa knew, it was only a matter of time before the interrogation became sentence. Thus man was robbed of the right to self-determination — before he had managed to possess himself of it. For Sachs this was a "life under threat." Twenty years later Imre Kertész would call the condition "fatelessness."

**TEXT** Letter to Euler 09/18/1956, ASachs · "Att leva under hot," *Vår lösen*, 1955, no. 10, 259–261 · "Leben unter Bedrohung," NSW:IV · Kertész, *Sorstalanság*, Budapest 1973 | **IMAGE 30** Nelly Sachs, "Leben unter Bedrohung," *Ariel*, 1956, no. 3

## THE FISHES, THE GLOVE, AND ASHES IN THE MOUTH

Among the personal experiences hinted at in "Leben unter Bedrohung" is a visit by SA and SS soldiers. The sound of jackboots approaching can be found in other texts as well — among them the programmatic poem "Auf daß die Verfolgten nicht Verfolger werden" (So That the Persecuted Shall Not Become Persecutors) from the end of the 1940s. It is likely that this is based on experiences from the forced sale of the house on Lessingstraße in 1939. In connection with the later application for damages Sachs listed what pieces of furniture, carpets and tapestries, paintings, sets of china, jewelry, rock and book collections the apartment had contained. Then she added, regarding the forced sale: "When it became known, people from the SA and the SS turned up with their wives and laid their hands on whatever took their fancy, telling us all the while that we had them to thank for the as yet relatively favorable conditions which obtained between us and the tenants." In a similar letter she was more specific: "In the general looting which took place, people claiming to be from the Storm Command or the SS and the SA seized whatever took their fancy. And since we were constantly living with the threat of being informed on or deported we did not dare protest. What then remained of heavy furniture, for example a Rococo bedroom of Italian walnut a similar drawing room in silk velvet and silk curtains hand-painted tables with bronze

Unsere Wohnung im Hause Lessingstr.33 dessen Besitzerin meine verstorbene Mutter war die Witwe Frau Margarete Sachs geb. Karger war ausgestattet mit einer Reihe kostbarer antiker orientalischer Teppiche die mein Vater gesammelt hatte . Darunter befand sich ein antiker Saalteppich, mehrere alte Buchara, Keschans, mittelalterliche Gebetteppiche, Seidenteppiche mit eingearbeiteten Figuren u.s.w. Dann eine Gemäldesammlung enthaltend alte und moderne Kunst. Darunter ein kleines Ölbild darstellend die Kriegsfurie was nach wissentschaftlicher Untersuchung ein Teilabschnitt aus Rubens großem Gemälde der " Krieg" darstellte. Mehrere niederreinische gotischen Madonnen, Kreuzigungen teilweise auf Holz gemalt . Die moderne Sammlung enthielt die schönsten Hauptgemälde des süddeutschen Malers Villroider Landschaften u.a. Französische Guachemalerein, Miniaturensammlung, Bronzekandelaber gezeichnet Thomire Paris, eine französische Bronze Empire Urn. Minckgefäße( persisch) eine Steinsammlung und Drusen, antike Möbel, Renaissance alle ausParis noch von meinem Großvater stammend Gobelins, Schränke voll Glas, außer Gebrauchsglas viele antike Stücke sowie Porzallane alt Meißen, xxxxxxxx alt englisch Service und Figuren. Bei einer Generalplünderung von Leuten die sich ausgaben vom Sturmkommando oder SS und SA. zu kommen wurde das was ihnen gefiel mitgenommen. Und da wir immer unter der Drohung von Anzeigen und Deportation lebten wagte man keinen Einspruch zu erheben . Was dann an schweren Möbeln beispielsweise ein Rockokoschlafzimmer in italienisch Nußbaum ein gleicher Damensalon mit Lioner Sammet und Seidendraperien bronzebeschlagenen handgemalten Tischen wurde dann von sogenannten Händlern die von der Straße kamen mit ganz geringer Bezahlung fortgeschleppt. Wir haben dann das letzte halbe Jahr bis zu unserer Auswanderung nach Schweden in einem möblierten Zimmer in Charlottenburg gewohnt.

Was den abgegebenen Schmuck betrifft, so war er besonders wertvoll und reichhaltig da der verstorbene Juwelier Eugen Marcus Unter den Linden, Berlin, mein Onkel war . Unter anderem gab meine Mutter ab: eine ganz mit Brillianten besetzte goldene Armbanduhr einen goldenen Armreif mit einem großen Solitärbrillianten, eine Platinkette mit Brillianten besetzt( Halskette) 4 Brilliantringe darunter einen mit einem großen Smaragd, verschiedene Schmuckagraffen und Broschen alle mit edlen Steinen und Brillianten besetzt, von meinem verstorbenen Vater zwei goldene Uhren mit Kette, sogenannte Frackhemdenknöpfe mit großen Brillanten einen Ring mit einem seltenen Brillianten der ein blaues Feuer sprühte. Zwei große Silberkästen, der eine noch von meinen Großeltern stammend einzelkästen mit Dessertbestecken Moccalöffeln Silberbechern u.s.w. Silberne Fruchtschalen, Brotkörbe, Leuchter. Alles aufnotierte ist nur der kleine Teil der mir im Augenblick besonders im Gedächnis haftet .

Stockholm d.3 Februar 1952 Leonie (Nelly) Sachs

31

Kurzer Lebenslauf während der Zeit der nazionalsozialistischen Verfolgungen .

Während der Zeit 1933-1940 in Berlin waren meine Mutter und ich, die inzwischen verstorbene Witwe Frau Margarete Sachs vielfachen Verfolgungen und Erpressungen ausgesetzt gewesen . Dabei handelte es sich meistenteils um einige Mieter des Hauses Lessingstr.33 dessen Besitzerin meine Mutter war . Man nahm jeden xxxxxxx jeden neuen Tag neuen Anlass uns zu erpressen und zu drohen zahlte keine Miete oder verlangte immer weitere Reduzierung so das wir,da wir als Juden keinen Hauszinssteuererlass bekamen , immer mehr Mühe hatten die Steuern aufzubringen . Man wollte uns ruinieren . Die Erpressungen gingen soweit das man auch mit Hilfe des Sturmbandführers nicht nur uns sondern auch meine Freundin und ihre Familie die keine Juden waren ins Konzentrationslager bringen wollte . Meine Freundin wohnte damals in Berlin und versuchte mutig uns vor den Erpressungen zu schützen . Sie wohnt jetzt in Dresden und heißt nach ihrer Verheiratung Gudrun Dähnert Dresden A. Reitzerstr. 42. Sie kann dies alles nach bestem Wissen und Gewissen bestätigen . Auch das meine Mutter schwer krank von den Aufregungen wurde und ich selbst drei Tage die Sprache verlor als man uns besonders peinigte .

Meine schriftstellerische Tätigkeit mußte ich natürlich aufgeben. Sie bestand damals meistens in Beitragen für die Berliner Tageszeitungen und Literaturzeitschrfiten. Der Föiltonredakteur des Berliner Tageblatts war damals Leo Hirsch der auch sein Leben in einem Koncentrationslager verlor. Er hatte auch schon eine Sammlung meiner Gedichte zur Herausgabe fertiggestellt , die nicht mehr erscheinen konnte . Im Jahre 1940 wurden meine Mutter und ich in letzter Minute von Selma Lagerlöf mit der ich von Kindheit auf im Briefwechsel stand nach Schweden gerettet .

Stockholm d.3 Februar 1952

32

fittings was dragged away by so-called traders from the street against very little payment."

It is open to question whether the relationship between the tenants and the former landlords was as favorable as the plunderers claimed. In a vita presented together with her application for damages, Sachs described attempts at blackmail by "Aryan" tenants. She mentions that the tenants had tried to have her and her mother deported and "that my mother became seriously ill from the emotional upset and I myself lost the ability to speak for three days." In "Leben unter Bedrohung" the experiences of terror were extended by two days and turned into an event with considerable repercussions in her writing: "For five days I lived speechless during a witch-hunt. My voice had fled to the fishes. Fled, without bothering with the other limbs, which stood in the salt of fear. My voice fled, since it no longer had any reply and since 'speaking' was prohibited."

In an era when people were being denied the right to speak because of their descent, muteness offered the only available sanctuary. For Sachs, the fish became its emblem. Its proximity to the Christian faith — in which the Greek word for "fish," *ichtys*, forms an acrostic of *Iesous Christos Theou Yios Soter* (Jesus Christ, God's Son, the Savior) — might make the symbol seem inappropriate. But for Sachs, who was not unreceptive to any part of the Bible, the animal's muteness and its solidarity with salt — the mineral of thirst and thus also of need — was probably of greater significance than the New Testament's belief in resurrection. From the 1940s onwards, fishes (and salt too) make frequent appearances in her work, where they usually represent the mute victims who cannot express their pain any other way than negatively, through silence or refusal. The escape to their element becomes both a salvation attempt and a confirmation that language can no longer achieve anything in a world where giving orders has replaced other forms of address.

Another key experience is described thus: "To live under threat: to molder in an open grave without dying. The brain no longer understands. The final thoughts center on that black glove that stained the entrance number to the Gestapo and almost cost a life. The sweat of anxiety ought to be invisible." The scene goes back to a visit Sachs paid to the Gestapo, where she had been summoned for what was probably a routine interrogation. In her memoir, Dähnert guesses that her friend was being forced to register as a Jew. She accompanied her to the large building and then waited anxiously for her to emerge again. When Sachs at last did emerge she smiled, surprisingly enough, and told her friend that everyone had been given little tickets with their queue number. Her anxiety had made her sweat through her black glove, which had stained the ticket. A policeman had shouted at her because the number had become blurred, but when she was taken to the office where the interrogation was to be held a senior official had comforted her. "You are afraid, I take it?

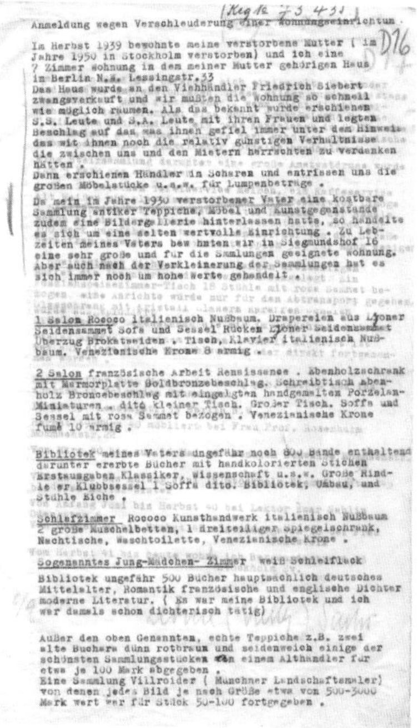
(Reg Nr 73 431)

Anmeldung wegen Verschleuderung einer Wohnungseinrichtung.

D16

Im Herbst 1939 bewohnte meine verstorbene Mutter (im Jahre 1950 in Stockholm verstorben) und ich eine 7 Zimmer Wohnung in dem meiner Mutter gehörigen Haus in Berlin N.W. Lessingstr.33
Das Haus wurde an den Viehhändler Friedrich Siebert zwangsverkauft und wir mußten die Wohnung so schnell wie möglich räumen. Als das bekannt wurde erschienen S.S. Leute und S.A. Leute mit ihren Frauen und legten Beschlag auf das was ihnen gefiel immer unter dem Hinweis das wir ihnen noch die relativ günstigen Verhältnisse die zwischen uns und den Mietern herrschten zu verdanken hätten.
Dann erschienen Händler in Scharen und entrissen uns die großen Möbelstücke u.s.w. für Lumpenbeträge.

Da mein im Jahre 1930 verstorbener Vater eine kostbare Sammlung antiker Teppiche, Möbel und Kunstgegenstände zudem eine Bildergallerie hinterlassen hatte, so handelte es sich um eine selten wertvolle Einrichtung. Zu Lebzeiten meines Vaters bewohnten wir in Siegmundshof 16 eine sehr große und für die Sammlungen geeignete Wohnung. Aber auch nach der Verkleinerung der Sammlungen hat es sich immer noch um hohe Werte gehandelt.

1 Salon Rococo italienisch Nußbaum. Drapereien aus Lyoner Seidensammet Sofa und Sessel Rücken Lyoner Seidensammet Überzug Brokatseiden. Tisch, Klavier italienisch Nußbaum. Venezianische Krone 8 armig.

2 Salon französische Arbeit Renaissance. Ebenholzschrank mit Marmorplatte Goldbronzebeschlag. Schreibtisch Ebenholz Broncebeschlag mit eingelegten handgemalten Porzelan-Miniaturen. dito kleiner Tisch. Großer Tisch. Soffa und Sessel mit rosa Sammet bezogen. Venezianische Krone fumé 10 armig.

Bibliotek meines Vaters ungefähr noch 800 Bände enthaltend darunter ererbte Bücher mit handkolorierten Stichen Erstausgaben Klassiker, Wissenschaft u.s.w. Große Rindleder Klubbsessel 1 Soffa dito. Bibliotek, Umbau, und Stühle Eiche.

Schlafzimmer Rococo Kunsthandwerk italienisch Nußbaum 2 große Muschelbetten, 1 dreiteiliger Spiegelschrank, Nachtische, Waschtoilette, Venezianische Krone.

Sogenanntes Jung-Mädchen- Zimmer weiß Schleiflack

Bibliotek ungefähr 500 Bücher hauptsächlich deutsches Mittelalter, Romantik französische und englische Dichter moderne Literatur. (Es war meine Bibliotek und ich war damals schon dichterisch tätig)

Außer den oben Genannten, echte Teppiche z.B. zwei alte Buchara dünn rotbraun und seidenweich einige der schönsten Sammlungsstücken an einem Althändler für etwa je 100 Mark abgegeben.
Eine Sammlung Villroider (Münchner Landschaftsmaler) von denen jedes Bild je nach Größe etwa von 500-3000 Mark wert war für Stück 50-100 fortgegeben.

33

You don't need to be afraid." The man gave her his telephone number and promised to provide advice if she was ever in danger — a rather incredible act which would turn out to be of decisive importance.

Both these events — the visit by SA and SS soldiers, and Sachs' own visit to the Gestapo — are, in their way, about vicarious death. The writer who flees to the fishes throws in her lot with the victims who lost their lives. The queue number which became illegible from anxiety sweat anticipates, for its part, the numbers that would be tattooed on so many arms as well as suggesting that there is no longer a place for the visitor in a world where people are bearers of names and memories and have not been reduced to a matter of logistics. This ambivalence — which returns in the definition of "living under threat" as "moldering in an open grave without dying" — gives the text an uncanny character. Written after the catastrophe, it is directed at a time past which paradoxically is part of the writer's present. With the help of empathy, Sachs tries to find her way about a place that will have nothing of her. Or as the text has it, in a historical present which shows that what is being recalled is by no means past: "There is nothing here to understand anymore, not here! But a white-hot explosion — ashes in the mouth — eyes blinded by being here — and the universe of the invisible — only with the soul's constellations — these letters written in the dark — addressed far beyond the milestone where death died."

If the supreme wish on earth is to be allowed to die without being murdered, the milestone at which "death died" marks the place where Jews and others were stripped of the right to dispose of their own deaths and thereby became "fateless," in Kertész' words. Anyone who wants to speak for these victims can only do so with ashes in the mouth — in a historical present which for Sachs was marked by emptiness.

**TEXT** "Anmeldung wegen Verschleuderung einer Wohneinrichtung" (D16), Akte 73 435, Margarete Sachs, 01/26/1956, Landesamt für Bürger- und Ordnungsangelegenheiten, Abt. I (EBB) · "Auf daß die Verfolgten nicht Verfolger werden," S (NSW:I) · "Unsere Wohnung in der Lessingstraße 33," NSW:IV · "Kurzer Lebenslauf während der Zeit der nationalsozialistischen Verfolgungen," NSW:IV · "Leben unter Bedrohung," NSW:IV · Dähnert, 238 | **IMAGE 31** "Unsere Wohnung in der Lessingstraße 33," typescript (KBS) · **32** "Kurzer Lebenslauf während der Zeit der nationalsozialistischen Verfolgungen," typescript (KBS) · **33** "Anmeldung wegen Verschleuderung einer Wohneinrichtung," typescript (EBB)

## TO THE SWEDISH KING!

The story of how Margarete and Nelly Sachs managed to flee has the stuff of adventure films. It's easy to imagine pictures in shades of gray, tracking shots through a Berlin with flags waving from the façades, where evil deeds are done on a large scale and misdeeds on a small scale... Possibly the plot will have to be rearranged and condensed, so the love story can coincide with the

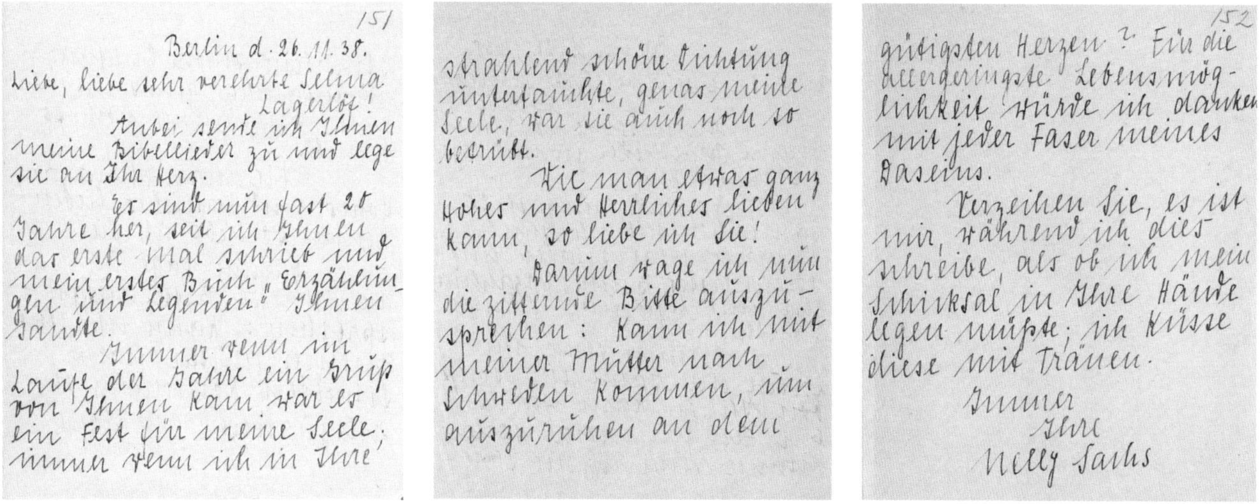
151

Berlin d. 26.11.38.

Liebe, liebe sehr verehrte Selma Lagerlöf!

Anbei sende ich Ihnen meine Bibellieder zu und lege sie an Ihr Herz.

Es sind nun fast 20 Jahre her, seit ich Ihnen das erste Mal schrieb und mein erstes Buch „Erzählungen und Legenden" Ihnen sandte.

Immer wenn im Laufe der Jahre ein Brief von Ihnen kam, war es ein Fest für meine Seele; immer wenn ich in Ihre strahlend schöne Dichtung untertauchte, genas meine Seele, war sie auch noch so betrübt.

Wie man etwas ganz Hohes und Herrliches lieben kann, so liebe ich Sie!

Darum wage ich nun die zitternde Bitte auszusprechen: Kann ich mit meiner Mutter nach Schweden kommen, um auszuruhen an dem

152

gütigsten Herzen? Für die allergeringste Lebensmöglichkeit würde ich danken mit jeder Faser meines Daseins.

Verzeihen Sie, es ist mir, während ich dies schreibe, als ob ich mein Schicksal in Ihre Hände legen müßte; ich küsse diese mit Tränen.

Immer
Ihre
Nelly Sachs

34

preparations for escape. But on the whole, events can be retold in the order they where experienced. The opening sequence might run as follows:

Early morning in July. The milkman's bottles are heard rattling as he bicycles along the deserted cobblestone streets in Charlottenburg. Otherwise it's as quiet as the calm before the storm. When the milkman has turned the corner we see the leafy apple trees sway in a morning light just a tad too bright. Two women emerge from the blur of the background. They're approaching along the pavement, wearing hats and carrying suitcases. They are Ilka Grüning in the role of "Marianne Sara Bartholdi," with Elfriede Borodkin as the daughter, "Nell Sara." Judging from their laborious progress, they are tired, most likely afraid. They've just been visited by some SS officers and their wives, who have plundered their apartment and in putative kindness given them one hour to leave it. They've spent the night on a park bench, fearful that their caper — two Jews on a bench for Aryans — would be discovered. When they reach the camera, which hasn't moved, the younger woman takes out a piece of paper and checks the house number. Then she nods to her mother and picks up the cases again. This is it. Number 22. A minute later they are entering the house of a stern widow of a professor, played by Dame May Whitty in a worn cardigan and a brooch on her bosom. With barely restrained hostility she counts the notes the women hand her — three months' advance rent. Then she points at the necklace the younger tenant is wearing. "As security," she sniggers. Elfriede Borodkin looks with shining eyes at Ilka Grüning who lowers her gaze, then places the gift from her beloved "Peter" in the widow's hand.

Another cut. A few hours later. Now the street is bustling: a couple of children are playing hopscotch on the pavement, a car sounds its horn, men in brown shirts salute a woman, who nods awkwardly. She is young, blonde, and

35

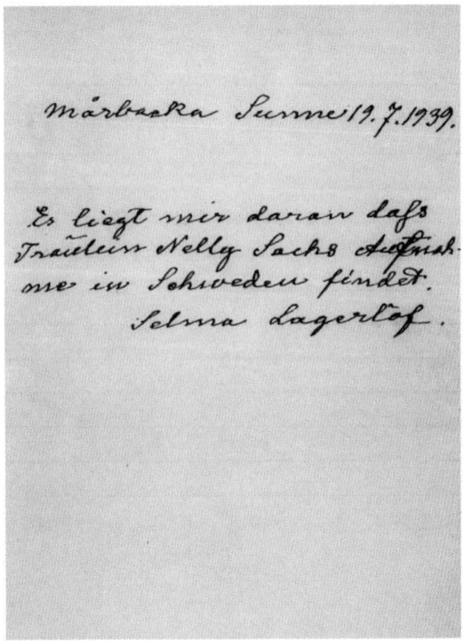

Mårbacka Sunne 19.7.1939.

Es liegt mir daran daß Fräulein Nelly Sachs Aufnahme in Schweden findet.

Selma Lagerlöf.

36

athletic — perhaps played by Kaaren Verne, possibly by Ingrid Bergman. Now we see that she is walking with difficulty, using a cane. Apparently she has an injured leg, but seems to be on the way to recovery. After joking with the children she reaches Mommsenstraße 22 and makes her way laboriously up the stairs. The audience doesn't know it yet, but the woman's name is "Gertrud Dannert" and she is a physiotherapist. It is not until she rings the doorbell on the second floor that the audience realizes that she doesn't live in the building, but is visiting "Frau Rosenheid, Furnished Rooms to Let." Another cut. When we see Dannert again she has put her cane away and is spreading out a map on a bed. There is also a ticket and some Swedish money on the bedspread. A voice that seems to be coming from the window says: "You must be careful, Gertrud." The camera moves slowly from northern Europe to the speaker. While we look into Elfriede Borodkin's pale face gazing down into the street outside the visitor behind her is heard replying: "I promise, Nell. I will save you." The picture and sound are toned out and replaced by the film's title: "To the Swedish King!"

The true story of Nelly Sachs' "life-saver" was considerably less kitschy, but equally as incredible as an antiwar film from 1942 with elements of fairy tale and *noir*. Many years later — at the beginning of the 1970s — Dähnert described her friend's "escape from Germany." Sachs had recently died and there was reason to retain memories of a forty-year-long, exceptional friendship. After the Olympic Games of 1936, the situation for the country's Jews came to a head. Gone were the cosmetic improvements carried out during a few late summer weeks in Berlin, when the country was visited by foreigners from near and far and the propaganda machinery was spinning in top gear. The so-called Jew passes were introduced and the "Aryanization" of businesses and firms was completed. On the night of November 9, 1938, Jewish shops were looted and set on fire, a couple of days later "non-Aryans" were banned from visiting theaters and cinemas, attend public events, or watch sporting events. "How might Lichen flee with her mother?" Dähnert asked herself. "We knew of no possibility. But just as unexpected solutions often appear in fairy tales, the idea of Selma Lagerlöf came to Lichen." On November 26, Sachs sent a letter to the Nobel laureate at Mårbacka: "Could I and my mother come to Sweden, to seek respite with the kindest of hearts? For the very smallest opportunity to life I would be grateful with every fiber of my being."

Sweden was at this time closed to refugees. Only those known as "transmigrants" — on their way to a third country — could hope for a temporary residence permit. When Sachs received no reply, she realized that her chances were limited. Someone close to her and trusted would have to travel to Mårbacka and appeal to Lagerlöf. Neff was unable to, as she had to look after her mother who was ill with cancer. That left Dähnert. Shortly after the new year she visited Vera Lachmann in Berlin-Dahlem. Familiar with issues concerning emigration, her friend explained the conditions to her. On her way home, however, Dähnert was hit by a bus which dragged her along for about forty meters, and she had to be taken to hospital for surgery. Valuable time was lost while she was recuperating. On January 26, 1939, Sachs made a last desperate attempt, writing to Lagerlöf: "And if I may repeat my diffident supplication, which to you may seem to be on bended knees: Would you, who have been a symbol of love and goodness all my life, would you help my mother and myself to open the gate to Sweden, a land to which we so fervently long, by allowing me to put your ever-valued name as a reference on the question form at the Swedish consulate here? This is our only hope of obtaining a residence permit in Sweden."

37

Still no reply. Only a few days later Hitler declared that in the event of war the Jewish race would be eradicated in Europe. In April Dähnert was finally released from the hospital. In June the cast was removed; she could now walk with a support splint and canes. A journey to Sweden no longer seemed an impossibility. To be able to afford the return ticket to Stockholm via Göteborg and Sunne, she sold her furniture. Neff "gave me a further few words on my way: 'For Lichen one must go all the way to the king of Sweden!'"

After having spent the night with relatives in Kullavik outside Göteborg, Dähnert visited a contact Sachs had conveyed: since 1935 the philosopher Ernst Cassirer, a cousin of her old neurologist Richard Cassirer, was a professor at the city's university. (After the German invasions of Denmark and Norway he felt unsafe in the country where he and his wife had become citizens, and they moved to America.) Despite good contacts, however, Cassirer was unable to offer any help. The only thing left to do was to visit the author of *The Wonderful Adventures of Nils*. Unfortunately the meeting did not go as hoped. Hard of hearing, Lagerlöf sat on her terrace with a shawl around her head. Hammering workmen were in the process of relaying the roof. Although Dähnert raised her voice she did not manage to make herself understood. In the end she had to leave Mårbacka with her business unfinished. "And it was on this we had pinned our hopes! I sat down at the edge of the wood, among the wild raspberries in the lovely green landscape. Saw all this beauty with a weight in my heart. Now there was only Stockholm left to try, which everyone regarded as utterly futile."

After a restless night in Sunne she decided to make one last attempt. "The thing was that Selma Lagerlöf had become an old woman who could hardly hear and probably also had difficulties reading. But maybe she would be able to recognize very large lettering." Dähnert wrote a letter in great block letters and returned to Mårbacka. On arrival she was told that the lady of the house had traveled to Falun. "My heart almost stopped." However, when she walked through the garden the maid suddenly called out to her. This time she was taken up to the study. And there she suddenly was, "the person our hopes had

Ett varmt tack
från 80åringen för all
visad vänlighet.
1 aug. 1945.
38

clung to. There was no hammering on the roof now. She was not wearing a shawl around her ears. And now I could speak, even in German, to her." Lagerlöf agreed to writing a brief recommendation to the government (it would read: "It matters to me that Miss Sachs is received in Sweden"). With that her German visitor could continue to Stockholm — relieved but as yet with unfinished business.

Helene Herrmann's niece Eva Ebert and her family had been living in the Swedish capital for a few years. Together with them, Dähnert deliberated about how Sachs might be saved. An audience with the king was out of the question, but the king's brother, the "Painter Prince" Eugen, might receive the visitor. Already the following day Dähnert made a request for an audience at Waldemarsudde, which led to the prince conveying the contact to the Foreign Ministry, where matters regarding refugees were processed. At the ministry in Arvfurstens Palace by Gustaf Adolfs Torg, Dähnert was asked to fill in forms. Even if recommendations from both a member of the royal family as well as a member of the Swedish Academy carried weight, there were regulations to follow. Sweden could only serve as transit country if there was an affidavit guaranteeing that her subsistence in America had been secured. Swedish entry regulations constituted a further obstacle. Since refugees were not issued work permits, a certificate was required guaranteeing a sufficient income of 200 to 225 Swedish kronor per month.

Dähnert visited the Jewish congregation, where she was received by the lawyer Wilhelm Michaeli, who had emigrated from Berlin in 1933 and worked on refugee issues. At the time of the visit he was in conversation with professor Hans Guggenheimer, who had also fled from Berlin. Guggenheimer knew the Sachs family and could vouch for them, after which Michaeli announced that he was prepared to guarantee 100 kronor. A visit to Enar Sahlin, who worked at a school in Solna, a northern suburb of Stockholm, and knew Lagerlöf from his secondary school years in Falun, led to another 25 kronor per month being secured. The publisher Karl Otto Bonnier pledged to contribute an equal amount if his writer in Värmland would also help. In a letter to Lagerlöf late in the autumn of 1939 Sahlin, who had taken charge of the matter, asked: "Can these two unfortunate women now hope for financial support from and through Mårbacka?" They could.

**TEXT** Dähnert, 242–252 · Letter of recommendation from Lagerlöf 07/19/1939, ASachs · Letters from Sachs to Lagerlöf 11/26/1938 and 01/26/1939, and letter from Sahlin 11/07/1939, Selma Lagerlöf's collection, KBS · In a letter from the Jewish congregation 02/07/1940 to Kungliga Socialstyrelsen it is confirmed that "Nelly and Margarete Sachs' maintenance costs in this country, up to a monthly sum of 150 kronor, have been put at their disposal by private entities and individuals," ASachs | **IMAGE 34** Letter from Nelly Sachs to Selma Lagerlöf 11/26/1938 (KBS) · **35** Mårbacka in the 1930s (Photo David Holmquist, the Mårbacka Foundation's archive) · **36** Selma Lagerlöf's letter of recommendation 07/19/1939 (KBS) · **37** Gudrun Dähnert, 1945 (Kurt Kehrwieder's collection, Bochum) · **38** Prince Eugen, 1945 (Photo Anna Riwkin, KBS)

## DENOUEMENT

After Dähnert's return to Berlin, the Sachses began preparing for their departure. In the spring of 1939 tenancy rights for Jews were suspended, and it was only a matter of time before they would lose the apartment in Lessingstraße. Furniture, carpets, and paintings were sold off at laughable prices; the heavy taxes imposed on Jews were paid with difficulty. Of particular assistance in this connection was OTTO SCHEURMANN (1897–1975), who ran a private bank on Behrenstraße 7 in Mitte and was one of few Germans permitted to handle money matters for Jews. After the war Sachs wrote of him in a letter to her cousin Toni Seemüller: "He had then during our last year in Berlin, where he was recommended by friends (he was at that time still the only person allowed to manage Jewish fortunes), together with the lawyer Flemming taken care of us and proved to be excellent." Scheurmann helped them in the forced dissolution of the apartment, paid the so-called Reich flight tax in 1940, and also supported the refugees during their first years abroad. Preserved documents show that until November 28, 1942, the banker managed capital amounting to 4,536.40 reichsmark and 16.20 reichsmark for Margarete and Nelly respectively. After the war, too, he helped — for example with transfers of smaller sums to Dähnert and Neff, and not least with the application for damages. Towards the end of the 1940s Sachs wrote: "We have never forgotten your kindness back then. You were one of the few brave and upright people when it came to attending to the wretched victims of Hitler." Her gratitude was so great that she invited the banker and his daughter to the Nobel Prize festivities in 1966.

From the middle of the 1930s the tenants in Lessingstraße no longer had to pay rent, which put the Sachses in increasingly dire straits. The situation was not alleviated by the fact that as landlords they were still obliged to pay not just for the building's upkeep, but also steep capital taxes and other charges directed at "non-Aryans." In 1939 Margarete Sachs was listed for the last time as owner in Berlin's *Adreßbuch*, after which the property passed into the hands of Friedrich Siebert, a cattle trader. The following year Margarete was listed as a tenant under the name "M. Sara." A letter from the Reich Finance Ministry to the chairman of the city council dated November 1939 lays down that "the de-Judaification [*Enteignung*] of the property NW. 87, Lessingstraße 33" must have been completed no later than August 17. The letter furthermore rejected "the present plaints [. . .] as lacking any foundation."

During the spring Erika Weigand managed to get her father, the Germanist Hermann J. Weigand, to sign an affidavit for the two women. With this crucial document they were able to apply for a visa at the American consulate in Bellevuestraße. On October 20 Sahlin described the progress in a letter to Lagerlöf, who three days later thanked him for the news and added: "I don't know any of them personally, but Leonie is a dainty writer of children's verse and short

39

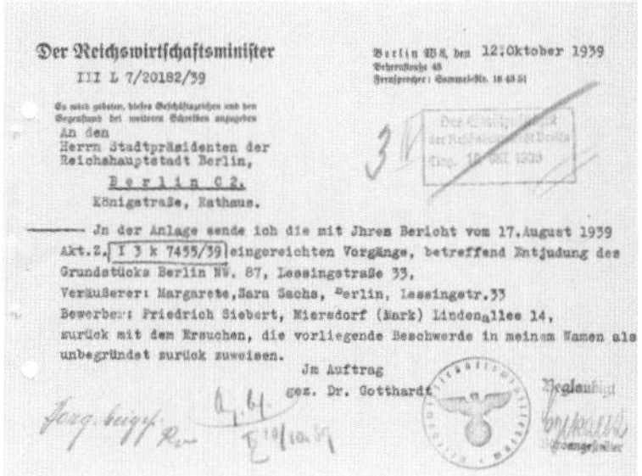

Der Reichswirtschaftsminister
III L 7/20182/39

Berlin W8, den 12.Oktober 1939
Behrenstraße 43

An den
Herrn Stadtpräsidenten der
Reichshauptstadt Berlin,
Berlin C 2,
Königstraße, Rathaus.

Jn der Anlage sende ich die mit Jhrem Bericht vom 17.August 1939 Akt.Z. I 3 k 7455/39 eingereichten Vorgänge, betreffend Entjudung des Grundstücks Berlin NW. 87, Lessingstraße 33,
Veräußerer: Margarete,Sara Sachs, Berlin, Lessingstr.33
Bewerber: Friedrich Siebert, Miersdorf (Mark) Lindenallee 14,
zurück mit dem Ersuchen, die vorliegende Beschwerde in meinem Namen als unbegründet zurück zuweisen.

Jm Auftrag
gez. Dr. Gotthardt

Beglaubigt

40

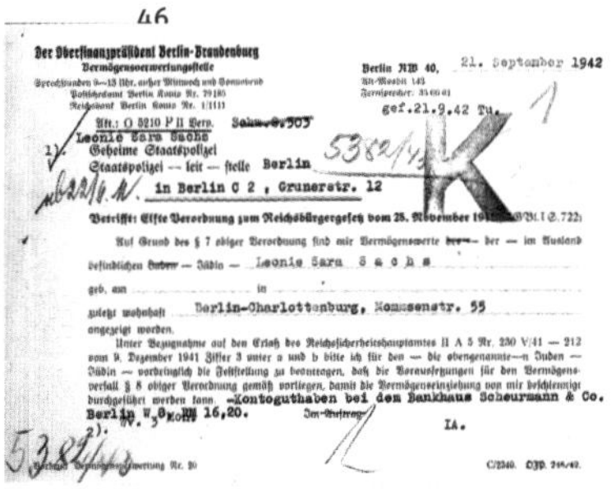

46

Der Oberfinanzpräsident Berlin-Brandenburg
Vermögensverwertungsstelle

Berlin NW 40, 21. September 1942
Alt-Moabit 143

gef.21.9.42

Leonie Sara Sachs
1) Geheime Staatspolizei
Staatspolizei — leit — stelle Berlin
in Berlin C 2, Grunerstr. 12

Betrifft: Elfte Verordnung zum Reichsbürgergesetz vom 25. November 1941

Auf Grund des § 7 obiger Verordnung sind mir Vermögenswerte der — im Ausland befindlichen — Jüdin — Leonie Sara Sachs
geb. am ... in ...
zuletzt wohnhaft Berlin-Charlottenburg, Mommsenstr. 55
angezeigt worden.

Unter Bezugnahme auf den Erlaß des Reichssicherheitshauptamtes II A 5 Nr. 230 V/41 — 212 vom 9. Dezember 1941 Ziffer 3 unter a und b bitte ich für den — die obengenannte—n Juden — Jüdin — vordringlich die Feststellung zu beantragen, daß die Voraussetzungen für den Vermögensverfall § 8 obiger Verordnung gemäß vorliegen, damit die Vermögenseinziehung von mir beschleunigt durchgeführt werden kann. -Kontoguthaben bei dem Bankhaus Scheurmann & Co. Berlin W 8, RM 16,20.

IA.

41

Sachs, Leonie

AMERIKANISCHES GENERALKONSULAT
BERLIN

AMERICAN CONSULATE GENERAL
MAR - 8 1939
BERLIN, GERMANY

Datum des Poststempels

Das Generalkonsulat teilt Ihnen hierdurch mit, dass Sie auf der deutschen Warteliste unter den folgenden Nummern eingetragen sind:

60218

Es kann zur Zeit noch nicht angegeben werden, wann Sie mit einer Berücksichtigung Ihrer Angelegenheit rechnen können; jedoch wird Ihnen diesbezüglich rechtzeitig eine weitere Mitteilung zugehen.

AMERIKANISCHES GENERALKONSULAT

Falls Sie mehrere Male Ihre Nummer bestätigt erhalten haben, gilt selbstverständlich nur die niedrigste Nummer.

42

43

44

fairy-tale plays for children. I should think she deserves to be helped." However, the women's high numbers at the American consulate — "60,000 + x and y," as Sahlin informed Lagerlöf — meant that their turn would only come in a couple of years. Which made it that much more important that they were allowed into Sweden for a transitional period as soon as possible.

Although the application for residence permits as "transmigrants" was sent to the National Board of Health and Welfare on August 5, and although it was supplemented in the fall with financial guarantees from the Jewish congregation as well as from Bonnier, Sahlin, and Lagerlöf, a response was not forthcoming. At this point the war had broken out and the Wehrmacht looked invincible. On August 14 Sachs thanked Lagerlöf for her letter of recommendation. Shortly thereafter she and her mother were forced to leave Lessingstraße and move to rented accommodations. On November 15 she was able to inform Sahlin that Lachmann was going to leave the country later in the month and travel to New York by way of Göteborg. She included a poem for Lagerlöf on her eighty-first birthday. On Christmas Day, expressing her anguish about the state of the older woman's health, she took the opportunity to add: "Dear, most highly esteemed Dr. Sahlin, do you think that we might still hope to receive the residence permit?" Nothing appeared to be happening at the Foreign Ministry in Stockholm. When the Germans marched into Denmark and Norway in the spring of 1940, and the occupation of France and Holland was imminent, Sachs' days too seemed numbered.

In April Dähnert rushed to Berlin from Dresden to aid her friend. On April

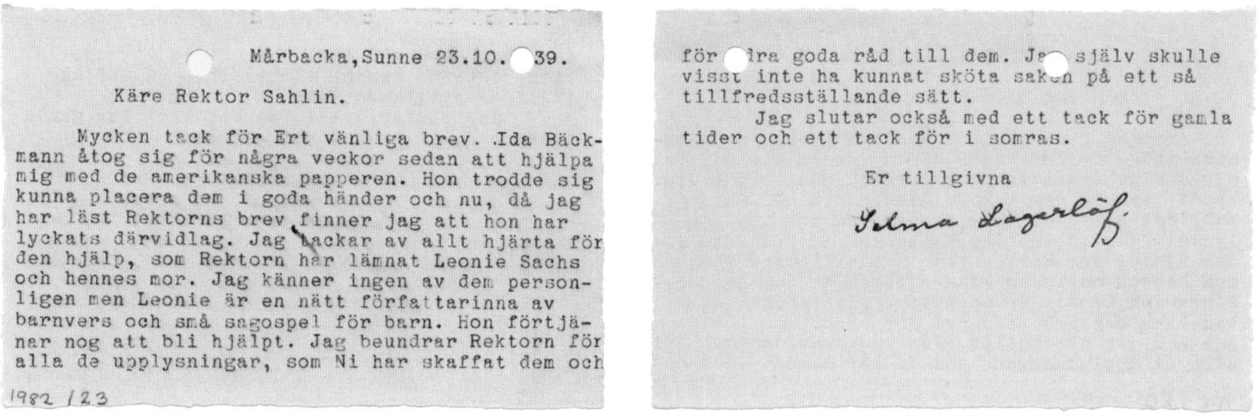

Mårbacka,Sunne 23.10. 39.

Käre Rektor Sahlin.

Mycken tack för Ert vänliga brev. Ida Bäckmann åtog sig för några veckor sedan att hjälpa mig med de amerikanska papperen. Hon trodde sig kunna placera dem i goda händer och nu, då jag har läst Rektorns brev finner jag att hon har lyckats därvidlag. Jag tackar av allt hjärta för den hjälp, som Rektorn har lämnat Leonie Sachs och hennes mor. Jag känner ingen av dem personligen men Leonie är en nätt författarinna av barnvers och små sagospel för barn. Hon förtjänar nog att bli hjälpt. Jag beundrar Rektorn för alla de upplysningar, som Ni har skaffat dem och för era goda råd till dem. Jag själv skulle visst inte ha kunnat sköta saken på ett så tillfredsställande sätt.

Jag slutar också med ett tack för gamla tider och ett tack för i somras.

Er tillgivna

Selma Lagerlöf

1982/123

45

25 an "emigration fee" was paid, corresponding to a tenth of their remaining capital, 11,240 reichsmark, and the following day yet another fee, this time "Reich flight tax" of 9,297 reichsmark. On the same day that Sachs received an order to present herself for transportation to a labor camp, Neff visited the Swedish consulate at Wallstraße 5–8. It turned out that the longed-for visas had been waiting for them for about a fortnight. Sachs immediately contacted the Gestapo official who had offered to help her and asked him what she should do with the order. The man advised her: "Tear up that order and fly to Stockholm with your mother now, today." When she told him that she'd bought train tickets the official replied: "You won't get through that way any longer. Change your tickets to airplane tickets right away." Which they did. After that no more obstacles stood in their way.

46

47

**TEXT** Letter to Seemüller 07/14/1949, ASachs · "Rep. 36 A II, nr. 32700" (documents concerning Leonie Sachs) and "Rep. 36 A II, nr. 32702" (documents concerning Margarete Sachs) (BLA) · For letter to Scheurmann 07/14/1949, see Briefe 62 · Stadtpräsident der Reichshauptstadt Berlin, no. 677: "Enteignung jüdischen Grundbesitzes / (Straßen L)" (LAB) · Dähnert, 250–252 · Copy of affidavit from Hermann J. Weigand 09/13/1939, ASachs · Letters from Sahlin 10/20 and 11/07/1939, Selma Lagerlöf's collection, KBS · Letters from Lagerlöf to Sahlin 10/23/1939, and from Sachs 11/14 and 12/25/1939, ASahlin | **IMAGE 39** Otto Scheurmann in the 1960s (Photo Klaus Peter Bier, Hans-Jürgen Laborn's collection, Berlin) · **40** "Enteignung jüdischen Grundbesitzes / (Straßen L)," 10/12/1939 (LAB) · **41** "Anträge zum Verfallen des Vermögens im Bankhaus Scheurmann wegen Ausreise der Kontoinhaberinnen," September 1942 (Brandenburgisches Landeshauptarchiv [BLHA], Rep. 36A Oberfinanzpräsident Berlin-Brandenburg [II] Nr. 32700) · **42** Copy of Nelly and Margarete Sachs' queue number at the American Consulate General in Berlin, 07/31/1939 (KBS) · **43** Nelly Sachs, 1940 (DLA) · **44** Margarete Sachs, 1940 (DLA) · **45** Letter from Lagerlöf to Sahlin 10/23/1939 (KBS) · **46** Siegmundshof, 1935 (LAB) · **47** Siegmundshof burning, 1940 (Photo Wolfgang Krueger, LAB)

48

49

## LUGGAGE

At the beginning of the summer of 1940 Tempelhof Airport, which was in the process of being expanded, had temporarily been opened for civilian traffic. The two "non-Aryans" who checked in for the flight to Stockholm on May 16 owned the clothes on their backs, the five marks they were allowed to take out the country, a thermos flask containing fennel tea for Margarete's health, and the contents of a brown suitcase measuring 74 x 21 x 44 centimeters. The case had been secured with a pair of leather straps and contained, besides clothes, manuscripts, and photographs, objects of sentimental value — including some of Nelly's father's medals, the music box, and the scrapbook. A letter to the "currency office" of the Finance Ministry from the beginning of the month indicates that the passengers had left the following at the main customs office: "2 lamps for bedside tables, 1 summer dress, 2 medals, 1 summer dress, approx. 110 books, manuscripts, since no recommendation from the Reich Authors' Chamber is as yet to hand."

As the red plane left German airspace Margarete announced contentedly: "I've hidden another five marks." If the money had been discovered at the airport control, it could have cost them their departure.

**TEXT** Dähnert, 252 · Transcript of letter from Margarete Sachs 05/03/1940 to the Oberfinanzpräsident Berlin (Devisenstelle), ASachs · Information about the concealed money, interview with Margaretha Holmqvist 03/17/2009 | **IMAGE 48** Tempelhof in 1934 (LAB) · **49** Eastern airfield of Tempelhof, 1940 (F.-Herbert Wenz, Airbus Bremen) · **50** The Sachs' brown suitcase (from a private collection)

50

# IN PEACEFUL SWEDEN

## FROM DREAM-KISSED THROAT

For the women aboard the plane that landed at Bromma Airport in May 1940, arrival meant a longed-for delivery from persecution. In Nelly Sachs' case, it was also a dream coming true. In the late summer of 1921, a few months before her first book had been published, she had written to Lagerlöf and asked permission to visit Mårbacka with her parents. Nothing is known of any reply, but Lagerlöf later sent Sachs a copy of the German edition of her childhood memoir from the Mårbacka estate. It is not unlikely that *Mårbacka* meant quite a lot to the writer of the prose story "Chelion," which made a similar inventory of childhood. When the political situation had worsened, with German Jews' possibilities of leaving the country curtailed, Sachs sent a birthday poem to the estate outside of Sunne. It ended with the verses:

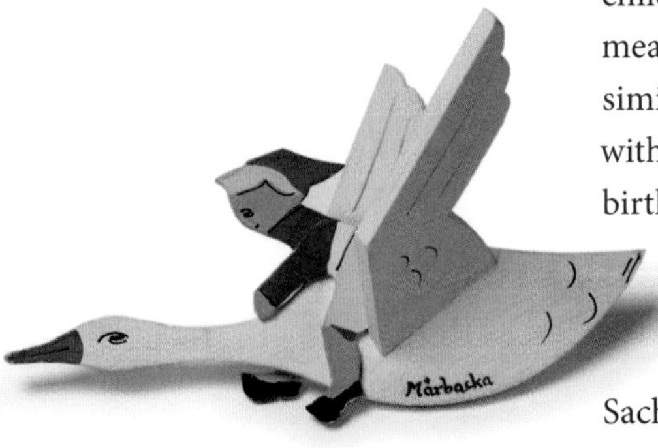

1

> Selma Lagerlöf, the One / Sang softly to us from her soul, / A dream-kissed throat, / And the stones sighed.

Sachs asked to have well-wishes conveyed on Lagerlöf's seventieth birthday, adding that at home by her reading lamp she was still visited by "the frail Elsalill, the sweet Elisabeth Dona and all the splendid men and women" who peopled Lagerlöf's childhood — "not forgetting the billy goat and the wild goose."

Geese and goats were all very well, but the true incarnation of the relief the refugee must have felt at Bromma Airport is another character from Lagerlöf's gallery. At least there is not likely to be a more apt symbol of the craft that saved Sachs than that diminutive globetrotter wearing clogs and a red woolen cap: Nils Holgersson. Sachs' literary estate at Kungliga Biblioteket in Stockholm still includes a painted wooden doll sitting astride a goose which, as far as can be judged, appears to have been hung from a length of string. The real relief, however, resided in the throat that Sachs herself after the flight no longer had to use in the manner of fishes. Kissed into new life by a dream which had improbably come true, she would come to abandon the kitschy fairy tales and romantic sceneries. Instead she would give voice to the brothers and sisters who had not been lucky enough to escape. From her throat would henceforth speak voices that had been denied the right to use words.

**TEXT** Letter to Lagerlöf 08/17/1921, Selma Lagerlöf's collection, KBS · For letter to Lagerlöf 11/18/1937 with the birthday poem "Oben, im verschneiten Wald," see Briefe 3 | **IMAGE 1** Wooden Nils Holgersson doll in Sachs' possession (KBS)

2

**STONES THAT SIGH**

After the move to the new apartment in 1948 Sachs informed her friend in Dresden: "I have laid out a little indoor rock garden of sheer longing." The minerals were intended to recall her father's precious collection in Berlin — a resurrected memorial.

For those attentive, the stones that sighed in the birthday poem to Lagerlöf could still be heard twenty years after Sachs' arrival in Sweden, for instance in a letter to Dagrun Enzensberger in which she emphasized that life after the improbable rescue was radically different. Gone were the terror and arbitrariness, but gone was also the security which had once made it possible to write risk-free rhymes about hearts breaking. Living conditions by the Spree Canal and Lake Mälaren's southern shores were not linked by some conciliatory dash, but separated by an irrevocable slash. If there is one single theme in Sachs' writings that persists from her early Berlin verses through the terse poems of the 1960s, it is, paradoxically, that of separation. The difference between the time before and the time after the flight was so fundamental that the escape from one country to the other made any other continuity an impossibility. The escape implied a breaking off and breaking up. That is: metamorphosis. Touching ground in Sweden, only the most elementary things were of any importance in Sachs' life. "Once one has, in the course of an escape, caressed a stone," she pointed out to Enzensberger, "because it was the first thing one sat down on in a free country — one will never again have a close relationship to anything that doesn't directly serve one's existence."

If anything, the stones that stilled the longing for what had been lost were tombstones.

**TEXT** For letter to Dähnert 05/17/1949, see Briefe 61 · Letter to Dagrun Enzensberger 01/22/1959, ASachs | **IMAGE** **2** Nelly Sachs' rock and shell collection (KBS)

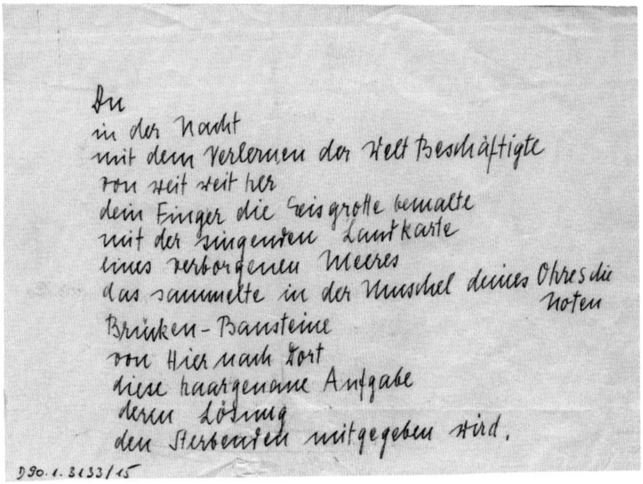

Du
in der Nacht
mit dem Verlernen der Welt Beschäftigte
von Zeit Zeit her
dein Finger die Eisgrotte bemalte
mit der singenden Landkarte
eines verborgenen Meeres
das sammelte in der Muschel deines Ohres die Noten
Brücken-Bausteine
von Hier nach Dort
diese haargenaue Aufgabe
deren Lösung
den Sterbenden mitgegeben wird.

D90.1.3133/15

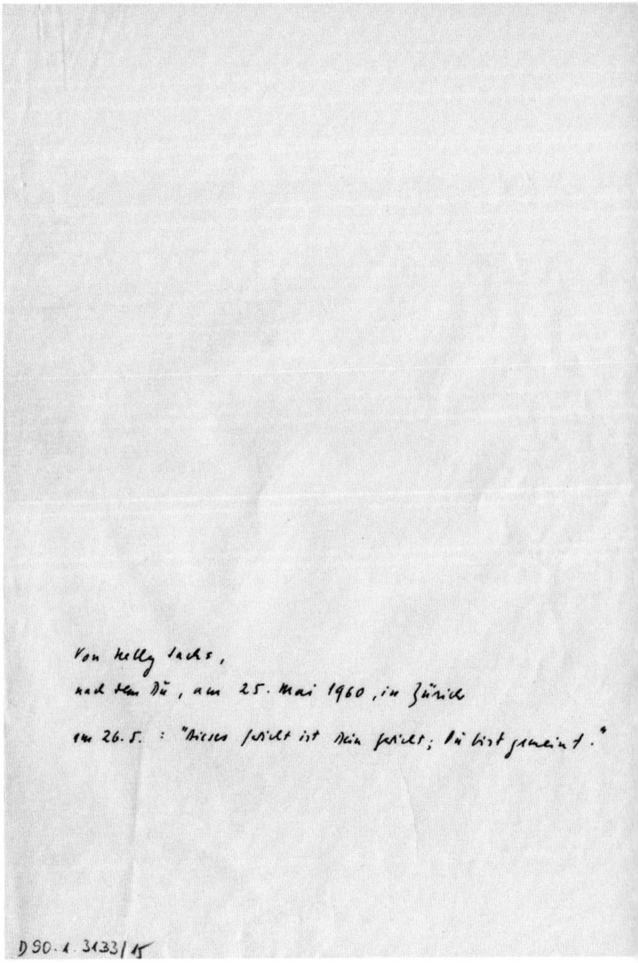

Von Nelly Sachs,
nach dem Du, am 25. Mai 1960, in Zürich
am 26.5.: "Dieses Gedicht ist Dein Gedicht; Du bist gemeint."

D90.1.3133/15

3

## FROM HERE TO THERE

If parting was one of the principal themes already in Sachs' early writing, transformation became another fundamental theme in her mature works. From the 1950s onwards, the dust readied itself for flight, set to begin a journey for which there was no fixed course. A simple formula for this transformation might be: "From Here to There." Sachs explored the relationship between the known, which had been left, and the unknown, which was sought in many ways — not always with the same intent, but almost always within the emotional register of longing. Even the poetry from before she was forced to leave her homeland dealt with the relationship as a separation in time and space. One of the poems "to the distant one" from the second half of the 1930s, entitled "Abschied, du Nachtigallenwort" (Farewell, You Nightingale-word), brings together distance with poetry's basic condition:

> Farewell, you nightingale-word / That sang itself to God / You tear-ewer in which a sobbing / Here and there drowned. // Do a pair of swallows in you kiss / As they are sundered? / Does death divide you, a hair's breadth / As the lover from love?

The poem is considered a vessel filled with the beloved's tears — which both confirms love and attests to the beloved's absence. Even if the abandoned one should drown in this grail of sobs, the vessel contains equal parts of "here" and "there." Thus the farewell is a clandestinely whispered welcome — a hushed invitation to the rendezvous called poetry.

The choice of imagery may seem trite, but on closer inspection Sachs accomplished something remarkable in these eight lines. The appeal to "Farewell" invokes a separation by which the text is born as poetry. For the speaker poetry seems to require such sharing, since otherwise there would be no reason to write. Scrutinized closely, the poem reveals a voice which is not directed to the distant beloved, but to the *word* attesting to his absence. This logic is captured most clearly in the question of whether a pair of swallows parting might still be able to kiss each other. The difference between "here" and "there" is like the birds' dash in the air — thin and silent, a hair's breadth from the void. Death is necessary in order for poetry to be separated from love. But in Sachs' universe poetry constitutes the very boundary, and thus becomes a dividing in a double sense, which by invoking the farewell preserves what romance could not save.

In the suite "Die Elegien von den Spuren im Sande" (The Elegies about the Tracks in the Sand), written after a few years in the new country, this theme is spun further:

> And the maiden by the spinning wheel / Has taken a thread of star's gold / And spun it. For she has confused Here and There / So wrapped up is she in your game / And since everything is so closely entwined / The eternal kisses: Here and There.

And in the programmatic poem "Land Israel" (Land of Israel) in *Sternverdunkelung* from 1949, where the address is broadened from the intimate you to embrace a whole people and its "width," the idea returns in the "narrow alley [which] runs between Here and There / where he gave and took as neighbor." The clearest formulation of the relationship between the two poles of longing, however, is found in the cycle "Fahrt ins Staublose" (Journey into a Dustless Realm). Here, the poem "You" sums up the condition in four effective lines:

> from Here to There / this hair-thin task / whose solution / the dying have with them.

Twenty years after landing at Bromma Airport, in May 1960, Sachs revisited a country which in the meantime had become abroad for her. The visit took place in connection with her receiving the city of Meersburg's Droste Prize for Women Poets. At the airport in Zurich on the other side of the Bodensee she was met by Paul Celan, among others. The following day, when the two of them saw each other on the terrace of the Zum Storchen Hotel, she handed him a handwritten version of "You" with the dedication: "This poem is your poem, it is about you." A couple of years later Sachs' friends Bengt and Margaretha Holmqvist were given a transcription of the same poem with the note: "This is my mother's death poem. Tomorrow, the 9th of June, is her birthday, I have transcribed it from the book with my love and my thanks to you." Clearly Sachs saw no contradiction in using one and the same pronoun for different people. And why should she? It was in the nature of direct speech that the "you" could change for every new thing said. What's more, a lot could happen in the course of the journey from "here" to "there"…

Following the poem's imagery, the movement of longing from one pole to the other is in fact a "task" much like that of the single hair itself: it continues to grow even after the addressee's death. The you is transient, separation eternal. For Sachs this meant that, in the end, the only thing that remained was sharing — this contradictory relation based on separation. Or, with words from the poem: "bridge-building stones."

**TEXT** "Abschied, du Nachtigallenwort," FG, 260 · "Die Elegien von den Spuren im Sande," NSW:I · "Land Israel," S (NSW:I) · "Fahrt ins Staublose," FiS (NSW:II) · Comments on the poem "Du," NSW:II | **IMAGE 3** "Du," manuscript with a conversation note by Paul Celan 05/25/1960 on the back (DLA)

## A BODY AND ITS FACTS

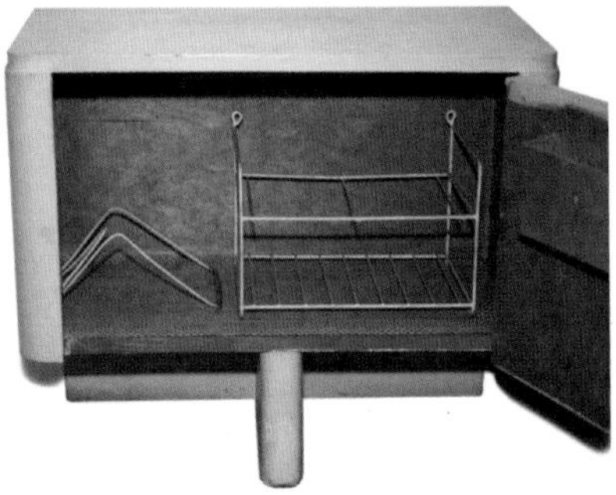

4

When Sachs set foot on Swedish soil she was at least 154 centimeters tall. There is no information available about her weight, but judging from photographs of the period a reasonable guess would be 50 kilos. Her shoe size was, and remained, 34. During the first weeks she slept in a child's bed. When she was admitted to the emergency ward at Södersjukhuset twenty years later, on August 8, 1960, her height was never measured but her weight was 36 kilos. Her body mass index at this time was about 16, which is equivalent to life-threatening underweight. The doctors feared she wouldn't make it (as a consequence of marasmus). When she applied for and received a new Swedish passport a few years later, her height was given as 148 centimeters. The photograph shows that she had put on weight.

Fact: during her first quarter century in the new country Sachs grew six centimeters shorter.

**TEXT** The information about Sachs' height in 1940 appears on her application for an alien's passport 02/14/1942, ASachs · Medical records from Södersjukhuset and Beckomberga · Passport 03/16/1965, ASachs | **IMAGE 4** Nelly Sachs' shoe cabinet (KBS)

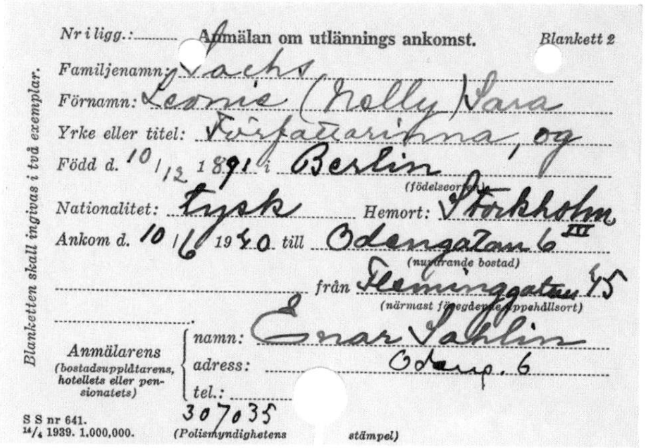

Blanketten skall ingivas i två exemplar.

Nr i ligg.: ........ Anmälan om utlännings ankomst. Blankett 2

Familjenamn: Sachs

Förnamn: Leonie (Nelly) Sara

Yrke eller titel: Författarinna, og

Född d. 10/12 1891 i Berlin (födelseort)

Nationalitet: tysk Hemort: Stockholm

Ankom d. 10/6 1940 till Odengatan 6 III (nuvarande bostad)

från Fleminggatan 45 (närmast föregående uppehållsort)

Anmälarens (bostadsupplåtarens, hotellets eller pensionatets) namn: Einar Sahlin adress: Odeng. 6 tel.: 307035

S S nr 641. 14/4 1939. 1,000,000. (Polismyndighetens stämpel)

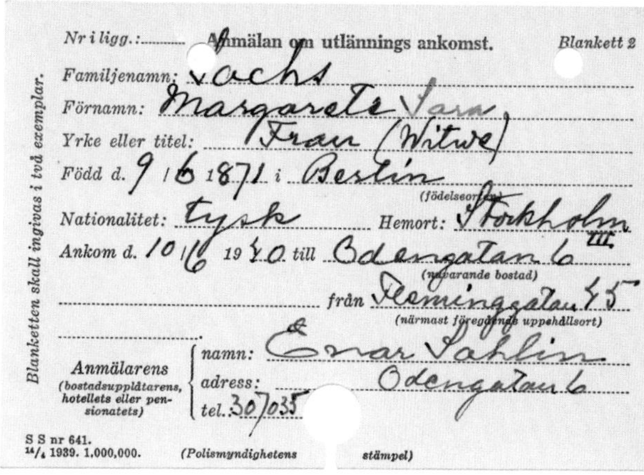

Blanketten skall ingivas i två exemplar.

Nr i ligg.: ........ Anmälan om utlännings ankomst. Blankett 2

Familjenamn: Sachs

Förnamn: Margarete Sara

Yrke eller titel: Frau (Witwe)

Född d. 9/6 1871 i Berlin (födelseort)

Nationalitet: tysk Hemort: Stockholm

Ankom d. 10/6 1940 till Odengatan 6 III (nuvarande bostad)

från Fleminggatan 45 (närmast föregående uppehållsort)

Anmälarens (bostadsupplåtarens, hotellets eller pensionatets) namn: Einar Sahlin adress: Odengatan 6 tel. 307035

S S nr 641. 14/4 1939. 1,000,000. (Polismyndighetens stämpel)

5

## SOON BETTER

Roughly half a million people managed to escape the terror of Nazi Germany. Of these a tenth had been persecuted because of their politics, the rest because they were "non-Aryans." About one per cent, or around 5,000 people, found refuge in the Nordic countries. When Denmark and Norway were attacked in the spring of 1940 these refugees were once again at risk, and most tried to make it to neutral Sweden. As Helmut Müssener has shown, Sweden soon became the Nordic center for German political and cultural emigration. But even if politicians such as Willy Brandt and Bruno Kreisky, scientists such as Max Hodann, Käte Hamburger, and Ernst Cassirer, writers such as Kurt Tucholsky, Bertolt Brecht, and Peter Weiss, or artists such as Lotte Laserstein found a new home in northern Europe and many of them later made their way to Sweden, the German refugees — between four and six thousand people — were characterized by unknown names. In this instance "you can," maintains one scholar (Einhart Lorenz), "really talk about an exile of the little people." Nelly and Margarete Sachs belonged to this anonymous group whose protection Swedish authorities would long view not as an onus so much as a nuisance.

6

During the first weeks after their arrival the pair stayed with the widow Elisabeth Müller-Winter at Fleminggatan 15 in the Kungsholmen district. On June 10 they moved to an apartment on the third floor at Odengatan 6 in

7

Vasastaden. The report filed on the foreigners' arrival shows that one Charlotta Goldstein, who had fled from Berlin-Lichterfelde, was also housed in the apartment. The owner was Lagerlöf's friend Enar Sahlin, who was spending the summer in the country and didn't need the apartment until school began again. The following day Sachs wrote her first letter in Swedish: "My esteem Herr Senior Master Sahlin! Now I want try write a letter at my esteem teacher point about what I learn. I fear which I have me to ashame. My esteem teacher have do his trouble such, but I do many mistakers. I apologize. I should hope that one shall being soon better."

The educationalist and politician ENAR SAHLIN (1862–1950), who had a doctorate in philosophy and had become a senior lecturer in the subject in 1888, had made Lagerlöf's acquaintance in 1899 after he had taken up the post of headmaster at the main state secondary school in Falun, where the author had moved a few years earlier. He arranged social events and also invited Lagerlöf to talk about her works. Among other things, she read the first chapters of *The Wonderful Adventures of Nils*. The titles of some of Sahlin's writings testify to the humanistic and emancipatory inclination of his interests: *Om J. G. Fichtes idealism* (On J. G. Fichte's Idealism [1888]), *Flickskolereformen i Preussen* (The Girls' School Reform in Prussia [1908]) and *Jean-Jacques Rousseau* (1912). For a time he was a member of the Riksdag's second chamber, where his main involvement was with morality issues. From 1911 he was Senior Master at the state upper secondary school in Stockholm's Östermalm district, but when Dähnert contacted him during her visit in the summer of 1939 he was working at a school by Brunnsviken in Solna, north of Stockholm. Sahlin was also active within the refugee aid services. A photograph from the same year shows an elderly man with noble features and a resolute air. It is no surprise that, at seventy-eight, he applied for duty with the volunteer corps in Finland — "willingly at the lowest rank." Or that he corrected and returned the letters that Sachs would write him in Swedish …

"So good and true are also your words about my first works," the refugee wrote in her reply to Sahlin's reactions after reading her. "Of course I had as a child and from fairy tales seen everything far too much in either white or black. And you, highly esteemed Herr Senior Master, are also right in that one should try and send these first stories, so wonderfully translated by you to your beautiful Swedish, to newspapers and magazines. [---] If you should happen to think that the works are felicitous, it would perhaps be possible to persuade Herr Bonnier or another publisher. But in that case I must sincerely ask you to demand the share that your work with the translation has cost from the publisher in question. As for myself, I neither can nor wish to demand anything, as it would already make me very happy if a publisher should take the risk, and I would furthermore feel fortunate in being allowed to offer an ever so small gesture of thanks to the beautiful country that is Sweden."

During a later conversation with Fritsch-Vivié, Sahlin's daughter Margit reported that the refugees had seemed nervous, even overcome with anxiety. Margarete Sachs was not used to household work, and Enar Sahlin is said to have been perplexed that the two ladies with whom he was trying to converse about the Old Testament did not seem to know the texts. With time, however, the fear subsided. Sachs began making new acquaintances, among them the literary historian and member of the Swedish Academy, Martin Lamm (Wilhelm Michaeli of the Jewish congregation had conveyed the contact). A couple of weeks after Sahlin had lent them his apartment, he received "a small selection" of poems and fairy plays. In the covering letter Sachs added: "How dearly would I not want to show myself grateful and worthy before the lovely country of Sweden which has so hospitably opened its doors to my mother and myself." The envelope also contained a transcript of Hirsch's letter of recommendation, which she hoped would facilitate contacts with Swedish publishers. Except for a few isolated publications in Swedish magazines, however, these efforts came to nothing.

At the beginning of July Sachs received the last sign of life from her advocate: "Finally I have your address," Hirsch wrote, "and finally I can write to you. When your farewell note arrived — wonderful and as a surprise doubly wonderful — you were already gone, and I had to tell myself constantly that it is meaningless to write long letters and produce the most beautiful words when you don't know where they are bound." Now the dramaturge, who was suffering from cancer, knew where letters could be sent and expressed his most heartfelt wish: "I do very much hope that you will gain a foothold in your inner self too." After the drastically worsened living conditions in Berlin, Stockholm meant new ground under Sachs' feet. The many letters with enclosed poems or stories that she carried to the mailbox during the first few years were building blocks with which she tried to lay the foundations of a new life also in her "inner self." With their help a bridge would be built to an unfamiliar, perhaps unthreatened but far from comfortable existence.

Otherwise life during those first few weeks looked something like this: "I shall tell you, what I am doing today. After we have rised up, and order the room, I must go to shopping. It is often to laugh. But shopkeepers help me if I cannot show with my spreach. At evening if I have peace, I begin to write my story and poem. Sometimes I painting the little flowers."

**TEXT** For the most detailed account of German-speaking emigrants in Sweden, see Helmut Müssener, *Exil in Schweden. Politische und kulturelle Emigration nach 1933*, Munich 1974 · Einhart Lorenz, "Exilforschung in Skandinavien," *Exilforschung. Ein internationales Jahrbuch*, ed. Claus-Dieter Krohn et al., Munich 1996, 119 · The information about the first addresses in Stockholm appears in document D17 from Sachs' later application for war damages on her mother's behalf, Akte 73 435, Margarete Sachs, 01/26/1956, Landesamt für Bürger- und Ordnungsangelegenheiten, Abt. I (EBB) · Entry declaration for foreign nationals 06/10/1940 and letter from Sachs 06/11/1940, ASahlin · On Sahlin's application as a volunteer, email message from Erland Bohlin 08/27/2009 · For letter to Sahlin 06/26/1940, see Briefe 7 · Fritsch-Vivié, 83 · Letter from Sachs 06/19/1940, ALamm · Letter from Hirsch 07/05/1940, ATegen | **IMAGE 5** Entry declaration for foreign nationals 06/10/1940 for Margarete and Nelly Sachs, and Charlotta Goldstein (KBS) · **6** Enar Sahlin in 1939 (Erland Bohlin's collection, Örebro) · **7** Stockholm, a view over Riddarholmen and Gamla Stan, 1949 (Photo Lennart Petersens, SSM)

## IN THE MIRROR OF HOMESICKNESS

Among the first poems after Sachs' flight are two cycles with Swedish themes: "Schwedische Elegien" (Swedish Elegies) and "Miniaturen um Schloß Gripsholm" (Miniatures around Gripsholm Castle). Just before moving, in August 1940, from Odengatan to Alströmergatan 16 in Kungsholmen — where Charlotta Goldstein had rented an apartment and mother and daughter could take a room — Sachs sent a sample to Sahlin. "It will allow you to understand how heavy my heart is, not just with the new suffering of my brothers and sisters, but now with everything that can no longer live in love." This is the first time she uses the formula "my brothers and sisters." A few years later it would return in

8

9

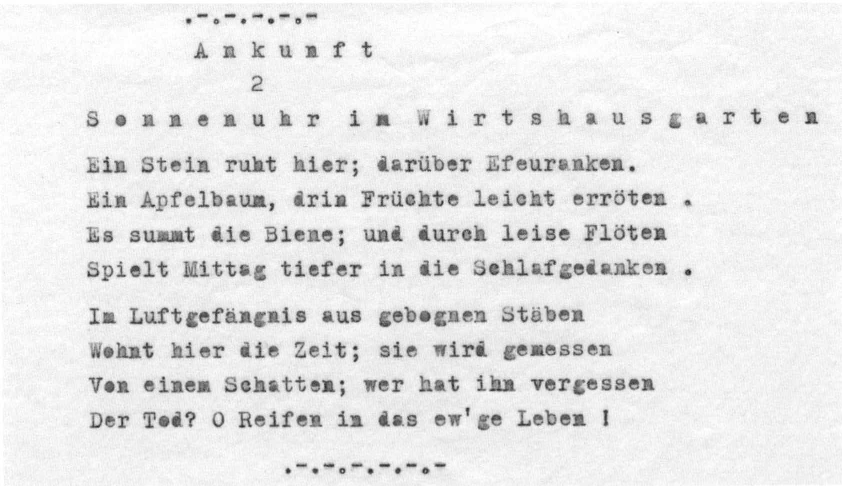

.-.-.-.-.-

A n k u n f t

2

S o n n e n u h r i m W i r t s h a u s g a r t e n

Ein Stein ruht hier; darüber Efeuranken.
Ein Apfelbaum, drin Früchte leicht erröten .
Es summt die Biene; und durch leise Flöten
Spielt Mittag tiefer in die Schlafgedanken .

Im Luftgefängnis aus gebognen Stäben
Wohnt hier die Zeit; sie wird gemessen
Von einem Schatten; wer hat ihn vergessen
Der Tod? O Reifen in das ew'ge Leben !

.-.-.-.-.-.-

the dedication of her first collection of poetry *In den Wohnungen des Todes*. Stylistically, however, the new elegies still belonged to the prewar poetry:

> From one treetop to another, / The wind sings and sings — / The spruce would wander / The sky rings. // It shakes its branches / And raises them to dance — / With silence I tie / A wreath of forest blooms.

The tone is unmistakable: here is a writer who specializes in lyrical commonplaces like deer, wells, and fall leaves. The clouds scud past "in the mirror of homesickness," swallows trace the familiar lines of parting across the sky. Sachs may have moved physically, but she has yet to arrive in literary terms.

At the beginning of July an unknown "lady" took her and her mother on a steamboat ride to Drottningholm outside Stockholm. "So lovely, so lovely," Sachs exclaimed in a letter to Sahlin, and recalled dreams in which she had seen nature manifest itself in a similar way — "light green, rocky islets, water and wind." The correspondence shows that she sought echoes of Germany in Sweden. The young Margit Sahlin's description of the village where she spent the first summer of the war prompted Sachs to tell her about an old village in Silesia that she had visited only three years earlier. Walks with her mother to the nearby Lilljans Wood brought back memories of the Bohemian landscapes which Adalbert Stifter had portrayed in *Bunte Steine* (Motley Stones) and *Studien* (Studies), works from Sachs' Berlin library that would only partly be saved through the box of books that friends sent her during the war.

10

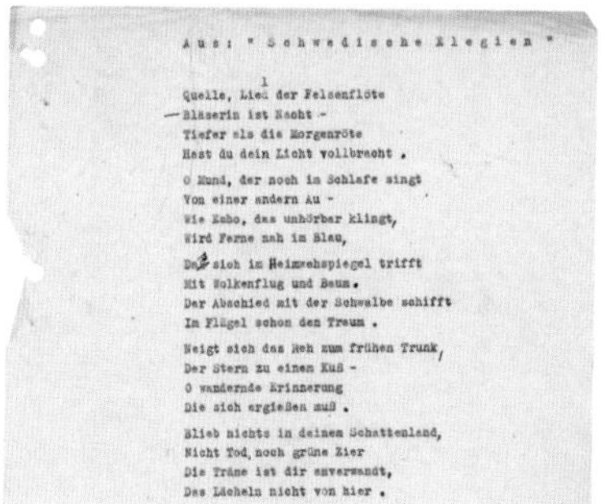

Aus: " Schwedische Elegien "

1

Quelle, Lied der Felsenflöte
Bläserin ist Nacht -
Tiefer als die Morgenröte
Hast du dein Licht vollbracht .

O Mund, der noch im Schlafe singt
Von einer andern Au -
Wie Echo, das unhörbar klingt,
Wird Ferne nah im Blau,

Daß sich im Heimwehspiegel trifft
Mit Wolkenflug und Baum.
Der Abschied mit der Schwalbe schifft
Im Flügel schon den Traum .

Neigt sich das Reh zum frühen Trunk,
Der Stern zu einem Kuß -
O wandernde Erinnerung
Die sich ergießen muß .

Blieb nichts in deinem Schattenland,
Nicht Tod, noch grüne Zier
Die Träne ist dir anverwandt,
Das Lächeln nicht von hier .

11

In a similar fashion, the elegies served to imbue the foreign with a sense of familiarity. The miniatures from Gripsholm are reminiscent of the sentimental images of excursions to Brandenburg, Thuringia, and Silesia. A boat ride on Lake Mälaren is described in twelve reverential tableaux — including arrival, sightseeing tour, and departure. Moss-covered wells and heraldic halls, magic spells and dolls with princess' faces — the poems are replete with the props of yore. Clearly the poet was seeking to make herself comfortable in exile. (In a letter to Lamm she says of Sahlin: "This good man has really made Sweden a homeland for us.")

> I see two swallows practice / The farewell, and see the tree / By the wall obscure / The sun with nightly dream.

When it came to her poetry, not even partings were missing from the new homeland...

**TEXT** "Schwedische Elegien" and "Miniaturen um Schloß Gripsholm," NSW:I · For letters to Sahlin 07/07 and 08/08/1940, see Briefe 8 and 9 respectively · Information about the box of books appears in a letter to Alfred Andersch 07/17/1959, DLA · Letter to Lamm 06/19/1940, ALamm | **IMAGE** **8** Martin Lamm in the 1950s (JMS) · **9** Poem from "Miniaturen um Schloß Gripsholm," typescript (KBS) · **10** Gripsholm Castle, 1947 (Photo Lennart Petersens, SSM) · **11** Poem from "Schwedische Elegien," typescript (KBS)

12

13

## WINDOWS ON THE BACKYARD

After spending two years living out of a suitcase, Margarete and Nelly Sachs moved to their own apartment in October 1941. Sahlin expressed his willingness to bear a large part of the cost of setting up the new home. Overwhelmed by his generosity, Sachs wrote a few weeks after the move: "It was for us as if 'He' had sent us his angels who, far from the homeland, had arranged for us this little home, this warm nest, so that we might thank and serve 'Him.'" The headmaster with the Old Testament under his arm, who had discontinued his translation services but carried on aiding the pair until his death in 1950, had been promoted from helper to guardian angel. Now he belonged to the same band of confederates as Dähnert, Neff, and Lagerlöf.

A new life began in a one-bedroom apartment with windows on the back yard at Bergsundsstrand 23. The building was owned by the Warburg Foundation and managed by the Jewish congregation, which placed most of the apartments at the disposal of refugees. GUNNAR JOSEPHSON (1889–1972), bookseller, chairman of the congregation, and active within the Swedish refugee aid services, was particularly obliging and would later help Sachs with housing matters. The Berliners who moved in on the ground floor were exempt from paying rent and allowed to inherit some furniture from "brothers and sisters" who had gone on to America or other countries. Circumstances were difficult. The pair hardly had money for food or clothes, and were forced to depend on handouts and the modest support the congregation had pledged on paper, but which had to be collected each month. During the winter the building's heating malfunctioned, and the indoor temperature frequently dropped below 10° C. From later documents it emerges that mother and daughter were also plagued periodically by a stench of sewers from the yard. In addition, Margarete's frail health required care and medication, which cost money they didn't have.

One of the first visitors was the poet and translator JOHANNES EDFELT (1904–1997), who had been called up for emergency military service and arrived at the apartment late in the autumn of 1941, wearing a uniform. He found Sachs in the kitchen, where she was sitting under dripping washing hung on lines across the kitchen, writing. She did not want to disturb her mother, who was sleeping. Edfelt had received a letter in which Sachs asked his permission to translate a few poems. Seeking contacts, she had sent similar letters to many writers and members of the literary community. The acquaintance led almost immediately to the two poets beginning to translate each other; soon a friendship evolved.

Over the following years Sachs would include poems by Edfelt in the two anthologies she compiled in German, and in 1956 she published a separate volume of translations entitled *Der Schattenfischer* (The Shadow-Fisher). Edfelt, for his part, began by translating various poems for magazines (the first ones were published in the 1941 Christmas issue of *Vi*), then presented the writer in articles and also reviewed Sachs' first German books in the Swedish press. He emerges as a friend and admirer of an idiom that was close to his own, in which the legacy of the great German poets was preserved in the wary knowledge of later catastrophes. Under the heading "She Should Have Been a Famous Poetess" he summed up one of his articles thus: "It is against a Swedish backdrop, it is in exile that Nelly Sachs has reached her beautiful maturity as a poet. Here she wrote her strange, delicate Epitaphs, filled with the frail ringing of bells, shimmering butterflies and the inscrutable shadow of death. These poems are like a brave, graceful dance before the flame that burns and consumes."

When the piece was published in the periodical *Idun* in 1947, *In den Wohnungen des Todes* had been released, and Sachs had found the poetic language that she would refine over the following years. In the accompanying photograph she is seated in her home with her hair coiffed and wearing a pearl necklace, leaning against a pillow. But when Edfelt paid her his first visit, a year or two remained before the tragedy would reveal its full scope. Sachs was still writing derivative poetry; she had not yet discovered the aesthetically radical strain in Swedish poetry. To the extent that she was interested in the new country's literature, she seems to have been drawn to early modernists and classicists such as Edfelt, Anders Österling, and Hjalmar Gullberg. One of the first texts from the period in Bergsundsstrand is entitled "Verwandlung" (Transformation). It was written at the Karolinska Hospital early in 1942 and dedicated to Sahlin "with thanks beyond words":

> Before my window the tree / Turns in to the night, in the dream — / It almost grows into eternity / With other greenery, other attire? // Only the night knows of love — / But as the light slowly fades / — A star remained among the branches — / The darkness rises in mute songs / And becomes a spruce of light — / Wanderers before His visage / Are we in the night when love speaks!

The verses show that the transformation which one year later would lead to the "Grabschriften in die Luft geschrieben" (Epitaphs Written in the Air) had begun, but was still in its nascent stage. The imagery is conventional, the meter tied up in tradition, the rhymes predictable. The stanzas in which a tree grows up into divine eternity is not so much saddled with disquiet or uncertainty as with something more fatal to poetry: faith.

**TEXT** Shopping receipts and "Verwandlung," ASahlin · For letter to Sahlin 10/26/1941, see Briefe 11 · For information about a stench of sewers, see "Weitere Aufzeichnungen," NSW:IV · JE (NSW:IV) · Edfelt, "Hon skulle ha varit berömd skaldinna," *Idun*, 1947, no. 21, 11 · The information about Edfelt's visit included in an email message from Margaretha Holmqvist 11/10/2009, who nevertheless has doubts about his recollection and assumes that the first visit took place while Sachs was still lodging with Goldstein | **IMAGE 12** Johannes Edfelt in the 1940s (Photo Harald Borgström, ABFS) · **13** Edfelt, *Der Schattenfischer* 1956

## TABLEAU WITH MOTHER AND DAUGHTER

Until Margarete Sachs' death in 1950, frailty and isolation contributed to making the already strong bond between mother and daughter grow stronger. For her mother's seventieth birthday on June 9, 1941, Nelly wrote a birthday poem — "Meinem Liebsten auf der Welt!" (To My Most Beloved in the World!) — whose intimacy was likely dictated by the solemn occasion, but also hints at a relationship with traits of symbiosis. (The word is Edfelt's, from a memorial article a few years after Sachs' death: "I don't think I have ever seen a more complete symbiosis between mother and daughter than the one that existed between Nelly and her mother.") One stanza reads:

> You are home for me and evening / Sweet calm and deep affection / And my mouth reading fairy tales / Feels love only in silence.

For a reader unaware of who these lines are intended for, it would be easy to think they were a declaration from one lover to another. Sachs often used the qualifier "Most beloved" for her mother, which doesn't exactly lessen the impression of an unusually intimate relationship. Among the photographs from this period are a handful that show them on a summer's day near water. They were probably taken during a visit to the country. In the first picture Nelly poses alone, standing next to an empty chair; in the second are two unknown women beside mother and daughter — which would seem to indicate that there was (at least) a fifth person present on the occasion. Perhaps the unknown women were also refugees — possibly one of them is Charlotta Goldstein. The third photograph shows Margarete Sachs with her hands clasped, sitting on the same chair next to which Nelly posed. She is wearing dark clothes and a white polka-dot blouse. Her wavy hair is streaked with gray, her gaze direct and attentive, with a hint of amusement. It may be that age has forced her to sit down and rest, but nothing in the image suggests she is infirm or ill. Standing next to her is her daughter, also dressed in a cardigan and with wavy, still dark hair. Her posture is one of anticipation, her gaze friendly. On her left wrist is a watch. These are not women living under threat. Even if they appear drawn more towards each other than towards the camera lens, it looks as if they feel at ease in the soft afternoon light.

It is the fourth photograph that is the interesting one.

Now the person behind the camera has taken a step forward and lowered the line of view. The angle is not very flattering for those posing. Margarete has her eyes closed, while Nelly has placed one hand protectively on her shoulder and turns her face to one side so that the sun highlights her apple-round cheek. If it was Margarete who was at the center of the previous image — self-assured and seated, confident that her daughter will follow her lead — the relationship has changed in this one. Margarete is still at the center, but

14

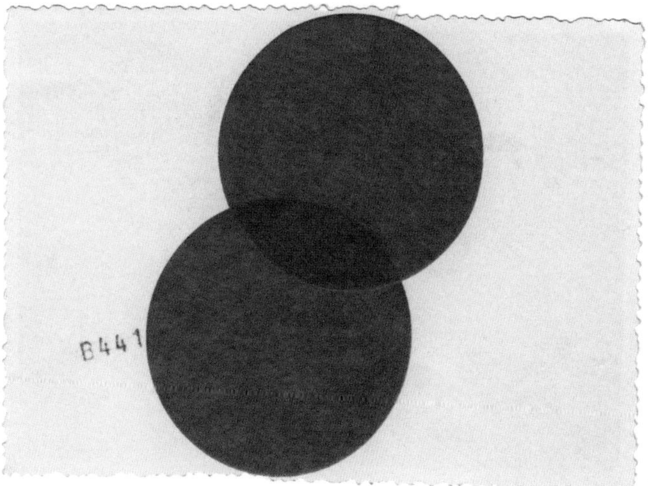


15

the perspective, her closed eyes, and above all her daughter's controlling hand make her appear aged, in need of help and protection.

At some point the photograph was cut into two and then taped together again. The cut is along Margarete's left side, separates her daughter's hand from the rest of her arm, and continues up through the tree in the background and into the summer sky. It is impossible to say why they were cut apart and put back together again. Perhaps one of them needed a picture of herself? In that case it ought to have been Margarete, since Nelly posed alone in another picture. Or was one them unhappy with what she looked like in the picture (eyes closed, too shiny a cheek)? Hard to say. All that is certain is this: the separation failed.

**TEXT** Edfelt, "Nelly Sachs på nära håll", *Svenska Dagbladet* 03/19/1974 · "Meinem Liebsten auf der Welt!", ASahlin | **IMAGE 14** Three photographs of Margarete and Nelly Sachs, early 1940s (DLA) · **15** Front and back of a photograph of mother and daughter, cut into two and then stuck back together again (DLA)

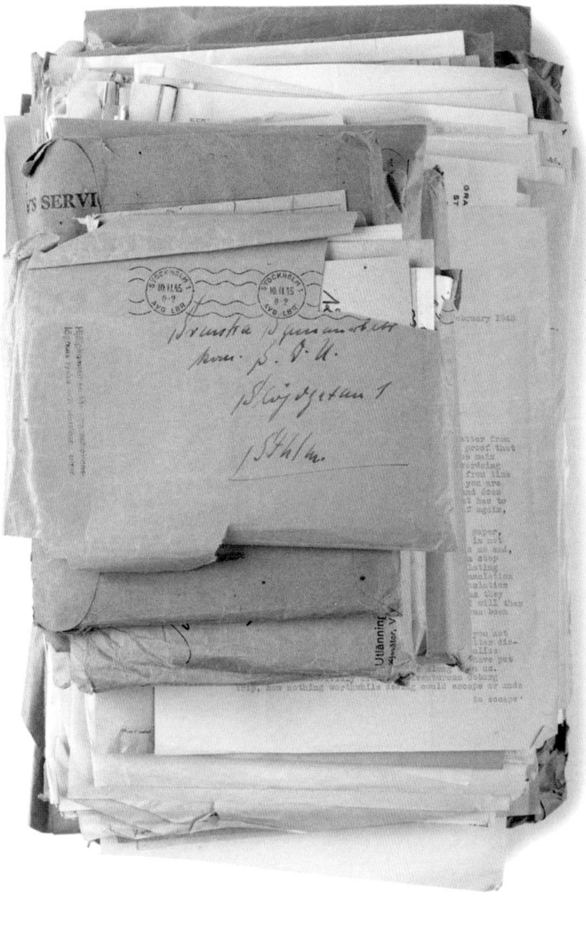

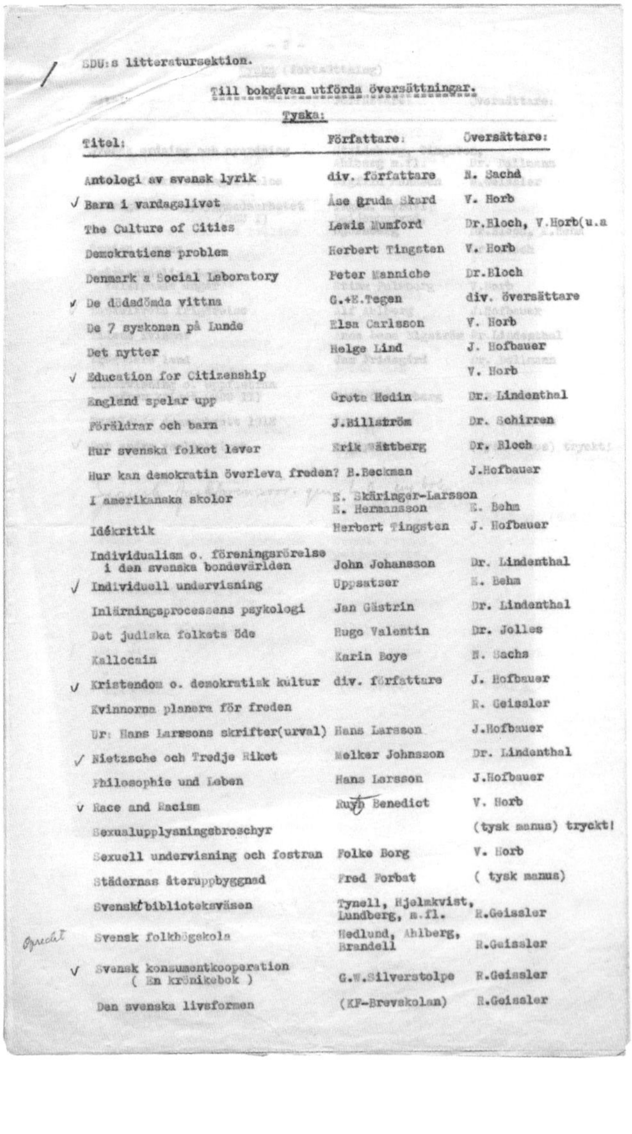

SDU:s litteratursektion.

Till bokgåvan utförda översättningar.

Tyska:

| Titel: | Författare: | Översättare: |
|---|---|---|
| Antologi av svensk lyrik | div. författare | N. Sachs |
| ✓ Barn i vardagslivet | Åse Gruda Skard | V. Horb |
| The Culture of Cities | Lewis Mumford | Dr.Bloch, V.Horb(u.a |
| Demokratiens problem | Herbert Tingsten | V. Horb |
| Denmark a Social Laboratory | Peter Manniche | Dr.Bloch |
| ✓ De dödsdömda vittna | G.+E.Tegen | div. översättare |
| De 7 syskonen på Lunde | Elsa Carlsson | V. Horb |
| Det nytter | Helge Lind | J. Hofbauer |
| ✓ Education for Citizenship | | V. Horb |
| England spelar upp | Greta Hedin | Dr. Lindenthal |
| Föräldrar och barn | J.Billström | Dr. Schirren |
| Hur svenska folket lever | Erik Wästberg | Dr. Bloch |
| Hur kan demokratin överleva freden? | B.Beckman | J.Hofbauer |
| I amerikanska skolor | E. Skäringer-Larsson E. Hermansson | E. Behm |
| Idékritik | Herbert Tingsten | J. Hofbauer |
| Individualism o. föreningsrörelse i den svenska bondevärlden | John Johansson | Dr. Lindenthal |
| ✓ Individuell undervisning | Uppsatser | E. Behm |
| Inlärningsprocessens psykologi | Jan Gästrin | Dr. Lindenthal |
| Det judiska folkets öde | Hugo Valentin | Dr. Jolles |
| Kallocain | Karin Boye | N. Sachs |
| ✓ Kristendom o. demokratisk kultur | div. författare | J. Hofbauer |
| Kvinnorna planera för freden | | R. Geissler |
| Ur: Hans Larssons skrifter(urval) | Hans Larsson | J.Hofbauer |
| ✓ Nietzsche och Tredje Riket | Melker Johnsson | Dr. Lindenthal |
| Philosophie und Leben | Hans Larsson | J.Hofbauer |
| ✓ Race and Racism | Ruyh Benedict | V. Horb |
| Sexualupplysningsbroschyr | | (tysk manus) tryckt! |
| Sexuell undervisning och fostran | Folke Borg | V. Horb |
| Städernas återuppbyggnad | Fred Forbat | ( tysk manus) |
| Svenskt biblioteksväsen | Tynell, Hjelmkvist, Lundberg, m.fl. | R.Geissler |
| Svensk folkhögskola | Hedlund, Ahlberg, Brandell | R.Geissler |
| ✓ Svensk konsumentkooperation ( En krönikebok ) | G.W.Silverstolpe | R.Geissler |
| Den svenska livsformen | (KF-Brevskolan) | R.Geissler |

16

17

**A DEPENDABLE WOMAN AND HER HUSBAND**

In his letter of the summer of 1940 Leo Hirsch did not merely express the relief he felt about the fact that Sachs had safely got away to distant Sweden, but also conveyed a contact to a publisher and writer "who was here then and is a dependable woman." The contact would prove decisive.

The woman's name was GUNHILD TEGEN (1889–1970), née Nordling. She had met the editor of the *Berliner Tageblatt* during a trip abroad. Having completed her training as a primary school teacher in 1910, she enrolled at Uppsala. She returned to her hometown of Sundsvall, however, where she got a job teaching at a girls' school. Using the pseudonym "Tor Tilja" she participated in 1929 in a literature contest for the best short story in a university setting. She won, and made her debut with *Eros i Uppsala och annorstädes* (Eros in Uppsala and Elsewhere), a collection of prose pieces published in the same year. At that point she was forty years old. Several novels would follow, including the most important one, *Slavar* (Slaves) from 1936, which dealt with Tegen's central theme, female sexuality, and caused something of a stir because of its outspokenness. In an article Johannes Edfelt summarized the prevalent impression among the literati of the era: "She is an irreproachable and wise storyteller, but for some reason her stories fail to exercise any real power of suggestion. Among other things, she lacks stylistic originality. What she has to say is important and in some cases enlightening as psychology. It is not wanting for warmth and sensitivity, but it does lack verve and charm." In other words: Tegen was a judicious person but a poor writer.

Possibly her strength lay elsewhere, in the extensive popular and adult education activities she also devoted herself to, and which eventually would take on a distinctly political character, not least with the screenplay *En judisk tragedi* (A Jewish Tragedy) in 1935. At that point Tegen had long been married to the philosopher and sociologist EINAR TEGEN (1884–1965), whom she had met at Uppsala and wed in 1914. Four years later her husband gained his doctorate with a thesis on Kant's critical theory of knowledge and shortly thereafter became a senior lecturer in the same subject. After an extended period at Lund he took up a professorship at Stockholm University in 1937. During the first two years of the war, Tegen was in America pursuing studies in social psychology, but on his return he became involved with helping refugees. In 1943 his wife left the Social Democratic Party, as she felt it acted too cautiously on refugee issues. When representatives of the Cooperative Union, the Trades Union Confederation, the Peace College Foundation, and World Assembly for Peace founded what came to be called the Cooperation Committee for Democratic Re-Edification (abbreviated SDU in Swedish) on June 4, 1944, Einar Tegen was appointed chairperson with Alva Myrdal as vice-chairperson. The purpose of the new organization was "to awaken interest in and support spiritual and cultural re-edification efforts in Central Europe after the war." It

18

19

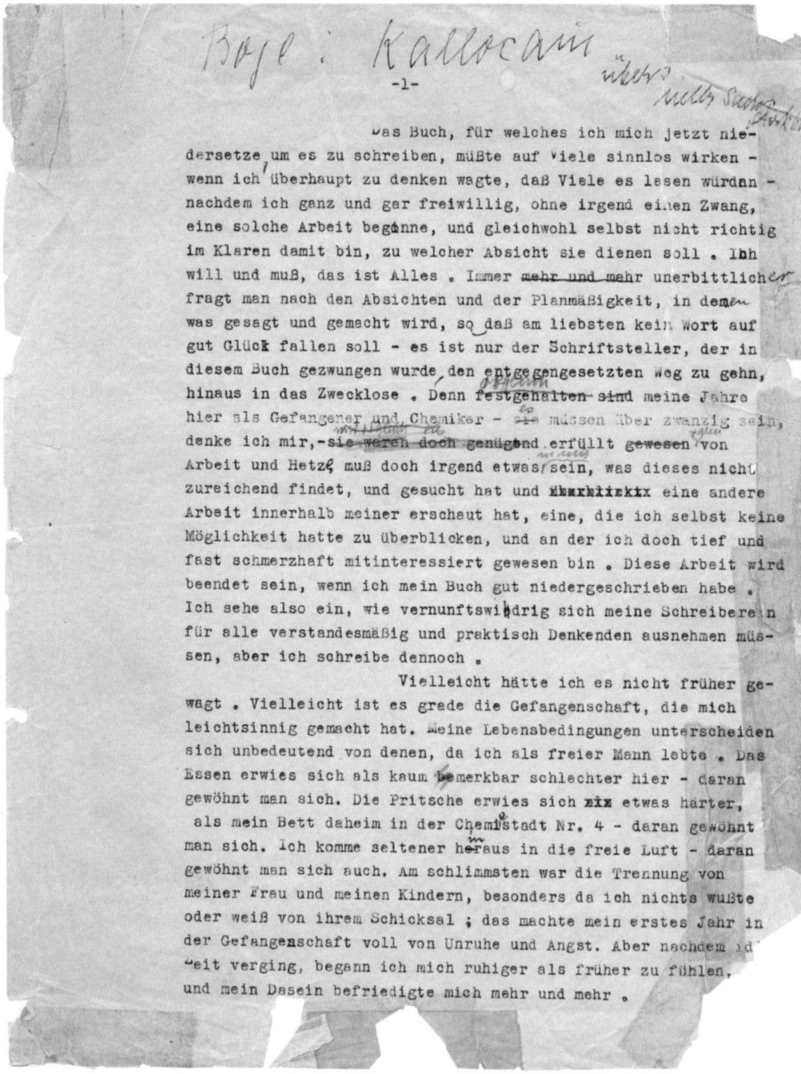

Boje: Kallocain

-1-

Das Buch, für welches ich mich jetzt niedersetze, um es zu schreiben, müßte auf Viele sinnlos wirken – wenn ich überhaupt zu denken wagte, daß Viele es lesen würden – nachdem ich ganz und gar freiwillig, ohne irgend einen Zwang, eine solche Arbeit begänne, und gleichwohl selbst nicht richtig im Klaren damit bin, zu welcher Absicht sie dienen soll. Ich will und muß, das ist Alles. Immer mehr und mehr unerbittlicher fragt man nach den Absichten und der Planmäßigkeit, in denen was gesagt und gemacht wird, so daß am liebsten kein Wort auf gut Glück fallen soll – es ist nur der Schriftsteller, der in diesem Buch gezwungen wurde, den entgegengesetzten Weg zu gehn, hinaus in das Zwecklose. Denn festgehalten sind meine Jahre hier als Gefangener und Chemiker – sie müssen über zwanzig sein, denke ich mir, – sie waren doch genügend erfüllt gewesen von Arbeit und Hetze; muß doch irgend etwas sein, was dieses nicht zureichend findet, und gesucht hat und eine andere Arbeit innerhalb meiner erschaut hat, eine, die ich selbst keine Möglichkeit hatte zu überblicken, und an der ich doch tief und fast schmerzhaft mitinteressiert gewesen bin. Diese Arbeit wird beendet sein, wenn ich mein Buch gut niedergeschrieben habe. Ich sehe also ein, wie vernunftswidrig sich meine Schreiberei für alle verstandesmäßig und praktisch Denkenden ausnehmen müssen, aber ich schreibe dennoch.

Vielleicht hätte ich es nicht früher gewagt. Vielleicht ist es grade die Gefangenschaft, die mich leichtsinnig gemacht hat. Meine Lebensbedingungen unterscheiden sich unbedeutend von denen, da ich als freier Mann lebte. Das Essen erwies sich als kaum bemerkbar schlechter hier – daran gewöhnt man sich. Die Pritsche erwies sich etwas härter, als mein Bett daheim in der Chemiestadt Nr. 4 – daran gewöhnt man sich. Ich komme seltener heraus in die freie Luft – daran gewöhnt man sich auch. Am schlimmsten war die Trennung von meiner Frau und meinen Kindern, besonders da ich nichts wußte oder weiß von ihrem Schicksal; das machte mein erstes Jahr in der Gefangenschaft voll von Unruhe und Angst. Aber nachdem die Zeit verging, begann ich mich ruhiger als früher zu fühlen, und mein Dasein befriedigte mich mehr und mehr.

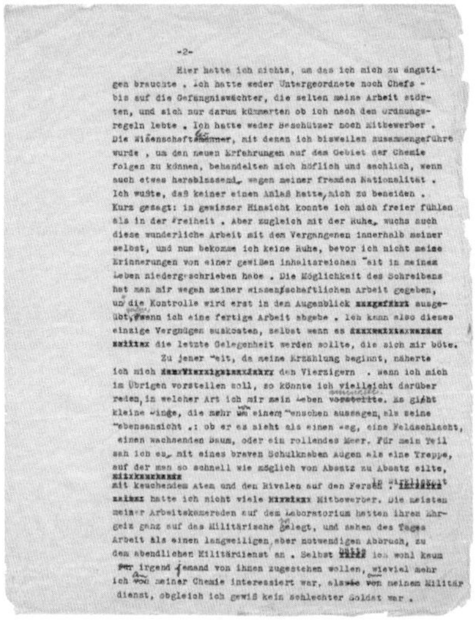

-2-

Hier hatte ich nichts, um das ich mich zu ängstigen brauchte. Ich hatte weder Untergeordnete noch Chefs – bis auf die Gefängniswächter, die selten meine Arbeit störten, und sich nur darum kümmerten ob ich nach den Ordnungsregeln lebte. Ich hatte weder Beschützer noch Mitbewerber. Die Wissenschaftler, mit denen ich bisweilen zusammengeführt wurde, um den neuen Erfahrungen auf dem Gebiet der Chemie folgen zu können, behandelten mich höflich und sachlich, wenn auch etwas herablassend, wegen meiner fremden Nationalität. Ich wußte, daß keiner einen Anlaß hatte, mich zu beneiden. Kurz gesagt: in gewisser Hinsicht konnte ich mich freier fühlen als in der Freiheit. Aber zugleich mit der Ruhe, wuchs auch diese wunderliche Arbeit mit dem Vergangenen innerhalb meiner selbst, und nun bekomme ich keine Ruhe, bevor ich nicht meine Erinnerungen von einer gewißen inhaltsreichen Zeit in meinem Leben niedergeschrieben habe. Die Möglichkeit des Schreibens hat man mir wegen meiner wissenschaftlichen Arbeit gegeben, und die Kontrolle wird erst in dem Augenblick ausgeübt, wenn ich eine fertige Arbeit abgebe. Ich kann also dieses einzige Vergnügen auskosten, selbst wenn es die letzte Gelegenheit werden sollte, die sich mir böte.

Zu jener Zeit, da meine Erzählung beginnt, näherte ich mich den Vierzigern. Wenn ich mich im Übrigen vorstellen soll, so könnte ich vielleicht darüber reden, in welcher Art ich mir mein Leben vorstellte. Es gibt kleine Dinge, die mehr von einem Menschen aussagen, als seine Lebensansicht: ob er es sieht als einen Weg, eine Feldschlacht, einen wachsenden Baum, oder ein rollendes Meer. Für mein Teil sah ich es, mit eines braven Schulknaben Augen als eine Treppe, auf der man so schnell wie möglich von Absatz zu Absatz eilte, mit keuchendem Atem und den Rivalen auf den Fersen. In Wirklichkeit hatte ich nicht viele Mitbewerber. Die meisten meiner Arbeitskameraden auf dem Laboratorium hatten ihren Ehrgeiz ganz auf das Militärische gelegt, und sahen des Tages Arbeit als einen langweiligen, aber notwendigen Abbruch, zu dem abendlichen Militärdienst an. Selbst hätte ich wohl kaum irgend jemand von ihnen zugestehen wollen, wieviel mehr ich an meiner Chemie interessiert war, als an meinem Militärdienst, obgleich ich gewiß kein schlechter Soldat war.

20

was in this area that the Tegens would make their most significant contribution.

Of particular importance were the interviews conducted as part of a project which had originally been suggested by the politically and socially engaged Uppsala resident Dory Engströmer: as many as possible of the former concentration camp prisoners rescued by Sweden were to be interviewed about their experiences. After a visit to a refugee compound at Mo Gård in Östergötland, where 1,500 Polish women were staying, Alva Myrdal noted in a proposal "re: specified activities for concentration camp prisoners, etc. transferred from Germany to Sweden": "It does not need to be pointed out that this is a unique opportunity for science, which will hopefully never present itself again." Engströmer interviewed French-speaking prisoners while Gunhild Tegen took on the German speakers and Einar Tegen applied for financial support from the ministries of Social Affairs and Ecclesiastical Affairs. They were turned down everywhere, however, even by Folke Bernadotte at the Swedish Red Cross. The majority of the interviews carried out would remain unpublished. Yet in the late autumn of 1945 the Tegens were at least able to publish *De dödsdömda vittna* (Testimonies of the Condemned), a selection of some twenty of a total of six hundred plus interviews and survey replies from named individuals, which had been edited and given an introduction. As late as 1947 they were still hoping to be able to present the project in a scientific context, but following rejections from academic sponsors as well, it was shelved.

By that time Sachs had become good friends with the dependable woman and her husband. Their correspondence was extensive, particularly during the 1940s, and they soon adopted the informal mode of address and began formulating affinities in the same effusive way as the "sisters" had in Berlin. Shortly after the war Tegen was portrayed thus in a letter to Dähnert in Dresden: "She got me my maintenance through translations, and in her I have an ardent supporter of my work, and admirer of the Jewish people." Between September 1943 and December 1947 Sachs was employed as an archivist. In practice, the job meant that she could look after her mother at home while translating Swedish literature — mainly poetry, but some prose too — in preparation for the extensive cultural re-edification work which it was presumed would be necessary. In this way she compiled, for example, the anthology *Von Welle und Granit* (Of Wave and Granite), but also completed a first version of Karin Boye's *Kallocain*, which she dubbed "the most important anti-fascist novel in Sweden" in a letter to Willi Weismann Verlag in Munich. According to Berendsohn the translation came about at Myrdal's initiative, but had its publication blocked by the Allies. Judging from the manuscript, the numerous misunderstandings and translation errors probably contributed to its disfavor as well. Moreover, a German translation by Helga Clemens had already been published by Büchergilde Gutenberg in Zurich a year earlier.

**TEXT** Letter from Hirsch 07/05/1940, ATegen · Edfelt, "Oskuld och kloster," *Bonniers litterära magasin*, 1941, no. 5, 394 · For further information about SDU, see Pia-Kristina Garde, *Mina föräldrars kärlek*, Växjö 2008 · TegenD · See e.g. letters from Sachs to Gunhild Tegen 08/11/1944, 07/01/1946, 01/05 and 03/27/1947, UUB · For letter to Dähnert 05/18/1946, see Briefe 16 · VWuG (NSW:IV) · On Boye's *Kallocain* in letter to Willi Weismann Verlag 05/05/1948, DLA · "Kallokain," ATegen · Berendsohn, 151, footnote 3 | **IMAGE 16** Documentation for Einar and Gunhild Tegen, *De dödsdömda vittna*, 1945 (KBS) · **17** Minutes from SDU, with information about translated literature (KBS) · **18** Gunhild and Einar Tegen in 1941 (Photo Anna Riwkin, Andreas Tegen's collection, Stockholm) · **19** Gunhild Tegen in 1941 (Photo Anna Riwkin, Andreas Tegen's collection, Stockholm) · **20** Pages from Sach's translation of Karin Boye's *Kallocain* (KBS)

## HURLED OUT

In the autumn of 1939 Sachs had begun studying Swedish. Encouragement came from Sahlin, but also from friends. It was necessary to prepare for the new circumstances if she and her mother would be allowed to leave Germany. Her preserved library includes a copy of *Langenscheidts Universalwörterbuch. Schwedisch-deutsch und Deutsch-schwedisch* with the ominous publication year 1933. The flyleaf has a handwritten dedication: "To my small swallow, / to my beloved, / with many kisses! / 'Wendelin.'"

The person behind the grammatically slightly incorrect inscription in Swedish — which has *min liten svala* for "my small swallow" instead of *min lilla svala*, and whose author may have been aware of the role that swallows played in Sachs' poetry at the time — is likely to have been Neff. After arriving in a foreign country "which words cannot sufficiently praise," as Sachs wrote to Manfred George after the war, she could employ the Langenscheidt to find her way about a literature which, with the exception of Lagerlöf, was unknown to her. Despite not mastering the new language — even towards the end of her life she would make elementary mistakes — she began translating almost immediately. The first proven translation from her exile, however, is a rendering into Swedish of one of her own poems. In a letter to Sahlin in July 1940 Sachs enclosed an almost incomprehensible version of "Mittsommernacht" (Midsummer's Night) — perhaps because she herself had just celebrated that well-known festivity for the first time. "I expect everything is wrong in it," she added, "but I send it all the same." She was not mistaken.

Soon she was trying to make a name for herself as a translator. The money from the Jewish congregation covered the bare essentials. But Sachs had no proper work permit and had to look after her ailing mother. Translation commissions that could be completed in the home did not require government approval. In a later interview she recalled: "Already during the first year in Stockholm I began on the lyrical anthology of Swedish poems which has now

21
22

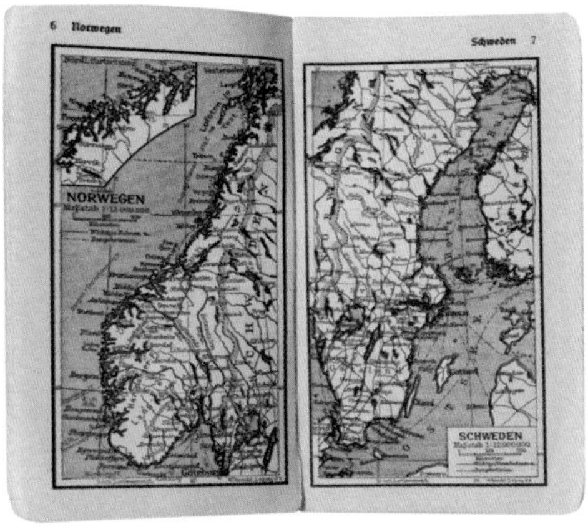

been published in Germany, *Von Welle und Granit*. [---] But my progress is slow, as I also take care of our little household and of my ailing mother. While I wash up and make the beds, and late in the night, I try to concentrate and to interpret the great suffering of the Jewish people without bitterness." At first she translated form-conscious poets such as Edfelt, Gullberg, and Österling, Karin Boye and Edith Södergran. In the late summer of 1943, when Sachs' own poetry was in a transitional phase, she contacted the composer and music critic Moses Pergament, as he had published an article in *Afton-Tidningen* which she had read with interest. "At the moment I am busy with Anders Österling, to be followed by Pär Lagerkvist and then by another two poets. Compiled into an anthology, this material will be submitted to a Swiss publishing house as a modest thank-you to Sweden." She wrote similar things in other letters, one to Fogelklou-Norlind among them. She never found a publisher in Switzerland, however, and another four years would pass before the planned anthology could be published by Aufbau Verlag in East Berlin. In the meantime she kept in touch with established colleagues more or less her age, which in some cases led to her poems being translated into Swedish.

Towards the end of her life Sachs claimed in a letter to the Germanist Peter Sager that she hadn't learned anything from Swedish poetry. But as has been pointed out, she was referring on this occasion to her existential sources, German romanticism and Jewish mysticism, and not to nuances of style or the radical changes in Swedish poetry during the 1930s and 1940s. Particularly during her first few years in exile, her own poetry was strongly transformed — at the same time as she was learning a foreign language and exploring its modern literature. As Erhard Bahr has noted, "it can hardly be denied that Nelly Sachs owes her translation activities to her encounter with modernism, which she had avoided during the twenties. In Stockholm she made up for what she had neglected in Berlin." The affinity between the texts selected for translation and the translator's own work was no coincidence. There are clear

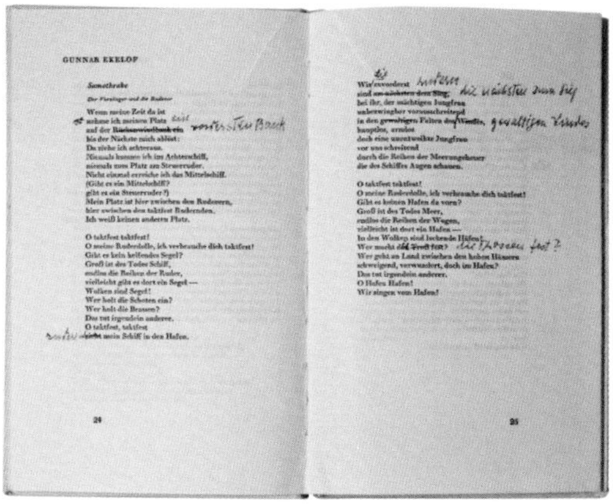

23

24

linguistic as well as thematic similarities. The ecstatic-hymnic, elegiac-painful tone, as well, is recognizable in what Swedish colleagues were writing during the same period. One might even venture to claim that Sachs' poetry turned modernist the moment modernism made its breakthrough with the Swedish public — primarily with the help of the "40s generation." The observation has been made by Anders Olsson, who has carried out the most thorough analysis of Sachs' translation work to date, and who asks the legitimate counter-question: "Where else would she have got the impulse for the modernist manner of writing?"

The transformation that Sachs' work went through during the war was not unconnected with what went on around her. She may have felt socially secluded, but she wasn't isolated in terms of either aesthetics or literature. During her first few years in Sweden she discovered and translated virtually every important exponent of Swedish modernism — among them some "exploded sonnets" from Erik Lindegren's *mannen utan väg* (The Wayless Man) from 1942, which would later enter the canon. Over the following thirty years she published three anthologies and another four volumes of works by individual poets which she had translated either on her own or together with others. Additionally, her estate includes large amounts of hitherto unpublished material. Taken together, this body of work shows not just how Sachs' poetry was strongly influenced by contemporaneous writing, but also and above all that she regarded her translating as an integral part of her work — the very writing that was required for survival. Although she would never regard herself as bilingual, and although German remained her "abode," it wasn't until she experienced the painful transition from one culture to another that her poetry found its form. Translating became the literary correlate of exile.

Her relationship to Lindegren provides an illustrative example. During her work on the selection that was published in the early 1960s, Sachs described how she had found a copy of the rare first edition of *The Wayless Man* in a bookshop and had immediately translated four of the texts. Her interest was due to more than mere attraction. She was drawn "somnambulistically" to

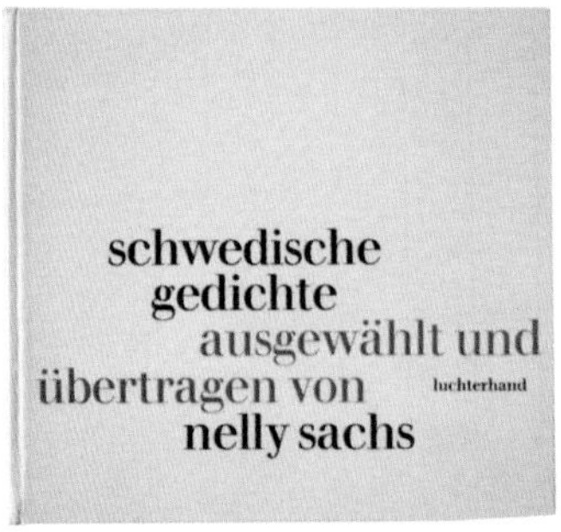

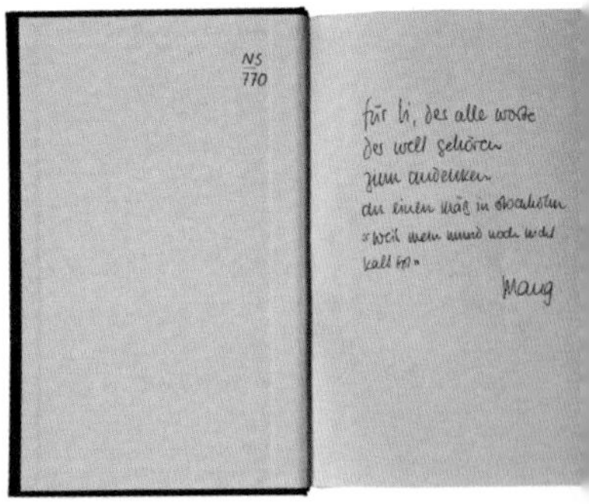


25
26
27
28

Lindegren's exploded sonnets, she was attracted by the attempt to renew an ossified idiom by means of drastic shifts between figurative and concrete elements, and she was overwhelmed by the elliptical syntax and rhetorically charged atmosphere. Furthermore it was difficult for her not to recognize the desperate humanistic credo of lines like "to the slain dead the murdered dead / and the screams of the wounded speak for mankind." Put simply: Sachs identified with the texts.

Of the thirty-odd poets she translated it was only Edfelt's, Harry Martinson's, and Gunnar Ekelöf's writing that exercised a similar attraction on her. The combination of rhythmic calm and melancholy moods that drew her to Edfelt was replaced through her discovery of Lindegren by a bolder imagery whose visionary scope held an immediate appeal for a poet seeking a voice for the many dead. Martinson's space epic *Aniara*, a visionary "revue about humankind in time and space" from 1956, became important for Sachs as she sought a poetry of cosmic proportions towards the end of the same decade, while Ekelöf's influence is most apparent in the condensed poetry from 1960 onwards, its concretion tinged with mysticism and its attempts to render the breakthrough to another dimension. Tellingly, it appears that Sachs' view of Ekelöf was initially influenced by Lindegren. For example, in the short preface to the first anthology she mentions that Ekelöf had embarked on "a kind of instrumentalist poetry" — a description lifted directly from Lindegren's article "On the Way to an Instrumentalist Poetry," published in *Aftonbladet* on New Year's Day 1945 and in which two of the poems that would be included in *Von Welle und Granit* were quoted as examples: the war poems "Jarrama" and "Samothrace."

The thematics in these and other texts show that the significance of Swedish poetry for Sachs' work was not limited to single motifs or metaphors, but was also reflected in the relationship with an uncertain age. In the postscript to the second anthology Sachs describes "Samothrace" as a poem "arising from a most deeply perceived vision of time" — a characterization that could apply just as well to the translator's own work. In addition, the title of the anthology is emblematic: *Aber auch diese Sonne ist heimatlos* (But Also This Sun Is Homeless). The themes of the outsider and of exile that Sachs found in Södergran, Lindegren, and Ekelöf, and which her poems linked to individual experiences, were portrayed by Karl Vennberg — who provided the title for the selection — as an ecstatic-cosmic homelessness whose universal claims would find an echo in 1950s poetry. It may be that the striving for a world beyond the visible is missing in Vennberg's poetry, and that in Sachs, conversely, the reader looks in vain for the skeptical irony that was his trademark. Furthermore, exile, which can only be understood in a figurative sense in Vennberg, was recontexualized by his German colleague and given an unmistakably personal resonance. But Sachs' words about modern Swedish poetry nonetheless apply to

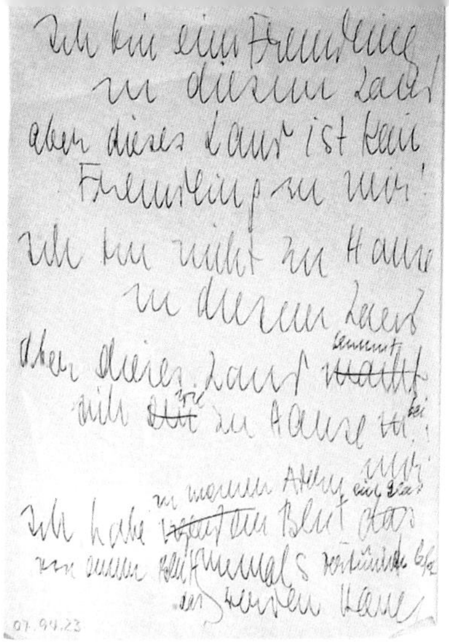

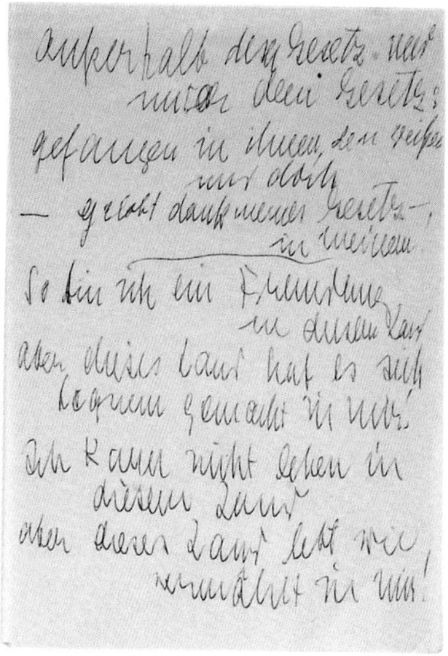

29

30
31
32

her own: "During humanity's past ignominious years, Swedish poets experienced an explosive 'hurling out into outer space,' this despair of no longer finding a straw to clutch at anywhere."

After Sachs had been hurled out of an existential context made up of people who would no longer have anything to do with her, Swedish poetry offered the straws she needed to clutch at in order to gain her footing as a poet and fashion herself a nest. The "small swallow" who had packed Langenscheidt's Universal Dictionary in her suitcase twenty years earlier aptly enough gave her Lindegren selection the title *Weil unser einziges Nest unsere Flügel sind* (For Our Wings Are Our Only Nest).

**TEXT** For letters to George 01/27/1946 and Pergament 08/05/1943, see Briefe 25 and 14 · Letter with the poem "Mittsommernacht" to Sahlin 07/07/1940, ASahlin · The signature "brodjaga," "Selma Lagerlöf hjälpte tyska till Sverige," *Dagens Nyheter* 01/21/1947 · Letter to Sager 07/15/1969, ASachs · Bahr, 193 · Anders Olsson, "Nelly Sachs, exilen och den svenska modernismen," *Aiolos*, 2007, no. 30–31, 79 · Lindegren, "På väg till instrumentallyriken," *Aftonbladet* 12/31/1945 · AadSih and EL (NSW:IV) | **IMAGE 21** Sachs' copy of *Langenscheidts Reisedolmetscher Schwedisch* 1937 · **22** Sachs' copy of *30 Stunden Schwedisch für Anfänger* 1941 · **23** *Von Welle und Granit* 1947 · **24** *Aber auch diese Sonne ist heimatlos* 1956 · **25** Erik Lindegren, *Weil unser einziges Nest unsere Flügel sind* 1963 · **26** *Schwedische Gedichte* 1961 · **27** Karl Vennberg, *Poesie* 1965 · **28** "Für Li, der alle Worte der Welt gehören zum Andenken," dedication by Hans Magnus Enzensberger in *Svensk-tysk ordbok* 1960 (KBS) · **29** "Ich bin ein Fremdling" (I Am a Stranger), draft manuscript for translation of Gunnar Ekelöf's poem "non serviam" (DLA) · **30** Gunnar Ekelöf in the 1950s (Photo Berndt Klyvare, ABFS) · **31** Erik Lindegren, n.d. (Photo Anna Riwkin, MMS) · **32** Harry Martinson in 1940 (Photo Anna Riwkin, MMS)

## THROWN INTO AN "OUTSIDE"

In August 1948 mother and daughter could at last leave the cold, smelly one-room apartment on the ground floor and move to a slightly bigger place with a kitchen and a dining alcove two floors up in the same building. "Just think," Sachs wrote to Dähnert before the move, "to be able once again to see and feel the stars was not something we dared hope for at all after 7 years of darkness and cold." The previous occupants — a mother and daughter from Hamburg

— were moving to Jamaica to join the remaining family. For the first time since the Sachses' arrival in Sweden, the concept of homeliness appeared possible. Through the windows overlooking the southern waters of Lake Mälaren the world opened up again and became accessible.

Circumstances, however, were as meager as before. With Dähnert's help, Sachs had begun to investigate the possibility of being awarded damages by the Federal Republic. But it would take another decade before a modest compensation was paid. And Margarete grew progressively worse. Already during the final years in Berlin, she had shown signs of frail health. After their arrival in Sweden her condition deteriorated; periodically she appears to have suffered from fainting spells. Now her daughter wrote: "I got my dear little mother back when she was almost gone. [---] Now my day is divided into care, household chores, my translations and my own work. You will notice that it hasn't been possible without nighttime work. In fact, almost all of my own things I have written at night, and in the dark, in order not to disturb mother." Comparing photographs from the first half of the 1940s with those taken towards the end of the same decade, the deterioration of Margarete's health becomes evident. The snapshots from the country outing show a woman of around seventy, with set hair and an attentive gaze; Anna Riwkin's portrait shows her as a bright and cheerful lady, obviously *compos mentis*. In a photo taken near the pair's home in Södermalm, however, she is seated on a park bench, looking vacant and listless, while her daughter, sporting the same hairstyle as in the other photos from the end of the 1940s, is wearing practical clothes and an obliging air. In another image they are standing arm in arm, but Margarete's arms are hanging limply at her sides and her gaze looks tired. Nelly is not just daughter, but has become nurse too.

33

During these years when it was only possible to write at night, when Margarete was asleep and the lights were out, the poems came about in an eruptive fashion, almost as if through no action of the writer, like a volcano or a hemorrhage. In a later letter to Abenius, Sachs would return to this primordial setting: "This life at night, many sleepless years and constantly thrown into an 'outside,' really having known death anew every night, since I watched the last beloved creature I had become enveloped by a distant unknown, I was compelled by every sight of the sufferer towards the words which later implied my poems and dramatic attempts." The scene of the action was the four-square-meter alcove she had christened her "cuddy" due to its view over the boats and the factories in Liljeholmen on the other side of the water. Under pressure from external circumstances — night, sleeplessness, suffering — "words" were brought forth which would only later be identifiable as "poems and dramatic attempts." Less a wordsmith than a mouthpiece, the poet who emerged in this version of history neither wanted nor chose to speak, but was obliged to do so.

The contradictory formulation "thrown into an 'Outside'" can serve as a paradigm for the view of writing poetry that Sachs would espouse after her flight. Through the act of writing, repeated every night as if for the first time, from an existential ground zero, she gradually made herself at home in exile. But it was an intimacy that could only be gained at the cost of estrangement. In the small hours of the night, Sachs was driven into social, but also lingual isolation — thrown into an "Outside" — which forced her repeatedly to revisit the siblings, these "dead brothers and sisters" to whom the first book was dedicated. Fear and compassion were indivisibly bound together in this attempt to voice what the mind was barely able to assimilate. Thus was born a work whose main task was literally to familiarize the reader with the "dwellings of death." (Tellingly, the first poems to be published in the emigrants' magazine *Der Aufbau* after the war were given the collective title "Verse des Mitleids von Nelly Sachs" [Verses of Compassion by Nelly Sachs].) In later conversations with critics and commentators — among them Gisela Dischner on June 12, 1966 — Sachs would stress: "Death was my master tutor." Her poetry was born in the involuntary meeting with this fearsome pedagogue. In the beginning was the Shoah.

**TEXT** For letters to Dähnert 08/14/1948 and 05/18/1946, Abenius 03/17/1958, and Lindegren 10/16/1963, see Briefe 30, 54, 125, and 202 respectively · "Verse des Mitleids von Nelly Sachs," *Der Aufbau*, 04/24/1945, 23 · Dischner, "Das verlorene und wieder gerettete Alphabet," NSzE:2, 108 | **IMAGE 33** Mother and daughter at the end of the 1940s, probably in the vicinity of Bergsundsstrand (DLA) · **34** Portrait photos of Margarete Sachs from the first half of the 1940s (Photo Anna Riwkin, DLA)

## ASCENT ON FEBRUARY 7, 1950

In May of 1949 Sachs wrote to her "most beloved heart," Gudrun Dähnert, telling her how much she would like to hold her hand. Just under a year earlier her friend had become engaged to the musicologist Ulrich Dähnert, and now they were newly wed. "You have your kind husband of course [---] and I have my darling, and yet my longing for you is infinitely great." Sachs felt lonely and forlorn, perhaps betrayed. Dähnert had set up a new life, former acquaintances were in other countries, the refugees she had got to know in Sweden moved on. "For me life is but leave-taking." To counter the sense of emptiness she arranged her "indoor rock garden" — "out of sheer longing," as she pointed out, possibly with a barb at her friend whose attention she must from now on share with her husband. The arrangement of minerals was a replica, albeit smaller, of her father's precious collection. But unlike near and dear ones, they wouldn't leave her. Maybe they even breathed.

Am 7. Februar starb meine
über alles geliebte Mutter
Margarete Sachs
geb. Karger.
In namenlosem Schmerz:
NELLY SACHS
Stockholm
Bergsundstrand 23

35

Only six months later, on February 7, 1950, disaster struck. On what would have been her father's ninety-first birthday, Margarete died. She was eighty, and had been cared for by her daughter around the clock. Two days later

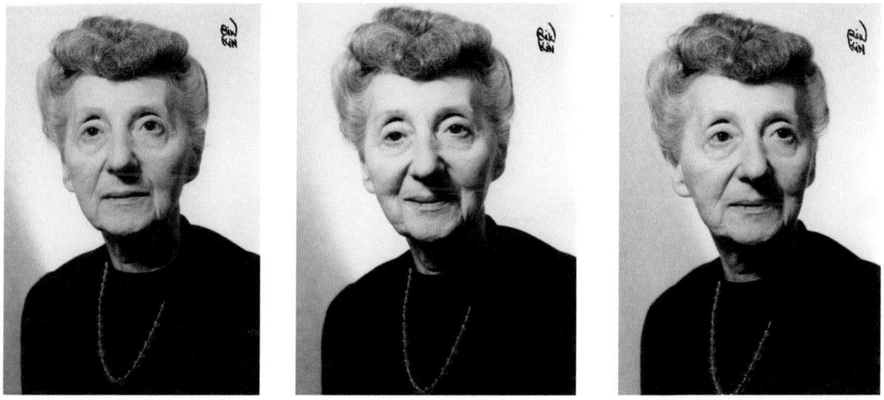

34

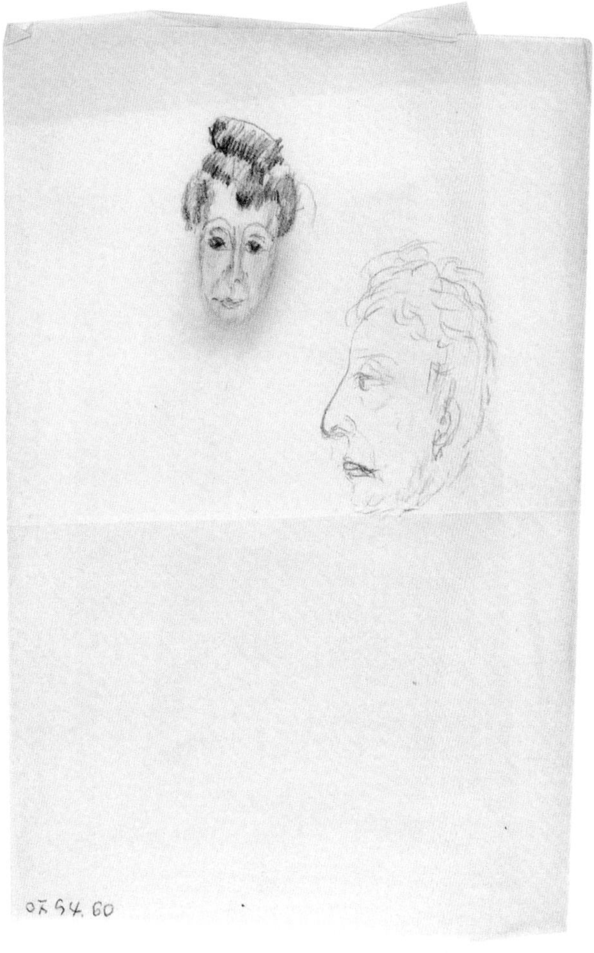

36

Sachs sent a short message to Dähnert which ended with the words "Think of me" and was signed "Li." She was a tad fuller in her letter to Manfred George: "My mother has died. My joy, my home, my all." A week later there was an obituary in *Der Aufbau*: "On the 7th of February my most highly beloved mother, Margarete Sachs née Karger, died. In nameless grief: Nelly Sachs Stockholm Bergsundsstrand 23." Almost sixty years old, she was alone for the first time.

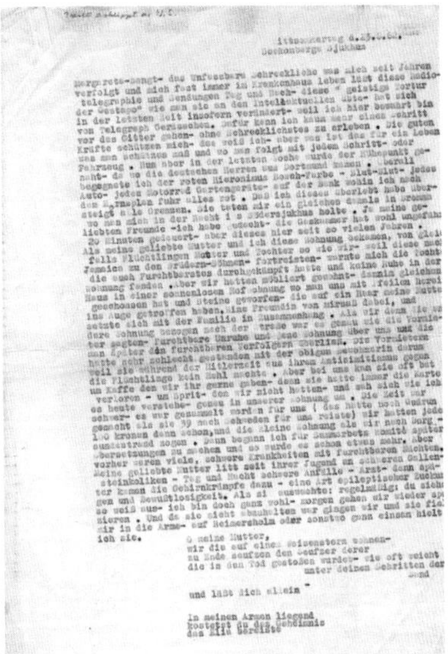

37

Among the many testimonies to the unusually close relationship between mother and daughter which thereby ended, two will suffice. In a letter to Berendsohn written a few years before Margarete's death, Sachs admitted: "Perhaps, despite this love, it would once have been possible more easily to untie the bonds between us, if death had not dealt so horrendously with our kin, and now she is the only one who ties me to this world at all." And ten years after her mother's death she declared to Domin: "We loved each other far more than just as mother and child." In the later letter she also described her mother's illness and drew parallels with herself: "I think she died every night again and again into unconsciousness, and I with her. The appalling thing came — she collapsed, shaking and unconscious, spoke to another world and returned, smiling, to me." Medical records from Södersjukhuset from the beginning of the 1960s contain statements by unnamed friends who were present at Sachs' internment (probably Dähnert, possibly Rosi Wosk as well) which suggest, however, that she was unaware of the fact that her mother must have suffered from persecution mania. She preferred to talk about "brain cramps" — "a kind of epileptic cramps and unconsciousness," as she wrote in a letter to the Holmqvists. Thus symptoms of senile dementia were elevated to the same "falling sickness" as the hero of *Simson fällt durch Jahrtausende* suffers from. Or phrased in terms of mythology: her mother's illness was due to excessive lucidity. The epileptic seizures indicated that she, being in clandestine collaboration with the past, touched upon the mystery of creation. Like Samson, Margarete was a "'human' among standard people," elected by a tragic fate.

After her mother's death Sachs wrote an account of her life and person which is characterized by the same strong idealizing as the earlier descriptions of her father. She recounts how Margarete during her final days was helped to the window of the apartment and commented on the sunset: "that I was still allowed to behold this." Sachs calls her mother — whose blithe soul had ascended to Him — an "enraptured admirer of His creation," fascinated by the clouds that formed and were dissolved on the firmament, and gentle in the way of children. "This childlike ability to receive, to be delighted and captivated by each moment, was her truest, innermost essence." Equally as interested in flowers as in animals, she would attract young people to her side and this "ability to make existence magic" rubbed off on all living things. Margarete lightened the existence of her "very serious" husband, she brought "her daughter with melancholic tendencies" to the point "where the difficult things are no longer difficult, since their innermost secret essence has been brought singing and dancing into the light."

The account ends with the words: "Thus she had opened the home for her daughter as a cloak under which times of persecution, estrangement, and all human gloominess were swept and flattened in an agreeable way. This veined butterfly soul, now so full of the dark pain of the world, and which had long been prepared for departure and anxiously beat her wings and waited for the sake of a single person, withered away. Many of those who knew her will perhaps feel how a warming benevolent spirit left them. But for her daughter, whose spirit's path she filled with a light that reached into its smallest ramifications, the cloak of home has fallen away and no consolation in the world is sufficient for this dispossession."

The imagery would return in the invocations of flight and metamorphosis of her 1950s poetry. Suffice it here to highlight the paradox that Hölderlin once summed up with the words: "One may also *fall* on high, as into the deep." Margarete Sachs, who had suffered from falling sickness, had ascended to heaven.

**TEXT** For letters to Dähnert 05/17/1949 and 02/09/1950, and to Holmqvist 06/23/1962, see Briefe 61, 65, and 194 respectively · Letter to George 02/09/1950 (Frank D. George's collection) · Letter to Berendsohn 12/04/1948, AberendsohnD · For letter to Domin 02/04/1960, see BDomin, 220 · "Anhang," ZiS (NSW:III) · "Margarete Sachs, geborene Karger, geboren den 9. Juni 1871, gestorben den 7. Februar 1950 am Geburtstag ihres verstorbenen Mannes," NSW:IV · Hölderlin, "Reflexion," *Sämtliche Werke und Briefe*, Munich 1970, vol. I, 855 | **IMAGE 35** Margarete's obituary in *Der Aufbau* 02/17/1950 (DLA) · **36** Nelly Sachs' pencil portrait of her mother, end of the 1940s (DLA) · **37** Letter to Margaretha and Bengt Holmqvist 06/23/1962 (KBS) · **38** "Margarete Sachs, geborene Karger," typescript (DLA)

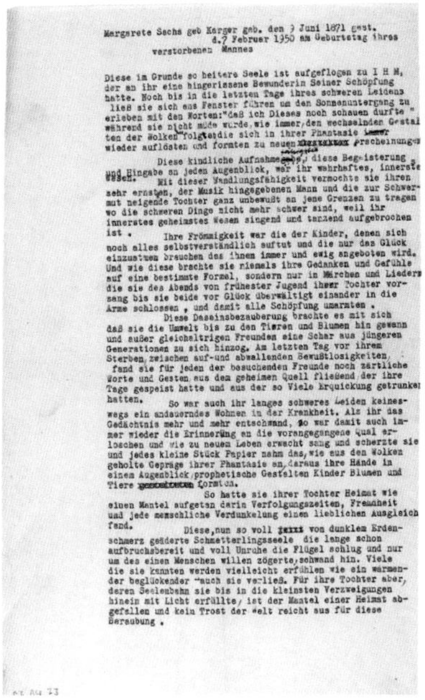
Margarete Sachs geb Karger geb. den 9 Juni 1871 gest.
d.7 Februar 1950 am Geburtstag ihres
verstorbenen Mannes

Diese im Grunde so heitere Seele ist aufgeflogen zu I H M, der an ihr eine hingerissene Bewunderin Seiner Schöpfung hatte. Noch bis in die letzten Tage ihres schweren Leidens ließ sie sich ans Fenster führen um den Sonnenuntergang zu erleben mit den Worten:"daß ich Dieses noch schauen durfte " während sie nicht müde wurde, wie immer, den wechselnden Gestalten der Wolken folgte, die sich in ihrer Phantasie immer wieder auflösten und formten zu neuen Erscheinungen

Diese kindliche Aufnahmegabe, diese Begeisterung und Hingabe an jeden Augenblick, war ihr wahrhaftes, innerstes Wesen. Mit dieser Wandlungsfähigkeit vermochte sie ihren sehr ernsten, der Musik hingegebenen Mann und die zur Schwermut neigende Tochter ganz unbewußt an jene Grenzen zu tragen wo die schweren Dinge nicht mehr schwer sind, weil ihr innerstes geheimstes Wesen singend und tanzend aufgebrochen ist . Ihre Frömmigkeit war die der Kinder, denen sich noch alles selbstverständlich auftut und die nur das Glück einzuatmen brauchen das ihnen immer und ewig angeboten wird. Und wie diese brachte sie niemals ihre Gedanken und Gefühle auf eine bestimmte Formel, sondern nur in Märchen und Liedern die sie des Abends von frühester Jugend ihrer Tochter vorsang bis sie beide vor Glück überwältigt einander in die Arme schlossen , und damit alle Schöpfung umarmten .

Diese Daseinsbezauberung brachte es mit sich daß sie die Umwelt bis zu den Tieren und Blumen hin gewann und außer gleichaltrigen Freunden eine Schar aus jüngeren Generationen zu sich hinzog. Am letzten Tag vor ihrem Sterben, zwischen auf-und abwallenden Bewußtlosigkeiten, fand sie für jeden der besuchenden Freunde noch zärtliche Worte und Gesten, aus dem geheimen Quell fließend, der ihre Tage gespeist hatte und aus der so Viele Erquickung getrunken hatten. So war auch ihr langes schweres Leiden keineswegs ein andauerndes Wohnen in der Krankheit. Als ihr das Gedächtnis mehr und mehr entschwand, so war damit auch immer wieder die Erinnerung an die vorangegangene Qual erloschen und wie zu neuem Leben erwacht sang und scherzte sie und jedes kleine Stück Papier nahm das, wie aus den Wolken geholte Gepräge ihrer Phantasie an, daraus ihre Hände in einem Augenblick, prophetische Gestalten Kinder Blumen und Tiere formten.

So hatte sie ihrer Tochter Heimat wie einen Mantel aufgetan darin Verfolgungszeiten, Fremdheit und jede menschliche Verdunkelung einen lieblichen Ausgleich fand. Diese, nun so voll von dunklem Erdenschmerz geäderte Schmetterlingsseele die lange schon aufbruchsbereit und voll Unruhe die Flügel schlug und nur um des einen Menschen willen zögerte, schwand hin. Viele die sie kannten werden vielleicht erfühlen wie ein wärmender beglückender Geist auch sie verließ. Für ihre Tochter aber, deren Seelenbahn sie bis in die kleinsten Verzweigungen hinein mit Licht erfüllte, ist der Mantel einer Heimat abgefallen und kein Trost der Welt reicht aus für diese Beraubung .

38

## ON TIPTOE

The death of her mother plunged Sachs into a crisis, in the course of which she wished for her own death. Members of the Jewish congregation feared for her health and sanity. According to later conversations with Berendsohn, she is said even to have destroyed several manuscripts in her grief. Three weeks after Margarete's death, Sahlin also died. After her final visit to her ailing guardian angel Sachs had a "nervous breakdown, after my really already ill soul had found some small amount of peace."

The statement comes from a letter to Berendsohn written on the same day that Sahlin died, March 2. As so often in the past, and in the future too, Sachs' salvation would be: words. After her crisis she started writing again. Or rather: she wrote her way out of the breakdown. The pain became her lifeline, her nerves were transformed into lines which — linked to the loss — could help and guide. During the first months after Margarete's death she wrote the cycle of poems entitled "Elegien auf den Tod meiner Mutter" (Elegies on the Death of My Mother). These texts were connected to the suite "Im Geheimnis" (In Secret) in *Sternverdunkelung* which had been published the year before, where the impending death had been outlined in foreboding tones. In part heavily reworked, eleven of the twenty-one poems would be divided between the collections *Und niemand weiß weiter* (And No One Knows Any Longer) from 1957 and *Flucht und Verwandlung* from 1959. As a coherent suite, however, they remained unpublished — most likely because Sachs, on closer scrutiny and with a few years' distance, found them too personal.

In December 1957 a letter arrived. "Highly esteemed, gracious," wrote Paul Celan and told her that her latest book stood "next to the truest books in my library." Might it be the case that his colleague had something unpublished lying around that she would like to publish in the Italian periodical *Botthege Oscure*, on whose editorial board he was, along with Ingeborg Bachmann among others? Sachs, pleased that her "things" would be given a "home," immediately put together a selection which also included some reworked elegies and added in her covering letter: "Notes and poems from my doom period lie hidden here, only means to rescuing the spirit from suffocation."

The elegies follow the same logic as the earlier songs about the distant beloved: they both address and invoke the deceased. She is part "clock of my time," part "blessed magnet mount" which the speaker's heart — a "compass" — points to. She is final kiss and silence, she is bygone gaze and memory, she is ashes and the searing pain that follows. In these documents all is "doom time." The hands of the clock as well as the needle of the compass have played themselves out; all that remains is departure:

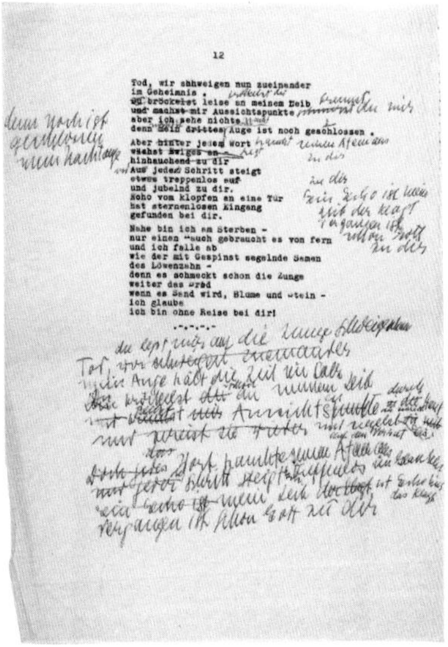
12

Tod, wir schweigen nun zueinander
im Geheimnis .
bröckelst leise an meinem Leib
und machst mir Aussichtspunkte
aber ich sehe nichts
denn Dein drittes Auge ist noch geschlossen .

Aber hinter jedem Wort
wächst Ewiges an -
hinhauchend zu dir
Aus jedem Schritt steigt
etwas treppenlos auf
und jubelnd zu dir.
Echo vom Klopfen an eine Tür
hat sternenlosen Eingang
gefunden bei dir.

Nahe bin ich am Sterben -
nur einen Hauch gebraucht es von fern
und ich falle ab
wie der mit Gespinst segelnde Samen
des Löwenzahn -
denn es schmeckt schon die Zunge
weiter das Erd
wenn es Sand wird, Blume und Stein -
ich glaube
ich bin ohne Reise bei dir!

39

> Once I shall seek / along the invisible starways / at the bends in the road, / where the angels' blind signals point across the border posts — // Soul, my mother's soul / I try, try as I stand on the tips of my toes / with my arms opened to the corners of the world / scanning amid drowning eyes / to break up from sheltered land —

The final stanza sums up the situation between epochs: a daughter on tiptoes, like a sixty-year-old child, ready to let herself into the clutches of the future — this motherless dimension of existence where earlier clockworks no longer will do.

**TEXT** Conversation with Berendsohn 01/11/1959, ABerendsohnD · For letter to Berendsohn 03/02/1950, see Briefe 68 · "Elegien auf den Tod meiner Mutter," NSW:I · For letters to Celan 12/13/1957 and 12/211957, see BCelan 2 and 3 respectively | **IMAGE 39** "Elegien auf den Tod meiner Mutter," typescript with corrections (DLA)

## A NEW ORDER OF TIME

During the first few months after her mother's death Sachs worked not only on the elegies, but also on the drama *Abram im Salz* which at this point was still called "Die Elegien an die Selige und das brennende Haar" (The Elegies to the Blessed and the Burning Hair). Additionally, she began an extensive prose work in which what she had termed "doom time" would eventually give rise to a new way of ordering time. Up until the summer of 1953 she wrote texts which at first bore the title "Nächtliche Aufzeichnungen" (Nightly Notes), later "Briefe aus der Mitternacht" (Midnight Letters), and finally "Briefe aus der Nacht." These thirty-odd texts in diary-like format chronicle a grieving process in which lyrical passages turn into reflections and personal or private musings are juxtaposed with deliberations on religious history. The tone shifts between longing and despair, the desperation is at once grandiose and bottomless.

"What an eloquent silence between us, beloved mother's soul," the text begins. "What an eloquent silence." For the mourner everything in existence has become significant and telling, even the silence after her mother's death. "Our eloquent silence," Sachs continues a few paragraphs later — and corrects herself: "Alas, it only goes from me to you, for humility forbids listening to the Elevated. And yet in moments touched by grace I know how the smile is born." In the partially dated notes which followed ("From the first months," "October 8," "5/4/1951," etc.), thoughts drift between reading impressions and sifted emotions, hope and despondency. Sachs reads the Bible, ruminates on the developing drama "Das Haar," and is plagued by insomnia. Not all the entries are about her mother, but Margarete remains their wellspring — a You that never says anything, at best shrouds herself in eloquent silence, and can only be addressed. Structurally speaking, the role of the deceased is similar to that of the bridegroom. Her death, too, breeds poetry. She is present with the same intensity with which she is missed. "We became one through ardor," reads a typical entry from March 1951.

In the same manner that Sachs' "letters" are addressed to an unreachable You as well as an uncertain future tense, she sought her way backwards in these texts — to memories and emotions that would not leave her in peace. "And I learn backwards," she writes at one point. Sachs learned the future backwards, so to speak — like a passing that doesn't stop disappearing, and therefore paradoxically harbors a future. Thus the text enables a peculiar temporality, perhaps literature's own, which may be seen as an infinite finitude, a tense linked to loss and passing and which for that very reason offers the writer a way of carrying on. Difficult to characterize, the most apt designation of this peculiar form of time might be precisely "doom time."

Many years later the young poet Peter Hamm, who was in the midst of a crisis-like situation that reminded Sachs of her own, would ask her advice. In a letter she replied: "The best thing, my dear, that you can do, at least what I did, and I only recommend what I have myself tried, so close to death — is to keep a diary. Not in the old sense — but, when you are unable to do anything else."

"Not in the old sense" but all the same turned "backwards": the texts brought about by her mother's death were no traditional diary. Written in the hours of darkness, they were more a *nocturnium* than a *diarium*, notes intimate with gloom and uncertainty, arising from the region of existence which Sachs named "this Nightly dimension." The writing appeared like ashes on paper. The loss remained the least common denominator of the fragments, and yet

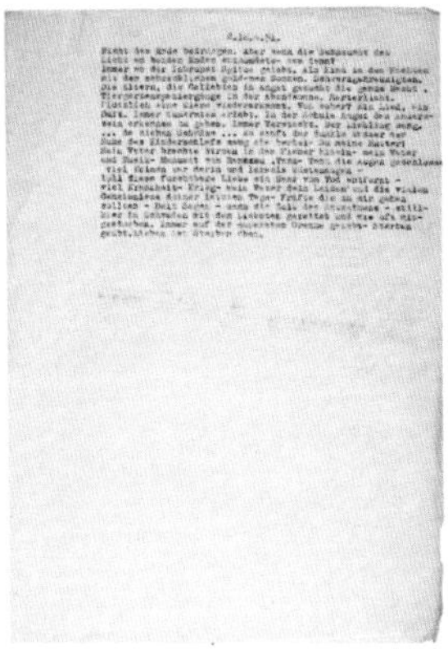

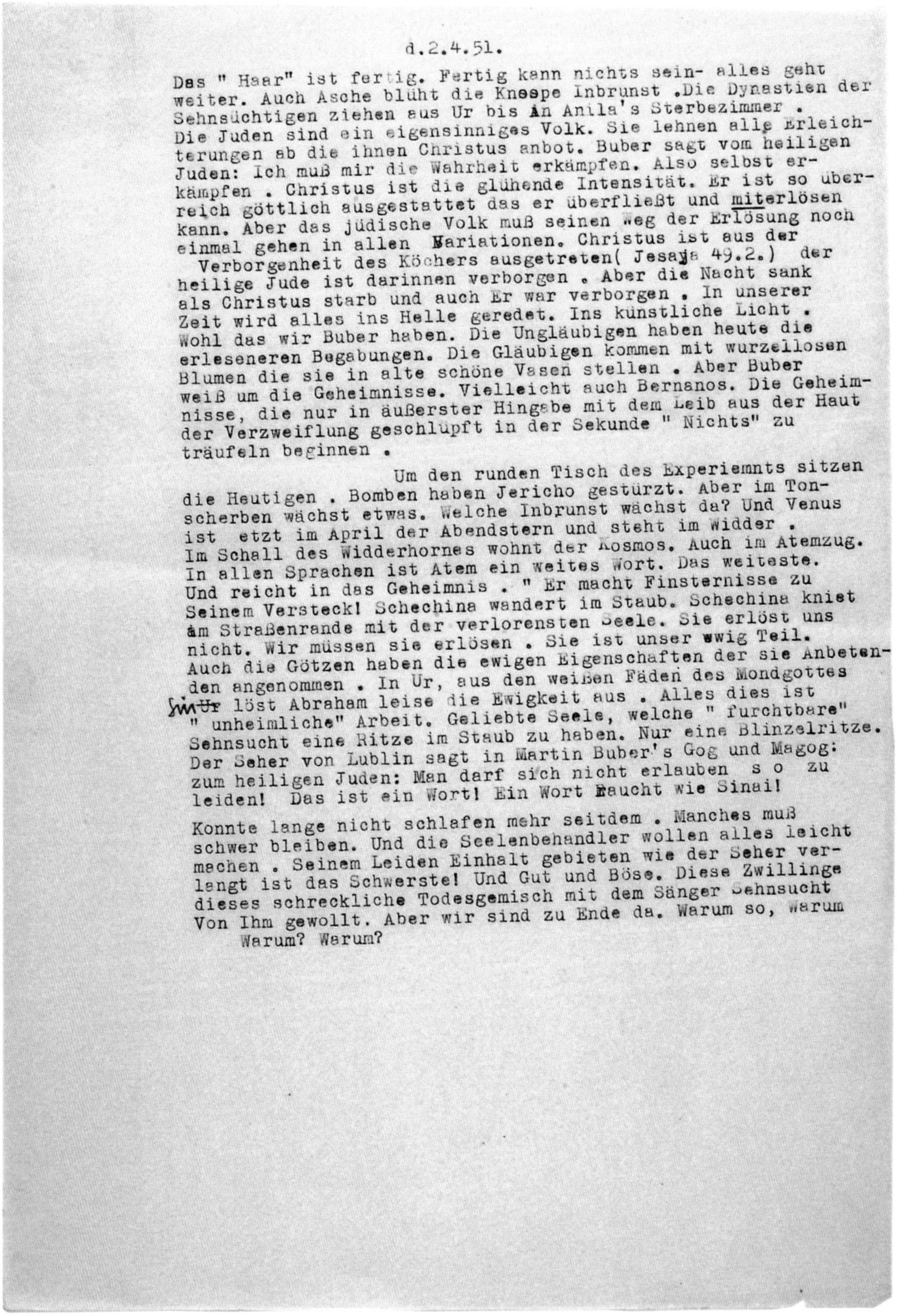

d.2.4.51.

Das " Haar" ist fertig. Fertig kann nichts sein- alles geht weiter. Auch Asche blüht die Knospe Inbrunst .Die Dynastien der Sehnsüchtigen ziehen aus Ur bis An Anila's Sterbezimmer . Die Juden sind ein eigensinniges Volk. Sie lehnen alle Erleichterungen ab die ihnen Christus anbot. Buber sagt vom heiligen Juden: Ich muß mir die Wahrheit erkämpfen. Also selbst erkämpfen . Christus ist die glühende Intensität. Er ist so überreich göttlich ausgestattet das er überfließt und miterlösen kann. Aber das jüdische Volk muß seinen Weg der Erlösung noch einmal gehen in allen Variationen. Christus ist aus der Verborgenheit des Köchers ausgetreten( Jesaja 49.2.) der heilige Jude ist darinnen verborgen . Aber die Nacht sank als Christus starb und auch Er war verborgen . In unserer Zeit wird alles ins Helle geredet. Ins künstliche Licht . Wohl das wir Buber haben. Die Ungläubigen haben heute die erleseneren Begabungen. Die Gläubigen kommen mit wurzellosen Blumen die sie in alte schöne Vasen stellen . Aber Buber weiß um die Geheimnisse. Vielleicht auch Bernanos. Die Geheimnisse, die nur in äußerster Hingabe mit dem Leib aus der Haut der Verzweiflung geschlüpft in der Sekunde " Nichts" zu träufeln beginnen .

Um den runden Tisch des Experiemnts sitzen die Heutigen . Bomben haben Jericho gestürzt. Aber im Tonscherben wächst etwas. Welche Inbrunst wächst da? Und Venus ist etzt im April der Abendstern und steht im Widder . Im Schall des Widderhornes wohnt der Kosmos. Auch im Atemzug. In allen Sprachen ist Atem ein weites Wort. Das weiteste. Und reicht in das Geheimnis . " Er macht Finsternisse zu Seinem Versteck! Schechina wandert im Staub. Schechina kniet am Straßenrande mit der verlorensten Seele. Sie erlöst uns nicht. Wir müssen sie erlösen . Sie ist unser ewig Teil. Auch die Götzen haben die ewigen Eigenschaften der sie Anbetenden angenommen . In Ur, aus den weißen Fäden des Mondgottes Sin ~~Ur~~ löst Abraham leise die Ewigkeit aus . Alles dies ist " unheimliche" Arbeit. Geliebte Seele, welche " furchtbare" Sehnsucht eine Ritze im Staub zu haben. Nur eine Blinzelritze. Der Seher von Lublin sagt in Martin Buber's Gog und Magog: zum heiligen Juden: Man darf sich nicht erlauben s o zu leiden! Das ist ein Wort! Ein Wort raucht wie Sinai!

Konnte lange nicht schlafen mehr seitdem . Manches muß schwer bleiben. Und die Seelenbehandler wollen alles leicht machen . Seinem Leiden Einhalt gebieten wie der Seher verlangt ist das Schwerste! Und Gut und Böse. Diese Zwillinge dieses schreckliche Todesgemisch mit dem Sänger Sehnsucht Von Ihm gewollt. Aber wir sind zu Ende da. Warum so, warum Warum? Warum?

40

the absence at their heart held the possibility of continuation. Or as the entry from March 7, 1951, reads: "Onward and onward, as all beings. Death, too, does bud."

**TEXT** *Abram im Salz*, ZiS (NSW:III) · "Briefe aus der Nacht," NSW:IV · Letter to Hamm 08/22/1958, DLA · Letter to Richard 01/30/1968 | **IMAGE 40** Pages from "Briefe aus der Nacht," typescript (DLA)

# EPITAPHS IN THE AIR

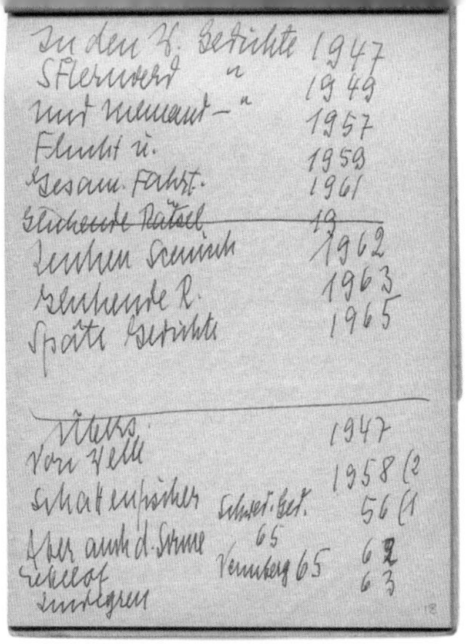

1

**IN THE BEGINNING WAS THE SHOAH**

At a reasonably safe distance from the horrors of the Second World War, Sachs wrote to the composer Moses Pergament (they were in the process of discussing a collaboration on *Eli*): "The Gripsholm songs and the songs of farewell and my first Bible songs were also still singing, but then — the inconceivable came, and the pounding just began against the secret: Why — ?"

The "inconceivable" was the news about what had happened to near and dear ones during the war. Sachs had herself been forced to experience the terror, and she knew about the labor camps. But it was only in the third year of the war, in the autumn and winter of 1942, that she had an intimation of the scope of the deportations and learned about the suffering in the quarries and the barracks. In the months that followed there were further accounts. In her literary estate there are only a few letters preserved from this period — and none which hint at when or even *if* she was notified of the death of the "bridegroom." It's likely that she also received word-of-mouth accounts from people who had succeeded in fleeing persecution. In her 1930s poems with biblical motifs she had still sung about the suffering of the Jews, but now? How could the "inconceivable" be captured in words that did justice to the suffering?

During her first years in Sweden Sachs was a custodian of epigonal poetry, writing about Gripsholm and steamboat trips on Lake Mälaren as if she were describing excursions to Silesia or sailing on the Wannsee. With time her acquaintance with modern Swedish literature would lead to a freer form, but the poems she wrote until 1943 show above all that she was keen to accommodate. The nature sceneries in particular emphasize correspondences between the countries and attempt to conjure something as fragile as a sense of home. As yet the exile experience shaped her life but not her literature. Socially and culturally Sachs was in another world, aesthetically, however, she remained in the old one. Then the news reached her about what was going on in "the Third Reich." In her youth she had translated the pain of being left into generalist poetic formulas and conventional imagery. Now the loss of people close to her led her to interpret her own vulnerability in a wider context. The consternation over the death of others gave her own suffering a deeper significance. With an inevitable paradox: through the Holocaust, Sachs was born as a poet.

This contradiction makes up one aspect of the answer to the important question which Bengt Holmqvist was the first to formulate: "How did a literary phenomenon like Nelly Sachs become possible?" Another aspect has to do with the very perception of time. In Sweden Sachs was struck by emotional jetlag. Her flight meant that she no longer had to live in a "time under dictate," as she wrote fifteen years later in the prose text "Leben unter Bedrohung." But the era of terror was by no means over. It lay at once behind her and was taking place while she looked after her mother or chatted to the neighbors in

Bergsundsstrand. The violations continued happening in a dimension of time from which she was only spatially separated. In Sweden Sachs discovered that she was both a part of the tragedy and removed from it — that is: as a poet, her trade was *Mit-Leid*, or "com-passion."

It is in this context one must understand her later attempts to fit her work into literary history. When Hans Magnus Enzensberger was about to edit the first select edition, *Fahrt ins Staublose* (Journey into a Dustless Realm) from 1961, she asked him: "Therefore I don't want you for a moment to misunderstand my turning away from the early things. But for me and for so many others a new aeon begins — an aeon of pain — with *In the Dwellings of Death*. Earlier there was Rameau dances and *other* tragedy, which follows an utterly secret line and is not there for anyone else." And when Berendsohn a few years later was preparing the bibliography for the *Festschrift* which was published in connection with her seventy-fifth birthday, she repeated her wish that "her entire work from before 1940 in Germany should be omitted." The urging that nothing written before her flight should be reprinted or even referenced bibliographically made it clear that Sachs found her calling as one "terribly struck by the dreadful events," as she had stated to Berendsohn in the autumn of 1957. Thus arose the view of her work which is predominant even today: in the beginning was the Shoah.

This view is supported by a number of texts, even if Sachs sometimes traced her work to other fateful events — primarily that "*other* tragedy" which she told Enzensberger about or called a "harsh fate, deep down" in a letter to Berendsohn in 1959. Both experiences — the general one she shared with all people of Jewish descent; the individual one which only affected the woman who loved "the distant one" — are crucial to her poetic universe. Occasionally they would be brought together, as when she told Dähnert after the war: "But my fate is to be alone, as it is the fate of my people." On the one hand there was the requirement to find a voice for people who had been denied language, on the other the need to assimilate the separation from the beloved with the help of poetry. Even if the experiences were different in character — here a people, there an individual — they shared a basic condition, which Sachs described thus to Berendsohn: "Everything which may lie accumulated in my poetry has only ever arisen in times of deepest despair, and only because of the need for help in carrying on living." Writing was about living on. Only in this way could death paradoxically become the condition for the "artistic rebirth," in Domin's phrase.

The letter to Berendsohn also described "an excellent little book about modern poetry" which she had recently been given by a young German colleague. The poet was PETER HAMM (born 1937), who had published his first poems in 1954 and contacted Sachs a few years later. The book was Beda Allemann's treatise *Über das Dichterische* (On the Poetic), published in 1957 by

Neske Verlag in Pfullingen, where Hamm worked as editor. Allemann's study, which is still extant in Sachs' library, offered an analysis of modern poetry based on the "unfruitful division between systematic and historical approaches." From the interplay of systematic and historical aspects a concept of style emerged that might do justice to the development which, in Sachs' words, went from "the verses which even in Rilke's time were still often overburdened with ornamental embellishment" to "the bold naked line of a young generation of poets." "Although their line often appears dispassionate," she added, "mine has come from the same seeking — even if it indicates the Laocoön line, bent in pain." The reference to Lessing — whose interpretation of the famous group of statues at the Vatican would lay the foundations for the modern view of the relationship between poetry and sculpture — was probably no coincidence. But more important than Sachs' having happened to live in Lessingstraße or being related to the Lessing family on her mother's side must have been that she understood her work in relation to the very categories of fear and compassion. In *Hamburgische Dramaturgie* (Hamburgian Dramaturgy) from 1767, which Max Herrmann had talked about during his open lectures before he was banned from practicing his profession, Lessing interpreted the Aristotelian doctrine of catharsis as a compassionate dread with the aim of bringing about a moral transformation in the viewer. Sachs' attempts at a poetic *Durchsmerzung*, or "working through of pain," of the world were based on the same interplay of fear and compassion, understood in the light of love's longing.

As a result of the news from Germany, an œuvre began which could no longer be linked to what had been written before the flight. The poetic "line" which had still been represented in the earliest Swedish poems — cycles such as "Schwedische Elegien" and "Miniaturen um Schloß Gripsholm" — could no longer be continued. The crime was too profound. No hyphen could withstand this rupture, only the acute slash was capable of intimating the catastrophe. With the texts she began to write in the winter of 1943, Sachs embarked on a new era whose elegiac tone would eventually become more terse and matter-of-fact, but no less drastic. Even if major changes soon appeared in terms of both material and style, there were nonetheless clear connections between the early and mature parts of her œuvre which were obscured by Sachs' wish to withhold bibliographic information about the Berlin years. For example, the works for puppet theater from the first two decades of the century show a pronounced interest in the gestural qualities of language as well as in the articulation of space, both of which return in her later dramatic works. Themes such as loss, guilt, and longing continue to be central, and both the early and the mature œuvre are shaped by the concept of unconditional, if unrequited, love. Separation remains the one thematic over more than fifty years of writing. Furthermore, Sachs' view of the role of poetry did not change to any notable degree after her treatment under Richard Cassirer — it was always a question of "surviving," which was her laconic reply to Olof Lagercrantz' question about whom she wrote for.

After the reports from the Third Reich, however, the conditions for writing changed. The *meaning* of the poems may have remained the same, but their *significance* shifted. What had originally been a poetry observing late-romantic conventions gained an urgency with the Shoah. This time it was an obligation that Sachs both wanted and was able to affirm in its radicalness. With reference to Paul Celan's acceptance speech "Der Meridian" (The Meridian) from 1960, in which the relevance of the past, the eternal, and the present are coordinated with different diacritic marks, one might claim that in her early works she had held forth with the help of the grave accent of retrospection. After the advent of "the inconceivable" she had to deploy the acute accent of trauma.

**TEXT** For letters to Pergament 04/22/1952, Enzensberger midsummer 1961, Berendsohn 10/30/1957 and 01/22/1959, and to Dähnert 08/14/1948, see Briefe 89, 186, 116, 131, and 54 respectively · Holmqvist, 23 · "Leben unter Bedrohung," NSW:IV · For the information about the selective bibliography, see NSzE:2, 222 · G, 114 · Allemann, 37 · Neff hints at the connection with Lessing in a letter to Dinesen 02/12/1982, ADinesen · "Schwedische Elegien" and "Miniaturen um Schloß Gripsholm," NSW:I · Reply to question from Lagercrantz, ASachs · Celan, *Der Meridian*, ed. Bernhard Böschenstein and Heino Schmull, Tübinger Ausgabe, ed. Jürgen Wertheimer, Frankfurt am Main 1999, 4 | **IMAGE 1** List of book publications, the 1960s (KBS)

## THE CROOKED LINE OF PAIN

One of the characteristic traits of Sachs' new poems was what drew her audience of the period into a pensive, painful silence, but is more likely to make today's readers squirm. That is: their tone. The poems' persona speaks with utter earnestness and without avoiding symbols which today, after sixty years of (over)use, easily come across as hackneyed. Marching boots, crying children, and murdering hands... If a poet were to use such imagery today, he would risk counteracting its purpose. The diagnosis would be evident: Holocaust kitsch. Possibly the most clichéd of all metaphors features in the poem with which Sachs' name is most often associated, even by readers who know about her only indirectly, as a representative of "German-Jewish destiny." The poem was written during the first winter after the war, at a time when most of the texts included in the collection had been completed. Nonetheless it was placed first in the book, which underscores its special position. On the one hand the poem would be the harbinger of the part of her œuvre which Sachs wished to be remembered for, on the other it sets the tone for what was to come:

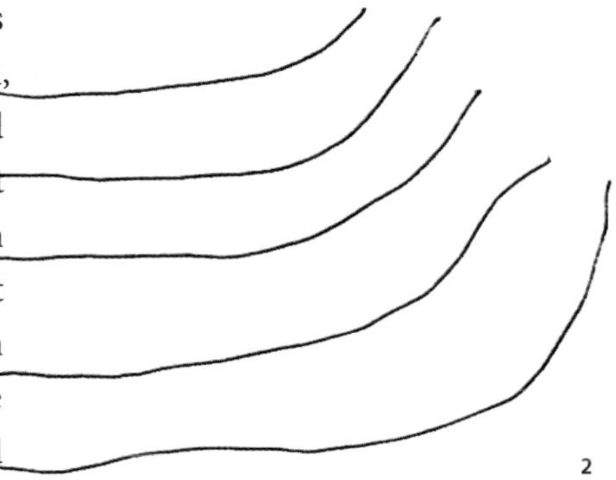

2

> O the chimneys / On the cleverly devised dwellings of death / When Israel's body dispersed in smoke / Drifted through the air — / A star like a chimney sweep gathered it / And blackened / Or was it a ray of sunlight? // O the chimneys!

/ Flues of freedom for the dust of Jeremiah and Job — / Who devised you and built brick for brick / The route for refugees of smoke? // O the dwellings of death, / Invitingly prepared / For the house's host, formerly guest — / O you fingers / Laying the threshold / Like a knife between life and death — / O you chimneys, / O you fingers, / And Israel's body drifting on the air!

The four stanzas contain several turns of phrase that might embarrass contemporary readers who prefer their passion in subdued form. Or who just favor imagery characterized by matter-of-factness rather than pathos — that is, a readership accustomed to "the bold naked line of a young generation of poets." What to do with the treatment of individual tragedies in the form of the collective "Israel's body"? Shouldn't the ambition be the opposite — to let the poem be a means of removing oneself from the overall identity and describe singular beings, unique fates? What to do with the references to Jeremiah and Job? Do these prophets of lamentation who were subjected to God-sent trials have anything in common with the peasants, burghers, and pacifists, children, cooks, and atheists who were herded together in cattle trucks and industrially executed without regard for anything except their ethnic background? Doesn't the parallel with the prophets suggest that the Holocaust was a trial for which there exists not just an explanation but a justification? And what to do with the chimney? Isn't the poem's chief symbol inconveniently over-explicit? Isn't the admonishing tone annoyingly imperative, the exclamation mark at the end of the poem overly emphatic? Above all: what to do with the notion that mechanically murdered prisoners are "refugees of smoke" — as if death were not an injustice but a liberation?

If zeitgeist can be defined as all that which we can take seriously at a given point in time, Sachs tests her present-day readers severely. On the one hand the text urges afterthought and gravitas, on the other the high-flown tone prevents true consternation. It may be that the poem's honor could be salvaged by pointing out that the chimney was hardly a symbol of the Holocaust when it was written. On the contrary, the image was new and poignant and did not appear anywhere else in German postwar poetry. Or one might note that the exalted tone with its five repeated *O*s was typical of the poetry of ruins written during the first years of peace, with only a year or two to go before the Cold War. Or that the invocation of Israel's body rising like smoke through the air effectively described the dispersion of the Jewish people. One could refer to Sachs' attempts to construct a historical context, at once biblical and current, to clarify what had happened — and that her ambivalent reply created a clarity as graspable as smoke. One could quote the poem's motto — "And after this my skin has been destroyed, yet in my flesh shall I see God" (Job 19:26) — and argue that the text dramatizes the conflict between despair and faith but doesn't (perhaps is even unable to) take sides. And one could refer to all the poems in which she later recycled these themes and metaphors, eliciting further significance from them. One could probably do more than that if one wanted to expound the poem's special position in the approach to Sachs' œuvre. Or, for that matter, if one wanted to analyze its importance for how the divided Germany dealt with its recent past.

Nonetheless the question remains whether the text's strengths are not to be found on a different level. Its cardinal metaphor — the chimney — is varied in a number of different ways. It is smoke column, ray of sunlight, finger, and knife — indeed, even exclamation mark. Of these different guises at least one travels in the opposite direction: in contrast with smoke, rising upwards, the ray of sunlight falls to earth. It comes from an eclipsed star and glows with the only energy that seems possible in this era of strife: an emphatic blackness with well-nigh unimaginable atomic weight. A couple of stanzas later the image is turned into a finger laid on the threshold "like a knife between life and death." Now the chimney is no longer vertical, instead it has become horizontal — the very boundary between motion and nothingness. In other words: a dividing line. Is it this characteristic that determines, on a deeper level, Sachs' choice of metaphors? In each case the smoke pillar constitutes a connecting link — between earthly existence and heavenly life, crematorium oven and freedom, life and death. And each time the guise is transitory. The smoke drifts through the air but doesn't last, it cannot be grasped and leaves nothing behind. Was it this nothingness that Sachs wanted to depict? In that case the poem's repeated *Os* would be the only thing remaining when the object of lamenting had departed life.

Many years later the poem "Der Umriß" would portray this relationship as a finger pulled out of a ring. What is left is merely an outline. But already in the tormented poetry Sachs began writing when "the inconceivable came," the apostrophe appeared as the governing figure. No doubt there are readers bothered by the sighs and exclamations, but if so, they are disregarding the fact that her *O* quite literally is a "crooked line of pain." Its curvature signals what was left for a poet who did not meet the same fate as her dead brothers and sisters: nothing. Put differently: an empty ring of lips demonstrating that everything said is dedicated to the dead. It is difficult to imagine a more naked line.

**TEXT** "O die Schornsteine," IdWdT (NSW:I) · For letter to Berendsohn 01/22/1959, see Briefe 131 · "Der Umriß," FiS (NSW:II) | **IMAGE 2** Doodles from a notebook (KBS) · **3** "O die Schornsteine," typescript (KBS) · **4** Original illustration by Rudi Stern for *In den Wohnungen des Todes* 1947

O die Schornsteine,
Auf den sinnreich erdachten Wohnungen des Todes,
Als Israels Leib zog aufgelöst in Rauch
Durch die Luft -
Als Essenkehrer ihn ein Stern empfing -
Oder war es ein Sonnenstrahl?

O die Schornsteine!
Freiheitswege für Jeremias und Hiobs Staub -
Wer erdachte euch und baute Stein auf Stein
Den Weg für Flüchtlinge aus Rauch?

O die Wohnungen des Todes,
Einladend hergerichtet
Für den Wirt des Hauses, der sonst Gast war -
O ihr Finger,
Die Eingangsschwelle legend
Wie ein Messer zwischen Leben und Tod -

O ihr Schornsteine,
O ihr Finger,
Und Israels Leib im Rauch durch die Luft !

.-.-.-.

3

4

It is unclear when Sachs heard about the suffering in the ghettos or understood the purpose of the camps in eastern Europe. With the invasion of Poland in September 1939, war became a reality. When the Wehrmacht continued eastwards, tore up the pact with the Soviet Union and attacked the country in June 1941, she was no less aware than any other "non-Aryan" of where it all might lead. In letters to Manfred George after the war she described how "our people were being deported [...] every day," and also that she had received a letter in the winter of 1942 from her cousin VERA SACHS (1905–1943), who had been in hiding at various addresses in Berlin before she was apprehended and murdered at Auschwitz. Vera, who was the daughter of William's younger brother Alfred, had informed her that her father had been deported that fall, "probably to Poland straight away, because we never had a message from Theresienstadt." The letter has not been preserved, but it may have contained information about other people as well. It is also quite possible that further letters have been lost. But Sachs' socializing with other refugees, her acquaintance with the Tegens, articles in the Swedish press, and not least her contacts with the Jewish congregation mean that she must have become aware soon enough of "that which happened," to use Celan's phrase for the cruelties of the Hitler years.

As Fritsch-Vivié has noted, the chief rabbi of Stockholm, Marcus Ehrenpreis, a Swedish-Bulgarian Judaist, spoke in a sermon held in the fourth autumn of the war about a "war of extermination" and three types of burnings: of books, of synagogues, of people. It is uncertain if Sachs heard the words or later read about them in the Swedish press. But neither is it very important if she did. For when Ehrenpreis spoke on Yom Kippur on October 9, 1943, she had already written some of the cycles of poems with which she would initiate the memorable part of her œuvre — including "Die Elegien von den Spuren im Sande." The title recalls a poem from the Berlin years, "Das Mädchen am Brunnen" (The Girl by the Well), in which traces in the sand refer to what remains of the distant beloved. The phrase occurs in other texts from the same period as well, for example in the poem "Dörfer im Spätsommer" (Villages in Late Summer), where Sachs states: "a trace in the sand leads to far away." If in the early texts the traces lead forwards, to the peculiar past that seems to lie in the future, the later traces are characterized instead by a definitive farewell to all that had been. Each tableau bears the secret caption: *Nevermore*.

The unpublished suite in two parts was written 1942–1943 and given the same motto from Job 19:26 that Sachs would use for "O the Chimneys." At the center is Israel, "you my people": "Now when it gets late, / And time bends down / Like a hand / That wants to fasten again / The lost star / In the sky — / I see your morning, my people." The poems meditate upon relationships of time, on late and early. Memory is that flexible medium in which yesterday and today may still touch one another, the traces in the sand are the former time's survival in the latter. Although Sachs celebrated her people's earliest experiences, the life of a tribe of herdsmen, with animals and rituals under a starry sky in the diaspora, the message she derived from it suggests a final parting. It may be that she asks: "who knows / When he bids farewell / If he is not already / On the threshold of home?" — a query which, if anything, cushioned the pain of parting with vague hope. In reality, however, the texts are about a crime so profound that it requires another tongue. Between night and morning a "cockcrow" is heard. Henceforth no day in Sachs' poetry would resemble earlier ones.

The elegies show how she was grappling with an idiom which she — possibly without yet realizing it — was about to abandon. In a certain sense, they may be read as a farewell to the comforting cadences of the old poetry. Sachs was still recycling phrases and metaphors — such as the image of the woman at the spinning wheel: "And the maiden by the spinning wheel / Has taken a thread of star's gold / And spun it. / For she has confused Here and There." But as these lines show, the realization has dawned that the new poetry cannot be spun from old yarn. A few stanzas later a lamb restlessly rummages around in its "'Whence,'" while an ass chewing the thistles of pain no longer wants to "return to the stable." Only the stag has eyes in which the rainbow stands out against the dark backdrop of parting — "They are my people's eyes!" As the poet of the Jewish people, Sachs took it upon herself to gaze with such eyes.

"Quiet, quiet," urges "Zwischen Gestern und Morgen" (Between Yesterday and Tomorrow), a later poem in the suite (with words later recycled in "Chor der Tröster" [Chorus of Consolers]):

> In / The depth of the gorge / Between / Yesterday and tomorrow / Stands the cherub, his wings painting / Golden bolts — / But his hands hold the scarps apart / Between yesterday and tomorrow — / Like the sides of a wound, which / Shall remain open, which / Must not yet heal . . .

The first and third lines were indented, which gives the stanza an unsettled air — as if Sachs no longer knew where to put her metrical feet down. The absence of rhyme and meter shows that the period of transition has arrived. The real difficulty was not in abandoning the harmonies of the end rhyme, but in finding a language for the wound that had opened — a language that did not bring about the healing of false reconciliation. The trauma must be made readable, despite all its inconceivableness. Consequently poetry should serve less as conciliator than as grist. A few lines later the poem's persona urges herself: "May no hand of dust try / To bridge / Yesterday and tomorrow!" At last Sachs had understood what the wound required: privation. The conclusion was obvious:

Neither shall you sing / As you have sung —

**TEXT** For letter to George 01/27/1946, see Briefe 25 · Celan, "Ansprache anläßlich der Entgegennahme des Literaturpreises der freien Hansestadt Bremen" (1958), *Gesammelte Werke*, ed. Beda Allemann and Stefan Reichert, Frankfurt am Main 1983, vol. III, 186 · Fritsch-Vivié, 87 · "Die Elegien von den Spuren im Sande," NSW:I · "Das Mädchen am Brunnen" and "Dörfer im Spätsommer," ASachs

## THESE THINGS

It was not until Sachs gave up her earlier idiom that she could find a new language. Paradoxically enough it also became a language in which she would gain access to loss. A few years after her flight she sent a selection of poems to MAX HODANN (1894–1946), a doctor and sexual pedagogue who was involved in socialist causes and who had fled in the mid-1930s, arrived in Sweden at the outbreak of the war, and was now active in immigrant circles. Among other things he was the chairman of the Freier deutscher Kulturbund, an association without party affiliations that organized lectures and readings in Stockholm. Hodann, however, had "no idea whatsoever" about what to do with the poems. Irresolute, he sent them to an émigré professor of German literature: WALTER A. BERENDSOHN (1884–1984). Berendsohn had presented his doctoral thesis in 1911 following German and Nordic studies as well as philosophy, and had nine years later obtained the right to teach at an institute of higher education. In 1926 he took up a professorship at the University of Hamburg, where he taught German and Scandinavian literature. As a member of the Social Democratic Party he became involved in the opposition against Nazi tendencies in Germany in the 1920s. When the National Socialists took power he immediately lost his post, and a few years later was stripped of both citizenship and property. He managed to avoid capture by fleeing to Denmark in 1936, where he began work on *Die humanistische Front* (The Humanist Front), the first volume of which would be published ten years later and lay the foundations of the new area of research eventually known as "exile literature." As a result of mounting persecution of the Danish Jewish population, he fled to Sweden in 1943.

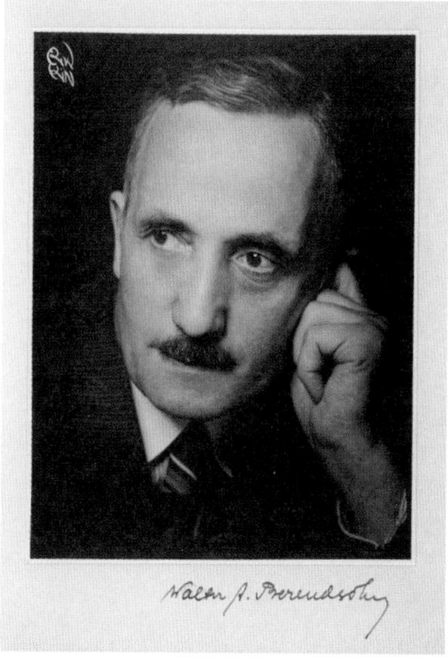

5

Berendsohn was resting at the Högsbo Sanatorium outside Falun in Dalarna when he received the poems. In a later recollection he wrote: "I felt that I held in my hands verse perhaps on a par with Rainer Maria Rilke, albeit of a different sort, less 'literary,' more primordial, and furthermore in a very gifted, unusual form which immediately made one prick up one's ears." Berendsohn summed up his impressions in a letter which Hodann forwarded to the poet. Thus began, in September 1944, an acquaintance that soon evolved into a friendship which would last, despite the odd misunderstanding, until Sachs' death in 1970. Berendsohn followed the development of his friend's writing at close range, wrote essays, and in 1951 ensured that a subscription edition of the drama *Eli* was published at private expense in Malmö. When the first awards came from Germany towards the end of the same decade and Sachs' fame grew both in Sweden and abroad, he prepared the first monograph on "the poet of Jewish destiny and her works." This understandable but reductionist perspective would lead to conflicts, but did not prevent Berendsohn from suggesting Sachs for the Nobel Prize in literature over several consecutive years. His interest and loyalty were crowned with an archive of manuscripts, cuttings, and correspondence set up at the Stadt- und Landesbibiliothek in Dortmund, as a result of the city instituting a Nelly-Sachs-Preis in 1961.

Sachs' first letter to the "Highly Esteemed Herr Professor" is suffused with the isolated writer's joy at receiving attention: "I want you to know that when I opened the letter and your name, long venerated, shone at me, I really had a moment of feeling at home." Pleasantries done, Sachs proceeded to give an account of her flight and also to express regret that Hodann had decided against organizing a reading of her poems: "It makes me sad, not for my own part, my name would be better kept in the dark, but that these things will not speak where they first ought to: to Jewish people." The "things" which were denied an audience were "Die Elegien von den Spuren im Sande" and "Grabschriften in die Luft geschrieben." Sachs admitted that the texts "came about as a great secret to myself" — for which reason she saw herself less as author than as mouthpiece. It was therefore logical not to change a single syllable: "I wrote them down as the night handed me them." The texts consisted less of outpourings than of inspirations — composed, or rather dictated, by a hidden entity. In her letter she also enclosed some earlier works so that her correspondent might "see the difference." Now that the flowers of the Berlin years had wilted and the poetic expression become naked, now that she had left the formal trepidation of the epigone behind but still sought a personal expression, she perceived herself as a medium. The night handed her secrets which must be passed on — bulletins from a world whose meaning remained ineffable even for the messenger. Poetry had acquired a mysterious dimension which it would never lose.

In a way the "old wound" Sachs had written about in the letter to Abenius had been ripped open again. But this time it was not about the loss of a person, it was the loss of a whole people. The trauma was too big, and it wasn't merely her own. She had neither the right nor the wish to close the wound. "These things" showed that it must remain unhealed.

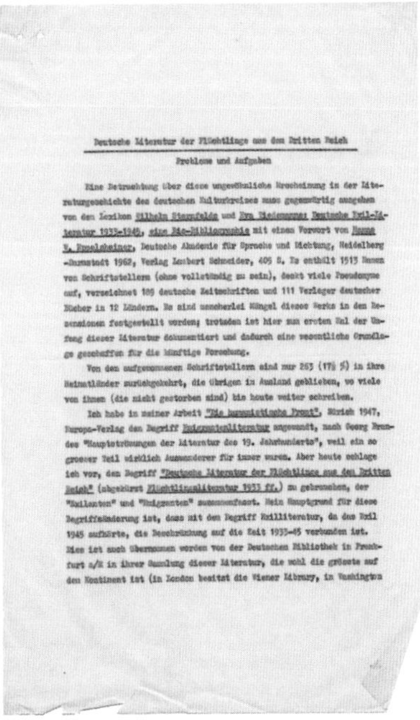

Deutsche Literatur der Flüchtlinge aus dem Dritten Reich

Probleme und Aufgaben

Eine Betrachtung über diese ungewöhnliche Erscheinung in der Literaturgeschichte des deutschen Kulturkreises muss gegenwärtig ausgehen von dem Lexikon Wilhelm Sternfelds und Eva Tiedemanns: Deutsche Exil-Literatur 1933-1945, eine Bio-Bibliographie mit einem Vorwort von Hanns W. Eppelsheimer, Deutsche Akademie für Sprache und Dichtung, Heidelberg-Darmstadt 1962, Verlag Lambert Schneider, 405 S. Es enthält 1513 Namen von Schriftstellern (ohne vollständig zu sein), deckt viele Pseudonyme auf, verzeichnet 189 deutsche Zeitschriften und 111 Verleger deutscher Bücher in 12 Ländern. Es sind mancherlei Mängel dieses Werks in den Rezensionen festgestellt worden; trotzdem ist hier zum ersten Mal der Umfang dieser Literatur dokumentiert und dadurch eine wesentliche Grundlage geschaffen für die künftige Forschung.

Von den aufgenommenen Schriftstellern sind nur 263 (17½ %) in ihre Heimatländer zurückgekehrt, die übrigen im Ausland geblieben, wo viele von ihnen (die nicht gestorben sind) bis heute weiter schreiben.

Ich habe in meiner Arbeit "Die humanistische Front", Zürich 1947, Europa-Verlag den Begriff Emigrantenliteratur angewandt, nach Georg Brandes "Hauptströmungen der Literatur des 19. Jahrhunderts", weil ein so grosser Teil wirklich Auswanderer für immer waren. Aber heute schlage ich vor, den Begriff "Deutsche Literatur der Flüchtlinge aus dem Dritten Reich" (abgekürzt Flüchtlingsliteratur 1933 ff.) zu gebrauchen, der "Exilanten" und "Emigranten" zusammenfasst. Mein Hauptgrund für diese Begriffsänderung ist, dass mit dem Begriff Exilliteratur, da das Exil 1945 aufhörte, die Beschränkung auf die Zeit 1933-45 verbunden ist. Dies ist auch übernommen worden von der Deutschen Bibliothek in Frankfurt a/M in ihrer Sammlung dieser Literatur, die wohl die grösste auf dem Kontinent ist (in London besitzt die Wiener Library, in Washington

6

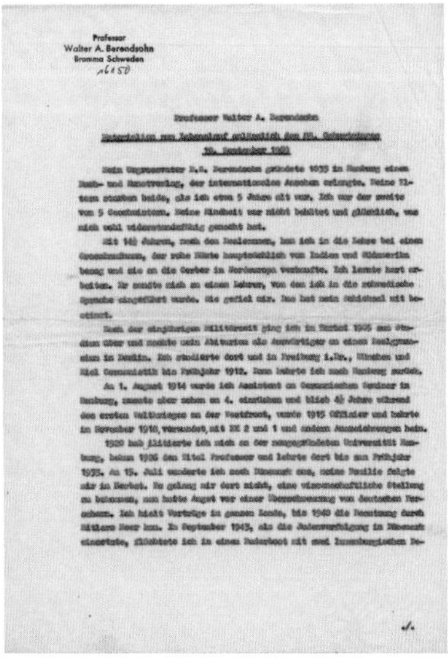

Professor
Walter A. Berendsohn
Bromma Schweden
6150

Professor Walter A. Berendsohn

7

**TEXT** Brev Letter from Hodann to Berendsohn 09/01/1944, ABerendsohnD · Berendsohn, 114 · For letter to Berendsohn 09/12/1944, see Briefe 22 | **IMAGE 5** Walter A. Berendsohn in the 1940s (Photo Anna Riwkin, MMS) · **6** Berendsohn, "Deutsche Literatur der Flüchtlinge aus dem Dritten Reich," typescript (KBS) · **7** Berendsohn, "Material zum Lebenslauf," 1969, typescript (KBS)

## EPITAPHS IN THE AIR

"Grabschriften in die Luft geschrieben" would be Sachs' first important work. The cycle consists of twenty-odd epitaphs on friends and acquaintances, of which thirteen were included in her first collection of poems in 1947. Letters indicate that the texts were written during the first half of 1943, which means that Sachs would probably have had word of the death of people close to her over the preceding eight or ten months. At the end of the year she sent Christmas and New Year's greetings to the Swedish writer, theologian, and Quaker EMILIA FOGELKLOU-NORLIND (1878–1972), whom she had become acquainted with through the circle around the writer Gunnar Beskow. The card showed a pair of deer in a snowy landscape, and the sender "Li" promised soon to send "a small collection of my latest poems" to the addressee, "Ili." Towards early summer she then sent a thank-you note for a joint outing to Djurgården, adding: "I am very happy that you consider me worthy of your friendship and that I could sit next to you on the grass and your beautiful, love-filled being immediately blossomed." The style of address is the same as with Sachs' women friends from the Berlin years, where pet names and declarations of affection provided rhetorical warmth. Along with a pressed four-leaf clover and a "daub" of flowers she included transcriptions of some early texts in the envelope, among them the poem "Miniatur aus Grunewald" (Miniature from Grunewald). Perhaps Sachs felt it important to retain the echo between times and countries, in order to invoke constancy. In the woods on Djurgården, memories of past excursions to mountain villages in Silesia returned to her. Despite the new tonalities which were beginning to emerge it was still possible to conjure up the past in the present.

8

Only a few months later, however, she sent another letter to Ili, posted in Stocksund north of Stockholm, where she and her mother were taking time off with the Beskow family. The tendency was similar: "Heartfelt thanks for your lovely and profound letter, whose every word really did fall like dew on my heart which is so often sad." But this time the correspondent was not talking about times past. Sachs had recently sent her friend a suite of "Inschriften" (Inscriptions), as she called her latest texts, and felt it necessary to inform her about the individuals behind the typified titles. The lines directed at the addressee were written by hand, while the explications of the poems were composed on a typewriter, suggesting that they might not have been intended (only) for Fogelklou-Norlind. In a letter that followed three weeks later "a further few inscriptions" were enclosed — four of them, probably newly written — with additional comments as well.

Of the thirty or so epitaphs, about half would be published. Why the thirteen which were included in *In den Wohnungen des Todes* were preferred over the rest is hard to say, though it is notable that most of the rejects were about relatives or identifiable people, unlike those chosen for publication. There is no

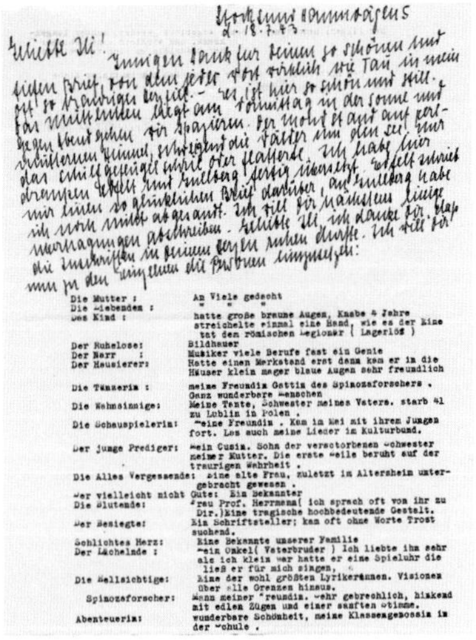

| | |
|---|---|
| Die Mutter : | An Viele gedacht |
| Die Liebenden : | " " " |
| Das Kind : | hatte große braune Augen, Knabe 4 Jahre streichelte einmal eine Hand, wie es der Eine tat dem römischen Legionär ( Lagerlöf ) |
| Der Ruhelose: | Bildhauer |
| Der Narr : | Musiker viele Berufe fast ein Genie |
| Der Hausierer: | Hatte einen Merkstand erst dann kam er in die Häuser klein mager blaue Augen sehr freundlich |
| Die Tänzerin : | meine Freundin Gattin des Spinozaforschers . Ganz wunderbare Menschen |
| Die Wahnsinnige: | Meine Tante, Schwester meines Vaters. starb 41 zu Lublin in Polen . |
| Die Schauspielerin: | Meine Freundin . Kam im Mai mit ihrem Jungen fort. Las auch meine Lieder im Kulturbund. |
| Der junge Prediger: | Mein Cusin. Sohn der verstorbenen Schwester meiner Mutter. Die erste Zeile beruht auf der traurigen Wahrheit . |
| Die Alles Vergessende: | Eine alte Frau, zuletzt im Altersheim untergebracht gewesen . |
| Der vielleicht nicht Gute: | Ein Bekannter |
| Die Blutende: | Frau Prof. Herrmann( ich sprach oft von ihr zu Dir.)Eine tragische hochbedeutende Gestalt. |
| Der Besiegte: | Ein Schriftsteller; kam oft ohne Worte Trost suchend. |
| Schlichtes Herz: | Eine Bekannte unserer Familie |
| Der Lächelnde : | Mein Onkel( Vaterbruder ) ich liebte ihn sehr als ich klein war hatte er eine Spieluhr die ließ er für mich singen, |
| Die Hellsichtige: | Eine der wohl größten Lyrikerinnen. Visionen über alle Grenzen hinaus. |
| Spinozaforscher: | Mann meiner Freundin. Sehr gebrechlich, hinkend mit edlen Zügen und einer sanften Stimme. |
| Abenteuerin: | wunderbare Schönheit, meine Klassengenossin in der Schule . |

9

noticeable difference in tone, rhetorical organization, or formal execution between them. Nor do the published texts appear to form a thematic context or follow any development of images or motifs which could not just as well have been done with the works that were not included. Some of the epitaphs are short, some are long, most of them rhyme but not always consistently so, many have more than two stanzas but a couple lack stanza breaks. All of them, however, employ the same pattern: the title provides a designation of the dead person's defining characteristic, followed by initials in square brackets. Among the published texts were "Der Spinozaforscher [H. H.]" (The Spinoza Researcher [H. H.]), "Die Tänzerin [D. H.]" (The Dancer [D. H.]), "Die Abenteuerin [A. N.]" (The Adventuress [A. N.]), and "Der Steinsammler [E. C.]" (The Rock Collector [E. C.]); among the unpublished "Die Wahnsinnige [M. M.]" (The Mad One [M. M.]), "Die Schauspielerin [E. L.]" (The Actress [E. L.]), "Der junge Prediger [H. M.]" (The Young Preacher [H. M.]), "Die Blutende [H. H.]" (The Bleeding One [H. H.]), "Der Lächelnde [A. S.]" (The Smiling One [A. S.]), "Der Pilger [L. H.]" (The Pilgrim [L. H.]), and "Die Hellsichtige [G. C.]" (The Far-Sighted One [G. C.]). In some transcripts sent to acquaintances including Lamm and Pergament, there was also the subtitle "To My Dead Brothers and Sisters," which shows that the writer regarded the suite as a portrait gallery of dead relatives, irrespective of whether they belonged to the Sachs family tree or not.

The first identifiable person is the age-mellowed Spinoza specialist — "my friend's husband. Very frail, with a limp, but with noble features and a mild voice," Sachs informed Fogelklou-Norlind. The man in question is Hugo Horwitz, whose destiny is described in verse and words reminiscent of the cadences of the Berlin years:

> You read and held a shell in your hand. / The evening came with tender farewell rose. / Your room became an intimate of eternity / And the music began in an old music box. // The candles burned in the evening glow; / You burned with the distant blessing. / The oak sighed from the heirloom / And the past kept its rendezvous.

In the original the poem has something of the lullaby dressed as epitaph. The melody is soft and the verse melancholy, with the rhymes putting pain to rest. The purpose is not to speak for the dead person, but to make him a gift of the sort of respite in which memory may be preserved in peace. If a term like "sanctity of the grave" has any place in a context marked by racist hatred, it is here: as the designation of the singular stillness surrounding Sachs' poems.

In the following inscription, dedicated to Horwitz's wife and Sachs' childhood friend Dora, the notion of parting's connection with eternity is further developed. The dancer wanders to "the edge" of a sarabande. In the course of her journey, however, her form changes and she becomes a butterfly, "the clearest sign of metamorphosis." Implied death transforms her friend into "a larva and pupa and already a thing," resting in God's safe hand. From this belief that death in Theresienstadt could be the final metamorphosis into a butterfly-like being fluttering in the palm of the Lord's hand, emerges Sachs' need to give senseless murder a higher meaning — or at least a glimmer of hope to alleviate despair. The unpublished epitaphs, too, are characterized by the wish to reinterpret murder into meaning, giving what would otherwise be inconceivable sacrifice a deeper significance. Sachs' epitaphs over the mad "M. M." (in a letter to Fogelklou-Norlind she is identified as an aunt who "died in 41 in Lublin, Poland"), the actress "E. L." (Erna Leonhard-Feld who "disappeared in May [1943] along with her boy"), the young preacher "H. M." (rabbi Heinz Meyer, "son of my mother's dead sister"), the bleeding "H. H." (Helene Herrmann, a "tragic and extremely important figure"), the smiling "A. S." (her uncle Alfred Sachs, who "had a music box which he let sing for me"), the pilgrim "L. H." (Leo Hirsch, who "really spread a glow of the Hasidic around him"), and the visionary "G. C." (Gertrud Kolmar, née Chodziesner, "probably one of the greatest lyricists") — these and other unpublished epitaphs demonstrate the same need to replace a historical frame of understanding with a metaphysical or even religious one.

The poem about Heinz Meyer is typical of Sachs' wavering between fact and wishful thinking:

> You have already slept in coffins / When the world offered you no other shelter. / Where are you resting now? / Gates shall be opened! / Your eyes relish other greenery / Known from childhood dreams, longing, pain, / Other scents bless you there / And meet you as memory. / The Hasids who illuminate their God in darkness / They have long since augured your home. / It turned late; and time / is dark with eternity.

From a letter to Alfred Andersch it emerges that her cousin for a time must have slept in and possibly also lain hidden in burial coffins. In later texts such as the dramatic poem *Nachtwache* Sachs returned to "the coffin [...] in which a beloved person long lay hidden." Her cousin also appears in one of the "glowing enigmas" from the 1960s, entitled "Vier Tage vier Nächte": "Four days four nights / a coffin was your hiding place / Survive breathed in — and out — to delay death —." The early epitaph turns this hiding place into an anticipation of eternal rest. Although the poem wonders where the dead preacher is resting now, it exudes confident hope: the gates to another greenery have been opened, the pious mystics are already heralding his "home." Even if the ambition to imbue the fate of the murdered with a deeper meaning paid scant heed to brutal fact, Sachs did not gloss over the circumstances. Rather, she refused to give the executioners' definition of the victims the last word. The religious interpretation with touches of sentimentality can be explained by the demands of the genre: as epitaphs, the poems must highlight the relationship between now and eternity, fire and ashes.

In the final analysis, then, the question is not so much why Sachs glorified the victims, but why she gave the epitaphs generalist titles. A present-day reader unwilling to give much credence to proxy statements in poetry is easily going to read as warning signals the empty shoes, the angels' veils, and halos decorating the figures and making them more archetypes than human beings. But even if Sachs understandably enough glorified the dead, she never rendered them anonymous. The initials specified unique individuals whose destinies were not interchangeable. In addition, the consistent apostrophe of an informal "you" — even of people with whom she used the formal "you" in letters — lent the tone a sense of intimate trust. As the epitaph on Dora Horwitz shows, Sachs wanted the poems to be vessels — or portable tombs — in which the memory of the disappeared was kept alive, covered by the glistening moss of eternity. At the same time the overall title of the suite made it clear that the texts were being written in the sky, and so were subject to shifts and impermanence. On the one hand life had regressed to the pupal stage, wrapped in the silk threads of eternity; on the other it amounted to dusty butterflies at the mercy of transience. A paradox of that order could hardly be more drastically summed up than in the image of epitaphs etched in air.

The unpublished poem "Die wahnsinnige Mutter sang [M. L.]" (The Mad Mother Sang [M. L.]) describes the same contradiction as "something like a bird's flight — / Is it a hair / Which was once on a child's head?" And in "Der Marionettenspieler [K. G.]" (The Puppet Player [K. G.]), whose title links the strings that make the puppet move to the hairs on a person's head, the paradox is deftly turned:

> The swallow built its nest in Elias' hair; / until he levitated in longing.

Of such transitions Sachs' epitaphs fashion a nest.

**TEXT** Christmas and New Year's greetings 1943 to Fogelklou-Norlind, GU · For letters to Fogelklou-Norlind 07/18/1943 and 08/06/1943, see Briefe 13 and 15 · "Grabschriften in die Luft geschrieben," NSW:I · Letter to Andersch 08/16/1958, DLA · *Nachtwache*, ZiS (NSW:III) · "Vier Tage vier Nächte," GR:III (NSW:II) | **IMAGE 8** Emilia Fogelklou-Norlind in 1945 (Photo Studio Håkan Lindqvist, Fogelklousällskapet) · **9** Letter to Fogelklou-Norlind 07/18/1943 (GU) · **10** Scrapbook pictures from "Das Oblatenalbum" (KBS)

10

# URPUNKT

PREMONITIONS BY THE KITCHEN WINDOW **160**

1

## PREMONITIONS BY THE KITCHEN WINDOW

The nest that Sachs lined after her mother's death in February 1950 was the refurnished one-room apartment with a dining alcove by the waters of southern Stockholm. Its 41 square meters would accommodate all that remained from her past: letters, manuscripts, and books, drawings and watercolors, the rock collection with which she tried to re-create her father's treasures in Siegmundshof, the postcards with images from religious legends and art history, the red album with scrapbook pictures from the turn of the century, the photographs of Margarete and William as children, betrothed, and parents, but also pictures of the "sisters" and "saviors," the seashells and the music box with its mechanical melody… The brown suitcase Sachs had fled with was joined by a smaller white one where she kept official personal documents. Reachable from her portable typewriter were pens and pencils, a paperknife and a magnifying glass. Two floors above the street she found shelter. A new table calendar made of black Bakelite reminded her that time still progressed.

After her breakdown in March 1950 Sachs was groping for support. She wrote elegies to her dead mother and sought contact with the world around her in a steady stream of letters. As indicated by the lyrical prose of the "Briefe aus der Nacht," which she began during these first weeks of feeling abandoned, she also delved deeply into the Jewish-mystical conception of the world with which she had become familiar partly through the lectures held by the religious philosopher Hugo Bergmann at Stockholm University in the winter of 1947–1948, partly through Martin Buber's editions of Hasidic tales and legends. In a letter to Bergmann, she stated: "The non-bound, the fluid, the ever-possible is, after all the terrible experiences, also the only thing that gives consolation, I believe." And continued: "How wonderfully you spoke of the transfusion from person to person as if in a common circulation system. Only one who has really experienced this absolute dedication, which can lead to miracles and secrets, is able to fathom the depths to which you delved with your words."

After her collapse she was given a gift by the new rabbi of the Jewish congregation, KURT WILHELM (1900–1965), who would help and support her until her death. Originally hailing from Breslau (present-day Wrocław), Wilhelm had left Israel in order to succeed Ehrenpreis a couple of years earlier. His gift would have a considerable impact on Sachs' view of the world, and also on her thoughts on poetry: it was Gershom Scholem's annotated translation of the first chapter of the most important document of the Kabbalah, *Zohar*. From a letter to Berendsohn sent in the fall of the same year it emerges that on October 25 she paid a visit to the congregation library in central Stockholm, where she consulted the Viennese Judaist Ernst Müller's analysis from 1920, *Der Sohar und seine Lehre* (The Zohar and Its Teachings). She confessed to having anxiously "read from the Kabbalah and taken in some of what is written in

Für meine geliebten Margareta und Bengt
Karfreitag/Sederabend 1965

In meiner Kammer
wo mein Bett steht
ein Tisch ein Stuhl
der Küchenherd
kniet das Universum wie überall
um erlöst zu werden
von der Unsichtbarkeit -
Ich mache einen Strich
schreibe das Alphabeth
male den selbstmörderischen Spruch an die Wand
an dem die Neugeburten sofort knospen
schon halte ich die Gestirne an der Wahrheit fest
da beginnt die Erde zu hämmern
die Nacht wird lose
fällt aus
toter Zahn vom Gebiß -

3

2

4

5

books about it, and I am once again happy to know the secret links." Here she found clues to the foundations of the cosmos.

Many of the letters that followed on this discovery bear witness to Sachs' involvement with *Zohar*. Already a few weeks after her visit to the library in Wahrendorffsgatan she told Fogelklou-Norlind that she "read a lot from the Kabbalah (Jewish mysticism). [...] Here one finds secret interpretations of the original beginning, quite beyond all the 'pipes' through which man otherwise tied to institutions imbibes the essential. Here one drinks at the open sea in self-forgetful 'devotion.'" The quoted words — and not least the somewhat tendentious interpretation — demonstrate what she considered important: the link between longing and origin. This secretive collaboration beyond social limitations and rituals suggested that Creation was pervaded by self-forgetful devotion. The message must have appealed to a writer who even in younger years had been unable to see any material differences between the task of the poet and unconditional love.

A few years later Sachs returned to the subject in a letter to Jacob Picard in New York: "I read a lot in Zohar, the Book of Splendor! And in the Hasids. The first is full of cosmic possibilities, the second of an everyday animated by the spiritual." The same themes appear in the poems from the period — for example, in the suite "Geheimnis brach aus dem Geheimnis" (Secret Broke Out of the Secret), which was included in *Und niemand weiß weiter* in 1957 but can be dated to the time before April 1952. The first stanzas of the opening poem, "Da schrieb der Schreiber des Sohar," establish the programmatic connection between world and script, astral bodies and letters, joined together in an enormous cycle:

> And then Zohar's writers wrote / and opened the veins and arteries of language / and infused the blood of stars, / orbiting invisibly, and lit / but of longing. // The corpses of the alphabet rose from their grave, / letter angels, ancient crystal, / with drops of water from Creation suspended / which sang — and through them one saw / ruby and hyacinth and lapis glimmer, / as the stone was soft / and sown like flowers.

The texts were written under the influence of the Kabbalah and of Buber's analyses, but also of Simone Weil's mystical impulses and Jakob Böhme's pious ecstasies, which eventually led to a poetry that was at once lighter and more concrete. After *In den Wohnungen des Todes* and *Sternverdunkelung*, in which the grief over those murdered had been borne by ash-colored pathos, Sachs took out a new course on the compass of longing. Here *Zohar* played the role of magnetic pole. Henceforth concepts and terms from Jewish and theosophic mysticism would be employed without excessive respect for the inscrutable thought edifices of the Kabbalists. When Lindegren asked her some questions in connection with his translations in the early 1960s, she soberly confessed:

ste [Stufe wird], und so eins zum andern, bis schließlich jede Stufe zur Schale für die nächste über ihr wird. Der Urpunkt ist ein innerliches Licht, dessen Reinheit, Feinheit und Klarheit mit keinem endlichen Maß erkennbar ist, bis eine Entfaltung aus ihm hervorging. Die Entfaltung dieses Urpunkts aber wurde zu einem Palast, indem jener Punkt sich mit einem Licht umkleidete, das der Größe seiner Klarheit wegen [noch immer] unerkennbar ist. Der Palast, der ein Kleid für jenen verborgenen Punkt ist, ist also unendliches Licht, und dennoch ist es nicht ebenso klar und fein wie jener verborgene und entrückte Urpunkt. Aus jenem ‚Palast' entfaltete sich dann weiterhin das ‚Urlicht' [des ersten Tages], und diese weitere Entfaltung ist ein Kleid für jenen ‚Palast', der noch feiner, klarer und innerlicher ist. Von dieser Stufe

6

“The Creation chapter from Zohar is in German by G. Scholem, and when I sent him my Zohar poems he wrote so beautifully about them, precisely because I had quite personally let them brand themselves into my inner self. They had again been moved to another inner dimension. My intellect is so inadequate that I cannot perceive everything the letters say — I have to transform it in my way, a situation I arrived at through extensive experiences of suffering.”

From later correspondence between Scholem and Dinesen it emerges that the charitable words were based on politeness more than anything else. Scholem described how Sachs after a lecture he had given in Stockholm in 1959 had approached him to thank him for a translation which had affected her “very deeply.” “That was all,” he noted. “Her poems I cannot evaluate. I certainly *do not* know what it is in them that could be called ‘Hasidic.’ We have not corresponded.” Sachs probably sensed something similar: everything she read she translated into her own experiences and ideas. It was never a question of importing the cerebrations of others, instead she sought and created something akin to a space for reverberations. Hidden quotations and allusions would be mere decoration; the only thing that mattered was the context which was revealed. One of the most important texts in this respect is the dramatic poem *Beryll sieht in der Nacht* from 1961. Its alternative title “Das verlorene und wiedergerettete Alphabet” (The Lost and Then Rescued Alphabet) shows that language itself constituted a “story of suffering.” In her annotation to the play, Sachs wrote: “The eternal cycle ever since the moment of creation ex- and inhaled in nature and people. From breath was born the letter and again new creation arises from the word. This is written in the Book of Splendor — Zohar’s book, the book of Jewish mysticism, where all the world’s mysticism converges.”

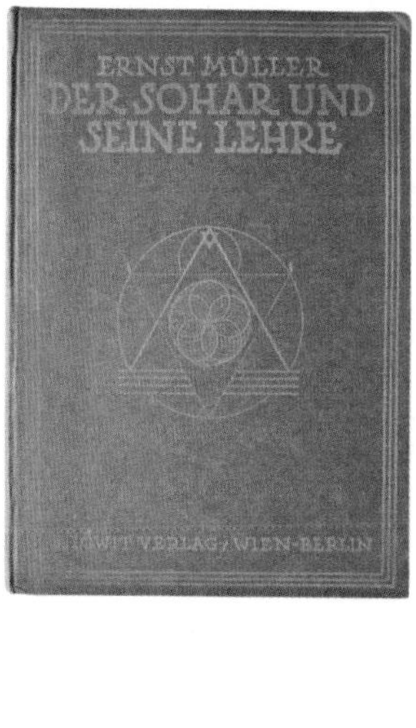

7

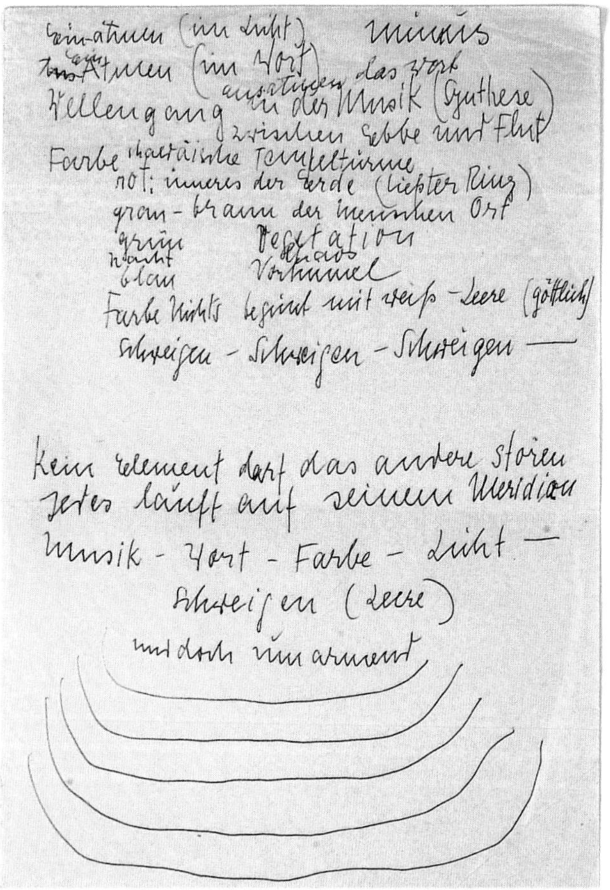

Ein-atmen (im Licht)   Nichts
Aus-Atmen (im Wort)   aussteigen das Wort
Wellengang in der Musik (Synthese)
zwischen Ebbe und Flut
Farbe chaldäische Tempeltürme
rot: inneres der Erde (tiefster Ring)
grau-braun der menschen Ort
grün   Vegetation
nacht   chaos
blau   Vorhimmel
Farbe Nichts beginnt mit weiß - Leere (göttlich)
Schweigen - Schweigen - Schweigen —

Kein Element darf das andere stören
jedes läuft auf seinem Meridian
Musik - Wort - Farbe - Licht -
Schweigen (Leere)
und doch umarmend

8

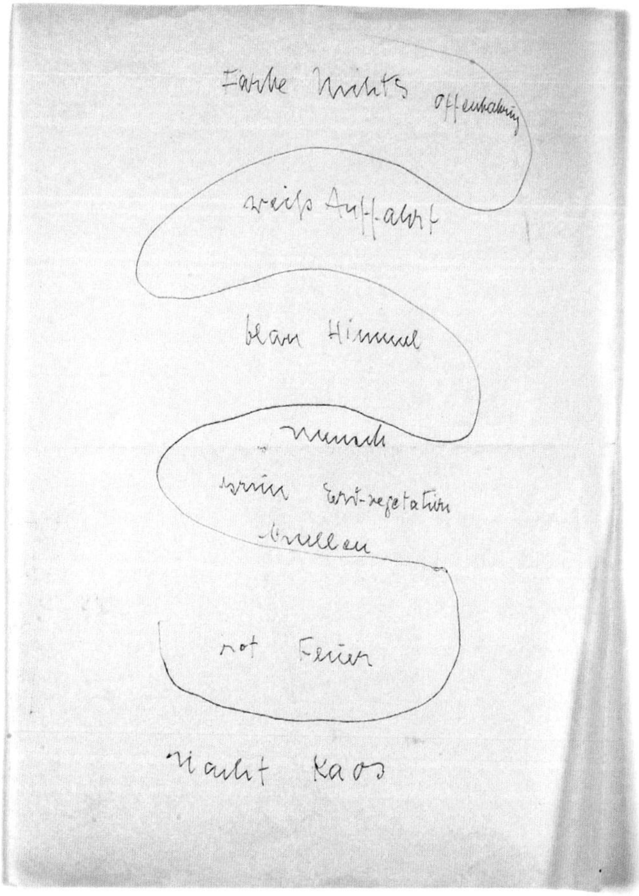

Farbe Nichts   Offenbarung
weiß Auffahrt
blau Himmel
mensch
grün Erd-vegetation
Quellen
rot Feuer
Nacht Kaos

She also mentioned the "primordial secret, concealed in the capsule of the *Urpunkt* and growing into the line." The final words would prove important.

The anonymous writer who in *Zohar* interpreted the story of creation in Genesis linked the concept of an *Urpunkt* to a theory of radiant emanations. In his introduction Scholem emphasizes that this point was the first to arise out of the Void — in a dimension that preceded even the beginning, without extension in time and space, when the only thing that existed was damp, radiant ether. From this original seed the universe developed and became a network of lines. While the Void is indicated by a pin on the tip of the original letter *jod* (י) in the Kabbalist tetragram, the beginning of the letter is reminiscent of a dot. In his annotation the author of *Zohar* states: "The *Urpunkt* is an inner light whose purity, fineness, and clarity isn't measurable with any finite measurement, before an evolution became discernible. However, the evolution of this *Urpunkt* became a palace because the point was surrounded by a light which is [still] immeasurable due to its great clarity."

In one of Sachs' two copies of the book — there are underlinings and comments in both of them, and each one still contains pressed flowers — she marked this particular passage with a big dot in the margin. That her marking might not be coincidental is confirmed by a typed three-page document entitled precisely "Urpunkt." The text bears no date, but the excerpts and paraphrases of which it mainly consists make a dating around the time of *Beryll sieht in der Nacht* likely. There are, for example, several themes that occur in the drama too, including a quote from Böhme's *Mysterium pansophicum* ("Nothing is a craving after Something"), words that are put in the mouth of the mute Netzach. Just like the excerpts, the play deals with the *Gedulah* (or "Greatness" of God) which is one of the ten original powers of the Kabbalah, also known as the *sephirot*. ("Netzach" corresponds to the eighth *sephirah* and means [Israel's] "Victory.") There is a "tree of tongues" in both texts, which has been replanted from Böhme's writings, and also a fallen angel named Asraela, who in Sachs' notes is called Lilit — a "female equivalent to Satan."

"Urpunkt" contains important DNA of the poetry Sachs would write from 1950 onwards. In addition to the quotes from *Zohar* as well as from Scholem's and Böhme's works, the occasionally elliptic notes also contain a number of excerpts, including some from the art historian Gustav Friedrich Hartlaub's studies of magical worldviews. Over three pages, interests were condensed into practice. Sitting in her alcove, surrounded by opened books and the fragments of a scattered life, Sachs collected seeds for her new existence as a poet. It is tempting to see the cuddy as a larger version of the "capsule" in which the "primordial secret" of existence was said to be hidden — and which, by means of poetry's lines of letters, formed growing lines. "The night begins early here," Sachs explained in a letter to Picard. "And then the constellations begin to drift past my window. And I might be standing in the kitchen drying the washing

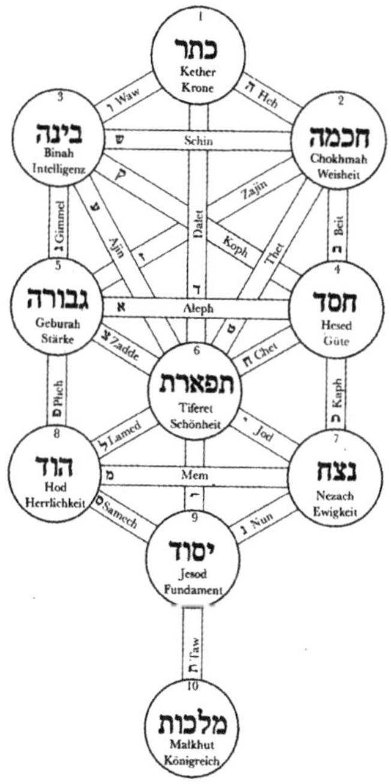


9

up, having premonitions, and the night slowly removes all the walls." Dimensions drifted into one another. What was outside and inside, cosmos and poetry, was no longer clear by the kitchen window in the wintry night.

10

In *Zohar* Sachs found a doctrine of the world's hidden connections that she could believe in, not least because it described a life situation she was able to identify with. After her flight from Germany, her life too had grown out of nothing. In addition, Sachs could link Kabbalistic doctrine to her notion of an invisible universe which it was poetry's task to reach, perhaps even release, in a movement where the significance of the past was located in the future — and the catastrophe consequently appeared as a kind of beginning. But the central work of Jewish mysticism also gave her the feeling that her poems were part of a larger context which extended through time and space. Their lines linked actual circumstances with those of legend, historical figures with mythical ones, and were able to interweave both dreams with waking experiences and the lost with the longed-for. In this vast system of coordinates, the cuddy was just a point, which (bearing in mind the term) was mobile to boot — a movable marker in a web of interconnections. But from Sachs' perspective as a writing person it became the very core of the world. Here the lines converged, from here they radiated. Or as she would write in "In meiner Kammer," a poem from the third cycle of *Glühende Rätsel* (Glowing Enigmas):

> In my room / where my bed is / a table a chair / the kitchen range / the universe kneels as everywhere / to be redeemed / from invisibility —

The poet's task was nothing less than to release the world. It comes as no surprise that the Kabbalists are said to have considered the *Urpunkt* a "hidden Eden"…

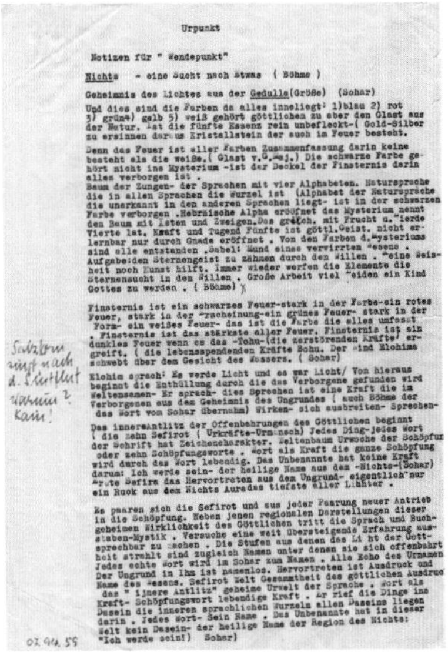
Urpunkt

Notizen für " Wendepunkt"

Nichts - eine Sucht nach Etwas ( Böhme )

Geheimnis des Lichtes aus der Gedulla(Größe) (Sohar)

Und dies sind die Farben da alles inneliegt: 1)blau 2) rot 3) grün 4) gelb 5) weiß gehört göttlichem zu aber den Glast aus der Natur. Ist die fünfte Essenz rein unbefleckt-( Gold-Silber zu ersinnen daraus Kristallstein der auch im Feuer besteht.

Denn das Feuer ist aller Farben Zusammenfassung darin keine besteht als die weiße.( Glast v.G.Maj.) Die schwarze Farbe gehört nicht ins Mysterium -ist der Deckel der Finsternis darin alles verborgen ist .
Baum der Zungen- der Sprachen mit vier Alphabeten. Natursprache die in allen Sprachen die Wurzel ist (Alphabet der Natursprache die unerkannt in den anderen Sprachen liegt- ist in der schwarzen Farbe verborgen .Hebräische Alpha eröffnet das Mysterium nennt den Baum mit Ästen und Zweigen.Das griech. mit Frucht u.Vierde Vierte lat. Kraft und Tugend Fünfte ist göttl.Geist. nicht erlernbar nur durch Gnade eröffnet . Von den Farben d.Mysteriums sind alle entstanden .Babel: Mund eines verwirrten Wesens . Aufgabe:den Sternengeist zu zähmen durch den Willen . Keine Weisheit noch Kunst hilft. Immer wieder werfen die Elemente die Sternensucht in den Willen . Große Arbeit viel Leiden ein Kind Gottes zu werden . ( Böhme) χ

Finsternis ist ein schwarzes Feuer-stark in der Farbe-ein rotes Feuer, stark in der Erscheinung-ein grünes Feuer- stark in der Form- ein weißes Feuer- das ist die Farbe die alles umfasst . Finsternis ist das stärkste aller Feuer. Finsternis ist ein dunkles Feuer wenn es das -Tohu-(die zerstörenden Kräfte) ergreift. ( die lebensspendenden Kräfte Bohu. Der Wind Elohims schwebt über dem Gesicht des Wassers. ( Sohar)

Elohim sprach: Es werde Licht und es war Licht/ Von hieraus beginnt die Enthüllung durch die das Verborgene gefunden wird Weltensamen- Er sprach- dies Sprechen ist eine Kraft die im Verborgenen aus dem Geheimnis des Ungrundes ( auch Böhme der das Wort vom Sohar übernahm) Wirken- sich ausbreiten- Sprechen-

Das innereAntlitz der Offenbahrungen des Göttlichen beginnt ( die zehn Sefirot ( Urkräfte-Urmensch) Jedes Ding-jedes Wort der Schrift hat Zeichencharakter. Weltenbaum Urwoche der Schöpfung oder zehn Schöpfungsworte . Wort als Kraft die ganze Schöpfung wird durch das Wort lebendig. Das Unbenannte hat keine Kraft darum: Ich werde sein- der heilige Name aus dem -Nichts-(Sohar) Erste Sefira das Hervortreten aus dem Ungrund- eigentlich nur ein Ruck aus dem Nichts Auradas tiefste aller Lichter .

Es paaren sich die Sefirot und aus jeder Paarung neuer Antrieb in die Schöpfung. Neben jenen regionalen Darstellungen dieser geheimen Wirklichkeit des Göttlichen tritt die Sprach und Buchstaben-Mystik . Versuche eine weit übersteigende Erfahrung aussprechbar zu machen . Die Stufen aus denen das Licht der Gottheit strahlt sind zugleich Namen unter denen sie sich offenbart Jedes echte Wort wird im Sohar zum Namen . Alle Echo des Urnamen Der Ungrund in Ihm ist namenlos. Hervortreten ist Ausdruck und Name des Wesens. Sefirot Welt Gesammtheit des göttlichen Ausdruck das " innere Antlitz" geheime Urwelt der Sprache . Wort als Kraft- Schöpfungswort lebendige Kraft . Er rief die Dinge ins Dasein die inneren sprachlichen Wurzeln allen Daseins liegen darin . Jedes Wort- Sein Name . Das Unbenannte hat in dieser Welt kein Dasein- der heilige Name der Region des Nichts: "Ich werde sein!) Sohar)

Salzkorn singt nach d. Sintflut warum? Kain!

02.94.55

11

TEXT For letter to Bergmann 12/18/1947, see Briefe 48 · For Wilhelm, see Hugo Valentin, "Kurt Wilhelm 50 år," *Judisk krönika*, 1950, vol. 23, 162 · For letter to Berendsohn 10/26/1950, see Berendsohn, 156 · Müller · For letters to Fogelklou-Norlind 11/06/1950, Picard 01/20/1952, and Lindegren 07/30/1963, see Briefe 78, 88, and 207 respectively · "Da schrieb der Schreiber des Sohar," Unww (NSW:II) · Letter from Scholem to Dinesen 01/13/1981, ADinesen · Zohar, 34 and 79 (underlining of "Netzach" on p. 90) · "Urpunkt," NSW:IV · Böhme, *Mysterium pansophicum* (1620), reprinted in *Sämtliche Schriften*, ed. Wil-Erich Peuckert, Stuttgart 1957 (orig. 1730), Part IV, first text · For Hartlaub, see *Das Unerklärliche. Studien zum magischen Weltbild*, Stuttgart 1951, which was part of Sachs' library · See also Hartlaub, *Chymische Märchen*, Ludwigshafen am Rhein 1955 · "In meiner Kammer," GR:III (NSW:II) · For the "hidden Eden," see Zohar, 32 | IMAGE 1 Sachs' apartment in Bergsundsstrand (Photo Harry Järv, KBS) · 2 Sachs in her apartment in Bergsundsstrand, 1960s (KBS) · 3 "In meiner Kammer," typescript with dedication to the Holmqvists, Easter 1965 (KBS) · 4 Kurt Wilhelm in 1953 (JMS) · 5 The synagogue in Stockholm in the 1950s (JMS) · 6 Cover of and page from Gershom Scholem, *Die Geheimnisse der Schöpfung* 1935 (copy B, KBS) · 7 Ernst Müller, *Der Sohar und seine Lehre* 1920 · 8 Sketches probably made during the work on *Beryll sieht in der Nacht* (DLA) · 9 Diagram from the Kabbalah · 10 Gunnar Josephson (Photo Anna Riwkin, Judiska församlingens arkiv, Stockholm) · 11 "Urpunkt," typescript (DLA)

# THE CAPILLARIES OF LANGUAGE

## BACKYARD DANCES

The visits to Bergmann's lectures and the Jewish congregation, the studies of *Zohar* and Buber's writings are testament to Sachs' affirmation of her Jewish cultural and religious heritage. With time this led to the transformation of what had previously been a negatively attributed identity into a positive one. Sachs never became a dogmatic believer. The rules of the synagogue did not offer the support she sought. But during her first decade of Swedish exile she — who had been brought up in an assimilated home where Christmas was celebrated and the holiest writ on the bookshelves was more likely to be the New Testament — found a framework that added a deeper dimension to personal experience. It was as if existence revealed patterns hitherto hidden. In November 1950 Sachs had her father's ashes transferred from the nondenominational cemetery at Berliner Straße in Wilmersdorf to share her mother's grave in the Jewish section of Stockholm's Northern Cemetery. Through the agency of his daughter, William Sachs would from now on rest in earth consecrated by Jews — a gesture hardly lacking in symbolic value. In a sense, Sachs' flight rearranged the letters of the additional name that Nazi bureaucrats had forced on her (and which, late in her life, would cause problems with the Swedish authorities): "Sara" became "Asra." With the words of the poem by Heine that the neurologist Cassirer had quoted to the seventeen-year-old forty years earlier, she could now affirm: "Your name I want to know, / Your homeland, your kin!"

In January 1957 Sachs sent a letter to her friend MOSES PERGAMENT (1893–1977). The Finno-Swedish composer of Jewish extraction, whom she had contacted after reading a newspaper article during the war, and his German wife ILSE PERGAMENT, née Kutzleb (1906–1960), had become her close friends. Now Sachs told them about some new poems she was in the process of compiling into a book. She also enclosed a poem of older date — as if to show that the tendency had been there as early as in the dark year of 1943, when the three of them had got to know each other and she was still looking after her ill mother in the apartment facing the backyard: "There are some strange poems laid out before me — for me that is, but I didn't dare show them. Now, however, when so much interest is being shown for precisely my transgressive things, I brought them out. 'Chassidischer Tanz' [Hasidic Dance] came about in my back room 14 years ago, when I saw a priv. Jewish assembly on the other side of the yard. Black silhouettes in a shadow play. There are several more left. Perhaps I will include them in the new collection, what do you think? There are after all only a precious few who know anything at all about 'the events' behind these things."

1

2

In a letter to Peter Hamm a few months later she returned to the dancing silhouettes: "Just now your dear letter arrived with your wonderful poem: Dylan Thomas. I am doubly moved, because for me, too, Dylan Thomas is the poet who with his every breath bodily experienced the mystery. In response I have transcribed 'The Hasids' for you. I saw them dance here, as if in the midst of fleeing, in a kitchen opposite mine, when I looked out across the yard. This was their religious service."

Spiritual affirmation in the middle of the dusky everyday: the service Sachs witnessed on the other side of the yard was a piece of emigrated Judaism. Whether there were really mystics dancing in connection with a private gathering or if what she saw were just the shadows of people who lived opposite and who shared her situation as a refugee is of less importance. In her eyes the kitchen on the other side of the yard had been transformed into a synagogue akin to a Platonic cave, in which the movements of vague figures hinted at a reality greater than the one in which existence was determined by malfunctioning heaters and the stench of drains. The religious service revealed an essence behind the order of things, a hidden world beyond the visible one. In one of the poems Sachs sent to Pergament, "Ausgewanderte Schritte" (Emigrated Steps, which would later be renamed "Auswanderer-Schritte Pulsreise-Schritte" [Emigré Steps Pulse Travel Steps] and included in *Und niemand weiß weiter*), she named this ability to behold contexts beyond the tangle of actions and objects that is existence:

> O how they travel / along the threads of sleep / with breathing's Adamic aspiration / away towards the mirrors / cleansed with blind ashes / for Balschem gazes, / before which God does not give way.

Israel ben Elieser, usually known as BAAL SHEM TOV (about 1700–1760), is traditionally regarded as the founder of Hasidism. According to legend, he was able to gaze from one end of the world to the other. Like Abraham and Sara, his parents had their longed-for child late, which was seen as a sign that their son had been chosen to bring the message of the Lord to the people. Born in what was then the southern Polish city of Okup (in present-day Ukraine), ben Elieser took an early interest in mysticism, was given free Talmud lessons after his parents had died, and trained as a rabbi. As the charismatic Baal Shem Tov he led the Jewish religious revivalism movement of the eighteenth century. A reaction against the sclerotic forms of institutionalized religion, Hasidism quickly gained the support of the peasant populations of Eastern Europe. In contrast with rule-bound Judaism, in which the link with God could only be achieved through the devoted study of scripture, it emphasized the importance of prayer and of the piousness of those who prayed. A poor person too had access to God, sometimes in a more heartfelt way than the learned men of the synagogue. Moreover he did not have to approach the Almighty through studies, but could do it just as well by means of song and dance — a way of ecstasy which did not deny the importance of the word, but neither did it overrate diligent reading at the expense of intuitive rapture.

It isn't difficult to understand why Sachs was drawn to a doctrine in which the intellect wasn't placed above feeling and the correct method didn't mean more than heartfelt sincerity. In addition, Hasidism's emphasis on devotion and its affirmation of dance as a medium must have appealed to someone who in her youth had improvised to her father's piano playing and who would later declare dancing her "element" in preference even to the word. Statements by Dähnert and Neff, as well as preserved books, indicate that Sachs was interested in Baal Shem Tov already during her Berlin years. It wasn't until her Swedish exile, however, that she became seriously absorbed by Hasidism. In this regard, Buber's introductions were the most important factor, primarily *Die Legende des Baalschem* (Baalschem's Legends), of which she owned the revised edition from 1955.

3

The impulse to take up this reading may have come from the German Jewish writer and publisher MAX TAU (1897–1976); at least he stimulated her interest. Following studies in Germanism which were concluded with a thesis on Theodor Fontane, the young Tau worked as editor for Bruno Cassirer's publishing house in Berlin, but was expelled from the Reich Literature Chamber in 1935 and fled to Oslo three years later. After the Germans had entered Norway he continued to Stockholm, where he met Sachs in 1944. As founder of Neuer Verlag, which through the agency of the Swedish publishing house Ljus was able to publish works by exiled writers such as Lion Feuchtwanger and Arnold Zweig, he supported and encouraged his new friend, and when the city of Dortmund in 1961 instituted a prize in her name, he became the first recipient of the prize after Sachs.

In the autobiographic *Ein Flüchting findet sein Land* (A Refugee Finds His Country) Tau described their first meeting: "I was seated in my office. The door opened and in stepped a woman whose appearance and unassuming presence did not at all seem to fit in with the times. She emitted a warmth which immediately captivated me. But it was as if she bore all the world's suffering on her shoulders. It wasn't really necessary for us to speak to one another. She had touched the untouchable in me. And it was as if her presence prompted in me the belief that everything could not be lost. The first sentence I heard her utter was: 'We must make sure that the persecuted do not become persecutors.'" The visitor gave Tau some poems held together with a safety pin, adjusted the unfashionable hat which had amused him and bid farewell. It wasn't until he began reading the texts and saw that they had been dedicated to the writer's dead brothers and sisters that he sought out her name: "It was as if the letters grew and came towards me: *Nelly Sachs*."

The account exhibits the same tendency to legend formation as Tegen's description of "Nell Bartholdi's" visit to "Huber" the editor or, for that matter, Dähnert's account of the woman she had met at her grandmother's house. In each case, reserve is associated with seriousness, beauty with anachronism. To some degree, Sachs' poetry is read into her person. Here is the pathos and the fragile splendor, the dormant experiences and the deep sincerity, the sorrow, the longing, and the need to put pain into words — all of it reflected in the writer's beautiful but restrained apparition. As a human being she appeared a vessel for greater forces, a biblical creature through which the destiny of a people spoke and behind whom powers perhaps not entirely carnal could be glimpsed. As the letter to Pergament shows, Sachs herself was hardly free from interpretations of this sort. The shadows stirring behind the windows on the other side of the yard pointed to an entity beyond things, which gave present-day events a dual quality: on the one hand they suggested human actions, on the other hand contexts of cosmic proportions. The quotidian was the handmaiden of legend.

4

This double optics was primed by the young Sachs' interest in stories about the lives of saints and also by her attempts to imbue ill-fated experiences with universal meaning. But it was not until she began her intensive reading of MARTIN BUBER (1878–1965) in the 1940s (which continued until the 1960s, as shown by some unpublished notes about "Messias" [Messiah]) that Sachs gained access to a worldview which ranged her interests in a broader frame of understanding. In her library are some ten preserved books by the German Jewish religious philosopher, including *Die Erzählungen der Chassidim* (The Stories of Hasidism). The edition is from 1949 and may be related to the poems Sachs began writing after the publication of *Sternverdunkelung* that same year, as well as the death of her mother a few months later. For Buber the world of the mystics was characterized by devotion. God did not constitute an authority graspable merely through diligent studies. On the contrary, it was possible to address Him directly, without diversion. By means of spontaneous "you-saying," the prayer confirmed the pious person's trust and willingness to transgress the limitations of the self, but God's "addressability" also made Him appear as reality. The relationship with the Creator immediately became a relationship to creation, for "God speaks to man in the things and the beings that He sends him in life." The almighty who encompassed the world nevertheless also dwelled in it…

5

This paradox was just one of several. Another concerned the issue of evil — an "error" which suggested that creation was imperfect and thus contradictory. From where does this "evil," this "imperfect" come in what was supposedly perfect? According to Buber the Hasids resolved the issue with reference to the Kabbalistic concept of the shattered vessels of creation. At the dawn of time the divine fire had overflowed the "original creations." The vessels were unable to resist or control the forces, and so were shattered in a firestorm whose flames spread to every corner of the world and also encapsulated the shards. Henceforth the dispersed but invisible parts of the vessels of creation were "imprisoned" and had to be freed. In his greatness God let man partake of this cosmic drama. "In truth man's living moment thus stands between creation and salvation." Man may not be sacred, but he was fashioned in His likeness — born flawed, sometimes even evil. The crux was "that man can fall means he can rise." That man could "bring ruin to the world" paradoxically meant that he was able to "bring it salvation" too.

The Hasids' view of the relationship between man and God, the flaws and marvels of creation and how the shards of times gone by could be brought together to save humanity on the last day and announce the arrival of the Messiah — these and other tenets of belief left many traces in Sachs' poetry. In Buber she found a worldview which — in Dinesen's observation — contained essential elements of her own religiousness. The world was animated; the intimate I/you relationship possessed a significance which, while going beyond the relationship between woman and man, nonetheless remained most clearly visible in it; by means of the hidden connections that reigned beyond the visible, a cosmic value could be adduced from personal suffering. In a letter to the Swiss poet Rudolf Peyer from the end of the 1950s, Sachs brought these aspects together under the sign of dance: "I breathe the You of each moment — of each moment — and when I dare to dress it in letters, it is written everywhere. In the kitchen where I am, too, as I cut parsley or boil a potato. The universe is ever also in our blood and our breathing. Didn't know that, when the Israelis said that 'The Dancer' dances to the Hasidic rhythm."

*Durchschmerzung*, "the working through of pain," was Sachs' own term for the transformation she sought with the help of poetry, and which would become the main theme of *Der magische Tänzer* (The Magical Dancer). At the bottom of one of the pages in Scholem's translation of the chapter from *Zohar*, there is a definition added by Sachs: "Attempt to make matter transparent using inner language." The Kabbalah emphasized that the relationship between Creator and creation was of a linguistic nature ("And God said: 'Let there be light'; and there was light," etc.). Each letter and diacritic had a meaning in a world beyond the alphabet. This in turn gave writing a significance far beyond the characters being hammered on a Mercedes Prima which sounded like a stone crusher. Beneath its keys an invisible cosmos was concealed, behind the pane of the misty window was eternity's radiance obscured, out of the kitchen faucet ran water from the springs of Israel.

"Black hats / God's lightning rods / stir up the sea / rock it / cease rocking it," Sachs wrote in the poem she sent to Hamm and Pergament in 1957. The religious mystics' hats danced behind the window on the other side of the yard like waves on the sea of eternity. Everything was in motion, everything was connected to the hidden forces. The world was simultaneously here and elsewhere, and therefore breathed with at least one "otherworldy lung." Whether Sachs really wrote the poem as early as 1943, as she asserted, or if it rather recalled experiences from that year, says less about its significance than about

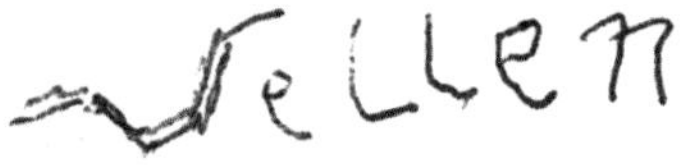


6

her need to locate her texts in a dimension where they could be historicized (and perhaps be made impervious to criticism). After all, times flowed through each other anyway. The "pulse travel steps" referred to in the other poem Pergament received lay embedded in exile — "far beyond the milestone, which keeps abandoned vigil in the daylight." The cosmic heart beat furtively. It was the task of poetry to harbor all the emigrated pulsations.

**TEXT** Heine, "Der Asra," *Romanzero*, Hamburg 1851 · Letter to Pergament 01/11/1957, APergament · Letter to Hamm 04/23/1957, DLA · "Auswanderer-Schritte Pulsreise-Schritte," Unww (NSW:II) · For information about Sachs' early reading of Buber, see letter from Neff to Dinesen 01/27/1982, ADinesen · Baalschem · Tau, *Ein Flüchtling findet sein Land*, Hamburg 1964, 220 · "Messias," NSW:IV · CErzählungen, xi, xiv, xix, xx, xxiv, and xxii respectively · Cf. Dinesen, 138-143; here 143 · For letter to Peyer 10/05/1959, see Briefe 151 · For the note in Zohar, see 29 · "Chassidim tanzen," NSW:II | **IMAGE 1** Moses Pergament in the 1950s (Photo Anna Riwkin, MMS) · **2** Ilse Pergament n.d. (KBS) · **3** Max Tau in 1964 (Photo Ursula Assmus, BDB) · **4** Martin Buber, n.d. (Photo Fred Stein, BPK) · **5** Martin Buber n.d. (Photo Fred Stein, BPK) · **6** Note by Sachs (KBS)

7

FOLKE BERNADOTTE
Slutet
Mina humanitära förhandlingar
i Tyskland våren 1945 och
deras politiska följder
NORSTEDTS

8

## STEP BY STEP

On September 17, 1948, the UN's negotiator in Palestine, Count FOLKE BERNADOTTE (born 1895), was murdered by Jewish terrorists. After having organized the exchange of prisoners during the war, he had returned to Germany in the spring of 1945 to help Danish and Norwegian political prisoners. In talks with Himmler, among others, he managed to extract permission to transport some 15,000 prisoners from the concentration camps. They were taken to safety in the early summer aboard the Swedish Red Cross' white buses, which would become legendary. A number of the prisoners who were placed in refugee facilities would be interviewed by Gunhild Tegen and her colleagues. Bernadotte himself described the rescue in his account *Slutet* (The End), published in June of the same year. Three years later the UN General Assembly appointed him negotiator in the conflict between Jews and Palestinians. Instead of opting for a proposal for a union between the two peoples, he suggested a solution based on two independent states. En route to a meeting with the military governor in Jerusalem, Dov Joseph, one Friday evening in September, Bernadotte's convoy was blocked by members of the so-called "Stern Gang." The Swedish negotiator and his French aide, André Sérot, were both shot and killed.

The news caused worldwide consternation. In Bergsundsstrand as well. In a letter to Dähnert a few weeks later, Sachs wrote: "Here we were so distraught because of Bernadotte. Indians and Jews, these peoples, who above all were bound by secret laws to reject murder of any kind, have both broken them this year." (On January 30, 1948, Mahatma Gandhi had been killed by a nationalistic Hindu.) With the murder of Bernadotte, her worst fears seemed to be coming true: victims could turn into perpetrators. In "Auf daß die Verfolgten nicht Verfolger werden," which had been published in *Sternverdunkelung* the

9

year before, she had voiced the thought: "Steps — / primordial game between executioner and victim, / persecutor and persecuted, / hunter and hunted —." Now the poem became reality.

In the play *Nachtwache* from the same period, Sachs depicted what she described in her adjacent comments as "the eternal game of the hunter and the hunted." The line of reasoning resonates with the poem. Yet while the play describes how one friend (Heinz) betrays another (Pavel) and is transformed from (co-)victim into perpetrator, the poem merely evokes the painful reversal and proclaims the open-ended questions of uncertainty. In six out of seven stanzas Sachs put the word *Schritte* (steps) first, alone on a line. This repetition recalls the portrayal in "Leben unter Bedrohung," where the tramp of approaching boots describes how soldiers force their way into the victims' apartment with regard for neither privacy nor religion. In the prose text from the 1950s the sound is associated with the perpetrators, whose boot-clad feet make them a part of a faceless collective that thinks in terms of "us" and "the others," whereas the relationship is rendered differently in the poem. The more frequently the footsteps recur, the clearer it becomes that they are not being caused by the persecutors but instead electing them as tormentors. The footsteps literally *precede* the division between executioner and victim. They distribute the roles — sometimes this way, sometimes that — providing the soundtrack for a "primordial game." In addition, the repetition imbues the word itself with the character of time — a steady tramping of boots that metes out humans' term on earth "with screams, sighs." The steps become "second hands in the passage of the world." Only the question remains: "what black moon wound it up so dreadfully?"

When Bernadotte was murdered the hands pointed to a black moon. People who had been persecuted revealed themselves to Sachs as murderers. Evidently the roles could be reversed. With time she became careful, therefore, to stress that she had never meant any concrete nation when she spoke of "Israel's body" (which moreover had not been in existence when she wrote the first poems). Sachs by no means denied the young state's right to exist, but "Israel" for her was less fact than notion — a vision, perhaps a destiny, which exceeded temporal circumstances. During the unrest that culminated in the murder of Bernadotte she remarked to Berendsohn, who expressed Zionist sympathies, that the country for her "means far more or also other things besides sowing and reaping, war and peace, science and art, and that its people are not just people like other people. [...] And for that reason alone nothing else is possible for me, as I am ever constituted, but to hang all that I think and do, and so too that which happens in the homeland, by the invisible umbilical cord called eternity."

It may be debated whether this umbilical cord could help two peoples who were in conflict with each other because of a third nation's war crimes. But there is no question that Sachs subordinated the game between victim and perpetrator under a higher authority. The gloomy lesson was that no state was ever just one of the two. Many years later she would write to Domin after having seen a performance of Sartre's *Les Séquestrés d'Altona* (The Condemned of Altona), which had just opened at the Royal Dramatic Theater in Stockholm. In the letter she returned to what was for her the basic conflict, allowing herself to dream of a step beyond destructive dialectics — a stride in the direction of liberation: "One must dare take the step in which executioner and victim are expunged as categories. Mankind cannot and must not remain standing there, if this star is not to perish spiritually. This experience is one I have truly had until the last drop of blood."

A first step was taken already in the 1940s, when Sachs wrote the play which still remains her best-known.

**TEXT** Bernadotte, *Slutet. Mina humanitära förhandlingar i Tyskland våren 1945 och deras politiska följder*, Stockholm 1945 · For letters to Dähnert 10/09/1948 and Berendsohn 03/24/1948, see Briefe 55 and 52 respectively · "Auf daß die Verfolgten nicht Verfolger werden," S (NSW:IV) · *Nachtwache*, ZiS (NSW:III) · "Leben unter Bedrohung," NSW:IV · For letter to Domin 12/14/1960, see BDomin 15 | **IMAGE 7** Count Folke Bernadotte with his family, 1945 (P. A. Norstedt & Söner) · **8** Folke Bernadotte, *Slutet*, 1945 · **9** White buses, 1945 (archive of the Swedish Red Cross)

## AFTER THE MARTYRDOM

In the winter of 1951 the sheets of a German publication were moving through the rollers at Forssells Boktryckeri AB, a printer's in Malmö. The limited edition of a 75-page "Mystery play about the suffering of Israel" was printed in two colors (black for running text, sky blue for headings and personal names), had marbled endpapers and also contained a vignette by the artist Esaias Thorén, a member of the Halmstad Group, which had introduced Surrealism to Sweden and was known for its engagement in social issues. Of the 200 numbered copies, signed by the author, three quarters were immediately dispatched to the subscribers who had financed the printing.

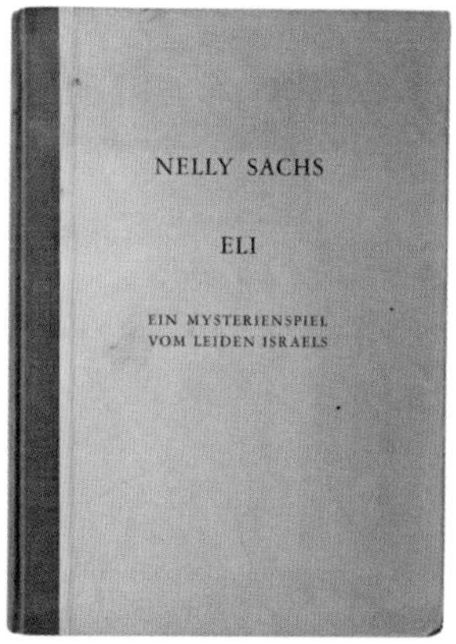

10

The initiative had been Berendsohn's. He had been involved for several years with the publication of the drama whose sky-blue cover print proclaimed the symbol-laden name *Eli*. With the reference to Jesus' last words on the cross — *Eli, Eli, lema sabachtani*, "My God, my God, why have you abandoned me?" — Sachs made it clear that her drama of suffering began where sacrificial death ended. Accordingly, the title page was followed by an indication that the era in which the action took place was the same as the one of which she had written epitaphs in the air: "AFTER THE MARTYRDOM." *Eli* brought its readers into a post-catastrophe epoch, from which the dreadful energies of the trauma could not be thought away. This was the time of the witnesses. But who were these witnesses? And what were they testifying about?

The first tableau paints a landscape of ruins, characterized by pain and loss

— "The square in a small Polish country town, where a few surviving Jews have assembled." At the center stands a symbolic well — the source of memory but also its open wound — around which the dramatis personae meet. By means of repetitions of words and phrases which have less to do with the singsong of folk tunes than with Yiddish turns of phrase, a world that Sachs had read about in Buber's anthologies is conjured. The very first exchange between a pair of washerwomen makes it clear that the drama has little to do with the structure and conflict resolution of classic theater. Here, rather, is a religious legend play rendered with Jewish overtones. "Your grandson's shirt I would like to bear to you," the first woman explains, and specifies: "Eli's shirt —." To which the other woman replies: "How was it, Gittel, that he became mute?" Thus the central issue has been formulated. The play is about a protagonist who is absent, hence its subject is less words than muteness. The text never portrays the murder of the shepherd boy Eli, however, but instead centers on what is neither said nor may be forgotten. In other words: the testimony is about the witness slain. At stake is the writing of history.

Eli incarnates Israel's suffering. When the young cobbler Michael, who in the drama's comments is designated *zaddik*, i.e., "one of the secret servants of God, thirty-six in all, who — quite unbeknownst to themselves — support the invisible universe," when this craftsman decides to go in search of the boy's murderer, he does so out of duty. An "inner calling" transforms him into a figure with limited influence over his own actions. Michael acts, but does so as if controlled by a higher power. He is a seeker of truth without vindictiveness, an administrator of justice minus the retaliation — or a puppet of sorts, without strings. With the arrow of God hidden in his quiver he wanders through "this true legend," finally sees the murderer's face cast its shadow across the boy's bloodied shirt and experiences "once again the bloody events of our lost times," "in a transcendental way." When the murderer — he is a young soldier who thought he was following a secret order — sees Michael's face, God-like in its radiance, he collapses and is dispersed like dust at his feet: "I am falling apart, falling apart — / I am but a stump, / sitting in the sand, / that was just now my flesh — / [...] / My hands, my hands — / O, my fingers, do not disappear —."

This apocalyptic scenario — "an image of regret" according to the comment — is preceded by speaking fingers ("the professor finger's voice," "the wildly gesticulating finger's voice," etc.) and culminates with a "voice" that speaks from above, through a "primordial light" that falls on Michael's forehead, takes hold of him, and carries him away. Now if not before it becomes clear that the play is not intended to reveal the offender or explain his actions. Nor is it about portraying the circumstances of the survivors, caught as they are between the need to remember and the wish for justice. On the contrary, Sachs has the murderer struck by remorse and disintegrate by his own doing into the dust of which everyone has come and will once again be. In other words: the play depicts an inner transformation with ethical overtones which, in essence, could apply to anyone. It is an attempt to take a step beyond the distinction between victim and perpetrator, where the offender realizes his guilt and perishes without external agency.

Latter-day reviewers have dismissed the text as "compensatory theater," but it would be truer to say that Sachs adopted Lessing's reinterpretation of the *katharsis* concept. In this respect, her shift from the designation "legend play" to "mystery play" is instructive. It occurred in the course of her work on the piece and can be followed in her correspondence. While the play's taking place "after the martyrdom" did mean that it portrayed existence in the shadow of the Holocaust, it also indicated that what was being portrayed constituted a testimony whose purpose was an ethical (and perhaps religious) transformation. The final genre specification underlines this. For Sachs the play was not just about the mystery of the Jewish people, or what at one point is termed "the enigma that is the Jew," but in itself also constituted a piece of Jewish liturgy projected onto a medieval Christian genre. As a "mystery play," the text should not just depict the transformation but — more importantly — carry it out. It wasn't enough to portray the change; it must be realized.

Nowhere is this ambition more clearly seen — or rather heard — than in connection with the play's salient symbol: the boy Eli's shepherd's pipe. Made from a bone, it is the actual reason he was murdered. Just before the soldier is turned to dust he confesses: "If he hadn't thrown back his head, / I wouldn't have killed him, / the milk tooth wouldn't have fallen out / together with the shepherd's pipe! / But — it was against the order — / to throw back one's head — / It had to be corrected." Eli's head thrown back doesn't respect the given anatomic-symbolic order. Instead of lowering his head in submission, or at least limiting himself to whistling for the animals, he turns with his mouth open towards the firmament, uttering the trilling sound that establishes a connection with an order greater than that of earthly life. Through the vertical line that thus runs along his spine and up through his throat, the ground he stands on is connected to the sky above his forehead. Thus is created an axis seemingly made for transcendence, based on the transient nature of sound. The murderer admits that it was this direct link between suffering on earth and a higher justice which he feared. The boy was killed not because he was a Jew, but because as a Jew he asserted a connection with divine powers:

> And to whom did he blow on his pipe? / A secret signal? / A sign through the air / — beyond all control — / Help, cobbler, / the milk tooth is growing out of the ground — / is starting to gnaw at me — / gnawing through my shoes — / my feet are falling apart — / becoming earth —

11

A present-day reader might feel bothered by the play's over-explicit symbols (well, shoes, shepherd's pipe). Or by the fact that the scenes are rarely allowed to rest and be sufficient in themselves, but instead must suggest a wider significance which can only be comprehended within a religious frame of interpretation. Some may be disturbed by what could be interpreted as shtetl romanticism, while others react to the author's statements in the postscript, ceremonial and controlling in equal measure. The information that this "mystery play came about following a horrific experience during the still-smoldering fires of the Hitler era, was written down during a few nights following the flight to Sweden," or that the text was penned "in a rhythm which also in terms of facial expressions must make the Hasidic-mystical glow clear to the interpreter," doesn't necessarily facilitate matters.

But such reactions, which are due to the fact that the demon *Zeitgeist* has left the stage, overlook the crucial point: the drama's character of mystery play. It's true that Sachs mystified the origin of the play. The first statement that "this play came about in 1943–44" (later reduced to "a few nights" and even "three nights," as she has it in a letter to Berendsohn) can hardly be correct. But why did Sachs change the dating of the play after the fact? Was it a question, in this case too, of locating the origin so far back in the past that the text could be historicized and thereby achieve a documentary value which would make objections look petty?

In another letter to Berendsohn, Sachs claimed that the play came about "in the feeling that I myself was going up in flames," and she confessed to the writer Paul Schallück in 1959 that the text had "once been written as if in flames." Nonetheless, both the material situation and correspondence with friends show that her work on the play could not have been carried out by divine command, blazing with the consuming fire of inspiration, but must have extended over a longer period of time and appears to have been difficult. What's more, it wasn't finished until November 1945 — a good two years later than the date ultimately given as the date of origin.

One can, as Dinesen does, interpret this stylizing of the poet struck by (heavenly) inspiration as a need to promote the similarities between the martyrdom portrayed and the writer's own role as witness to the fearsome forces of creation — that is, as an expression of an "Orphic ideology of poets." In light of events that were not over in 1943–1944, it appeared logical that a writer who received news about the ghettos and extermination camps would react strongly. When the atrocities were public knowledge two years later, the reaction appeared less prophetic — not to mention in 1951, when the play was first published.

Yet the paradox remains: Sachs wanted *Eli* to be read as a direct consequence of the Holocaust, nonetheless she dated it to a point in time when the systematic extermination of Jews was still going on — and in fact had not yet become

Westdeutsche Allgemeine 16.3.62

Kultur – Unterhaltung

# Tod und neues Leben

**Uraufführung in Dortmund: „Eli" von Nelly Sachs**

**Die Stadt Dortmund hat einen 1961 gestifteten Kulturpreis mit dem Namen einer Frau verknüpft, die in ihrem dichterischen wie in ihrem persönlich-menschlichen Rang Tragik und Größe jüngster Geschichte verkörpert. Nelly Sachs, 1891 in Berlin geboren, 1940 mit der Hilfe Selma Lagerlöfs vor den Schergen Hitlers nach Stockholm gerettet, durch schweres Leid in ihrer versöhnlichen Haltung nur gefestigt, ist die erste Trägerin dieser Auszeichnung.**

*Szene aus der Uraufführung von Nelly Sachs' Legendenspiel „Eli" in Dortmund.*
WAZ-Bild: Fanka

Im Schauspielhaus am Ostwall übergab Oberbürgermeister Keuning die Urkunde des mit 10 000 DM dotierten Preises, der alle zwei Jahre Künstlern zuerkannt werden soll, die dieses Vorbilds der Toleranz würdig sind, dem schwedischen Schriftsteller Johannes Edfelt, einem Freund der durch Krankheit am Erscheinen verhinderten Dichterin. Der Feier, an der auch Bundespräsident Lübke teilnahm, schloß sich die Uraufführung von Nelly Sachs' 1943/44 entstandenem Legendenspiel „Eli" an.

Wie in Else Lasker-Schüler, dem „schwarzen Schwan Israels", verbinden sich auch in Nelly Sachs untrennbar jüdisches Schicksal und sublimes deutsches Sprachgefühl.

Die zugleich mächtige und zarte Hymnik des Spiels, das eher eine Folge von Stationen als ein festgefügtes Drama darstellt, hat ihr eigenes Erdreich, ihre eigenen Bilder. Ihre sprachlichen Wurzeln reichen in die deutsche Romantik, der Nelly Sachs sich als junger Mensch besonders verbunden fühlte.

Darin dem großen Maler Marc Chagall vergleichbar, bewahrt die Dichterin das Erbe des im 18. Jahrhundert in der Ukraine entstandenen Chassidismus, dessen oberstes Gesetz freudig-impulsive Hingabe an Gottes Willen ist. Durch ihr Mysterienspiel, das sich unmittelbar nach dem zweiten Weltkrieg in Polen ereignet, geht der junge Schuhmacher Michael, einer der 36 Gerechten, die der chassidischen Legende zufolge jede Generation haben muß.

Dieser Michael hat „den ungebrochenen Blick ... von einem Ende der Welt zum anderen"; mit ihm findet er den Mörder des Knaben Eli, einen früheren deutschen Soldaten. Als dieser unter den Augen Michaels stirbt, von seinem Gewissen zerfressen, als Elis stummer Großvater die Sprache wiederfindet, schließt sich die zerschlagene Ordnung des Lebens neu zusammen.

Der poetischen Eigenwilligkeit des Spiels, das Baum, Stern, Fußspur und Mörderfingern Stimmen gibt, dem unirdisch-irdischen Klang der Sehnsucht, den es vernehmbar macht, kann nur ein distanziert-strenger Aufführungsstil angemessen sein. Ihn erreichte in Dortmund, wo Imo Wilimzig das Werk mit der Musik von Moses Pergament inszeniert hatte, nur der Bühnenbildner Carl Wilhelm Vogel. Er drückte das tiefste Wesen des Spiels großartig durch Sinnbilder einer zerbrochenen Schale aus, deren Farbgebung Projektionen veränderten. Von den nicht sehr glücklich geführten Schauspielern waren nur wenige zuweilen dem Geheimnis der Dichtung nahe.

WERNER TAMMS

12

public knowledge. The image she wished to project of herself as a writer was not just one of poetic, then, but also of prophetic inspiration, beyond the control and intentions of the writing subject. In this connection, the text becomes interesting even to readers who baulk at a static symbol drama of seventeen "pictures" in which the external events are only rarely characterized by something akin to drama. The play's proper purpose is to bring about an internal transformation of the kind propounded by Lessing. For Sachs it was important that the viewer was drawn into, indeed transformed by the play in a way that recalled the participant in medieval mystery plays, who was expected, after the performance, to return to his business a new man. Eli's shepherd's pipe was a shrill warning in a catastrophic era, but also a signal that could not be ranged within the prevailing system of signs. The sound remained "beyond all control," as the soldier says — possible to perceive in the world of humans, but not a part of its manner of signifying. In addition, as metaphor, the pipe probably referred to the ability of art to go beyond the limitations of earthly life and establish contacts with extrasensory forces.

The play returns to this idea at a central juncture. In the eighth picture, the praying assemble in the prayer tent and the rabbi intones what are known as the "shofar songs":

> THE RABBI'S VOICE
> Tekiah — *a drawn-out, monotone sound is heard.*
>
> A VOICE
> Shevarim — *three sounds follow on each other.*
>
> A VOICE
> Teruah — *a trilling sound.*

*Tekiah, shevarim, teruah*... Eli's signal is a diminutive form of the rabbi's intonations, the shepherd's pipe a miniature version of the horn with which the Jewish New Year is heralded. Originally made of a ram's horn, this shofar recalls both the animal Abraham sacrificed instead of his son Isaac (Genesis 22:13) and the seven horns that sounded before the capture of Jericho (Joshua 6:4). In Sachs, the three sounds clear the air of smoke, blood, and doubt: "The air is new — / gone is the smell of fires, / gone is the stench of blood, / gone is the scent of doubt — / the air is new!"

But between the Jewish New Year (Rosh Hashana) and the Day of Atonement (Yom Kippur) that follows it are ten days traditionally known as "the Days of Awe." Sachs' awareness of this designation is apparent from the lyrical prose notes "Briefe aus der Nacht," where the term is used. Was it during such days that she imagined the real drama in *Eli* taking place? In that case, the shepherd boy's head thrown back and his open mouth would have been a hint of what remained of the catastrophe: a last desperate sound, directed at the sky. After that, only silence was possible. Thus, in the final scene, the horizon opens up "to its widest periphery." And now there appears "a bleeding mouth like a sinking sun." A "voice" is heard:

> Samuel's muted mouth, / open!

A speaking mouth addresses a mute one, a voice urges another to enunciate. The setting sun shows that time has neared the end. Possibly a new time is about to begin. But between them lie the days of awe about which the silent Samuel must testify. Is that why the fourth tone, which according to Jewish custom should be sounded after *tekiah*, *shevarim* and *teruah*, is never mentioned in Sachs' play? *Tekiah gadola* is the designation of the final, very long tone, which is traditionally held until all breath has gone. In the Jewish New Year's ritual it symbolizes the return of the Lord. But in *Eli* it is missing. Or rather, is never heard. But does that mean that it is absent?

As Sachs' dating of the play shows, she wanted the time *after* the martyrdom to be seen as a part *of* it. Did she imagine the play as an enormous exhalation — one last, long, and lamenting silence that bore witness to the catastrophe and quietly transformed the viewers? That would explain why she changed the genre designation to "mystery play," and also why she spoke elsewhere of "cult theater." Her role as writer was far greater than simply being in charge of placing some characters on the stage and having them portray a tragic course of events. Rather, she was a ministrant, as it could not be enough to depict the ethical transformation on stage. The audience must be made part of the martyrdom, too, and leave the theater as other beings. The *Durchschmerzung* she strived for, this "thorough animation of dust" which would reveal "an invisible universe," did not suggest a course of events possible to represent with actions in external reality. It remained an inner development, intimately connected with suffering. In the final analysis, the temporal specification "after the martyrdom" may amount to this: the participating viewer was in a place after the end but before the rebirth — in a caesura in time reminiscent of the transition between ex- and inhalation that the play depicted. Only silence could do justice to this transitional period, these days of awe. Only thus would the audience become co-sufferers.

It is, moreover, hard to imagine that a writer who linked the play's themes so closely to her own fate, who saw herself as a poet with something of both the medium and the ministrant, and who in one place has a child sing in lament "ei, ei, ei" — that this writer did not, in Samuel's cry "Eli!" hear her own pet name ring as well.

**TEXT** *Eli*, ZiS (NSW:III) · For Sachs' comments on *Eli*, see "Anhang," ZiS (NSW:III) · For the term "compensatory theater," see Hellmut Geissner, "Sprache und Tanz (Versuch über die szenischen Dichtungen der Nelly Sachs)," DBdNS, 368 · For letter to Berendsohn 01/23/1957, see Briefe 104 · Letter to Berendsohn 09/07/1959, ABerendsohnD · Letter to Schallück 11/18/1959, DLA · Dinesen,

158 · "Briefe aus der Nacht," NSW:IV · Sachs speaks of "cult theater" e.g. in a letter to Andersch 10/30/1957 and about "thorough animation" in a letter to Abenius 12/30/1957, see Briefe 115 and 120 respectively | **IMAGE 10** *Eli* 1951 · **11** Stage images from a production of *Eli* at the Akademie der Künste in West Berlin, February 1969 (Stadtmuseum Berlin / Harry Croner) · **12** Review of the first performance of *Eli* in Dortmund in 1962 (KBS)

## LI AND THE HAIR

Names play an essential role in Sachs' œuvre. In the title of the prose piece "Chelion," she created a nearly perfect anagram of "Lichen." But more important than actual names, it appears, were individual syllables or letters. The most commonly used pet name for the girl who was baptized Leonie in Berlin-Schöneberg in 1891 — "Li" — crops up so often in the dramatic works that it can hardly be dismissed as coincidence. The syllable is not merely inserted into a boy's name like "E*li*," it also occurs in most of the important female roles: "*Li*li," "An*i*la," "Rosa*li*e," "*Li*litu," "De*li*lah" ... And in the other names it tends to survive as a trimmed but prominent *i* — as in "N*i*na," "Mar*i*na," and "Mar*i*e." The few female names that deviate from this rule are not far removed: "Maya" is used as a diminutive form for "Mar*i*a," while "Azraela" is related to the Bible's "*Lili*th" ...

If Sachs reserved the syllable *li* mainly for women, there are a few prominent cases in which men have names where other letters of the alphabet appear to possess a special significance. Several of the texts from the 1940s and onwards that represent the transition to another dimension thematize Sachs' unconditional view of love. A person who desires another does so with every fiber of her being; only absolute self-sacrifice holds the promise of transformation; only then can death seem a rebirth. The idea is hardly unique, yet is put to use with a consistency, particularly in the dramatic texts, which demonstrates that much must have been at stake for her personally. In this connection the alphabet's most elusive letter, the aspirated *h*, features prominently. It is one of the initials of "Hans Riese" in *Nachtwache*, who manages to escape death but immediately betrays his friend Pavel (and whose other initial, *R*, combined with the first and pronounced in German, amount to *Haar*, "hair"). In the unpublished torso "Das Haar," from which *Nachtwache* was extracted, "Heinz" features as an insurance agent, which he also does in the unpublished play "Der Stein und das Blut" (The Stone and the Blood) where, incidentally, his wife is named "Anila" and the secretary "Lili." But it is in the play *Abram im Salz*, which Sachs began shortly after *Eli* (but didn't complete until April 1951), that the letter is most clearly cast.

This play, too, is an instance of cult theater. During her work on it Sachs corresponded with Berendsohn, who warned her not to exaggerate the mythical element at the expense of real-life circumstances. A couple of months after having completed the text she defended herself: "We must quite simply help

13

lift the world of matter or thirst to the spiritualized world of longing. Of course this is not in itself a dramatic theme, but I went to some effort to find a form for it. After all there are so many good down-to-earth theater plays, might one not for once be allowed to work from the outside inwards?" The play's tendency is reflected in the framework, as the initial instruction makes clear: "During the excavations at Ur imprints of patterns and objects, completely dissolved into dust, were often found on the ground. It was the script of what had already become invisible they were attempting to read." *Abram im Salz* is — literally — a reading drama. From the traces of time past, new meanings will be invoked. Consequently the text begins with a prologue in which an archaeologist falls asleep, reading "patterns kissed into / the Bible of dust": "Music-playing constellations / rushed like wine / in Abram's ear / until he plunged backwards / drunk / struck / by a death / which is no death."

The play depicts this transformation. Once again the time is after the deluge. The ram's horn, however, proclaims that the shepherd boy Abram will rise up against the bloodthirsty tyrant. As yet, the hunter Nimrod's cult of the moon rules the snow-white lunar landscape of Ur, but the desire for another order has been awakened: "Fulfilled is one time / the other begins — / Longing from thirst —." When the fifteen-year-old Abram hears a celestial voice he emerges from the deathly cavern where he is being held prisoner and replies: "You have called me, Abram, / and I so long for you!" Against the tyrant, for whom the barren landscape and the ancient blood cults are enough, stands the young progenitor of the Jews, whose longing is born of the thirst "after a beyond," as Sachs' comments have it. The still-dominant power is self-sufficient, while Abram incarnates the hope of a principle greater than that which reigns in the earth's prison. The salt invoked both brings thirst and preserves the memory of life forms past. That is why Abram can plunge "backwards," hit by a death which will prove to amount to something other than extinguishment. For his coming destiny paradoxically enough lies hidden in the past, in the same way that the archaeologist in the prologue sought future significance in the traces of the past.

In order to illustrate this logic, Sachs repeatedly used the image of a hair. At the beginning of the play the "Mothers' choir" proclaims that "Someone comes / bringing greetings for us from afar / a hair burns on his head." Abram's own mother explains that a "hair shone upon your head" when he was younger. The hunter Nimrod (whom Sachs identified with Hitler) draws his attention to the Word "burning in a hair." And the dancing Lilitu sings about "an umbilical cord in salt" when the transformation finally begins… In short: Abram's metamorphosis is a close shave.

He himself pronounces to the higher power that exercises such a strange attraction: "You draw me / but not with any rope / and I long so for you!" Here the hair symbolizes the link between the lower and the upper, the human and

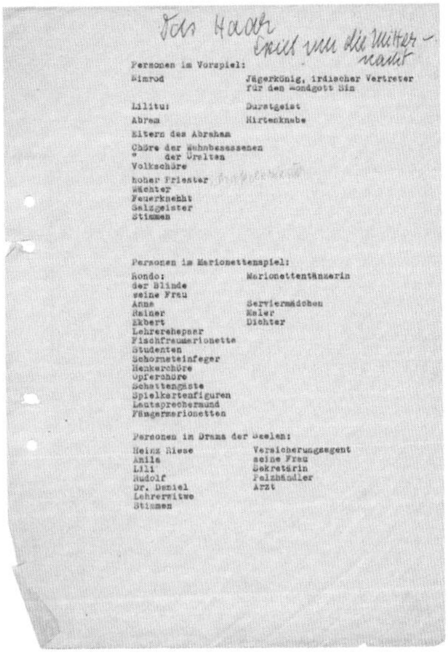
Das Haar

Personen im Vorspiel:

| | |
|---|---|
| Nimrod | Jägerkönig, irdischer Vertreter für den Mondgott Sin |
| Lilitu: | Durstgeist |
| Abram | Hirtenknabe |
| Eltern des Abraham | |
| Chöre der Wahnbesessenen | |
| " der Uralten | |
| Volkschöre | |
| hoher Priester | |
| Wächter | |
| Feuerknecht | |
| Salzgeister | |
| Stimmen | |

Personen im Marionettenspiel:

| | |
|---|---|
| Rondo: | Marionettentänzerin |
| der Blinde | |
| seine Frau | |
| Anne | Serviermädchen |
| Rainer | Maler |
| Ekbert | Dichter |
| Lehrerehepaar | |
| Fischfraumarionette | |
| Studenten | |
| Schornsteinfeger | |
| Henkerchöre | |
| Opferchöre | |
| Schattengäste | |
| Spielkartenfiguren | |
| Lautsprechermund | |
| Fängermarionetten | |

Personen im Drama der Seelen:

| | |
|---|---|
| Heinz Riese | Versicherungsagent |
| Anila | seine Frau |
| Lili | Sekretärin |
| Rudolf | Pelzhändler |
| Dr. Daniel | Arzt |
| Lehrerwitwe | |
| Stimmen | |

14

the divine spheres — or as it was phrased in *Eli*: "hair on the head, / to rise towards heaven in sweaty anguish." The statement suggests a literal interpretation of the Latin *religio*, meaning "bond" or "obligation." The hair is link without being line, instrument of capture without being arrow.

In the last scene Abram repeats his yearning words, and when the bodiless voice at last calls him again he replies: "I am coming!" Thereby the longing ends — what remains is rapture. For with that confirmation, the play concludes with a reply whose consequences cannot be represented within the framework given. In the final epilogue the archaeologist awakens, however, and explains with ponderous import, while the sand runs between his fingers: "Something fell away from me — / Something new has begun in me —." The end of the play is both a termination and a beginning. The act of reading has transformed the dreamy archaeologist, and Abram can become who he will be after his transformation into the progenitor of the Jews: Abra*ha*m.

The *h* of this new name — which in German is pronounced *ha* — ties the letter to *Haar*, or "hair." Unsurprisingly, Sachs gave the extensive dramatic work she was grappling with after *Eli* precisely the title "Das Haar." The play was to encompass several epochs, from prehistoric to contemporary times. It was completed but never published. Sachs' correspondence with friends and acquaintances, as well as "Briefe aus der Nacht," show how laborious the work occasionally was. Unable to come to grips with her "vast subject," as she wrote in a letter to the Swiss writer Max Rychner, she eventually decided to divide the material into free-standing parts, of which *Abram im Salz* and *Nachtwache* made up two. "Das Haar," too, aimed to portray an inner transformation which could only be accomplished with the help of external forces — or as the motto of the text, borrowed from *Zohar*, has it: "From the thread of mercy hangs abandonment." The hair was this "thread"; the *H* perhaps even a ladder of sorts. The play dealt with the same problems as the piece about the patriarch of the Jews, here in places still called "Aba." In a key scene, Nimrod cuts off his hair. The tyrant holds up his booty and asks Lilitu with scorn in his voice: "Are they also washing lines?" At which point the girl points towards the hunter's constellation in the firmament. "Perhaps arrow, / hair and skin / are already joined up there / into a new fabric of light." A few scenes later the context is clarified by the boy's mother: "O my son, my dear son / I believe in the glowing hair / I believe in the burning light / I believe in the new word / that issued from your throat." Hair — light — word: together they wove a constellation which for Sachs indicated a life beyond the martyrdom. Only those who had suffered loss could expect mercy.

With time she must have realized, however, that it wasn't possible to combine a prehistoric drama about hunters and scapegoats with a contemporary drama about executioners and victims without diluting what was particular in each epoch. Not even the surrealistic entr'acte with puppet dancers and playing cards (ace of spades, queen of hearts, jack of spades), which she had thought would alleviate the tension, managed to create a reliable transition. The text looked at risk of becoming an allegory that reduced specific circumstances to universal variables. In the section of “Das Haar” which was reworked and ultimately became *Nachtwache* the hair theme nevertheless survived in several statements. In contrast with the portrayal of Abram, here it was linked to Lilitu’s latter-day equivalent, Anila. “Don’t pull my hair,” she entreats her beloved Pavel at one point. “It so hurts my head.” Anila feels like a victim and likens herself to a fish — a relationship in which the hair serves as fishing line. Also a victim to begin with, the insurance agent Heinz Riese is gradually transformed into (Pavel’s) executioner, and returns repeatedly to a growth of hair which he associates with the Pleiades at one point and with “puppet strings” at another. As earlier, hair symbolizes the link between earthly and divine, loss and mercy, then and now. This time, however, it is also associated with the relationship between man and woman.

In her next play, which Sachs began writing five years later, the theme would be woven into a story about love and betrayal between the sexes. This time she followed Molnár’s example and took the help of the Bible’s story about Samson with the long hair and his seductress, Delilah. Yet there are many instances in her poetry as well where hairs are given special significance. In the cycle of poems “Die Engel sind stark in den Schwachen” (The Angels Are Strong in the Weak) from 1942, for example, an insane mother sings: “With my left hand I grasp something like a flock of birds — / Is it a hair / Which was on a child’s head?” (“Lied einer wahnsinnigen Mutter” [Song of an Insane Mother]). And the next poem in the cycle, entitled “Es gehen viele Stufen” (There Are Many Steps), proclaims: “Down there the soul cries, / Death flowers in its hair —.” In “Chor der verlassenen Dinge” (The Choir of Abandoned Things) from her 1947 collection of poetry she writes: “Are you a ribbon, plucked from a corpse’s hair [?]” In “Abschied” (Farewell) from *Sternverdunkelung* a couple of years later, reference is made to “human hair in a clawed hand / that reft —.” Towards the end of the next decade one of the poems in *Und niemand weiß weiter*, entitled “Was suchst du Waise” (What Are You Looking for, Orphan), pronounces: “The executioner / in the guilt-laden darkness / has hidden his finger / deep in the hair of the newborn.” While another text in the same book, entitled “Die Stunde zu Endor” (The Hour at Endor), declares: “Only a hair — licked by sparks — / shall remain / before David, eternity’s bolt.” The book also contains the poem “Haar, mein Haar,” an explicit summary of the significance of hair for the connection between life and death, childhood and rebirth:

> Hair, my hair, / spread in flashing bolts — / a bush of desert broom, / memory-sparked // Hair, my hair, / what ball of sunglow / has been brought to rest / in

your night? // In your ends a world dies! / God has gently tucked it in, / extinguished it / in a tear-steeped body // But also / in a child's longing's / harrowing wish / about the ever growing beginning / of its balls of fire.

The motto for Sachs' interest might be just that: "memory-sparked." Hair was the living proof of the link between the present and the past. Electrified by the brush, it moved upwards as if of its own will, evoking, paradoxically, something yet to come — an eternally growing, eternally ravaging beginning.

In another poem from *Und niemand weiß weiter*, written in February 1957, just before she finished work on the book, Sachs joined these themes to that of the mourner's adoration of her beloved. The poem is about her mother, and opens with seven stanzas all framed as questions. The first makes it clear that the link between writing and grief is essential: "What emerged from your body's white flowering / when I at the last breath / still called you mother?" The white sheet of paper becomes a body from which the words issue. "What abandoned longing remains on the sheet?" the poem's persona asks, relating the sheet of paper to the bed in which her mother lay as she breathed her last. After another five questions — which heighten the querying from a "time tormented through" to a "stairway of death" the persona wants to charge up the steps of — she remembers the "unearthly receptions" that the two of them were often invited to. "But now: she from love here disbanded / leaning over the tragedy of suffering and stones / brooding over the hair of divorce // and creating a time of the heart / where death is filled with breath / and then emptied again —."

All that is left is the fine marker of severance — an image Sachs used in the final scene of "Das Haar," where she had a distant voice announce after Anila's passing: "Ends with a hair on the pillow." The hair against the white linen became the epitaph of separation. As such, however, it created what the poem terms "a time of the heart." This was no temporality reserved for biological organs with limited duration, but a dimension able to withstand transience at the cost of breathing. It was less about survival than living on. By means of the epitaph, loss was bound to memory. The words' letters may be dead, but just like hair they augured another life. Poetry became the place "where death is filled with breath / and then emptied again" — the *H* being its distinguishing mark, this aspiration turned sign, this "stairway of death" leading up to heaven.

15

**TEXT** *Abram im Salz* and *Nachtwache*, ZiS (NSW:III) · "Das Haar" and "Der Stein und das Blut," NSW:III · Letter to Berendsohn 07/03/1951, ABerendsohnD · For letter to Rychner 10/06/1946, see Briefe 37 · "Lied einer wahnsinnigen Mutter" and "Es gehen viele Stufen," NSW:I · "Chor der verlassenenen Dinge," IdWdT (NSW:I) · "Abschied," S (NSW:I) · "Was suchst du Waise," "Die Stunde zu Endor," "Haar, mein Haar," and "Was stieg aus deines Leibes weißen Blättern," Unww (NSW:II) | **IMAGE 13** Scrapbook pictures from "Das Oblatenalbum" (KBS) · **14** Cast of characters in "Das Haar," typescript (KBS) · **15** Sachs' hairbrush (KBS)

## JUST A FEW LITTLE FLOWERS (COMPENSATION)

When Sachs placed a single strand of hair on the pillow in "Das Haar," not much remained of the Berlin she had left twelve years earlier. Her furniture and property had been bought for trifling sums by SS and SA soldiers; the things she and her mother had not been able to take had been arrogated by pawnbrokers or stolen by neighbors. The library was largely scattered, several of the manuscripts that had been entrusted to friends had disappeared or been destroyed for fear they might be incriminating. The buildings in Siegmundshof and Lessingstraße had been wrecked by Allied bombing. During the first summer after the war, Sachs wrote to Dähnert: "What you say about the house in Lessingstr. is interesting and distressing, just a few little flowers left of our dream garden. But it is also a symbol." The past lay shattered and smoldering. The question was if anything could grow in the ruins. Possibly a few symbolic flowers. The scene her friend conveyed contrasted with the view Sachs would have through the window of the new apartment. "From up here we see the river," she informed Dähnert after the move. The watercourse outside the window may have belonged to the present, but in all likelihood it reminded her more of what remained "after the deluge," to quote the specification in *Abram im Salz*.

When her new home had been repainted and furnished — "Decorating our little home has given me so much joy. Now it really is a home" — Sachs finally had a fixed point in her life. From now on she would be able to spend time on the painful procedure which would lead, several years later, to a modest compensation from the Federal Republic. Before the move she had asked Otto Scheurmann if he could help her with an application for damages in connection with the forced sale and wealth charges of the 1930s. But she had received no reply. In a PS at the bottom of the letter in which she expressed her despair over Bernadotte's death she asked Dähnert: "Has the application for damages been sent in?" At first her friend took care of the contacts with the authorities. Yet the task grew increasingly difficult as Dähnert had recently married and now lived in the "zone," the Soviet-occupied area east of Braunschweig. In letters to her cousin TONI SEEMÜLLER (1893–1972), née Sachs and the daughter of William's younger brother Alexis, and to her brother GUSTAV SACHS (1893–1957) and sister EMMA (1897–1985), whose married name in England was BRANDT, Sachs worked out the ownership picture for a garage lot in the Moabit district which had belonged to the family. When she finally made personal contact with Scheurmann in the summer she could have the matter formalized. The banker was given a power of attorney, a number of forms were filled out and annexes were presented along with the application.

Over the following years the matter was processed by the authorities. The correspondence most of all illustrates how the victims' difficulties weren't over just because the war had ended. How were the survivors to prove that they

- 2 -

II.

Aus der~~/den~~ zu Ziff. I. aufgeführten Entscheidung~~(en)/und/~~
~~gütlichen Einigung(en)~~ steh~~en~~t der Berechtigten nach Massgabe der §§ 14 bis 26 BRüG folgende(r) Anspruch~~/Ansprüche~~
zu:

**DM 24 600,--**

Der Anspruch vermindert sich gemäss § 23 BRüG
um DM -,--
auf DM -,--
Der hiernach insgesamt geschuldete Geldbetrag wird auf
DM 24.600,--
(i.W.: Vierundzwanzigtausendsechshundert Deutsche Mark)
festgestellt.

III.

Von dem zu Ziff. II. festgestellten Betrag sind nach
§ 32 BRüG zu zahlen:
1) bis spätestens zum 31. März 1959 DM 20.000,--
2) bis spätestens zum 31. März 1961 DM -,--
Der verbleibende Restbetrag von DM 4.600,--
ist grundsätzlich bis zum 31. März 1962 zu zahlen.
Im Falle des § 32 Abs. 5 BRüG vermindert sich der Restbetrag auf einen nach dieser Vorschrift zu ermittelnden Hundertsatz.

IV.

Der zu Ziff. II. festgestellte Geldbetrag ist im Rahmen des § 34 BRüG unter Zugrundelegung eines Zinssatzes von 4 vom Hundert vom 1. April 1956 ab zu verzinsen. Die im Rahmen des § 34 BRüG etwa zu erfüllenden Zinsansprüche werden bis zum 31. Dezember 1962 befriedigt.

- 3 -

16

17

had been forced to sell property when no documents could be taken out of the country? Were wealth charges legal just because they had been ratified by a popularly elected government? How were credit balances to be confirmed when accounts had either been frozen or looted by others? Or the consequences of losses be calculated which had arisen due to bans on practicing professions, life annuities and sickness insurance policies falling due, forced sales of personal property and art collections or personal objects with a sentimental value? Not to mention injuries from the time spent as a camp prisoner or slave laborer in the armaments industry... Following Adenauer's announcement in 1951 that the Federal Republic was prepared to pay compensation for the crimes, the Jewish Claims Conference was created to aid people who lived outside Israel. A "Damages Authority" was set up to meet the demands. As the German term *Wiedergutmachungsamt* suggests, damage could actually be "made good" and lost time be repaid. Over the years that followed the authority paid out a total of more than three and a half billion deutschmark as compensation for slave labor, persecution, and confiscated property.

In a letter dated December 14, 1956, which was enclosed with the application for "Damages for the Victims of National Socialism," Sachs described the consequences for her health and her work: "After seven years in Berlin under the rule of National Socialism during which we endured persecution, extortion tied to insufficient nourishment we were totally exhausted and also completely without means. A collection arranged by Swedish and foreign personalities helped us through the first period. Then I began to provide for our maintenance and also partially assumed responsibility for the household as we were living in a furnished room. To this was added daily and nightly care for my gravely ill mother, translations I did for a Swedish committee, and my own poetic work, of which three books were published after the war in Germany." The work was difficult and she was unaccustomed to it, which led to hemorrhages, requiring an operation the year after she had arrived. "However, our financial circumstances were so dire after this that it was impossible for me to take care of myself or recover in any way whatsoever. We were still dependent on what I earned from translations and on gifts given to us by the Jewish congregation and some friends. To consult a doctor was only possible in the most extreme emergency, I was really always working while ill or exhausted. I will not be able to achieve stable health in the future either."

When Sachs began her efforts to obtain compensation for lost property, her mother was still alive. Ten years later she received the notification that her requests as "rights successor" to the recently deceased Margarete Sachs had been granted. Sixteen years to the day after the Wannsee conference, on January 20, 1958, the "Estate and Property Administration" in Berlin finally informed her that she would receive 24,600 deutschmark. On April 1 of the same year she was told that the Federal Republic also intended to pay her a monthly "damages pension" of 550 deutschmark. But it was only seven years later, in April 1965, that she received personal compensation for damage inflicted.

**TEXT** For letters to Dähnert 05/18/1946, 08/14, and 10/09/1948, see Briefe 30, 54, and 55 respectively · *Abram im Salz*, ZiS (NSW:IV) · For the damages policy of the Federal Republic, see Constantin Goschler, *Wiedergutmachung. Westdeutschland und die Verfolgten des Nationalsozialismus, 1945–1954*, Munich 1992 · "Beilage zur Anmeldung von Ansprüchen gemäß Gesetz über die Entschädigung der Opfer des Nationalsozialismus," NSW:IV | **IMAGE 17** "Rückerstattungsrechtliche Geldverbindlichkeiten des Deutschen Reiches an Nelly Sachs" (Brandenburgisches Landeshauptarchiv [BLHA], Rep. 36A Oberfinanzpräsident Berlin-Brandenburg [II] Nr. 32700/32702) · **18** Otto Scheurmann in 1973 (KBS)

## THIRD TIME LUCKY

18

In February of 1942 Sachs applied to the Swedish Foreigners' Bureau, which was part of the Royal Board of Health and Welfare, for an extension of her "alien's passport including due visa thereof." In the entries for "earlier nationality" and "nationality" she stated, as earlier, "German." To the question "When and how did you lose your nationality?" however, she this time responded: "see attachment." The letter from the German embassy which she enclosed confirmed that she had been stripped of her citizenship on November 25, 1941, as a result of an ordinance. When she applied in February of 1942 for an extension of her alien's passport with a residence visa "pending emigration to another country," she had thus been stateless for six months. And would remain so for several years to come.

After the war, Sachs reapplied for an extension of her visa. This time, however, she also asked that her mother and she be approved "for settlement." She pointed out that they had not been able to set out on the planned journey to America and mentioned: (1) that Hermann J. Weigand's health had deteriorated and that he was unable to keep the promises in his affidavit (his daughter Erika had recently committed suicide); (2) that her mother had fallen ill due to "all the mental agitation and suffering"; (3) that returning to Germany after the persecution "has become unthinkable for us"; and (4) that she was now able to guarantee their subsistence thanks to her activities as translator and writer. "With reference to all this we ask for the gracious granting of our application, which would afford us a much longed-for sense of calm." The visa was granted.

Towards the end of the decade Sachs decided to apply for Swedish citizenship. Twice the application was turned down — the first time on November 28, 1950, the second on January 4, 1952, both times with the justification that her "maintenance possibilities appeared very uncertain." She submitted supplementary information, but seemed not to have high hopes. A letter to the Pergaments expresses her concern: "The whole business is nevertheless beginning to worry me slightly, so far I haven't taken it terribly seriously. But now I

19

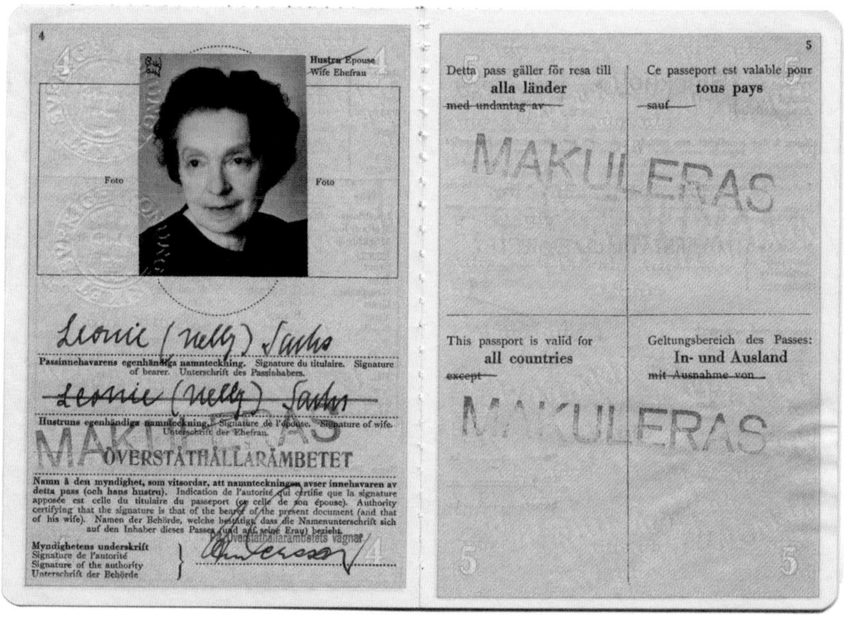


20

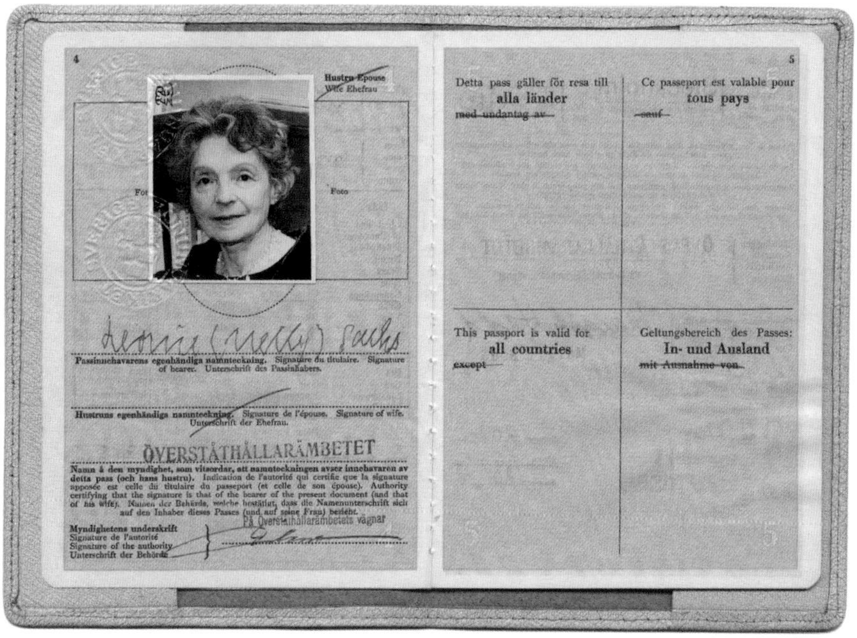


21

have two guarantors, the most excellent references from important people, and still I have heard nothing." Among the people referred to were Gunnar Josephson, Einar Tegen, Johannes Edfelt, and Anders Österling. Still Sachs feared the worst. Perhaps it would be in her disfavor that she had become acquainted with two German actors in connection with an evening of readings at the end of the war? One of them was CURT TREPTE (1902–1990), who had been in Sweden as a political refugee and then returned to the Soviet occupation zone to help with the reconstruction of a socialist German state. (In his luggage he had carried the manuscript of *In den Wohnungen des Todes*, which had been handed to Johannes R. Becher, who in turn had recommended it to Aufbau Verlag in East Berlin.) "Oh my dears," Sachs ended her letter, "if they really don't want me, they should say no. The short time which may still be given to me I can also spend without any nationality."

Three days later His Royal Majesty's government decided to admit her as a Swedish citizen. Germany had finally turned into a foreign country.

**TEXT** Extract from the Justice Ministry's documents regarding "Sachs, Leonie *10 / 12 1891 statsl.-tysk / m *Berlin kv.," ASachs · "Bilaga till ansökan om visering" 02/20/1948, ASachs · For letter to Pergament 04/22/1952, see Briefe 89 | **IMAGE 18** Curt Trepte in the 1940s (AAdK) · **19** Sachs' passport 04/19/1960 (KBS) · **20** Sachs' alien's passport 03/23/1942 (KBS) · **21** Sachs' passport 03/16/1965 (KBS)

## EVERYTHING WHICH HAS BEEN BREATHED INTO THE AIR

After six months as a Swedish citizen, Sachs wrote to Kurt Pinthus in New York: "But I will never again move anywhere from Sweden. For Israel it's too late." She added: "Tied to the German language, a person doesn't have much to hope for as a Jew. That's why everything uncertain must wait." (Literally the last sentence reads: "That is why everything must wait which has been breathed into the air" [*So muß alles warten was in die Luft geatmet wurde*].) The new homeland may be offering her a place to live, but a new *Heimat* it would never be. And Germany had ceased to be that for good. The break between the past and the present was too sharp. Sachs needed the language but not the country. What was left was the air, breathed by victims and perpetrators alike — which, transformed into poetry, nonetheless meant "rescue from suffocation." Although Sweden would never be a proper homeland, and although it had become too late for Israel, there was something still waiting. What this "everything" "breathed into the air" might have been she never explained. But it is likely it had to do with people which Sachs in the letter to Pinthus called "those left over, spread out."

Sachs' experiences as a refugee were colored by the tenet of Jewish theology which holds that the original vessel of creation was shattered. From Buber and Scholem she learned that the mystics gathered the shards that had been spread across the world under the term *Skekhinah*, literally God's "dwelling" in Israel, which was interpreted as indicating the Almighty's presence wherever his dispersed and banished were. Among the term's secondary meanings are "joy," "tranquility," and "peace." The foreword in one of Sachs' two copies of Scholem's translation from *Zohar* contains a number of highlightings and underlinings, pressed flowers, exclamation marks, and notes written in the margin. For example, she noted the various steps in the discourse of the ten emanations of the tree of life, underlining that the first of these *sephirot* was designated "NOTHINGNESS" and putting a point next to the statement that the second was "the point which at the beginning of time sprang from the source of

Nothingness." Following the account of the step-by-step dissemination of the divinity in Creation, she made notes until she came to the description of the tenth *sephirah* of the tree of life, which differed from the other nine in that it did not represent an active principle but a passive one. In the margin she highlighted the passage, and also marked individual words in it: "*Skekhinah* signifies nothing in and of herself, she is just the sea into which all the other emanations flow out and appear as a unit. No longer hidden or undeveloped, as in the *Urpunkt*, but realized and purer, one is tempted to say: become an act which is in itself a resting, like the sea."

Here Sachs found a theological model for her personal wish to find rest in the diaspora. Whether or not she shared the mystical view of a god's exile from himself, this belief in a divinity who left the origins before time and space in order to pervade Creation and who in all his serene enormity, all his restful splendor was represented by a female principle, may be an interesting query, but is not essential to the understanding of the poetic universe that Sachs established in *her* exile. The exegesis provided her with images that matched her own experiences. Despite the pantheistic credo that occasionally emerges in letters and poems, she neither wanted to nor could ignore the wound caused by twelve years of dictatorship. The texts which she accorded bibliographical status were based on this fundamental experience of loss. Death was the prerequisite of what grew in her poetry from 1943 onwards. The columns of smoke with which she had begun her first book of poetry were an emblem of the complex relationship between writing and transience, grieving and survival which appeared subsequently. The chimneys were tragically ironic signs: not only did they remain after the dead had been murdered and cremated in the camp ovens, thus marking their absence like cenotaphs, but they also contributed to this very disappearance. As black indicators or "fingers" they pointed to the threshold area where life and death passed into one another. This "route for refugees" was nonetheless *itself* "of smoke," suggesting that the only salvation for the dead lay in being dispersed in the same air that the living breathed.

"That is why everything must wait which has been breathed into the air," Sachs pointed out in her letter to Pinthus. By means of the chimney smoke her work had been begun with an image she later inverted in the notion of being thrown into "an 'Outside.'" In "O die Schornsteine" it wasn't the poet who was subjected to a threatened exterior, but rather the dead who were incorporated as foreign dust in the inner selves of the living. The only chance the murdered had of surviving the second death that being dispersed in the air amounted to, was to be harbored by the living. This obligation to incorporate something which nevertheless remains external and foreign is a recurring trope in Sachs' œuvre. From its contradictoriness she eventually derived a poetics of sharing, tuned in the keys of fear and compassion, which strived ever so slightly

22

23

24

22 Nelly Sachs and Margareta Lindh (Danneskiöld-Samsøe)
23 Nelly Sachs and Lenke Rothman
24 Lenke Rothman and Sivar Arnér
25 Alfred Andersch
26 Erwin Leiser
27 Artur Lundkvist
28 Peter Hamm and Elisabeth Borchers
29 Hella Appeltofft
30 Hermann Hesse

25

26

27

28

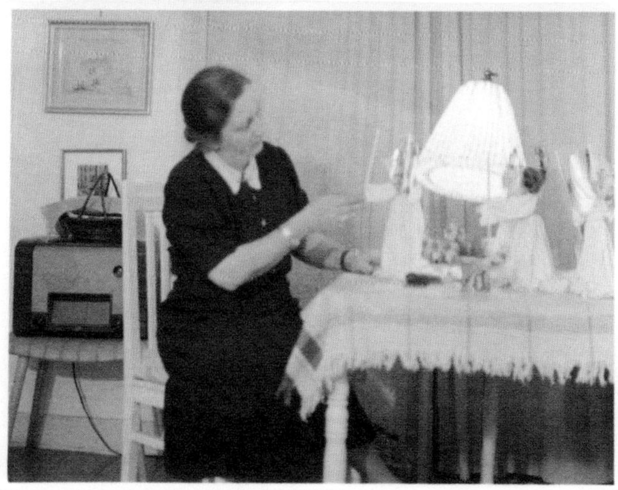

29

30

to have the dead and living exchange attributes in a transformation whose dimensions were as lyric as they were cosmic. The basic condition, however, remained the desperate awareness of vulnerability, as well as the conviction that the poetic word was governed by the death of the others — all those "who were like me, the others who were different from me and the same, the little siblings," as it is stated in a prose text by the sibling soul who would came to mean most for Sachs' later development: Paul Celan.

It is against the backdrop of such poetics that Sachs' repeated avowals that she did not miss a family must be seen. Although her father died in 1930 and her mother twenty years later, although she didn't have any siblings or children, and although many people who were near and dear to her disappeared in the camps, she eventually acquired both "sisters" and "brothers." That which conventional kinship ties could not provide, friendships would confer. After her mother's death Sachs built herself a community based not on principles of ethnic background or geographical domicile, that is, on *Blut* or *Boden*, but on the perception of vulnerability. To her "sisters" from the Berlin years were added, during her Swedish exile, women who were often of Jewish descent, including neighbors such as Grete and Elisabet Alsberg, Elisabeth Knoche, and Rosi Wosk. As her "brothers" she would eventually regard not just Swedish colleagues such as Edfelt, Lindegren, and Ekelöf, but also German poets such as Andersch, Celan, and Enzensberger — as well as distant outsiders such as Kafka and Beckett and historical or fictitious figures such as Abraham, Baal Shem Tov, and Saint Francis, the cobbler Michael, and the Great Anonymous.

31

The latter brothers make it clear that distances in time and space were no impediment to Sachs' view of kinship. Siblings were not something she had but something she chose — from among the living and the dead, from life, longing and literature, history, myth and religion. Often they were cast as chosen ones. Perhaps she even saw them as unknowing *zaddikim* on whose shoulders salvation rested, which in that case would suggest that the sharing she had in mind was of a community of pain, founded on the deaths of other siblings and the conviction that we know nothing, as a late poem has it, other "than that your loneliness / is not mine."

32

Nonetheless Sachs did make distinctions. The brothers, who for the most part were poets, critics, or literary historians, she turned to for support and encouragement in her literary work. Her sisters, on the other hand, did not necessarily have to be active in literature or the other arts, even if several were (including Brita Edfelt and Margaretha Holmqvist). With them she felt freer, was able to exchange confidences and give vent to her more everyday side. Phrased differently, she mainly found her female family members in social life, whereas the male members tended to be found in literary life. In the latter case it is possible that the Swedish habit of addressing professional colleagues as "brother" had some significance. The Swedish women writers with whom

Sachs had personal contact were Fogelklou-Norlind, Tegen, and (towards the end of her life) Birgitta Trotzig, but those who meant something for her literary development — such as Lagerlöf, Södergran, and Boye — she never met. And of the German colleagues, one was a fleeting acquaintance (Ingeborg Bachmann) and another was limited to correspondence (Hilde Domin). Only Ilse Aichinger and Elisabeth Borchers, who for some years was Sachs' publishing editor, really broke the pattern.

The new acquaintances that Sachs made in and through literature strengthened her identity as a new-born poet. To a degree rare among writers of her fairly advanced age, she developed a poetic idiom in dialogue with others' works. However, this was less a matter of the kind of intertextuality which is best described in terms of sources and influences, and more one of family likenesses. Only exceptionally did she use quotes and allusions consciously. Sachs' poetry was never "learned" in the conventional sense. She read avidly, but unsystematically and mainly in order to find meaning in existence. What she discovered in the course of this wide-ranging and intensive but also disordered reading were commonplaces, as Bengt Holmqvist has pointed out: "The very fact that they were commonplaces was her most important literary discovery." This explains, to a large extent, the representative, occasionally universal trait one finds in the early part of her œuvre and which distinguishes it from Celan's, for example. More intuitive in her relationship to other works, Sachs created a field of signification based on affinity, friendship, likeness.

This may be seen especially clearly in her correspondence as well as in her efforts as a translator. The latter was an activity which she characterized as "very close to my heart" in the "Vorwort" (Foreword) of her first anthology. While it was true that her choice of writers was based on the canonical names of Swedish modernist poetry, the selection of texts also revealed that this was not a translator who could just as well have been interpreting other poems. Titles such as "Als die Mutter starb" (When Mother Died), "Das Land, welches nicht ist" (The Land That Is Not), and "Nach dem Tode" (After Death), to pick but a few examples from the first third of the book, placed the translations firmly in the same thematic sphere that Sachs' own poems inhabited. In this manner a language economy was established between "siblings," which would have an effect not just on her recognition in literary Sweden, but also on the way in which she conceived of poetry as precisely sharing.

The four "exploded sonnets" from Lindegren's *mannen utan väg* which were included in *Von Welle und Granit* reminded readers familiar with the translator's own works of the drastic shifts between figurative and concrete elements, the elliptical syntax, and rhetorically charged atmosphere which would become her own poetic mark:

## *EN SYSTER TILL KAFKA*

*Nelly Sachs.*

Om man utöver hans tre köttsliga systrar vill söka Franz Kafka också en andlig sådan behöver man för närvarande inte gå långt för att finna henne. Hon bor på Reimers holme, är känd under namnet Nelly Sachs och utgör det senaste exemplet på att en särpräglad litterär begåvning fortfarande kan leva på undantag vägg i vägg med en reklamhungrig tid. Detta och sin judiska börd och tyska dialekt har hon gemensamt med sin store diktarfrände, men dessutom förenar dem en annan och närmare släktskap som det skulle behövas en hel liten avhandling för att rätt bestämma.

Sin diktsamling "In den Wohnungen des Todes" (Aufbau-Verlag 1947) har Nelly Sachs ägnat åt en mycket speciell om än inte alldeles unik situation i den judiska diasporan, ett massläge där all handling definitivt kringskurits av död och intighet: de tyska förintelselägren. Man måste säga det vore svårt att finna en mera värdig prövosten för den chassidiska moralen. Huruvida den i verkligheten bestod provet är en fråga för sig; att den i diktsamlingen gör det är i varje fall uppenbart, och det är tillräckligt för att ge Nelly Sachs verk ett omisskännligt drag av vad man plägar kalla för stor poesi.

Vad innehåll och motiv beträffar formar sig "In den Wohnungen des Todes" till en lyrisk triptyk. Det vänstra sidostycket därav ägnas åt lindandet och undergången, som tecknas i klart lysande bilder mot en bakgrund av sotsvart mörker. En klagande monoton smärta drar genom dessa dikter och kommer avdelningen "Gebete für den toten Bräutigam" att påminna om vissa partier av Garcia Lorcas "Blodsbröllop". Det högra sidostycket är en variation på samma tema, nu sett från trons och den paradoxala tillitens vinkel. Israels långa lidandesväg ser författarinnan fortsätta genom årtusendena, tåget genom öknen mynnar ut vid nutidens krematorieugnar och sveper i breda rökslöjor över himlen; men dessa "vägar av rök" bildar dock frihetsvägar för Jeremias och Jobs stoft. Här utvecklar lidandet all sin dialektiska förmåga; vad som än sker, så tycks meningen vara, äger människan ej att hängiva sig åt den bottenlösa smärtan. Den utestänger henne från en rätt överblick och begränsar hennes förståelse för de sammanhang vari hon ingår. I triptykens mittparti slutligen, en serie "Gravskrifter, skrivna i vatten och vind", sammanfattas och i viss mån upphäves de båda sidofälten. Ledsagat av något som påminner om Kafkas gåtfulla svala leende får det namnlösa lidandet namn och gestalt. Författarinnan liksom träder ett steg tillbaka från sina bilder i svart och vitt för att låta det mänskliga och begränsade intaga sin plats mellan det obegränsade och det ofattbara, medan erövrarna passerar i taktfast passo romana med sinaifolkets nedgående sol som en röd matta under fötterna. Här finner man några av samlingens bästa dikter, bland dem de prov på Nelly Sachs konst som Edfelt lämnat i "Nya tolkningar".

*Ragnar Thoursie.*

33

die Hand zittert im Schwindel auf der Würgungen Leiter / gierige Tränen prasseln in der Nachtigall leerem Bauer // schon die Trauer allein fordert mehrere Todesopfer / auch ein Eisenbahnunglück stammelt Verzeihung // ein abgeschältes Auge brennt; Kurzschluß und Einsamkeit / und das Schicksal photographiert noch eine verwunderte Leiche // das Feuer verheert auch das unversicherte Herz / und des Leidens Wächter fliehen zu einem Glaubensfond // anonyme Stacheln träumen sich zur Wirklichkeit / und schaukeln sich zum Dorn auf der Wirklichkeit Abhang // aber ein Ruf von Schmerz rollt einen Berg hinauf / und wirft sich auf eine Steile um zu zerschellen // grandios weilt des Schmerzes Flucht auf der Adler Tuch / während der Wind hübscher Gesichter Kartenspiel mischt

the hand trembles in stupor on the stranglers' rungs / greedy tears rustle in the nightingale's empty cage // the very fact of mourning claims several victims / a railway accident, too, stutters forgiveness // a stripped eye is burning: short-circuit and solitude / and fate photographs one more surprised corpse // fire ravages the unassured heart as well / and agony's wardens flee to a theme of faith // nameless prickles dream their way to reality / and sway into thorns on reality's slope // but a cry of pain rolls up a mountain / and throws itself off a precipice to shatter // pain's flight rests grandiose on the eagles' cloth / as the wind shuffles the deck of courteous faces

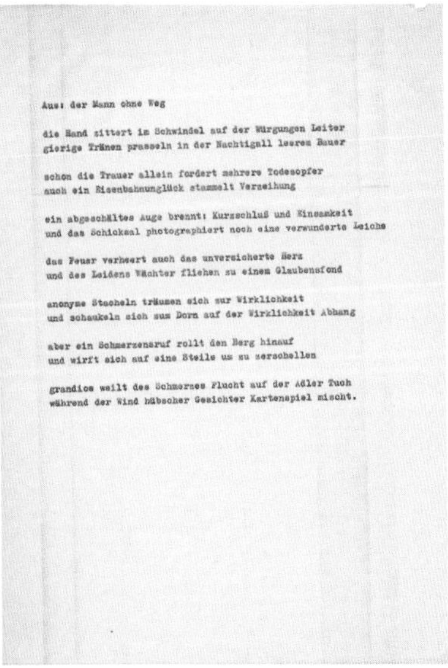

Aus: der Mann ohne Weg

die Hand zittert im Schwindel auf der Würgungen Leiter
gierige Tränen prasseln in der Nachtigall leerem Bauer

schon die Trauer allein fordert mehrere Todesopfer
auch ein Eisenbahnunglück stammelt Verzeihung

ein abgeschältes Auge brennt: Kurzschluß und Einsamkeit
und das Schicksal photographiert noch eine verwunderte Leiche

das Feuer verheert auch das unversicherte Herz
und des Leidens Wächter fliehen zu einem Glaubensfond

anonyme Stacheln träumen sich zur Wirklichkeit
und schaukeln sich zum Dorn auf der Wirklichkeit Abhang

aber ein Schmerzensruf rollt den Berg hinauf
und wirft sich auf eine Steile um zu zerschellen

grandios weilt des Schmerzes Flucht auf der Adler Tuch
während der Wind hübscher Gesichter Kartenspiel mischt.

34

The flight of pain in Lindegren signaled the same cosmic ambition that Sachs sought from *Sternverdunkelung* and onwards. Eventually it led to a radical transformation of the conditions of poetry and life, most effectively captured in the title of her last 1950s book, *Flucht und Verwandlung*. Texts such as "In der Flucht" (During the Flight) and "Hier ist kein Bleiben mehr" (No One Can Stay Here Any Longer) set the tone. The flight still took place in "the dwellings of death," yet these abodes were now regarded as a place of birth — or at the least as the place where the promise of another beginning could be discerned. The epitaphs were still being written in the air, but from now on the wind acted as a cosmic assistant. Sachs could even speak of a "rest on the flight" and claim, in a couple of lines frequently quoted: "In homeland's place / I hold the transformations of the world —."

Through those "left over, spread out" the foundations were laid for a growing network where new contacts were continuously being added. Located in the air, like a celestial sea of interconnections, this web brought together the living and the dead, realia and legends, and promised if not release then at least rescue. Or as Sachs wrote to Edfelt: "From a shattered reality to come close to the existing reality, despite all the slipping to try again and again, are things that don't wait for a publisher and a printing run. They are breaths through which one lives." The rest was stitches, void, and hope. Poetry wasn't about taming the uncertain or recapturing what had been lost, but about letting losses become an integral part of itself. In the air waited everything that had been exhaled.

**TEXT** For letter to Pinthus 10/02/1952, see Briefe 91 · Zohar, 31, 32, and 36 · Celan, "Gespräch im Gebirg" (1959), *Gesammelte Werke*, ed. Beda Allemann and Stefan Reichert, Frankfurt am Main 1983, Vol. III, 172 · "Immer ist die leere Zeit," GR:II (NSW:II) · Holmqvist, 29 · "Vorwort" and "Die Hand zittert im Schwindel auf der Würgungen Leiter," VWuG (NSW:IV) · "In der Flucht" and "Hier ist kein Bleiben mehr," FuV (NSW:II) · For letter to Edfelt 01/14/1953, see Briefe 92 | **IMAGE 22** Sachs and Margaretha Lindh (Danneskiöld-Samsøe) on Sachs' birthday in 1961 (Photo Anna Riwkin, KBS) · **23** Sachs and Lenke Rothman on Sachs' birthday in 1961 (Photo Anna Riwkin, KBS) · **24** Lenke Rothman and Sivar Arnér, 1959 (KBS) · **25** Alfred Andersch in 1965 (Annette Korolnik-Andersch's collection, Berlin) · **26** Erwin Leiser in 1951 (Stadtmuseum Berlin / Harry Croner) · **27** Artur Lundkvist in the 1950s (Photo Berndt Klyvare, ABFS) · **28** Peter Hamm and Elisabeth Borchers in the 1950s (KBS) · **29** Hella Appeltofft in the 1950s (KBS) · **30** Hermann Hesse in 1927 (With the kind permission of Suhrkamp Verlag, Frankfurt am Main / Berlin) · **31** Rosi Wosk in the 1950s (Bertil Wosk's collection, Järfälla) · **32** Saint Francis (KBS) · **33** Ragnar Thoursie, "En syster till Kafka," *Stockholms-Tidningen* 10/13/1947 (KBS) · **34** Sachs' translation of one of the sonnets in Lindegren's *mannen utan väg*, typescript (KBS)

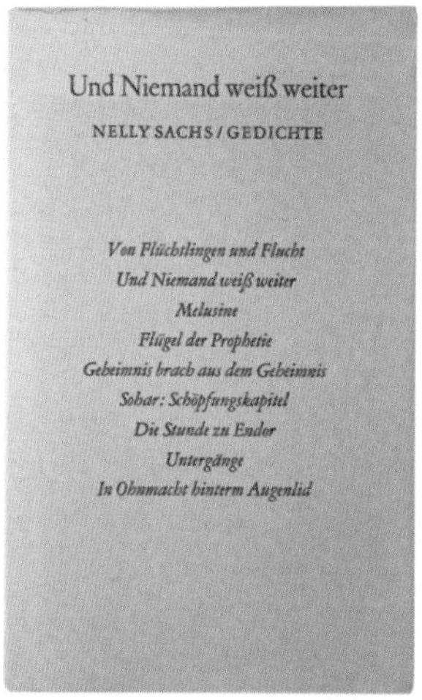


35

36

## *BUCHSTAUB*

The two poetry collections of the 1940s constitute the glowing core of Sachs' œuvre. Both were devoted to the consequences of Nazi terror. While the former book's choruses and epitaphs sang of the loss in an exalted, sometimes liturgical tone that converted biblical psalms of lament into modern poetry, the latter explored the dialectics between victim and perpetrator and what remained after the sun had burnt itself out. Dedicated to her father's memory, *Sternverdunkelung* had Sachs searching for a valid articulation of experiences which ultimately could perhaps only be expressed as refusal or absence. The poem brought that which was invoked to life, but this life was made up of the signs of death. Although smoke was no longer rising from the chimneys, the texts were written in the shadow of the Holocaust. As indicated by "Warum die schwarze Antwort des Hasses" (Why the Black Response of Hate), the era of the threat, moreover, had not ended: "Why the black response of hate / to your existence, Israel? // Stranger, you / a star from farther away / than the others / sold to this earth / so that loneliness be inherited."

Crucial to Sachs' view of the relationship between executioner and victim was their interchangeability. As the programmatic poem "Auf daß die Verfolgten nicht Verfolger werden" showed, there was always the danger that the persecuted would turn into a self-appointed administrator of justice. Yet *Sternverdunkelung* also contained poems whose Old Testament figures recalled the "Biblische Lieder" (Biblical Songs) from the 1930s, and some of which would return in the dramatic works — kings and prophets such as Abraham and Jacob, Job and Daniel. Israel featured, too, "once nameless, / still entwined in the ivy of death, / eternity worked secretly in you." In contrast to the previous book, the tribal name now indicated the people as well as the land. Primarily, however, it remained synonymous with a transhistorical promise — which was made clear in the poem that opened the book's fourth cycle: "Land of Israel / chosen starsite / for the heavenly kiss!" After this representative poetry,

37

where Sachs could appear as her people's "prophet" (with a designation from an unpublished poem), a new phase was begun, characterized by the engagement with Buber's writings, the discovery of *Zohar* and the tradition of religious mysticism to which Jakob Böhme and Master Eckhart belong. Additionally, texts about moral and religious issues by contemporary writers such as Albrecht Goes and Georges Bernanos, Graham Greene and Simone Weil played a significant role.

At the same time the mood in literary Germany was changing. The acute situation of the first postwar years made way for a more matter-of-fact but also increasingly severe tone, which was partly politically motivated and had as much to do with the divided country as with an incipient generation conflict. Roberto Rossellini had recently premiered his *Germania anno zero*, whose title suggested that it was a matter of starting again from scratch. Aptly enough, young literati with experiences from the front line were at the same time preparing to shake up the literary scene. Among the names in what would go down in history as "Gruppe 47" were several who ten or so years later would become important for Sachs — including Andersch and Enzensberger. A few words from a program article by the group's leader, Hans Werner Richter, summed up the situation such as it appeared to many: "The distinctive mark of our era is the ruin. It surrounds life. It is the outer symbol for man's inner uncertainty in our time. The ruin lives in us and we in it. It is our reality, which requires depiction."

Richter's proclamation was not directed at writers who had spent the war in external or internal exile, and even less at ex-camp inmates. The wavering quisling Gottfried Benn and the ambivalent Elisabeth Langgässer, or emigrants such as Döblin and Feuchtwanger, were not among the envisaged readers either. Nor were, for that matter, refugees such as Peter Weiss and Cordelia Edvardson from the younger generation. On the contrary Richter, a former prisoner of war, wanted to give a voice to the generation that had grown up under National Socialism and in many cases also taken part in the final stages of the war. He demanded a new realism, free of elegiac embellishments and encumbering pathos. Clean, straight, and chastened, it would find "behind reality the unreal, behind rationality the irrational." The internal emigrants' nature scenes, ruminating digressions, and tableaux from an increasingly shabby spiritual life were passé once and for all. The war had put the aesthetic pretensions to shame. If one just cleared away the high-flown pomposity, the wasteland would hold the promise of a new beginning. Young literature ought to brush off the past as if it were dust and rise from the devastation like a Phoenix from the ashes. Put differently: Richter's ruin was not Sachs'.

The literary climate which came to characterize Adenauer's republic evinced no particular interest in the poetry that spoke in *In den Wohnungen des Todes* and *Sternverdunkelung*. The first book was printed in 20,000 copies and widely

Am 17. Oktober wird Nelly Sachs in der Paulskirche zu Frankfurt/M. der Friedenspreis des deutschen Buchhandels überreicht.

5



Nelly Sachs.

Ekstatischer Aufstieg und künstlerische Entwicklung

Nelly Sachs hat im Winter 1943/44 die Gedichte der Sammlung "In den Wohnungen des Todes" und die dramatische Dichtung "Eli, ein Mysterienspiel vom Leiden Israels" geschaffen und in den folgenden Jahren die Gedichte der "Sternverdunkelung". Kaum eine Familie unter den europäischen Juden, die verstreut leben in allen Erdteilen, ist unbeteiligt an der Katastrophe des jüdischen Volkes im Dritten Reich. Sechs Millionen Menschen, alle unschuldig, die meisten wehrlos, sind auf mannigfaltige Weise umgebracht, vor allem aber in den Gasöfen des Ostens wie Abfall und Kehricht verbrannt. Nelly Sachs hat die gewaltige Totenklage um ihr Volk angestimmt, den Kindern, den Männern und Frauen, den greisen Menschen, die verstummt sind, Stimme gegeben, und läßt das ganze Universum, von den Steinen bis zu den Sternen, mitsingen in den riesigen Chören der Toten und der ~~wenigen~~ Überlebenden. Tag und Nacht werkten die Vernichtungsanstalten,und ihre Rauchfahnen verdunkelten das Licht der

38

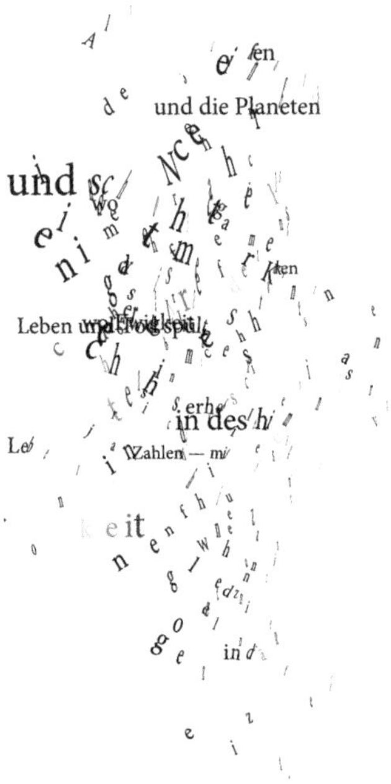


distributed, while the latter was published in a small edition and sold poorly to boot. After that Sachs had difficulty getting published. The Bermann-Fischer-Verlag announced that it was going to remainder the edition and that it didn't intend to publish any further titles by her. Eight years passed until *Und niemand weiß weiter* in 1957, during which Sachs' poems appeared sporadically in periodicals. Only *Eli* was published in this period — in a private subscription edition of 200 copies. The German book market was busy with other things than the experiences with which her name was associated. During these years Sachs worked on grandly conceived dramas which were technically difficult to stage, wrote some prose, and compiled a second anthology of translations, *Aber auch diese Sonne ist heimatlos* from 1957. Her work was at a crossroads: how to move on without abandoning (the memory of) the dead?

With the help of the Kabbalah she found an answer or rather a method: the purpose of poetry was to effect a comprehensive change to existence, on a par with the mystery plays. In an important letter to the literary critic MARGIT ABENIUS (1899–1970), whom she appreciated as an authority on Boye and Weil, Sachs maintained: "I believe in the working through of pain, in the dust's consummate animation as a labor in which we are part. I believe in an invisible universe, into which we write our unclear fulfillment." At around the same time she noted in her comments on Berendsohn's essay "Ekstatischer Aufsteig" that the notion of an invisible universe was "quite simply my own credo." The two books of poems with which Sachs would return to the public eye in the second half of the 1950s were about flight and arrival in a new world and time, but above all tried to stir up matter and transform the dust in the manner of the mystics. For *Und niemand weiß weiter*, death played the central role in this all-encompassing metamorphosis which seemed to know no limits; for *Flucht und Verwandlung* two years later, the same role was taken by life. "O meine Sonne" (O My Sun), the first book's opening poem — "Da du" (As You) — has it,

> I spin you into / my love's prison of falling stars / in the asylum for my breaths / this the quietest of suicide flocks.

Correspondingly, the opening poem of the second volume — "Wer zuletzt" (He Who Is the Last) — proclaims:

> He who is the last / to die here / will carry the seeds of the sun / between his lips / let the night thunder / in the death throes of decay.

It was surely no coincidence that both collections began with an image of the sun. In the former the poet was its keeper, perhaps even defender, but also the leader of the suicides. The poem was seen as a hiding place spun of oxygen for a celestial body that was lost and regained with every new breath. In the latter case, by contrast, the sun constituted the hope of survival for he who had died as the last of men — a seed borne where breaths (this multitude that freely chooses death) leave the body.

Even if Sachs partly renewed her imagery, it must have appeared overblown to readers like Richter. Was it not possible to cloak one's feelings in less cumbersome attire? Could the message not be formulated one size smaller? Such objections ignored the issue, however. For Sachs it wasn't about the sun in general, but about "my sun" — an irreplaceable life source behind which a specific person was standing who needed the poem's persona to be done justice. ("I was long doubtful as to whether I should publish such deeply private things at all," she pointed out when she sent a transcript of the poem to Borchers. "Then I thought: such a short time left, perhaps, on earth — it could be that someone else comes along and takes it up.") Only as "encapsulated love word" could the life principle be given form, embedded in language like the fly in amber. The poem's persona might be nothing without her sun, yet at the same time the sun would not be able to assert itself without the poem. When lips were pressed against the prayer's stone in the final stanza and kissed "lifelong death," this was done "until the singing gold seed / ruptures the rock of parting." For Sachs longing was lifelong. At least. In time and perhaps eternity the poem's persona hoped that with the aid of song, glowing with the fire of the other, she would break through to the concealed dimension of existence where farewells weren't definitive.

*Flucht und Verwandlung* opened with precisely this expectation: "He who is the last / to die here / will carry the seeds of the sun / between his lips." The end, it turned out, was not a culmination as much as a transition. For Sachs the gauges never pointed to zero. Lips that would one day be sealed for good held the seed of continuation. In the same way poems could glow with an inner magma which wasn't their own but nonetheless amounted to the reason they had been brought into being. In one copy of Scholem's translation Sachs underlined the word *Keruvim* and noted that it designated the forces that rise upwards in sacrificial smoke and are also known as "pillars of smoke." The strength of her own alphabet columns derived from the same transition. Dust, light, and love's prison of shooting stars: poetry was made of shimmering book dust. *Buchstaub.*

**TEXT** "Warum die schwarze Antwort des Hasses," "Israel," and "Land Israel," S (NSW:I) · For the unpublished poem, see Arch. 317, ABerendsohnD · Richter, "Die Literatur im Interregnum," *Der Ruf*, 03/15/1947 · For letter to Abenius 30/12/1957 and Borchers 06/07/1957, see Briefe 120 and 108 respectively · Comments on Berendsohn's "Ekstatischer Aufstieg," ASachs · "Da du," Unww (NSW:II) · "Wer zuletzt," FuV (NSW:II) · Zohar, 71 | **IMAGE 35** *Und niemand weiß weiter* 1957 · **36** *Flucht und Verwandlung* 1959 · **37** Rossellini shooting *Germania anno zero*, Berlin 1947 (Filmmuseum Berlin, Deutsche Kinemathek) · **38** Walter A. Berendsohn, "Ekstatischer Aufstieg," typescript (KBS)

## JOY, SORROWS, AND FRIENDS

In the summer of 1956 Sachs received a visit from ALFRED ANDERSCH (1914–1960). After having deserted during the final phase of the war, he had spent a year in American prisoner-of-war camps. On his return to Germany he founded the periodical *Der Ruf* with Richter and organized the meeting which is generally regarded as the launch of Gruppe 47. In the 1950s he became known for poems and short stories that centered on the question of the individual's freedom of choice. When Andersch visited Stockholm he was also a radio editor of growing influence and the editor of *Texte und Zeichen*. The contact had come about when Sachs had offered the periodical translations of Swedish poetry and prose. Andersch declined (to begin with), but mentioned his forthcoming trip to Sweden. At the end of May she replied: "I am really sorry that the Swedish poets do not appeal to you, I do think they have their very own manner of expression. Torn away to an utterly different world myself, I admire their spirit. Of course I would be delighted to receive you in my little apartment by Bergsundsstrand."

The meeting would have great significance and contribute to the growing interest for Sachs' works in what she called "the younger generation" — i.e., among people who had experienced but not created the madness of the 1930s and 1940s. When Andersch descended the stairs in Bergsundsstrand a few hours later he was carrying newly written poems and translations. The translations were published the following year in the first installment of *Text und Zeichen*, which Sachs called "the Sweden issue" and wished to see in every Swedish bookshop; the poems were published a few issues later. The friendship was sealed by Andersch's repeated wish to broadcast *Eli* as a radio play. Sachs' doubts were considerable at first, but she let herself be persuaded by Berendsohn, who had gone to some effort to have the play performed on Swedish radio. When she sent her manuscript to her young friend in Stuttgart she brought up her doubts: "But this is nothing for Germany, I know that and feel it. It is my firstling and was entirely written in the flames of a terrible suffering."

Was Sachs afraid that a play about "the enigma that is the Jew" would stir up ill feeling? Was she fearful of the retaliatory tones which could hardly be said to be absent from the German press and public debate at this time? Did she baulk at the transformation that the new medium would bring, which also meant that the text had to manage without the help of the reading eye? Or was her concern, rather, for Andersch and what might happen to him if he realized his plans?

There were likely several, and complicated, reasons. In her accompanying letter Sachs mentioned that a "composer" had already taken on *Abram im Salz* but had chosen a different route from the one she intended and turned the spoken word into song. Now she had handed the piece completely over to him, but perhaps one might consider something newly written for German

Upprinnelsen till mysteriespelet är en fruktansvärd [illegible] upplevelse under Hitlertiden. Det hedskrävs i Sverige efter min flykt hit. Syftet har varit att föra upp det över alla gränser lidandefyllda på ett trascendent plan för att göra det möjligt att uthärdas och för att trots allt låta ett skimmer av det gudomliga lysa ner i natten.

Stockholm i mars 1959.

39

radio? She herself imagined that the play *Nachtwache* would be well suited to a radio adaptation. Andersch, however, wanted *Eli*. Once in agreement, Sachs suggested that the composer mentioned could provide some background music — perhaps a lullaby or a dance reminiscent of the Hasids'? The composer in question was Moses Pergament. But in Stuttgart they managed just fine without specially composed music. Instead Sachs and Pergament collaborated on the libretto, for at the same time the Swedish Broadcasting System acquired the rights to what in its finished form would be an opera. The text was translated by Edfelt.

During the late winter Irmfried Wilimzig visited Stockholm. He had been entrusted with directing the German radio play and wanted to make changes in consultation with the author. On May 23, 1958, the drama had its first performance, on the Südwestdeutscher Rundfunk. Three days later a repeat was broadcast. And at the beginning of July Sachs took her seat next to the Israeli cultural attaché Jakob Horowitz and his wife Etschi in a Sveriges Radio studio, where they listened to a recording. That same night she wrote to Andersch: "I would never have believed that this poem, which is constantly taking off from the earth, would be so suited to a radio play. And now everything is there." Sachs' joy was unmistakable, also because the director had so carefully taken the spoken character of words into account. In a play set after the martyrdom, the characters couldn't sing as before — that is to say: as if nothing had happened. Andersch not only respected the author's intentions, he understood them too.

Less joy came from Sachs' impression of Pergament's opera. During the spring she tried to temper her friend's tendency to reinforce every statement with melody and vibrato. But the spoken parts à la Luigi Nono that she'd envisioned were turned into conventional singing parts. After having heard the German radio play she tried to influence the final work on the opera in a direction more consistent with her artistic convictions. "This is not primarily an external dramatic development," she clarified apropos of *Abram im Salz*, "but about a spiritual one. A dawning insight about an invisible concept of God amid a people still in a state of trance and seeking, surrounded by the darkness of night." The same thing applied to *Eli*. Sachs couldn't let voices which belonged in the Polish countryside, in a time following the catastrophe, risk any likenesses with the sounds once heard in the opera houses of Dresden or Bayreuth. Nor was she willing to accept that the secret servant of God, the cobbler Michael, who went "quietly, almost whisperingly [...] through this legend," was stylized as a triumphant avenger. "It is not my *Eli*, but in this version yours."

The last sentence came in the letter with which she congratulated Pergament on his success in connection with the airing of the opera by Radio Sweden on March 19, 1959. On the one hand she was pleased for her friend. Having endured many years of disdain in the Swedish public sphere — not without anti-Semitic overtones — he deserved every bit of positive attention. On the other hand, the sentence made it clear that the finished work had precious little to do with her original intentions. Behind the joy sorrow was concealed. And after having pondered a review in *Svenska Dagbladet* on the day after the premiere, she was beset by painful forebodings. For the reviewer, Kajsa Rootzén, the piece appeared to be just the sort of oratory of revenge that Sachs had wished to avoid. The pulse of the drama was on the inside — in the bond the words established with an empathic audience. The play did not proclaim revenge and Michael had nothing of the hero about him. In a letter to Edfelt, Sachs clarified her criticism. In Germany they had been "so careful with the word, I would even say they protected it, in order that it should reach people, and they resolutely refused to give preference to the music except in a few single themes. I had myself suggested to Moses that he might write the shofar songs and the old Jewish children's song — no more was really needed there. But now: the mother sings the child's death. Michael has been entrusted to a young heroic tenor — a cobbler's apprentice who seeks a murderer and at last finds him and finally feels a sort of triumph that he receives the righteous punishment. And to make matters worse, Kajsa Rootzén sees Michael's character as an avenger, whose hatred dissolves the murderer like acid." Pergament's opera had turned the victims into the last thing she wanted them to be: persecutors.

Over the next few weeks Sachs' health deteriorated. The problems with the opera were a nervous strain; in addition, she suffered a minor heart attack. Artistically speaking she felt not just misunderstood, but betrayed. Her relationship with Pergament was not improved by her having sent a letter to the editor of *Svenska Dagbladet* to explain her position, following the review. In it she repeated her thoughts from the letter to Edfelt and continued: "In this obscure world, where some sort of secretive balance appears to prevail all the same, innocence is always made victim. The child Eli and the murderer's child both die, as victims of evil. But never for a moment does the mystery play wish to portray either the murderer's end or his child's death as some kind of act of vengeance." To emphasize the personal nature of the subject she added: "The origin of the mystery play was a terrible experience during the Hitler era. It was written in Sweden after my flight here."

In the manuscript Sachs had originally mentioned "a terrible *event*" (*händelse*), but decided to cross out the noun and instead write "experience" (*upplevelse*). Did the difference matter? Perhaps not. Perhaps in this way: fateful events were bad enough, but what ultimately mattered for literature were the experiences. Or: for the poet the crucial thing was not the catastrophe in itself, but how one related to it. Or: *Eli* did not want to dramatize the actions which led to the main character's death, but show how they were perceived by those who came after. That is to say: the play was not about murder and reprisal, but about trauma and testimony. Eventually the portrayed experiences could possibly be transformed into events which affected the viewer. But for the audience as well as the witnesses on stage, the original was available only in the crossed-out state.

**TEXT** Letter to Andersch 05/29/1956, DLA · For "the Sweden issue," see e.g. letter to Andersch 01/08/1957, DLA · For the background to *Eli* as a radio play, see Sommerer, 67–79; see also Uwe Naumann, "Ein Stück der Versöhnung". Zur Uraufführung des Mysterienspiels *Eli* von Nelly Sachs," *Exilforschung*, ed. Thomas Koebner, Munich 1986, 98–114 · For letters to Andersch 10/30/1957 and 07/04/1958, and to Pergament 02/02 and 03/21/1959, see Briefe 115 and 127, and 133 and 135, respectively · For Rootzén's review, see *Svenska Dagbladet* 03/20/1959 · For letter to Edfelt 03/24/1959, see Briefe 136 · Sachs' clarification regarding *Eli* is dated "Stockholm in March 1959," ASachs | **IMAGE 39** Detail from Nelly Sachs' letter to the editor of *Svenska Dagbladet* in March 1959 (KBS)

40

41

**IN PURGATORY**

In the 1950s Sachs spent time at Sigtunastiftelsen (the Sigtuna Foundation) north of Stockholm on several separate occasions. These stays at the culturally oriented institution, initially run by Ungkyrkorörelsen (the Youth Church Movement), served for both work and rest. With access to a large library and surrounded by nature, she found peace and regained her strength. In his memoirs, the then director, minister, and writer OLOV HARTMAN (1906–1982) recalls that Sachs stayed in the guest house as early as in 1954. He cites the dedication in a copy of *Sternverdunkelung* in which she mentioned "the rare time of reflection at Sigtunastiftelsen," and describes how he unexpectedly ran into her one day. Behind the vault that separated the chapel's original building from an extension was "a protected place. Opposite it hung a crucifix in the gothic style, not there to mark the place where the conversation took place — it was there anyway for anyone who wished to see it." One day Hartman met Sachs, who stopped on her way to the exit, looked up towards the crucified one and declared, in German: "I, too, love Him."

The anecdote shows that the guest's religiousness was not limited to one doctrine. Sachs too could love the incarnation of the article of faith which had been laid down in the New Testament. After the war Hartman had traveled through divided Germany, and in 1956 his translation of Sachs' prose piece "Leben unter Bedrohung" would be published in the foundation's periodical *Vår lösen*. During the years that followed he published several texts by and about Sachs, among them one in which he noted that in "her poetry the Jewish and the Christian saints don't contradict each other." Baal Shem Tov could stand side by side with

Francis, the sand where Abraham found the murmuring shell of God's secret could carpet the ground under the feet of the apostles. The important thing was not individual Bible scenes or theological issues transformed into dogmas, but the suffering and compassion that characterized all religions. Hartman read the work as a "reason for soul-searching": "It is not in the public debate that these poems gain their true relevance, but in the soul's distress, where the surface of judgment ruptures and one asks the question for the ultimate reality." In such a situation, not many books retained their value, but Sachs' poems were among those he did not want to do without. "They have been in the crucible."

The assessment says something about the contemporary reception of Sachs' œuvre, but also something about Sachs' personal situation in the 1950s. Thought-wise she was still in the crucible, or at least in purgatory. The texts seemed both to beseech and evoke the pain. When Hartman sent her a copy of his religious play *Den brinnande ugnen* (The Burning Oven) she wrote back to thank him. The play "burns in my heart. This testimony speaks of ancient violence, calling to mind Bernanos' words dug up from the abyss of the human soul. So was it with me too, back in Sigtuna with your morning devotions — these hot, trembling attempts beyond the limits quaked in every word — and so it is included in each of your works with the ever new breath." She finished with an image which is recognizable from elsewhere: "My own things, always arising so close to death, meant for me merely the rescue from suffocation." Literature imparted a relief which it nonetheless threatened. It created an insightfulness which it simultaneously put in danger. The poems were written to allay the anxiety but came about in an eruptive fashion — like panting breaths or a "lung hemorrhage until extinction," as she confided to Ekelöf.

This paradox was to take concrete form at Sigtuna. A couple of weeks after Sachs' reaction to Pergament's opera she visited the foundation. A short time earlier she had written to Abenius to describe how she felt "thrown into an 'Outside'" but at last had begun to feel faith — not least at the thought of a younger generation that didn't view her poetry as modernist experiments but "as lyrical passion." The reason for the visit was one of the "poets' conferences" which were regularly held at the foundation and in which several younger colleagues were going to take part. As the patient sheet from her internment at Södersjukhuset two years later shows, however, Sachs was forced to flee the gathering head over heels. Among the participants she thought she had identified a Nazi spy. Purgatory wasn't over. On the contrary. Over the following years the situation would worsen.

**TEXT** Hartman, *Färdriktning*, Stockholm 1976, 306 and 55–56 respectively · Hartman, "Lovsång i Inferno. Några drag i Nelly Sachs diktning," *Vår lösen*, 1965, no. 5, 213 and 215 · For letters to Ekelöf 07/05/1965 and Abenius 03/17/1965, see Briefe 216 and 125 respectively · Hartman, *Den brinnande ugnen*, Stockholm 1959 · Letter to Hartman 01/01/1959, SSA | **IMAGE 40** Sigtunastiftelsen (SSA) · **41** Hartman in the 1950s (Photo Per Anders Thunqvist, SSA)

## CONFIDANTE OF THE NIGHT

Now as before, night offered Sachs the greatest sense of security. "Up here we are now fully shrouded in night from 3 pm," she informed Kurt Pinthus at the end of December 1959. "But that is good for work. This lack of images awakens one's own depths, and much rises that has slept during the light-filled summer." The only time she had been able to dedicate to poetry while her mother was still alive remained, ten years later, associated with work and trust. But the disagreement with Pergament and the events at the Sigtuna Foundation contributed to making her feel increasingly threatened, and soon even her nightly dimension could no longer provide shelter. The persecution she had experienced in Berlin had left its mark — and Sachs' knowledge of what had happened during the war didn't make it any easier for her to trust her environment. At the same time as public appreciation grew — not least in Germany, where in 1957 she had been made "corresponding member" of the German Academy for Language and Literature in Darmstadt, and in 1959 been awarded the German Industrial Federation's literature prize — the first clear symptoms of persecution anxiety appeared.

The illness would mark the remaining years of Sachs' life, in effect coinciding with the increased public attention. The opera version of *Eli* had shown not just that her artistic intentions might be misunderstood, but also that she couldn't have blind faith in her friends. When Berendsohn at around the same time announced that he intended to write a study of "the poet of Jewish destiny," she was pleased with the purpose but feared the outcome. After she had sent him her comments on the preliminary study "Ekstatischer Aufsteig" the pair spoke on the telephone. The aging literary historian confessed that Sachs' many deletions paralyzed him in his continued work. Writing a few days after the Lucia holiday in December 1959, she clarified: "Dear me, yes, it is difficult with my friends. Perhaps precisely because they know me, they all think they have the right to know my way in life." Then she continued: "Over the years I have told you much of my inner self — much more than I have told any of the others. That should make you realize how gratefully I receive your friendship. Of course I would not like for these things that I have said in confidence to be made public." Without wishing to, and without being able to help it, she felt threatened even by people close to her. At first Pergament and now Berendsohn. During their conversations she had come out of her shell, sharing intimate details about herself and her past. Suddenly these confidences were threatening to end up in the hands of an uncontrollable public. Poetry was one thing; life, after all, another. "My things I am putting out — now towards the end of my life — since the young generation wants them —, but as for myself I would like to disappear in darkness."

42

A similar worry is expressed in letters to KÄTE HAMBURGER (1896–1992). The literary historian had returned to Germany a few years earlier and had recently attended a lecture given by Berendsohn at the university in Stuttgart, where she was tenured. Sachs justified her interest in what had emerged with the remark: "I asked him a long time ago not to touch so much upon my private and earlier life. It is after all about my work and not about me. Otherwise I feel helplessly exposed. He means well of course, and I am always afraid to upset him bearing in mind his age, but for myself I would rather remain in darkness." As a writer she remained the confidante of night. During the dark hours she felt alone but safe. The absence of images afforded rest from external impressions, stirred up deeper strata, and brought the dregs to the surface. But when the movable patterns were illuminated from the outside, as in the case with Berendsohn, and traced to underlying formations at the bottom of the soul, Sachs recoiled. Only a properly protective blanket would help.

43

One of the poems in *Und niemand weiß weiter*, entitled "Salzige Zungen aus Meer" (Salty Tongues from the Sea), may be read as an allegory of the wish that the finds pulled from the deep be left alone by strangers' eyes:

> Salty tongues from the sea / lap at the pearls of our illness — / The rose on the horizon, / not of dust, / but of night, / sinks into your birth — / Here in the sand / grows its black / cipher wound in time / grows like hair / does even in death —

At the same time as the thirst for understanding licks the riches clean, the flowering night sinks towards the origins. The poem describes an inversion: the treasures lie glittering but inviolable while the text's guiding metaphor — this dome-shaped form that is perhaps the black sun of melancholy — glides through the nether darkness. In the end it is not the revelation of some hazardous truth but the secret in itself, this "cipher wound in time," that emerges. It is hard not to recall the word "event" which was replaced by "experience" in the letter to *Svenska Dagbladet*: the poem points to life's hidden occurrences, but wound up in the coded time of experiences. The cipher grows with every touch, like a rare but aberrant pearl. The significance, however, remains inaccessible. Or put differently: the coded gift of poetry broadens the horizon for what it is to understand. Its meaning includes the ungraspable too.

During the dark half of the day Sachs was closer to the lost than to the living, could become ill from memories and long herself to death. Yet when day arrived with its anecdotes and social obligations she would rather drain out of the poems like water. Just the sand, the salt, and the pearls need remain. The text had to survive by its own means, without reference to the domiciled citizen she was during chats on the stairs or the telephone. Only that way would what had been said carry on growing — even after what she described in her correspondence with Berendsohn as "the end of my life."

**TEXT** Letter to Pinthus 11/21/1959, DLA · For letter to Berendsohn 12/15/1959, see Briefe 155 · Letter to Hamburger 10/16/1959, DLA · "Salzige Zungen aus Meer," Unww (NSW:II) | **IMAGE 42** Käte Hamburger in the 1950s (Universitätsarchiv, Stuttgart) · **43** Bergsundsstrand at night (KBS)

# THE HELLS OF BOSCH AND BREUGHEL

## A MIND CAPSIZES (THE SACHS CASE)

The heart attack was an omen. As 1960 was about to begin, the strategies that Sachs had developed to protect herself from the threatening world around her began to totter too. Worrying reports from her former homeland reached Bergsundsstrand. War criminals were moving with impunity in the public sphere, pursuing careers and filling important functions in a democratic society. Shortly before Christmas the newspapers reported that the Bundestag had rejected a law against incitement to racial hatred. During the holidays members of the Deutsche Reichspartei desecrated the synagogue in Cologne by painting swastikas on its walls. A parliamentary debate was turned down on the grounds that anti-Semites could not be given a public forum. The Hamburg newspaper *Die Welt* played down the events and sided with Adenauer, who assumed that they were in fact actions planned by the twin country in the east, with the aim of destabilizing the Federal Republic. The editor-in-chief Hans Zehrer — who twenty years earlier had sat on the board of the Reich Literature Chamber — responded to critics by printing pictures of protesting writers such as Heinrich Böll and Paul Schallück (who was corresponding with Sachs at this time) alongside one of Cologne's rabbi Zvi Asaria in prominent profile. There was no mistaking the intention: the nose was the message.

While in Sachs' new homeland the brown sympathies from the war had been stowed away along with lapsed ration cards and filters for vehicles run on wood gas, Swedish newspapers still informed about neo-Nazi tendencies. In February, for example, it was reported that the Justice Ministry had toughened the laws against incitement to racial hatred after discovering that right-wing extremists were printing and distributing anti-Semitic pamphlets in the country. The problems in connection with Pergament and Berendsohn complicated the situation. Although it was hardly their intention, it turned out that her friends' involvement might constitute a threat both artistically and personally. Days and nights grew more uneasy, her insomnia increased. At the same time as the nightly writing opened the sluice gates, it became more and more difficult to maintain the boundary between the intimate sphere and the surrounding world. Sachs felt besieged.

Her gradual deterioration can be seen in the intermittent notes with which she resumed the lyrical prose diary from the beginning of the 1950s. In "Briefe aus der Nacht" she had written: "Holding on is like dying. My head is sick. The same illness as you my mother," and hinted that it was the same complaint that the main character in *Simson fällt durch Jahrtausende* suffered from. Between the spring of 1956 and the summer of 1965 she continued to make notes about places where life and poetry could not be separated. An entry in these "Weitere Aufzeichnungen" (Additional Notes), dated April 1956, includes a poem which was never published and which describes the very point of intersection. Here eternity turns out to be immersed in the present:

> Look the number "eight" in the eyes / the meandering snake's constellation // So too is life: never runs / into its end / but skin is no limit / for longing's meteors

On its side the 8 formed the sign through which Sachs wished to contemplate existence. For someone who regarded life through eternity's spectacles, barriers and boundaries could only constitute obstacles of a temporary sort. Actually there was neither an end nor any limits. The numeral was a line that tied existence to a dimension beyond transience — a "lasso thrown from outside" which incorporated the ephemeral beings in a world wider than that of earthly life.

One year later Sachs returned to the idea. "Geometrical eternity of colored dust breaks out," she wrote in the summer of 1957. Sachs was in the middle of her reinterpretation of the drama about Samson and Delilah and was pondering how the timeless related to the temporal. "Samson's power, the real power is in the hairs (paths of light through the millennia). He only used the force of the dust. Delilah's treason — treason against the divine force, she is killed when she holds the hair. [...] And suddenly everything into the present. Simply man, woman, secret." Eternity was part of the present, but could be severed from it by the definitive slash of treason. Then the uncovered presence was transformed, its meaning coded and turned into a "secret." Sachs usually associated this mystery with the nightly hours and concealed contexts of existence. But even if the nightly dimension communed with unearthly forces, it might inhibit. "Torment me — torment me," an entry from July 1959 has it: "Out — out — like the magic dancer. Take me — take me — midnight is no hour — midnight is maturity." The stroke that turned one day into the next was really a splitting of time — the moment when the night was separated from itself and the self plunged into eternity's abyss. Sachs longed to achieve "maturity," the coveted moment when the writer had become ready, like Samson, to fall "through millennia." Both the Bible's long-haired judge and her own mother had suffered from "falling sickness"; was she not their kin? Although she felt her grip loosening progressively, the critical stage had not yet arrived: "I am not falling yet — still not — 'The sinking is there for the sake of the rising — here is no longer a lasting stead.'"

One year later it happened, however. In the summer of 1960 Sachs did what Samson had done. And her mother. She fell. The next diary entry is from October of the same year and was made in Ward 29 at the Beckomberga mental hospital. Behind her lay eight weeks of inferno. Now she wasn't wishing herself away but home — to an existence far from lies and delusions: "'Prayer' about no longer falling so far away from the truth —." Again she cited the words about the hidden purpose of falling which so many years ago had been used as a motto for one of the poems in her first collection of poetry, "Einer war, der blies den Schofar" (Someone Blew the Shofar): "'The sinking happens for the sake of the rising' — But by now using all force — all courage to continue the *Durchschmerzung* of the darkness —." A letter to Dähnert explained the quote by pointing out that "the path is an inner one — the path everyone must walk." Then she reproduced some words of Master Eckhart (probably quoted from Buber's *Ekstatische Konfessionen* [Ecstatic Confessions]) and added: "The way of the mystics is described thus in the Song of Songs: I have gone beyond all mountains — and my entire ability, all the way to the Father's dark force. Then I heard without sound, then I saw without light, then I knew smells without scent, then I tasted that which was not, then I perceived that which did not exist. Then my heart became baseless, my soul loveless, my intellect shapeless and my nature featureless. And so I begin anew each day this rising — I fall — I try." The inner drama had begun.

What happened between the summer of 1959 and the following one? What made Sachs abandon the thought of breaking out of the night and sinking through the millennia in the hope of being caught and borne by the present? Although she regarded existence as a heaving sea, the fall caused her anguish. Something made her lose faith in life's unsteady craft — or at least in the 41 square meters with a view of Lake Mälaren. Why did she tell Ilse Pergament in May 1960: "this apartment has become such a great dread for me, that I can no longer remain there"? What was threatening the cuddy and making her mind capsize?

**TEXT** For an account of the political climate in the Federal Republic in 1960, see Barbara Wiedemann, "Das Jahr 1960," *Paul Celan: Biographie und Interpretation – Biographie et interprétation*, ed. Andrei Corbea-Hoisie, Konstanz, Paris, and Bucharest 2000, 44–46 · For the information about the Justice Ministry, see Dinesen, 301–302 · "Weitere Aufzeichnungen," NSW:IV · The poem in IdWdT is entitled "Einer war, der blies den Schofar" (NSW:I) · For letters to Dähnert 10/20/1960 and Pergament 05/10/1960, see Briefe 175 and 161 respectively · Martin Buber, *Ekstatische Konfessionen*, Jena 1909, 15–16

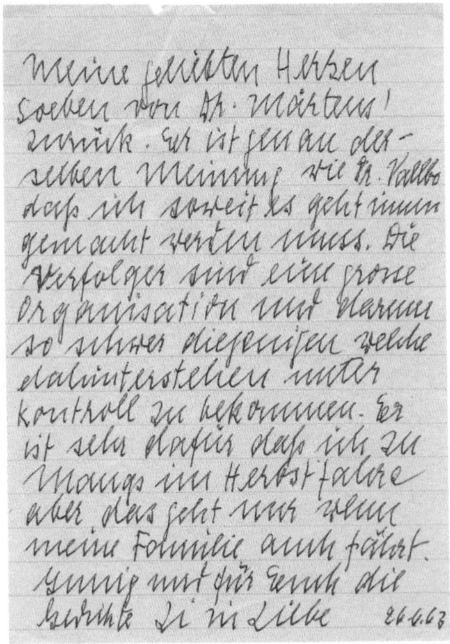
Meine geliebten Herzen
soeben von Dr. Märtens!
zurück. Er ist genau der-
selben Meinung wie Dr. Vallbo
dass ich soweit es geht immun
gemacht werden muss. Die
Verfolger sind eine grosse
Organisation und darum
so schwer diejenigen welche
dahinterstehen unter
kontroll zu bekommen. Er
ist sehr dafür dass ich zu
Mangs im Herbst fahre
aber das geht nur wenn
meine Familie auch fährt.
Innig mit dir Euch die
Gedichte Li in Liebe 26.6.63

1

## MATHEMATICS À LA SATANE

One answer is given by one of the rare texts Sachs wrote in Swedish, "Sedan omkring ett år" (Since about one year). The document lacks proper title and date, but appears to have been written to Hälsovårdsnämnden, the Public Health Board (or possibly to Gunnar Josephson), as a plea for help in a situation which was threatening to overwhelm her. Similar turns of phrase occur in a typescript in German that Moses Pergament marked "March 1960" and "Nelly on her suffering in her home." It also mentions a certain "Fräulein Lindgren von der Hälsovårdsnämnden," which makes it likely that the Swedish text was written at about the same time. "Since about one year," Sachs explained in imperfect Swedish, "a carving sound can be heard by the faucet in the kitchen. It could first not be localized if it was over or under my apartment — but one did not get the impression that it had to do with daily household work. — This noise went on throughout the day with a few intervals. Late in the evening it began again and continued during the night in a different manner."

The walls no longer protected against the encroachments of the outside world, the plumbing and wiring made such a methodical racket that she could only interpret it as coded signals. A machine seemed to be operating in the apartment above "and all night clickings and bangings are heard at different intervals making a sleep impossible." There was hammering, too, "then there is clicking in the kitchen and the room i.e. everywhere." Could such an organized din be a coincidence? No workmen worked both day and night, did they? "Since there is not any peace in the apartment not in the day not in the night my health and literary work is seriously threatened. As I also work at home I must be suffering even more than other tenants who are away for most of the day." Sachs drew the logical conclusion: it was a case of systematic terror.

Her neighbors — retired policeman Stig Svensson and his wife Signe — averred that not even the water which flowed from the faucets was safe. "On Good Friday 'the motor' has apparently gone out of order that even my neighbors the Svenssons became aware of this loud noise and told me that they now and then had got such things as an electric shock by the faucet." The conscientiously placed quotation marks around "the motor" demonstrate not just that Sachs was searching for the correct word in Swedish, but also that she suspected that the sounds were more than a coincidence. Somewhere in the building was a machine the purpose of which was to upset existence. The methodical din was directed at a writer who happened to be of Jewish descent. Or was it mere chance that the motor went awry precisely on the longest, loneliest day of the year? And that it electrified water, this cleansing element? No, the terror Sachs had experienced twenty years earlier wasn't over. It had just changed face and method. In letters to friends and acquaintances she threw her final caution to the wind. "A workshop has secretly infiltrated the apartment above mine," Rudolf Peyer was informed in May 1960. "They are young, probably unemployed people and they give me no peace during either day or night. The worst thing about this is that so many people are involved in it that I am utterly helpless. Am no longer able to sleep, have to do so in a neighbor's apartment. In human terms I have had this experience, a Hitler crowd in miserable and immense cowardice." One week later she concluded in a letter to Ilse Pergament: "My apartment was the telegraph center with Morse signals and all the devices. I have pledged to keep quiet about it, and will so do."

For the vulnerable Sachs there was nothing to do but grin and bear it. Hopefully her silence would be interpreted as untouchableness. At any rate, her attempts to bring the terror to the attention of the authorities and administration of the building failed. Worse: people close to her appeared to doubt the veracity of her claims. Either they didn't believe her or else they tried to downplay the significance of the noises and interpret the causes on a different tack. Were the radiators playing up? Was it a matter of building works? Renovations? Perhaps the alcoholic lady who lived upstairs, and who Sachs feared, simply received unusually noisy company at night? For the writer in the apartment below such explanations smacked of subterfuge. Gallingly, her own past experiences were given no credit in this context. Actual experiences were dismissed with reference to misinterpreted noise. Did they in fact distrust her intentions? In that case it was best to remain silent. Perhaps her friends' reactions were hypocritical pretexts, which ultimately could only mean that people she had hitherto trusted had turned against her. When the scales fell from her eyes, Sachs saw the truth: she was surrounded by "a small-time Hitler crowd."

2 

In September two years later, when her hospital stays had made her a "case," she would write in "Diese Telegraphie mißt":

> This telegraphy sounds and gauges / with its mathematics à la satane / where my body rings most sensitive

The cuddy's inferno transformed her into one of the martyrs.

**TEXT** "Sedan omkring ett år," NSW:IV · For letters to Peyer 05/04/1960 and Ilse Pergament 05/10/1960, see Briefe 160 and 161 respectively · "Diese Telegraphie mißt," GR:I (NSW:IV) | **IMAGE 1** Notes about the signs of persecution, 1960s (KBS) · **2** Doodles from a notebook (KBS)

## LEAP INTO THE UNKNOWN

The Nazi command center on the third floor at Bergsundsstrand wasn't the only reason Sachs' health deteriorated during the winter and spring of 1960. Nor were the beams of moving car headlights, which shone from the street and traveled menacingly across the walls of the apartment, or the wretched traffic light by the pedestrian crossing — red as the blood of the butchers — enough to ruffle her by themselves. Not even the enormous sign which said "STRÄNGBETONG" ("bonded prestressed concrete," and the name of a Swedish factory

3

for its production established in Stockholm in 1942; the patent for the process, incidentally, was German) and glowed ever so threateningly on the other side of the water, could by itself make her fall. There were other reasons for the breakdown too. Among them a journey to her old homeland which she decided to undertake after asking doctors' advice.

In March Andersch again visited Stockholm, this time accompanied by his wife, Gisela. He asked for newly written material for the periodical *Blätter und Bilder* (Sachs gave him a few scenes from *Simson fällt durch Jahrtausende*) and could unofficially notify her that she was going to receive the Three Countries Prize. Recently instituted by representatives of the cultural establishments in Switzerland, Austria, and Germany, the prize was awarded every three years. The extract of the minutes arrived not long after: the German Jewish poet in Swedish exile would be celebrated in Meersburg by Lake Constance at the end of May. The prize recalled Annette von Droste-Hülshoff, who had died in the city's castle in 1848, and was awarded to women poets only. Sachs regarded the distinction as a source of both joy and fear. To Etschi Horowitz, who was in Tel Aviv, she confessed that "here was so much that made me happy and on the other hand still made me dreadfully upset." The reason for the ambivalence was spelled out in the observation that "I am no longer a private person at all, which makes me so sad." Even if fame brought welcome attention, it also meant that the person behind the work was pushed into the spotlight — just as her need to be left alone was greatest. But this merry disaster would not mean the end of either joy or sorrows. Sachs had not visited Germany since her flight. Now she was a Swedish citizen and was expected to embark on a journey to what remained, despite civil rights changes, a country with a history. She wrote to Celan and informed him that it "is the first time since the flight back then that I travel abroad from Sweden." The two had corresponded since the mid-1950s and were hoping to meet in person. Then she added: "I would probably never have done it if the doctor hadn't urgently insisted on

SVENSKA DAGBLADE

*Nelly Sachs' diktargärning belönas med treländerspris*

*Nelly Sachs i hemmet vid Bergsunds strand.*

**Som 14-årig flicka i Berlin läste Nelly Sachs "Gösta Berlings saga", trollbands av den fängslande berättelsen, började skriva brev till och fick svar från Selma Lagerlöf, som om Nelly Sachs bifogade sagoförsök skrev: jag skulle inte kunnat göra det bättre själv. Föga anade Nelly Sachs då att hon som utblottad flykting undan nazi-Tyskland genom Selma Lagerlöfs försorg skulle beredas en fristad i Sverige. Här har hon bott jämnt 20 år, och här har hela hennes poetiska och dramatiska livsverk kommit till. I dagarna har hon nåtts av meddelandet att hon av en enhällig jury från Tyskland, Österrike och Schweiz utsetts till årets diktarinna, som den 29 maj skall motta Meersburger Drostepriset på Schloss Meersburg.**

— Jag är överväldigad och glad att jag får detta treländers pris, som fått sitt namn efter Tysklands stora diktarinna Anette von Droste Hülshoff, säger Nelly Sachs, när hon tar emot Svenska Dagbladet i sitt hem vid Bergsunds strand. Kanske reser jag ned och tar emot priset personligen.

Spröd och bräcklig till det yttre, men en intensivt levande människa är Nelly Sachs. Hon skriver enbart på tyska. Till sin diktning är hon närmare besläktad med dagens unga diktargeneration än sina jämnåriga. Till hemmet i Stockholm vallfärdar unga tyska diktare, som söker kontakt och tankeutbyte med sin andligt jämnåriga.

Oändligt vänlig och anspråkslös med en air av rastlöshet, som hänger samman med djupa, outplånliga skador som nazisttidens upplevelser satt på hennes innersta nerv, berättar Nelly Sachs om sitt liv och sin diktning:

— Min första diktsamling "In den Wohnungen des Todes" skrev jag för att befria mig från allt det hemska jag upplevt. Jag måste helt enkelt skriva för att kunna överleva och hade aldrig en tanke på att publicera den.

Men när diktsamlingen kom ut i Tyskland 1947 blev mottagandet så varmt att Nelly Sachs fann mod att skriva vidare. Sedan dess har ytterligare tre av hennes diktsamlingar getts ut på olika förlag i Tyskland, nu senast "Flucht und Verwandlung". Det enda av hennes verk, som utkommit i Sverige, är mysteriespelet "Eli", som uppförts i svensk radio. Ett annat radiospel "Nattvaka" har uppförts av Alfred Andersch i hans avantgardistiska program i Radio Stuttgart. Här kommer också hennes allra nyaste radiospel "Simson faller genom årtusendena" att för första gången uppföras i höst.

— I mina dramatiska försök går jag från den jordiska upplevelsen men söker ge det universella perspektivet, säger Nelly Sachs. Just nu håller jag på med ett dramatiskt mimiskt verk med kör "Abram i Salz" till vilket Moses Pergament gör musiken. Det är ett försök till förnyelse av den gamla kultteatern.

**ÖVERSÄTTER SVENSKA DIKTER**

Svenska diktare i tysk översättning har Nelly Sachs också presenterat för tyska läsare. Hittills har hon gett ut två antologier "Von Welle und Granit" och "Auch diese Sonne ist heimatlos". I diktsamlingarna finns dikter av bl. a. Karin Boye, Anders Österling, Pär Lagerkvist, Hjalmar Gullberg, Johannes Edfelt, Erik Lindegren, Karl Vennberg, Harry Martinson, Artur Lundkvist, Gunnar Ekelöf, Ragnar Thoursie och Bo Setterlind. Inom kort kommer den tredje antologin, som bl. a. kommer att innehålla åtskilligt av Erik Lindegrens penna samt 50-talisterna. Nyligen utkom en volym med Edfelt-dikter, och för närvarande arbetar Nelly Sachs på en bok med Ekelöf-dikter.

Samtalet kring dikter förmår till sist Nelly Sachs att spontant plocka fram en översättning av Erik Lindegrens "Hamlets himmelsfärd". Med känsla och nerv läser hon dikten och fortsätter sedan att läsa några av sina egna dikter ur "Flucht und Vorwandlung". För Nelly Sachs är diktandet ett absolut livsvillkor.

MARJA

4

Switzerland. So then I have the Meersburg day in between, on this leap into the unknown."

The doctor's advice calmed her. By sleeping at a hotel in Zurich, Sachs would not have to spend the night on German soil. Instead she could take the ferry across the water, and her first steps together with Dähnert, who had been granted en exit visa from East Germany. The visit may have been a "leap into the unknown," but at least she had company. Accompanying her on the journey would be EVA-LISA LENNARTSSON (1910–1999), who held evening courses in reading poetry and whom Sachs in a letter to Domin the same year had named "the best reciter of modern Swedish poetry." They had become acquainted in connection with the celebration of the state of Israel's fifth year, held at Stockholm's Skansen Park in May 1953, when Lennartsson had been asked to read "O die Schornsteine" in Pergament's Swedish translation. Three years later the friendship was sealed in the course of a meeting at Bergsundsstrand. With Eva-Lisa by her one side and Gudrun by her other, nothing could happen. Moreover, the Andersch couple, the Celan family, Ingeborg Bachmann, and Max Frisch were all going to come. Even Sachs' friend HELLA — or, more properly, Helena — APPELTOFFT (1901–1969), whom she'd got to know in the 1940s and who worried about her health, would be traveling with her.

"Our journey began on the 25th of May, 1960, at 8:10 am," Lennartsson reported in a personal travel memoir a quarter of a century later. The destination was Zurich, with a stopover at Düsseldorf. "Aboard the plane I asked Li if she had ever flown before. 'Ja, natürlich!' — 'When?' — 'When my dear little mother and I fled to Sweden on an American plane.'" Waiting to receive her in Switzerland was, besides Bachmann and the Celan family, HANS RUDOLF HILTY (1925–1994), who ran Tschudy Verlag in St. Gallen and published the periodical *Hortulus*. Eric Celan, five years old at the time, extended a bouquet of roses to Sachs, who reported in a letter to the Pergaments: "Everyone embraced me, unforgettable." The flowers, the friends, and the appreciation showed that she was in safe hands. Or, as she also wrote to Pergament: "Am in a fairy tale, nothing surprises me any more."

The festivities took place a few days later. After having spent the night at Hilty's in St. Gallen, the party crossed Lake Constance to Meersburg in the late morning of May 28. There Dähnert was waiting with her husband, Ulrich, who had not been granted permission to visit Switzerland. "Just think," Sachs' oldest friend wrote to Pergament, "I had no way of knowing on which boat she'd be coming, I think I thought she was coming by car. I stood there confused and thought: 'Well, so what's the fastest way of finding her?' Just then a boat arrived, and I saw my Lichen on board. Now I could immediately embrace her and take her ashore." The reunion immediately took on an air of legend. Enveloped in the mist of fairy tales, Sachs' "savior" helped her off the boat. No harm could come to her. When Hilty finished his tribute with what was no doubt a well-meaning but misplaced "Shalom," the prize winner with the German, Jewish, and Swedish, but hardly Israeli, identity could relax. Even if she was being greeted in a language she didn't speak and which moreover emphasized that she came from a foreign cultural context, she heard the good intentions behind the word. "Everything was recorded on tape," she reported to Pergament with obvious satisfaction.

5

The acceptance speech Sachs held in a school assembly hall on a rainy Sunday morning was entitled "Wir alle sind Betroffene" (We Are All Afflicted). The five short paragraphs recycled images and turns of phrase from other texts — both prose and poetry. By way of introduction she proclaimed the necessity of grasping the word by the roots "and beseechingly making it grow across the earth." Addressing "the enormous task" of making an invisible universe "readable [...] for a divine eye," she returned to the days when she had lived without language, when her voice had fled to the fishes and her limbs bathed "in the salt of fear." She also mentioned the beloved person who had been torn away from her and how the earth's trajectory through space forever had been tied to the longing "that each work of death bequeaths to its eternity." All people on earth were "afflicted," what one had to do was try to "suffuse the suffering of this star — love it through."

The speech condensed important themes of Sachs' poetics. The poem she chose to read in closing underlined the vicarious role of the poet in the cosmic drama sketched. It was the same text that had opened *Und niemand weiß weiter* in 1957. The final lines made it clear that life and death, song and release were inextricably linked to one another: "With lips against the prayer's stone / I kiss lifelong death, / until the singing gold seed / ruptures the rock of parting." Something in these considerations ought to have been alluded to in the award statement which was then read out. In it the "presiding committee of the Lake

6

7

8

9

Constance Club" thanked "the poetess for her lyrical works, which with incontestable linguistic power extend her reach from the prophecy of the Old Covenant to the spheres of experience of our times." It celebrated the Jewess of German descent who by using the language of the executioners showed that it could also be a "vessel of mercy," it paid tribute to the translator who had made meetings possible "beyond the borders," and it honored the poet for her "testimony of urgent truth and blessing love" — righteous words which didn't say much about the work itself.

Grounds for the judgments could indeed be derived from the acceptance speech. But the remarkable thing about Sachs' address was not the quotations from or allusions to what was at this point a considerable œuvre. What was remarkable was that she began by expressing her appreciation of "my sisters and brothers who are gathered here." Towards the end she returned to this heartfelt concern: "My sisters, my brothers, continue to grant me the courage that you give me today and which has helped me overcome my reserve." For the first time since the dedication in her first book of poetry from 1947 she used the sibling formula, but this time it didn't refer to dead brothers and sisters but to living ones. The strength required to write "after the martyrdom," and which she had so long drawn from the grief over murdered relatives (real or not), could also come from people with whom she shared time and space. Most likely, Sachs was alluding primarily to her friends and colleagues in the assembly hall, but the universalist apostrophe made it clear that the rest of audience could feel included too. While it was true that without the catastrophes there would never have been any poems of the sort she was being honored for, readers were needed as well. Indeed, it was only with the recipients, "far away, and yet there," that there was the promise of "a new prospect." It wasn't just the visit to the new abroad which was a "leap into the unknown"; so was the faith in poetry's unknown addressee.

Despite the radical break which had led to Sachs' reinventing herself in the diaspora, she remained true to the fairy-tale gospel of the Berlin years. Country, friends, and family, context, property, and foothold — all had been lost, still there was hope. Before her she saw "a good dream — which will be realized in our hearts" ... *Etiam amor vincit omnia.*

**TEXT** For letter to Horowitz 03/24/1960, see Briefe 157 · Letter to Celan 04/304/1960, BCelan 29 · For letter to Domin 04/07/1960, see BDomin, 223 · For letter to Pergament 05/26 (the dating, it should be noted, is by Moses Pergament) and 05/30/1960, see Briefe 162 and 163 respectively · Dähnert's letter to Pergament 06/01/1960 is quoted in Briefe, 248, footnote 2 · "Wir alle sind Betroffene," NSW:IV · "Da du," Unww (NSW:II) · The record of the Three Countries Prize, AHolmqvist | **IMAGE 3** Alfred and Gisela Andersch in the 1960s (Photo Monique Jacqot, Annette Korolnik-Andersch's collection, Berlin) · **4** The signature Marja, "Nelly Sachs' diktargärning belönas med treländerspris," *Svenska Dagbladet* 03/30/1960 · **5** Sachs and Eva-Lisa Lennartsson in 1966 (KBS) · **6–7** Sachs and Hella Appeltofft in Meersburg, 1960 (KBS) · **8** Sachs in Ascona, 1960 (Photographer unknown) · **9** Hans Rudolph Hilty in 1986 (Photo Christine Hilty, Schweizerische Nationalbibliothek, Bern)

## BROTHER PAUL (ALREADY TODAY, ALREADY TOMORROW)

In the spring of 1954 PAUL CELAN (1920–1970) asked his publisher to send *Mohn und Gedächtnis* (Poppy and Memory) to Sachs in Stockholm. The year before he had read three poems by her in the Franco-German periodical *Documents*, including "Chor der Waisen" (The Orphans' Choir). In May the following year Sachs thanked him for the gift. After offering a brief characterization which could just as well have applied to her own view of poetry — "You see much of the spiritual landscape which is hidden behind all things temporal, and have the strength to capture the secret that slowly reveals itself" — she wondered if she might ask her own publisher to send *Sternverdunkelung* to Paris.

Until their respective deaths (Sachs died on the same day that Celan was buried) they would exchange over a hundred letters, telegrams, and greetings conveyed by friends and acquaintances. During this period which was marked by both success and setback, and which included confidences as well as misunderstandings, the book titles ended up providing catchwords. In the stellar eclipse the Holocaust became visible, this black epoch when hope's sun seemed to have been extinguished, but also the somber period that followed it, when the colors of the sky were homeless and the survivors lacked roots. "Where to we vestiges of stellar eclipse?" as the poem has it from which the book's name was taken. The same painful tension between Then and Afterwards was evident in the title of Celan's book. Poppies were the seeds of oblivion, but were also sprinkled on the breads baked for Jewish feasts, e.g. the Sabbath bread (*challah*), while memory represented the need to remember everything that had been lost (including oblivion). The symbolically charged words of the title were taken from a poem entailing stars, "Corona" (Corona), in which the self descends "to the loved one's sex" and declares: "we love one another as poppy and memory."

Star and eclipse, oblivion and recollection: the far from harmonious dynamic between these principles was dealt with in the works of both poets. On one occasion it would appear as loss and grief, on another as hope and extinction. The correspondence, with its forty-odd letters before and about ninety items after the meeting in Zurich, shows a mutual need to define such commonalities. Or as Sachs wrote in October 1959, a year before the central word in her sentence would be used in the title of the most quoted poetic declaration of the German postwar era, Celan's acceptance speech "Der Meridian" (The Meridian): "Between Paris and Stockholm runs the meridian of pain and solace." During the ten-odd years that their contact was frequent and "the truth" traveled along the imaginary longitude between Sweden and France they sought support from each other, exchanged news and poems. While shared interests and concerns deepened the understanding of each for the distinctive nature of the other's work, their friendship was nevertheless also tested. To begin with it didn't show. During the critical years around 1960 both lived up to the high expectations they had of each other as "brother" and "sister." But with time there were misunderstandings. What was not said eventually became as important as what was — until the silence filled with questions as unspoken as their answers were unutterable. Or as Celan remarked before the complications hampered the passage of truth between capitals: "All the unanswered questions of these dark days. This ghost-like, mute not-yet, this even more ghost-like and mute no-more and yet-again, and in between them the unpredictable, already tomorrow, already today." The words described a situation he wanted to spare Sachs, but in the light of what would follow they appear prophetic.

10

An important aspect of the friendship's psychogram was the correspondents' relationship with the public sphere of literature, another the ever-greater role that illness came to play in their respective lives, a third what ultimately must be traced back to fundamental divergences in their views of poetry. The meeting in Zurich was important in all these respects. After having told him that Dähnert would be coming from Dresden and that she intended to visit the Andersch couple in connection with the awards ceremony, Sachs wondered if there was any chance of seeing Celan. He had just had a visit by Inge Wærn Malmqvist, a close friend of Sachs' who had been asked to seek him out and convey her regards. Celan agreed to a meeting in Zurich and also wondered if Sachs would like to continue to Paris. In his letters he had not declined to mention the accusations of plagiarism recently leveled at him by the widow of the French surrealist Ivan (or Yvan) Goll, born Isaac Lange, who had written in both French and German and to whom Celan had been close for a period. But now he merely hinted that not everyone he had tried to summon to his defense had behaved honorably (including Andersch, even if he was never mentioned by name).

Although Sachs had hinted at difficulties in her own life, she too observed decorum: "Be calm: you are maintaining your balance." The letter, dated May 12, was followed by a further two. The last was sent just under a week before her departure: "Here in peaceful Sweden I am going through something quite dreadful — no nothing to do with literature — a shady party amusing themselves with persecution techniques. In Zurich 1 room has been reserved at hotel Storchen Weinplatz 2 for the 25th." The contents of the second sentence are not the continuation of the import of the first, but show how close hope was to despair.

A dinner had been arranged at Kronenhalle on the evening of Sachs' and Lennartsson's arrival. During it Celan accounted for Goll's accusations and the equally unfounded but regrettably not unpremeditated articles that had started appearing in the German press. He smelled, with a certain accuracy, an anti-Semitic attempt to diminish his poetry as the work of an epigone —

derivative, bloodless, fragile. In Celan's case, too, growing fame coincided with a mounting sense of persecution: during consultations with friends about how he should react to the insinuations, the Darmstadt Academy's chairman Hermann Kasack informed Celan on May 11 that he had been designated that year's Büchner Prize winner. On the day after the dinner with Sachs, at which Ingeborg Bachmann and Max Frisch were also present and Sachs, who was thirty years older than Celan, suggested that they adopt the informal mode of address, the pair met alone. The time: 4 pm on Ascension Day. The place: the terrace restaurant at Hotel Zum Storchen, with a view over the Limmat and the church towers on the other side. The meeting would be portrayed in one of Celan's most famous poems, which was written immediately afterwards and sent to Stockholm on May 30:

ZÜRICH, ZUM STORCHEN

*For Nelly Sachs*

Of too much we spoke, of
too little. Of you
and yet-you, of
clouding of clarity, of
Jewishness, of
your god.

There-
of.
On the day of an ascent, the
Minster stood on the other side, it brought
some gold across the water.

Of your god we spoke, I spoke
against him, I
let the heart, which I had,
hope:
for
his final, muddled, his
quarrelsome words —

11

Your eye looked at me, looked away,
your mouth
spoke with the eye, I heard:

We
really don't know, you know,
we
really don't know
what counts.

12

The text was published a few months later in *Neue Zürcher Zeitung*, alongside Sachs' poem "Mund" (Mouth), which she had sent her friend back in February of the same year. In thirty-odd lines, he summed up the congruities but also the differences between two of the most prominent German postwar poets. The poem suggests that their conversation touched on *Das Buch Hiob und das Schicksal des jüdischen Volkes* (The Book of Job and the Destiny of the Jewish People) by the German Jewish writer MARGARETE SUSMAN (1872–1966), who lived in Zurich and who had begun her study of the difficulty of speaking about Auschwitz with the reflection: "In the face of these events, every word will be too much and too little." Perhaps Rilke's fifth Duino Elegy was also significant, "where the pure Too little / inexplicably transformed —, shifts / to the empty Too much." The ambivalence between the said and the perceived, what was withheld and what could be gleaned from between the lines returns in what "we" can really claim to know. In his notes after the conversation on the terrace Celan recorded: "Nelly Sachs, alone. 'But I am a believer.' When I remarked that I hoped to be able to blaspheme until the end: 'One doesn't know, of course, what counts.'" The poem points to what is perhaps the decisive difference between the two poets: where Sachs at least thought she knew that she didn't know what counts, Celan didn't even want to hear about such negative sort of knowledge. Against his friend's hope he posited blasphemy.

Late the next morning they went together to the station, where Sachs caught a train to Hilty in St. Gallen, from where she would continue to Meersburg. Celan did not attend the awards ceremony, but instead returned home with his family. Two weeks later, on the afternoon of June 13, Sachs and Lennartsson landed at Orly. They were coming from an extended stay at Bellinzona in Ticino, where they had spent time with the Andersch family. There Sachs had tried unsuccessfully to meet with the ageing Hermann Hesse, who lived in nearby Montagnola and with whom she had corresponded in her youth. Now she was going to spend four days and nights in Paris and stay in a hotel in the sixteenth arrondissement which Celan had booked — "five to seven slow pedestrian minutes" from where he lived, as he noted in a letter. Notes made after the meeting show that the days were spent sightseeing — in the Quartier Latin and the Jardin du Luxembourg, in Montmartre and at Heinrich Heine's grave, the Place des Vosges and the Musée Carnavalet. They also met Enzensberger, who was visiting and wanted to know more about the Goll affair. On several occasions the guests paid visits to the host family's home on the fifth floor at 78, rue de Longchamp. During one of these visits Sachs and Celan saw a golden light glimmer in an adjacent room, reminding them of the gold from the twin towers of Zurich's famous Minster Cathedral being reflected in the water by the hotel terrace where they had been sitting.

And then there was the incident at the Café aux Deux Magots …

In his notebook Celan only wrote in parentheses: "Incident with Max Ernst, who didn't even offer Nelly a chair." Lennartsson was more comprehensive. After having described Celan's agony over the plagiarism accusations, she noted in her memoir of the visit that his well-intentioned attempts to make Sachs see the dangers surrounding them had the opposite effect. Then she portrayed the host's bitterness and the pain which resurged on several occasions during their walks together, while the guest from Stockholm grew more and more anxious. "In such mood we are walking [...] on Boulevard Saint Germain. When we pass Saint Germain des Prés, Paul spots the artist Max Ernst sitting at a table." Since Ernst had been a good friend of Lennartsson's recently deceased husband, she went up to greet him. "I wanted to prove that not all intellectuals in Paris were against Paul." The artist invited her to sit down, but she motioned to her waiting friends — and Ernst immediately invited them too. "I go to get Li and Paul. They are pleased. When we return to Max Ernst's table and he sees my Jewish friends, he stiffens, turns to his companion, pretends as if we don't exist. We left. Silence. After a while Paul says tiredly: 'You see, Eva-Lisa.'"

As to whether the dismissive gesture had to do with racist antipathies or with the fact that Ernst, who had been a close friend of Paul Éluard, recalled Celan's ambivalent elegy "In memoriam Paul Éluard" from 1952, in which he reflected on the communist poet's refusal to protest against the death sentence that the Stalinist regime in Czechoslovakia had issued against his surrealist colleague Zavis Kalandra — who knows? The experience of his action was real enough. And confirmed painful presentiments. After the incident at the Deux Magots, Sachs discovered that their hotel had been a Gestapo headquarters during the occupation. Celan, who knew nothing about it, investigated the matter — and could verify it. In the course of a separate conversation on the night before their departure Lennartsson finally told Celan about Sachs' persecution mania and the reactions his allusions were causing. The following day they went to the airport. Celan expressed regret over his words about the National Socialist resentment barely papered over in the tributes at Meersburg. They were just figments brought about by his pathological suspiciousness of a country and a culture that had not come to terms with its past. "But Li was silent. Withdrawn. Introverted. As if she was hiding her anguish and pain in a frozen absence." Perhaps Sachs already missed a family she had come to regard as sacred. "Now she was going back to loneliness again." And the hells of Bosch and Breughel began. Already tomorrow, already today.

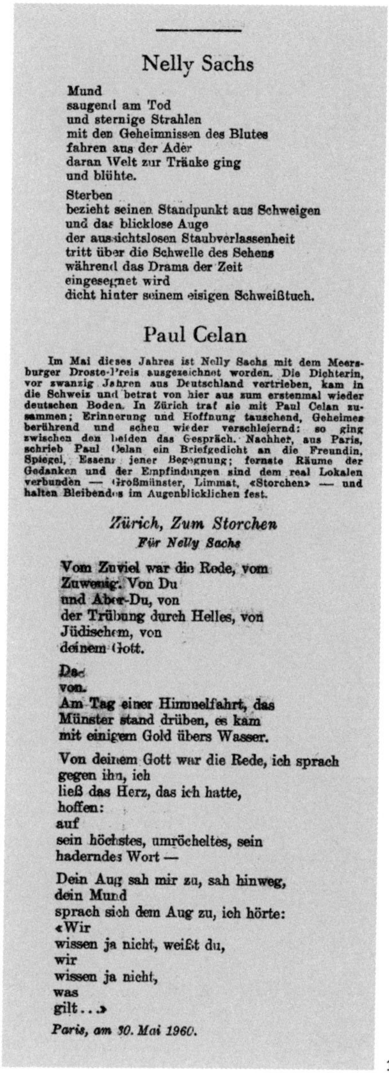

Nelly Sachs

Mund
saugend am Tod
und sternige Strahlen
mit den Geheimnissen des Blutes
fahren aus der Ader
daran Welt zur Tränke ging
und blühte.

Sterben
bezieht seinen Standpunkt aus Schweigen
und das blicklose Auge
der aussichtslosen Staubverlassenheit
tritt über die Schwelle des Sehens
während das Drama der Zeit
eingesegnet wird
dicht hinter seinem eisigen Schweißtuch.

Paul Celan

Im Mai dieses Jahres ist Nelly Sachs mit dem Meersburger Droste-Preis ausgezeichnet worden. Die Dichterin, vor zwanzig Jahren aus Deutschland vertrieben, kam in die Schweiz und betrat von hier aus zum erstenmal wieder deutschen Boden. In Zürich traf sie mit Paul Celan zusammen; Erinnerung und Hoffnung tauschend, Geheimes berührend und scheu wieder verschleiernd: so ging zwischen den beiden das Gespräch. Nachher, aus Paris, schrieb Paul Celan ein Briefgedicht an die Freundin, Spiegel, Essenz jener Begegnung; fernste Räume der Gedanken und der Empfindungen sind dem real Lokalen verbunden — Großmünster, Limmat, «Storchen» — und halten Bleibendes im Augenblicklichen fest.

*Zürich, Zum Storchen*
*Für Nelly Sachs*

Vom Zuviel war die Rede, vom
Zuwenig. Von Du
und Aber-Du, von
der Trübung durch Helles, von
Jüdischem, von
deinem Gott.

Da-
von.
Am Tag einer Himmelfahrt, das
Münster stand drüben, es kam
mit einigem Gold übers Wasser.

Von deinem Gott war die Rede, ich sprach
gegen ihn, ich
ließ das Herz, das ich hatte,
hoffen:
auf
sein höchstes, umröcheltes, sein
haderndes Wort —

Dein Aug sah mir zu, sah hinweg,
dein Mund
sprach sich dem Aug zu, ich hörte:
«Wir
wissen ja nicht, weißt du,
wir
wissen ja nicht,
was
gilt ...»

*Paris, am 30. Mai 1960.*

13

**TEXT** Celan, "Corona," *Mohn und Gedächtnis*, Munich 1952 · "Chor der Waisen," IdWdT (NSW:I) · For letters to Celan 05/10/1954, 10/28/1959, 05/11, 05/18, and 02/27/1960, see BCelan 1, 19, 35, 37, and 27 respectively · For letters from Celan 05/30/1958 and 06/08/1960, see BCelan 10 and 42 · "O die heimatlosen Farben des Abendhimmels," S (NSW:I) · For an account of the plagiarism accusations, see *Paul Celan – die Goll-Affäre. Dokumente zu einer 'Infamie'*, ed. Barbara Wiedemann, Frankfurt am Main 2000 · For an account of Celan's life and work at the time of Sachs' visit, see

Barbara Wiedemann, "Das Jahr 1960," *Paul Celan: Biographie und Interpretation – Biographie et interprétation*, ed. Andrei Corbea-Hoisie, Konstanz, Paris, and Bucharest 2000, 44–59 · "Zürich, Zum Storchen," *Die Niemandsrose*, Frankfurt am Main 1963, 12–13 · For a commentary on Celan's poem, see Thomas Sparr, "'Das Gespräch im Gedicht'. Paul Celan's poem 'Zürich, Zum Storchen,'" *Neue Zürcher Zeitung* 11/23/1990 · "Mund," FiS (NSW:II) · Margarete Susman, *Das Buch Hiob und das Schicksal des jüdischen Volkes*, Zurich 1946 · Rainer Maria Rilke, "Die fünfte Elegie," *Sämtliche Werke*, Frankfurt am Main 1976, vol. 2, 704 · For Celan's notes about the meetings in Zurich and Paris, see BCelan, 40–41 and 46–47 respectively · Lennartsson, 90 and 94 respectively · For a comment on the incident with Max Ernst in the light of the relationship between Celan and Éluard, see John Felstiner, *Paul Celan: Poet, Survivor, Jew*, New Haven 1995, 66–67 | **IMAGE 10** Paul Celan in the 1960s (Photo Wolfgang Oschatz) · **11** Hotel Zum Storchen, Zurich, 1960 (Hotel Zum Storchen, Zurich. S. Fischer Verlag) · **12** Margarete Susman in the 1960s (Gidal-Bildarchiv, Salomon Ludwig Steinheim-Bildarchiv für deutsch-jüdische Geschichte, Duisburg) · **13** *Neue Zürcher Zeitung* 08/06/1960

14

## 8/8/

Upon her return to Stockholm Sachs thanked Celan for the time in Paris: "After the parting and then the journey through the air and then getting out, confused — but you had hurried ahead, the grass on the Swedish side for a moment golden green as in childhood dreams." The passage recalls the addressee's manner of corresponding. But it also resounds with the past she had learned to celebrate both in youthful dream images and the adult person's elegies. The principal word was still *Abschied* (parting), the key verb *abgerissen* (torn apart). After the landing at Bromma, the disquiet returned. It took practice to get used to existence again — "so difficult to take hold of life outside when one after such a long time again has felt so at home." During her weeks abroad Sachs had felt more at home than for a long time. Now she was once again "outside" and didn't trust the security. But "the little apartment entered in fear was silent and remains for now without evil signs in the air." To be on the safe side she took some talismans, including a letter from Gisèle Celan-Lestrange and a photo of brother Paul. These objects were placed next to the others which had taken on a special value in her life: the rock collection and the pictures of her parents, the photos of friends, and a postcard of Saint Francis… After which she dared sleep.

Two weeks later she wrote to him again. Now the tone was agitated. "Things are not good in this building, but the Jew. congregation has allowed me to change." The she added: "It is difficult to part and part-ing [*Ab-schied*] is a severing word of which a part was left behind at the railway station." During the weeks after her return the situation had quickly got worse. Even the language was now being torn apart by what it described. As the summer progressed Sachs became increasingly convinced that neo-Nazis were pursuing her. Sometimes she left the apartment accompanied by Lennartsson (always wearing ear muffs or a scarf around her head, mostly both). But in the planes that could be seen in the sky she sensed spies, following and photographing them. Newspaper headlines were coded and really directed at her, which was confirmed by Morse signals through the walls, telephone taps, and gas being released into the apartment. Celan replied: "We think, as every day, over to you" — as if the severed connection could be reestablished with the intimate counter-transference of friendship.

For a while Sachs stayed with Inge Wærn, but then her friend had to go to the country. At the end of July she again wrote to Paris and described how "a Nazi spiritualist gang is pursuing me awfully sophisticatedly with a radio telegraph, they know everything about where I set foot." It seemed that there was no longer any safe place in existence. Celan immediately replied that he hoped the evil had dispersed to "a little pile of nothing." To soothe her angst he included a strip of bark from a plane tree. "One holds it between thumb and forefinger, presses it really hard and thinks about something good. But — I cannot keep it secret from you — *poems*, especially yours, are *even better* than plane tree bark. I beg of you, do write again. And let it travel to our fingers." Where Sachs saw partings and broken connections, Celan tried to restore the links by encouraging the only thing that helped in the long term: a poetry that repaired the severed bonds and drew meridians between points of pain. To be on the safe side he also enclosed a piece of a window pane that his son had painted on. If the bark couldn't carry across the turbulent waters of angst, surely the glimmer of the glass would.

15

Towards the end of July Sachs asked Lennartsson to help arrange police protection. (At the same time Dähnert was embarking on a journey to Stockholm. Her exit was facilitated by the fact that the East German authorities regarded the persecution of a Jewish friend as proof the class enemy in the west wasn't as democratic as it claimed.) "We were wonderfully lucky," Lennartsson reports in her memoir: "One of the participants in one of my poetry courses was a policewoman and a trained nurse. A woman full of warmth and life experience." The woman's name was Astrid Ivarsson, and she agreed to letting the increasingly paranoid Sachs stay with her. Hopefully the arrangement would have a calming effect. Although the first signs were positive, the illness was nevertheless far advanced. And when Sachs decided to attend the preview of Erwin Leiser's documentary *The Bloody Time*, also known as *Mein Kampf*, she lost possession of herself. The film, which portrayed Hitler's route to power, she interpreted as an accusation directed at her personally.

Dähnert arrived the same day. Yet she too was unable to calm her friend. When Ivarsson was slicing the breakfast bread the following morning, Sachs was unwilling to rule out the possibility that the police nurse was doing the murderers' work. On the same day she wrote to Celan: "Gudrun is with me and a dark net has been drawn around me." The mesh of threats descended quickly. She was caught in it and became less and less contactable. When she tried to lock herself in a closet, her friends asked RUTH ETTLINGER (1920–2009) to

16

come. A psychiatrist in private practice and of Jewish descent herself, Ettlinger knew about Sachs from her work as acting head physician at Södersjukhuset. She informed them that coercive committal was not permitted under Swedish law. The patient must consent to care, which Sachs as yet refused to do. Lennartsson was also called. In her memoirs she relates how she sat down with the ailing Sachs (whether this was at Ivarsson's or in Bergsundsstrand is unclear). "I held Li's hand. For how long we sat that way I don't know. It was outside of time. [---] Suddenly in the silence I hear Li's weak whisper: 'Yes.'"

In the end Sachs had confirmed the parting. Now Ettlinger could telephone for a car. *Within* time it was Monday August 8.

**TEXT** For letters to Celan 06/18, 07/03, 07/25, and 08/08/1960, see BCelan 44, 47, 50, and 53 respectively · For letter from Celan 07/20 and 07/28/1960, see BCelan 48 and 51 respectively · Lennartsson, 97 | **IMAGE 14** Inge Wærn in the mid-1960s (Inge Wærn's collection, Stockholm) · **15** Stills from Erwin Leiser's film *The Bloody Time*, 1960 (Minerva Film, Stockholm) · **16** Ruth Ettlinger in the 1950s (The Ettlinger-Hollander collection, Stockholm) · **17** Södersjukhuset in the 1960s (Södersjukhuset, Stockholm) · **18–21** Beckomberga, about 1938 (Photo Nils Åzelius, SSM)

17

18

19

20

21

**THE HELLS OF BOSCH AND BREUGHEL, OR, INTERVIEW WITH DR. F.**

When the worst was over Sachs described her "hells of Bosch and Breughel" in a letter to Domin. She was referring to the inferno she had been forced to go though. In the home of Dr. F. are the clinical documents of the case. We meet one spring day in 2009.

*Before us lies what could be regarded as the black box after Sachs' passage through the valley of the shadow of death: her medical records. How would you characterize the case from a psychiatrist's perspective after having read the material (which we neither can nor want to quote from)?*

DR. F.: Sachs was treated at three different institutions during the 1960s. These are the records from two of them: Södersjukhuset and Beckomberga. In August of 1963 she was transferred to Rålambshovs Hospital, as it had been discovered that she had not been a Swedish citizen in the calendar year in which she turned fifty-nine, and therefore was not entitled to care at the city's mental hospital...

22

The first thing that can be noted is that the additional name ordained on her by the Nazis, "Sara," lives on in the material — an example of tactlessness to say the least, which can probably only be explained with reference to the general lack of a sense of history and the gullibility of the Swedish authorities. Then it should be noted that Södersjukhuset only practiced voluntary care. Coercive committals with institutional psychiatric care was the remit of the mental hospitals. When Sachs arrived on August 8, 1960, it was thus after having consented to hospitalization. An older colleague has told me how it is likely to have happened. Sachs had for a time been staying with the police nurse Astrid Ivarsson, but had moved back home as it had become impossible to take care of her. She was introverted and terror-stricken, fragmented in her way of communicating. As we know she was afraid in her home, she perceived threats from neighbors and Nazis. Among other things she interpreted normally occurring noises from the plumbing as telegraphy. In the end she agreed to asking Ruth Ettlinger to come. Ettlinger looked around, knocked on the pipes in the apartment and said that something clearly wasn't right. It was actually perfectly understandable that Sachs felt unsafe. At Södersjukhuset things were safer. If Sachs wanted, she could come along to the hospital. There she would at least have peace and quiet.

This mild suggestion got her to consent. When she arrived at the hospital, her name, date of birth, and address were routinely taken down, but also her Jewish background and the persecution in Germany in the 1930s, her contacts with Lagerlöf and Prince Eugen...

23

*Unidentified friends report that her mother was said to have suffered from a similar paranoia.*

DR. F.: It was probably Dähnert who provided that information. Sachs is unlikely to have told them. For so many years she had been looking after her ill mother. When she died the illness manifested itself expressively in her daugh-

24

ter. In a way it was transferred from the mother. The records show that the first signs appeared already in 1953. In other words it took seven years for the paranoia to develop from indications to debilitating disease.

In other respects the anamnesis is good and thorough: The Droste Prize and Paul Celan are mentioned, there's a description of the type of obsessions she suffers from, her neighbors report on her living situation … Even the incident at Sigtunastiftelsen is there. The patient is depicted as gentle and friendly in contact but also chatty. It was especially difficult, for example, to engage in a dialogue. That's typical of paranoiacs. There can be no doubt, every sign of uncertainty is seen as a potential threat, objections or other viewpoints are never allowed to sink in. The patient drones on and shuts out, which can be understood as the world — or at least the patient's concept of the world — having come under threat.

*In Bergsundsstrand the intrusions were performed by means of Morse signals, gas, and electrified water. As long as the besieged Sachs could speak at least she was protecting her poor head.*

DR. F.: Yes, the stream of language formed an armor of words. In company she was ordered, but in reality her interlocutors made no contact, as she refused to enter into a dialogue. Normally a pause of between three and six seconds is perceived as a sign that the word has been handed over to the other speaker. A person in Sachs' situation cannot allow herself these interruptions, or to relinquish the initiative. It emerges from the records that she described the perceived threats in detail, but also that she wished Celan would come. During this first period the nursing staff did not manage to get her to eat or take her medicine to any notable extent — which is also a typical sign. Her BMI dropped to 14, in other words, she was so emaciated that her life was in danger. In the end Södersjukhuset was unable to help her. On September 9 a certificate for institutional psychiatric care was written and she was transferred to Beckomberga.

*What's your assessment of the medication?*

DR. F.: That it was normal. On arrival she was given large doses of tranquilizers in order to be able to sleep. With the exception of the insulin treatment, which is no longer carried out but was one of many routine measures back then, the medicines were all standard stuff. At Beckomberga they added electroshock treatment — about fifteen times in all. Sachs seems to have responded well. Distinctly positive effects were noted already after two treatments. Her inhibitions were overcome and she came to life, started eating and no longer spurned those around her. But the paranoia didn't go away — after all, the electroshock treatment isn't done to cure the delusions. Still, now she wanted to know what was going on in the world and worried more about her friends than about herself. By all accounts Sachs was an empathic human being. She felt for people. Caring pervaded her character.

*One of the neighbors, Mrs. Alsberg, described her as egocentric but not egotistic.*

DR. F.: That's right. An odd lady who cared.

*Or a writer…*

DR. F.: Usually electroshock treatment is given three times a week, between ten and twenty times in total. The time from when the patient is anaesthetized until she or he wakes up again is about fifteen minutes. The effects vary, but a patient who is deeply depressed or catatonic will often be brought out of the apathetic state. In Sachs' case the reaction was immediate. Her spirits were high, she talked to the other patients, began writing. After less than two months, in November, she was discharged and then spent a few weeks at a rest home while the apartment was being repainted and made habitable again. Later she contacted Beckomberga when her anxiety grew and the insecurity returned — the following spring for instance, when she herself asked to be taken in. She said she didn't want to burden the neighbors. This time she arrived with a packed suitcase. Subsequently Beckomberga became a haven where she could write in a protected environment. But that didn't mean the paranoia was past. She complained that her name was being dragged into the dirt, that friends suffered for it and in some cases had turned against her, that the spiritualists continued their infernal attacks… Here the records begin to grow sparser, however.

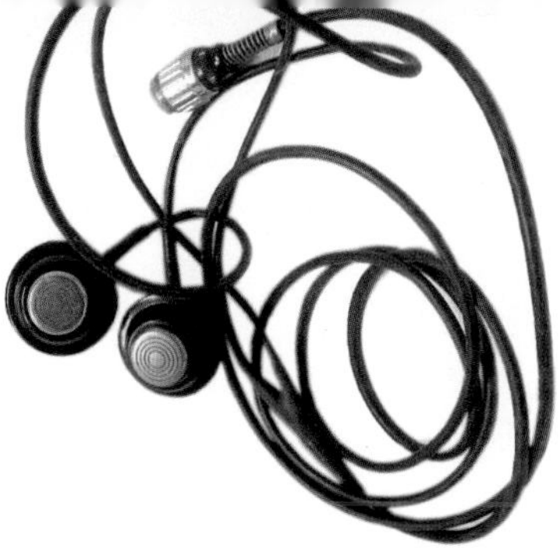

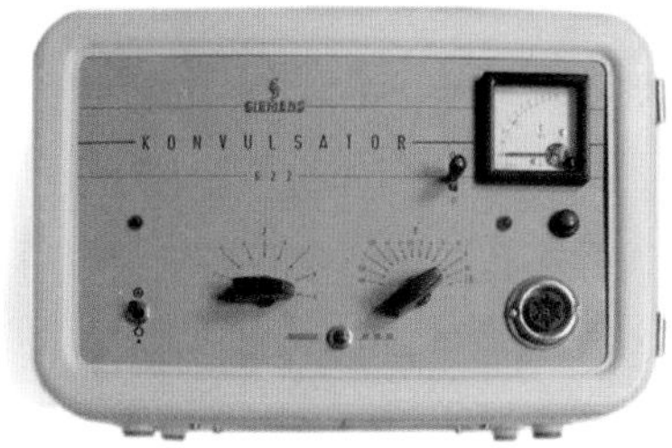


25

*To what extent was Sachs aware of her illness?*

DR. F.: My guess is to a fairly limited extent. The records as well as what close friends such as the Holmqvists have recounted suggest that she wasn't capable of assessing the situation. Anyone who tried to talk to her about the obsessions was soon forced to abandon the subject. She was convinced that her persecution was real. And yet the symptoms were twofold: people who are ill in this way feel that there is something seriously wrong with them, but almost all of them view the cause as being outside of themselves. Then there are quite often lacunae of lucidity, islands of certainty, but these are often associated with such pain that they can hardly be endured. The hidden agenda is to be given help. If psychiatry is the place where you get treated with the most respect, it's not strange if that becomes the place you voluntarily seek out when your surroundings begin to appear threatening. Even if everyone wants to harm me, at least the hospital will help me — Sachs' reasoning could have gone something like that. It's also possible that she was urged by friends to turn to Beckomberga when they noticed that she was losing her grip on reality.

26

*Are there any indications that she tried to defend herself against being hospitalized?*

DR. F.: Anyone can be overcome by emotions or situations in which they lose their foothold. Paranoia might be compared to something as "banal" as jealousy. Usually it is rooted in something real, but the upshot for the person affected is that he or she slowly begins to become paranoid. They start to see

27

hidden meanings in everything that is done or said — or, for that matter, everything that is not done or said. If the patterns are repeated, it can drive even the best of us mad. In Sachs' case there *were* precedents. Think of the man who left her in her youth, "the dead bridegroom." Think of her experiences of the Nazi era or of her mother's infirmity, which we know so little about. That last thing is something I wish there was more comprehensive documentation about. I have a feeling that there's a lot we don't know about Margarete Sachs.

*Despite Sachs' privileged upbringing, circumstances weren't altogether favorable. At first her father decided about her schooling and education. After the First World War she was a young woman who became "marriageable" at the same age as her mother had been when she gave birth to Nelly, and it might have been expected that she would leave the family to form her own. But then the financial crisis arrived, and shortly thereafter William Sachs became ill with cancer. Now the illness decided how his daughter should use her time. There was no space for her in which to make herself independent. Only poetry offered freedom — on paper…*

*After the death of her father, her mother took over the role as the center of existence. She became the needy one. And the situation didn't improve after 1933. On the contrary. Nelly and Margarete were forced to stick together in order to survive. While the flight to Sweden saved them, it also meant that this situation was pushed to extremes. In the foreign country they literally had only each other. Margarete spoke no Swedish, her health deteriorated steadily, and she required around-the-clock care. Margaretha Holmqvist has related that an estate owner proposed to Sachs not long after her arrival in Stockholm. They had lunch in Djurgården. Suddenly air raid sirens wailed and Sachs immediately wanted to return home to her mother. That says a lot… Between thirty-five and sixty years of age, a period during which most of us lead a more or less autonomous adult life, hers seems to have been run by her parents — first by her father's illness, then by her mother's. Irrespective of whether "the dead bridegroom" existed or not, or was one person or several, the attempted breakout failed.*

*It would be odd if a life situation like that didn't give rise to great sorrow. These are of course purely speculations, but possibly the difficulties in breaking free produced resentment. At the same time Sachs knew the reasons, which made the feelings guilt-ridden and prevented her from creating a distance between herself and those closest to her. Instead she over-compensated, idealizing her parents. Her father, who had composed military marches, was cast as an aesthete; her mother became her "most beloved." The presumed lover was turned into a "bridegroom" in death. And later suitors were left with the bill… No matter how you look at it, we're talking strong tobacco, as the Germans say. When Sachs at the age of sixty at last only had herself to think about, the only thing that was left was language with its veins and arteries, its* Aderwerk. *When even this network*

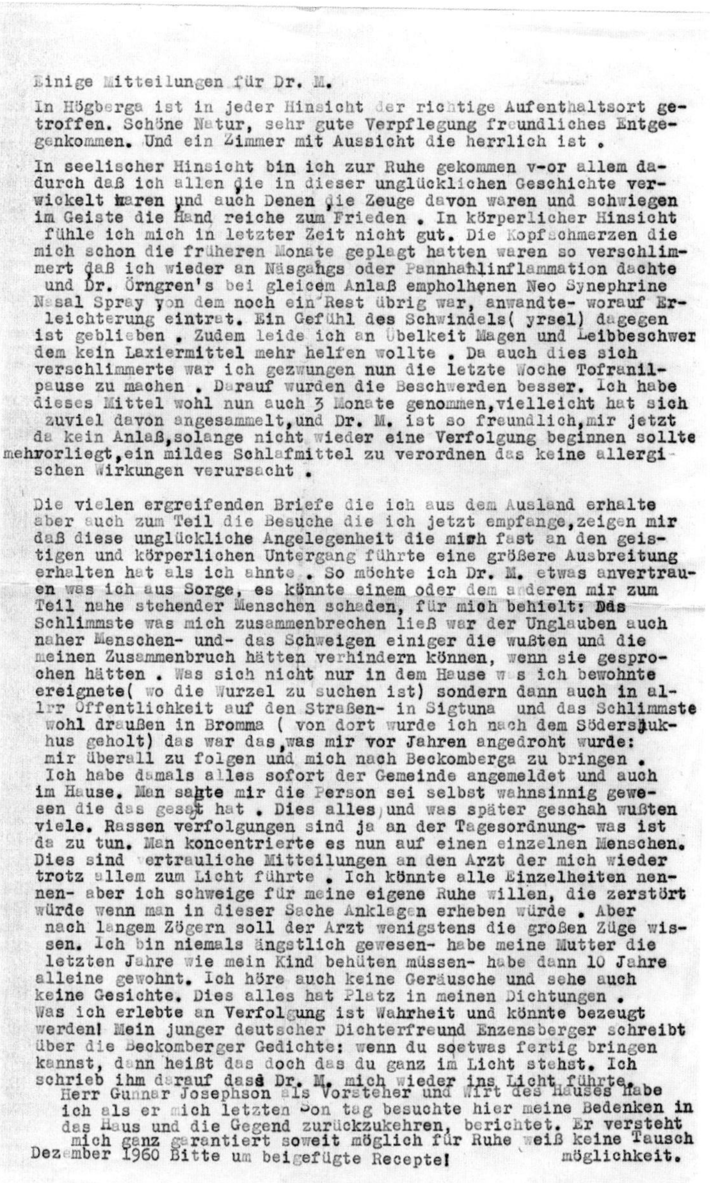

Einige Mitteilungen für Dr. M.

In Högberga ist in jeder Hinsicht der richtige Aufenthaltsort getroffen. Schöne Natur, sehr gute Verpflegung freundliches Entgegenkommen. Und ein Zimmer mit Aussicht die herrlich ist .

In seelischer Hinsicht bin ich zur Ruhe gekommen v-or allem dadurch daß ich allen die in dieser unglücklichen Geschichte verwickelt waren und auch Denen die Zeuge davon waren und schwiegen im Geiste die Hand reiche zum Frieden . In körperlicher Hinsicht fühle ich mich in letzter Zeit nicht gut. Die Kopfschmerzen die mich schon die früheren Monate geplagt hatten waren so verschlimmert daß ich wieder an Näsgahgs oder Pannhahlinflammation dachte und Dr. Örngren's bei gleicem Anlaß empholhenen Neo Synephrine Nasal Spray von dem noch ein Rest übrig war, anwandte- worauf Erleichterung eintrat. Ein Gefühl des Schwindels( yrsel) dagegen ist geblieben . Zudem leide ich an Übelkeit Magen und Leibbeschwer dem kein Laxiermittel mehr helfen wollte . Da auch dies sich verschlimmerte war ich gezwungen nun die letzte Woche Tofranilpause zu machen . Darauf wurden die Beschwerden besser. Ich habe dieses Mittel wohl nun auch 3 Monate genommen,vielleicht hat sich zuviel davon angesammelt,und Dr. M. ist so freundlich,mir jetzt da kein Anlaß,solange nicht wieder eine Verfolgung beginnen sollte mehrvorliegt,ein mildes Schlafmittel zu verordnen das keine allergischen Wirkungen verursacht .

Die vielen ergreifenden Briefe die ich aus dem Ausland erhalte aber auch zum Teil die Besuche die ich jetzt empfange,zeigen mir daß diese unglückliche Angelegenheit die mich fast an den geistigen und körperlichen Untergang führte eine größere Ausbreitung erhalten hat als ich ahnte . So möchte ich Dr. M. etwas anvertrauen was ich aus Sorge, es könnte einem oder dem anderen mir zum Teil nahe stehender Menschen schaden, für mich behielt: Das Schlimmste was mich zusammenbrechen ließ war der Unglauben auch naher Menschen- und- das Schweigen einiger die wußten und die meinen Zusammenbruch hätten verhindern können, wenn sie gesprochen hätten . Was sich nicht nur in dem Hause was ich bewohnte ereignete( wo die Wurzel zu suchen ist) sondern dann auch in aller Öffentlichkeit auf den Straßen- in Sigtuna und das Schlimmste wohl draußen in Bromma ( von dort wurde ich nach dem Södersjukhus geholt) das war das,was mir vor Jahren angedroht wurde: mir überall zu folgen und mich nach Beckomberga zu bringen . Ich habe damals alles sofort der Gemeinde angemeldet und auch im Hause. Man sagte mir die Person sei selbst wahnsinnig gewesen die das gesagt hat . Dies alles,und was später geschah wußten viele. Rassen verfolgungen sind ja an der Tagesordnung- was ist da zu tun. Man koncentrierte es nun auf einen einzelnen Menschen. Dies sind vertrauliche Mitteilungen an den Arzt der mich wieder trotz allem zum Licht führte . Ich könnte alle Einzelheiten nennen- aber ich schweige für meine eigene Ruhe willen, die zerstört würde wenn man in dieser Sache Anklagen erheben würde . Aber nach langem Zögern soll der Arzt wenigstens die großen Züge wissen. Ich bin niemals ängstlich gewesen- habe meine Mutter die letzten Jahre wie mein Kind behüten müssen- habe dann 10 Jahre alleine gewohnt. Ich höre auch keine Geräusche und sehe auch keine Gesichte. Dies alles hat Platz in meinen Dichtungen . Was ich erlebte an Verfolgung ist Wahrheit und könnte bezeugt werden! Mein junger deutscher Dichterfreund Enzensberger schreibt über die Beckomberger Gedichte: wenn du soetwas fertig bringen kannst, dann heißt das doch das du ganz im Licht stehst. Ich schrieb ihm darauf dass Dr. M. mich wieder ins Licht führte. Herr Gunnar Josephson als Vorsteher und Wirt des Hauses habe ich als er mich letzten Sonntag besuchte hier meine Bedenken in das Haus und die Gegend zurückzukehren, berichtet. Er versteht mich ganz garantiert soweit möglich für Ruhe weiß keine Tausch möglichkeit.

Dezember 1960 Bitte um beigefügte Recepte!

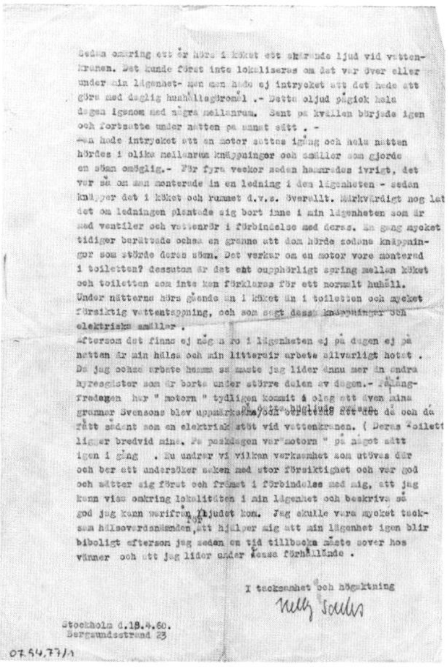

Sedan omkring ett år hörs i köket ett skärande ljud vid vattenkranen. Det kunde först inte lokaliseras om det var över eller under min lägenhet- men man hade ej intrycket att det hade att göra med daglig hushållsgöromål .- Detta oljud pågick hela dagen igenom med några mellanrum. Sent på kvällen började igen och fortsatte under natten på annat sätt . -
Man hade intrycket att en motor sattes igång och hela natten hördes i olika mellanrum knäppningar och smällar som gjorde en sömn omöglig.- För fyra veckor sedan hamrades ivrigt, det var så om man monterade in en ledning i den lägenheten - sedan knäpper det i köket och rummet d.v.s. överallt. Märkvärdigt nog lat det om ledningen plantade sig bort inne i min lägenheten som är med ventiler och vattenrör i förbindelse med deras. En gang mycket tidiger berättade ochsa en granne att dom hörde sodona knäppningor som störde deras sömn. Det verkar om en motor vore monterad i toiletten? dessutom är det eht oupphörligt spring mellan köket och toiletten som inte kan förklaras för ett normalt hushåll. Under nätterna hörs gående än i köket än i toiletten och mycket försiktig vattentappning, och som sagt dessa knäppningar och elektriska smällar .
Eftersom det finns ej någon ro i lägenheten ej på dagen ej på natten är min hälsa och min litterair arbete allvarligt hotat . Da jag ochsa arbete hemma sa maste jag lider ännu mer än andra hyresgäster som är borta under större delen av dagen.- Påskangfredagen har " motorn " tydligen kommit å olag att även mina granner Svensons blev uppmärksamma/och berättade att det då och då fått sådant som en elektriak stöt vid vattenkranen. ( Deras toilett ligger bredvid mina. På paskdagen var"motorn " på något sätt igen i gång . Nu undrar vi vilken verksamhet som utöves där och ber att undersöker saken med stor försiktighet och var god och sätter sig först och främst i förbindelse med mig, att jag kann visa omkring lokalitäten i min lägenhet och beskriva så god jag kann varifrån ljudet kom. Jag skulle vara mycket tacksam hälsovardsnämnden,för att hjälper mig att min lägenhet igen blir biboligt eftersom jag sedan en tid tillbacka måste sover hos vänner och att jag lider under dessa förhållande .

I tacksamhet och högaktning

Nelly Sachs

Stockholm d.18.4.60.
Bergsundsstrand 23

07.54.77/1

28

29

*was threatened, by spiritualist gangs that used the same methods but for converse purposes, that is to say ensnared her with their mesh of evil signals, her feeling of vulnerability must have been massive.*

DR. F.: With a clinical picture like Sachs' you could possibly choose the degree of vulnerability — that is, make it more or less permeable, for example with the help of medication. In "fortunate" cases the patient herself can be in charge of the dosage. If the dose becomes too high she'll be unable to do certain things — think normally, maintain regular body functions — but in return she will not feel that the threats are looming over her. If the dose on the other hand becomes too low she might be able to work to a limited extent, but in return she risks becoming more ill. The ability to self-administer is a sign of insight. When one has accepted whatever it is that's going on, that is, acknowledged that there is something there that might be called "illness," it becomes possible to control it to some extent. Often it's easier to acknowledge one's insight to the doctor than to friends. The doctor, if he or she is good, will be on your side. Friends and acquaintances understand that there is something pathological there too, but the doctor is also aware that the ideas in themselves are a threat to the person's integrity and existence. People close to the patient usually can't handle the paranoid situation for very long. They try to make her or him get a grip, realize the facts, stop misinterpreting. It's easier to admit the pathological sides to a doctor, and moreover you need to connect with that side of the problem in order to create an alliance that leads to improved health.

Evidently Sachs knew that with the help of medication she could keep herself well enough to be able to write. Perhaps it is the case that her writing was more charged and that she wrote more poems after becoming ill, but I wonder if her "madness" itself can be seen as a driving force behind this. The only thing she seems to have managed to write when she was really ill are fragmented letters. It may be that the acceptance of medication can be seen as the artist choosing to work, but that doesn't mean that the person admits that she is ill or resolves to get better.

*Although perhaps not original, there is a notion in Sachs' view of the world which is central to her work. I'm thinking of the idea that behind — or rather* in *— the visible world there is another dimension which remains invisible but can be felt. It is the task of man — in particular perhaps of the poet — and most of all probably of the mystic — to reach this world through what she terms* Durchschmerzung, *the "working through of pain." This relation is structurally reminiscent of paranoia, which also presupposes a dimension parallel to the one we normally inhabit. For the paranoiac, however, there is an evil force that systematically terrorizes the self, while in the mystic's case the self wants and tries to break through to the other dimension. As a poet Sachs' associated herself with this desire to break through, considering it her "credo," as she says at one point. But because of the persecution during the 1930s, that is, as a consequence of actual historical events, the paranoia superimposed itself on this — giving everything an ambivalent character. Disastrous.*

DR. F.: That's interesting. There are critics who have speculated that Sachs may have tried to attain a state of heightened perception, which is also one of the defining symptoms of a psychosis. Many times you meet patients who seem to be totally unaware of what is going on around them. Usually, though, they will afterwards be able to give you very precise descriptions of what was going on. The patient has in fact observed everything. As a psychiatrist I take exception to the interpretation that Sachs would have sought such a situation. A psychosis with a crippling dread for one's life is not something a person

REPORTAGEBILD
KLARA S. KYRKOGATA 18 - TEL. 20 69 77
STOCKHOLM - SWEDEN
COPYRIGHT
Für Dozent Sten Mårtens
der mich viele Male rettete
im Gedenken an den 10.12.1966
Nelly Sachs

30

voluntarily exposes herself to. Still, there is something interesting in this connection. In trance cultures people collectively send themselves into such states at ritual gatherings. The goal is to meet a divinity of some form. The question is how the individual artist is to achieve the desired state. How can you see *the other*? How should one stand before God? This is at the core of Hasidism, which Sachs also studied in *Zohar*. It's not about standing before the *idea* of God, not before the *altar*, not before the *ark*. It's about standing before God. How can a person do that without going mad?

*Perhaps this is a duality that cannot be resolved? The one, release, cannot be attained without risking the other, destruction. The mystic has his assurance, the ill person her paranoia, but what does the poet have? Is she the one who "no longer knows," as one of the titles of Sachs' books has it? Utterly uncertain about what awaits her she still tries to break out or rather through… That would be one way of understanding Sachs' wish as a writer to disappear behind the work — an "extinguishing" which didn't eliminate the private individual, but allowed her to live on in the shelter of darkness, "this Nightly Dimension."*

DR. F.: Sachs blurred the boundaries. Her mother forced her to stay alive until 1950. When she died Nelly became defenseless and gradually lost her grip on existence. There was an incident reported from her second stay at Beckomberga. She is said to have sought out some of the places where she had previously perceived threatening signs. Why did she do that? Did she expose herself to the danger in order to produce a heightened sense of presence or was she trying to convince herself that the threat had blown over? Perhaps a little of both. For me, however, it seems brave above all. Apparently she felt secure enough that she dared try to find out what it was all about. Possibly the doctor had asked her what she believed would ensue if she sought out these charged places. Would something really happen?

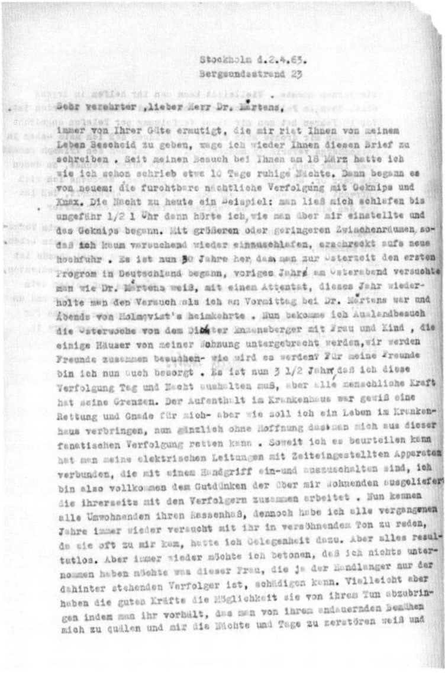
Stockholm 4.2.4.63.
Bergsundsstrand 23

Sehr verehrter ,lieber Herr Dr. Mårtens,

immer von Ihrer Güte ermutigt, die mir riet Ihnen von meinem Leben Bescheid zu geben, wage ich wieder Ihnen diesen Brief zu schreiben . Seit meinen Besuch bei Ihnen am 18 März hatte ich wie ich schon schrieb etwa 10 Tage ruhige Nächte. Dann begann es von neuem: die furchtbare nächtliche Verfolgung mit Geknips und Knax. Die Nacht zu heute ein Beispiel: man ließ mich schlafen bis ungefähr 1/2 1 Uhr dann hörte ich, wie man über mir einstellte und das Geknips begann. Mit größeren oder geringeren Zwischenräumen, sodaß ich kaum versuchend wieder einzuschlafen, erschreckt aufs neue hochfuhr . Es ist nun 30 Jahre her, daß man zur Osterzeit den ersten Progrom in Deutschland begann, voriges Jahr am Osterabend versuchte man wie Dr. Mårtens weiß, mit einen Attentat, dieses Jahr wiederholte man den Versuch als ich am Vormittag bei Dr. Mårtens war und Abends von Holmqvist's heimkehrte . Nun bekomme ich Auslandbesuch die Osterwoche von dem Dichter Enzensberger mit Frau und Kind , die einige Häuser von meiner Wohnung untergebracht werden, wir werden Freunde zusammen besuchen- wie wird es werden? Für meine Freunde bin ich nun auch besorgt . Es ist nun 3 1/2 Jahr, daß ich diese Verfolgung Tag und Nacht aushalten muß, aber alle menschliche Kraft hat seine Grenzen. Der Aufenthalt im Krankenhaus war gewiß eine Rettung und Gnade für mich- aber wie soll ich ein Leben im Krankenhaus verbringen, nun gänzlich ohne Hoffnung daß man mich aus dieser fanatischen Verfolgung retten kann . Soweit ich es beurteilen kann hat man meine elektrischen Leitungen mit Zeiteingestellten Apparaten verbunden, die mit einem Handgriff ein-und auszuschalten sind, ich bin also vollkommen dem Gutdünken der über mir Wohnenden ausgeliefert die ihrerseits mit den Verfolgern zusammen arbeitet . Nun kennen alle Umwohnenden ihren Rassenhaß, dennoch habe ich alle vergangenen Jahre immer wieder versucht mit ihr in versöhnendem Ton zu reden, da sie oft zu mir kam, hatte ich Gelegenheit dazu. Aber alles resultatlos. Aber immer wieder möchte ich betonen, daß ich nichts unternommen haben möchte was dieser Frau, die ja der Handlanger nur der dahinter stehenden Verfolger ist, schädigen kann. Vielleicht aber haben die guten Kräfte die Möglichkeit sie von ihrem Tun abzubringen indem man ihr vorhält, das man von ihrem andauernden Bemühen mich zu quälen und mir die Nächte und Tage zu zerstören weiß und

31

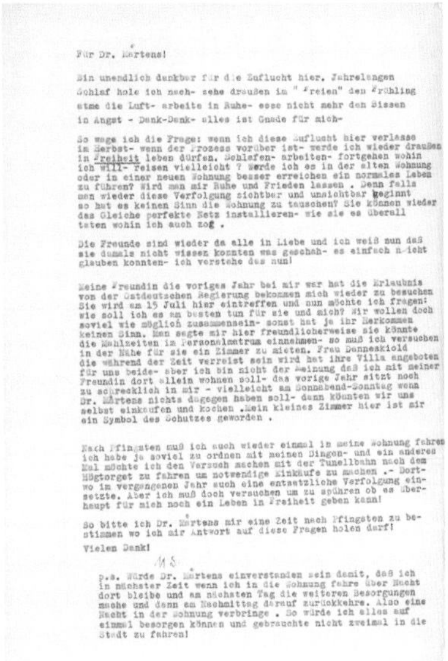
Für Dr. Mårtens!

Bin unendlich dankbar für die Zuflucht hier. Jahrelangen Schlaf hole ich nach- sehe draußen im " Freien" den Frühling atme die Luft- arbeite in Ruhe- esse nicht mehr den Bissen in Angst - Dank-Dank- alles ist Gnade für mich-

So wage ich die Frage: wenn ich diese Zuflucht hier verlasse im Herbst- wenn der Prozess vorüber ist- werde ich wieder draußen in Freiheit leben dürfen. Schlafen- arbeiten- fortgehen wohin ich will- Reisen vielleicht ? Werde ich es in der alten Wohnung oder in einer neuen Wohnung besser erreichen ein normales Leben zu führen? Wird man mir Ruhe und Frieden lassen . Denn falls man wieder diese Verfolgung sichtbar und unsichtbar beginnt so hat es keinen Sinn die Wohnung zu tauschen? Sie können wieder das Gleiche perfekte Netz installieren- wie sie es überall taten wohin ich auch zog .

Die Freunde sind wieder da alle in Liebe und ich weiß nun daß sie damals nicht wissen konnten was geschah- es einfach nicht glauben konnten- ich verstehe das nun!

Meine Freundin die voriges Jahr bei mir war hat die Erlaubnis von der Ostdeutschen Regierung bekommen mich wieder zu besuchen Sie wird am 15 Juli hier eintreffen und nun möchte ich fragen: wie soll ich es am besten tun für sie und mich? Wir wollen doch soviel wie möglich zusammensein- sonst hat ja ihr Herkommen keinen Sinn. Man sagte mir hier freundlicherweise sie könnte die Mahlzeiten im Personalmatrum einnehmen- so muß ich versuchen in der Nähe für sie ein Zimmer zu mieten. Frau Danneskiold die während der Zeit verreist sein wird hat ihre Villa angeboten für uns beide- aber ich bin nicht der Meinung daß ich mit meiner Freundin dort allein wohnen soll- das vorige Jahr sitzt noch zu schrecklich in mir - vielleicht am Sonnabend-Sonntag wenn Dr. Mårtens nichts dagegen haben soll- dann könnten wir uns selbst einkaufen und kochen .Mein kleines Zimmer hier ist mir ein Symbol des Schutzes geworden .

Nach Pfingsten muß ich auch wieder einmal in meine Wohnung fahren ich habe ja soviel zu ordnen mit meinen Dingen- und ein anderes Mal möchte ich den Versuch machen mit der Tunellbahn nach dem Högtorget zu fahren um notwendige Einkäufe zu machen .- Dortwo im vergangenen Jahr auch eine entsetzliche Verfolgung einsetzte. Aber ich muß doch versuchen um zu spühren ob es überhaupt für mich noch ein Leben in Freiheit geben kann!

So bitte ich Dr. Mårtens mir eine Zeit nach Pfingsten zu bestimmen wo ich mir Antwort auf diese Fragen holen darf!

Vielen Dank!

M S

p.s. Würde Dr. Mårtens einverstanden sein damit, daß ich in nächster Zeit wenn ich in die Wohnung fahre über Nacht dort bleibe und am nächsten Tag die weiteren Besorgungen mache und dann am Nachmittag darauf zurückkehre. Also eine Nacht in der Wohnung verbringe . So würde ich alles auf einmal besorgen können und gebrauchte nicht zweimal in die Stadt zu fahren!

32

33

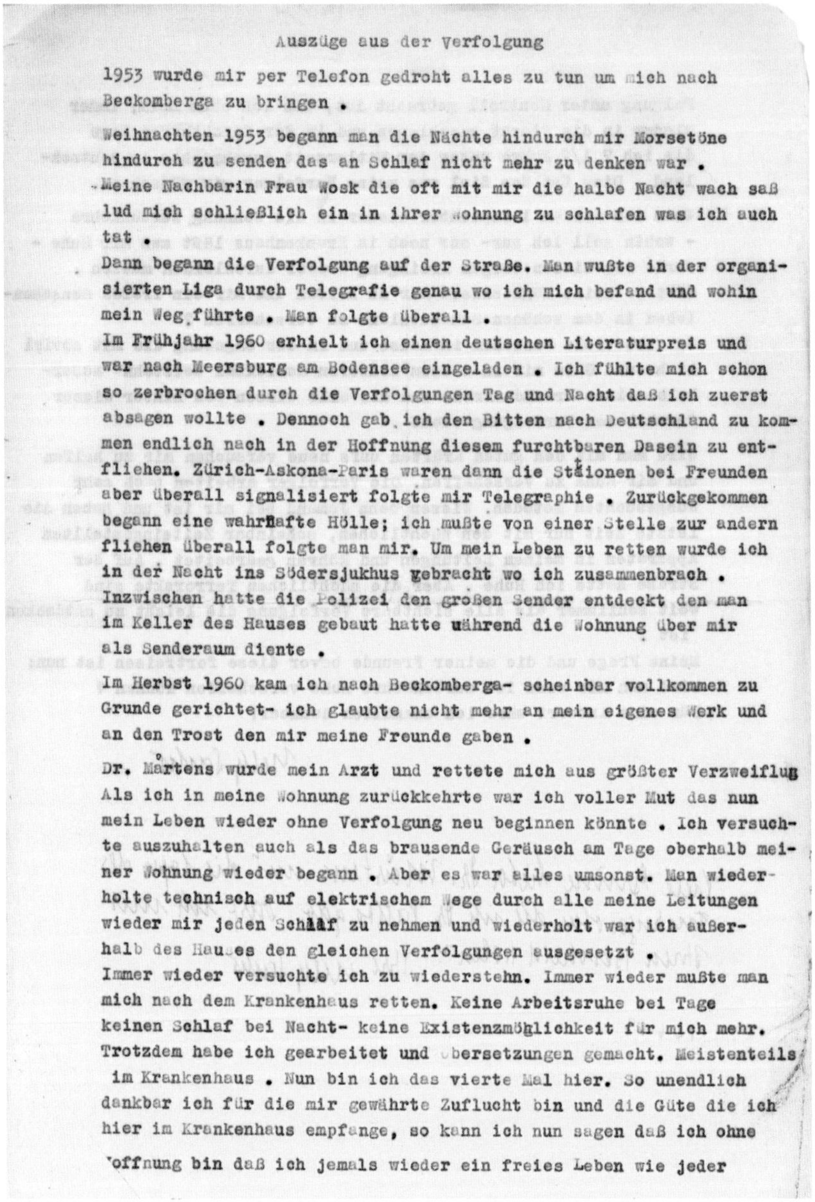
Auszüge aus der Verfolgung

1953 wurde mir per Telefon gedroht alles zu tun um mich nach Beckomberga zu bringen .

Weihnachten 1953 begann man die Nächte hindurch mir Morsetöne hindurch zu senden das an Schlaf nicht mehr zu denken war .
Meine Nachbarin Frau Wosk die oft mit mir die halbe Nacht wach saß lud mich schließlich ein in ihrer Wohnung zu schlafen was ich auch tat .
Dann begann die Verfolgung auf der Straße. Man wußte in der organisierten Liga durch Telegrafie genau wo ich mich befand und wohin mein Weg führte . Man folgte überall .
Im Frühjahr 1960 erhielt ich einen deutschen Literaturpreis und war nach Meersburg am Bodensee eingeladen . Ich fühlte mich schon so zerbrochen durch die Verfolgungen Tag und Nacht daß ich zuerst absagen wollte . Dennoch gab ich den Bitten nach Deutschland zu kommen endlich nach in der Hoffnung diesem furchtbaren Dasein zu entfliehen. Zürich-Askona-Paris waren dann die Stationen bei Freunden aber überall signalisiert folgte mir Telegraphie . Zurückgekommen begann eine wahrhafte Hölle; ich mußte von einer Stelle zur andern fliehen überall folgte man mir. Um mein Leben zu retten wurde ich in der Nacht ins Södersjukhus gebracht wo ich zusammenbrach .
Inzwischen hatte die Polizei den großen Sender entdeckt den man im Keller des Hauses gebaut hatte während die Wohnung über mir als Senderaum diente .
Im Herbst 1960 kam ich nach Beckomberga- scheinbar vollkommen zu Grunde gerichtet- ich glaubte nicht mehr an mein eigenes Werk und an den Trost den mir meine Freunde gaben .

Dr. Mårtens wurde mein Arzt und rettete mich aus größter Verzweiflung
Als ich in meine Wohnung zurückkehrte war ich voller Mut das nun mein Leben wieder ohne Verfolgung neu beginnen könnte . Ich versuchte auszuhalten auch als das brausende Geräusch am Tage oberhalb meiner Wohnung wieder begann . Aber es war alles umsonst. Man wiederholte technisch auf elektrischem Wege durch alle meine Leitungen wieder mir jeden Schlaf zu nehmen und wiederholt war ich außerhalb des Hauses den gleichen Verfolgungen ausgesetzt .
Immer wieder versuchte ich zu wiederstehn. Immer wieder mußte man mich nach dem Krankenhaus retten. Keine Arbeitsruhe bei Tage keinen Schlaf bei Nacht- keine Existenzmöglichkeit für mich mehr. Trotzdem habe ich gearbeitet und Übersetzungen gemacht. Meistenteils im Krankenhaus . Nun bin ich das vierte Mal hier. So unendlich dankbar ich für die mir gewährte Zuflucht bin und die Güte die ich hier im Krankenhaus empfange, so kann ich nun sagen daß ich ohne

Hoffnung bin daß ich jemals wieder ein freies Leben wie jeder

*Who was* STEN MÅRTENS *(1924–2007) — or "Dr. M." as Sachs called him in a letter? She was so appreciative of his treatment that she gave him copies of her books with personal dedications, as well as a number of poems.*

DR. F.: Mårtens was a strict chief physician whom Sachs had every reason to trust. I sought him out in around 2005 in order to learn more about her period of illness. He was firmly dismissive when I explained my interest. "Why should I talk to you about a patient?" His reaction made me refrain from any further attempt, since he so clearly saw himself as the guardian of her memory. Then he sent me an account of his time with Sachs anyway. Obviously he had decided to trust that I was interested in her medical history without any sensationalist bent. Mårtens' summary of the illness closely tallies with the trajectory described in the records. In 1968 he moved abroad — first to Switzerland, I think, and then to Ireland and France. A few years ago he returned to Sweden, but soon died from a serious disease. We never met.

*I've had access to the twenty-odd letters and fifty or so poems that Sachs gave or sent to Mårtens during the 1960s. Her appreciation and gratitude are unmistakable. After the Nobel awards ceremony she gave him a photograph of the event in Konserthuset. On the back she wrote: "To Senior Physician Sten Mårtens / who has saved my life many times / in remembrance of December 10, 1966 / Nelly Sachs."*

*The material, which has been preserved by Mårtens' widow, also contains descriptions of the perceived persecution. There is quite a lot of repetition, but there are also interesting details. For example, Sachs herself dates the start of the persecution to 1953–1954 — which is of course many years before the illness became manifest. She regarded her stays at Beckomberga as a "refuge," as she writes in a letter in the late winter of 1962. Or as a "mercy," as she has it on April 2. In a missive of May 17 the following year she talks about a "haunted time" in which only "the flight" to the hospital can save her. In the April letter she also traces the persecution back to the terror inflicted on her former homeland: "It is now 30 years since the pogroms began in Germany around Eastertime." The fact that it happened during Easter, this time of sacrifice, seemed important to her. Sachs saw a pattern. "On Holy Saturday last year they tried an attack, as Dr. Mårtens knows, this year they repeated the attempt." A few months later, on May 22, she calls the motors that the Nazi gang has installed in the apartment above hers "instruments of torment." With its etymological connection to martyrdom the German word —* Marterapparate *— suggests that Sachs inscribed the agony in a frame of understanding which had to do precisely with the will to sacrifice and belief. "With this endless suffering which no longer lets me lead a dignified human life, I serve no one — can help no one — save no one. Until now I always believed that I was fulfilling a deeper intention with this suffering — during the last years that always gave me the courage to hold out, but now I no longer see any point to sustaining evil by patient endurance. I feel caught in a trap."*

*The letters testify to Sachs' great faith in Mårtens and to an evident will to come to terms with the situation. In a letter dated January 13, 1962, she remarks: "This clear-sightedness has now become a necessity for me." But the letters also show how fatally trapped Sachs remained by certain delusions. It is as if the very insight she so fervently sought prevented her from seeing clearly. Was she perhaps even fearful that the poems would lose something if it turned out that the clarity they reached for was based on self-deception? Impossible to say. Sachs was at least aware that medicines could help, but at the same time afraid that they would prevent her from working. In an account in Swedish — "Some observations during the time from middle of May to beginning of June 63" — she writes, unidiomatically but tellingly: "Haldol is a good medicament, but if it can make me immune against such terror during the night without to take at the same time all my life feeling and possibilities of writing is perhaps not possible."*

*Why do you think Mårtens wrote his account all those years later?*

DR. F.: The purpose is explained in the introduction: it was a reaction to the frequently unreliable publicity occasioned by the centenary commemorations in 1991. Perhaps he was planning something bigger, like a book — never written, in that case. Mårtens had great respect for his patient, and also for her work. In the report he summarizes the history of her illness, but also makes an attempt to go through Sachs' poetry. He was no literary historian. What we get is the reflections of a clinical psychiatrist on the art of poetry. He notes such things as the volume of text before and after the onset of illness, and concludes that Sachs produced twice as many poems during her period of illness than before it. It would be safe to assume that he was justifiably proud to have been able to help her. In any event, Sachs was fond of Mårtens. And felt such faith in him that she asked him to escort her when she went to receive the Nobel Prize. Perhaps the gesture was a way of thanking him — precisely because he had saved her life.

**TEXT** For letter to Domin 10/03/1960, see BDomin 12 · Letters to Mårtens 01/311 and in the late winter of 1962, and 04/02, 05/17, and 05/22/1963, Beth Mårtens' collection · "Några iakttagande under tiden mitten av mai till början av Juni 63," Beth Mårtens' collection | **IMAGE 22** Hilde Domin in the 1960s (KBS) · **23** Gudrun Dähnert (Kurt Kehrwieder's collection, Bochum) · **24** Sachs' medical records from Beckomberga · **25** Siemens ECT machine for electroshock therapy from the 1960s · **26** Proofing notes to Erik Lindegren, *Weil unser einziges Nest unsere Flügel sind* 1963 (KBS) · **27** Sten Mårtens in 1958 (Beth Mårtens' collection, Stockholm) · **28** "Einige Mitteilungen für Dr. M.," typescript (DLA) · **29** "Since about one year," typescript (DLA) · **30** Gustaf VI Adolf applauds the Nobel laureate, with a dedication to Sten Mårtens (Photo Reportagebild, Beth Mårtens' collection, Stockholm) · **31** Letter to Mårtens 04/02/1963 (Beth Mårtens' collection, Stockholm) · **32** Undated letter to Mårtens, spring 1963 (Beth Mårtens' collection, Stockholm) · **33** "Auszüge aus der Verfolgung" (Extracts from the Persecution), typescript (Beth Mårtens' collection, Stockholm)

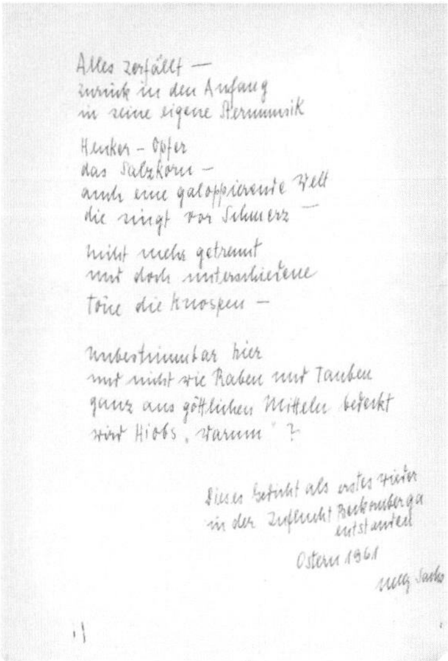
Alles zerfällt —
zurück in den Anfang
in seine eigene Sternmusik

Henker — Opfer
das Salzkorn —
auch eine galoppierende Welt
die singt vor Schmerz —

nicht mehr getrennt
und doch unterschiedene
Töne die Knospen —

Unbestimmbar hier
und nicht wie Raben und Tauben
ganz aus göttlichen Mitteln bedeckt
wird Hiobs „warum" ?

Dieses Gedicht als erstes wieder
in der Zuflucht Beckomberga
entstanden

Ostern 1961

Nelly Sachs

34

## INDETERMINABLE HERE

Among the many texts that Mårtens received during the 1960s — poetry, prose, drama — is a hitherto unpublished poem, entitled "Alles zerfällt —"(Everything Is Falling Apart —). Terse, bordering on the elliptical, it captures the dynamic between crumbling and asylum in fourteen lines divided into four stanzas. It is as if Sachs not only sought, but wished to transform poetry into a place beyond the dialectics of executioner and victim, ravens and doves — "indeterminable here":

> Everything is falling apart — / back to the beginning / in its own star music // Executioner — victim / the grain of salt — / even a galloping world / singing from pain — // No longer separate / yet different / tones the buds — // Indeterminable here / and not as ravens and doves / wholly in divine means' haven / is Job's "Why?"

The poem is followed by the addendum: "This poem was written as the first again in the refuge of Beckomberga / Easter 1961 / Nelly Sachs."

**TEXT** "Alles zerfällt –," Beth Mårtens' collection | **IMAGE 34** "Alles zerfällt –," manuscript (Beth Mårtens' collection, Stockholm)

## (AN AFFAIR IN PARENTHESES)

The express letter that Sachs sent the same day she was interned at Södersjukhuset was opened twenty-four hours later. Following the main theme — the dark net that was being drawn together — Celan wrote back immediately: "The net, the dark one, has been pulled away —isn't that right, Nelly, you can see it now."

He did not yet know that his "sister" had been hospitalized. During the first week of August Celan had visited his friends Klaus and Nani Demus in Vienna, to discuss a rebuttal to Goll. On his return to Paris he informed the philosopher Otto Pöggeler, who had sided with him, and recounted recent events: "We had a troubled holiday: we had very worrying news about Nelly Sachs from Sweden. Nelly Sachs is our sisterly friend in the truest sense of the word — I thought that I must immediately go to Stockholm to see her: the night, the dark had invaded her ecstatic soul." The same afternoon Rosi Wosk telephoned. Now he was informed of what had happened. The net had been drawn together. Sachs was in psychiatric care, but was asking after her "brother" and his family. A couple of days later Celan thanked her for her concern on two postcards: "Thank you, my good and sisterly friend, thank you from the heart for being close to us and with us!" To which Sachs replied: "Warm thanks for the two postcards and the two consoling angels. I am not yet free Paul, the net of fear and dread they have thrown over me is not yet lifted off. But Gudrun is here to console me. And you are well. With these two means of solace as my only medicine I hope to overcome all that still remains for me of suffering, or to find a peaceful release, I long so for my beloved dead."

The roles had been distributed. Although both siblings suffered from real as well as possibly imaginary harassments, the sister was the needy one, the brother the helper. As long as Dähnert remained nearby and could spend the night at the hospital Sachs felt reasonably safe. Towards the end of the month her friend had to return to Dresden, however, and Sachs' hopes that the dark net would be lifted were not high. Around the middle of the month she wrote again, this time to ask if Celan wanted to take over from Dähnert. Several express letters and telegrams were exchanged, then she wrote with considerable emphasis: "You will be heartily welcome no matter what day you come. We must at last speak to each other to have clarity! Take a taxi straight from the railway station to Södersjukhuset. Wire your reply immediately." That was on August 29. Three days later Celan arrived at Stockholm Central. Due to a trade fair in the city all hotels were full. Friends were consulted, among them the photographer Anna Riwkin and her husband Daniel Brick. According to reports he stayed first with the Edfelts and then with Wærn.

Both of Sachs' biographers emphasize that she never received her brother — either because she was too ill and didn't recognize him, or because she wished to protect him from the evil forces. The account can be traced back to Lennartsson, who in her memoir maintains: "Paul wasn't allowed in. Li refused to see him. Paul wanted to give Li his support through his friendship. He had made the journey in vain. He returned to Paris. Desolated." Thus was born a legend which has contributed to the picture of a friendship in distress. They may have regarded each other as sibling souls, but the consequences of the persecution in the 1930s and the accusations of plagiarism couldn't conceal the fact that their differences were profound and that their respective appraisals of being in the public eye remained far apart. "Everything broke. For her and for him," Celan's friend, the philologist Jean Bollack, declared many years later.

Letters and notes indicate, however, that Celan did visit his ailing sister, possibly on a daily basis. On September 5 he wrote to his wife about the latest developments in the Goll affair — "Angry emotions, coming from a thousand directions, far away and near." Then he added: "What can I say about Nelly? She is suffering a lot. Does not want to hear more about her poems — 'I just want to' — and here she joins the thumb and forefinger of her right hand to make a circle — 'keep this little light.'" All that remained was an outline.

The continuation of Celan's missive shows how close to each other the events that dominated his life were at this time — the plagiarism charges, the Büchner Prize, the sick "sister": "In reference to a letter sent by Ingeborg [---], in which I had enclosed a pair of white gloves, Nelly remarked: 'White gloves, but that means: "je lave mes mains dans l'innocence" — I wash my hands in innocence — so it's *proof of falsity*'!!!" The envelope bore the sender's address: "Celan c/o Mme Sachs, Stockholm / Soedersjukhuset, Avd."

At this time — torn between Sachs who interpreted every sign as a threat, and a scandal where he no longer felt that he could trust close friends — Celan stayed in Östermalm. The poem "Die Schleuse" (The Sluice), which was published in the same book as "Zürich, Zum Storchen" a few years later, partly recalls the daily journey via Slussen (a sluice and reference point in central Stockholm) to the hospital in Södermalm: "Through / the sluice I have to go, / to salvage the word back / and forth and across the salt river: / *Yizkor*." The Hebrew word designates the Jewish death prayer directed to God in the hope of remembrance. At the actual *Yizkor* only those who have lost one or both parents take part. The quiet prayer also recalls the Jewish martyrs, in particular those who died in the Holocaust. Why did Celan end his poem with such a word?

A first draft was made a few days after his return to Paris, on September 13. At that point the text still bore the title "Stockholm, Linnégatan 12." That was

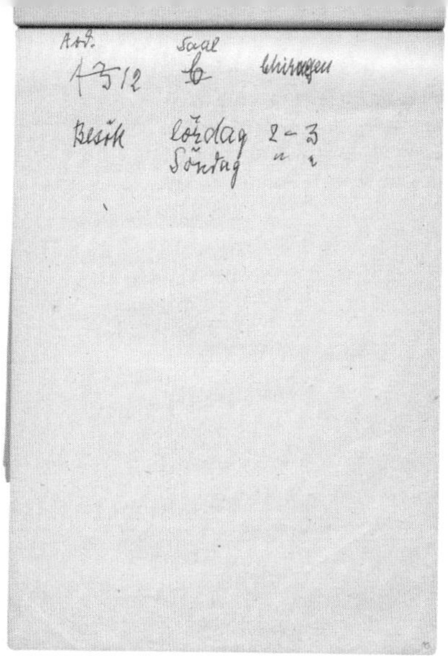


35

the address at which he stayed during the latter part of his visit, in an apartment rented by INGE WÆRN (1918–2010). The German actress and director was the daughter of a mother of Jewish descent and a Swedish father who worked as an agronomist in Germany before abandoning the family when the child was two years old. Wærn was born in the old Swedish regions on Usedom near the Baltic coast, but moved to Berlin with her young mother and grandmother at the end of the 1920s. The family lived in Greifswalderstraße not far from Alexanderplatz; her mother, who had acting ambitions, found a job with a theater company while her grandmother ran a pension. The young Inge was cast in children's roles on tours throughout the country. In 1930 her mother remarried and the family moved to Vienna, where Wærn was accepted at Max Reinhardt's theater school. The famous director had led the program since 1929, mainly from Berlin, but had fled in connection with the Nazi takeover. The student was fifteen years old when she enrolled.

Just three years later she was employed by the Deutsches Theater in Prague, where she quickly made a career and was fêted as the new starlet. She played Luise in *Kabale und Liebe* (Cabal and Love), Gretchen in *Faust* and Ophelia in *Hamlet*. She got to know Max Brod who reviewed several performances, but felt increasingly vulnerable as a half-Jewess — particularly after the Munich Agreement in 1938, in which Czechoslovakia ceded the Sudetenland. Thanks to her father she had Swedish citizenship and could travel freely through Europe in the winter of the same year. After the 1939 New Year she settled in a country whose language she had yet to master. There she became acquainted with Sandro Malmqvist, who was the director of Malmö's city theater from 1944 to 1947, married and started a family. A series of roles followed on Swedish stages, including ones in theater works directed by Ingmar Bergman. But eventually she changed profession, becoming a director herself and opening a school of mime arts based on Étienne Decroux's theories about controlling the body and exact expression.

Wærn had become acquainted with Sachs through poems she had read on Swedish radio. Not long thereafter they met personally — in the elevator up to a party at the home of Brick and Riwkin. Wærn did readings of Sachs' poetry later as well, and in the 1980s she staged *Der magische Tänzer* in Stockholm. "I think I connected with her first of all as a human being," she explained in a late interview with Anders Olsson — and only after that "as the great poet she is. You know, a person can read Tranströmer every day of the week. You can't do that with Nelly. Her work is far too powerful. [---] As a person Nelly had something sweet and very charming about her, and she enjoyed being surrounded by young, attractive people. She could also be very funny. But her gaze could suddenly shift and become absolutely piercing, as with Picasso. Nelly had a tremendous longing for closeness, as there was no man in her life."

In conjunction with a trip to Paris in 1960, Sachs had asked Wærn to visit the Celan family. She checked in to the Hotel Orfila, known from Strindberg's day, and was invited to dinner at Celan's home on the rue de Longchamp. During the evening she spoke German to the host, while the hostess mostly listened. "As the evening progressed he suddenly started speaking very openly and nakedly about Jewishness, about the Holocaust, and about the situation in the present. It was as if he was talking to a relative from the same central European family, and I felt quite shaken when I got up to leave and bade them goodbye." The following day Wærn worried that Celan, who was known for his integrity, had been upset by the open-heartedness and telephoned him. They arranged to meet at the Closerie des Lilas the next day. The meeting would be both carefree and vertiginously deep, marked by humor as well as reflection. And attraction. "When we parted I felt it was as inevitable as fate that we would meet again. The vibrations between us were giddying."

At Linnégatan 12 the couple began an affair which would go on for the next few years. They met again in Paris and when Celan had readings abroad — in Hamburg and Copenhagen, for example. At least four of the poems published in *Atemwende* (Breathturn) in 1967 were sent in various versions to Wærn and contain important details from their encounters: "Wenn du im Bett" (When You Are in Bed), "Hafen" (Harbor), "Schwarz" (Black), and "In Prag" (In Prague). Of the four texts, all of them love poems, the last is the only known text in which Celan mentions a place he had never visited. Otherwise he was careful to write only about things and places he himself had experienced. This exception to the rule becomes easier to understand when recalling Wærn's background at the Deutsches Theater and that she during a stroll with Celan

36

37

in the arcades of the Place des Vosges looked up to the ceiling and discovered an image of two crossed swords there — a detail which recalls the poem's "two rapiers, / sewn to heaven-stones." To Anders Olsson, who has noted these and other correspondences, the ageing Wærn pointed out in conversation: "Paul Celan said that 'no love poem even gets close to reality. I want you to know that. I have only written about places that I have experienced myself, except in the poem "In Prague." I have never been to Prague.'" When asked why she thought he had chosen to write about the city anyway, she replied: "I guess it was written through me."

To write *through* another person: this, exactly, happens in "Die Schleuse." The first version, which had not yet been given the transitory title "Stockholm, Linnégatan 12," includes a stanza that Celan put in parentheses. After some editing, which among other things removed the brackets, it read in published form:

> By a mouth, / that had it as a thousandword, / I lost — / I lost a word / which had remained: / sister.

In a poem whose title was taken from a passage between water levels and in which the place alluded to also marks the spot where the sweet waters of Lake Mälaren flow into the salty waters of Saltsjön, it is probably no coincidence that the loss of a dear word appears in what was originally a parenthesis. Here, it turns out, Celan is literally writing through Sachs. "Sister" was the term for the sibling soul who was in agony in Ward 14 at Södersjukhuset and who so urgently had asked him to come — him specifically, brother Paul Celan and no one else. "Sister" was the complement to a mode of address Sachs had used in their correspondence as early as November 1959, but Celan did not begin to use it until he wrote the intimate postcards in August the following year — by which time they had met in person — using the words "My good and sisterly friend." "Sister" was a special word; "sister" could only be used for an irreplaceable person.

But when Celan arrived in Stockholm he found Sachs surrounded by people who all laid claim to the title. The word turned out to have come from "a mouth that didn't count," as the first draft of the poem has it. In reality it was a "thousandword" that could just as well be used in the relationship with Dähnert and Wosk as in connection with Borchers and Domin. And of course when addressing the hospital staff. All of which suggested in turn that Celan was not in fact a single soulmate, a unique "brother," but must expect that Andersch, Enzensberger and Hamm, Edfelt and Lindegren all belonged to Sachs' band of brothers. As an indication of their relationship the word robbed the friendship of what made it unique. (It is moreover difficult to say with certainty whether Celan really met Sachs during his visit to Stockholm. He *can* have invented the hospital visits in his letters to his wife in order to cover up

38

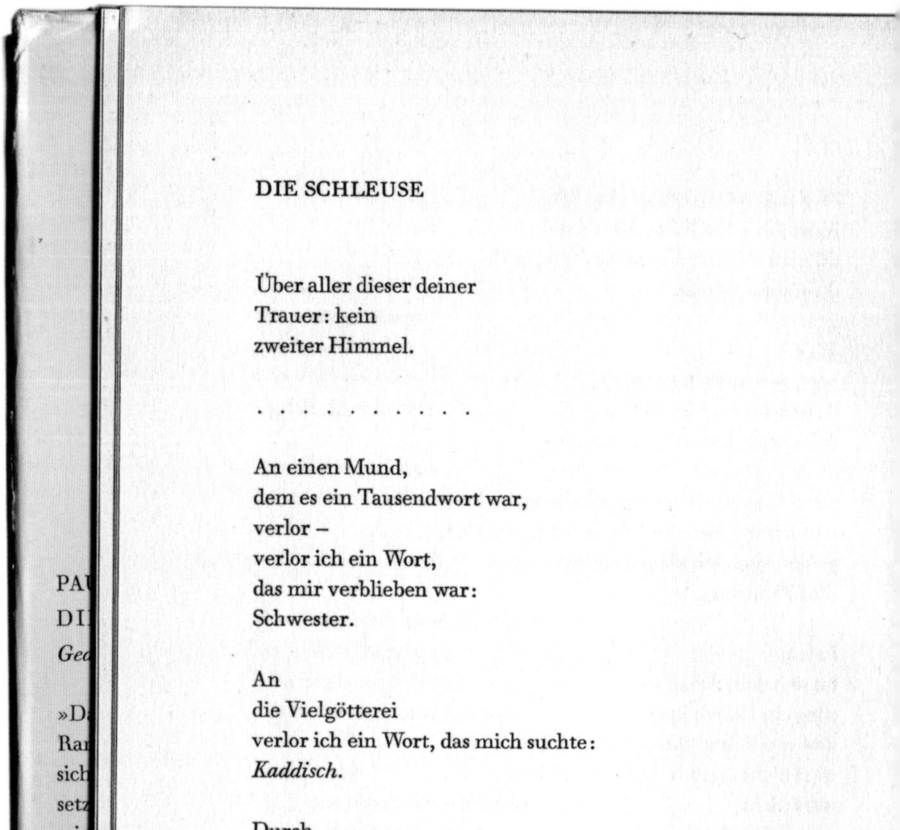

DIE SCHLEUSE

Über aller dieser deiner
Trauer: kein
zweiter Himmel.

. . . . . . . . . . .

An einen Mund,
dem es ein Tausendwort war,
verlor –
verlor ich ein Wort,
das mir verblieben war:
Schwester.

An
die Vielgötterei
verlor ich ein Wort, das mich suchte:
*Kaddisch.*

Durch
die Schleuse mußt ich,
das Wort in die Salzflut zurück –
und hinaus- und hinüberzuretten:
*Jiskor.*

20

39

his infidelity and explain why he chose to remain longer in the city than he'd planned. It's more doubtful, however, that he would have thought it necessary to feign statements by Sachs for the same reason. Or, for that matter, maintain the fiction in his personal notebooks.)

That there was something more behind Celan's wounded sensitivities is indicated by a diary-like poem written during a serious depression five years later. The text reacted to an article which had brought back memories of the Goll affair, going through various phases of the harassment. In addition, an "absolute Jewess" is mentioned, who willingly abided by the "new concept" of the postwar literary establishment in which one's ethnic background was used to invoke the hope of reconciliation. "'It may be', she pronounced, / 'that my people's faith / shines on me.' / It may be. / And yet how? / But that which / shone out of herself / they killed." Once more Celan was reacting against the public's utilization of Sachs and its inability to see the particular and not the general. Yet again he was turning against what he saw as his sister's willingness to (let herself) be identified as a representative of an entire people's suffering. For Celan every human being was exceptional, and his or her words therefore irreplaceable. The German institutions hid their guilty conscience by celebrating a poet who was called a queen or a prophet, but whose poetry there was reason to believe they didn't take at its word. And moreover: "of what / was her purple red?" Heart or blushing, sentiment or cosmetics?

40

> Who and what / drove Nelly Sachs to madness? / Who / taught her / deceit and arrogance? // In Stockholm I heard her say: / "Those in Auschwitz / did not suffer what I am suffering." / Others heard it too, among them / Lenke Rothmann. / Who supported this? And / what guilt / raged behind it?

The sentence was harsh but not groundless. (In a note made on September 10 it read: "hubris of pain.") Celan ended the poem with the same row of lone full stops that appears between the first and second stanza of "Die Schleuse" — as if the passage between the poets was set with stones. In the latter poem three stanzas followed which all ended with a lone word: "Schwester" (sister), "*Kaddish*," and "*Yizkor*," italicized in the first and last case. After the loss of the first word, which had proven to be so worn out and unreliable that it seemed a "thousandword," the term for the Jewish prayer for the dead was mentioned. Because of "the polytheism," however, the poem's self lost this word as well, although it had sought him out. What remained was the hope for a final word — the quiet prayer's reminder of those who had sacrificed their lives. These nameless ones did not wear the purple of royalty. No survivor could match their suffering.

In the first drafts Celan wrote "the sluices," as if he was referring to several. But Slussen was and remained the same. It was just the journey that changed direction — "back / and forth and across." When he left Stockholm on September 7, after a parenthesis in time which had turned out to contain the beginning of another affair, he did so as a friend. The letters which remained to exchange until the winter of 1969 exhibit an undeceived friendship. But the blind faith of siblingship had been broken.

Over all this sorrow / of yours: no / second sky. / . . . . . . . . . .

**TEXT** For letters from Celan 08/09, 08/11, and 08/19/1960, see BCelan 54, 55, and 57 respectively · For the friendship between Celan and the Demus couple, see Paul Celan, Klaus and Nani Demus, *Briefwechsel*, Frankfurt am Main 2009 · For letter from Celan to Pöggeler 08/09/1960, see *Paul Celan — die Goll-Affäre. Dokumente zu einer 'Infamie'*, ed. Barbara Wiedemann, Frankfurt am Main 2000, 506 · For letters to Celan 08/16 and 08/29/1960, see BCelan 56 and 63 respectively · For the information about Celan's lodging in Stockholm: interview with Inge Wærn 03/05/2009 · Dinesen, 310–311 · Fritsch-Vivié, 117 · Lennartsson, 99 · Jean Bollack, *Dichtung wider Dichtung. Paul Celan und die Literatur*, ed. and trans. from the French by Werner Wögerbauer, Göttingen 2006, 82 · Paul Celan and Gisèle Celan-Lestrange, *Briefwechsel*, Frankfurt am Main 2001, vol. I, 110 · Celan, "Die Schleuse," *Die Niemandsrose*, Frankfurt am Main 1963, 20 · Interview with Inge Wærn 11/26/2008, 03/05, and 03/20/2009 · Anders Olsson, "Möten. Inge Wærn, Nelly Sachs och Paul Celan," *Bokstäverna jag färdas i*, ed. Anders Olsson, Stockholm 2001, 119–134; here 121–123 and 131 respectively · Celan, *Atemwende*, Frankfurt am Main 1967 · Celan, "Die ihn bestohlen hatten," Celan and Celan-Lestrange, *Briefwechsel*, vol. I, 204 · For the note about "hubris of pain," see Celan, *Werke*, ed. Bonner Arbeitsstelle für die Celan-Ausgabe, Frankfurt am Main 2006, vol. 11, 269 | **IMAGE 35** Note by Sachs about visiting hours (KBS) · **36** Inge Wærn in 1936 (Inge Wærn's collection, Stockholm) · **37** Inge Wærn during a theater performance in the 1940s (Inge Wærn's collection, Stockholm) · **38** Caricature of Wærn at Max Reinhardt's in the Deutsches Theater in Prague, 1930s (Inge Wærn's collection, Stockholm) · **39** Celan, "Die Schleuse," *Die Niemandsrose* 1963 (S. Fischer Verlag) · **40** Paul Celan around 1960 (Photo Gisèle Celan-Lestrange, Paris, rue de Longchamp, 1958 © Eric Celan and Editions du Seuil, Paris)

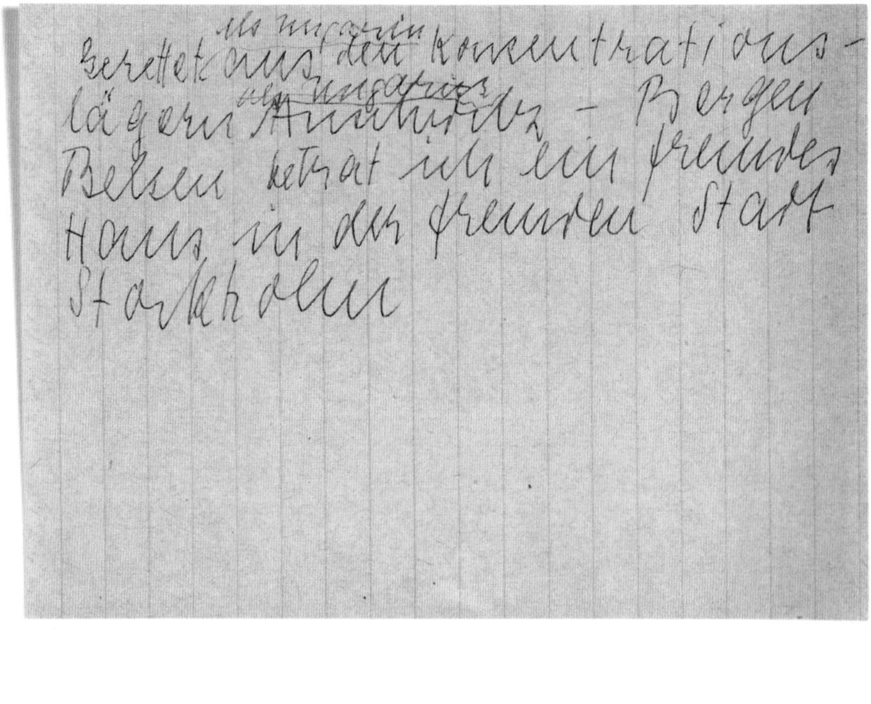

41

**A FRIEND AMID THE DESOLATION**

42

Celan and Lenke Rothman weren't the only ones to react to Sachs' comparison of her own suffering with that of the victims in camps like Dachau, Mauthausen, or Sobibór. Her neighbor on the second floor, ROSE WOSK (1916–2004), née Press and usually called "Rosi," also wondered.

In an undated note from the 1960s, Sachs took on another person's fate and wrote: "Saved as a Hungarian from the concentration camps Auschwitz–Bergen-Belsen I entered a strange house in the strange city of Stockholm." Possibly she was thinking of Rothman (who had also been at Guben), possibly of Wosk. Her neighbor was the daughter of a Hungarian Jewish firewood and coal wholesaler from Budapest. Before she was deported she had trained as a hairdresser. During her time in Auschwitz she was introduced to Joseph Mengele three times. After the Americans had liberated Bergen-Belsen she made it onto one of the white buses to Sweden, where she arrived gravely undernourished (weighing 33 kilos) and strapped by serious tuberculosis. She spent the first months in hospital, then two years in a convalescent home in Ulricehamn. Later on she would wed Henry Wosk, who was of Polish Jewish descent, had been at Auschwitz, and had also been saved on the buses. They married in 1949, and two years later their son Benjamin, later called Bertil, was born. In 1953 the family moved into the apartment next to Sachs'. (Shortly thereafter the couple divorced and the husband emigrated to America.) A few floors higher up in the building, Lenke Rothman would move in with the writer Sivar Arnér. Wosk herself described her acquaintance with her neighbor thus in a tribute on her seventieth birthday: "It was in a strange city, in a strange country and in a completely strange house. I was a refugee, full of uncertainty and despair. Right away on the first day a small, delicate and amiable lady came over to my apartment. She simply said: Good day and a warm welcome. I hope you will like it here. We're neighbors. This delicate and very amiable woman was Nelly Sachs."

At first the women met only sporadically, but from the end of the 1950s and onwards Wosk in effect became Sachs' factotum. Always ready to help, she was both neighbor and nurse, secretary and confidant. In contrast with Rothman, in whom Sachs claimed to see her own mother as a young woman, Wosk assumed tasks which Sachs herself had shouldered in the role of daughter. She answered the telephone, kept an eye on the calendar, and arranged for friends and acquaintances to pay visits. She ran errands, made sure the larder was stocked, and provided calm and security particularly during the periods of illness. When her angst attacks made existence unbearable in her own apartment, Sachs went over to Wosk's. Many times her son Bertil had to move so that the ageing lady could spend the night in his bed. The ten-year-old boy's doubts about moving in together most probably contributed to Sachs turning down the apartment that the Swedish Academy placed at her disposal after the second stay at Beckomberga in 1962. Despite the microphones and the electric water, Bergsundsstrand had a working system of care she didn't dare give up.

Wosk became Sachs' friend in desolation. After her arrival in Sweden she had begun jotting down thoughts and impressions in a spiral-bound notebook. The first diary is written in Hungarian and begins in January 1946. In it she expressed her grief over relatives who had been murdered, hopes that her two younger brothers would turn out to have survived, and worries about her fiancé Zoli, who wrote to her regularly from Hungary but lacked the money to come and visit her. She commented on the Nuremberg trials and lamented the fact that it wasn't possible to talk about the time in the camps with Swedes as they didn't have such experiences. Mainly, however, she described the complications of her tuberculosis and the routine as a patient at Sjö-Gunnarsbo Sanatorium. There followed a fifteen-year hiatus before Wosk once again took up her diary. The first of the four spiral-bound notebooks that followed was begun on April 4, 1960. In it, as in the following notebooks, Wosk wrote in a broken German acquired in the camps. The very first entry makes it clear that this time she didn't want to retain thoughts about her own life, but instead protocol life with her neighbor: "Li was so exhausted, really looked very tired, she said she couldn't create since there is a pecking all night and it drives her mad — as she said — and she can't bear it. I told her that she was welcome to

43

44

sleep in my apartment in order to rest a bit. Yes, she said, all her friends had already asked her to come and stay with them but she didn't want to. Yes, I said, but we live so close that you're really still in your own house and then it's not such a big thing, so come and sleep in my apartment."

Up until the last entry on June 28, 1971 — where Wosk in Swedish reports a visit by Olof Lagercrantz — she would fill a couple of hundred pages with impressions of the person she had characterized in her birthday tribute in 1961 as having a "big soul" and a "warm heart." The spiral-bound notebooks described Sachs' angst and persecution manias, how she ate and slept, when she wrote or read out new poems. Wosk became a female version of Eckermann, perhaps employed by the Post Office but really on her neighbor's service, who noted down what this *grande dame* said and did — a Mrs. Goethe who measured 1.48 m in stockings and had seven years of schooling.

The minutes-like character of the entries gives rise to repetitions: on most pages the ailing holds forth in monologues, sees threatening signs and infers conspiracies behind seemingly innocent phenomena. She returns persistently to key experiences in a past which has anything but had its day and at times expresses a strong mistrust of friends and acquaintances she assumes have allied themselves with an "organized gang." On July 13, 1960, Wosk jotted down a monologue that shows how close events of fifty years ago were to the present for Sachs. Here, inner and outer events blend into each other: "Was I not equal to the love here. The time when it tore me to pieces and my mother helped me. I believe in an inner cycle. And even if people destroy this world: the inner cycle continues. Neither is it the people. We are all. I myself did one thing and another. I omitted and failed. It goes into the inner cycle. A sick place here and there. Who knows."

In this inferno of agony and recrimination, trauma and turbidity, a particular event came to play the dominant role: the kidnapping of former SS-Obersturmbannführer ADOLF EICHMANN (1906–1962) in Buenos Aires on May 11, 1960, only a few weeks before Sachs traveled to Meersburg. Her journey abroad was overshadowed by the case, which she could follow in the papers and the broadcast media. Just three days before her departure, the man who had organized the deportation of millions of Jews was flown in secret to Israel, where one of the century's most widely watched trials would begin the following year. Sachs came to interpret her perceived persecution as revenge for Eichmann's capture. Six months later, when the delusions had again become severe, Wosk reported: "Suddenly! Today an article in the paper about Eichmann, I know, I know it, they telephoned me in Bromma, that time. He had been arrested and I must suffer, because of him too — I wanted to say something — but they didn't let me — you don't need to say, I know it."

That was on March 17, 1961. A few days later Enzensberger was lecturing in Stockholm and Sachs wanted to arrange a dinner party for her friend at her

45

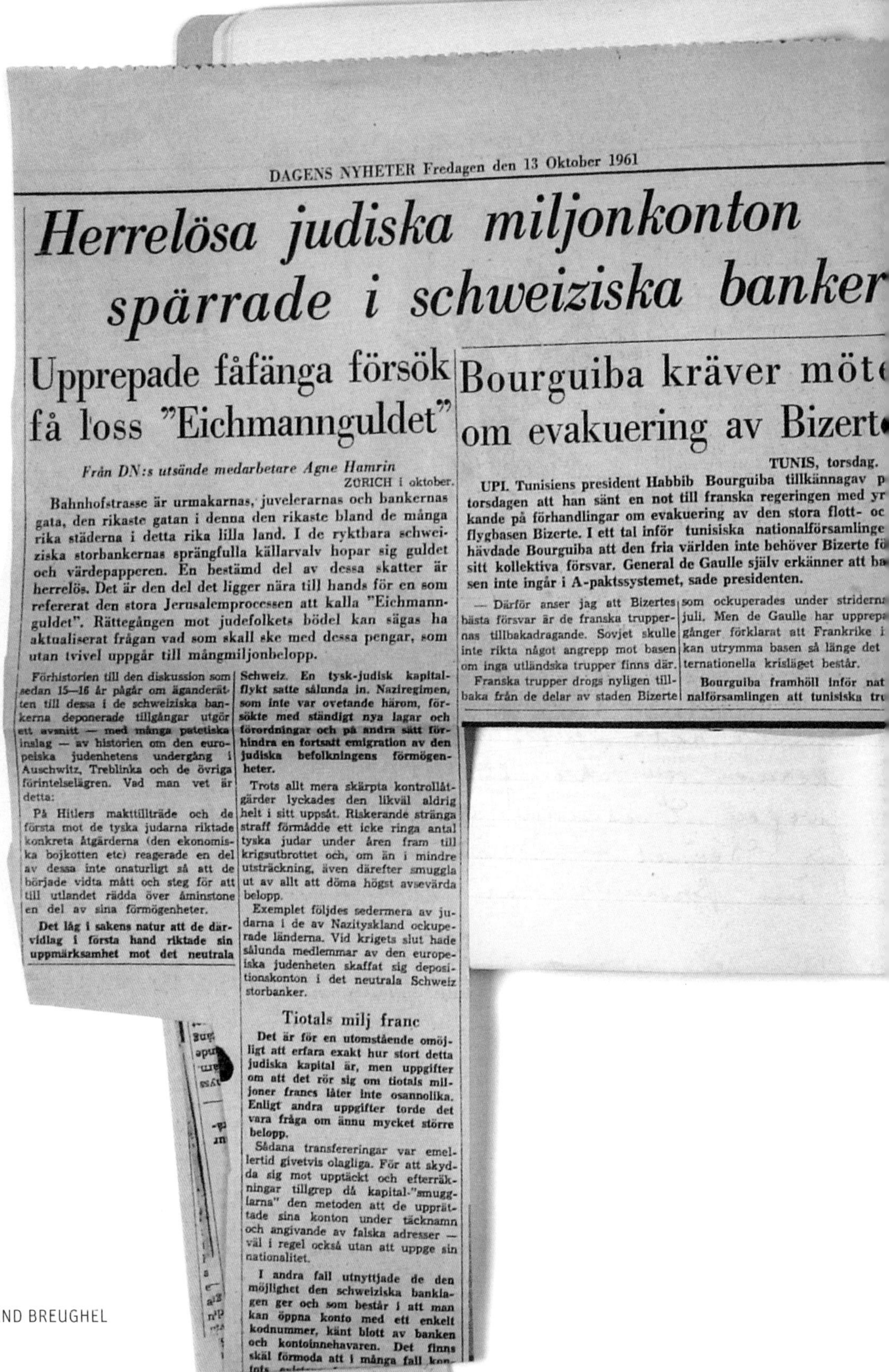

DAGENS NYHETER Fredagen den 13 Oktober 1961

# Herrelösa judiska miljonkonton spärrade i schweiziska banker

## Upprepade fåfänga försök få loss "Eichmannguldet"

*Från DN:s utsände medarbetare Agne Hamrin*

ZÜRICH i oktober.

Bahnhofstrasse är urmakarnas, juvelerarnas och bankernas gata, den rikaste gatan i denna den rikaste bland de många rika städerna i detta rika lilla land. I de ryktbara schweiziska storbankernas sprängfulla källarvalv hopar sig guldet och värdepapperen. En bestämd del av dessa skatter är herrelös. Det är den del det ligger nära till hands för en som refererat den stora Jerusalemprocessen att kalla "Eichmannguldet". Rättegången mot judefolkets bödel kan sägas ha aktualiserat frågan vad som skall ske med dessa pengar, som utan tvivel uppgår till mångmiljonbelopp.

Förhistorien till den diskussion som sedan 15—16 år pågår om äganderätten till dessa i de schweiziska bankerna deponerade tillgångar utgör ett avsnitt — med många patetiska inslag — av historien om den europeiska judenhetens undergång i Auschwitz, Treblinka och de övriga förintelselägren. Vad man vet är detta:

På Hitlers makttillträde och de första mot de tyska judarna riktade konkreta åtgärderna (den ekonomiska bojkotten etc) reagerade en del av dessa inte onaturligt så att de började vidta mått och steg för att till utlandet rädda över åminstone en del av sina förmögenheter.

**Det låg i sakens natur att de därvidlag i första hand riktade sin uppmärksamhet mot det neutrala Schweiz. En tysk-judisk kapitalflykt satte sålunda in. Naziregimen, som inte var ovetande härom, försökte med ständigt nya lagar och förordningar och på andra sätt förhindra en fortsatt emigration av den judiska befolkningens förmögenheter.**

Trots allt mera skärpta kontrollåtgärder lyckades den likväl aldrig helt i sitt uppsåt. Riskerande stränga straff förmådde ett icke ringa antal tyska judar under åren fram till krigsutbrottet och, om än i mindre utsträckning, även därefter smuggla ut av allt att döma högst avsevärda belopp.

Exemplet följdes sedermera av judarna i de av Nazityskland ockuperade länderna. Vid krigets slut hade sålunda medlemmar av den europeiska judenheten skaffat sig depositionskonton i det neutrala Schweiz storbanker.

### Tiotals milj franc

**Det är för en utomstående omöjligt att erfara exakt hur stort detta judiska kapital är, men uppgifter om att det rör sig om tiotals miljoner francs låter inte osannolika. Enligt andra uppgifter torde det vara fråga om ännu mycket större belopp.**

Sådana transfereringar var emellertid givetvis olagliga. För att skydda sig mot upptäckt och efterräkningar tillgrep då kapital-"smugglarna" den metoden att de upprättade sina konton under täcknamn och angivande av falska adresser — väl i regel också utan att uppge sin nationalitet.

**I andra fall utnyttjade de den möjlighet den schweiziska banklagen ger och som består i att man kan öppna konto med ett enkelt kodnummer, känt blott av banken och kontoinnehavaren. Det finns skäl förmoda att i många fall konton ...**

## Bourguiba kräver möt om evakuering av Bizert

TUNIS, torsdag.

**UPI. Tunisiens president Habbib Bourguiba tillkännagav p torsdagen att han sänt en not till franska regeringen med yr kande på förhandlingar om evakuering av den stora flott- oc flygbasen Bizerte. I ett tal inför tunisiska nationalförsamlinge hävdade Bourguiba att den fria världen inte behöver Bizerte fö sitt kollektiva försvar. General de Gaulle själv erkänner att ba sen inte ingår i A-paktssystemet, sade presidenten.**

— Därför anser jag att Bizertes bästa försvar är de franska truppernas tillbakadragande. Sovjet skulle inte rikta något angrepp mot basen om inga utländska trupper finns där.

Franska trupper drogs nyligen tillbaka från de delar av staden Bizerte som ockuperades under striderna juli. Men de Gaulle har upprep gånger förklarat att Frankrike i kan utrymma basen så länge det ternationella krisläget består.

**Bourguiba framhöll inför nat nalförsamlingen att tunisiska tr**

nach geschrien das alles ist wegen
Eichmans verhaftung, eigentlich nach
ihre meinung sollte man die ganze
Proces nicht machen, mit Böse kann
man Böses nicht bekämpfen
– auf mein frage wie so, alle
Verbrecher soll ohne Straf weiter
auf ihrer Verbrecherweg weiter gehen
sagte sie andere Verbrecher muss man
isolieren, aber Eichmans Schuld ist so
groß, und sie meint gegen 6.000.000
Menschen ist eine nicht zu Straffen
das ist Natürlich ein Teori, dass man
nur verbluft sein.
Erst besingt sie in ihre Dichtung
Verhöhnung des "Todes" die Martyrinnen
und jetzt will sie für jeder
Henker verzein

46

27 Okt. 67

~~Ei~~ Paar Tage her, hat Ky ein Band Gedichte in Manuskript von ein Dr X aus Deutschland mit der Titel „Tema über Gedichte von N. S. Sie ist sehr empört und als Beispiel erwehnte sie, dass wie „Clara Gool" Geschichte davon gemacht, auch dass Paul Célan ein Vers von ihr verstorbenen mans Gedichte als eigenes Publiziert hat — und dazu ist Paul Célan ein grosser Dichter — nicht so wie der hier, und welche Kritiker Kampanj davon geworden ist.

Es ist interessant zu erinneren, dass 1959-60, wann ihre „Vervolgungsmanie" ~~an~~ an die höhe sprung — die Zeit bevor sie im Södersjukhuset kam — hatte sie mir unzeligesmal wiedergeholt, dass eben so wie sie ist auch P. Célan vervolgt, zu dise Zeit war

home. But the illness intervened and she feared that the guests would be subjected to terror attacks. Instead the dinner party was held at Wosk's home. After that Sachs' health deteriorated rapidly. Enzensberger left on March 25. Already the following day Sachs prepared to return to Beckomberga. On March 27 Wosk noted: "I have just come from Li's, with a mental agitation I know so well in her, she says: 'My fate hinges on the Eichmann affair!' — and that is the reason she flees to the hospital. One day she said — I can't risk being at home, then they could tell me at Easter that they want blood. You do know, she says to me — histories bloodbath. Can you understand, she says, 'in the fall when I was in the depths of Dante's hell in Bromma, that was when Eichmann was taken away (kidnapped) and then they also wanted to take me away, from Bromma, when I had to flee to Södersjukhuset, but I was struck dumb and couldn't speak — but now I see things clearly.'"

Alongside the continuous reporting on Sachs' illness, the diaries also contain newspaper clippings. One article discusses what was referred to as the "Eichmann gold," that is, the capital — later inaccessible — that Jews had transferred to Swiss banks before being deported; in another Sten Mårtens is quoted in an account of Swedish mental health care; a third reports that Moses Pergament has started work on a new opera entitled *Abram* whose text was written "by the German writer Nelly Sachs" and was about "man's first contact with the invisible god." One clipping announces that a prize in Sachs' name has just been instituted in Dortmund, while another contains poems by Gunnar Ekelöf. The material shows how intimately Wosk followed Sachs and that she tried to re-create the contexts of her neighbor's statements and actions. At the same time that her friend was being written about in the papers, she was being treated by "Dr. M." and was translating poems by Gunnar Ekelöf. However, the judicial process against Eichmann increasingly appeared to be the prism through which all of existence and its signs were being seen. "The core of her conversation," reads a note made on March 7, 1961, "was that she was being held hostage because of Eichmann. As she said in Bromma already, they shouted at her that everything is due to Eichmann's arrest, in her opinion the trial should really not be held, you can't fight evil with evil."

Naturally enough, Wosk — who unlike Sachs had experienced the camps from the inside and also lost close relatives — saw the situation differently: "To my question, What, should all criminals be allowed to continue their criminal pursuits without punishment? she replies that other criminals must be isolated, but that Eichmann's guilt is too vast, and she doesn't think one person can be punished for 6,000,000 people. That is of course a theory, one can only be stunned. First she celebrates martyrdom in her poems in 'The Dwellings of Death,' and now she wants to forgive all executioners." Like Rothman and Celan, Wosk was left wondering at Sachs' attitude. How could she, who might have been persecuted but had avoided deportation, permit herself to represent moral standpoints which should be reserved for the murdered? Did a person who had herself managed to survive have the right to decide for those who hadn't? Surely no one could forgive in the name of the victims? And why this stylizing of herself as a suffering savior figure?

To Wosk, Sachs' attitude appeared an expression of the same "hubris of pain" that Celan had diagnosed. Or as she noted on January 9, 1962, a couple of weeks after Eichmann had been sentenced to death and Sachs had held a morning-long monologue: "She spoke constantly about how dreadful it was that she yet again is being persecuted in this peaceful country. It isn't dangerous just for her, but for all of Sweden. Everyone knows that she is no private individual, that she is a poet and now so much is being written about her everywhere. In short: megalomania!"

Despite the objections, and despite her personal experiences, Wosk remained loyal — even when Sachs, over the following months, tried to persuade the Israeli government to reverse the decision. On March 27 Sachs sent a letter from Beckomberga to David Ben-Gurion: "Most honored Mr. President, with words that have matured in deepest suffering I would like to inform you of what moves me most deeply. [---] Do not carry out the death sentence against Eichmann — in Germany, too, there are just people — for their sakes let there be mercy." The Israeli head of state, however, was not moved to clemency. On May 29 the sentence was upheld on appeal and two days later Eichmann was hanged. A month later, on Midsummer's Day, Sachs, who was still at Beckomberga, experienced strong anxiety. To her new friends Bengt and Margaretha Holmqvist she explained: "It can't just have been bloodthirsty avengers of Eichmann who made the day red and before and afterwards — and why this lynching atmosphere against me? Will I have to leave this country? But where to? Who can yet save me?"

Illness prevented her from considering a thought she had quoted already in "Briefe aus der Nacht": "One cannot allow oneself to suffer *so*!" The phrase occurs in Martin Buber's historical novel *Gog und Magog* (Gog and Magog), which stood on one of the shelves in Sachs' library. In it he portrayed, based on Ezekiel 38-39, two Hasids during the Napoleonic wars at the end of the eighteenth century. For the main character Jaakob Yitshak, known as "the Jew," God is a god of freedom. It follows that evil is anything that subjects man to compulsion. That in turn means that there is a false way of suffering — namely, if suffering is turned into a force that suppresses and enslaves, thus threatening freedom. He who lets himself be overwhelmed by his own suffering effectively relinquishes freedom, and thereby God. "This is a word! A word smokes like Sinai!" Sachs commented in "Briefe aus der Nacht." A decade later she was too unwell to realize that the torment she associated with her life could be seen as Wosk and Celan were inclined to consider it: as a dispossession of freedom. And thus as wrong. The illness turned everything into its opposite.

47

What were delusions appeared as affirmations of genuine insight. Oddly enough, it was in madness that the definitive truth lay hidden. Or as it is stated in one of Sachs' most disturbing poems, "Überall Jerusalem" (Everywhere Jerusalem), which was given the motto "In grief" and was dated the same day that the Eichmann trial began, April 11, 1961:

> There / in the illness / fermented to lucidity / the prophetess stabs her staff / at the soul's riches // There is gold hid in the confusion —

**TEXT** Personal data on Rosi Wosk were provided by Bertil Wosk in an interview 09/29/2008 and an email message 10/22/2009 · "Gerettet als Ungarin," AWosk · Wosk, "Dem Menschen Nelly Sachs zum 70. Geburtstag," AWosk · Wosk's diaries, AWosk · The article about the "Eichmann Gold," *Dagens Nyheter* 10/13/1961, the article about Swedish mental health care, *Dagens Nyheter* 11/22/1961, the article about Pergament's new opera, *Svenska Dagbladet* 04/12/1961; the items about the newly instituted prize in Dortmund and Ekelöf's poems, respectively, have no stated sources · Buber, *Gog und Magog*, Frankfurt am Main and Hamburg 1957 (orig. 1941) · Letter to Ben-Gurion 03/27/1962, Dinesen, 338 · "Überall Jerusalem," NfTdL (NSW:II) | **IMAGE 41** "Als Ungarin gerettet," manuscript (DLA) · **42** The Sjö-Gunnarsbo Sanatorium in Ulricehamn (Leif Gustafsson's collection, Älvsjö) · **43** Sachs with Wosk and the Svenssons (KBS) · **44** Sachs with Rosi Wosk and Signe Svensson, 1965 (KBS) · **45–46** Pages from Wosk's diaries (DLA) · **47** Eichmann during the trial in Jerusalem, 1961 (BPK)

## FROM GOLD TO GLOW

The hospital stays were not just spent on misguided attempts at alchemy, but also on quiet work in seclusion. Around 1960 Sachs' poetry took a new turn. From now on she would not just delineate and conjure silence, but try to transform it into a structural element of the texts themselves. The two principles she had named in the title *Flucht und Verwandlung* radicalized her poetry and freed it from the last remnants of the so-called "poetry of ruins" (*Trümmerlyrik*). The rhetorical pathos disappeared, the over-burdened vocabulary was abandoned. The poems were given a steeper syntax and a metaphorical terseness which moved them ever closer to the "silence" that the last book of the 1950s declared "a new land."

"Silence is the abode of the victims," she argues in one of the poems ("Gefangen überall" [Captive Everywhere]) written during the first half of the 1960s. But if silence was regarded as a domicile — that other side of speech which poetry could never fully incorporate without at the same time affirming its estrangement — that also meant that Sachs did not just want to speak for the dead, but also speak their language. Finally she freed herself from the representative poetics which had characterized her œuvre. If her earlier poems conveyed the impression that the texts amounted to a poetic labor of grief whose ultimate purpose was to become reconciled with the catastrophes of the past, her ambition now appeared more radical: by applying silence poetically, the pain was allowed to continue having its effect. The object — as the poem "Immer wieder neue Sintflut" (Always a New Deluge) from September

1962 has it — was to "make the wound readable." Only in this manner could the false reconciliation be avoided which would otherwise subject the victims to the threat of dying a second time, thus being turned into "the slain dead the murdered dead," in the words of one of Lindegren's sonnets Sachs had translated. To this end, she gradually reduced the discursive strain in favor of an articulation of silence, which by virtue of its ambiguity remained open and permeable. By incorporating non-verbal modes of expression she tried to "write the first letter / of the wordless language." With such silence only the respect for the dead could be restored. As earlier, Sachs regarded poetry as a "guide towards the unprotected," in the unforgotten words from the poem "Abraham" in *Sternverdunkelung*. But now she could also proclaim: "All words refugees / in their immortal hiding places."

The latter lines are taken from a text Sachs sent to Celan in November 1963 (with the salutation: "I am homesick for you!"). The poem would be included in the second of the four cycles she dedicated herself to during the hospital stays, and later gave the overall title *Glühende Rätsel* (Glowing Enigmas). The first suite was included in *Ausgewählte Gedichte* (Selected Poems), compiled by Enzensberger in 1963, the last in the posthumous collection *Suche nach Lebenden* (Searching for the Living), published by her friends the Holmqvists in the year after her death. With these four suites Sachs reached the summit of her writing life. In a single gesture, she succeeded in both condensing and simplifying the poetic statement. The earlier tendency to proclamation had vanished, the wish to persuade was gone, what remained were images characterized by a simplicity which was as great as their complexity was intimate.

In these darkly glowing verses Sachs substituted biblical contexts for despair's sensory concretion. The awareness of being chosen as poet was in no way diminished, but she no longer appeared as prophet. Neither announcing nor compounding the cause of suffering, she was now a sufferer herself. Finally, the pain didn't have to be proxied for. It was enough to rely on the perilous energies of her own experiences. The poems came about suddenly and in an eruptive manner, as if by fits and starts; the act of writing turned into a repeated dying in miniature. Yet at the same time the voice that spoke didn't wish to assert itself or emphasize the significance of an overall destiny. "The hells of Bosch and Breughel" had shown Sachs the fortuity of existence. She needed no Abraham to discern her own Mount Moriah. Or as she wrote to Ekelöf in the summer of 1965: "Poems come suddenly as a hemorrhage until annihilation, all the way to death. One trembles, one begs for them to stop, but one must succumb, one is a 'battleground.'"

If madness brooded on riches of the soul that Sachs, in her illness, had regarded as "gold," she now realized that poetry contained a dimension which glowed and shimmered yet never relinquished its mystery. Such treasures didn't have to be concealed beneath layers of imagery and rhetoric. If they made up an essential part of the poem itself, inseparable from its manner of articulation, they could glimmer in full light of day without risking diffusion. This is possibly the secret of the "secret" that Sachs so often summoned. As a consequence, that which may be termed "understanding" in her late texts must be conceived of as something other than a treasure or meaning unearthed. The poems provide a disguised form of elucidation. Just like love such as Sachs imagined it, they offer illumination without explanation, catch without spoils. In the words of "Lichterhelle kehrt ein":

> Glimpse of light comes into the dusky verse / flying the flag Comprehension / In gray dread I shall leave to search / Finding is elsewhere —

**TEXT** "Es springt," FuV (NSW:II) · "Gefangen überall," GR:III (NSW:II) · "Immer wieder neue Sintflut," GR:I (NSW:II) · EL (NSW:IV) · "Wer weiß, wo die Sterne stehn," Unww (NSW:II) · "Abraham," S (NSW:I) · For letter with poem to Celan 11/04/1963, see BCelan 93 · For the poem to Celan, see "Als der große Schrecken kam," GR:II (NSW:II) · SnL (NSW:II) · For letter to Ekelöf 07/05/1965, see Briefe 216 · "Lichterhelle kehrt ein," GR:I (NSW:II)

## NO HIDE AND SEEK

Several of Sachs' "glowing enigmas" make use of motifs from a hospital environment. There are tableaux with nurses, portraits of fellow patients, and snapshots from an institutionalized daily life. Yet the tone is simpler than in the cosmically expansive poems from the 1950s, the choice of imagery at once more drastic and concrete. Nor do they lack a contrary sense of humor or a tendency towards "absolute" metaphorical language, where the reliable transfer from figurative to literal no longer works in an established manner. The opening poem, "Diese Nacht" (This Night), is typical of the strangely heightened calm that pervades the cycles:

> Last night / I walked a dark side street / turned the corner / Then my shadow lay itself / across my arm / This wearied garment wanted / to be borne / and the color Nothing spoke to me: / *You are on the Other side!*

With seemingly plain means — a street corner, a piece of clothing, Nothing — Sachs portrays the passage to another world as if it were both obvious and natural. Yet what is obvious, or natural for that matter, in a nightly dimension where the shadow can't be distinguished from the darkness? And is not the shadow something a person always carries with her, whether she wants to or not? In Sachs' late poetic universe the surroundings resemble normal ones with their post office boxes and traffic lights, but in fact they obey different laws. It wasn't until now, however, when she had turned the corner, that the difficult-to-grasp rules emerged in her poetry.

In the poem "Vergessenheit" (Forgetfulness), published in the volume with which Sachs a few years earlier had begun the late phase of her œuvre, she found a formula for the longing to take the step into another world. She speaks there of being "on blood's / last tongue of land." A little later she returned to the notion in the cycle of poems "Noch feiert Tod das Leben" (Still Death Celebrates Life), in which the self moves out towards "the furthest tip of the tongue of land." The point alluded to is at once the place where the ground beneath one's feet ends and the tip of the tongue whence words leave their dwelling in the mouth. Language and land were still associated magnitudes — not because this was implied by terms like *Blut* and *Boden*, but because both ephemeral being and alphabetical creature strove for the outermost point where existence passed into another. In both cases the aim was to achieve the ultimate — the tip or point beyond which no one knew anymore. In the late 1950s poems Sachs had discovered that parting need no longer be mourned as in the Berlin years, but could be affirmed. For Berendsohn (and Celan) she appeared, by and large, as an ecstatic — a poet who tried to transcend the given boundaries of existence and through affirmation become part of a greater reality. The observation is reasonable. Yet Sachs could just as well be regarded an intense poet. In effect it wasn't so much the preposition *out of*, but *through* which indicated her striving. Already in "Briefe aus der Nacht" she noted: "Only intensity keeps the world going." The central term *Durchschmerzung*, "the working through of pain," refers to this. It is not a question of applying some religiously or poetically justified method to step out of oneself, leaving suffering and uncertainty behind, but about going through the inevitable pain to reach another, perhaps longer-lasting dimension of existence. For Sachs the very precondition for this striving was the fundamental uncertainty about the outcome.

In Baudelaire's words from the prose poem about the "artist's confession" (which Celan quoted from in the book that also included "Zürich, Zum Storchen") she could now say that "there are certain delicious perceptions whose vagueness doesn't exclude intensity." Possibly the word "delicious" should be replaced in Sachs' case, but the rest of the confession belonged to a doctrine she was familiar with. The 1960s poetry spoke with an immediacy which no longer needed to dramatize the meaning of what was being portrayed. From now on Sachs moved, as the poem "Grad hinein in das Äußerste" has it:

> Straight into the Utmost / not playing hide and seek with pain

**TEXT** "Diese Nacht," GR:I (NSW:II) · "Vergessenheit," Unww (NSW:II) · "Auf der äußersten Spitze der Landzunge," NfTdL (NSW:II) · "Briefe aus der Nacht," NSW:IV · "Grad hinein in das Äußerste," GR:II (NSW:II)

48

49

## THE HIDDEN RESERVES OF SIBLINGSHIP

All the same — or perhaps precisely because of this directness — Sachs felt a great need for protection. Beckomberga provided an asylum in the best sense of the word. While the clinic could offer no home, it was a refuge — "indeterminable here." Even if the doubts persisted and she seems never to have rid herself entirely of the suspicions of persecution, she had little reason to believe that the hospital was wiretapped or the staff in cahoots with murderers. In her room in Ward 29 Sachs wrote more poems than she had in a long time, and also translated Swedish colleagues. The correspondence shows that her contact with the outside world was periodically intensive. Books were planned, queries from readers and researchers answered, friends informed of the latest news.

During the first half of the 1960s GUNNAR EKELÖF (1907–1968) became particularly important. One of the brightest stars in Swedish poetry at this time, he had recently been elected to the Swedish Academy, and with *Opus incertum* from 1959 — which Sachs had spontaneously begun translating — had continued the anti-poetry commenced with *Strountes* five years earlier. In 1960 the polyphonic poetry collection *En Mölna-elegi* (A Mölna Elegy) was published. Yet to come were the three volumes which would make up the "Diwan" trilogy and constitute the byzantine portal to his œuvre. Sachs had translated Ekelöf during her earliest years in Sweden. She followed what was written about him and also cut out newly published texts from the papers. Yet it wasn't until she began planning a third anthology of translations that she seriously took on her colleague's work. The planned collection volume grew to such a size, however, that the publishers baulked, and when Rowohlt Verlag turned it down citing a negative verdict by a reader (Peter Rühmkorf, whose comments included: "the translation does not proffer poetry, but corrupt German"), the plans were finally abandoned. Instead sections of the material were excerpted and published in separate volumes dedicated to Edfelt, Lindegren, and Vennberg. In Ekelöf's case the redistribution meant that Suhrkamp Verlag published a representative sample in a bilingual edition entitled *Poesie* (Poetry) in 1962. The initiative was Enzensberger's: a few years earlier he had included seven of Sachs' translations in his milestone in the German history of poetry translation, *Museum der modernen Poesie* (Museum of Modern Poetry).

The work led to a remarkable exchange. Sachs and Ekelöf had met for the first time in connection with a dinner party she asked Eva-Lisa Lennartsson to arrange at Eastertime in 1962, as the Enzensberger family was visiting. Later they saw each other at dinner parties at the Holmqvist residence, among other occasions. Both the letters and the poems Sachs wrote over the following years are testament to a strong sense of kinship. By the time of Ekelöf's death from cancer in 1968 she had translated around sixty poems, many of which were never published, while her friend translated the first cycle of *Glühende Rätsel* in connection with the Nobel Prize in 1966. In January 1961

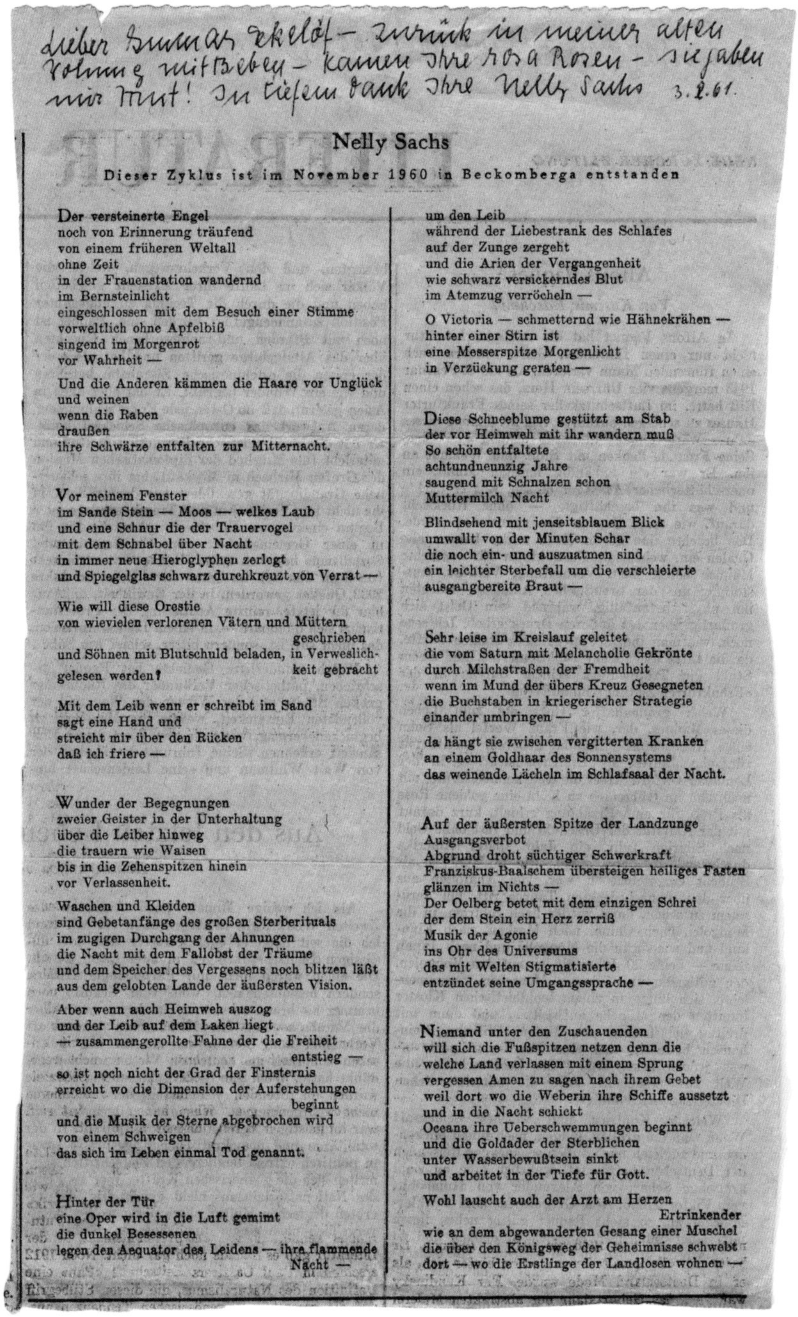

Lieber Gunnar Ekelöf — zurück in meiner alten Wohnung [illegible] — kamen Ihre rosa Rosen — sie gaben mir Mut! In tiefem Dank Ihre Nelly Sachs 3.2.61.

## Nelly Sachs

**Dieser Zyklus ist im November 1960 in Beckomberga entstanden**

Der versteinerte Engel
noch von Erinnerung träufend
von einem früheren Weltall
ohne Zeit
in der Frauenstation wandernd
im Bernsteinlicht
eingeschlossen mit dem Besuch einer Stimme
vorweltlich ohne Apfelbiß
singend im Morgenrot
vor Wahrheit —

Und die Anderen kämmen die Haare vor Unglück
und weinen
wenn die Raben
draußen
ihre Schwärze entfalten zur Mitternacht.

Vor meinem Fenster
im Sande Stein — Moos — welkes Laub
und eine Schnur die der Trauervogel
mit dem Schnabel über Nacht
in immer neue Hieroglyphen zerlegt
und Spiegelglas schwarz durchkreuzt von Verrat —

Wie will diese Orestie
von wievielen verlorenen Vätern und Müttern geschrieben
und Söhnen mit Blutschuld beladen, in Verweslichkeit gebracht
gelesen werden?

Mit dem Leib wenn er schreibt im Sand
sagt eine Hand und
streicht mir über den Rücken
daß ich friere —

Wunder der Begegnungen
zweier Geister in der Unterhaltung
über die Leiber hinweg
die trauern wie Waisen
bis in die Zehenspitzen hinein
vor Verlassenheit.

Waschen und Kleiden
sind Gebetanfänge des großen Sterberituals
im zugigen Durchgang der Ahnungen
die Nacht mit dem Fallobst der Träume
und dem Speicher des Vergessens noch blitzen läßt
aus dem gelobten Lande der äußersten Vision.

Aber wenn auch Heimweh auszog
und der Leib auf dem Laken liegt
— zusammengerollte Fahne der die Freiheit entstieg —
so ist noch nicht der Grad der Finsternis
erreicht wo die Dimension der Auferstehungen beginnt
und die Musik der Sterne abgebrochen wird
von einem Schweigen
das sich im Leben einmal Tod genannt.

Hinter der Tür
eine Oper wird in die Luft gemimt
die dunkel Besessenen
legen den Aequator des Leidens — ihre flammende Nacht —
um den Leib
während der Liebestrank des Schlafes
auf der Zunge zergeht
und die Arien der Vergangenheit
wie schwarz versickerndes Blut
im Atemzug verröcheln —

O Victoria — schmetternd wie Hähnekrähen —
hinter einer Stirn ist
eine Messerspitze Morgenlicht
in Verzückung geraten —

Diese Schneeblume gestützt am Stab
der vor Heimweh mit ihr wandern muß
So schön entfaltete
achtundneunzig Jahre
saugend mit Schnalzen schon
Muttermilch Nacht

Blindsehend mit jenseitsblauem Blick
umwallt von der Minuten Schar
die noch ein- und auszuatmen sind
ein leichter Sterbefall um die verschleierte
ausgangbereite Braut —

Sehr leise im Kreislauf geleitet
die vom Saturn mit Melancholie Gekrönte
durch Milchstraßen der Fremdheit
wenn im Mund der übers Kreuz Gesegneten
die Buchstaben in kriegerischer Strategie
einander umbringen —

da hängt sie zwischen vergitterten Kranken
an einem Goldhaar des Sonnensystems
das weinende Lächeln im Schlafsaal der Nacht.

Auf der äußersten Spitze der Landzunge
Ausgangsverbot
Abgrund droht süchtiger Schwerkraft
Franziskus-Baalschem übersteigen heiliges Fasten
glänzen im Nichts —
Der Oelberg betet mit dem einzigen Schrei
der dem Stein ein Herz zerriß
Musik der Agonie
ins Ohr des Universums
das mit Welten Stigmatisierte
entzündet seine Umgangssprache —

Niemand unter den Zuschauenden
will sich die Fußspitzen netzen denn die
welche Land verlassen mit einem Sprung
vergessen Amen zu sagen nach ihrem Gebet
weil dort wo die Weberin ihre Schiffe aussetzt
und in die Nacht schickt
Oceana ihre Ueberschwemmungen beginnt
und die Goldader der Sterblichen
unter Wasserbewußtsein sinkt
und arbeitet in der Tiefe für Gott.

Wohl lauscht auch der Arzt am Herzen Ertrinkender
wie an dem abgewanderten Gesang einer Muschel
die über den Königsweg der Geheimnisse schwebt
dort — wo die Erstlinge der Landlosen wohnen —

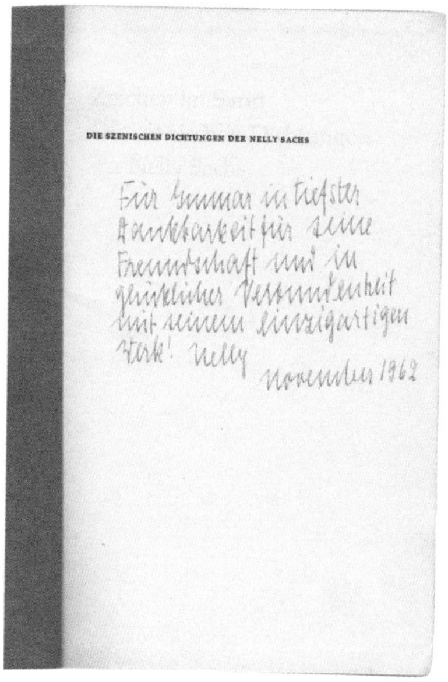


50

51

the *Neue Zürcher Zeitung* published some new texts with the heading "Dieser Zyklus ist im November 1962 entstanden" (This cycle was written in November 1969 at Beckomberga). A week later Sachs mailed the clipping to Ekelöf with thanks for the pink roses he had sent her on her return from the hospital. Thereafter words and objects would be regularly exchanged between the periodically insecure poet in Bergsundsstrand and her gradually more ailing colleague in Sigtuna.

For Sachs, new periods of illness brought special significance to a handful of objects. Besides the pictures of her parents, friends, and saints that she distributed like guardian angels throughout the apartment, there was the strip of plane tree bark that Celan had sent her and the painted piece of window pane from his son Eric. Other objects with a special charge included her father's old music box, her parents' wedding rings, a large colorless piece of crystal, as well as the rock collection. And then there was an icon …

During the intensive phase of the translation Sachs kept Ekelöf informed of her progress, but also expressed concern and anguish, not least about the Eichmann trial. To give her some relief her friend lent her an icon. With an allusion to the Virgin in the "Diwan" trilogy he was in the process of writing, he called the Madonna *panayia*, "the Pain-filled." In February of 1962 Sachs was once again at Beckomberga and wrote back to thank Ekelöf: "She is with me, the 'Protectress,' day and night. When she arrived — enveloped in your hand and then taken out by me and again bedded down — the Precious thing in the drawer of my bedside table — and the sacred eyes in which dearest memory lives — then there is calm on the flight in the room. The most moving thing: that you lend her to me in a moment of despair, when all my attempts at reconciliation had run aground yet again, that you catch this moment, in which I two years ago disappeared into night — that is the unforgettable thing." The icon, which was later exchanged for another, was immediately imbued with magical powers. In reality it was less a prayer image than a protective talisman. Henceforth the Virgin would not be absorbed by reading as in the "little garden of paradise" of the Berlin years, but would be a Madonna that personified a real story of suffering.

Shortly before the publication of Ekelöf's *Poesie* Sachs again wrote him from the hospital. After having described the bloody Bosch scenes she had experienced, she told him about the feeling of abandonment which had come over her after the torment. "But this time it's different — I have you my dear friends — 'the Pain-filled' is with me next to the photographs of my dear deceased." A few weeks later she informed him: "*Panayía*, the Pain-filled — is by my side throughout the time of martyrdom." And the following month: "Gunnar, dear brother — as I transcribe to you in bad, tired handwriting a sister to your icon the Pain-filled from my book — the door opens and a nurse comes in with your package, I open it and immediately love her." In the package was the icon that is still preserved at the Royal Library in Stockholm.

The descriptions show how Sachs established links between different dimensions of existence. She wasn't merely a "sister" and "brother" with Ekelöf, nor was she merely in an institution where "sisters" took care of her, but now the first borrowed icon had also got a "sister." The question is whether the poem she was in the process of copying when the nurse brought in the package, entitled "Im eingefrorenen Zeitalter der Anden," doesn't offer the best model for the sort of exchange that seems to have been on Sachs' mind. The first lines read: "In the ice-bound era of the Andes / the princess in the sarcophagus of ice / embraced by all the world's love / resurrection-ready." The poem had been written the year before, after Sachs had read about a discovery in the Andes. There, archaeologists had found a preserved corpse encased in ice. It was the body of a twelve-year-old girl, possibly a princess, who had been sacrificed to the gods half a millennium earlier, apparently without offering any resistance. In Sachs' eyes this South American Snow White, embedded in ice like an insect in amber, was an image of self-sacrificing love that outlives time and space. Faithful to the gods not just until the end but far beyond that, the virgin reminded her of Ekelöf's Madonna: in the ice casket as well as the icon, absolute devotion lay hidden — visible to the eyes of all, but inaccessible.

With the term "resurrection-ready" Sachs may have wanted to signal that it was enough to press one's lips against the ice for the bound and yet limitless love to be reawakened. The human imagination, with its capacity for passion and empathy, became the medium in which siblingship could be affirmed beyond time and space. Or as the stage directions read for the unpublished drama "Eisgrab, oder, Wo Schweigen spricht" (Ice Grave, or, Where Silence Speaks), which was based on the same item of news:

> An old Indian legend tells of the ice grave in Chile high in the Andes. Many thousands of years ago a princess was buried here, it is said. When the grave was discovered she was fresh as life and yet dead. In this realm between life and death or in a dimension which has already arisen somewhere else, this space tale shall take place — without any other space than that which the human imagination holds —

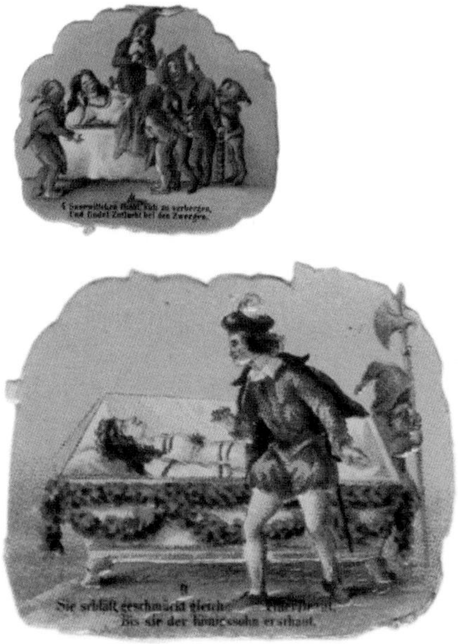

52

**TEXT** For Rühmkorf's assessment, see letter to Enzensberger 06/30/1961, ASuhrkamp · Cf. also Rühmkorf, *Die Jahre, die ihr kennt*, Reinbek bei Hamburg 1972, 129–130 · GE · "Dieser Zyklus ist im November 1962 entstanden," *Neue Züricher Zeitung* 01/29/1962 · For letters to Ekelöf 02/22, 06/25, and 08/24/1962, see Briefe 191, 195, and 200 respectively · Letter to Ekelöf 07/17/1962, the Gunnar Ekelöf collection, UUB · "Im eingefrorenen Zeitalter der Anden," NfTdL (NSW:II) · "Eisgrab," NSW:III | **IMAGE 48** Icon, gift from Gunnar Ekelöf (KBS) · **49** Crystal (KBS) · **50** Cycle of poems written at Beckomberga in 1960, published in *Neue Zürcher Zeitung* 01/21/1961, with a dedication to Gunnar Ekelöf (UUB) · **51** "For Gunnar in deepest gratefulness for his friendship and in happy solidarity with his singular work! Nelly in November 1962," dedication to Ekelöf in *Zeichen im Sand*, 1962 (from a private collection) · **52** Scrapbook pictures from "Das Oblatenalbum" (KBS)

53

## PLASTIC TALISMAN

Among the objects to which Sachs ascribed magical powers was also an item with a decidedly higher kitsch factor than Ekelöf's icon. It does not depict a Madonna or a princess in a frozen tomb but a Swedish manor preserved behind transparent plastic. A postcard has been mounted in a frame of reflecting metal foil decorated with little tassels. The picture is of a two-storey Palladian

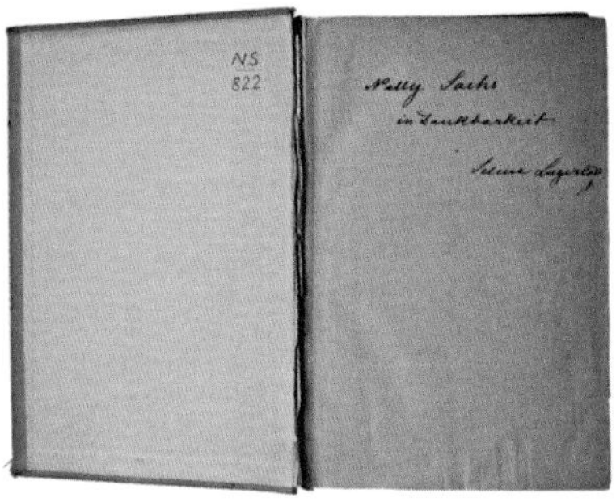

54

residence with a yellow façade and cornice. The four columns around the entrance are decorated with capitals, the windows shaded by awnings, and the steps flanked by pedestals with flowers in large pots. Two flagpoles are hung with banners in the Swedish and what might be the American colors. In front of the building is a large pond edged by clipped lawns. In the foreground there are the obligatory plants and flowers.

The postcard is of the model for Ekeby Manor, where Gösta Berling lives in Lagerlöf's novel: Rottneros Manor in Värmland. Sixty years after the story of the defrocked vicar awakened a fifteen-year-old Berlin girl's passion for the land in the north, the theme came back to Sachs. In connection with the announcement of the Nobel Prize in 1966, the plastic gift was handed to her by the neighbor she most feared — the alcoholic woman on the floor above whom she suspected of collaborating with the Nazis. Did the neighbor know anything of Sachs' early love of an imagined Sweden? Had blessed chance arranged it so that one of her enemies showed her reverence — perhaps even offered her friendship — at the same time that she received the ultimate confirmation that she was a *Schriftstellerin*?

Impossible to say. But as long as the object remained on the shelf in the cuddy no evil could happen. In its sealed state Rottneros Manor continued to exert a magical influence. Indirectly, the gift celebrated the origins of so many of Sachs' own stories. Protected by plastic, the only thing that meant anything survived: the belief that love conquers all.

55

**IMAGE 53** Selma Lagerlöf, *Gösta Berling*, German trans. Mathilde Mann, 1921 · **54** Nelly Sachs' copy of *Mårbacka. Jugend-Erinnerungen*, 1923, sent to her by Selma Lagerlöf in December 1923 (KBS) · **55** Plastic object with postcard of Rottneros Manor in Värmland (KBS)

## SCISSORS IN AUGUST

In a note made in the summer of 1957 Sachs returned to one of the leitmotifs of her œuvre: "Cutting of hair: sign from another world which gives force." She was alluding to the myth of Samson and Delilah, which she was trying to reinterpret for the stage. "Samson's power, the real power, is in the hairs themselves. (Paths of light through the millennia.)" At a higher level Delilah's treachery was a betrayal of the divine power. When she cut off the man's hair she was violating the very life which had animated the universe for aeons. Everything in the play happened on two parallel planes. The man and woman on stage were at the same time constellations in the sky, their everyday doings were also events on the firmament. The question was only how to portray this duality without turning the play into a mechanical allegory. If every action had to be read in two registers, then no room was given for individual freedom. Didn't the whole thing look a little like the sort of puppet theater she had performed in Berlin? It may be that the strings making the puppets dance weren't visible, but if every action was dictated by an invisible yet larger course of events, perhaps the freedom of movement was illusory anyway?

After having pondered the title — at this point it was still "Im Schlafleib" (In Sleeplife) — Sachs imagined that voices would whisper "in sleepwater like music." The sky was turned metaphorically into a sea where eternity was a water filled with purling dreams; events in the present only rippled the surface. Thus the sky was given a dimension of depth and Samson's fall "through millennia" could be interpreted as a fall through all the dreams, conversations, and memories on which human existence was built — or rather floated. "And suddenly everything into the present. Simply man, woman, the secret"...

Whether these deliberations solved any problems of dramatic composition is safest left unsaid. Yet it bears noting that Sachs saw the relationship between the individual and the general, the present and eternity as the very axis of the drama. She was not trying to portray the timeless message behind the coincidences of reality, but neither did she want to celebrate the transient love between man and woman at the expense of what went on behind the inscrutable backdrop of the sky. On the contrary, she regarded the connections between dimensions as the play's basic precondition and actual subject. The secret, in other words, was in the hair. It followed that a "revelation" wasn't possible until Samson had been shorn and the force released. In his sense, he was a puppet: only when Delilah cut off the strings to the higher will did he regain the freedom to fall through the aeons. That made the scissors an ambiguous instrument. On the one hand it took Samson's power from him, on the other hand that power was thereby bequeathed to another world. His death meant a new but different sort of life, for "hair grows after death"...

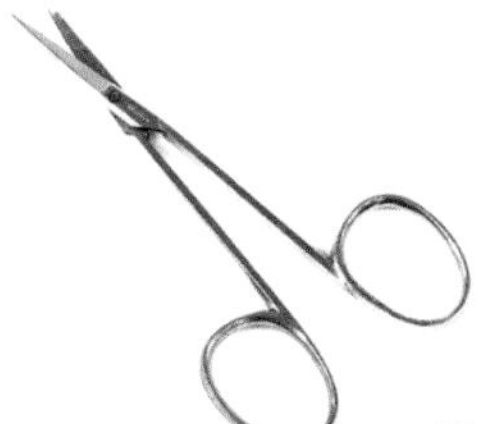
56

Delilah may be a traitor, nonetheless the scissors beg the question: did she betray love in all respects? At the beginning of the play a woman's voice "who once was Delilah" speaks: "Actually I just want to scratch the universe a little / with my questioning, scratch open a hole / for curiosity plagues me so — to peer in behind the force —." Inquisitiveness is usually considered a mortal sin, particularly if its arrogance is directed at ultimate causes. Judging from Sachs' specification, the woman spoke after having lost her identity as Delilah. Curiosity has already taken its tribute, then: she was no longer who she had been. Or put differently: the scissors sealed her fate. Perhaps it isn't so remarkable that a writer — who preferred to give the female characters in her plays names in which her own pet name featured — through the encounter with a new language thus became aware of the ambivalence not of her first but of her *last* name.

During the difficult year of 1962, most of which was spent at Beckomberga, Sachs made some notes in which despair is mixed with bewilderment. In these lines, insight is tough to distinguish from delusion, the wish to heal with words is hard to extricate from the compulsion to see ominous tidings in the

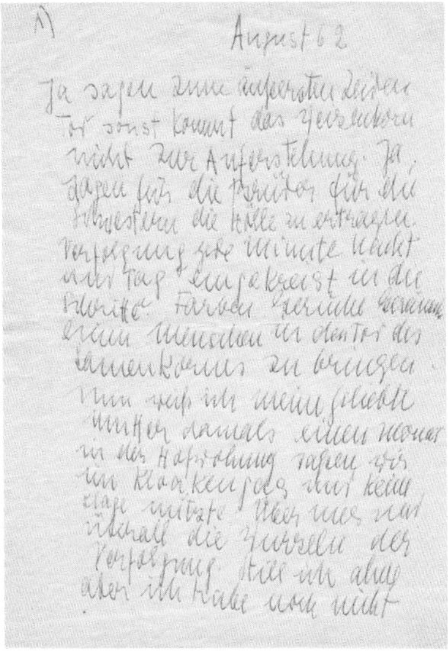
August 62

57

signs. In a manuscript dated "August 62" which is partly difficult to decipher, she noted among other things:

> I glow the words in the night to you my beloved. My throat was clogged with fear I was mute with dread. My name means scissors in Swedish written with airplanes on the sky the crossed knives on the crafts' walls —

Mentally ill, Sachs elevated herself to the role of savior of the beloved. She was simultaneously the person whose words glowed in the night, like signaling stars, and the woman whose throat had seized up during the terror of the 1930s. Then and now lay next to each other, the roles of savior and victim could not be separated. Instead they were like the twin blades on one and the same pair of scissors. During a stroll with Margaretha Holmqvist by Runstensplan in Bromma she thought she could read her surname in the intersecting vapor trails of two airplanes. According to Holmqvist, Sachs also thought of the swastikas that were painted on the planes of the Third Reich — as if her own name was being written into the very signature of terror.

Later she wrote out the notes on the typewriter, demonstrating how seemingly spontaneous impressions and stray thoughts were condensed into material for literary work. Now she linked the quoted passage with a direct allusion to the very origins of her œuvre:

> To you my beloved I extend these words in the night. My name (Sachs — means scissors [*sax*] in Swedish) with smoke — a pair of scissors painted on the blue sky (above Runstensplan)
> O you chimneys — — — — —

58

Here Sachs literally gives herself *as* word, and *in* translation, to the beloved dead. Like Delilah she could say that she was the woman "who once was Sachs." Her last name was inscribed as smoke across the sky, translated into epitaph. Thus she would continue to live, growing beyond her own death, like vapor. Or rising smoke. Like hair.

Perhaps Sachs did not see it as a coincidence that the two ringed handles of the instrument of parting formed — an infinity sign.

**TEXT** "Weitere Aufzeichnungen," NSW:IV · For a different examination of Sachs' surname, see Ruben Frankenstein, "Nelly Sachs, eine Randbemerkung," *Lichtersprache aus den Rissen. Nelly Sachs – Werk und Wirkung*, ed. Ariane Huml, Göttingen 2008, 181–184 | **IMAGE 56** Nelly Sachs' scissors (KBS) · **57** "August 62," manuscript (KBS) · **58** Sachs in her apartment, 1964 (Photo Eva Mohr, KBS)

# DUST, RIPE FOR FLIGHT

1

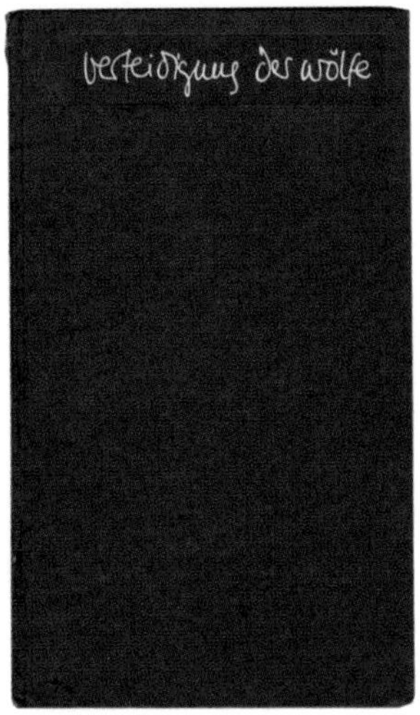


2

### FAME BURGEONS

With the recognition of Sachs as one of the postwar era's most important German-language poets came both a heightened sense of exposure and new friendships, principally in literary circles. An important role in the latter respect was played by HANS MAGNUS ENZENSBERGER (*1929), who after having worked as editor at Süddeutscher Rundfunk published his first collection of poetry, *verteidigung der wölfe* (The Wolves' Defense) in 1957. In January of the following year he got to know Sachs. In her earliest extant letter she thanks Enzensberger for the poetry collection he has given her, adding that she immediately passed it on to Swedish colleagues. "It will now travel from Sivar [Arnér] to Karl Vennberg, with whom you, I think, have much in common. Also with Ragnar Thoursie." Enzensberger's poems must immediately circulate and also be translated. The newly acquainted adopted the informal mode of address straight away and used the pet names "Li" and "Mang." Her friend's Norwegian wife, DAGRUN, née Kristensen (*1930), quickly became a close friend as well. One year into their acquaintance, Sachs fantasized about sleeping on the kitchen bench in her friends' home on the island of Tjörne in the Bay of Oslo. "You know," she explained to Dagrun, "at home I also sleep in the kitchen, simply because I feel more at home there than in the living room, where the furniture is inherited from other refugees." The Celan family had been named "the holy family," now the Enzensbergers were given an equally exemplary role. Her friends had recently had a child, TANAQUIL (*1958). Mother, father, daughter — for Sachs it was a familiar constellation.

In 1960 Enzensberger was hired as editor at Suhrkamp. He immediately made efforts to have Sachs' poems published by his new employer. Recently released from Beckomberga, she replied: "Yes, I would be more than happy to give you everything for your Suhrkamp publisher." The rights to old texts were purchased, a contract was signed in November, and work on a first collection volume could commence. Over the following months Sachs made suggestions for a selection, advised against including her Berlin poems, assembled and wrote out the new texts since *Flucht und Verwandlung*. In time for her birthday the following year *Fahrt ins Staublose* was published along with the *Festschrift Nelly Sachs zu Ehren* (In Honor of Nelly Sachs), to which Andersch, Bachmann, Celan, Domin, Enzensberger, and Hamm among others contributed texts. More distant acquaintances, too, supplied poems or essays, including Günter Eich and Johannes Bobrowski, Beda Allemann and David Rokeah.

The context made it clear which generation was closest to Sachs: the younger one. The dust jacket text of the collection indirectly explains why: "Nelly Sachs, the great Jewish poet with German as her mother tongue, today, at seventy, lives in Stockholm. Little is known about her life: she was born in Berlin in 1891. Her early works have disappeared without a trace, lost in the gloom of the Hitler era. Shortly before the outbreak of war she managed to flee to

Sweden [---]. Nelly Sachs' whole *œuvre* is a 'journey into a dustless realm.' But this journey begins in ourselves, in 'the dust that blocks the light'; it begins 'in the dwellings of death.'"

As a social creature Sachs was forty years older than her tribute-paying colleagues, but as a writing person she was in effect of the same age. Although she didn't pen the dust jacket text herself, she is likely to have approved it. There are no signs, however, that she tried to correct the misleading information about the year of the flight or the manuscripts that had been lost. Or that she protested when, at the end, her poems were described by Kurt Pinthus as "the German-language finale of the three thousand-year-old line that began with the psalmists and the prophets" (an estimation which did not please Celan, who incidentally was aware of Pinthus' friendship with Goll). The dust jacket text confirmed the view of her œuvre that Sachs herself wanted to convey. For the writer, the year of birth was 1947.

3

At the same time that Sachs was suffering from mental stress an image began to form in the public eye that would eventually take on the traits of legend. In the same year that Sachs reached seventy biblical years of age, the city of Dortmund instituted its literature prize in her name. Behind the initiative were, among others, the writer and translator EGON KÖTTING (1914–1987), who had spent the war in Sweden and was active within the Deutsch-Schwedische Gesellschaft, as well as the councillor for culture of Dortmund, the Social Democrat ALFONS SPIELHOFF (1912–1987). The prize was to be awarded every two years; Sachs was the first recipient. The criteria for the prize made it clear what was associated with her name: "To honor and promote persons who by means of exceptional creative achievements in the literary and intellectual area strive particularly to improve the cultural links between peoples; who in a distinctive way have undertaken to further cultural exchange between countries as a new and unifying element between peoples; who through their life and work in an exemplary way have advocated spiritual tolerance and reconciliation between peoples." Not without reason Sachs was seen as a model for the mediation between cultures; more problematic was the wish to read her works under the sign of reconciliation.

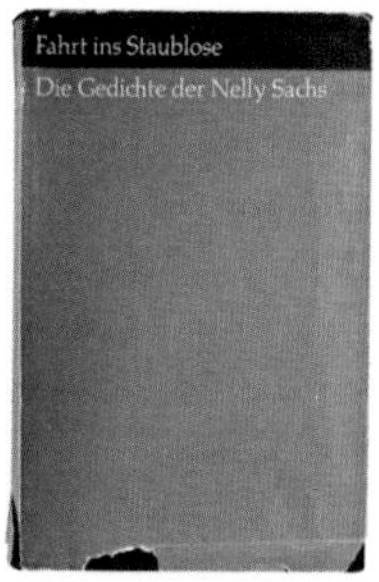

4

5

Since Sachs' health was too frail for her to travel, a delegation was dispatched to Stockholm under the leadership of Dortmund's Social Democratic mayor EWALD GÖRSHOP (1887–1962). The visit coincided with Sachs' birthday and was celebrated at the home of her friend MARGARETA DANNESKIÖLD-SAMSØE, née von Sneidern (later remarried Lindh), in the suburb of Bromma, north of the city. A reception was arranged for the late morning of December 12. In the evening the guests were joined by "the Swedish poets and their wives," as Sachs wrote to Dähnert. Among those present were not just Artur Lundkvist, the Lindegrens, Edfelts, and Holmqvists, but also Enzensberger and Rothman, Erwin Leiser and Peter Weiss. The editor-in-chief of

6

7

*Judisk krönika*, DANIEL BRICK (1903–1987), was there with his wife, the Russian-born photographer ANNA RIWKIN (1908–1970), who documented the festivities with her camera. In her short speech Sachs expressed her thanks above all because the prize gave her the courage to carry on working for understanding between people with the help of words. "For what else can we do with the word here, other than to pull it up by its roots and beseechingly let it sweep across the globe, so that it carries out its secret conquest on earth, which does not beget tears but smiles — the conquest of peace."

Four years later, when she received the German book trade's "peace prize," she expressed her thanks for the honor with near enough identical words. On the last day of the book fair in 1965, before about a thousand guests in Paulskirche in Frankfurt am Main, she asked rhetorically: "And all of us, what can we do with the word that was given to us, but pull it up by its roots and beseechingly let it sweep across the globe, so that it lends its secret, uniting power to a conquest — the only conquest on earth that does not beget tears, that begets smiles: the conquest of peace." The image conjured in the presence of President Heinrich Lübke, among others, was so significant to Sachs that she felt inclined to repeat it. Her œuvre would conquer readers' hearts in peace. Yet this peaceful conquest required that the word was grasped at its base. Unlike the many tongues of cultures, the language of poetry was homeless by principle. Like a vast network of links, its rootlets were drawn across the globe, giving the planet poetry's own longitudes and latitudes. If the speech expressed

6 Lenke Rothman, Nelly Sachs, Margareta Lindh (Danneskiöld-Samsøe)
7 Artur Lundkvist, Nelly Sachs, Erik Lindegren
8 Egon Kötting, Karl Hansmeyer, Nelly Sachs, Ewald Görshop
9 Nelly Sachs with Ewald Görshop and Karl Hansmayer, among others

8

9

a will to reconciliation, this wasn't based on repression but on remembrance. Poems didn't redraw the map, but were a continuing attempt to make the topography of pain and landscape of loss visible.

The jury's statement in Frankfurt was reminiscent of the one in Dortmund. Among other things, it highlighted that Sachs' works "speak for the Jewish destiny in an era of inhumanity and reconcile the German and the Jewish without contradictions." In the acceptance speech, however, the word "reconciliation" was never used, nor were there any speculations about differences between the German and the Jewish. Sachs' belief in the homeless but not rootless poetry as an abode tried, rather, to broaden the understanding of identity as something that could not be captured in narrow categories such as "German" and "Jewish." Overcoming her reserve following a long period of illness, she noted that she was visiting her former homeland in order to "tell the new German generation" that she "believed in it." Thereby she emphasized first the cost of overcoming her reservations, second that she was turning to young people who, even if they had hardly escaped the horrors, had not created the conditions for them. The addressee had not been born in places like Braunau am Inn in 1889 or Munich in 1900, that is, did not belong to Hitler's or Himmler's vintage, which Sachs had to assume were represented in the audience, but to the less implicated age groups who in the worst case had been called up during the final phases of the war.

Although a red *J* had been stamped in the prize winner's passport in the

10

11

1930s, and although the identity document which now made it possible for her to travel bore the Swedish national coat of arms, if she belonged anywhere it was in the stateless republic of poetry. Sachs spoke as poet. And as such she suggested a searching approach to life "tormented by anxiety and doubt." In one of the poems the prize recipient read at the end of her address, and which was later printed in a booklet along with the award statement and the other speeches, she noted: "During the flight / what a splendid reception / along the way —." Together with the concluding lines — "Instead of a homeland / I hold the world's transformations" — these stanzas may well be considered the national anthem of a poet without a country.

12

The trip to Germany in 1965 went under the sign of a "young" nation. The previous fall Gruppe 47 had chosen Sigtuna for their annual conference abroad. Following private meetings with poets from the younger generation, Sachs had met representatives of the leading group in German cultural life. Even if neither Andersch nor Bachmann, Ilse Aichinger nor Günter Eich were able to attend, she was pleased about the visits at Bergsundsstrand and moved by the atmosphere at the foundation. Reporting to Elisabeth Borchers that the tone at the readings had been a bit too critical for her taste, she nonetheless enthused that the reception had been "so touching." Surrounded by German and Swedish colleagues, Sachs had "a strong sense of home." "Pulled out of my loneliness into the great world of literature, everything to me seemed dream-like."

The following year's trip abroad went to this world of books and memories rather than to a nation which was just experiencing an "economic miracle." While she couldn't feel at home in the reconstructed financial metropolis on the Main, Sachs could in literature. All the same, this time she was unable to avoid sleeping on German soil. For support she was accompanied by the Finno-Swedish literary critic and historian BENGT HOLMQVIST (1924–2002) and his wife MARGARETHA, née Lindblom (*1926), a translator of German literature. Although they had known of each other for some time, they had not started socializing until Enzensberger had brought Sachs along to a dinner party on March 19, 1961. The visit would lead to the firmest friendship of the remaining years of her life. The Holmqvists had children too (two daughters), but unlike Celan and Enzensberger, they lived in the same city as Sachs, who quickly ordained them her family. She was content with the role as child between the daughters and "transferred her need for fatherly authority on Bengt, and for motherly care on Margaretha," as Dinesen notes. Possibly it was not unimportant that the latter bore the same name as Sachs' own mother. During the last ten years of Sachs' life they were in daily contact. When they couldn't see each other they spoke on the phone, they organized joint excursions, and much of the poet's public life, particularly in connection with literary prizes, was regulated by the Holmqvists.

The traits Sachs ascribed to her friends came in handy during the twelve days

13

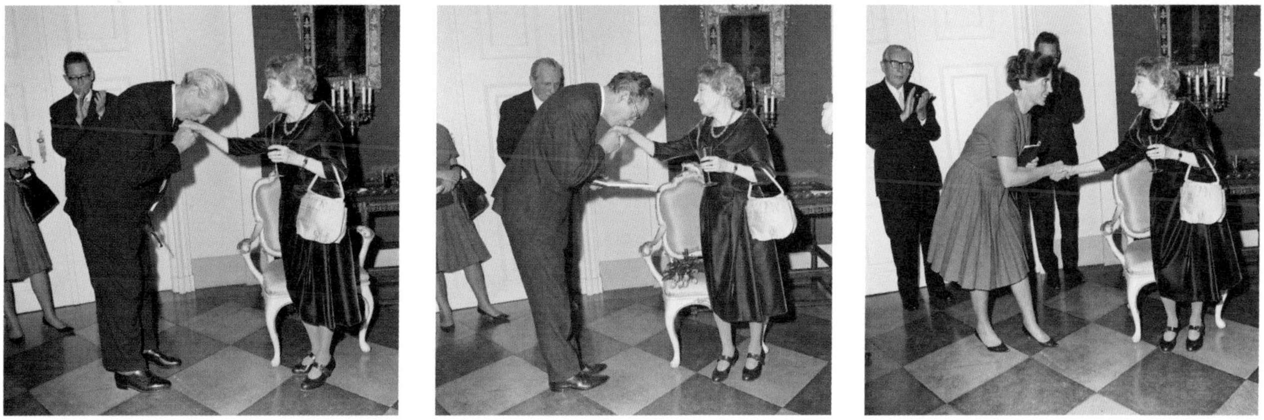

14

15

16

in Germany — from to October 15 to 27. Bengt and Margaretha gave her support on literary matters, but also protected her against unwelcome attention. Not without pride, she reported to Dähnert: "Now I also must tell you [...] that thousands of people will be assembled (for the awards ceremony alone they have distributed 1,000 tickets). After the church I will be stormed by a number of film people and reporters, as they are making a Europe film, then I will be put in a car and driven to the great banquet. Then it's back to the hotel for a few hours' rest, where Margaretha and Bengt will guard me like lions, and then in the evening there will be the possibility of speaking to me personally at the big reception that my publisher, Dr. Siegfried Unseld from Suhrkamp, is arranging at his home." By film she meant Eurovision, which broadcast the whole ceremony. But Sachs was also interviewed for Swiss television by WERNER WEBER (1919–2005), a literary critic and professor at the University of Zurich, who delivered the speech of tribute at the awards ceremony. The interview turned into a meditation on poetry as pain management — best summed up when Sachs, in words reminiscent of the letters to Ekelöf, explained to the taciturn, probably touched interviewer: "Very close to death, the words came. If I were to ask myself who had taught me to reach these words, I can only say, again and again: death. [---] When I experienced something horrific, and was close to death, then these poems, these ... in the last part ... broke forth yet again — with such violence in the language. And this I felt so enormously strongly that it almost threw me against the limit of my life. I was seriously ill, felt a deep sorrow ... The words came and broke forth in me — to the edge of annihilation."

Following receptions, signings, and a visit to the book fair, and not least meetings with friends and acquaintances — including Neff and the Gymnasium teacher Dorothée Zimmermann, who had visited Bergsundsstrand a couple of years earlier — Sachs and the Holmqvists were driven to Stuttgart by the publisher SIEGFRIED UNSELD (1924–2002). There new friends awaited, including the writers Walter and Inge Jens, the chairman of the Darmstadt Academy, Hermann Kasack, the writer Karl Schwedhelm, and Käte Hamburger. On October 21 it was time to board the plane to Berlin. When Sachs praised the fine weather, the flight controller commented: "That's how it is when angels fly." At the airport in the former capital the reception committee included Marie Hirsch, who was responsible for cultural affairs in West Berlin, as well as the journalist INGEBORG DREWITZ (1923–1986), whom Sachs had got to know a few years earlier. They were lodged in the Hotel am Zoo, where a posse of journalists was waiting. Hirsch effectively pushed the press people aside, but Sachs had time to see an elderly man bow to her as she stepped out of the car. The gesture of respect meant much for the calm which characterized the days that followed. As earlier, Bengt and Margaretha occupied the rooms on either side of their friend's — a safety precaution: if Sachs felt anxious she had to be able to go into Margaretha's room.

The visit to Sachs' hometown turned into an exciting experience. The day after their arrival Drewitz took the party around Sachs' old neighborhood by car. Hardly anything was left, yet she was pleased to see Rousseauinsel and Neuer See in Tiergarten, and she recognized the rowing boats from the old days. Following lunch, a nap, and a reading at the College of Fine Arts there was a reception in Sachs' honor at Charlottenburger Schloß. The next day the friends were driven to Grunewald, visited Pfaueninsel and Schlachtensee, and had lunch at the residence of the Swedish consul, Sven Backlund.

A couple of years after her return to Sweden — on July 14, 1967 — Sachs was officially named an honorary citizen of Berlin. On this occasion too, the statement spoke of "a woman who through her artistic work has found a universal expression for the persecuted person's suffering and reconciliation with his or her destiny and homeland." The official announcement ended with the city council thanking the German poet with a Swedish passport for "feeling linked to her hometown, although she had been unjustly driven away from it." In connection with the announcement a plaque was mounted on the façade of Maaßenstraße 12, where Sachs had been born three-quarters of a century earlier. The artist Helga Tiemann painted an oil portrait based on a photograph, which was hung in the gallery of the town hall in Schöneberg. The object of the tribute was unable to attend. In March 1967 she had another heart attack, after which she was told to rest.

**TEXT** For letters to Hans Magnus Enzensberger 02/01/1958 and in October 1960, to Dagrun Enzensberger 01/22/1959, and Dähnert 11/29/1961, see Briefe 122, 169, 130, and 189 respectively · FiS (NSW:II) · NSzE:1 · "Danksagung zur Verleihung des ersten Nelly-Sachs-Preises der Stadt Dortmund," NSW:IV · "Danksagung zur Verleihung des Friedenspreises des Deutschen Buchhandels," NSW:IV · *Ansprachen anläßlich der Verleihung des Friedenspreises des deutschen Buchhandels*, Frankfurt am Main 1965 · "In der Flucht," FuV (NSW:II) · For letters to Borchers 09/14/1964 and Dähnert 08/13/1965, see Briefe 211 and 217 respectively · Dinesen, 283 · Interview with Werner Weber on Swiss television 11/10/1965 · Interview the Holmqvists in Ralph Giordano's documentary *Sterben ohne gemordert zu werden*, West German Broadcasting (WDR) 1981 · Margaretha Holmqvist, diary entries 10/15-24/1965 · Thorsten Müller, *Berlins Ehrenbürger*, Berlin 1968, 152 | **IMAGE 1** Hans Magnus Enzensberger in the 1960s (ASuhrkamp) · **2** Hans Magnus Enzensberger, *verteidigung der wölfe* 1957 · **3** *Nelly Sachs zu Ehren*, ed. Suhrkamp Verlag, 1961 · **4** *Fahrt ins Staublose* 1961 · **5** *Zeichen im Sand* 1962 · **6** Sachs with Margaretha Lindh (Danneskiöld-Samsøe) and Lenke Rothman in 1961 (Photo Anna Riwkin, KBS) · **7** Sachs with Artur Lundkvist and Erik Lindegren in 1961 (Photo Anna Riwkin, KBS) · **8** The gentlemen from Dortmund: Egon Kötting, Karl Hansmeyer, and Ewald Görshop, 1961 (Photo Anna Riwkin, KBS) · **9** Sachs with Görshop and Hansmeyer in 1961 (Photo Anna Riwkin, KBS) · **10** Sachs with Unseld at the book fair, Frankfurt am Main, 1965 (Photo K.-E. Sundqvist, KBS) · **11** Sachs with Enzensberger, Peter Weiss, Erwin Leiser, and Dorothee Bjelvestam in 1961 (Photo Anna Riwkin, KBS) · **12** Sachs with Günter Eich at Unseld's, Frankfurt am Main, 1965 (Photo Gisela Dischner, Gisela Dischner's collection, Hannover) · **13** Sachs with the Holmqvists, Frankfurt am Main 1965 (Photo Ursula Assmus, BDB) · **14** Sachs, honorary reception by the city of Berlin, 1965 (Stadtmuseum Berlin / Harry Croner) · **15** Sachs in Paulskirche, Frankfurt am Main, 1965 (Photo Klaus Meier-Ude, BDB) · **16** Sachs during a TV interview with Werner Weber, Frankfurt am Main, 1965 (KBS)

17

18

**FINALLY A FAMILY**

In Bengt and Margaretha Holmqvist, Sachs found a family with whom spending time together wasn't complicated by geographical distances. In November 2009, Margaretha Holmqvist answered some questions about their friendship:

*Do you recall your first impressions of Sachs when she visited you and Bengt together with Enzensberger that day in March 1961?*

M.H.: Bengt had reviewed Nelly before, but for me she was a completely new acquaintance. The first thing I saw were her eyes, large, dark, and very beautiful, but melancholy. Then the delicate figure; she was almost as small as my children. Nelly later described the meeting as "written in the stars." It felt that way for me too, and for the whole family.

*Sachs quickly came to regard you as her family. In a way she behaved as if she was a third daughter — despite being a little older than both of your children, well, in fact she was two or three decades older than their parents. How is one to picture your time together?*

M.H.: When we met, Nelly was still interned at Beckomberga. Now and then, she was given permission to leave. I visited her regularly at the hospital and she often came to see us. She longed for a sense of security and felt tranquil with "her" family. She didn't need to hold up a shield with us, she could let go of the attitude which she otherwise preferred to present in interviews, for example. She could laugh and joke, show her childish side, listen to music. Incidentally, her taste in music was quite advanced and she liked to listen to new music. Perhaps it corresponded to her inner disquiet. We had visits by composers like György Ligeti and Ingvar Lidholm, and she was very interested and a lively participant in the conversation. Ligeti was an entertaining storyteller of course, and his stories amused Nelly. But like many of the great composers he wasn't interested in complicated texts.

*Until Sachs' death nine and a half years later, you were in contact with each other practically on a daily basis — either in person or on the telephone. What role did these exchanges play for her?*

M. H.: We spoke every day when she wasn't in the hospital or we were on a holiday. Almost always I was the one who rang. Sometimes she would beat me to it. The conversations lasted about an hour. Usually they were about everyday things, and quite often she would tell me about her childhood. About her fear of being abandoned. She would often return to such instances from childhood. Once her mother had met a friend outside a department store and followed her in, and somehow Nelly lost contact with them. She had become completely hysterical and the memory of the event pursued her for the rest of her life. When her parents left her at a boarding school in the country she panicked. That too became a traumatic experience. When her parents were out and the servants left her on her own was another story she would return to — for example in 1965, when we were in Berlin and staying at the Hotel am Zoo. We had been given rooms overlooking the courtyard so that Li wouldn't be disturbed by noises from the street. When we walked down the long corridors she gripped my arm and said: "This is like my childhood." She remembered her despair when she ran screaming down the corridors of her home, abandoned by both parents and servants. But all our conversations weren't about fear, of course.

*On a number of occasions Sachs recited newly written poems to you. You and Bengt became her first audience.*

M. H.: On almost every visit she read out new poems to the whole family, including "Granny," as she used to call my mother (eight years younger than Nelly). Li's mother had the same name as me; I guess that contributed to her feeling for me. And the natural thing then was for Bengt to become her father and the children her younger siblings. When she read her poems to us we sat and listened in silence. And showed our admiration. When the poems then were going to be compiled Bengt would sometimes help her out. (He used to do that with Ekelöf and Lindegren as well.) The poems she left behind I compiled. Bengt wrote the foreword. Her poems were always complete from the outset. Alterations were only ever made exceptionally.

Nelly wrote her poems by hand on small notepads. I remember that it was extremely difficult, if not impossible, to date them after her death, for the posthumous edition eventually entitled *Teile dich Nacht* (Part Yourself, Night). Once I asked her about her copious use of dashes. She replied: "That's because

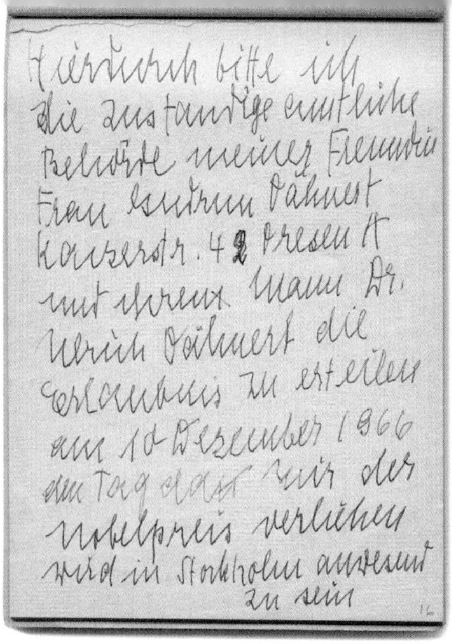
Hierdurch bitte ich die zuständige amtliche Behörde meiner Freundin Frau Gudrun Dähnert Kaiserstr. 42 Dresden mit ihrem Mann Dr. Ulrich Dähnert die Erlaubnis zu erteilen am 10 Dezember 1966 am Tag dass mir der Nobelpreis verliehen wird in Stockholm anwesend zu sein
16

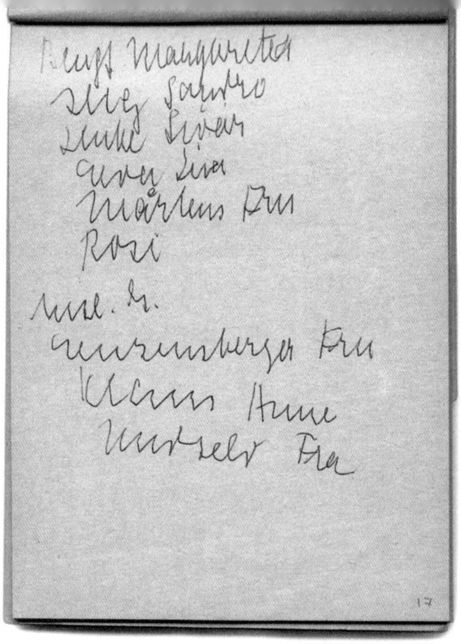
Bengt Margaretha
Rosi
17

19
20

I've never learned punctuation." On occasion Ekelöf and Lindegren would ask me about difficult metaphors in her texts. Gunnar was doing *Glühende Rätsel* and got stuck on "The timescreen with all of the four worldfolds" for example. For Nelly that was simply the TV screen. She didn't have a set of her own, but she used to pop in to Rosi's when she wanted to watch something.

*How would you describe her voice?*

M.H.: You can hear it on the recording Bengt made at our house on his Tandberg, which served as the basis for the record Suhrkamp released. Her poetry reading voice was the same voice she used in interviews or among people she didn't know very well. At home she was more relaxed and not nearly as plaintive.

*In October 1965 you traveled to Germany, where Sachs received the book trade's so-called peace prize. How did the official reception strike you?*

M.H.: In the situation where Bengt and I found ourselves, I think we were mostly concerned with how the person at the center of it all would handle the ceremonies without collapsing — at least I was. As usual Nelly spoke of reconciliation and of the new Germany and of the youth her hopes were on. I think we were the ones who were annoyed by the formulation rather than her. Incidentally, the Nobel Prize formulation was no better in that respect…

*From Frankfurt you went on to Stuttgart and finally to Berlin — the secret destination of the trip.*

M.H.: The days in Germany were intense, but I think they were happy too. Everywhere Li was met with appreciation, warmth, and interest. After dinner on the last night, melancholy came. She bid farewell to Berlin. At Kastrup everything was back to normal again. Back in Stockholm we could breathe a sigh of relief having dropped her off, tired but happy, at Bergsundsstrand. During the period that followed the state of Li's health was quite good. Strangely enough she didn't become tired, instead she lived on in the bubble of her happiness.

*When did you learn about her past? Most of her friends — including Dähnert — describe how Sachs hinted at traumatic experiences which she nonetheless preferred not to talk about. What was written between the lines, in invisible ink?*

M. H.: Can I quote from my notes? This is from 1966, without a more precise date:

> Li stayed in a room in Bercka near Weimar where the door had the following inscription: "Here lived Her Excellency Frau Christiane von Goethe with her chambermaid."
>
> When Gudrun was in Sweden asking for money for Li's upkeep she was turned down by the Jewish congregation. Only Josephson said yes. He and Professor Guggenheimer contributed materially to making it possible for Li to come to Sweden.
>
> Probably in 1940 a landowner proposed to her. They had lunch at Bellmansro. Then the air raid sirens went off and Li wanted to return home to her mother right away. The man always rang Li's landlady. He wrote about Lagerlöf.
>
> Before 1944 Li had a guaranteed income of 150 kronor to live on. In 1944 she was paid 200 kronor for translations for the Cooperation Committee.
>
> Li was fourteen when she fell in love the first time. He was a pupil at the dance school and his surname was Herpich. "A typical blond lad," she said. His father was a furrier in Unter den Linden.
>
> When Li was in Marienbad at sixteen she met a man who called her "Libelle," "dragonfly."
>
> Li's classmate Alix Neufeld features in the epitaph "Die Abenteuerin." She is also mentioned in Musil's diaries, by the way. She was the daughter of a wealthy industrial magnate. Li was jealous of her stylish clothes. "Very haughty, got involved with men."
>
> On the swimming jetties by the Baltic were stalls where they sold things like red velvet purses with mother-of-pearl. And penholders with a little glass eye through which you could see a painted landscape. It was on such a seaside stay that her father had brought Flock the dog to cure its cold. The dog broke free and made its way into a theater performance Li's father was attending. Big commotion. But her father could also be dark and frightening, even if he was very protective of his family. Like that time in Marienbad when he climbed out of the window to fetch a doctor for Li's aching ears. The neighbors, Countess Tolstoya with her daughters Olga and Tatyana, banged loudly on the wall, but Li's father explained in French that Li was in such pain.
>
> When her mother grew old she became Li's child and stood in her pink dressing gown with the keys in a ribbon around her neck, waiting for Li. The dressing gown Li had bought cheaply because it was a bit faded. She bought it with her first earnings.

*The German word for "dragonfly,"* Libelle — *Li, Liebe, Belle... A telling pet name. How did your collaboration work in practice?*

M.H.: Nelly wanted me to translate her plays. She chose the titles herself. For instance, she decided that *Nachtwache* was to be called *The Road Is a Hand* in Swedish. I suppose you could say that the translation is authorized, since she reviewed and approved it. Her interest in Maria Volkonskaya, incidentally, is reflected in *Nachtwache*. Among her papers I found an article from a German paper about the Decabrists and Volkonskaya. Like Lagerlöf, Nelly got ideas from newspaper articles. "In the Ice-Bound Era of the Andes," for example, is based on an item from *Dagens Nyheter* about the discovery of an Indian woman frozen in the ice up in the Andes. Otherwise she often talked about her favorite writers, about Günderrode, whom she wanted me to translate, about Bettina von Arnim, Stifter, and Fontane. *Effi Briest* moved her deeply. "My mother was so cheerful, but also a bit of an Effi Briest," she once said. She mentioned Buber, too. Through him she learned about Baal Shem Tov, whom she often came back to in conversation. His special kind of Hasidism appealed to her, the light and playful kind, not the kind that today's "black" Hasids in Jerusalem adhere to. The fact that she also appreciated Beckett wasn't so surprising, really. Both of them liked Fontane, by the way. During our visit to Berlin we wrote a postcard to Beckett. Bengt knew him.

*The year after your return from Germany it was announced that Sachs would share the Nobel Prize in literature with Agnon.*

M.H.: In my notes from the autumn of 1966 I wrote, two days before the announcement: "Li is going to get the Nobel Prize and seems to be the only one who doesn't know it. There are rumors in the press about Agnon, and that makes her sad. In fact the prize is going to be shared by her and Agnon." The following day, October 19, I noted: "Li is beside herself and we can't say a thing. But a TV appearance has already been booked. Lots of people ringing and everything is upside down." And the next day: "Li rang at half past eight and said that Gierow had telephoned. And at half past twelve we brought her here for TV. Bengt spoke about her on *Aktuellt* and interviewed her for *Studio 66*. Reception at Li's for thirty-odd journalists. Afterwards we brought her here for dinner. Erik and Lo Lindegren came later. Champagne."

And that was just the beginning... Every day there was something happening. Bengt and I became seriously worried about how Li would fare amid the chaos. We were in contact with Mårtens, who prescribed various pills. We accompanied her to one reception after another and she was delighted with all the acclaim and didn't even seem tired. As of now Li wasn't answering the telephone, instead all matters were dealt with via us and Rosi. Interviews, letters, often begging letters, people imploring her and even threatening her in order to get a place at the Nobel ceremony. Visits to dressmakers and furriers and shoemakers. Since Li wore size 34 shoes she had to have shoes specially made. Revisits and fittings.

*Describe the day of the ceremony. It was Sachs' birthday, as well.*

M.H.: On December 10 it was pouring with rain. At eleven in the morning there was a rehearsal at Konserthuset. We fetched Li and Rosi. Li was radiant during the ceremony and not in the least nervous. She carried herself with a naturalness that only a good upbringing can instill. With calm and dignity. In between there was a short rest at the Hotel Carlton. Then to the banquet. There we parted ways. When it was time she gave her speech. After that she could finally relax, and so could we, together with her friends Dähnert, Mang, Werner Weber, and Siegfried Unseld (and Scheurmann with his daughter, I think). Li stayed late at the banquet.

*The years that followed the Nobel Prize were marked by old age and increasing illness. In March 1967, for example, Sachs had another heart attack. She didn't write much new material. The significant part of her œuvre seemed to be behind her.*

M.H.: In the late winter of 1967 her health began to deteriorate again. On March 19 she felt unwell, and on the twentieth her speech was slurred and she could hardly speak. I rang Södersjukhuset and Dorothée Zimmermann, who was visiting, drove her there. Her blood pressure was more than 210. A partial heart attack. On the twenty-second she had another attack, but not as powerful. Diagnosis: angina pectoris. In May she had an abdominal X-ray which didn't show anything worrying. The war between Israel and the Arab states had begun and we were concerned about how Li would react. But she appeared calm. She had many visitors, including Gudrun. We went for walks as well, to Reimersholme for example, where she had used to take walks with her mother. She thought the view from there towards Långholmen reminded her of Pfaueninsel. And she was often invited out. In November we saw García Lorca's play *Así que pasen cinco años* (When Five Years Pass). She talked about a trip to Israel after a visit by the Israeli ambassador. But nothing ever came of it.

In January 1968 she began showing signs of paranoia again. They grew gradually worse. On March 12 I rang Mårtens. He wanted her to come in for a consultation, but she didn't want to. "He's just a friend, as a doctor he's never been able to do anything with his pills." The persecution she perceived continued. Ekelöf's death on March 16 was hardly touched upon between us. At times she revived, though. But on April 22 Rosi rang already at eight in the morning. Bengt contacted Mårtens and at three Rosi and I took Li to Rålambshov. She seemed pleased. "Here I can write," she said. This fleeing into illness as an instigator of poems! "After all, everything was written at Beckomberga."

On the last day of May Lindegren died. In the summer Gudrun again came to visit. Emmy and Toby Brandt came, too. Li wrote regularly but not very much. Towards the end of the year the conspiracy theories escalated and we suspected that she had stopped taking her medicine. After a visit to Mårtens it seemed as if he had got her to take the pills again. She felt better and could spend time among friends and move about the city, but not alone. During the spring of 1969 Li complained of pain. She was hospitalized in April and fears were confirmed: colon cancer. Her final year was marked by the illness. After the operation things seemed to be under control. No metastases. She went from dying to being fresh as a daisy. But then she began spitting her medicine out again and the paranoia returned. She hardly ate anything. When she was admitted to St. Eriks Hospital in September 1969 she weighed 28.7 kilos. Slowly her appetite returned. She particularly liked air-cured ham, which I used to take her. For the Orthodox Jews who occasionally visited it must have felt strange …

*When Sachs was dying in May 1970 she was reportedly told that her friend Celan had sought "voluntary death," as the Germans say. Shortly after that she died.*

M.H.: At the end of April it was discovered that the cancer had come back. Li was very ill and was taken to St. Görans Hospital. Bengt and I visited her, but then I caught a cold and didn't dare risk passing on the infection. On one of the days during that final period Li received a visit by Gisela Dahinten, who was married to the then director of the Goethe Institute, Egon Dahinten. I think she was the one who told her that Celan was dead. I don't know how Li took the news, but possibly there was some consolation in the fact that he had gone before her. On May 12 I was called to the hospital at seven o'clock in the morning. Li's condition had worsened during the night and she was unconscious. Rosi was already there. At 1:14 pm Li passed away, at last freed forever from her agony.

The funeral took place a week later, on May 19. Emmy and Toby Brandt came to pick us up. We sat for a while and listened to Li's voice on a record. Then we went to Norra kyrkogården and the Jewish burial ground there. Leo Rosenblüth sang Kaddish, Chief Rabbi Morton Narrowe conducted the funeral ceremony. All the men, in hats or kippahs, shoveled three lots of earth on the white wooden coffin. In the chapel it was covered with a black cloth and only decorated with the Star of David. There were lots of wreaths — an exception made for the Christian participants. Li was interred a few meters from her parents' grave. Only a smallish group of people accompanied her to her grave. Among her friends they were, besides Rosi, Gudrun, Emmy and Toby, Dorothée Zimmermann, Brita and Johannes Edfelt, Martina and Olof Lagercrantz, Unseld, and Peter and Gunilla Weiss. Representatives from the German embassy and Hermann Kant from the East German authors' union were also among the guests.

*After the estate inventory it was decided that the contents of the estate should be transferred to the Royal Library. Eventually a Nelly Sachs Room was set up — at first next to an emergency exit, and later four floors underground. The place is* unheimlich, *or "uncanny," in the classical Freudian sense. You and Bengt organized the move.*

M.H.: After the funeral I discovered to my horror that Li had appointed me the executrix of her will. Immaterial rights were bequeathed to Enzensberger, the material estate to Bengt and me. National Librarian Uno Willers expressed an interest in preserving the interior of the apartment at the library. At the beginning of July Harry Järv, who was deputy national librarian, began the move after having photographed the apartment in its intact state. The move itself took place on July 21. Remaining items were left to friends and acquaintances. The objects I kept as memories have been handed over to the library. The most important objects — the Nobel Prize plaque along with Nelly's parents' wedding rings and a lock of her mother's hair — have been given to the Jüdisches Museum in Berlin. The room was inaugurated on December 10, 1970, in the presence of Olof Palme among others. When I visit the new room in the basement now, which is much nicer than the old one by the emergency exit, it feels familiar.

21

**TEXT** Interview with Margaretha Holmqvist 10/04/2009 | **IMAGE 17** Sachs with Bengt Holmqvist in the mid-1960s (KBS) · **18** Margaretha Holmqvist, n.d. (KBS) · **19** Draft for an application for exit visas for Gudrun and Ulrich Dähnert, 1966 (KBS) · **20** Guest list for the Nobel awards ceremony, 1966 (KBS) · **21** *Das Buch der Nelly Sachs*, ed. Bengt Holmqvist, 1968

## ONE DAY IN OCTOBER, ONE DAY IN DECEMBER

Prior to Swedish municipal elections in September 1966 Sachs, like the rest of the electorate, received a ballot paper. The addressee was given as "Leonie Sara Sachs." Something similar had happened seven years earlier, when she had applied for a passport in connection with receiving the German industry's literature prize and was issued with a document which included the additional name forced upon her by the Nazis. The reason in both cases was the Swedish population register, which was still administered by the country's parish churches. On both occasions Sachs was dismayed and couldn't rule out that it was a conscious provocation. Margaretha Holmqvist informed Högalid parish, where her friend was registered. The minister seemed surprised. Why the change? "Sara is such a pretty name." "Yes, but not if you were given it by Hitler." For an official change, however, a certificate from Germany was required. On November 17 the population registration office in Berlin-Schöneberg could at last confirm that Sachs had not been baptized "Sara."

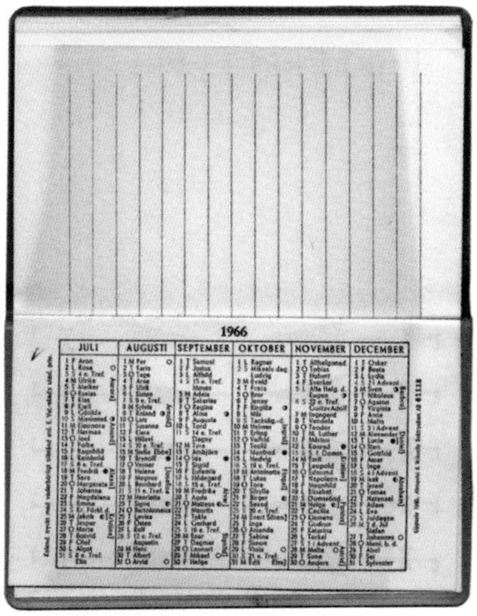

22

Between these two events lay an announcement which in its way had to do with the questioned identity. On October 20 the Permanent Secretary of the Swedish Academy, the poet and playwright Karl Ragnar Gierow, announced that the Nobel Prize in literature for that year would be shared for the third time in the history of the award. It had been decided that the award would go to "the German Jewish writer Nelly Sachs and the Israeli novelist Josef Agnon." The Galician-born Agnon was being rewarded for his "profoundly character-

23

ful narrative art with themes from the life of the Jewish people," while the Swedish citizen Sachs was given the same award for her "distinguished lyrical and dramatic poetry, which interprets Israel's destiny with poignant force." At this time the eighteen-member Swedish Academy included friends such as Ekelöf and Lindegren, who had both translated and also been translated by Sachs, as well as Pär Lagerkvist, Harry Martinson, and Anders Österling, whose works she had translated earlier. The basis for the decision most likely took statements by Berendsohn into account, who had recommended her over the past three years. The late date of the announcement suggests that the academy had had difficulty coming to a unanimous decision. With the shared prize, it was recognizing representatives of a Jewish people that encompassed but wasn't limited to Israel's borders or the linguistic boundaries of Hebrew and German respectively. The very prerequisite for a shared prize — that both recipients were deserving of it for themselves — nonetheless made it clear that the academy was in no doubt that both Agnon and Sachs were being rewarded as writers.

In an item on Swedish television the same evening, Sachs could be seen arriving by car to Bergsundsstrand, escorted by Bengt and Margaretha Holmqvist. She sat in the back, wearing a shawl and a hat as usual, glowing. In front of the entrance to her building twenty or so reporters and photographers were assembled. Over the following days the images would feature in press coverage both in Sweden and abroad. The same item also included an extract from an interview recorded at the home of Sachs' friends in Tantogatan. "Since this morning I only know it," the laureate explains in Swedish. "And it is almost like a dream for me that I have been given after so much suffering and darkness one so wonderful happiness … Now when I am old."

Over the following weeks Sachs was showered with messages of congratulations. Bergsundsstrand 23 would turn into a site of pilgrimage. She was forced to disconnect the telephone and hand all contact with the outside world over to the Holmqvists. Her doctor ordered two weeks complete rest. Wosk took care of the daily shopping. A letter to Dähnert towards the end of the month describes "heaps of letters, telegrams, flowers, interviews, television, etc. You can't imagine what a prize like this brings from all over the world." Despite her tiredness, the letter spoke of joy and expectation. "Dress, coat, shoes, everything is being made to measure. Full dress, and full-length of course." What was more, "curtsy before the king and much else" had to be rehearsed. The maiden who had read saints' legends in the garden of paradise at Lessingstraße had become a poet in an evening gown, who with self-mocking assurance saw her reflection in the mirror as "half lady of society, half angel."

The tasks in connection with the awards ceremony included providing the Nobel Foundation with a vita, the length of which was the laureate's choice. Sachs' contribution comprises three sentences, written down in a notebook:

24

25

26

27

Eure Majestät, Eure Königliche Hoheiten, meine verehrten Zuhörer:

Im Sommer 1939 reiste meine deutsche Freundin nach Schweden um Selma Lagerlöf aufzusuchen und um ihre Hilfe zu bitten eine Freistatt für meine Mutter und mich in Schweden zu erwirken .

Ich hatte das Glück seit meiner Jugend mit Selma Lagerlöf im Briefwechsel zu stehn. Aus ihrem Werk erwuchs mir die Liebe zu ihrem Heimatland .

Der Malerprinz Eugen und die Dichterin setzten sich für das Rettungswerk ein .

Im Frühjahr 1940 nach qualvoller Zeit trafen wir in Stockholm ein. Die Besetzung Dänemarks und Norwegens war schon geschehn. Die große Dichterin trafen wir nicht mehr am Leben .
Ohne die Sprache zu verstehn oder einen Menschen zu kennen atmeten wir die Freiheit ein

Heute nach 26 Jahren gedenke ich der Worte meines Vaters, die er an jedem 10 Dezember in meiner Heimatstadt Berlin äußerte: Nun feiern sie in Stockholm das Nobelfest.

Dank der Wahl der schwedischen Akademie befinde ich mich jetzt mitten in dieser Feier. Es will mir scheinen als wäre ein Märchen Wirklichkeit geworden .

In der Flucht
welch großer Empfang
unterwegs -

Eingehüllt
in der Winde Tuch
Füße im Gebet des Sandes
der niemals Amen sagen kann
denn er muß
von der Flosse in den Flügel
und weiter -

Der kranke Schmetterling
weiß bald wieder vom Meer -
Dieser Stein
mit der Inschrift der Fliege
hat sich mir in die Hand gegeben -

An Stelle von Heimat
halte ich die Verwandlungen der Welt -

28

Mit Freundesgrüßen
Walter B.

20. Januar 1964

Schwedische Akademie

Gamla Börshuset
<u>S t o c k h o l m  C</u>

Für den Nobelpreis in Literatur 1964 schlage ich die <u>Dichterin jüdischen Schicksals Nelly Sachs</u> vor.

In der künstlerischen Entwicklung dieser Dichterin kann man drei Perioden unterscheiden:

1.

Ehe sie im Jahre 1940 als Flüchtling nach Schweden kam, war sie in Deutschland schon eine angesehene Lyrikerin, deren Gedichte von Ende der 20er Jahre an von berufenen Männern beachtet und veröffentlicht wurden. Die Vossische Zeitung, Berlin, druckte 1929, das Berliner Tageblatt 1933, die "Jugend", München, 1933 und in den folgenden Jahren, die jüdische Zeitschrift "Der Morgen", Berlin, 1936-38 und einige andere jüdische Zeitschriften in Berlin und München 1936-37 Gedichte unter ihrem Namen. Stefan Zweig, dem ein Freund des Hauses zwei Gedichte zugeschickt hatte, schrieb ihr, daß Frauenlyrik meist zur runden Formung neige, während ihre Lyrik eine ekstatisch aufsteigende Linie zeige, ein prophetisches Kritikerwort. Ich besitze etwa 100 Gedichte aus dieser Frühzeit, die z.T. aus de Nachlaß Selma Lagerlöfs ans Licht gekommen sind, mit der Nelly Sachs seit 1921 in Verbindung stand und die bei ihrer und ihre Mutter Rettung nach Schweden mitgewirkt hat. Ihre damalige Dichtung zeigt schon ein persönliches Profil, ist aber gebunden in traditionellen Formen. Alle Gedichte sind gereimt; sie

29

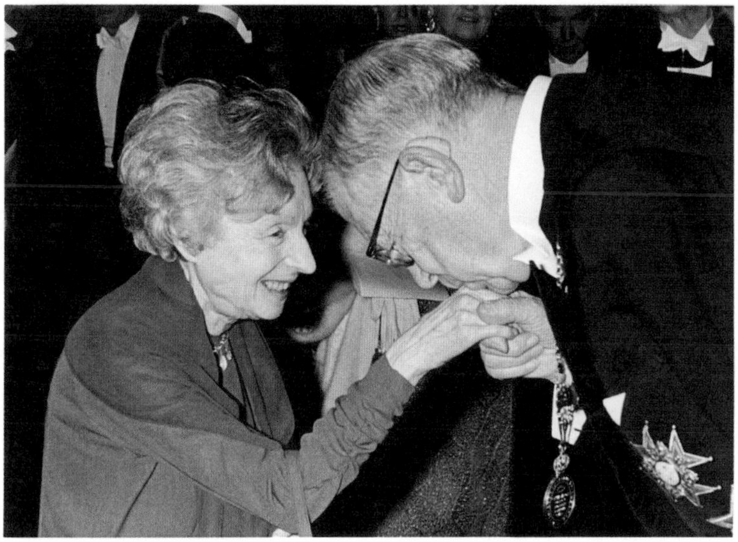

30

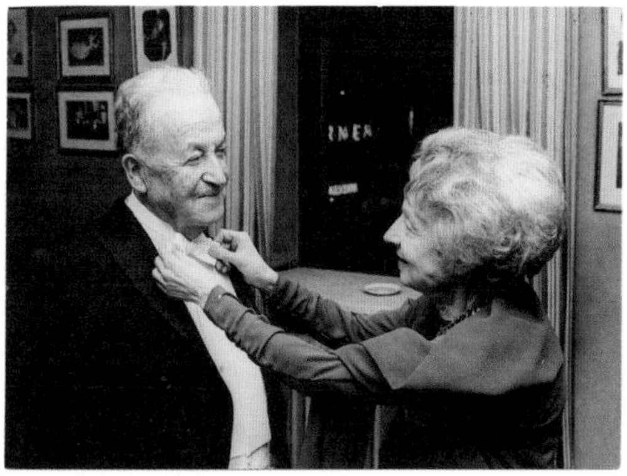

31

32

33

"Nelly Sachs, born December 10, 1891, in Berlin. Arrived in Sweden as a refugee with her mother on May 16, 1940. Lives in Stockholm since 1940, where she works as a writer and translator." The terse description — simply entitled "Nelly Sachs" — made it clear that from the laureate's perspective there was nothing more to add about the person who had just shared the greatest award in the literary world. If etiquette had allowed for it, she would probably have preferred to disappear entirely behind her œuvre.

On that gray Saturday, December 10, 1966, it was seventy years since the founder, Alfred Nobel, had passed away. The awards ceremony was boycotted by diplomatic representatives of the Arab nations, who, like tribute holder Österling, viewed the writers as representatives of "Israel's message in our time." Before the celebrations in Konserthuset's main hall at 4:30 pm (sleet, darkness already fallen) Sachs was picked up by the Holmqvists. The Italian-born hairdresser Pia Zanetti had done her hair and taken several photographs. Wosk, who had been invited to the ceremony, also documented the departure. A snapshot taken as Sachs was getting into the car, her eyes half shut and one gloved hand held to her shawl to protect her hair, captures her halfway inside, halfway outside — an emblematic image for a poet who extolled movement and transformation, who saw everywhere and nowhere as her home. The awards ceremony featured musical elements, including the prelude to Lars-Erik Larsson's lyrical suite *Förklädd Gud* (Disguised God) with words by the recently deceased academy member Hjalmar Gullberg, and Pergament's chamber music piece *Nu samlar Gud i sin hand* (Now God Gathers in His Hand) with words by Bengt Anderberg. After Pergament's piece Österling stepped up to the microphone. First he thanked the Israeli writer whom Sachs with affectionate cheek called her "little cousin," then he turned to the female laureate: "You have long lived in our country, at first as an unnoticed stranger and then ..."

At the City Hall banquet, which as usual was being reported by the gossip press, Sachs was seated between King Gustaf VI Adolf and Prince Bertil. The speech she gave, "Rede anläßlich des Nobelbanketts," was preceded by a short tribute by the historian and academy member Carl Ingvar Andersson. Then Sachs spoke. She began by describing her flight to Sweden, which had been made possible by a "German woman friend" and by support from the Swedish court as well as an academy member. In closing she added: "Today after 26 years I think of my father's words, repeated every December 10th in my hometown, Berlin: Now they are celebrating the Nobel festivities in Stockholm. Thanks to the Swedish Academy's choice, I am now in the middle of those festivities. It seems to me as if a fairy tale has come true." The writer who had penned legends in prewar Berlin was finally in one herself, surrounded by nobility and visiting dignitaries.

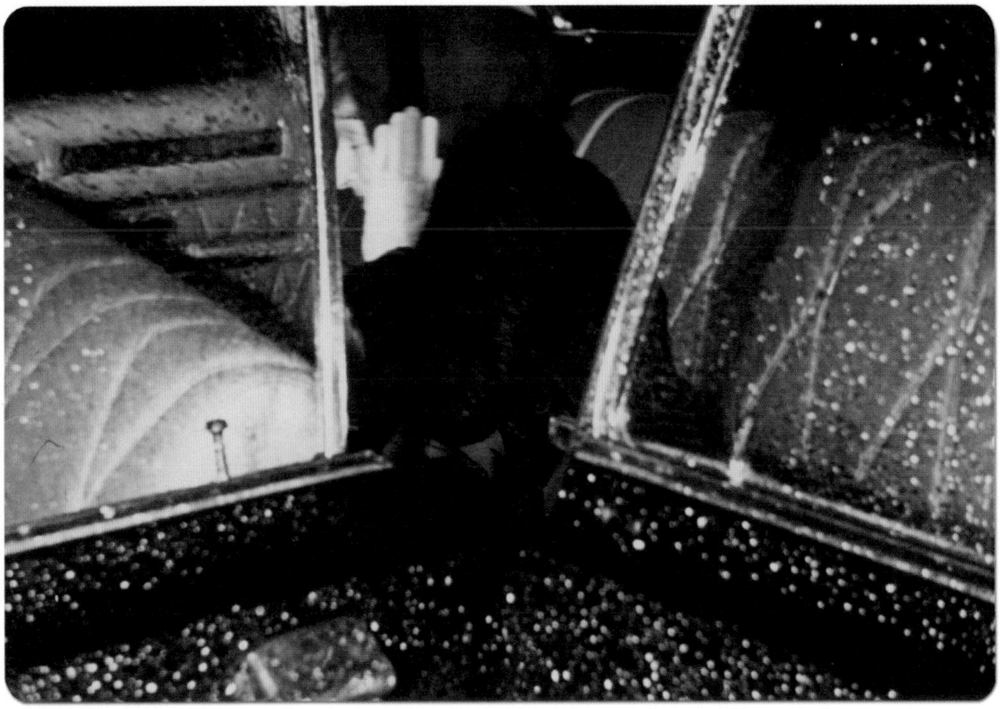

34

**TEXT** Statements by Berendsohn 1964–1966, ABerendsohnD · For letter to Dähnert 10/31/1966, see Briefe 219 · The self-characterization "half lady of society, half angel" is quoted in Ralph Giordano, *Sterben ohne gemordert zu werden*, West German Broadcasting (WDR) 1981 · "Nelly Sachs," vita, ASachs · "Rede anläßlich des Nobelbanketts," NSW:IV | **IMAGE 22** Nelly Sachs' pocket calendar for the second half of 1966 (KBS) · **23** Sachs before the Nobel awards ceremony, 1966 (Photo Pia Zanetti, KBS) · **24–25** Before leaving for Konserthuset (Photo Pia Zanetti, KBS) · **26–27** With Rosi Wosk before the Nobel festivities, 1966 (Photo Pia Zanetti, KBS) · **28** Sachs' speech at the City Hall banquet, 1966 (KBS) · **29** Walter A. Berendsohn, recommendation for the Nobel Prize in literature, 1964 (KBS) · **30** King Gustav VI Adolf offers his congratulations (KBS) · **31** With Samuel Josef Agnon in 1966 (KBS) · **32** With the king (KBS) · **33** Sachs arriving at Bergsundsstrand after the announcement about the Nobel Prize in literature, October 1966 (KBS) · **34** Sachs climbs into the car which will take her to the awards ceremony (KBS) · **35** Vita, notes (KBS)

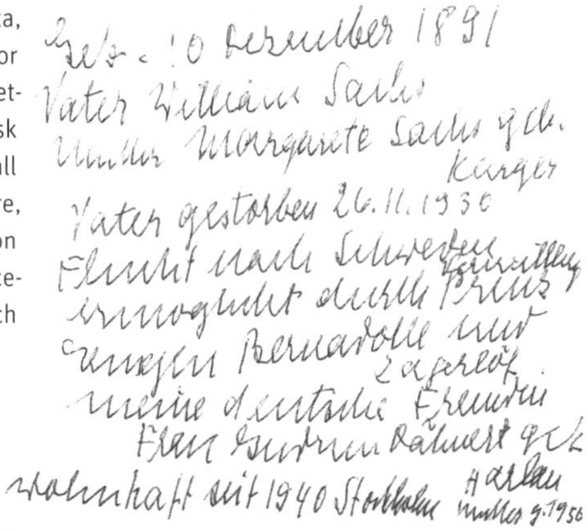


35

## WHEN ONE HAS TURNED SEVENTY-FIVE

The months following the awards ceremony were mostly spent resting. In March 1967 Sachs had a heart attack and was briefly hospitalized. A short time earlier she had received a reporter from the membership magazine of the Red Cross. The new Nobel laureate in literature — who was dubbed "sibyl, child, friend of life and death, the little sister of loneliness and pain" — replied with surprising candor to the journalist's questions. To the query "Do you enjoy living now?" she declared: "No-o … I wouldn't call it that. But now I am *able* to live with my sorrow — I have good friends. *Doch, Ich bin aufbruchsbereit* [Still, I am ready to depart]."

Whether Eckermann's book of conversations with Goethe was part of the seventy-five-year-old laureate's reading matter is impossible to say. Her per-

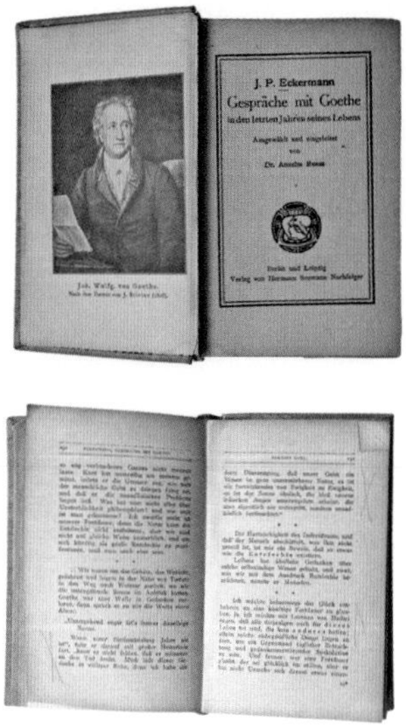


36

sonal copy contains many highlightings and underlinings, however, including in the section on "Goethe's God." In one place Sachs has highlighted the description of how the two men on their way back to Weimar were discussing what the philosophers of antiquity termed "entelechy," which is the characteristic of bearing one's end within oneself — as the pupa harbors the butterfly or the larva the dragonfly. For Goethe, nature could not manage without this principle. He recalled a line from the Greek poet Nonnus: "Setting it is always the same sun." In the same way that the basic principle of the universe only seemed to set but in actual fact shone interminably, the soul continued to act from one eternity to another.

For someone like Sachs, who had begun writing poetry on the theme of parting and who saw the basis for her work in the Holocaust, the quoted maxim from Nonnus cannot have been without importance — particularly as it was cited in connection with Goethe's belief in man's continued existence. She marked the statement: "[']When one is seventy-five years old,' he then continued with great mirth, 'it cannot be denied that one occasionally thinks about death.[']" In an unpublished poem from the middle of the 1950s, entitled "Fliehend in der Liebe" (Escaping in Love), when Sachs was still ten years younger than Goethe was as he uttered those words, she had declared that "all sunsets / are bridges to the sunrises." And in the poem "Mit Wildhonig die Hinterbliebenen" (With Wild Honey the Left Ones) from *Und niemand weiß weiter* she portrayed the dead whose "emigrated pulses" were bathed with date wine: "But you, / but you, / how do I feed you? // Love surmounts / all of dust's milestones, / like the beheaded sun / in the pain / only seeks extinction. // With my extinction / I feed you —." Ultimately only love for a you guaranteed continued life — even if it cost the physical self its extinction.

In connection with her convalescence following the heart attack ten years later, Sachs wrote a poem in which she returned to this motif. A second version was sent to the Holmqvists with the comment: "Thus I felt death (new version 18/4/67)." Describing a death experience, the poem, "So leuchten zwei Hände in der Nacht," would read in its final form:

> Thus glow two hands in the night / Your hands / moonless / only because the agony / of death's and love's embrace / leads to the truth // Veins and arteries swollen blue / like the solar system's sudaria / before the explosion / to discover new worlds / these signs / in which release lives

The longing for a you may have been the only way for the self to endure after death. But for the departure-ready Sachs not even the solar system guaranteed subsistence. Rather, the embrace of love and dying hinted that a final unveiling still remained. The universe with its planetary orbits turned out to be an enormous sudarium that covered an ultimate truth. Behind, in a dimension where the categories of time and space no longer applied, one could glimpse

Utgivarkorsband
Nr 3/67

ÖPX II B-a/.

101





**TILL POSTPERSONALEN**
Om adressen är felaktig var vänlig sänd Bl 288 A till VRK. Registeravdelningen, Fack, Stockholm 14.

**TILL VRK:s LÄSARE**
Vid adressändring var god meddela till posten eller lokalorganisationen. (Se medlemskortet eller girotalong på inbet. avgift.) Meddela titel, namn, gamla och nya adressen (gata, postbox, gårdsnamn e dyl samt postanstalt).

Anmäl också till lokalorg om Ni får dubbelexemplar. Ange alla adressuppgifter på det exemplar som skall ändras.

Vårt röda kors

# Samtal med Nelly Sachs den 15/3 1967

Av MARIANNE RAPPE

*"Att bli övergiven är för henne att älska vidare för två."*

Den snålgrå marsdagen silas genom rummets stillhet. En vass vind därutanför tvingar Mälarens isflak till sång. Nelly Sachs, sibylla, barn, vän med livet och döden, ensamhetens och smärtans lilla syster:

- När det är svårt då blir jag lugn. När oron stiger, när jakten går, då blir jag stilla.

**Hur förblir man enkel och öppen, utlämnad till förföljelse och övergivenhet?**

— Jag var inte ensam när jag kom hit våren 1940. Jag hade min lilla mamma med mig. Vi tog aldrig ett steg utan varandra. Hon var 69 år då — den mest älskade människan i livet. För henne levde jag. Det var bara vi två — nästan helt isolerade i ett litet rum. På dagen vårdade jag mamma, som var svårt sjuk, skötte hushållet och gjorde prosaöversättningar. Ofta behövdes nattläkare. Pengarna ville inte räcka. På nätterna försökte jag skriva eget. Jag skrev mycket litet på den tiden. Skräcken släppte inte.

— Men vi var så lyckliga att vara tillsammans. Min lilla mamma hade svåra anfall om nätterna. På morgonen hade hon glömt det. "Vi måste gå ut och spatsera. Du ser så blek ut."

— Vårt rum var mörkt och kallt och låg åt gården. Mamma upplevde bara ett år i den här lägenheten.

— Hon visste ofta ingenting om svårigheterna, ekonomiska och andra. I sådant var hon ett barn. Hon hade en underbar karaktär. Allt hade hon fått lämna, sitt vackra hem, sina vänner, allt.

— Men hon kunde ändå glädja sig: "Vi har ju syrenerna!" Mamma var inte beroende: "Vi har ett rum, vi har oss båda — vi vill inte ha mera!"

— Emilia Fogelklou kunde säga: "Ni är två sagobarn, ni båda."

**Hur får man styrka att leva hand i hand med upplevelser som sprängt alla värderingar? Hur blir man vän med lidandet?**

"Man måste tro att lidandet har en mening.
Det har ej med tro att göra.
Det är bara nödvändigt."

Orden är min befrielse — döden och orden. Utan orden vet jag inte hur det hade gått. Att kunna ge uttryck åt min smärta — då lever den bredvid mig som en vän.

**Känner Ni Er alltid som flykting?**

— Ja, jag är alltid starkt medveten om det. Andra flyktingar förtvivlade. Mamma och jag kunde trösta dem.

— Jag skrev kontinuerligt 1949—1957, men jag ville inte publicera vad jag skrev. Jag kunde inte lämna mina dikter ifrån mig.

Hennes spröda leende lyser i galghumor.

**Äldre människor har ofta svårt att förstå Era dikter. Hur tar man språnget över två generationer?**

— Ungdomen säger ofta: "Du talar vårt språk." Sönderbruten och sjuk började jag forma min egen dikt. Jag måste våga skapa detta nya språk.

— Utan mina fruktansvärda upplevelser hade jag aldrig vågat. De gav mig ett eget språk. Våldet lyfte fram en individ. Att själv börja se sig själv . . .

— Jag är flykting. — Jag är jagad. — Döden är bara en början . . .

— Då min mor dött önskade jag mig döden. Ordet blev ett redskap mot skräck och förtvivlan. Att skriva blev att vittna för dem som kommer efter mig.

**Ni talar i Era dikter om "såret mellan dag och natt". Och "träffad till liv och död av såret Gud"?**

— Jag har själv stark erfarenhet av den timme på morgonen då natten övergår till dag: en ödesdiger timme kände jag redan som barn; förvandlingen från död till liv. Den timme då många föds, många dör . . . självmördarnas timme. "Die Stunde ist die Wunde zwischen Nacht und Tag."

**Nelly Sachs, kanske är det Er närhet till lidande, övergivenhet och död som slår bryggan över till de nya generationerna? Ni översätts nu till de flesta kulturspråk.**

— Jag är lycklig att nå ungdomen i andra länder: det judiska folkets lidande är ställföreträdande för alla människor som lider.

*Nelly Sachs, nobelpristagarinna 1966, mottar sin utmärkelse av kung Gustaf VI Adolf.*

**Och bitterheten, har den sjunkit undan?**

— Jag känner ingen bitterhet. Alla goda människor som hjälpt mig . . . Jag har goda vänner.

**Tycker Ni om att leva nu?**

— Neej . . . Det är för mycket sagt. Men nu kan jag leva med min sorg — jag har goda vänner. Doch, Ich bin aufbruchbereitet.

**Jag tror att dagens ungdom delar den känslan av uppbrottsberedskap. Idag är idag, om imorgon vet vi ingenting. Där ligger kanske brännpunkten för deras idenfikation med Er diktning?**

— Ur denna uppbrottsberedskap föddes det nya språket. Tidens upplevelser har brutit sönder vårt gamla språk. Det kan inte längre vara som förut: stilla, fredligt, låst vid konventionerna.

**Och det nya språket?**

— Man måste lära det nya språket. Som Olof Lagercrantz sagt:

"En diktare i vår tid är nu som en skärvsamlare: Som en Job bland ruinerna av sitt liv och sin tillit söker han skapa nya symboler av skärvorna från sin barndoms språk.

— Det är nödvändigt att tiden förvandlas! Det går ett snitt genom tillvaron sedan förföljelserna under förra kriget — som en århundradens, en årtusendens klyfta.

**Ja, den vetskapen tror jag präglar många ungas attityd?**

— Det finns en stor längtan hos unga människor. De vet det kanske inte, men i grund och botten längtar de efter något annat.

— Ett slags uppbrottsberedskap finns där omedvetet — en oro som ibland stegras: Det finns ett främmande varför i tiden.

— Ungdomen har blivit annorlunda. Vi måste försöka förstå . . .

**Hur var det att komma tillbaka till Tyskland?**

— Det var inte lätt för mig. Men jag ville tala till ungdomen. Jag blev djupt gripen av deras gensvar. Jag är mycket lycklig att ungdomen förstår min dikt.

**Birgitta Trotzig har sagt: "Lidandet är ett sår som bör hållas öppet. En motsägelse som inte får jämnas ut."**

— Ja, som Bernanos. Och som jag själv uttryckt det:
". . . liksom kanterna på ett sår
som måste stå öppet
som ännu inte får läkas."

**Har alla flyktingar det svårt?**

— Ja, alla. Men särskilt de gamla. De kan inte ställa om sig till ett nytt sätt att leva. De plågas ständigt av isolering och ensamhet.

— Utom i mitt arbete med samarbetskommittén under kriget levde jag helt isolerad. Men min lilla mamma räckte för mig. Sedan, efteråt, när det var som värst för mig, kom alla skalderna — de goda vännerna.

**Skriver Ni nu?**

Nelly Sachs ler ljust — självironiskt.

— Just nu är det omöjligt för mig. Jag får så många brev. Jag har inte hjärta att inte svara. Jag måste ge dem tröst. De tror att jag kan svara på allt — också oviktiga frågor. Tjugo brev om dagen skriver jag. Sedan är jag slut.

Med mjuka steg rör hon sig i rummets blida dager. Hon är vacker, Nelly Sachs, tidlöst, tyngdlöst ung.

Genom slöjan av år och vemod lyser hon av ömhet, klarhet och styrka.

— Jag vet, mina kolleger svarar inte. Men den unga människan som sänt mig sin dikt väntar och väntar.

Hon ler igen.

— Kanske är mina brev en del av min uppbrottsberedskap.

**Man får vad man ger . . . Hur känns det att få ett alldeles nytt och annat liv vid slutet av livet?**

— När man upplever det fruktansvärda tänker man: Solen måste sluta skina. Livet måste stanna. Det gör det inte . . .

"Och solen och månen har fortsatt sin spatsertur —
två skelögda vittnen som ingenting sett."

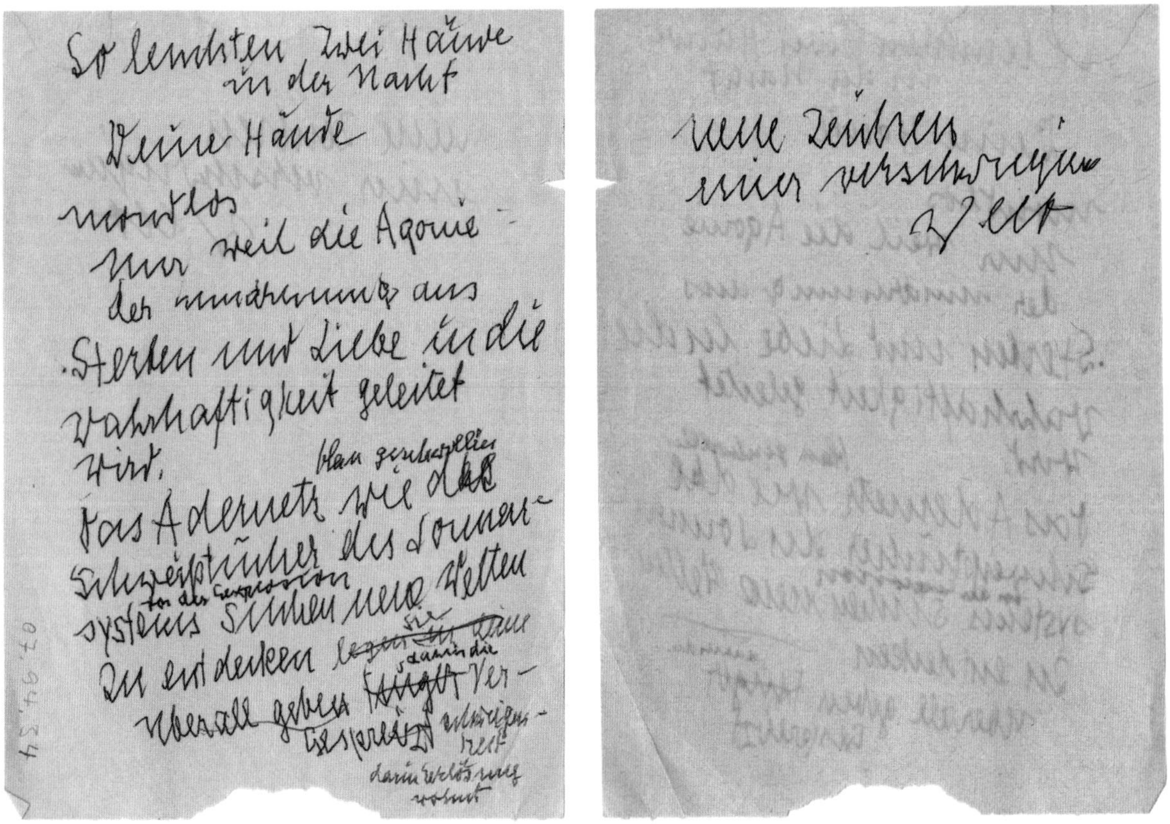

38

release (in another version it is "the secret"). That this transformation, as grandiose as it was definitive, was associated for Sachs with poetry's ability both to live through and live on — in short: to "traverse pain" — is indicated by an attached note. It reads, in the poet's characteristic hand: "You darlings, to you: still the scrawl with which one would pull the universe into the wretched bloodstream." In Sachs' eyes the swollen veins that crisscrossed the backs of the poem's hands were reminiscent of a ballpoint pen's sprawling writing. Only poetry's scribble tore away the veil from existence so that release could occur…

"Such boldness!"

39

**TEXT** Marianne Rappe, "Samtal med Nelly Sachs den 15/3 1967," *Vårt röda kors*, 1967, no. 3, 12 · Johann Peter Eckermann, *Gespräche mit Goethe in den letzten Jahren seines Lebens*, selection and introduction by Anselm Ruest, Berlin ca. 1918, 290 · "Fliehend in der Liebe," NSW:II · "Mit Wildhonig die Hinterbliebenen," Unww (NSW:II) · "So leuchten zwei Hände in der Nacht," TdN (NSW:II) · Letter to the Holmqvists 04/26/1967 (dating uncertain), ASachs | **IMAGE 36** Sachs' copy of Eckermann, *Gespräche mit Goethe*, ca. 1918 (KBS) · **37** "Samtal med Nelly Sachs den 15/3 1967," *Vårt röda kors*, 1967 · **38** "So leuchten zwei Hände in der Nacht," manuscript (DLA) · **39** Sachs' hands, 1965 (KBS)

## ATTEMPTED BREAKOUT

The longing for the cosmic breakthrough is formulated in many of Sachs' late texts. Where poetry had to rely on scarce, sometimes elliptical means — immense occurrences compressed into dashes, rapid shifts between then and now, abrupt montages of figurative and literal elements — the stage poems could portray the metaphysical drama in (at least) three dimensions. Dance, mime, and music were added as elements, and Sachs had direct access to what she called, in a letter to Andersch, "this silent complement before and after the word." This ambition also to include that which precedes and follows on the word is probably most consistently illustrated in *Der magische Tänzer*.

The subtitle of the play is "Attempt at Breaking Out." The cast — "two people and two puppets" — shows not just that Sachs' interest in theatrical interpretation from the Berlin years wasn't a thing confined to the past, but also that the dynamics between the animated and the mechanical remained a central issue. Moreover, as the main title indicates, dance didn't merely amount to a form of expression among others, but provided the very theme of the text. Incidentally, one of the puppets has a tape recorder hanging from a cord around his neck, which in the comments to the piece was explained such that the machine symbolizes "the mechanical process of our everyday existence." The technological accessory introduced a new element to Sachs' œuvre. Together with the occasionally sarcastic, almost slang-like use of language it made the play feel more modern than previous works. The props from the former mystery plays were mothballed, but without doing away with the attempt to dramatize the relationship between the visible and the invisible.

The ingredients from a world defined by goods and advertising can be interpreted in light of Sachs' admiration for Samuel Beckett, whose plays were increasingly being staged in Sweden during the 1950s. The ten or so titles extant in her library suggest that his œuvre was significant, which is also corroborated by the later statement that Beckett was an "exceptional brother in suffering." In connection with Sachs' first meeting with Enzensberger in January 1958 she had seen a production of *Endgame* at the Marsyas Theater, a basement stage in the Old City of Stockholm which had opened five years earlier. The headlines in the evening papers warned that a bloody rag would cover the face of one of the actors and a prominent reviewer is said to have attended the performance with his back to the stage. "Was fearsome and poignant with big perspectives," Sachs reported to Hamm (i.e., not to Clov's master in the play, but to her poet-friend in Stuttgart). *Krapp's Last Tape*, which introduced the tape recorder on stage, had recently premiered at the Royal Court Theatre in London as a prelude to *Endgame*. In her collection *Zeichen im Sand* (Signs in the Sand) from 1962 Sachs stated that *Der magische Tänzer* had been written eight years earlier, that is, in 1955, but there is good reason to call the dating into question. In July 1959 she sent a first clean copy to Andersch — a couple

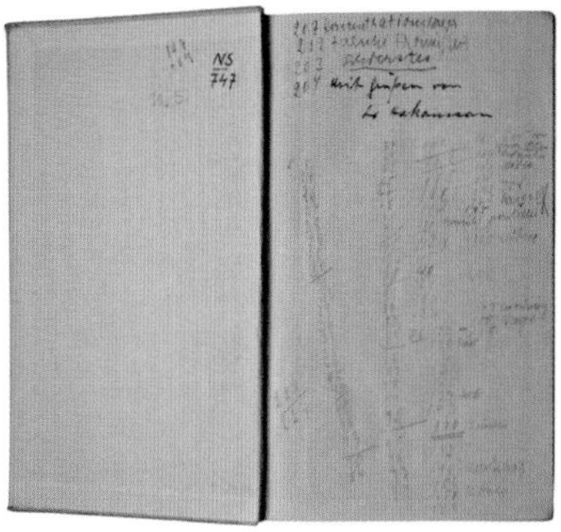
40

41

of scenes were to be published in the Swiss publication *Hortulus* — and a month later she informed Edfelt: "Last spring I wrote some short scenes, 'The Magic Dancer.'"

Whether Sachs knew about the tape recorder handled by Krapp in Beckett's play is uncertain, but also of subordinate importance. Her own tape recorder is part of a dramaturgical new departure, in which Beckett's stripped-down scenic space and physical expression played the more important role. The basic ambition — staging as transformation — had not been abandoned, but the registers of expression had been both broadened and sharpened. It is likely that developments in contemporary Swedish dramatic art — for example the choreographer Birgit Åkesson's collaborations with poets such as Lindegren and Martinson and composers such as Karl-Birger Blomdahl — had a certain influence too. Sachs wasn't merely trying to modernize her dramatic poetry, but also to create a work that contained all forms of expression (words, dance, mime, music, drama). Possibly the real locus of the action imagined by her was that dimension she termed an "intermediary realm" in the directions to the unpublished drama "Eisgrab."

*Der magische Tänzer* is played out in a realm with marked similarities to an invisible universe: "The whole space as dematerialized as possible." The main character, the dancer David, "unwinds from himself — symbol turned into action — the washing lines which have been transformed into meridians. The linen garments flap in the chamber turned into globe-like countries at the call of the cosmic wind; a breaking out from the private to the universe." (Faced with such directions, it is easy to sympathize with Wærn, who wanted to stage the play in Margaretha Holmqvist's translation but was looking for a technically feasible method. When she asked Sachs how she imagined it she received the reply: "But that's up to you, my dear!") Against this cosmic backdrop the magic dancer performs — a puppet who has little in common with earlier dolls on strings and who, according to the comment, is an "incarnation of David's, the human dancer's, past." A "built-in audio tape" explains:

> Touch me — made entirely of magic. / Developed straight from the meridians. / Larva, pupa, butterfly. / Go ahead, go ahead — *he bows in all directions, while David writhes.* / Out of the tangle — out I say — / David, David — the skin is no limit / break it — break it!

The desire to break through to another world could hardly be portrayed more starkly. Earthly life was made up of fetters, the skin was a prison, the meridians ropes that tied fast. The paradoxical form of creation that would ensue, akin to what Simone Weil terms *décréation* in *Gravity and Grace* — "I pull the degrees off you / the meridians off you" — this inverted coming-into-being is, more properly, a de-creation. In the final scene it reaches its climax:

> It is the large sack Zero — Zero — Zero — meridian / There is the cat in the bag / I haul, haul the zero meridian / The whole world entwined in the zero meridian — / Must get out — out — out — / Must get out — out — out — out — / Where the dead are living —

Birth as destitution, conception as denouement… "Where the dead are living": that can only mean a dimension of existence where the ultimate transformation of compassion has become possible. "Always to the utmost," Sachs wrote in a letter to Rudolph Peyer a year or two after having seen *Endgame*, "always to the cessation of time and space." The play she herself wrote announced a magical act of similarly cosmic proportions, whose ultimate purpose was to shake off the shackles and do away with the limitations that prevented the dead from becoming living — yet living in the manner of the dead. "But the hair," David proclaims with words by now familiar, it "grows after death —"…

**TEXT** *Der magische Tänzer* and "Anhang," ZiS (NSW:III) · Letters to Andersch 01/29 and 07/17/1959, and to Hamm 01/28/1958, DLA · The statement about the Marsyas Theater appears in Leif Zern, "Det är Becketts förtjänst att vi miste oskulden," *Dagens Nyheter*, 04/13/2006 · For letter to Edfelt 08/25/1959, see Briefe 148 · For an analysis of the background to *Der magische Tänzer*, see Ruth Dinesen, "Den magiske dansaren. Inge Wærns Inszenierung des 'magischen Tänzers' in Stockholm 1980/81," *Lichtersprache aus den Rissen. Nelly Sachs – Werk und Wirkung*, ed. Ariane Huml, Göttingen 2008, 283-297 · The description of Beckett as a "brother" appears in a letter dated 02/14/1968, ASachs · DS (NSW:II) · "Eisgrab," NSW:III · Interview with Inge Wærn 11/26/2008 · For letter to Peyer 10/05/1959, see Briefe 151 · Simone Weil, *Schwerkraft und Gnade*, German trans. Friedhelm Kemp, Munich 1952 (*Gravity and Grace*, English trans. Arthur Wills, New York 1952) | **IMAGE 40** Sachs' copy of Simone Weil, *Schwerkraft und Gnade* 1952 (KBS) · **41** Pictures of Inge Wærn's production of *Der magische Tänzer* in Stockholm 11/25–12/07/1980 (KBS. By permission of Inge Wærn)

## LOOPED ANGEL

For Sachs the expansion before and after the word was symbolized by hair. People were born with hair on their head, but it also continued to grow after their death. In *Versteckspiel mit Emanuel* from 1955 this figure was given concrete form. The play portrays Marie's longing for the love of her youth who went to sea but never came back. In this "delirium of loneliness" parting is definitive. It may be that its *nevermore* might be repeated in the same manner as in Poe's poem, but unlike a farewell it didn't contain any implicit promise of a reunion — rather, it confirmed a fundamental loss. Towards the end of the play Marie's voice changes. Suddenly it sounds like a "deep male" voice. It turns out to be Emanuel speaking *through* the hallucinating girl. The voice urges her to observe a sign which is beginning to appear on the wall: "See the two zeroes chained together / See, they open their eyes / and the night flows —." Across the wallpaper an infinity sign is now visible. The delirious Marie asks her beloved to hoist her lungs: "Hoist my chest up the mast / hoist — hoist — how it stings —." Stretched out and set like a sail, her chest is at the same time a "salt coffin." Expansion remains inextricably linked with death. Now Marie can finally drink "up the whole / divorce —":

> Empty, the zeroes have flown — arm in arm / counts — doesn't count — counts for all eternity — / all walls through the emptiness // *singing:* // through — through / through my golden ring –

Sachs considered the infinity sign the presence of the dead in the text. By means of an ongoing processing of grief in poetic form — which could be sober and matter-of-fact but also become delirious, be a sign of health yet vent pathologies as well — links were created that turned nothingness into something which might be shared and thereby counted "for all eternity." The meridian was at once the route of the poem and an infinite loop that proclaimed the endless communion of suffering. In a way she had found poetry's equivalent to her father's Expander.

In "Bin in der Fremde" (Am in a Foreign Land) from the third cycle of *Glühende Rätsel* the figure returns as guardian angel:

> Am in a foreign land / it is protected by 8 / the holy looped angel / He is always on his way / through our flesh / inciting unrest / and readying the dust for departure –

The sign is familiar from one of the most famous poems of Swedish modernism, Ekelöf's "apoteos" (Apotheosis) from his debut collection *sent på jorden* (Late on Earth), which Sachs translated and included as "Apotheose" in her bilingual selection from 1962. The closing lines read: "four compass points stand empty around the bier / and the angels' muslin is magically / transformed / into nothing / ∞." In Sachs' German translation: "Vier Himmelsrichtungen stehn leer um die Bahre herum / und der Engel Musselin verwandelt sich / durch einen Zauberschlag / in Nichts [ / ∞]." Even if the sign was missing from the Suhrkamp edition, it returned in her own poetry from the same period: upright, more precisely, as if she wanted to indicate a significance which, although non-alphabetical, was no less readable — in two registers simultaneously: on the one hand graphically, as numeral, on the other in verbalized form. Eternity was literally attended to, or in *Acht genommen* as German parlance has it, and thus activated — that is to say: actualized. The foreign region in whose light Sachs viewed poetry was protected by a holy "looped angel." ("Like the infinity sign, the 8 is formed by a loop," she points out in a letter to Jürgen P. Wallmann.) In this intersection between the two fundamental categories of time, now and eternity, the poem's self lost its status as pronoun, but lived on as verbal entity, transformed to an "unrest" about which an earlier version of the poem claimed it meant one was "on eternity's way."

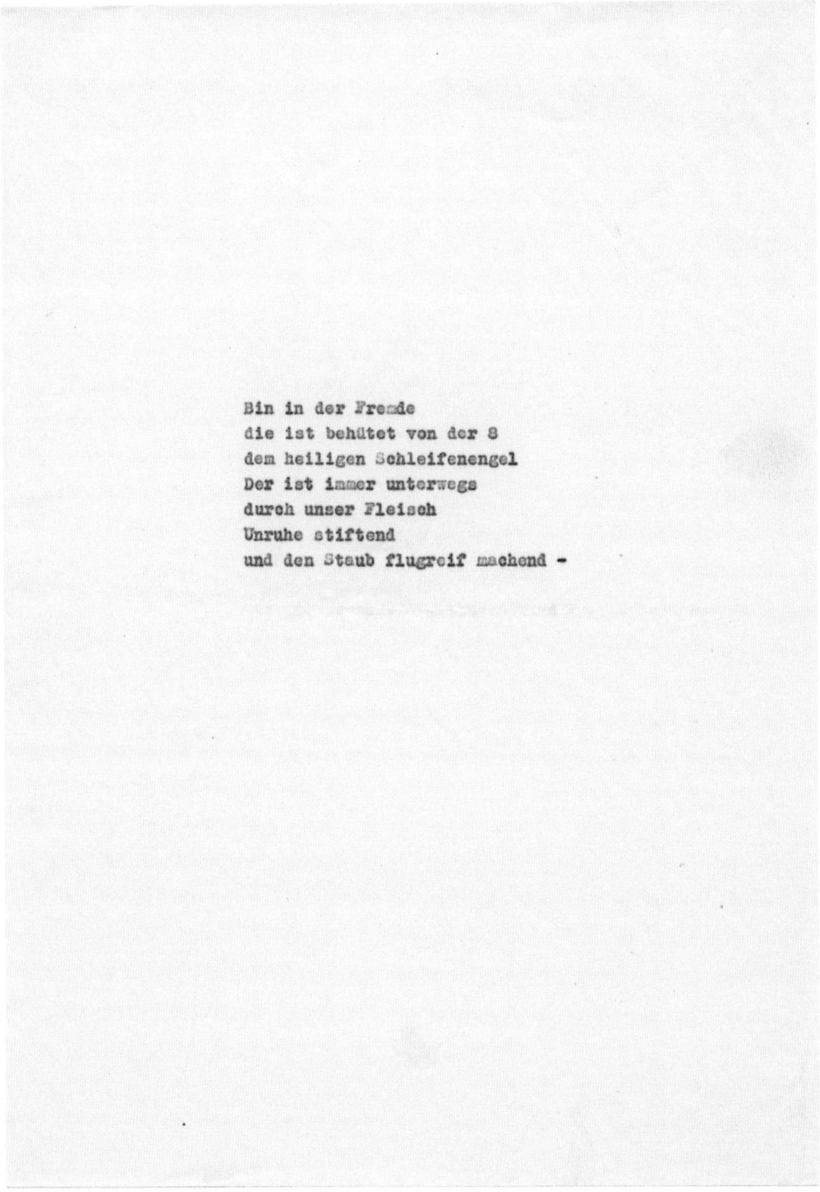
Bin in der Fremde
die ist behütet von der 8
dem heiligen Schleifenengel
Der ist immer unterwegs
durch unser Fleisch
Unruhe stiftend
und den Staub flugreif machend -

42

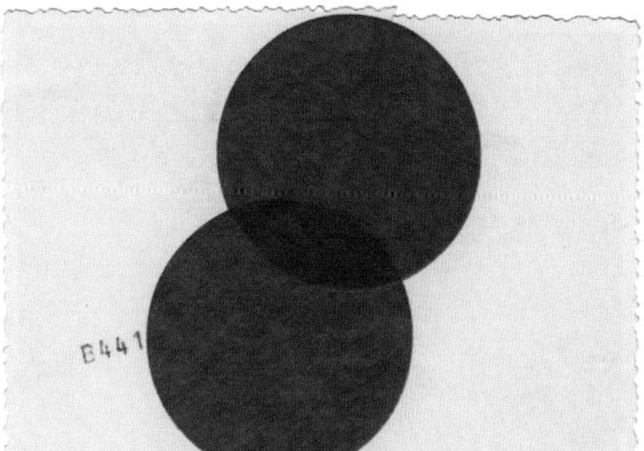


43

**TEXT** *Versteckspiel mit Emanuel*, ZiS (NSW:III) · Edgar Allan Poe, *The Complete Tales and Poems*, New York 1975, 943–946 · "Bin in der Fremde," GR:III (NSW:II) · "Apotheose," GE (NSW:IV) · Copy of a letter to Wallmann 06/24/1966, ASachs | **IMAGE 42** "Bin in der Fremde," typescript (KBS) · **43** The back of a photograph of Nelly and Margarete Sachs (DLA)

## OUTSIDE

44

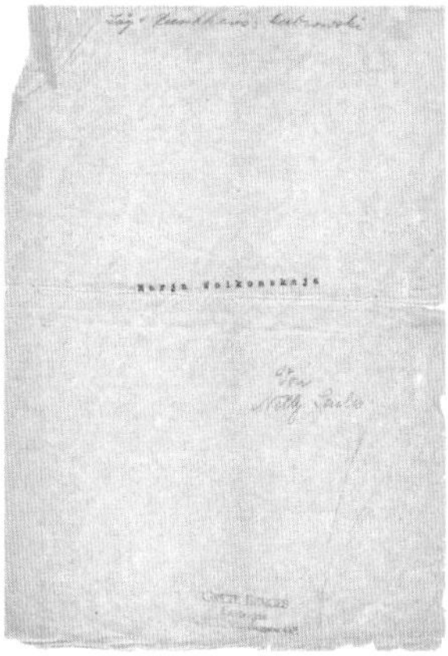


45

The consistency with which Sachs linked themes such as the loop, the line, and the hair with the coordinates of longing and passion can be seen in her interest in MARIA VOLKONSKAYA, née Rayevskaya (1806–1863). As a young woman the Russian countess married Sergei Grigoryevich Volkonsky, a general who was eighteen years her senior and one of the richest men in the tsar's empire. Participating in the Decabrist revolt in December 1825, her husband was found out, stood trial, and was sentenced to twenty years of forced labor. His wife chose to leave the couple's only child behind and accompany him to Siberia. The conditions for doing so, however, were that she relinquish all rights to money and property, and also promise that any further children would become serfs. In short: destitution was to be absolute. For nearly thirty years Volkonskaya lived close to her husband's camp and instituted, among other things, a functioning social welfare program in the region.

For Sachs the socially engaged countess appeared the incarnation of unconditional devotion. In one of her first letters after her flight to Sweden she informed Enar Sahlin that she had material in her possession "woven of truth and fiction" which she had kept "for years" and which was about "one of these heroines of silent love." She wasn't exaggerating. Turned into a prose piece with dramatic elements, the material was given the title "Marja Wolkonskaja" but never published — most likely because the story was still wrought with the same mixture of pathos and prudishness that characterized Sachs' early poetry. In her comments on the dramatic works, twenty years later, she explained that one of the texts harked back to a work from her youth devoted to this "seventeen-year-old who was loved by Pushkin and given the name 'The Girl from the Ganges' by him." Her identification with the countess was evidently so powerful that historical facts were of lesser concern: not only had Pushkin's reference been to Zinaïda Volkonskaya, a relative of Maria's, but the countess had also been almost twenty when she followed her husband into banishment — unlike Sachs, who indeed had been seventeen or eighteen when she was struck by earth-shattering love . . .

The idea for the text came from two articles published in the *Berliner Tageblatt* before and after New Year 1913/1914, which Margaretha Holmqvist found among her friend's belongings after her death and which Sachs must have packed into her brown suitcase before her flight. Under the headline "Die Fürstin Marja Wolkonskaja" (Countess Maria Volkonskaya), Paul Barchan described the Russian woman's will to sacrifice. Images and themes from the

46

articles reappear in texts of up to half a century later — most clearly in the unfinished dramatic poem "1825," in which the future is said only to exist "in the lines of the hand / and there but once and / never more." But also in the cycle of poems *Die Suchende*, published in connection with the Nobel Prize and likely intended as a continuation of *Glühende Rätsel*, Sachs returned to Volkonskaya. In three lines she summarized her model's extreme situation with terse simplicity: "Where she stands / the world is ended / The unknown pulls in where a wound is."

The line that Sachs' poetry drew between the "flowering" lit by beyond in the early poems and "wind's bloomstraws" of the late texts, as *Und niemand weiß weiter* has it — partly concealed, partly exposed — links terrible and passionate, disclosed and withheld experiences. Only through the gaps in the web of the veins and arteries of language, its *Aderwerk*, were the wounds made readable. That these ambiguous omissions have something to say about a writer who herself wanted to disappear behind her work seems inevitable. "Where is the picture of her," the fragment "1825" asks. The reply:

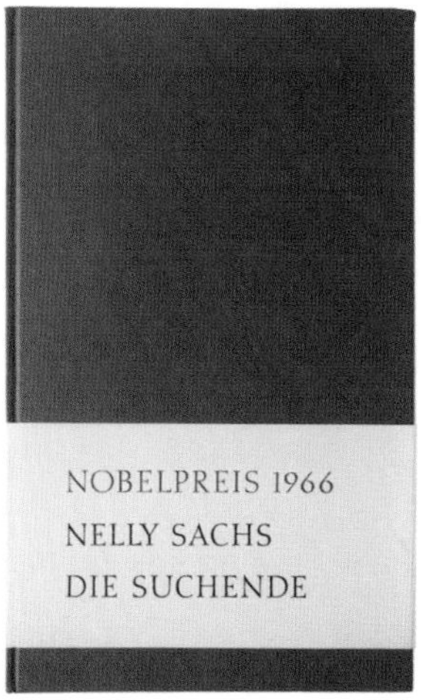


47

> where unreality begins / this line / drawn outside

**TEXT** For letter to Sahlin 06/26/1940, see Briefe 7 · "Marja Wolkonskaja," NSW:IV · "Anhang," ZiS (NSW:III) · Barchan, "Die Fürstin Marja Wolkonskaja," *Berliner Tageblatt* 12/30/1913 and 01/12/1914 · "1825," NSW:IV · DS (NSW:II) · "Zur Ruh," FG · "Vergessenheit" and "Da schrieb der Schreiber des Sohar," Unww (NSW:II) | **IMAGE 44** J.K. Dmitrijev, painting of Maria Volkonskaya after historical original (Insel Verlag, Frankfurt am Main) · **45** "Marja Wolkonskaja," typescript (KBS) · **46** Sachs in front of her bookshelves in the 1960s (Photo Margaretha Holmqvist, KBS) · **47** *Die Suchende* 1966

## OUT OF SILENCE

That which precedes and follows on the word — this "outside" singular to poetry — must consist of silence. In "Chelion" from the 1930s Merlin professes at one point: "This my magic wand cannot show. That which breathes here, is made out of silence." The wizard is referring to the impossibility of unveiling the very principle behind creation. He may have been capable of conjuring mountains, seas, clouds, and butterflies… But before the very foundation of such splendor and riches he too must come to a halt. The *Urpunkt* wasn't available even to wizards.

On a scrap of quadrille paper Sachs returned to the notion. The note has neither date nor context, but judging from the paper as well as the handwriting it was made towards the end of her life — perhaps in connection with the unpublished play "Eisgrab" with its alternative title "Wo Schweigen spricht" (Where Silence Speaks); perhaps during her last year. The three words on the piece of paper don't say much, almost nothing. But what they say about almost nothing contains the stuff of the invisible universe Sachs wished to conjure in her works. In retrospect, it is difficult not to read them as the credo of a writer whose voice once fled to the fishes and who, out of the feeling of suffocation, wrought a poetry in which "breathing continues building a room made only of crossed thresholds." The proper basis of the poem is on the other side of the threshold, where the reader could only enter as if into an Outside. For Sachs the goal amounted to tying together the beginning and the end of that eternal loop of flight and metamorphosis, I and you, of which poems were made. She wrote herself *out* of silence, but also onward *with* it. This is what the scrap of quadrille paper says. Three penciled words:

> *Aus dem Schweigen*
>
> Out of silence

**TEXT** "Chelion," ASachs · "Eisgrab," NSW:III · "In einer Landschaft aus Musik," Unww (NSW:II) · "Aus dem Schweigen," from a private collection | **IMAGE 48** "Aus dem Schweigen," manuscript (from a private collection)

48

# APPARATUS

1

**ACKNOWLEDGEMENTS**

In the beginning — which is to say 1986 — was an academic study that got shelved. It would probably have remained in the dusty attic of memory if it hadn't been for my former bosses, ambassadors Carl Tham and Ruth Jacoby, who encouraged me to do something about what they identified as an aching conscience. Many thanks...

Eventually those measures led to an annotated four-volume works edition, an exhibition, as well as a CD with previously unknown recordings. Thank you to Göran Blomkvist, Dan Brändström, Frederik Lundmark, and Maria Wikse of Riksbankens Jubileumsfond, who made it possible to devote the necessary time to the project and who have also given support to the exhibition. Thank you to National Librarian Gunnar Sahlin, who agreed to host the project, and to his colleagues at the Swedish Royal Library: Håkan Adenkrantz, Sara Bengtzon, Andrea Davis Kronlund, Eva Dillman, Jan-Eric Ericsson, Johanna Fries Markiewicz, Jens Gustafsson, Agneta Holmenmark, Peter Olin, Jerker Rydén, Therese Scotte, Pelle Snickars, Ingrid Svensson, and Leena Uusitalo. Special thanks to their former colleague Kristina Eriksson, who has done more than anyone for the organization of Sachs' estate. Thomas Sparr and Wolfgang Kaußen at Suhrkamp Verlag accompanied the German version of this book with care and curiosity. The same applies to Anna Bengtsson and Ola Wallin at Ersatz, who not only took on the Swedish version, but also believed that a CD with sound recordings was needed. Harald Krewer and Vera Teichmann at speak low produced the CD. With admirable ease Tomas Tranæus translated the text into English. Keenly and judiciously, Emily Jane Cohen and her team at Stanford University Press — Sarah Crane Newman, Richard Gunde, Judith Hibbard, and Mary Katherine Maco — turned it into a publishable book.

Thank you to my friends at gewerk design GmbH — Birgit Schlegel, Jens Imig, Thilo Albers, Andreas Baumbach, Klaus Fermor, Christine Kitta, Natascha Roshani, and Marten Suhr — who designed both book and exhibition and also managed the project funds. Thank you to speak low, as well as Martin Kamratowski at Artavi, who took care of everything to do with sound in the exhibition, and to Paul Klier who did the carpentry work. Early on, Michael Blumenthal, Helmut Braun, and Cilly Kugelmann at the Jüdisches Museum in Berlin showed contagious enthusiasm. Thank you to my friends at the Jewish Theatre in Stockholm: Pia Forsgren, Elisabeth Secher Svenstedt, and Robert Weil, who brought many new ideas to the project — not least in terms of dramatic representation. And thank you to my former colleagues at the Swedish embassy in Berlin, Kerstin Poehls and Grit Thunemann, as well as to my successor as counsellor for cultural affairs, Ulrika Holmgaard.

Thank you to Kulturstiftung des Bundes in Halle and Klassenlotterie der Berliner Lotto-Stiftung, which provided financial support. In the former case Hortensia Völckers and Friederike Tappe-Hornbostel must be mentioned; in the latter André Schmitz and Klaus Wowereit, mayor of Berlin, who additionally was kind enough to take on the role of *Schirmherr*. His Swedish counterpart, Sten Nordin, shouldered the same role in Stockholm. Thank you to Horst Claussen on the staff of the minister of state for culture, Bernd Neumann, who saw to it that this book did not remain a pious hope. The Swedish embassy in Berlin provided much appreciated financial support. The Swedish Academy contributed both monies and goodwill, as did its German counterpart, the Akademie für deutsche Sprache und Dichtung in Darmstadt. Special thanks to the former permanent secretary Horace Engdahl and secretary-general Bernd Busch. Roman Hess, who manages Museum Strauhof in Zurich, was the first to receive the exhibition; Ulrich Moeske, Hans-Georg Schulz, and Wolfgang Weick of Kulturbetriebe in Dortmund hopefully not the last.

This book is the product of extensive research in archives and libraries. No one interested in Sachs' life and work, however, can afford to neglect her biographers. Ruth Dinesen, whose many years of work in the archives laid the foundations for the research, filled in the gaps in my knowledge whenever and wherever necessary. Gabriele Fritsch-Vivié, who has written a useful monograph, conveyed appreciated points of view. Without their respective studies, much of what follows would have turned out differently. In Ariane Huml and Matthias Weichelt I have had reliable colleagues during the work on the works edition. Katharina Erben and Sabine Salzmann helped with the archive work. Katharina also organized the pictorial material for this book, for which I am greatly indebted to her. Sara Danius, Ruth Dinesen, Margaretha Holmqvist, Anders Olsson, and Mikael van Reis commented on early drafts of the text; Anna Bengtsson and Ola Wallin on late ones. Thank you also to Paul Berf, who besides translating the text into German contributed interesting points of view. So did Daniel Frydman, a psychiatrist and psychoanalyst in private practice who was formerly director and senior medical physician at Södermalm's psychiatric emergency and outpatient ward. A couple of panel discussions with Ulrich von Bülow, who heads the manuscripts department at the Deutsches Literaturarchiv in Marbach, made thoughts grow clearer. He and his colleagues — Jan Bürger, Thomas Kemme, Rosemarie Kutschis, Jochen Mayer, and Ulrich Raulff — provided practical assistance throughout the course of the project. The same applies to Jens-André Pfeiffer, who manages the Nelly-Sachs-Archiv at the Stadt- und Landesbibliothek in Dortmund, and to Amir Eshel and Roland Hsu of the Forum for Contemporary Europe at Stanford University, who allowed me to speculate out loud during a talk. Conversations with a number of friends brought me forward: among them Barbara Agnese (Vienna), Werner Hamacher (Frankfurt am Main), Levke Harders (Berlin and Bielefeld), Beth and Karl Mårtens, Daniel Pedersen, Inge Wærn Malmqvist, and Bertil Wosk (all Stockholm), as well as Peter Waterhouse (Vienna) and Mai Wegener (Berlin). Suggestions and viewpoints have also been received from Erland Bohlin (Stockholm), Maria Gazetti (Frankfurt am Main), Harald Harlan (Hamburg), Leif Jonsson (Sigtuna), Lionel Richard (Paris), and Leif Zern (Stockholm).

The students who took part in my seminars on "Die szenische Dichtungen der Nelly Sachs" and "Darstellung der Literatur" at the Freie-Universität Berlin in the winter of 2008–2009 contributed observations and finds. Participants in the former seminar were: Agnes Gerstenberg, Lisa Kempter, Verena Reiß, Nele Ana Riepl, Rina Schmeller, and Katharina Zegers. In the latter: Rosa Baumgartner, Luca Beisel, Tanja Bertele, Marie Bickmann, Isabel Bredenbröker, Judith Daute, Dilan Dülec, Michaela Engelbrecht, Kirstine Rosalia Fenger, Janna Fießelmann, Naomi Fukuzama, Dennis Grabowsky, Nele Grampner, Anna Hansch, Dörte Herwig, Manuela Klotz, Lena Kollender, Bettina Kracht, Maria Mushtieva, Tabea Nagel, Anton Pluschke, Christine Ringer, Daniel Schebesta, Liane Schlumberger, Lea Schneider, Kim Schnitzer, Maria Schrade, Thomas Streidl, Ulla Tommerup, Hannah Vogt, Stefanie Waldow, Sarah Wiltschek, and Julia Wischniowski.

Special and emphatic thanks to the holder of the rights to Sachs' works, Hans Magnus Enzensberger. The same applies to all the individuals and institutions who have granted us permission to reproduce and/or exhibit documents, photographs, and objects. Names are given in connection with each exhibit. (Abbreviations are explained in the Bibliography.)

Finally and fundamentally Margaretha Holmqvist must be thanked. She and her late husband, Bengt, were Nelly Sachs' close friends between 1961 and 1970. Anyone interested in Sachs' life and work, and most things between the two, has a judicious conversation partner in Margaretha, as well as a good friend.

This book was written in August and October of 2009.

## BIBLIOGRAPHY

This bibliography covers all first editions of Sachs' books, as well as publications quoted more than once. It also lists abbreviations for archives and rights owners of images and reproduced objects.

The first time a publication by Sachs is mentioned in the text its title is given in both German and English, thereafter only in German. If the text in question has been translated, and that translation is used, this is recorded in the bibliographical note at the end of each section. References to Nelly Sachs *Werke*, an annotated edition of four volumes edited by Aris Fioretos (Berlin: Suhrkamp, 2010–2011), are to NSW, followed by a colon and a Roman numeral for the volume. If a reference is preceded by a comma, it is to the page number, or otherwise the ordinal number. (Thus "Dähnert, 226" refers to the page number while "Briefe 226" refers to the ordinal number.)

Language errors in quotations from Sachs' texts in Swedish have been translated only conservatively into English. [...] indicates up to five omitted words in a quote; [---] up to five omitted sentences.

### Archives, Estates, Collections

| | |
|---|---|
| AAdK | Archiv der Akademie der Künste, Berlin |
| ABFS | Albert Bonniers Förlag, Stockholm |
| ASuhrkamp | Archiv des Suhrkamp Verlags, Marbach am Neckar |
| BDB | Börsenverein des deutschen Buchhandels, Berlin |
| BLH | Brandenburgisches Landeshauptarchiv, Potsdam |
| BPK | Bildarchiv Preußischer Kulturbesitz, Berlin |
| CM | Compact Memory, www.compactmemory.de |
| DLA | Deutsches Literaturarchiv, Marbach am Neckar |
| AWosk | Nachlaß Rosi Wosk |
| DPMA | Deutsches Patent- und Markenamt, Berlin, Jena and München |
| DTA | Deutsches Theaterarchiv, München |
| EBB | Entschädigungsbehörde, Berlin |
| GU | Göteborgs universitetsbibliotek |
| AFogelklou | Emilia Fogelklous samling |
| HMM | United States Holocaust Memorial Museum, Washington |
| HUB | Humboldt-Universität, Berlin |
| JFS | Judiska församlingen, Stockholm |
| JMB | Jüdisches Museum, Berlin |
| JMS | Judiska museet, Stockholm |
| KBS | Kungliga biblioteket, Stockholm |
| ABerendsohn | Walter A. Berendsohns arkiv |
| ADähnert:I | Gudrun Dähnert's Nelly Sachs collection I |
| ADähnert:II | Gudrun Dähnert's Nelly Sachs collection II |

| | |
|---|---|
| ADinesen | Ruth Dinesen: Material regarding Nelly Sachs |
| AHolmqvist | Bengt and Margaretha Holmqvist: Material by and about Nelly Sachs |
| ALamm | Greta and Martin Lamm's papers regarding Nelly Sachs |
| ALennartsson | Eva-Lisa Lennartsson's posthumous papers |
| APergament | Moses Pergament's collection regarding Nelly Sachs |
| ASachs | Nelly Sachs collection |
| ASachsS | Nelly Sachs: Sonette |
| ASahlin | Enar Sahlin's papers regarding Nelly Sachs |
| ASahlinB | Enar Sahlin: Letters from Nelly Sachs |
| ATegen | Gunhild Tegen's papers regarding Nelly Sachs |
| AWærn | Inge Wærn Malmquist's papers |
| LAB | Landesarchiv, Berlin |
| MMS | Moderna museet, Stockholm |
| RAS | Riksarkivet, Stockholm |
| SBB | Staatsbibliothek zu Berlin |
| SLD | Stadt- und Landesbibliothek, Dortmund |
| ABerendsohnD | Nachlaß Walter A. Berendsohn im Nelly-Sachs-Archiv, SLD |
| SSA | Sigtunastiftelsens arkiv, Sigtuna |
| SSB | Stiftung Stadtmuseum, Berlin |
| SSM | Stockholms stadsmuseum |
| UUB | Uppsala universitetsbibliotek |

## Nelly Sachs: Writings and Selected Letters

| | |
|---|---|
| AG | *Ausgewählte Gedichte*. With an afterword by Hans Magnus Enzensberger. Frankfurt am Main: Suhrkamp 1963. |
| Briefe | *Briefe der Nelly Sachs*. Published by Ruth Dinesen and Helmut Müßener. Frankfurt am Main: Suhrkamp 1984. |
| Briefregister | *Nelly Sachs Briefregister*. 3 454 letters in microfiches. Edited by Ruth Dinesen. Stuttgart: Akademischer Verlag 1989. |
| BCelan | Paul Celan and Nelly Sachs, *Briefwechsel*. Edited by Barbara Wiedemann. Frankfurt am Main: Suhrkamp 1993. |
| BSchwedhelm | Karl Schwedhelm, Nelly Sachs. *Briefwechsel und Dokumente*. Edited and annotated by Reinhard Kiefer and Bernhard Albers. Aachen: Rimbaud 1998. |
| BDomin | Hilde Domin, Nelly Sachs, Briefwechsel. From: *Nelly Sachs – "an letzter Atemspitze Lebens"*. Published by Birgit Lermen and Michael Braun. Bonn: Bouvier 1998, 217–254. |
| DS | *Die Suchende*. Frankfurt am Main: Suhrkamp 1966. |
| E | *Eli. Ein Mysterienspiel vom Leiden Israels*. Malmö: Forssells Tryckeri AB 1951. |
| FG | "Frühe Gedichte". From: LuEN, 243–262. |

| | |
|---|---|
| FiS | *Fahrt ins Staublose*. Frankfurt am Main: Suhrkamp 1961. |
| FuV | *Flucht und Verwandlung*. Stuttgart: Deutsche Verlags-Anstalt 1959. |
| G | *Gedichte*. Published and provided with an afterword by Hilde Domin. Frankfurt am Main: Suhrkamp 1977. |
| GR | *Glühende Rätsel*. Frankfurt am Main: Insel 1964. |
| GR:I | "Glühende Rätsel", I. From: AG, 70–81. |
| GR:II | "Glühende Rätsel", II. From: GR, 35–54. |
| GR:III | "Glühende Rätsel", III. From: SG, 199–216. |
| GR:IV | "Glühende Rätsel", IV. From: TdN, 67–74. |
| IdWdT | *In den Wohnungen des Todes*. Berlin: Aufbau-Verlag 1947. |
| L | *Landschaft aus Schreien*. Selection and afterword by Fritz Hofmann. Berlin and Weimar: Aufbau 1966. |
| LuE | *Legenden und Erzählungen*. Berlin: Friedrich Wilhelm Mayer 1921. |
| LuEN | New edition with a facsimile of LuE. From: Ruth Dinesen, *"Und Leben hat immer wie Abschied geschmeckt". Frühe Gedichte und Prosa der Nelly Sachs*. Stuttgart: Akademischer Verlag 1987, 123–242. |
| NeW | "Nur eine Weltminute". From: *Aus aufgegebenen Werken*. Published by Suhrkamp Verlag. Frankfurt am Main: Suhrkamp 1968, 143–147. |
| NfTdL | "Noch feiert Tod das Leben". From: FiS, 345–386. |
| Richard | "Briefe und Dokumente". 20 annotated letters from Nelly Sachs to Lionel Richard. With further documents arranged by Michael Kessler. From: Kessler, 309–372. |
| S | *Sternverdunkelung*. Amsterdam: Bermann-Fischer/Querido; Wien: Bermann-Fischer; Berlin: Suhrkamp 1949. |
| SfdJ | *Simson fällt durch Jahrtausende und andere szenische Dichtungen*. München: Deutsche Verlags-Anstalt 1967. |
| SG | *Späte Gedichte*. Frankfurt am Main: Suhrkamp 1965. |
| SnL | *Suche nach Lebenden*. Utgiven av Margaretha Holmqvist och Bengt Holmqvist. Frankfurt am Main: Suhrkamp 1971. |
| TdN | *Teile dich Nacht*. Edited by Margaretha Holmqvist and Bengt Holmqvist. Frankfurt am Main: Suhrkamp 1971. |
| Unww | *Und niemand weiß weiter*. Hamburg and München: Ellermann 1957. |
| V | *Verzauberung*. Frankfurt am Main: Suhrkamp 1970. |
| ZiS | *Zeichen im Sand*. Frankfurt am Main: Suhrkamp 1962. |

## Nelly Sachs: Translations


AadSih — *Aber auch diese Sonne ist heimatlos. Schwedische Lyrik der Gegenwart*. Translation and selection by Nelly Sachs. Darmstadt: Georg Büchner 1956.

AL — Artur Lundkvist, *Gedichte*. Edited by Peter Hamm. Translated by Friedrich Ege, Peter Hamm, Ilmar Laaban, Nelly Sachs and A. O. Schwede. Köln and Berlin: Kiepenheuer & Witsch 1963.

EL — Erik Lindegren, *Weil unser einziges Nest unsere Flügel sind*. Selection and translation by Nelly Sachs. Neuwied am Rhein and Berlin: Luchterhand 1963.

GE — Gunnar Ekelöf, *Poesie*. Edited by Hans Magnus Enzensberger. Translated by Nelly Sachs. Frankfurt am Main: Suhrkamp Verlag 1962.

JE — Johannes Edfelt, *Der Schattenfischer*. Translation and selection by Nelly Sachs. Darmstadt: Georg Büchner 1958.

KV — Karl Vennberg, *Poesie*. Edited by Hans Magnus Enzensberger. Translation by Nelly Sachs and Hans Magnus Enzensberger. Frankfurt am Main: Suhrkamp 1965.

SchwG — *Schwedische Gedichte*. Selection and translation by Nelly Sachs. Neuwied and Berlin: Luchterhand 1965.

VWuG — *Von Welle und Granit. Querschnitt durch die schwedische Lyrik des 20. Jahrhunderts*. Selection and translation by Nelly Sachs. Berlin: Aufbau 1947.


## Publications about Nelly Sachs


Bahr — Erhard Bahr, *Nelly Sachs*. München: C. H. Beck and Edition Text + Kritik 1980.

Berendsohn — Walter A. Berendsohn, *Nelly Sachs. Einführung in das Werk der Dichterin jüdischen Schicksals*. Darmstadt: Agora 1974.

BerendsohnE — "Ekstatischer Aufstieg". From: *Mitteilungsblatt* (supplement to *Irgûn Ôlê Merkaz Êrôpa*, Tel Aviv), 15 October 1965, no. 42, 4–5.

Dähnert — Gudrun Dähnert, "Wie Nelly Sachs 1940 aus Deutschland entkam. Mit einem Brief an Ruth Mövius". From: *Sinn und Form*, 2009, nr 2, 226–257.

DBdNS — *Das Buch der Nelly Sachs*. Edited by Bengt Holmqvist. Frankfurt am Main: Suhrkamp 1968.

Dinesen — Ruth Dinesen, *Nelly Sachs. Eine Biographie*. Translated from Danish by Gabriele Gerecke. Frankfurt am Main: Suhrkamp 1994.

| | |
|---|---|
| DinesenU | *"Und Leben hat immer wie Abschied geschmeckt". Frühe Gedichte und Prosa der Nelly Sachs.* Stuttgart: Akademischer Verlag 1987. |
| Fritsch-Vivié | Gabriele Fritsch-Vivié, *Nelly Sachs.* Reinbek bei Hamburg: Rowohlt 1993. |
| Holmqvist | Bengt Holmqvist, "Die Sprache der Sehnsucht". From: DBdNS, 7–70. |
| Kessler | *Nelly Sachs. Neue Interpretationen.* Edited by Michael Kessler and Jürgen Wertheimer. Tübingen: Stauffenberg Verlag 1994. |
| Lagercrantz | Olof Lagercrantz, *Den pågående skapelsen. En studie i Nelly Sachs diktning.* Stockholm: Wahlström & Widstrand 1966. |
| Lennartsson | Eva Lisa Lennartsson, "Nelly Sachs och hennes vänner: mina personliga minnen". From: *Fenix,* 1984, no. 3, 46–133. |
| NSzE:1 | *Nelly Sachs zu Ehren. Gedichte · Prosa · Beiträge.* Band 1. Published by Suhrkamp Verlag. Frankfurt am Main: Suhrkamp 1961. |
| NSzE:2 | *Nelly Sachs zu Ehren. Gedichte · Beiträge · Bibliographie.* Band 2. Published by Suhrkamp Verlag. Frankfurt am Main: Suhrkamp 1966. |
| Sager | Peter Sager, *Nelly Sachs. Untersuchungen zu Stil und Motivik ihrer Lyrik.* Bonn: Rheinische Friedrich-Wilhelms-Universität 1970. |
| Schubert:1 | Lina Schubert, "Rückblick wie ich das Leben sah! Bei der Familie Sachs! im Jahre 1929", L90:6:6, ASachs. |
| Schubert:2 | Lina Schubert, "Wie ich das Leben im Hause William Sachs sah im Jahre 1930", L90:6:6, ASachs. |
| Schubert:3 | Lina Schubert, "Erinnerungen an das Jahr 1931 im Hause der Dichterin ›Nelly Sachs‹!", L90:6:6, ASachs. |
| Sommerer | Gerald Sommerer, *"Aber dies ist nichts für Deutschland, das weiß und fühle ich". Nelly Sachs – Untersuchungen zu ihrem szenischen Werk.* Würzburg: Königshausen & Neumann 2008. |

### Other Publications

| | |
|---|---|
| Baalschem | Martin Buber, *Die Legende des Baalschem.* Zürich: Manesse Bibliothek der Weltliteratur 1955 [1907]. |
| CBücher | Martin Buber, *Die Chassidischen Bücher.* München: Jakob Hegner 1928. |
| CErzählungen | Martin Buber, *Die Erzählungen der Chassidim.* Zürich: Bibliothek der Weltliteratur 1949. |

Müller — *Der Sohar und seine Lehre. Einleitung in die Gedankenwelt der Kabbalah*. Berlin and Wien: R. Löwit 1920.

SachsW — William Sachs, *Die Heilgymnastik im Hause*. Berlin n. d.

Scholem — Gershom Scholem, *Die jüdische Mystik in ihren Hauptströmungen*. Frankfurt am Main: Metzner 1957.

TegenD — Einar and Gunhild Tegen, *De dödsdömda vittna. Enquêtesvar och intervjuer*. Stockholm: Wahlström & Widstrand 1945.

TegenJ — Gunhild Tegen, *Jakobs skugga*. Stockholm: Författarens förlag 1953.

Zohar — *Die Geheimnisse der Schöpfung. Ein Kapitel aus dem Sohar*. Translation and introduction by Gershom Scholem. Berlin: Schocken 1935.

## INDEX OF PERSONS

This index of persons lists all historical persons mentioned in the text, with the single exception of Nelly Sachs. Names given in the Acknowledgments are not included. Italicized page references indicate that the person's background is presented in greater detail.

## INDEX OF TEXTS

This text index covers all mentioned or quoted works by Nelly Sachs. Official documents are also included. The letters are in a separate section. Where recipients have received letters both individually and together with a spouse, the spouse's name is given in brackets. Only the titles of books and published plays are italicized. The titles of all other texts are in standard font and without quotation marks.

#### LETTERS TO:

**TEXTS:**

2

**IMAGE 1** Sachs with Johannes and Brita Edfelt and Anna Riwkin, among others, probably in the 1950s (KBS) · **2** Sachs' calendar, opened to the day after her death (KBS) · **3** Sachs in the apartment in Bergsundsstrand in the 1960s (KBS)